T0180636

Communications
in Computer and Information Science   1794

Rationale

The CCIS series is devoted to the publication of proceedings of computer science conferences. Its aim is to efficiently disseminate original research results in informatics in printed and electronic form. While the focus is on publication of peer-reviewed full papers presenting mature work, inclusion of reviewed short papers reporting on work in progress is welcome, too. Besides globally relevant meetings with internationally representative program committees guaranteeing a strict peer-reviewing and paper selection process, conferences run by societies or of high regional or national relevance are also considered for publication.

Topics

The topical scope of CCIS spans the entire spectrum of informatics ranging from foundational topics in the theory of computing to information and communications science and technology and a broad variety of interdisciplinary application fields.

Information for Volume Editors and Authors

Publication in CCIS is free of charge. No royalties are paid, however, we offer registered conference participants temporary free access to the online version of the conference proceedings on SpringerLink (http://link.springer.com) by means of an http referrer from the conference website and/or a number of complimentary printed copies, as specified in the official acceptance email of the event.

CCIS proceedings can be published in time for distribution at conferences or as post-proceedings, and delivered in the form of printed books and/or electronically as USBs and/or e-content licenses for accessing proceedings at SpringerLink. Furthermore, CCIS proceedings are included in the CCIS electronic book series hosted in the SpringerLink digital library at http://link.springer.com/bookseries/7899. Conferences publishing in CCIS are allowed to use Online Conference Service (OCS) for managing the whole proceedings lifecycle (from submission and reviewing to preparing for publication) free of charge.

Publication process

The language of publication is exclusively English. Authors publishing in CCIS have to sign the Springer CCIS copyright transfer form, however, they are free to use their material published in CCIS for substantially changed, more elaborate subsequent publications elsewhere. For the preparation of the camera-ready papers/files, authors have to strictly adhere to the Springer CCIS Authors' Instructions and are strongly encouraged to use the CCIS LaTeX style files or templates.

Abstracting/Indexing

CCIS is abstracted/indexed in DBLP, Google Scholar, EI-Compendex, Mathematical Reviews, SCImago, Scopus. CCIS volumes are also submitted for the inclusion in ISI Proceedings.

How to start

To start the evaluation of your proposal for inclusion in the CCIS series, please send an e-mail to ccis@springer.com.

Mohammad Tanveer · Sonali Agarwal ·
Seiichi Ozawa · Asif Ekbal · Adam Jatowt
Editors

Neural
Information Processing

29th International Conference, ICONIP 2022
Virtual Event, November 22–26, 2022
Proceedings, Part VII

Springer

Editors
Mohammad Tanveer
Indian Institute of Technology Indore
Indore, India

Seiichi Ozawa
Kobe University
Kobe, Japan

Adam Jatowt
University of Innsbruck
Innsbruck, Austria

Sonali Agarwal 🆔
Indian Institute of Information Technology -
Allahabad
Prayagraj, India

Asif Ekbal
Indian Institute of Technology Patna
Patna, India

ISSN 1865-0929   ISSN 1865-0937 (electronic)
Communications in Computer and Information Science
ISBN 978-981-99-1647-4   ISBN 978-981-99-1648-1 (eBook)
https://doi.org/10.1007/978-981-99-1648-1

Preface

Welcome to the proceedings of the 29th International Conference on Neural Information Processing (ICONIP 2022) of the Asia-Pacific Neural Network Society (APNNS), held virtually from Indore, India, during November 22–26, 2022.

The mission of the Asia-Pacific Neural Network Society is to promote active interactions among researchers, scientists, and industry professionals who are working in neural networks and related fields in the Asia-Pacific region. APNNS has Governing Board Members from 13 countries/regions – Australia, China, Hong Kong, India, Japan, Malaysia, New Zealand, Singapore, South Korea, Qatar, Taiwan, Thailand, and Turkey. The society's flagship annual conference is the International Conference of Neural Information Processing (ICONIP).

The ICONIP conference aims to provide a leading international forum for researchers, scientists, and industry professionals who are working in neuroscience, neural networks, deep learning, and related fields to share their new ideas, progress, and achievements. Due to the current situation regarding the pandemic and international travel, ICONIP 2022, which was planned to be held in New Delhi, India, was organized as a fully virtual conference.

The proceedings of ICONIP 2022 consists of a multi-volume set in LNCS and CCIS, which includes 146 and 213 papers, respectively, selected from 1003 submissions reflecting the increasingly high quality of research in neural networks and related areas. The conference focused on four main areas, i.e., "Theory and Algorithms," "Cognitive Neurosciences," "Human Centered Computing," and "Applications." The conference also had special sessions in 12 niche areas, namely

1   International Workshop on Artificial Intelligence and Cyber Security (AICS)
2. Computationally Intelligent Techniques in Processing and Analysis of Neuronal Information (PANI)
3. Learning with Fewer Labels in Medical Computing (FMC)
4. Computational Intelligence for Biomedical Image Analysis (BIA)
5   Optimized AI Models with Interpretability, Security, and Uncertainty Estimation in Healthcare (OAI)
6. Advances in Deep Learning for Biometrics and Forensics (ADBF)
7. Machine Learning for Decision-Making in Healthcare: Challenges and Opportunities (MDH)
8. Reliable, Robust and Secure Machine Learning Algorithms (RRS)
9. Evolutionary Machine Learning Technologies in Healthcare (EMLH)
10 High Performance Computing Based Scalable Machine Learning Techniques for Big Data and Their Applications (HPCML)
11. Intelligent Transportation Analytics (ITA)
12. Deep Learning and Security Techniques for Secure Video Processing (DLST)

Our great appreciation goes to the Program Committee members and the reviewers who devoted their time and effort to our rigorous peer-review process. Their insightful reviews and timely feedback ensured the high quality of the papers accepted for publication.

The submitted papers in the main conference and special sessions were reviewed following the same process, and we ensured that every paper has at least two high-quality single-blind reviews. The PC Chairs discussed the reviews of every paper very meticulously before making a final decision. Finally, thank you to all the authors of papers, presenters, and participants, which made the conference a grand success. Your support and engagement made it all worthwhile.

December 2022

Mohammad Tanveer
Sonali Agarwal
Seiichi Ozawa
Asif Ekbal
Adam Jatowt

Organization

Program Committee

General Chairs

M. Tanveer   Indian Institute of Technology Indore, India
Sonali Agarwal   IIIT Allahabad, India
Seiichi Ozawa   Kobe University, Japan

Honorary Chairs

Jonathan Chan   King Mongkut's University of Technology
                                                 Thonburi, Thailand
P. N. Suganthan   Nanyang Technological University, Singapore

Program Chairs

Asif Ekbal   Indian Institute of Technology Patna, India
Adam Jatowt   University of Innsbruck, Austria

Technical Chairs

Shandar Ahmad   JNU, India
Derong Liu   University of Chicago, USA

Special Session Chairs

Kai Qin   Swinburne University of Technology, Australia
Kaizhu Huang   Duke Kunshan University, China
Amit Kumar Singh   NIT Patna, India

Tutorial Chairs

Swagatam Das   ISI Kolkata, India
Partha Pratim Roy   IIT Roorkee, India

Finance Chairs

Shekhar Verma   Indian Institute of Information Technology
                               Allahabad, India
Hayaru Shouno   University of Electro-Communications, Japan
R. B. Pachori   IIT Indore, India

Publicity Chairs

Jerry Chun-Wei Lin   Western Norway University of Applied Sciences,
                               Norway
Chandan Gautam   A*STAR, Singapore

Publication Chairs

Deepak Ranjan Nayak   MNIT Jaipur, India
Tripti Goel   NIT Silchar, India

Sponsorship Chairs

Asoke K. Talukder   NIT Surathkal, India
Vrijendra Singh   IIIT Allahabad, India

Website Chairs

M. Arshad   IIT Indore, India
Navjot Singh   IIIT Allahabad, India

Local Arrangement Chairs

Pallavi Somvanshi   JNU, India
Yogendra Meena   University of Delhi, India
M. Javed   IIIT Allahabad, India
Vinay Kumar Gupta   IIT Indore, India
Iqbal Hasan   National Informatics Centre, Ministry of
                               Electronics and Information Technology, India

Regional Liaison Committee

Sansanee Auephanwiriyakul   Chiang Mai University, Thailand
Nia Kurnianingsih   Politeknik Negeri Semarang, Indonesia

Md Rafiqul Islam	University of Technology Sydney, Australia
Bharat Richhariya	IISc Bangalore, India
Sanjay Kumar Sonbhadra	Shiksha 'O' Anusandhan, India
Mufti Mahmud	Nottingham Trent University, UK
Francesco Piccialli	University of Naples Federico II, Italy

Program Committee

Balamurali A. R.	IITB-Monash Research Academy, India
Ibrahim A. Hameed	Norwegian University of Science and Technology (NTNU), Norway
Fazly Salleh Abas	Multimedia University, Malaysia
Prabath Abeysekara	RMIT University, Australia
Adamu Abubakar Ibrahim	International Islamic University, Malaysia
Muhammad Abulaish	South Asian University, India
Saptakatha Adak	Philips, India
Abhijit Adhikary	King's College, London, UK
Hasin Afzal Ahmed	Gauhati University, India
Rohit Agarwal	UiT The Arctic University of Norway, Norway
A. K. Agarwal	Sharda University, India
Fenty Eka Muzayyana Agustin	UIN Syarif Hidayatullah Jakarta, Indonesia
Gulfam Ahamad	BGSB University, India
Farhad Ahamed	Kent Institute, Australia
Zishan Ahmad	Indian Institute of Technology Patna, India
Mohammad Faizal Ahmad Fauzi	Multimedia University, Malaysia
Mudasir Ahmadganaie	Indian Institute of Technology Indore, India
Hasin Afzal Ahmed	Gauhati University, India
Sangtae Ahn	Kyungpook National University, South Korea
Md. Shad Akhtar	Indraprastha Institute of Information Technology, Delhi, India
Abdulrazak Yahya Saleh Alhababi	University of Malaysia, Sarawak, Malaysia
Ahmed Alharbi	RMIT University, Australia
Irfan Ali	Aligarh Muslim University, India
Ali Anaissi	CSIRO, Australia
Ashish Anand	Indian Institute of Technology, Guwahati, India
C. Anantaram	Indraprastha Institute of Information Technology and Tata Consultancy Services Ltd., India
Nur Afny C. Andryani	Universiti Teknologi Petronas, Malaysia
Marco Anisetti	Università degli Studi di Milano, Italy
Mohd Zeeshan Ansari	Jamia Millia Islamia, India
J. Anuradha	VIT, India
Ramakrishna Appicharla	Indian Institute of Technology Patna, India

He Chen	Hebei University of Technology, China
Hongxu Chen	University of Queensland, Australia
J. Chen	Dalian University of Technology, China
Jianhui Chen	Beijing University of Technology, China
Junxin Chen	Dalian University of Technology, China
Junyi Chen	City University of Hong Kong, China
Junying Chen	South China University of Technology, China
Lisi Chen	Hong Kong Baptist University, China
Mulin Chen	Northwestern Polytechnical University, China
Xiaocong Chen	University of New South Wales, Australia
Xiaofeng Chen	Chongqing Jiaotong University, China
Zhuangbin Chen	The Chinese University of Hong Kong, China
Long Cheng	Institute of Automation, China
Qingrong Cheng	Fudan University, China
Ruting Cheng	George Washington University, USA
Girija Chetty	University of Canberra, Australia
Manoj Chinnakotla	Microsoft R&D Pvt. Ltd., India
Andrew Chiou	CQ University, Australia
Sung-Bae Cho	Yonsei University, South Korea
Kupsze Choi	The Hong Kong Polytechnic University, China
Phatthanaphong Chomphuwiset	Mahasarakham University, Thailand
Fengyu Cong	Dalian University of Technology, China
Jose Alfredo Ferreira Costa	UFRN, Brazil
Ruxandra Liana Costea	Polytechnic University of Bucharest, Romania
Raphaël Couturier	University of Franche-Comte, France
Zhenyu Cui	Peking University, China
Zhihong Cui	Shandong University, China
Juan D. Velasquez	University of Chile, Chile
Rukshima Dabare	Murdoch University, Australia
Cherifi Dalila	University of Boumerdes, Algeria
Minh-Son Dao	National Institute of Information and Communications Technology, Japan
Tedjo Darmanto	STMIK AMIK Bandung, Indonesia
Debasmit Das	IIT Roorkee, India
Dipankar Das	Jadavpur University, India
Niladri Sekhar Dash	Indian Statistical Institute, Kolkata, India
Satya Ranjan Dash	KIIT University, India
Shubhajit Datta	Indian Institute of Technology, Kharagpur, India
Alok Debnath	Trinity College Dublin, Ireland
Amir Dehsarvi	Ludwig Maximilian University of Munich, Germany
Hangyu Deng	Waseda University, Japan

Mingcong Deng	Tokyo University of Agriculture and Technology, Japan
Zhaohong Deng	Jiangnan University, China
V. Susheela Devi	Indian Institute of Science, Bangalore, India
M. M. Dhabu	VNIT Nagpur, India
Dhimas Arief Dharmawan	Universitas Indonesia, Indonesia
Khaldoon Dhou	Texas A&M University Central Texas, USA
Gihan Dias	University of Moratuwa, Sri Lanka
Nat Dilokthanakul	Vidyasirimedhi Institute of Science and Technology, Thailand
Tai Dinh	Kyoto College of Graduate Studies for Informatics, Japan
Gaurav Dixit	Indian Institute of Technology Roorkee, India
Youcef Djenouri	SINTEF Digital, Norway
Hai Dong	RMIT University, Australia
Shichao Dong	Ping An Insurance Group, China
Mohit Dua	NIT Kurukshetra, India
Yijun Duan	Kyoto University, Japan
Shiv Ram Dubey	Indian Institute of Information Technology, Allahabad, India
Piotr Duda	Institute of Computational Intelligence/Czestochowa University of Technology, Poland
Sri Harsha Dumpala	Dalhousie University and Vector Institute, Canada
Hridoy Sankar Dutta	University of Cambridge, UK
Indranil Dutta	Jadavpur University, India
Pratik Dutta	Indian Institute of Technology Patna, India
Rudresh Dwivedi	Netaji Subhas University of Technology, India
Heba El-Fiqi	UNSW Canberra, Australia
Felix Engel	Leibniz Information Centre for Science and Technology (TIB), Germany
Akshay Fajge	Indian Institute of Technology Patna, India
Yuchun Fang	Shanghai University, China
Mohd Fazil	JMI, India
Zhengyang Feng	Shanghai Jiao Tong University, China
Zunlei Feng	Zhejiang University, China
Mauajama Firdaus	University of Alberta, Canada
Devi Fitrianah	Bina Nusantara University, Indonesia
Philippe Fournierviger	Shenzhen University, China
Wai-Keung Fung	Cardiff Metropolitan University, UK
Baban Gain	Indian Institute of Technology, Patna, India
Claudio Gallicchio	University of Pisa, Italy
Yongsheng Gao	Griffith University, Australia

Yunjun Gao	Zhejiang University, China
Vicente García Díaz	University of Oviedo, Spain
Arpit Garg	University of Adelaide, Australia
Chandan Gautam	I2R, A*STAR, Singapore
Yaswanth Gavini	University of Hyderabad, India
Tom Gedeon	Australian National University, Australia
Iuliana Georgescu	University of Bucharest, Romania
Deepanway Ghosal	Indian Institute of Technology Patna, India
Arjun Ghosh	National Institute of Technology Durgapur, India
Sanjukta Ghosh	IIT (BHU) Varanasi, India
Soumitra Ghosh	Indian Institute of Technology Patna, India
Pranav Goel	Bloomberg L.P., India
Tripti Goel	National Institute of Technology Silchar, India
Kah Ong Michael Goh	Multimedia University, Malaysia
Kam Meng Goh	Tunku Abdul Rahman University of Management and Technology, Malaysia
Iqbal Gondal	RMIT University, Australia
Puneet Goyal	Indian Institute of Technology Ropar, India
Vishal Goyal	Punjabi University Patiala, India
Xiaotong Gu	University of Tasmania, Australia
Radha Krishna Guntur	VNRVJIET, India
Li Guo	University of Macau, China
Ping Guo	Beijing Normal University, China
Yu Guo	Xi'an Jiaotong University, China
Akshansh Gupta	CSIR-Central Electronics Engineering Research Institute, India
Deepak Gupta	National Library of Medicine, National Institutes of Health (NIH), USA
Deepak Gupta	NIT Arunachal Pradesh, India
Kamal Gupta	NIT Patna, India
Kapil Gupta	PDPM IIITDM, Jabalpur, India
Komal Gupta	IIT Patna, India
Christophe Guyeux	University of Franche-Comte, France
Katsuyuki Hagiwara	Mie University, Japan
Soyeon Han	University of Sydney, Australia
Palak Handa	IGDTUW, India
Rahmadya Handayanto	Universitas Islam 45 Bekasi, Indonesia
Ahteshamul Haq	Aligarh Muslim University, India
Muhammad Haris	Universitas Nusa Mandiri, Indonesia
Harith Al-Sahaf	Victoria University of Wellington, New Zealand
Md Rakibul Hasan	BRAC University, Bangladesh
Mohammed Hasanuzzaman	ADAPT Centre, Ireland

Takako Hashimoto	Chiba University of Commerce, Japan
Bipan Hazarika	Gauhati University, India
Huiguang He	Institute of Automation, Chinese Academy of Sciences, China
Wei He	University of Science and Technology Beijing, China
Xinwei He	University of Illinois Urbana-Champaign, USA
Enna Hirata	Kobe University, Japan
Akira Hirose	University of Tokyo, Japan
Katsuhiro Honda	Osaka Metropolitan University, Japan
Huy Hongnguyen	National Institute of Informatics, Japan
Wai Lam Hoo	University of Malaya, Malaysia
Shih Hsiung Lee	National Cheng Kung University, Taiwan
Jiankun Hu	UNSW@ADFA, Australia
Yanyan Hu	University of Science and Technology Beijing, China
Chaoran Huang	UNSW Sydney, Australia
He Huang	Soochow University, Taiwan
Ko-Wei Huang	National Kaohsiung University of Science and Technology, Taiwan
Shudong Huang	Sichuan University, China
Chih-Chieh Hung	National Chung Hsing University, Taiwan
Mohamed Ibn Khedher	IRT-SystemX, France
David Iclanzan	Sapientia Hungarian University of Transylvania, Romania
Cosimo Ieracitano	University "Mediterranea" of Reggio Calabria, Italy
Kazushi Ikeda	Nara Institute of Science and Technology, Japan
Hiroaki Inoue	Kobe University, Japan
Teijiro Isokawa	University of Hyogo, Japan
Kokila Jagadeesh	Indian Institute of Information Technology, Allahabad, India
Mukesh Jain	Jawaharlal Nehru University, India
Fuad Jamour	AWS, USA
Mohd. Javed	Indian Institute of Information Technology, Allahabad, India
Balasubramaniam Jayaram	Indian Institute of Technology Hyderabad, India
Jin-Tsong Jeng	National Formosa University, Taiwan
Sungmoon Jeong	Kyungpook National University Hospital, South Korea
Yizhang Jiang	Jiangnan University, China
Ferdinjoe Johnjoseph	Thai-Nichi Institute of Technology, Thailand
Alireza Jolfaei	Federation University, Australia

Ratnesh Joshi	Indian Institute of Technology Patna, India
Roshan Joymartis	Global Academy of Technology, India
Chen Junjie	IMAU, The Netherlands
Ashwini K.	Global Academy of Technology, India
Asoke K. Talukder	National Institute of Technology Karnataka - Surathkal, India
Ashad Kabir	Charles Sturt University, Australia
Narendra Kadoo	CSIR-National Chemical Laboratory, India
Seifedine Kadry	Noroff University College, Norway
M. Shamim Kaiser	Jahangirnagar University, Bangladesh
Ashraf Kamal	ACL Digital, India
Sabyasachi Kamila	Indian Institute of Technology Patna, India
Tomoyuki Kaneko	University of Tokyo, Japan
Rajkumar Kannan	Bishop Heber College, India
Hamid Karimi	Utah State University, USA
Nikola Kasabov	AUT, New Zealand
Dermot Kerr	University of Ulster, UK
Abhishek Kesarwani	NIT Rourkela, India
Shwet Ketu	Shambhunath Institute of Engineering and Technology, India
Asif Khan	Integral University, India
Tariq Khan	UNSW, Australia
Thaweesak Khongtuk	Rajamangala University of Technology Suvarnabhumi (RMUTSB), India
Abbas Khosravi	Deakin University, Australia
Thanh Tung Khuat	University of Technology Sydney, Australia
Junae Kim	DST Group, Australia
Sangwook Kim	Kobe University, Japan
Mutsumi Kimura	Ryukoku University, Japan
Uday Kiran	University of Aizu, Japan
Hisashi Koga	University of Electro-Communications, Japan
Yasuharu Koike	Tokyo Institute of Technology, Japan
Ven Jyn Kok	Universiti Kebangsaan Malaysia, Malaysia
Praveen Kolli	Pinterest Inc, USA
Sunil Kumar Kopparapu	Tata Consultancy Services Ltd., India
Fajri Koto	MBZUAI, UAE
Aneesh Krishna	Curtin University, Australia
Parameswari Krishnamurthy	University of Hyderabad, India
Malhar Kulkarni	IIT Bombay, India
Abhinav Kumar	NIT, Patna, India
Abhishek Kumar	Indian Institute of Technology Patna, India
Amit Kumar	Tarento Technologies Pvt Limited, India

Nagendra Kumar	IIT Indore, India
Pranaw Kumar	Centre for Development of Advanced Computing (CDAC) Mumbai, India
Puneet Kumar	Jawaharlal Nehru University, India
Raja Kumar	Taylor's University, Malaysia
Sachin Kumar	University of Delhi, India
Sandeep Kumar	IIT Patna, India
Sanjaya Kumar Panda	National Institute of Technology, Warangal, India
Chouhan Kumar Rath	National Institute of Technology, Durgapur, India
Sovan Kumar Sahoo	Indian Institute of Technology Patna, India
Anil Kumar Singh	IIT (BHU) Varanasi, India
Vikash Kumar Singh	VIT-AP University, India
Sanjay Kumar Sonbhadra	ITER, SoA, Odisha, India
Gitanjali Kumari	Indian Institute of Technology Patna, India
Rina Kumari	KIIT, India
Amit Kumarsingh	National Institute of Technology Patna, India
Sanjay Kumarsonbhadra	SSITM, India
Vishesh Kumar Tanwar	Missouri University of Science and Technology, USA
Bibekananda Kundu	CDAC Kolkata, India
Yoshimitsu Kuroki	Kurume National College of Technology, Japan
Susumu Kuroyanagi	Nagoya Institute of Technology, Japan
Retno Kusumaningrum	Universitas Diponegoro, Indonesia
Dwina Kuswardani	Institut Teknologi PLN, Indonesia
Stephen Kwok	Murdoch University, Australia
Hamid Laga	Murdoch University, Australia
Edmund Lai	Auckland University of Technology, New Zealand
Weng Kin Lai	Tunku Abdul Rahman University of Management & Technology (TAR UMT), Malaysia
Kittichai Lavangnananda	King Mongkut's University of Technology Thonburi (KMUTT), Thailand
Anwesha Law	Indian Statistical Institute, India
Thao Le	Deakin University, Australia
Xinyi Le	Shanghai Jiao Tong University, China
Dong-Gyu Lee	Kyungpook National University, South Korea
Eui Chul Lee	Sangmyung University, South Korea
Minho Lee	Kyungpook National University, South Korea
Shih Hsiung Lee	National Kaohsiung University of Science and Technology, Taiwan
Gurpreet Lehal	Punjabi University, India
Jiahuan Lei	Meituan-Dianping Group, China

Pui Huang Leong	Tunku Abdul Rahman University of Management and Technology, Malaysia
Chi Sing Leung	City University of Hong Kong, China
Man-Fai Leung	Anglia Ruskin University, UK
Bing-Zhao Li	Beijing Institute of Technology, China
Gang Li	Deakin University, Australia
Jiawei Li	Tsinghua University, China
Mengmeng Li	Zhengzhou University, China
Xiangtao Li	Jilin University, China
Yang Li	East China Normal University, China
Yantao Li	Chongqing University, China
Yaxin Li	Michigan State University, USA
Yiming Li	Tsinghua University, China
Yuankai Li	University of Science and Technology of China, China
Yun Li	Nanjing University of Posts and Telecommunications, China
Zhipeng Li	Tsinghua University, China
Hualou Liang	Drexel University, USA
Xiao Liang	Nankai University, China
Hao Liao	Shenzhen University, China
Alan Wee-Chung Liew	Griffith University, Australia
Chern Hong Lim	Monash University Malaysia, Malaysia
Kok Lim Yau	Universiti Tunku Abdul Rahman (UTAR), Malaysia
Chin-Teng Lin	UTS, Australia
Jerry Chun-Wei Lin	Western Norway University of Applied Sciences, Norway
Jiecong Lin	City University of Hong Kong, China
Dugang Liu	Shenzhen University, China
Feng Liu	Stevens Institute of Technology, USA
Hongtao Liu	Du Xiaoman Financial, China
Ju Liu	Shandong University, China
Linjing Liu	City University of Hong Kong, China
Weifeng Liu	China University of Petroleum (East China), China
Wenqiang Liu	Hong Kong Polytechnic University, China
Xin Liu	National Institute of Advanced Industrial Science and Technology (AIST), Japan
Yang Liu	Harbin Institute of Technology, China
Zhi-Yong Liu	Institute of Automation, Chinese Academy of Sciences, China
Zongying Liu	Dalian Maritime University, China

Jaime Lloret	Universitat Politècnica de València, Spain
Sye Loong Keoh	University of Glasgow, Singapore, Singapore
Hongtao Lu	Shanghai Jiao Tong University, China
Wenlian Lu	Fudan University, China
Xuequan Lu	Deakin University, Australia
Xiao Luo	UCLA, USA
Guozheng Ma	Shenzhen International Graduate School, Tsinghua University, China
Qianli Ma	South China University of Technology, China
Wanli Ma	University of Canberra, Australia
Muhammad Anwar Ma'sum	Universitas Indonesia, Indonesia
Michele Magno	University of Bologna, Italy
Sainik Kumar Mahata	JU, India
Shalni Mahato	Indian Institute of Information Technology (IIIT) Ranchi, India
Adnan Mahmood	Macquarie University, Australia
Mohammed Mahmoud	October University for Modern Sciences & Arts - MSA University, Egypt
Mufti Mahmud	University of Padova, Italy
Krishanu Maity	Indian Institute of Technology Patna, India
Mamta	IIT Patna, India
Aprinaldi Mantau	Kyushu Institute of Technology, Japan
Mohsen Marjani	Taylor's University, Malaysia
Sanparith Marukatat	NECTEC, Thailand
José María Luna	Universidad de Córdoba, Spain
Archana Mathur	Nitte Meenakshi Institute of Technology, India
Patrick McAllister	Ulster University, UK
Piotr Milczarski	Lodz University of Technology, Poland
Kshitij Mishra	IIT Patna, India
Pruthwik Mishra	IIIT-Hyderabad, India
Santosh Mishra	Indian Institute of Technology Patna, India
Sajib Mistry	Curtin University, Australia
Sayantan Mitra	Accenture Labs, India
Vinay Kumar Mittal	Neti International Research Center, India
Daisuke Miyamoto	University of Tokyo, Japan
Kazuteru Miyazaki	National Institution for Academic Degrees and Quality Enhancement of Higher Education, Japan
U. Mmodibbo	Modibbo Adama University Yola, Nigeria
Aditya Mogadala	Saarland University, Germany
Reem Mohamed	Mansoura University, Egypt
Muhammad Syafiq Mohd Pozi	Universiti Utara Malaysia, Malaysia

Anirban Mondal   University of Tokyo, Japan
Anupam Mondal   Jadavpur University, India
Supriyo Mondal   ZBW - Leibniz Information Centre for
                                   Economics, Germany
J. Manuel Moreno   Universitat Politècnica de Catalunya, Spain
Francisco J. Moreno-Barea   Universidad de Málaga, Spain
Sakchai Muangsrinoon   Walailak University, Thailand
Siti Anizah Muhamed   Politeknik Sultan Salahuddin Abdul Aziz Shah,
                                   Malaysia
Samrat Mukherjee   Indian Institute of Technology, Patna, India
Siddhartha Mukherjee   Samsung R&D Institute India, Bangalore, India
Dharmalingam Muthusamy   Bharathiar University, India
Abhijith Athreya Mysore   Pennsylvania State University, USA
   Gopinath
Harikrishnan N. B.   BITS Pilani K K Birla Goa Campus, India
Usman Naseem   University of Sydney, Australia
Deepak Nayak   Malaviya National Institute of Technology, Jaipur,
                                   India
Hamada Nayel   Benha University, Egypt
Usman Nazir   Lahore University of Management Sciences,
                                   Pakistan
Vasudevan Nedumpozhimana   TU Dublin, Ireland
Atul Negi   University of Hyderabad, India
Aneta Neumann   University of Adelaide, Australia
Hea Choon Ngo   Universiti Teknikal Malaysia Melaka, Malaysia
Dang Nguyen   University of Canberra, Australia
Duy Khuong Nguyen   FPT Software Ltd., FPT Group, Vietnam
Hoang D. Nguyen   University College Cork, Ireland
Hong Huy Nguyen   National Institute of Informatics, Japan
Tam Nguyen   Leibniz University Hannover, Germany
Thanh-Son Nguyen   Agency for Science, Technology and Research
                                   (A*STAR), Singapore
Vu-Linh Nguyen   Eindhoven University of Technology, Netherlands
Nick Nikzad   Griffith University, Australia
Boda Ning   Swinburne University of Technology, Australia
Haruhiko Nishimura   University of Hyogo, Japan
Kishorjit Nongmeikapam   Indian Institute of Information Technology (IIIT)
                                   Manipur, India
Aleksandra Nowak   Jagiellonian University, Poland
Stavros Ntalampiras   University of Milan, Italy
Anupiya Nugaliyadde   Sri Lanka Institute of Information Technology,
                                   Sri Lanka

Anto Satriyo Nugroho	Agency for Assessment & Application of Technology, Indonesia
Aparajita Ojha	PDPM IIITDM Jabalpur, India
Akeem Olowolayemo	International Islamic University Malaysia, Malaysia
Toshiaki Omori	Kobe University, Japan
Shih Yin Ooi	Multimedia University, Malaysia
Sidali Ouadfeul	Algerian Petroleum Institute, Algeria
Samir Ouchani	CESI Lineact, France
Srinivas P. Y. K. L.	IIIT Sri City, India
Neelamadhab Padhy	GIET University, India
Worapat Paireekreng	Dhurakij Pundit University, Thailand
Partha Pakray	National Institute of Technology Silchar, India
Santanu Pal	Wipro Limited, India
Bin Pan	Nankai University, China
Rrubaa Panchendrarajan	Sri Lanka Institute of Information Technology, Sri Lanka
Pankaj Pandey	Indian Institute of Technology, Gandhinagar, India
Lie Meng Pang	Southern University of Science and Technology, China
Sweta Panigrahi	National Institute of Technology Warangal, India
T. Pant	IIIT Allahabad, India
Shantipriya Parida	Idiap Research Institute, Switzerland
Hyeyoung Park	Kyungpook National University, South Korea
Md Aslam Parwez	Jamia Millia Islamia, India
Leandro Pasa	Federal University of Technology - Parana (UTFPR), Brazil
Kitsuchart Pasupa	King Mongkut's Institute of Technology Ladkrabang, Thailand
Debanjan Pathak	Kalinga Institute of Industrial Technology (KIIT), India
Vyom Pathak	University of Florida, USA
Sangameshwar Patil	TCS Research, India
Bidyut Kr. Patra	IIT (BHU) Varanasi, India
Dipanjyoti Paul	Indian Institute of Technology Patna, India
Sayanta Paul	Ola, India
Sachin Pawar	Tata Consultancy Services Ltd., India
Pornntiwa Pawara	Mahasarakham University, Thailand
Yong Peng	Hangzhou Dianzi University, China
Yusuf Perwej	Ambalika Institute of Management and Technology (AIMT), India
Olutomilayo Olayemi Petinrin	City University of Hong Kong, China
Arpan Phukan	Indian Institute of Technology Patna, India

Chiara Picardi	University of York, UK
Francesco Piccialli	University of Naples Federico II, Italy
Josephine Plested	University of New South Wales, Australia
Krishna Reddy Polepalli	IIIT Hyderabad, India
Dan Popescu	University Politehnica of Bucharest, Romania
Heru Praptono	Bank Indonesia/UI, Indonesia
Mukesh Prasad	University of Technology Sydney, Australia
Yamuna Prasad	Thompson Rivers University, Canada
Krishna Prasadmiyapuram	IIT Gandhinagar, India
Partha Pratim Sarangi	KIIT Deemed to be University, India
Emanuele Principi	Università Politecnica delle Marche, Italy
Dimeter Prodonov	Imec, Belgium
Ratchakoon Pruengkarn	College of Innovative Technology and Engineering, Dhurakij Pundit University, Thailand
Michal Ptaszynski	Kitami Institute of Technology, Japan
Narinder Singh Punn	Mayo Clinic, Arizona, USA
Abhinanda Ranjit Punnakkal	UiT The Arctic University of Norway, Norway
Zico Pratama Putra	Queen Mary University of London, UK
Zhenyue Qin	Tencent, China
Nawab Muhammad Faseeh Qureshi	SU, South Korea
Md Rafiqul	UTS, Australia
Saifur Rahaman	City University of Hong Kong, China
Shri Rai	Murdoch University, Australia
Vartika Rai	IIIT Hyderabad, India
Kiran Raja	Norwegian University of Science and Technology, Norway
Sutharshan Rajasegarar	Deakin University, Australia
Arief Ramadhan	Bina Nusantara University, Indonesia
Mallipeddi Rammohan	Kyungpook National University, South Korea
Md. Mashud Rana	Commonwealth Scientific and Industrial Research Organisation (CSIRO), Australia
Surangika Ranathunga	University of Moratuwa, Sri Lanka
Soumya Ranjan Mishra	KIIT University, India
Hemant Rathore	Birla Institute of Technology & Science, Pilani, India
Imran Razzak	UNSW, Australia
Yazhou Ren	University of Science and Technology of China, China
Motahar Reza	GITAM University Hyderabad, India
Dwiza Riana	STMIK Nusa Mandiri, Indonesia
Bharat Richhariya	BITS Pilani, India

Pattabhi R. K. Rao	AU-KBC Research Centre, India
Heejun Roh	Korea University, South Korea
Vijay Rowtula	IIIT Hyderabad, India
Aniruddha Roy	IIT Kharagpur, India
Sudipta Roy	Jio Institute, India
Narendra S. Chaudhari	Indian Institute of Technology Indore, India
Fariza Sabrina	Central Queensland University, Australia
Debanjan Sadhya	ABV-IIITM Gwalior, India
Sumit Sah	IIT Dharwad, India
Atanu Saha	Jadavpur University, India
Sajib Saha	Commonwealth Scientific and Industrial Research Organisation, Australia
Snehanshu Saha	BITS Pilani K K Birla Goa Campus, India
Tulika Saha	IIT Patna, India
Navanath Saharia	Indian Institute of Information Technology Manipur, India
Pracheta Sahoo	University of Texas at Dallas, USA
Sovan Kumar Sahoo	Indian Institute of Technology Patna, India
Tanik Saikh	L3S Research Center, Germany
Naveen Saini	Indian Institute of Information Technology Lucknow, India
Fumiaki Saitoh	Chiba Institute of Technology, Japan
Rohit Salgotra	Swansea University, UK
Michel Salomon	Univ. Bourgogne Franche-Comté, France
Yu Sang	Research Institute of Institute of Computing Technology, Exploration and Development, Liaohe Oilfield, PetroChina, China
Suyash Sangwan	Indian Institute of Technology Patna, India
Soubhagya Sankar Barpanda	VIT-AP University, India
Jose A. Santos	Ulster University, UK
Kamal Sarkar	Jadavpur University, India
Sandip Sarkar	Jadavpur University, India
Naoyuki Sato	Future University Hakodate, Japan
Eri Sato-Shimokawara	Tokyo Metropolitan University, Japan
Sunil Saumya	Indian Institute of Information Technology Dharwad, India
Gerald Schaefer	Loughborough University, UK
Rafal Scherer	Czestochowa University of Technology, Poland
Arvind Selwal	Central University of Jammu, India
Noor Akhmad Setiawan	Universitas Gadjah Mada, Indonesia
Mohammad Shahid	Aligarh Muslim University, India
Jie Shao	University of Science and Technology of China, China

Nabin Sharma	University of Technology Sydney, Australia
Raksha Sharma	IIT Bombay, India
Sourabh Sharma	Avantika University, India
Suraj Sharma	International Institute of Information Technology Bhubaneswar, India
Ravi Shekhar	Queen Mary University of London, UK
Michael Sheng	Macquarie University, Australia
Yin Sheng	Huazhong University of Science and Technology, China
Yongpan Sheng	Southwest University, China
Liu Shenglan	Dalian University of Technology, China
Tomohiro Shibata	Kyushu Institute of Technology, Japan
Iksoo Shin	University of Science & Technology, China
Mohd Fairuz Shiratuddin	Murdoch University, Australia
Hayaru Shouno	University of Electro-Communications, Japan
Sanyam Shukla	MANIT, Bhopal, India
Udom Silparcha	KMUTT, Thailand
Apoorva Singh	Indian Institute of Technology Patna, India
Divya Singh	Central University of Bihar, India
Gitanjali Singh	Indian Institute of Technology Patna, India
Gopendra Singh	Indian Institute of Technology Patna, India
K. P. Singh	IIIT Allahabad, India
Navjot Singh	IIIT Allahabad, India
Om Singh	NIT Patna, India
Pardeep Singh	Jawaharlal Nehru University, India
Rajiv Singh	Banasthali Vidyapith, India
Sandhya Singh	Indian Institute of Technology Bombay, India
Smriti Singh	IIT Bombay, India
Narinder Singhpunn	Mayo Clinic, Arizona, USA
Saaveethya Sivakumar	Curtin University, Malaysia
Ferdous Sohel	Murdoch University, Australia
Chattrakul Sombattheera	Mahasarakham University, Thailand
Lei Song	Unitec Institute of Technology, New Zealand
Linqi Song	City University of Hong Kong, China
Yuhua Song	University of Science and Technology Beijing, China
Gautam Srivastava	Brandon University, Canada
Rajeev Srivastava	Banaras Hindu University (IT-BHU), Varanasi, India
Jérémie Sublime	ISEP - Institut Supérieur d'Électronique de Paris, France
P. N. Suganthan	Nanyang Technological University, Singapore

Derwin Suhartono	Bina Nusantara University, Indonesia
Indra Adji Sulistijono	Politeknik Elektronika Negeri Surabaya (PENS), Indonesia
John Sum	National Chung Hsing University, Taiwan
Fuchun Sun	Tsinghua University, China
Ning Sun	Nankai University, China
Anindya Sundar Das	Indian Institute of Technology Patna, India
Bapi Raju Surampudi	International Institute of Information Technology Hyderabad, India
Olarik Surinta	Mahasarakham University, Thailand
Maria Susan Anggreainy	Bina Nusantara University, Indonesia
M. Syafrullah	Universitas Budi Luhur, Indonesia
Murtaza Taj	Lahore University of Management Sciences, Pakistan
Norikazu Takahashi	Okayama University, Japan
Abdelmalik Taleb-Ahmed	Polytechnic University of Hauts-de-France, France
Hakaru Tamukoh	Kyushu Institute of Technology, Japan
Choo Jun Tan	Wawasan Open University, Malaysia
Chuanqi Tan	BIT, China
Shing Chiang Tan	Multimedia University, Malaysia
Xiao Jian Tan	Tunku Abdul Rahman University of Management and Technology (TAR UMT), Malaysia
Xin Tan	East China Normal University, China
Ying Tan	Peking University, China
Gouhei Tanaka	University of Tokyo, Japan
Yang Tang	East China University of Science and Technology, China
Zhiri Tang	City University of Hong Kong, China
Tanveer Tarray	Islamic University of Science and Technology, India
Chee Siong Teh	Universiti Malaysia Sarawak (UNIMAS), Malaysia
Ya-Wen Teng	Academia Sinica, Taiwan
Gaurish Thakkar	University of Zagreb, Croatia
Medari Tham	St. Anthony's College, India
Selvarajah Thuseethan	Sabaragamuwa University of Sri Lanka, Sri Lanka
Shu Tian	University of Science and Technology Beijing, China
Massimo Tistarelli	University of Sassari, Italy
Abhisek Tiwari	IIT Patna, India
Uma Shanker Tiwary	Indian Institute of Information Technology, Allahabad, India

Alex To	University of Sydney, Australia
Stefania Tomasiello	University of Tartu, Estonia
Anh Duong Trinh	Technological University Dublin, Ireland
Enkhtur Tsogbaatar	Mongolian University of Science and Technology, Mongolia
Enmei Tu	Shanghai Jiao Tong University, China
Eiji Uchino	Yamaguchi University, Japan
Prajna Upadhyay	IIT Delhi, India
Sahand Vahidnia	University of New South Wales, Australia
Ashwini Vaidya	IIT Delhi, India
Deeksha Varshney	Indian Institute of Technology, Patna, India
Sowmini Devi Veeramachaneni	Mahindra University, India
Samudra Vijaya	Koneru Lakshmaiah Education Foundation, India
Surbhi Vijh	JSS Academy of Technical Education, Noida, India
Nhi N. Y. Vo	University of Technology Sydney, Australia
Xuan-Son Vu	Umeå University, Sweden
Anil Kumar Vuppala	IIIT Hyderabad, India
Nobuhiko Wagatsuma	Toho University, Japan
Feng Wan	University of Macau, China
Bingshu Wang	Northwestern Polytechnical University Taicang Campus, China
Dianhui Wang	La Trobe University, Australia
Ding Wang	Beijing University of Technology, China
Guanjin Wang	Murdoch University, Australia
Jiasen Wang	City University of Hong Kong, China
Lei Wang	Beihang University, China
Libo Wang	Xiamen University of Technology, China
Meng Wang	Southeast University, China
Qiu-Feng Wang	Xi'an Jiaotong-Liverpool University, China
Sheng Wang	Henan University, China
Weiqun Wang	Institute of Automation, Chinese Academy of Sciences, China
Wentao Wang	Michigan State University, USA
Yongyu Wang	Michigan Technological University, USA
Zhijin Wang	Jimei University, China
Bunthit Watanapa	KMUTT-SIT, Thailand
Yanling Wei	TU Berlin, Germany
Guanghui Wen	RMIT University, Australia
Ari Wibisono	Universitas Indonesia, Indonesia
Adi Wibowo	Diponegoro University, Indonesia
Ka-Chun Wong	City University of Hong Kong, China

Kevin Wong	Murdoch University, Australia
Raymond Wong	Universiti Malaya, Malaysia
Kuntpong Woraratpanya	King Mongkut's Institute of Technology Ladkrabang (KMITL), Thailand
Marcin Woźniak	Silesian University of Technology, Poland
Chengwei Wu	Harbin Institute of Technology, China
Jing Wu	Shanghai Jiao Tong University, China
Weibin Wu	Sun Yat-sen University, China
Hongbing Xia	Beijing Normal University, China
Tao Xiang	Chongqing University, China
Qiang Xiao	Huazhong University of Science and Technology, China
Guandong Xu	University of Technology Sydney, Australia
Qing Xu	Tianjin University, China
Yifan Xu	Huazhong University of Science and Technology, China
Junyu Xuan	University of Technology Sydney, Australia
Hui Xue	Southeast University, China
Saumitra Yadav	IIIT-Hyderabad, India
Shekhar Yadav	Madan Mohan Malaviya University of Technology, India
Sweta Yadav	University of Illinois at Chicago, USA
Tarun Yadav	Defence Research and Development Organisation, India
Shankai Yan	Hainan University, China
Feidiao Yang	Microsoft, China
Gang Yang	Renmin University of China, China
Haiqin Yang	International Digital Economy Academy, China
Jianyi Yang	Shandong University, China
Jinfu Yang	BJUT, China
Minghao Yang	Institute of Automation, Chinese Academy of Sciences, China
Shaofu Yang	Southeast University, China
Wachira Yangyuen	Rajamangala University of Technology Srivijaya, Thailand
Xinye Yi	Guilin University of Electronic Technology, China
Hang Yu	Shanghai University, China
Wen Yu	Cinvestav, Mexico
Wenxin Yu	Southwest University of Science and Technology, China
Zhaoyuan Yu	Nanjing Normal University, China
Ye Yuan	Xi'an Jiaotong University, China
Xiaodong Yue	Shanghai University, China

Aizan Zafar	Indian Institute of Technology Patna, India
Jichuan Zeng	Bytedance, China
Jie Zhang	Newcastle University, UK
Shixiong Zhang	Xidian University, China
Tianlin Zhang	University of Manchester, UK
Mingbo Zhao	Donghua University, China
Shenglin Zhao	Zhejiang University, China
Guoqiang Zhong	Ocean University of China, China
Jinghui Zhong	South China University of Technology, China
Bo Zhou	Southwest University, China
Yucheng Zhou	University of Technology Sydney, Australia
Dengya Zhu	Curtin University, Australia
Xuanying Zhu	ANU, Australia
Hua Zuo	University of Technology Sydney, Australia

Additional Reviewers

Acharya, Rajul	Doborjeh, Maryam
Afrin, Mahbuba	Dong, Zhuben
Alsuhaibani, Abdullah	Dutta, Subhabrata
Amarnath	Dybala, Pawel
Appicharla, Ramakrishna	El Achkar, Charbel
Arora, Ridhi	Feng, Zhengyang
Azar, Joseph	Galkowski, Tomasz
Bai, Weiwei	Garg, Arpit
Bao, Xiwen	Ghobakhlou, Akbar
Barawi, Mohamad Hardyman	Ghosh, Soumitra
Bhat, Mohammad Idrees Bhat	Guo, Hui
Cai, Taotao	Gupta, Ankur
Cao, Feiqi	Gupta, Deepak
Chakraborty, Bodhi	Gupta, Megha
Chang, Yu-Cheng	Han, Yanyang
Chen	Han, Yiyan
Chen, Jianpeng	Hang, Bin
Chen, Yong	Harshit
Chhipa, Priyank	He, Silu
Cho, Joshua	Hua, Ning
Chongyang, Chen	Huang, Meng
Cuenat, Stéphane	Huang, Rongting
Dang, Lili	Huang, Xiuyu
Das Chakladar, Debashis	Hussain, Zawar
Das, Kishalay	Imran, Javed
Dey, Monalisa	Islam, Md Rafiqul

Jain, Samir
Jia, Mei
Jiang, Jincen
Jiang, Xiao
Jiangyu, Wang
Jiaxin, Lou
Jiaxu, Hou
Jinzhou, Bao
Ju, Wei
Kasyap, Harsh
Katai, Zoltan
Keserwani, Prateek
Khan, Asif
Khan, Muhammad Fawad Akbar
Khari, Manju
Kheiri, Kiana
Kirk, Nathan
Kiyani, Arslan
Kolya, Anup Kumar
Krdzavac, Nenad
Kumar, Lov
Kumar, Mukesh
Kumar, Puneet
Kumar, Rahul
Kumar, Sunil
Lan, Meng
Lavangnananda, Kittichai
Li, Qian
Li, Xiaoou
Li, Xin
Li, Xinjia
Liang, Mengnan
Liang, Shuai
Liquan, Li
Liu, Boyang
Liu, Chang
Liu, Feng
Liu, Linjing
Liu, Xinglan
Liu, Xinling
Liu, Zhe
Lotey, Taveena
Ma, Bing
Ma, Zeyu
Madanian, Samaneh

Mahata, Sainik Kumar
Mahmud, Md. Redowan
Man, Jingtao
Meena, Kunj Bihari
Mishra, Pragnyaban
Mistry, Sajib
Modibbo, Umar Muhammad
Na, Na
Nag Choudhury, Somenath
Nampalle, Kishore
Nandi, Palash
Neupane, Dhiraj
Nigam, Nitika
Nigam, Swati
Ning, Jianbo
Oumer, Jehad
Pandey, Abhineet Kumar
Pandey, Sandeep
Paramita, Adi Suryaputra
Paul, Apurba
Petinrin, Olutomilayo Olayemi
Phan Trong, Dat
Pradana, Muhamad Hilmil Muchtar Aditya
Pundhir, Anshul
Rahman, Sheikh Shah Mohammad Motiur
Rai, Sawan
Rajesh, Bulla
Rajput, Amitesh Singh
Rao, Raghunandan K. R.
Rathore, Santosh Singh
Ray, Payel
Roy, Satyaki
Saini, Nikhil
Saki, Mahdi
Salimath, Nagesh
Sang, Haiwei
Shao, Jian
Sharma, Anshul
Sharma, Shivam
Shi, Jichen
Shi, Jun
Shi, Kaize
Shi, Li
Singh, Nagendra Pratap
Singh, Pritpal

Singh, Rituraj
Singh, Shrey
Singh, Tribhuvan
Song, Meilun
Song, Yuhua
Soni, Bharat
Stommel, Martin
Su, Yanchi
Sun, Xiaoxuan
Suryodiningrat, Satrio Pradono
Swarnkar, Mayank
Tammewar, Aniruddha
Tan, Xiaosu
Tanoni, Giulia
Tanwar, Vishesh
Tao, Yuwen
To, Alex
Tran, Khuong
Varshney, Ayush
Vo, Anh-Khoa
Vuppala, Anil
Wang, Hui
Wang, Kai
Wang, Rui
Wang, Xia
Wang, Yansong

Wang, Yuan
Wang, Yunhe
Watanapa, Saowaluk
Wenqian, Fan
Xia, Hongbing
Xie, Weidun
Xiong, Wenxin
Xu, Zhehao
Xu, Zhikun
Yan, Bosheng
Yang, Haoran
Yang, Jie
Yang, Xin
Yansui, Song
Yu, Cunzhe
Yu, Zhuohan
Zandavi, Seid Miad
Zeng, Longbin
Zhang, Jane
Zhang, Ruolan
Zhang, Ziqi
Zhao, Chen
Zhou, Xinxin
Zhou, Zihang
Zhu, Liao
Zhu, Linghui

Contents – Part VII

Applications II

An Interpretable Multi-target Regression Method for Hierarchical Load Forecasting

Zipeng Wu[1], Chu Kiong Loo[1], Kitsuchart Pasupa[2(✉)] (iD), and Licheng Xu[1]

[1] Faculty of Computer Science and Information Technology, University of Malaya, 50603 Kuala Lumpur, Malaysia
{s2013980,s2011558}@siswa.um.edu.my, ckloo.um@um.edu.my
[2] School of Information Technology, King Mongkut's Institute of Technology Ladkrabang, Bangkok 10520, Thailand
kitsuchart@it.kmitl.ac.th

Abstract. Accurate energy load forecasting provides good decision support for energy management. Current energy load forecasts focus more on forecast accuracy without exploring the similar patterns and correlations of energy load demand between regions. Our proposed interpretable hybrid multi-target regression approach provides more explanatory abilities for each region's energy load prediction. After combining the correlation between forecast targets and hierarchical forecast information, our model achieves a high forecast accuracy in that the mean square error is reduced by three quarters compared to LightGBM's independent prediction for each region on the GEFCom 2017 dataset.

Keywords: Multi-target prediction · Interpretable machine learning · Energy load prediction

1 Introduction

In recent years, changing market competition, aging infrastructure, and the requirement for integrating renewable energy sources have made probabilistic load forecasting increasingly crucial to planning and operating energy systems. Since the Global Energy Forecasting Competition (GEFCom) series was held, load forecasting has received more attention from researchers. The related work can be divided into two categories according to the modeling methods used. One is the use of traditional methods such as Auto-regressive model, Auto-regressive Integrated Moving Average, Kernel Density Estimation, and Error, Trend, Seasonal (ETS) [2,11], which have the advantage of simple model structures and focus on pre-processing the data to improve model accuracy, such as removing outliers, decomposing components of the series data, and extracting seasonal features. Traditional methods can also achieve good results in short-term prediction, but the prediction performance is limited because of the lack of other external features. Another category is machine learning methods, such as Quantile Regression [5,8,17,18], Linear Regression, and Gradient Boosting

© The Author(s), under exclusive license to Springer Nature Singapore Pte Ltd. 2023
M. Tanveer et al. (Eds.): ICONIP 2022, CCIS 1794, pp. 3–12, 2023.
https://doi.org/10.1007/978-981-99-1648-1_1

Machine (GBM) [12,13], where the accuracy of these models depends on the feature selection [7] and feature generation components. These machine learning methods are more suitable for long-time series and are the most accurate load prediction methods. Neural network models [1], although prevalent today, are still a relatively new approach to the load forecasting problem. From the GEF-Com 2017 competition results, neural network model methods did not make the top five among 177 teams [3]. In addition, energy load hierarchical forecasting can better meet the practical needs of power decision-making, and the forecasting model that combines hierarchical information can obtain higher forecasting accuracy.

However, they have two limitations: (i) They did not consider the relationship between prediction targets. For example, the nearby city's energy load demand may have the same pattern of changing due to the same external environment and the same style of life. (ii) Traditional energy load prediction improves overall prediction accuracy, but they are not interpretable. Interpretable machine learning techniques can give the corresponding explanation to make the model's prediction more reliable. In addition, it can better extract and interpret the patterns present in the data in a more intuitive way, e.g., visualize the extent to which temperature and calendar feature variables positively or negatively impact a specific sample.

To overcome the above limitations, we propose a new hybrid interpretable multi-target regression model for energy load demand prediction. The proposed model carries two novelties. First, we combine the LightGBM [6] with the Dynamically Adjusted Regressor Chain [16] with Shapely value [9] methods to offer a new interpretable multi-target regression model. Second, the model can achieve a higher prediction accuracy than the single output model by making good use of the relationship between the energy load of each zone and also can get the specific strong or weak similarities of each area.

This paper makes two main contributions as follows.

1. This paper proposes the Dynamically Adjusted LightGBM Regressor Chain model (DALightGBMRC), which provides an interpretable method with a chained LightGBM model. The proposed model can generate a target correlation matrix and features importance and interaction dependency. With this improved model interpretability, the model provides valuable information for energy load demand prediction, dew point, dry-bulb temperature, day of year, and hour of the day. Their interactions are found to have significant impacts on energy load demand prediction.

2. The proposed model concerns the complex and dynamic nature of the energy load in a different area. It uses a dynamic adjusted chain structure to transform the single regression algorithms into a multi-target regression model to increase the accuracy by making good use of the relationship between prediction targets. Also, the structure of our algorithm makes use of hierarchical prediction information. The experimental results show that the proposed model is superior to single LightGBM regression in overall prediction accuracy.

2 Methods

The basic idea of the proposed DALightGBMRC is to design a multi-target model that combines interpretable and multi-target regression models. The DALightGBMRC has several advantages compared to the load prediction models. It does not use one model for all the prediction targets, which not only can make good use of the target's dependency but also can build a sub-model for every prediction target, which could make the specific interpretation for these prediction targets. In addition, the traditional time series prediction does not consider the other essential features like temperature; the proposed model can take these features into modeling consideration, even if it discovers the relationship among targets.

The proposed algorithm's first step is to generate the correlation matrix of prediction targets based on Spearman's rank correlation coefficient. The second step is to rank the targets to be predicted, and other targets strongly correlated with each predicted target are selected as features to expand the feature space of the sub-model, just like a feature selection based on correlation level among targets. The third step is to train a regressor chain for these targets based on the target's order and feature space extension in the second step. The final step uses the Shapely value to explain model features and dependency and the specific precision sample.

2.1 Data and Problem Definition

Data is eight bottom-level zones and two aggregated zones in New England as used in the direct track of the GEFCom 2017 [4]. Massachusetts (MASS) consists of three bottom-level zones: Southeast Massachusetts (SEMASS), Western/Central Massachusetts (WCMASS), and Northeast Massachusetts (NEMASSBOST). The bottom-level zones are Maine (ME), Connecticut (CT), New Hampshire (NH), Rhode Island (RI), and Vermont (VT). The sum of all eight bottom-level zones is designated "TOTAL". Forecasting loads for multiple regions is a multivariate time series forecasting problem. Hierarchical load forecasting is a dynamic and complex problem, as load demand is influenced by many factors, such as seasonality, temperature, holidays, weekdays, etc.

The data is a time series starting at 00:00 on March 1, 2003, and ending at 23:00 on April 30, 2017, with a frequency of hours and a total of 124,171 data (a complete sequence of this period would have 124,200 time-points of data). There are 29 time points with missing data, and the missing time points are all at 1:00 am, which should be the missing data caused by the scheduled power outage. In addition to the electricity load demand data for these ten regions, the data also contains data on the meteorological variables corresponding to these regions. Dew point and dry bulb temperature variables are included in the data.

The ratio of our training and test datasets is 9:1. We use the training set for five-fold cross validation training, thus reducing the risk of over-fitting. The names of the feature variables of the data can be divided into two categories: (i)

Calendar Feature Variables—'hour', 'month', 'dayofmonth', 'dayofyear', 'weeko-fyear', 'weekday', 'quarter', 'year', 'holiday', 'weekend' and (ii) Temperatures Feature Variables—dry bulb and dew point temperature for each zone.

2.2   Correlation Coefficient Calculating

We use Spearman correlation coefficient for each pair of target variables y_a and y_b, $y_a = \{y_1, \ldots, y_N\}$ is a time series of loads for a region, e.g. y_{V_T} is the load time series data for the VT region. Then we obtain a correlation coefficient matrix $COE_{m \times m} = \text{coefficient}\,(y_1, \ldots, y_m)$, where m is the number of region's load, here $m = 10$. We sum each row to obtain the cumulative sum of the correlations of this target variable to all the target variables. The targets are sorted in descending order according to their cumulative correlation coefficients, $c = \{c_1, \ldots, c_m\}$. c_1 is the first target variable that obtains the largest cumulative maximum correlation in the list.

2.3   Dynamically Adjusted LightGBM Regressor Chain

The Regressor Chain (RC) method has received extensive attention due to its simple concept and excellent performance [10,15]. Dynamically Adjusted Regressor Chain (DARC) is a new variant of the RC [16]. The training process of the RC is to train sub-model one by one with specific output target order. We choose LightGBM as the sub-model (also can call base model). The prediction input is an extension of the early prediction of targets. The process of DARC is the same as RC, with the difference that DARC gives the RC a chain order c of maximum correlation. For each sub-model, the variables with weak correlation are eliminated based on the value of the correlation matrix $COE_{m \times m}$. LightGBM regression model h_j is built for each region's load according to the chain order c. We obtains a target variable set $Y_{c_j}^{MC_{m \times m}} = \left\{\hat{y}_1, \ldots, \hat{y}_{c_{j-1}}\right\} (1 < j < m)$ that is highly correlated with the j_m^{th} target according to the correlation matrix $COE_{m \times m}$. When $j > 1$ in the j_m^{th} model of RC, the model h_i is learned on the transformed training set $D_j = \left\{(x_1, y_j^1), \ldots, (x_N, y_j^N)\right\}$. All of the raw input spaces have been expanded by the values of the all previous target $Y^p = \left\{\left(y_{c[1]}^1, \ldots, y_{c[j]}^1\right)^{\top}, \ldots, \left(y_{c[1]}^N, \ldots, y_{c[j]}^N\right)^{\top}\right\}$ whose correlation coefficient with the output target is lower than θ has been deleted. $y_{C[j]}^N$ is the value of the jth predicted target variable for the Nth sample data. N is the number of samples. To form an extended input space $X' = \{x_1, \ldots, x_N\}$, x_N denotes the feature vector of the Nth data sample.

During the RC prediction process, since the true value of the target variable is not available, the previously obtained predicted values $\hat{y}_1, \ldots, \hat{y}_{j-1}(1 < j < m)$ are continuously used as additional input variables to extend the input space. The pseudocode of the DALightGBMRC is shown in Algorithm 1.

Algorithm 1: Dynamically Adjusted LightGBM Regressor Chain

Data: Training dataset D, Threshold θ
Result: Chained LightGBM regression $h_j, j = \{1, \ldots, m\}$
$COE_{m \times m} = \text{coefficient}(Y)$;
$c_l = \sum(COE(:,l)), l = \{1, \ldots, m\}$;
$c = \text{sort}(\{c_1, \ldots, c_m\}, \text{decreasing})$;
$D'_{c[1]} = \left\{ \left(\boldsymbol{x}_1, y^1_{c[1]}\right), \ldots, \left(\boldsymbol{x}_N, y^N_{c[1]}\right) \right\}$;
$h_1 : D'_{c[1]} \to \mathbb{R}$;
for $j = 1$ *to* $m - 1$ **do**
$\quad Y^p = \left\{ \left(y^1_{c[1]}, \ldots, y^1_{c[j]}\right)^\top, \ldots, \left(y^N_{c[1]}, \ldots, y^N_{c[j]}\right)^\top \right\}$;
$\quad$ **for** $i = 1$ *to* $c[j]$ **do**
$\quad\quad$ **if** $COE[c[j+1]][i] \le \theta$ **then**
$\quad\quad\quad \mid$ Delete i^{th} row from Y^p
$\quad\quad$ **end**
$\quad$ **end**
$\quad X' = \begin{bmatrix} X \\ Y^p \end{bmatrix}$;
$\quad D'_{c[j+1]} = \left\{ \left(\boldsymbol{x}'(:,1), y^1_{c[j+1]}\right), \ldots, \left(\boldsymbol{x}'(:,N), y^N_{c[j+1]}\right) \right\}$;
$\quad h_{j+1} : D'_{c[j+1]} \to \mathbb{R}$;
end

2.4 SHapley Additive exPlanation (SHAP)

SHAP is a model-independent "model interpretation" package developed in Python [9]. It constructs an additive explanatory model inspired by cooperative game theory, where all features are considered "contributors". For each prediction sample, the model generates a prediction value, and the SHAP value is the value assigned to each feature in that sample.

3 Experiment Framework

The DALightGBMRC was implemented to predict the energy load demand for all regions. It was compared with a single GBM regression, our baseline, because three GBM appeared in the top five among 177 teams in the GEFCom 2017. Some interpretations of the corresponding RC's sub-models for each region are presented using SHAP. The results are evaluated by several prediction accuracy criteria: (i) Mean Squared Error—MSE $= \frac{1}{m}\sum_{j=1}^{m}\left(\widehat{y}^t_j - y^t_j\right)^2$, (ii) Root Mean Squared Error—RMSE $= \sqrt{\frac{1}{m}\sum_{j=1}^{m}\left(\widehat{y}^t_j - y^t_j\right)^2}$, and (iii) Mean Absolute Percentage Error—MAPE $= \frac{100\%}{m}\sum_{t=1}^{m}\left|\frac{\widehat{y}_t - y_t}{y_t}\right|$. Smaller values of them indicate more accurate predictions of the model.

4   Results and Discussions

4.1   Correlation Matrix

Figure 1 is the heat map drawn from the Spearman correlation coefficient matrix, with higher values indicating more consistent monotonicity. We can see that there is a strong correlation between almost all regions in terms of electrical loads.

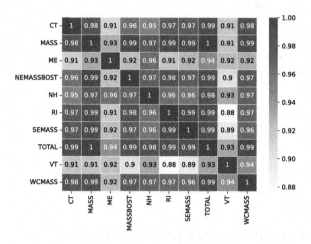

Fig. 1. Heat map of the Spearman's rank correlation coefficient matrix between electrical loads for all zones

According to Table 1, our proposed method is better than the single Light-GBM, indicating that combining correlations between targets improves prediction performance. Figure 2 shows the squared difference between the predicted values—by the proposed and the baseline models—and the actual values in seven days. We can see that the values of the squared error of the proposed model are generally lower than that of the baseline model. Figure 3 shows the cumulative sum of the correlations of the corresponding target variable to all other target variables. It give the following order listed in c: 'TOTAL' ≻ 'MASS' ≻ 'WCMASS' ≻ 'NEMASSBOST' ≻ 'NH' ≻ 'CT' ≻ 'SEMASS' ≻ 'RI' ≻ 'ME' ≻ 'VT'. TOTAL and MASS are ranked first and second as two aggregation regions. The later sub-models are able to use the higher-level information of TOTAL, and the later sub-regions of MASS can also use the higher-level information of MASS, thus also using the information of hierarchical prediction to get a better prediction accuracy. TOTAL obtains the same results because TOTAL is the first in the order of the regressor chain and does not treat the targets as features to extend the feature space. Thus, it is equivalent to both being independent predictions of LightGBM and should obtain the same results.

Table 1. Performances of the proposed model, DALightGBMRC, and the baseline, LightGBM on predicting load demand for eight regions and two aggregation regions. Bold indicates best

Zones	Single LightGBM			DALightGBMRC		
	MSE	RMSE	MAPE	MSE	RMSE	MAPE
CT	15230.33	123.41	0.025	**3020.01**	**54.95**	**0.0112**
MASS	35163.99	187.52	0.021	**2839.94**	**53.29**	**0.0052**
ME	1307.39	36.16	0.022	**1032.14**	**32.13**	**0.0188**
NEMASSBOST	12975.95	113.91	0.027	**611.06**	**24.72**	**0.0060**
NH	1847.12	42.98	0.024	**509.44**	**22.57**	**0.0120**
RI	952.26	30.86	0.023	**141.83**	**11.91**	**0.0091**
SEMASS	4922.76	70.16	0.029	**403.84**	**20.10**	**0.0088**
TOTAL	**206530.70**	**454.46**	**0.023**	206530.70	454.46	0.0230
VT	300.71	17.34	0.020	**203.67**	**14.27**	**0.0166**
WCMASS	3743.79	61.19	0.024	**435.46**	**20.87**	**0.0083**

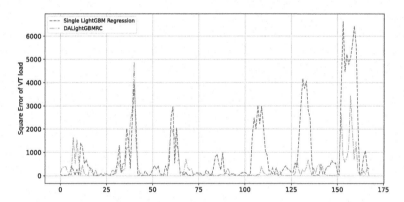

Fig. 2. The squared difference between the predicted values by the considered model and the actual values in seven days

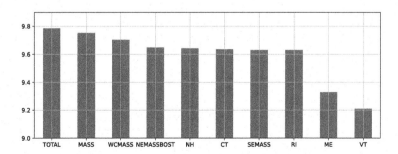

Fig. 3. Cumulative sum of the correlations of the corresponding target variable to all other target variables

4.2   Model Interpretability

Due to article length constraints, we chose the last region VT as our example because its model contains information on the correlations of all previous regions. There has been related work demonstrating the importance of temperature and calendar features for prediction by statistical methods [14], while this paper focuses on extracting the relationship between the prediction targets. The advantage of SHAP values is that, compared with the traditional feature importance that does not show positive and negative effects. SHAP can not only reflect the importance of features in each sample but also show positive and negative effects. Figure 4 is a summary of the modeled SHAP values for VT. The SHAP value of WCMASS is the highest due to that VT is physically located close to WCMASSBOST. The SHAP values of CT and RI and SEMASS and MASS are all relatively low. The SEMASS, CT, and RI are also farther from VT. Two physically close areas will have a higher correlation or similarity in their electricity loads. Moreover, we can see from the SHAP Partial Dependence plot[1] as shown in Fig. 5 that the feature that interacts most with both day of month and day of the year is the dew point temperature of the VT region. When the dew point temperature is low and the day of the year is at the beginning and end of the year, they have a very high impact on the forecast results. We can obtain a pattern where the dew point temperature is low from November to February, and the electricity load demand is forecast to increase under these conditions.

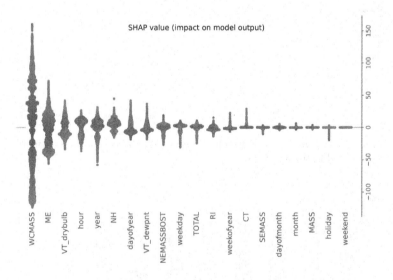

Fig. 4. SHAP value of VT prediction model

---

[1] A partial dependence plot shows the marginal effect of one or two features on the predicted outcome of a machine learning model.

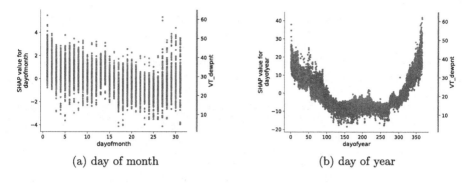

(a) day of month   (b) day of year

Fig. 5. SHAP Partial Dependence plot

5   Conclusion and Future Work

We conclude that there is a correlation between the energy loads of the various regions of the New England states, and our methods take advantage of this correlation to improve our predictive performance further. We interpreted the model in conjunction with the SHAP method. We obtained the features that influence the importance of energy loads in each region, for example, the day of the year, the week of the year, the dry bulb temperature of the corresponding location, etc. Also, the pattern of influence of some factors' interaction on electricity load was obtained; for example, if the dew point temperature is shallow from November to February, the electricity load demand will rise. Our future work will explore further and summarize the specific patterns of power load variation in each region. We will continue to use SHAP to examine the causes of some power load peaks.

References

1. Dimoulkas, I., Mazidi, P., Herre, L.: Neural networks for GEFCom2017 probabilistic load forecasting. Int. J. Forecast. **35**, 1409–1423 (2019). https://doi.org/10.1016/j.ijforecast.2018.09.007

2. Haben, S., Giasemidis, G., Ziel, F., Arora, S.: Short term load forecasting and the effect of temperature at the low voltage level. Int. J. Forecast. **35**, 1469–1484 (2019). https://doi.org/10.1016/j.ijforecast.2018.10.007

3. Hong, T., Xie, J., Black, J.: Global energy forecasting competition 2017: hierarchical probabilistic load forecasting. Int. J. Forecast. **35**, 1389–1399 (2019). https://doi.org/10.1016/j.ijforecast.2019.02.006

4. Hong, T., Xie, J., Black, J.: Global energy forecasting competition 2017: hierarchical probabilistic load forecasting. Int. J. Forecast. **35**(4), 1389–1399 (2019). https://doi.org/10.1016/j.ijforecast.2019.02.006

5. Kanda, I., Veguillas, J.M.: Data preprocessing and quantile regression for probabilistic load forecasting in the GEFCom2017 final match. Int. J. Forecast. **35**, 1460–1468 (2019). https://doi.org/10.1016/j.ijforecast.2019.02.005

6. Ke, G., et al.: LightGBM: a highly efficient gradient boosting decision tree. In: Advances in Neural Information Processing Systems (2017)
7. Khamparia, A., Gupta, D., Nguyen, N.G., Khanna, A., Pandey, B., Tiwari, P.: Sound classification using convolutional neural network and tensor deep stacking network. IEEE Access **7**, 7717–7727 (2019). https://doi.org/10.1109/ACCESS.2018.2888882
8. Landgraf, A.J.: An ensemble approach to GEFCom2017 probabilistic load forecasting. Int. J. Forecast. **35**, 1432–1438 (2019). https://doi.org/10.1016/j.ijforecast.2019.02.003
9. Lundberg, S.M., Lee, S.I.: A unified approach to interpreting model predictions. In: Advances in Neural Information Processing Systems (2017)
10. Melki, G., Cano, A., Kecman, V., Ventura, S.: Multi-target support vector regression via correlation regressor chains. Inf. Sci. **415–416**(November), 53–69 (2017). https://doi.org/10.1016/j.ins.2017.06.017
11. Nowotarski, J., Liu, B., Weron, R., Hong, T.: Improving short term load forecast accuracy via combining sister forecasts. Energy **98**, 40–49 (2016). https://doi.org/10.1016/j.energy.2015.12.142
12. Roach, C.: Reconciled boosted models for GEFCom2017 hierarchical probabilistic load forecasting. Int. J. Forecast. **35**, 1439–1450 (2019). https://doi.org/10.1016/j.ijforecast.2018.09.009
13. Smyl, S., Hua, N.G.: Machine learning methods for GEFCom2017 probabilistic load forecasting. Int. J. Forecast. **35**, 1424–1431 (2019). https://doi.org/10.1016/j.ijforecast.2019.02.002
14. Sobhani, M., Hong, T., Martin, C.: Temperature anomaly detection for electric load forecasting. Int. J. Forecast. **36**, 324–333 (2020). https://doi.org/10.1016/j.ijforecast.2019.04.022
15. Spyromitros-Xioufis, E., Tsoumakas, G., Groves, W., Vlahavas, I.: Multi-target regression via input space expansion: treating targets as inputs. Mach. Learn. **104**(1), 55–98 (2016). https://doi.org/10.1007/s10994-016-5546-z
16. Wu, Z., Lian, G.: A novel dynamically adjusted regressor chain for taxi demand prediction. In: Proceedings of the International Joint Conference on Neural Networks (2020). https://doi.org/10.1109/IJCNN48605.2020.9207160
17. Zhao, T., Wang, J., Zhang, Y.: Day-ahead hierarchical probabilistic load forecasting with linear quantile regression and empirical copulas. IEEE Access **7**, 80969–80979 (2019). https://doi.org/10.1109/ACCESS.2019.2922744
18. Ziel, F.: Quantile regression for the qualifying match of GEFCom2017 probabilistic load forecasting. Int. J. Forecast. **35**, 1400–1408 (2019). https://doi.org/10.1016/j.ijforecast.2018.07.004

Automating Patient-Level Lung Cancer Diagnosis in Different Data Regimes

Adam Pardyl[1]([✉])[iD], Dawid Rymarczyk[1][iD], Zbisław Tabor[2][iD], and Bartosz Zieliński[1][iD]

[1] Faculty of Mathematics and Computer Science, Jagiellonian University, 6 Lojasiewicza Street, 30-348 Kraków, Poland
{adam.pardyl,dawid.rymarczyk}@student.uj.edu.pl,
bartosz.zielinski@uj.edu.pl
[2] AGH University of Science and Technology, 30 Mickiewicza Avenue, 30-059 Kraków, Poland
ztabor@agh.edu.pl

Abstract. As the leading cause of cancer-related mortality, lung cancer is responsible for more deaths than colon, breast, and prostate cancer put together. Screening with low-dose computed tomography detects cancer at an early stage and reduces mortality. However, it requires the tedious work of radiologists to obtain malignancy scores, which additionally are very subjective. That is why many researchers worked on methods automating lung cancer classification, usually using the publicly available LIDC-IDRI dataset for training. However, most of those methods consider only node-level classification and provide poor results for patient-level diagnosis. In this paper, we fill this gap by introducing an end-to-end methods with a CT scan on the input and the patient-level diagnosis on the output. We consider three approaches for three different data regimes to examine how stronger and weaker supervision influences the model performance.

Keywords: Multiple Instance Learning · Autoencoders · Medical Imaging · Computer Tomography

1 Introduction

The most common cause of death among men is lung cancer. To effectively diagnose the disease in an early stage, low-dose lung CT screening is employed because reliable and accurate screening tests can substantially reduce the mortality rate and reduce the costs of further diagnostic tests such as histopathology examinations. However, analyzing CT scans is time-consuming and requires highly trained radiologists. Additionally, doctors can be biased and not always agree with each other. That is why they should find a consensus before giving a final diagnosis.

Acknowledge support of National Center for Research and Development (NCBR, Poland) under grant no. POIR.01.01.01-00-1666/20. This research was supported by PLGrid Infrastructure (ACC Cyfronet AGH).

Table 1. We consider three weakly supervised methods dedicated to three different training data regimes. While DEEPLUNG introduced in [25] requires information about nodule location and malignancy, our AUTOLUNG needs only information about patient-level malignancy.

METHOD	NODULE-LEVEL		PATIENT-LEVEL
	LOCATION	MALIGNANCY	MALIGNANCY
DEEPLUNG	✓	✓	✓
MILLUNG		✓	✓
AUTOLUNG			✓

Due to laborious CT-based lung cancer diagnosis, its automation has been a subject of much research [8] and one of the Kaggle competitions [11]. However, due to the limited availability of Kaggle data, most of the works employ the LIDC-IDRI dataset [2] and its preprocessed version LUNA16 [18], using conventional or deep learning methods. The former extracts morphological features to generate image representation passed to a shallow classifier to obtain a prediction. The latter employs convolutional neural networks, either 3D or 2D, to learn image representation and its label simultaneously. However, existing methods operate on a patch from the CT scan (nodule-level). That is why they require a set of suspicious regions for which they predict the malignancy. It can be obtained using conventional methods, like voxel clustering or pixel thresholding, or with deep methods employing detection networks such as FASTER R-CNN [15]. To conclude, all of the aforementioned methods focus on nodules detection [9,24], segmentation [14,19,20], and classification [3,16,23]. However, before applying a model dedicated to nodules, one needs to identify which patients should be included in a detailed examination. Ergo, perform a screening to decide if a patient should be further diagnosed. According to our knowledge, the only work considering this (patient-level) problem on the LIDC-IDRI dataset is proposed in [25].

In this work, we consider three weakly supervised methods dedicated to three different training data regimes, as presented in Table 1. Each of them is an end-to-end method with a CT scan on the input and the patient-level diagnosis on the output. The first method, called DEEPLUNG, assumes that the information about nodule-level location and nodule and patient-level malignancy are available during training. In comparison, the second method, called MILLUNG, does not require nodules' locations. Finally, the last method, called AUTOLUNG, needs only patient-level malignancy. As we present in our experiments, each method has its own strengths and weaknesses: DEEPLUNG obtains the highest AUC, MILLUNG is more transparent than other methods, while AUTOLUNG can be trained on the most general labels. This, together with other conclusions described in Sect. 5 can be a valuable guideline for the medical image analysis community. Our contributions can be summarized as follows:

- introducing novel end-to-end screening algorithms for lung cancer detection, with accuracy comparable with experienced radiologists,
- incorporating interpretability component into the automation of the lung cancer diagnosis process,
- providing guidelines on using different types of methods depending on the training data regime.

2 Related Works

Our work focuses on a patient-level diagnosis of lung cancer using low-dose CT scans. From this perspective, it relates to the LIDC-IDRI dataset [2], containing more than a thousand CT lung scans, its subset LUNA16 [18] containing preprocessed patches with nodule candidates, and a high-scale dataset from Kaggle competition [11] with a restricted usage license. When it comes to existing methods, many of them address either nodule detection, classification, or segmentation. Conventional methods for those problems are described in [13], [1] and [6,19], respectively. Deep methods use FASTER R-CNN [5,25] for detection, U-NET [17,20] for detection and segmentation, and multi-scale convolutions and transfer learning [3,18,21,22] for classification. Moreover, most recent models employ self-supervision for the representation learning phase [9,24], exploiting the information about the anatomical structure of lungs. Despite multiple approaches to nodule detection, classification, and segmentation, end-to-end methods for patient-level assessment are missing. To the best of our knowledge, only Zhu et al. [25] consider this problem using the LIDC-IDRI dataset, introducing a two-step deep learning algorithm with FASTER R-CNN and 3D-CNN for detection and classification steps, respectively. In this paper, we introduce novel end-to-end approaches trained on the LIDC-IDRI dataset.

3 Method

In this section, we consider three weakly supervised end-to-end methods, returning patient-level diagnosis based on a lung CT scan, dedicated to three different training data regimes. All methods are presented in Fig. 1 and briefly described in the successive subsections.

3.1 DeepLung

DEEPLUNG consists of two components, nodule detection (identifying the locations of candidate nodules) and classification (classifying candidate nodules into benign or malignant). Nodule detection is obtained by employing 3D FASTER R-CNN [15]. Then, 3D Dual Path Network [4] is used to extract deep features from the detected and cropped nodules. Finally, the fusion of the features from gradient boosting machine [7], deep features, detected nodule size, and raw

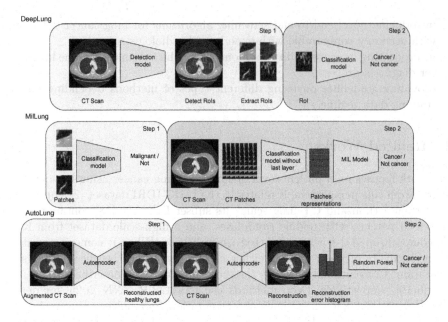

Fig. 1. We consider three end-to-end methods with a CT scan on the input and the patient-level diagnosis on the output. Each method is trained with a two-step procedure but with different components and training set regimes, as defined in Table 1.

pixels is employed for final classification. Patient-level diagnosis can be achieved by aggregating the classification results of detected nodules. Due to the usage of the FASTER R-CNN detector, DEEPLUNG requires both information about patches malignancy and location to train the encoder of the patches.

3.2   MilLung

During the training phase, MILLUNG first teaches a nodule-level classifier based on 3D patches or 2D slides with and without nodules (malignant and nonmalignant). Such a classifier without the last layer f is used to generate patches' representations. Then, we train a patient-level classifier composed of MIL aggregator and multilayer perceptron. In the evaluation phase, a normalized 3D CT scan is divided into 3D patches or 2D slides. The patches or slides overlapping the lung area are then passed to f to generate their representations. Such representations are aggregated with a patient-level classifier to generate scan representation and provide final malignancy prediction.

We preprocess CT scans using z-normalization as described in [25] and use a standard sliding window with 50% patches overlapping. Moreover, a nodule-level classifier can be replaced with a nodule-level regressor with a malignancy score at an output. Finally, as a MIL operator of patient-level classifier, we use Attention-based Multiple Instance Learning (ABMIL) [10] or Dual-Stream Multiple Instance Learning (DSMIL) [12].

3.3 AutoLung

AUTOLUNG generates a patch representation in a fully unsupervised way. First, the lung CT scans of healthy patients are normalized and preprocessed as in Sect. 3.2. Then, we crop a random 3D patch p from a lung area of such CT scans and augment it p_{aug} with a small ellipsoid generated with parameters $r_1, r_2, r_3 \in (5, 15)$ and filled with 1 s. Then, p_{aug} is passed to the autoencoder to obtain reconstruction p_{rec}. The model is trained by minimizing the reconstruction loss $MSE(p, p_{rec})$. This way, the autoencoder learns to remove the rounded objects (also nodules) from the input patch.

When the autoencoder is trained, we generate reconstructions for each scan from the dataset and calculate the differences $d = x_{rec} - x$ between the reconstructed and original scan. Due to the autoencoder loss function, the values of d in the area of nodules should be negative, and those values are used to calculate a histogram of differences. Finally, such histogram is normalized and passed to a RANDOM FOREST classifier trained to distinguish between patients with and without cancer.

4   Experimental Setup

4.1   Dataset

In the experiments, we aim to evaluate the proposed approach on the publicly available LIDC-IDRI dataset. We compare our results with the DEEPLUNG method [25]. Therefore, we use a similar experimental setup. We perform a 10-fold cross-validation using a random split. For each experiment, we use 8 of 10 subsets as the training set and the two remaining subsets as the validation set and testing set, respectively. We run experiments using folds 1, 2, 3, 4, and 5 and report results as average performance for those folds. We use nodule annotations and lung segmentations provided with the LIDC-IDRI dataset. Because the LIDC-IDRI contains annotations made by four doctors, we average the malignancy scores assigned by them for each nodule. If a given nodule was not annotated by all doctors, it is treated as annotated by them with a score of 0 (meaning not a nodule). Nodules with average malignancy equal to 3 (uncertain about malignant or benign) are treated as neutral (ignored for classification). Nodules with score greater than 3 are considered *positive* and those score lower than 3 as *negative*. On the patient-level, we label a scan as positive if and only if it contains at least one nodule labeled as positive.

4.2   Preprocessing and Augmentation

We clip raw CT image data into the range of $[-1200, 600]$ and transform that range linearly into $[0, 1]$. As the scans in the LIDC-IDRI dataset were produced by different CT devices with different slice thicknesses, we normalize the slice thickness to 1 mm using linear interpolation. For encoder training, we preprocess the dataset extracting $96 \times 96 \times 96$ patches for training. For positive samples, we extract all nodule regions centered on those nodules. Negative samples are uniformly sampled from regions not containing nodules, with 20 samples per scan. During training, we crop $64 \times 64 \times 64$ patches from preprocessed ones, randomly shifted. For classifier training, we drop random patches from each image to provide augmentation and increase training data.

4.3   Hyperparameters of the Models

In the case of DEEPLUNG we follow the training procedure described in [25][1]. The 3D RESNET18 for MILLung experiments was trained using Adam optimizer with default parameters, batch size of 4, learning rate of $1e-3$, and no weight decay for 300 epochs. In the experiments on 2D slices, the 2D RESNET18 pretrained on ImageNet was trained using Adam optimizer with default parameters, batch size 4 and weight decay 0.001 for 1000 epochs with early stopping window 25. The dataset consisted of slices without any nodule or slices centered in z axis and shifted by $\pm 20\%$ of nodule size. To evaluate the classifier, we performed a hyperparameter grid search with the following properties: learning rate in $[1e-3, 2e-4, 1e-4, 5e-5]$, weight decay in $[5e-3, 1e-4, 1e-5]$, model dropout in $[0, 0.1, 0.2]$, and patch augmentation dropout in $[0, 0.1, 0.2]$. The model with the best performance on the validation set was chosen for evaluation on the test set for each experiment. The batch size is set to 1 due to the variable size of a MIL bag. In the case of AutoLung, we implement the autoencoder as a denoising autoencoder with a hidden dimension of $4 \times 4 \times 320$ and 3 convolution and 3 upsampling layers. It is trained with a batch size 4, learning rate 10^{-2}, SGD optimizer with Nesterov momentum 0.99 for 1000 and dropout probability of 0.5. For reconstruction error distribution representation, we use a normalized histogram with 10 bins on negative values. For a RANDOM FOREST classifier, we use grid search with the following parameters: the number of estimators in $[200; 2000]$, maximum depth in $[2, 10]$, and gini criterion.

5   Results

In this section, we present the results of each scenario and discuss the parameters of each model. We compare representation learned by classification and regression model and we compare them with scores obtained from experienced radiologists. Lastly, we discuss the interpretability component of the MILLUNG approach.

---

[1] We used the code from: https://github.com/wentaozhu/DeepLung.

Table 2. Results of three considered methods, including various modifications of MIL-LUNG method.

SCORE	METHOD	STEP 1	STEP 2	AUC
MALIGNANCY > 3	DEEPLUNG	FASTER R-CNN	3D DPN	**0.83 ± 0.04**
	MILLUNG CLASSIFICATION	3D RESNET18	ABMIL	0.75 ± 0.05
			DSMIL	0.77 ± 0.04
		2D RESNET18	ABMIL	0.82 ± 0.03
			DSMIL	0.82 ± 0.02
	MILLUNG REGRESSION	3D RESNET18	ABMIL	0.82 ± 0.02
			DSMIL	**0.83 ± 0.03**
	AUTOLUNG	AUTOENCODER	RANDOM FOREST	0.80 ± 0.01
MALIGNANCY > 0	DEEPLUNG	FASTER R-CNN	3D DPN	**0.86 ± 0.04**
	MILLUNG CLASSIFICATION	3D RESNET18	ABMIL	0.73 ± 0.11
			DSMIL	0.77 ± 0.09
		2D RESNET18	ABMIL	0.82 ± 0.02
			DSMIL	0.84 ± 0.02
	MILLUNG REGRESSION	3D RESNET18	ABMIL	0.81 ± 0.05
			DSMIL	0.82 ± 0.06
	AUTOLUNG	AUTOENCODER	RANDOM FOREST	0.71 ± 0.05

In Table 2, we present the results for all considered methods for malignancy $M > 3$ and for $M > 0$. The former can be used to find patients needing immediate treatment. The latter is considered a screening system to identify patients needing further diagnosis. AUC of most models for $M > 0$ is comparable with $M > 3$. The except is AUTOLUNG, which is less effective for $M > 0$, most probably because of the smaller size of non-malignant nodules.

We also test how the choice of the MIL method in MILLUNG influences the final model performance. We observe, that results between ABMIL and DSMIL are comparable, but in favor of DSMIL. Additionally, we check if 3D information is beneficial in the case of classification. One can observe that the system using 3D RESNET18 on 3D patches performs worse than the 2D RESNET18 pretrained on ImageNet and finetuned on slices. However, the latter performs on par to MILLUNG with a 3D RESNETs trained on a regression task. We present the detailed analysis of regression and classification RESNETs in the following subsection. Notice that we do not train a regression model on slices since it is difficult to determine to which slice of the nodule one should assign a malignancy score.

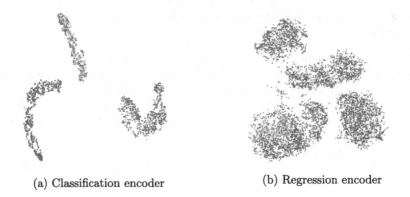

(a) Classification encoder   (b) Regression encoder

Fig. 2. t-SNE visualization of the patch embeddings for encoders trained in a classification (a) and regression (b) mode. Blue dots represent patches without nodules, while other colors represent different nodule malignancy levels, such as pink (highly suspicious), red (moderately suspicious), and other colors (non-malignant nodules available only for regressional encoder). (Color figure online)

Overall, the best performing model is DEEPLUNG, especially in detecting patients with malignant nodules. Its effectiveness comes from the utilization of the biggest amount of information. However, the drop in AUC for MILLUNG and AUTOLUNG is not that significant, taking into consideration that they use significantly limited information.

5.1   Malignancy Classification or Regression?

We present the latent spaces obtained for those two approaches to understand the differences between models trained on 3D patches in regression and classification setup. In Fig. 2, one can observe that the classification encoder divides the hidden space into three clusters, blue, red-pink, and mixed. Each color corresponds to a different malignancy score, blue the smallest and red the highest. This visualization shows that the classification encoder can separate malignant and benign nodule patches, but one-third of them are still mixed, which confuses the model. At the same time, the regression encoder divides the data into a higher number of well-separated clusters. It shows that the malignancy scores are not independent, and their order carries additional information that increases the model's effectiveness (see Table 2).

5.2   Comparison with Experienced Doctors

Here, in Table 3, we present the comparison between the best models obtained in each of the scenarios with experienced doctors[2]. As they are only for nodules,

---

[2] Radiologists annotations are taken from https://github.com/wentaozhu/DeepLung/blob/master/nodcls/annotationdetclssgm_doctor.csv.

Table 3. Comparison between the best variation of the three methods with the scores obtained from the experience radiologists. CONSENSUS corresponds to the average over scores provided by four radiologists.

	DR 1	DR 2	DR 3	DR 4	AVERAGE	CONSENSUS
CONSENSUS	81.88%	79.95%	77.78%	61.32%	77.23%	100.00%
DEEPLUNG	72.73%	72.36%	72.10%	65.12%	70.57%	80.65%
MILLUNG	74.13%	74.52%	70.92%	62.02%	70.45%	78.32%
AUTOLUNG	54.79%	54.79%	55.48%	44.52%	52.40%	73.20%

we present this analysis only on conditions for malignancy higher than three. The accuracy is calculated only on patients with annotated nodules, and the number of annotations equals four and only on the test set patients.

In Table 3, we take the best variation of the three methods for $M > 3$ and compare their results with the scores obtained from the experienced radiologists. The accuracy is calculated only on patients from testing set with nodules annotated by four radiologists. One can observe that the average agreement between particular doctors and a consensus (average over scores provided by four radiologists) is around 77.23%. Among the methods, DEEPLUNG achieves the best agreement with the particular doctors and their consensus (70.57% and 80.65%, respectively). At the same time, MILLUNG achieves worse agreement in both cases (analogically, 70.45% and 78.32%). Finally, AUTOLUNG, which does not use nodule level labels at all in the training phase, achieves 70.45% and 78.32% agreements, respectively. It is better than the result obtained by DR 4 (who agree with consensus in 61.32%) but worse than the accurateness of the other doctors. We conclude that the deep learning model's performance is similar to a single medical expert. However, training an ensemble on models trained on individual doctors' annotations can lead to a higher agreement with a consensus. However, the current version of LIDC-IDRI datasets does not allow to reliably train a model for each of the doctors separately since the annotations are collected only for detected nodules and not the whole CT scans.

5.3   Explainability

Within tested models, only the MILLUNG allows for patient-level interpretability of the classification results. As both ABMIL and DSMIL are based on instance attention, we can visualize the importance of single patches for the score of the entire scan. In Fig. 3, we show 2D slices of example attention maps for correctly classified positive and negative samples, as well as for false positive and false negative ones. We observe that for scans classified as positive by our method, the attention map highlights patches presumed to contain malignant nodules, allowing a radiologist to narrow down the area of interest when verifying method prediction.

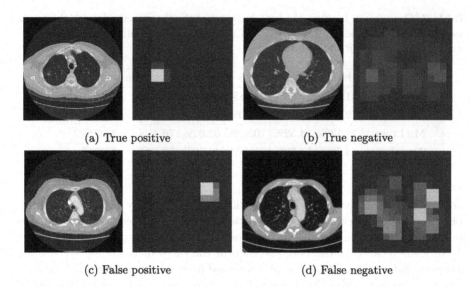

(a) True positive   (b) True negative

(c) False positive   (d) False negative

Fig. 3. Sample attention maps returned by MiLLung (3D ResNet18 regression + DSMIL). For each sample on the left image, a slice of the input CT scan is shown. Red overlay marks malignant nodules as labeled by doctors. On the right image, a patch importance map is shown, as generated by the DSMIL attention mechanism. We observe that for scans classified as *positive* the attention mechanism focuses on distinct regions presumed to contain malignant nodules. For *negative* samples, the attention weights are distributed all over the slide.

6   Conclusions

In this work, we show how different data regimes influence the performance of deep learning for patient-level lung cancer diagnosis using CT scans. As expected, the more information is provided during model training, the more effective it is. However, interestingly, two weakly supervised methods (MiLLung and AutoLung) obtain results only slightly worse than the DeepLung. It shows that a reliable system can also be built with limited data. Additionally, in an ablation study, we show that regression learning of malignancy scores is more beneficial than simple classifier, and we discuss interpretable aspects of the methods. In future works, we plan to analyze how data regimes influence digital pathology and exploit active learning techniques to improve the overall performance of the patient screening system.

References

1. Aerts, H.J., et al.: Decoding tumour phenotype by noninvasive imaging using a quantitative radiomics approach. Nat. Commun. **5**(1), 1–9 (2014)
2. Armato, S.G., III., et al.: The lung image database consortium (LIDC) and image database resource initiative (IDRI): a completed reference database of lung nodules on CT scans. Med. Phys. **38**(2), 915–931 (2011)

3. Asuntha, A., Srinivasan, A.: Deep learning for lung cancer detection and classification. Multimedia Tools Appl. **79**(11), 7731–7762 (2020)
4. Chen, Y., Li, J., Xiao, H., Jin, X., Yan, S., Feng, J.: Dual path networks. In: Advances in Neural Information Processing Systems, vol. 30 (2017)
5. Ding, J., Li, A., Hu, Z., Wang, L.: Accurate pulmonary nodule detection in computed tomography images using deep convolutional neural networks. In: Descoteaux, M., Maier-Hein, L., Franz, A., Jannin, P., Collins, D.L., Duchesne, S. (eds.) MICCAI 2017. LNCS, vol. 10435, pp. 559–567. Springer, Cham (2017). https://doi.org/10.1007/978-3-319-66179-7_64
6. Farag, A.A., Abd El Munim, H.E., Graham, J.H., Farag, A.A.: A novel approach for lung nodules segmentation in chest CT using level sets. IEEE Trans. Image Process. **22**(12), 5202–5213 (2013)
7. Friedman, J.H.: Greedy function approximation: a gradient boosting machine. Ann. Stat. **29**(5), 1189–1232 (2001)
8. Gu, Y., et al.: A survey of computer-aided diagnosis of lung nodules from CT scans using deep learning. Comput. Biol. Med. **137**, 104806 (2021)
9. Haghighi, F., Hosseinzadeh Taher, M.R., Zhou, Z., Gotway, M.B., Liang, J.: Learning semantics-enriched representation via self-discovery, self-classification, and self-restoration. In: Martel, A.L., et al. (eds.) MICCAI 2020. LNCS, vol. 12261, pp. 137–147. Springer, Cham (2020). https://doi.org/10.1007/978-3-030-59710-8_14
10. Ilse, M., Tomczak, J., Welling, M.: Attention-based deep multiple instance learning. In: International Conference on Machine Learning, pp. 2127–2136. PMLR (2018)
11. Kuan, K., et al.: Deep learning for lung cancer detection: tackling the Kaggle data science bowl 2017 challenge. arXiv preprint arXiv:1705.09435 (2017)
12. Li, B., Li, Y., Eliceiri, K.W.: Dual-stream multiple instance learning network for whole slide image classification with self-supervised contrastive learning. In: Proceedings of the IEEE/CVF Conference on Computer Vision and Pattern Recognition, pp. 14318–14328 (2021)
13. Lopez Torres, E., et al.: Large scale validation of the M5L lung cad on heterogeneous CT datasets. Med. Phys. **42**(4), 1477–1489 (2015)
14. Pang, S., Du, A., He, X., Díez, J., Orgun, M.A.: Fast and accurate lung tumor spotting and segmentation for boundary delineation on CT slices in a coarse-to-fine framework. In: Gedeon, T., Wong, K.W., Lee, M. (eds.) ICONIP 2019. CCIS, vol. 1142, pp. 589–597. Springer, Cham (2019). https://doi.org/10.1007/978-3-030-36808-1_64
15. Ren, S., He, K., Girshick, R., Sun, J.: Faster R-CNN: towards real-time object detection with region proposal networks. In: Advances in Neural Information Processing Systems, vol. 28 (2015)
16. Riquelme, D., Akhloufi, M.A.: Deep learning for lung cancer nodules detection and classification in CT scans. AI **1**(1), 28–67 (2020)
17. Ronneberger, O., Fischer, P., Brox, T.: U-Net: convolutional networks for biomedical image segmentation. In: Navab, N., Hornegger, J., Wells, W.M., Frangi, A.F. (eds.) MICCAI 2015. LNCS, vol. 9351, pp. 234–241. Springer, Cham (2015). https://doi.org/10.1007/978-3-319-24574-4_28
18. Setio, A.A.A., et al.: Validation, comparison, and combination of algorithms for automatic detection of pulmonary nodules in computed tomography images: the LUNA16 challenge. Med. Image Anal. **42**, 1–13 (2017)
19. Sharma, M., Bhatt, J.S., Joshi, M.V.: Early detection of lung cancer from CT images: nodule segmentation and classification using deep learning. In: Tenth International Conference on Machine Vision (ICMV 2017), vol. 10696, pp. 226–233. SPIE (2018)

20. Shaziya, H., Shyamala, K., Zaheer, R.: Automatic lung segmentation on thoracic CT scans using U-Net convolutional network. In: 2018 International Conference on Communication and Signal Processing (ICCSP), pp. 0643–0647. IEEE (2018)
21. Shen, W., et al.: Learning from experts: developing transferable deep features for patient-level lung cancer prediction. In: Ourselin, S., Joskowicz, L., Sabuncu, M.R., Unal, G., Wells, W. (eds.) MICCAI 2016. LNCS, vol. 9901, pp. 124–131. Springer, Cham (2016). https://doi.org/10.1007/978-3-319-46723-8_15
22. Shen, W., Zhou, M., Yang, F., Yang, C., Tian, J.: Multi-scale convolutional neural networks for lung nodule classification. In: Ourselin, S., Alexander, D.C., Westin, C.-F., Cardoso, M.J. (eds.) IPMI 2015. LNCS, vol. 9123, pp. 588–599. Springer, Cham (2015). https://doi.org/10.1007/978-3-319-19992-4_46
23. Xu, Y., Zhang, G., Li, Y., Luo, Y., Lu, J.: A hybrid model: DGnet-SVM for the classification of pulmonary nodules. In: Liu, D., Xie, S., Li, Y., Zhao, D., El-Alfy, E.S. (eds.) International Conference on Neural Information Processing, vol. 10637, pp. 732–741. Springer, Cham (2017). https://doi.org/10.1007/978-3-319-70093-9_78
24. Zhou, Z., et al.: Models genesis: generic autodidactic models for 3D medical image analysis. In: Shen, D., et al. (eds.) MICCAI 2019. LNCS, vol. 11767, pp. 384–393. Springer, Cham (2019). https://doi.org/10.1007/978-3-030-32251-9_42
25. Zhu, W., Liu, C., Fan, W., Xie, X.: DeepLung: deep 3D dual path nets for automated pulmonary nodule detection and classification. In: 2018 IEEE Winter Conference on Applications of Computer Vision (WACV), pp. 673–681. IEEE (2018)

Multi-level 3DCNN with Min-Max Ranking Loss for Weakly-Supervised Video Anomaly Detection

Snehashis Majhi[1], Deepak Ranjan Nayak[2(✉)], Ratnakar Dash[1], and Pankaj Kumar Sa[1]

[1] Department of CSE, National Institute of Technology, Rourkela, India
[2] Department of CSE, Malaviya National Institute of Technology, Jaipur, India
drnayak.cse@mnit.ac.in

Abstract. Video anomaly detection in real-world surveillance systems is challenging due to the unavailability of large annotated data, visual challenges like partial occlusion and illumination change, and the untrimmed nature of videos. In this paper, we propose a method that mitigates the above challenges. The proposed method adopts a weakly-supervised learning paradigm to address the scarcity of temporally annotated data. In this, only video-level supervision is required for learning, but precise temporal locations of anomalies are detected during testing. To effectively learn from weak supervision, a Min-Max ranking loss is proposed with the objective to maximize the margin of separation between anomaly and normal instances and to minimize the separation among the normal instances simultaneously. Further, to handle the visual challenges in real-world scenarios, a multi-level feature combination strategy from 3DCNN is proposed to extract the fine lower-level representation of the input video sequences. An efficient temporal dependency encoding is utilized further to capture the sharp change in untrimmed surveillance videos. The proposed method is evaluated on a widely used benchmark anomaly detection dataset, UCF-Crime. The results demonstrate that the proposed method achieves competitive performance compared to recently reported anomaly detection methods.

Keywords: Video anomaly detection · Weakly-supervised learning · 3DCNN

1 Introduction

Keeping public safety in mind, a massive number of surveillance cameras have been installed in public areas such as shopping malls, banks, railway stations, etc. These surveillance cameras constantly observe the scene on a 24×7 basis. Since no intelligence is associated with the surveillance system, huge manpower

S. Majhi—This work is done at National Institute of Technology, Rourkela as a part of Master's Thesis.

is required for monitoring. These cameras generate petabytes of video data every minute, which is difficult to investigate through human efforts. Thus, to avoid the waste of human labor and time, the development of computer vision-based anomaly detection algorithms is a pressing need.

Anomaly detection in real-world videos is an active domain in computer vision society. Computer vision algorithms for solving anomaly detection task comprise of two major steps *i.e.*, *extraction of discriminative feature representations and choice of learning mechanism to distinguish anomaly instances from normal ones.* In the last decade, several methods [2,6,13,21] have been reported based on hand-crafted feature extraction strategy. These methods manually compute the inherent properties of video frames which vary with the change in scene associated with the anomaly detection task. Moreover, the difficulties involved in obtaining tracks and trajectories as well as the shallow representation of global motion patterns leads to unreliable feature vectors. Since no feature learning is associated with hand-crafted feature extraction strategy, these methods are not promising in recent anomaly detection task. The deep convolutional neural networks (CNN) like VGG16, GoogleNet, C3D [19] are most popular among the researchers due to its capability of learning feature representation by itself. As these architectures are most successful in image and video classifications task and they are pre-trained on large scale datasets such as ImageNet [8] and Sports1M [7], authors in [15] claim that the pre-trained CNNs can be good feature extraction backbone for any other computer vision task. Following this, authors in [17,25] utilized the pre-trained 3DCNNs as a feature extractor backbone for solving anomaly detection task. They have extracted the features from the penultimate layer *i.e., fc6* of the C3D model for every 16-frame video sequence. Although CNNs are successful in image and video classification tasks, they still have limited robustness to anomaly detection in surveillance videos. This is due to the challenges (*i.e.,* change in illumination, partial occlusion, high intra class variation) involved in the task. Moreover, extraction of penultimate CNN layer features only provides the higher-level abstraction of the input video sequences. Hence they fail to address the above mentioned challenges. Recent studies [23] demonstrate that the intermediate layers of CNN provide lower-level feature representation of the input, which is robust in handling partial occlusion, variation in illumination etc. Inspired by this, the lower layer 3DCNN features are utilized for solving anomaly detection task. Moreover, a single intermediate layer is not sufficient for handling the above mentioned challenges. Thus, a multi-level feature combination strategy is proposed, which combines features from multiple intermediate 3DCNN layers.

In real world, the surveillance videos are untrimmed and of longer duration. Thus, modeling of motion pattern is a crucial task in anomaly detection. For this, authors in [26] combines the RGB features from C3D model with the optical flow feature from PWCNet [18] to model the global motion pattern in anomaly detection task. Since 3CDNN and Optical flow are capable of capturing the short-term motion dynamics only, long range temporal dependency modeling is required. Inspired by this, authors in [25] employ temporal convolution network (TCN) on top of C3D spatio-temporal features for long-range temporal modeling.

Following this, the proposed method also includes many-to-many long short term memory (LSTM) module top of the multi-level 3DCNN features for long range temporal dependency modeling.

The choice of learning mechanism plays a crucial role in video anomaly detection. Recently many approaches [1,3,5,10,16,20] have been reported based on unsupervised learning. These methods are optimized only from the normal examples for a given scene. Since it is difficult to define all types of normal examples, these methods raise higher false alarms in real-world scenarios. To combat the pitfall of unsupervised methods, recent studies [17,25,26] formulate video anomaly detection as the binary classification problem that takes both normal and anomaly examples into account during optimization. In order to learn from strong supervision similar to action detection tasks [22] in untrimmed videos, it requires huge temporally annotated data. Obtaining dense temporal annotations in long untrimmed videos for anomaly detection task is labor intensive and time consuming. Hence, authors in [17] proposed a multiple instance learning (MIL) framework to learn from weak-supervision. In this, video-level supervision is sufficient for training. In order to learn from weak-supervision authors in [17] proposed a hinge based ranking loss with the objective to maximize the separation between normal and anomaly instances.

Although several approaches have been reported in weakly-supervised video anomaly detection task, most of them rely on the penultimate features from 3DCNN and aims at maximizing the separation between normal and anomaly by ranking loss. Due to this, it has been observed that the detection performance is limited. To achieve an enhanced detection performance, a multi-level feature combination strategy is proposed in this work as shown in Fig. 1, which extracts features from lower-level abstraction of input video sequences. Along with this, a Min-Max ranking loss is proposed which not only ensures maximum separation between normal and anomaly instances but also ensures minimum separability among the normal instances to reduce false alarms in real-world scenarios.

To summarize, the contributions of the paper are in three folds:

- A multi-level feature combination strategy in 3DCNN is proposed with the objective to mitigate visual challenges like *partial occlusion, change in illumination* in anomaly detection task.
- A Min-Max ranking loss is proposed which maximizes the separation between anomaly and normal instances and minimizes the separation among the normal instances simultaneously.
- An extensive experimental evaluation is carried out on a large-scale widely used UCF-Crime [17] dataset to showcase the effectiveness of the proposed method compared to recently reported schemes.

2   Proposed Method

The proposed scheme consists of four different stages and are executed sequentially to detect the anomalies from untrimmed surveillance videos. The four

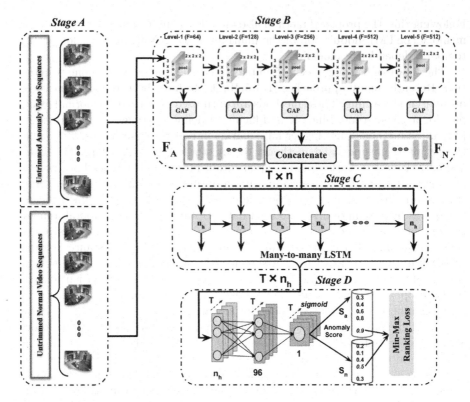

Fig. 1. Proposed Framework: It is comprises of four stages: *Stage A* divides long video sequences into T temporal segments. *Stage B* extracts the features from the proposed multi-level 3DCNN for each temporal segments. *Stage C* encodes the temporal dependencies among the video segments. *Stage D* performs anomaly detection task using multi-layer perceptrons (MLP) where the loss is calculated from a Min-Max Ranking loss.

different stages of the proposed scheme are shown in Fig. 1. Since the suggested scheme follows a weakly-supervised MIL approach, *stage A* divides the untrimmed videos into temporal segments *(say T)*. In *Stage B* spatio-temporal features are extracted from each temporal segments using multi-level 3DCNN. *Stage C* encodes the long range temporal dependency among the feature segments obtained from *stage B*. Finally, *stage D* performs the anomaly detection by the multi-layer perceptrons (MLP) which is trained by the proposed Min-Max ranking loss. In the following subsections, a complete description of each stage is provided.

2.1 Divide Video into Segments

In *stage A*, each untrimmed video V is divided into constant number *(say T)* of temporally disjoint segments $\{TS_1, TS_2, \ldots, TS_T\}$ to keep homogeneity among the variable length videos. Moreover, V can be an anomaly or normal video where the length of a temporal segment TS_i can differ in various video sequences, due to the accumulation of variable length videos.

2.2   Multi-level 3DCNN Feature Extraction

In *stage B*, spatio-temporal features are extracted from a suggested multi-level 3DCNN network. The suggested feature extractor is designed by utilizing the sequential 3D ConvNet, C3D [19] architecture which is pre-trained on Sports1M dataset [7]. Since C3D is a sequential 3DCNN and it has five levels of convolution and pooling layers, the spatio-temporal representation of the input 16-frames sequence can only be obtained after the fifth level. This obtained feature representation can be termed as penultimate layer features, which has limited robustness to challenges like *partial occlusion, high intra class variations and change in illuminations* involved in the task. Thus, a multi-level 3DCNN architecture is proposed which obtains the spatio-temporal feature representation from each level of the sequential C3D model. The proposed scheme allows to extract the feature representations from the inner layers instead of only from the penultimate layer. The multi-level 3DCNN shown in Fig. 1 uses only $3 \times 3 \times 3$ dimension convolution filters with ReLU activation and $2 \times 2 \times 2$ dimension Max pooling operator in all five levels. However, the difference between five levels is the number of convolution layers and the number of 3D convolution filters applied in each level. The first two levels *i.e. Level 1 and 2* of the multi-level 3DCNN has single convolution layers with ReLU activation followed by the pooling layers and it has 64 and 128 3D convolution filters respectively. But the Level 3, 4 and 5 have two consecutive convolution layers with ReLU activation followed by a pooling layer and it has 256, 512, 512 number of 3D convolution filters respectively. Similar to the sequential C3D model, the multi-level 3DCNN also requires 16-frames video sequence for spatio-temporal feature extractions. But in each level of the multi-level 3DCNN, the dimension of output feature map is significantly high, which increases the computational complexity. Thus to have a reduced dimension feature map, a global average pooling (GAP) operator is employed to compute average value of the feature map of each filter in a layer. As a result, the feature extracted each of Level-1, 2, 3, 4, and 5 has 64, 128, 256, 512, 512 dimensional feature vectors respectively, which is nothing but the number of convolutional filters employed in each of the levels. Moreover, extraction of spatio-temporal features from a single level is not sufficient for handling the above mentioned challenges. Thus, features are concatenated from each of the five levels of multi-level 3DCNN to obtain a single feature vector for a single 16-frames snippet. The resultant feature vector has dimension of 1472 *(=n)* as shown in Fig. 1, where $n = 64 + 128 + 256 + 512 + 512$. In addition, due to the unavailability of temporal annotations in the weakly-supervised anomaly detection task, it is difficult to fine-tune the proposed multi-level 3DCNN architecture. Hence, the pre-trained architecture which is trained in Sports1M [7] dataset is used to extract the off-the-shelf spatio-temporal features.

2.3   Temporal Modeling

Long range temporal dependency modeling is necessary in untrimmed videos for anomaly detection task. Thus, LSTM module is utilized in *stage C* to obtain the temporal encoding for a given video feature map. LSTMs are preferred over RNN since it can retain the relevant features and discard the irrelevant ones through it's internal gates. In this method, a many-to-many variant of LSTM $f()$ with β_h parameters is used for temporal dependency encoding. The LSTM $f()$ inputs the multi-level 3DCNN feature map $F_T \in \mathbb{R}^{T \times n}$ from *stage B* for a given video sequence. Here T corresponds to the number of temporal segments in a video and n is the feature vector dimension of each temporal segments. The LSTM has n_h internal neurons with *tanh* squashed that outputs $T \times n_h$ dimensional temporal encoding to be used for anomaly detection task in *stage D*. Hence, the LSTM output F_{ht} can be computed as:

$$F_{ht} = f(h_{T-1}, F_T; \beta_h) \tag{1}$$

2.4   Anomaly Detection

Stage D performs the anomaly detection task across the temporal segment for a query video sequence. As input to *stage D* is the temporal encoding F_{ht} with dimension $T \times n_h$, a `time-distributed` MLP network is used to process each temporal segment. The final layer of the MLP has single neuron with *sigmoid* activation to assign independent anomaly ranks (*scores*) to each temporal segments (TS).

2.5   Network Optimization with Min-Max Ranking Loss

The proposed framework is end-to-end trainable except the multi-level 3DCNN backbone. Since no temporal ground truths are provided during model optimization, a min-max ranking loss is proposed in this work to effectively optimize the network. The min-max ranking loss essentially overcome the drawbacks of the ranking loss function proposed by Sultani *et al.* [17] for weakly-supervised learning. The primary objective of the ranking loss function is to maximize the separation between anomaly and normal video segments. But identifying normal and anomaly video segments without temporal annotations is a difficult task. Thus to identify, authors in [17] assume that temporal segments (TS) gathered from an untrimmed anomaly video and normal video carry at least a single anomaly TS and no anomaly TS respectively. With this assumption, anomaly and normal TS can be identified in the score level since the *stage D* assigns independent scores to each TS. Two score bags (S_a) and (S_n) are created to accumulate the ranks of anomaly and normal videos respectively. Further, based on another assumption the maximum score of (S_a) is identified as the anomaly TS. Similarly, the maximum score of (S_n) is chosen as a normal TS to reduce the false positives. Thus, following is the MIL ranking loss formulated by [17].

$$L_{Ranking}(S_a, S_n) = \max\left(0, 1 - \max_{i \in S_a}(S_a^i) + \max_{i \in S_n}(S_n^i)\right) \tag{2}$$

where $N = T \times BatchSize$. From detailed investigation, it is found that the ranking loss in (2) only considers a single anomaly TS and normal TS for maximizing the margin between them. However, an anomaly video may contain multiple anomaly TS. So, considering only one TS from each of (S_a) and (S_n) through *max* operation may not be expressive. Thus motivated by this, the *mean* score of all TS gathered from normal and anomaly video sequences are considered for maximizing the margin. The improved ranking loss can be formulated as follows:

$$L_{Mean\ Ranking}(S_a, S_n) = \max\left(0, 1 - (\sum_i^N S_a^i)/N + (\sum_i^N S_n^i)/N\right) \tag{3}$$

Since the improved ranking loss in (3) considers all the TS present in anomaly and normal videos for margin maximization, this incorporates noise in the loss function. Consider an case where an untrimmed anomaly video has only one anomaly TS and rest all are normal TS. In this case the normal TS are dominant over the anomaly TS. Thus, the improved ranking loss in (3) may not maximize the margin of separation effectively. As an untrimmed anomaly video contains both normal and anomaly temporal segments. So a ranking loss function is required which not only maximizes the separation between normal and anomaly TS but also minimizes the separation among the normal instances. Motivated by this, a Min-Max ranking loss function is proposed which not only maximize the separation between *max* score of (S_a) and $(Sscriptn)$ but also bind together all the normal TS of (S_a) and (S_n) through minimization. The normal TS are chosen by taking the *min* score of (S_a) and (S_n). The proposed Min-Max ranking loss can be formulated as follows:

$$\begin{aligned} L_{Min-Max\ Ranking}(S_a, S_n) = {} & \max\left(0, 1 - \max_{i \in S_a}(S_a^i) + \max_{i \in S_n}(S_n^i)\right) \\ & + \min\left(0, 1 - \min_{i \in S_a}(S_a^i) + \min_{i \in S_n}(S_n^i)\right) \\ & + \lambda_1 \sum_i^{(N-1)} (S_a^i - S_a^{i+1})^2 + \lambda_2 \sum_i^N (S_a^i) \end{aligned} \tag{4}$$

where λ_1 and λ_2 denote the weighting factors of the temporal smoothing and sparsity constraints, respectively as proposed in [17].

3   Experiments

3.1   Dataset Description and Evaluation Metric

The experiments are performed on UCF-Crime dataset [17]. It is a large-scale diversified video anomaly detection dataset recorded in real-world scenarios like streets, shopping malls, corridors, roads etc. This diverse collection of videos with variable duration ranging from (1 min) to (*approx* 5 h) makes the anomaly detection task more difficult and challenging in this dataset. It has 1900 untrimmed videos, of which 950 videos are normal and the remaining are anomalies of 13

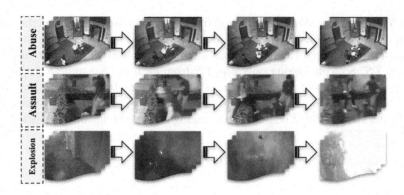

Fig. 2. Visualization of sample anomaly instances from UCF-Crime dataset.

types. For the experimentation and performance comparison the official train-test split provided by [17] has been followed. Following earlier works [17,25,26], we use frame-level receiver operating characteristics (ROC) and its corresponding area under the curve (AUC) to evaluate the proposed approach (Fig. 2).

3.2   Implementation Details

At first, videos are divided into 32 $(=T)$ temporal segments and then spatio-temporal features are extracted from the multi-level 3DCNN for every 16-frames snippets in each temporal segments. For feature extraction, the frames are resized into 128×170 and a center crop of dimension 112×112 is taken. As the multi-level 3DCNN outputs a 1×1472 dimensional feature vector for every temporal segments, for a given long untrimmed video a feature map of dimension 32×1472 is obtained from multi-level 3DCNN. Further, to encode the temporal dependency in video feature map, a LSTM module with 1024 hidden neurons $(= n_h)$ is used. Then a `time-distributed` two-layers perceptron with 96 and 1 neurons is used to detect anomalies. The network is trained up to 33000 iterations with Adam optimizer and 0.0001 learning rate. The hyper parameters λ_1 and λ_2 are kept to 8×10^{-5} in Min-Max ranking loss. The loss is computed by uniformly selecting 60 videos *i.e.* a *BatchSize* of 30 videos each from normal and

Table 1. Ablation study on features extracted from multi-level 3DCNN.

Method	AUC (%)
LEVEL-1 feature + LSTM	72.8
LEVEL-1 $\oplus$ 2 feature + LSTM	74.82
LEVEL-1 $\oplus$ 2 $\oplus$ 3 feature + LSTM	76.85
LEVEL-1 $\oplus$ 2 $\oplus$ 3 $\oplus$ 4 feature + LSTM	78.05
LEVEL-1 $\oplus$ 2 $\oplus$ 3 $\oplus$ 4 $\oplus$ 5 feature + LSTM	**79.03**

Table 2. Ablation study on the different loss functions.

Method	AUC (%)
Multi-level 3DCNN + $L_{Ranking}$ [Eq. 2]	79.03
Multi-level 3DCNN + $L_{Mean\ Ranking}$ [Eq. 3]	79.14
Multi-level 3DCNN + $L_{Min-Max\ Ranking}$ [Eq. 4]	**80.49**

Table 3. State-of-the-art anomaly detection performance comparison in terms of AUC on UCF-Crime dataset. Kindly Note that * marked AUC are reported by using multi-level 3DCNN backbone.

Methods	Feature Modality	AUC (%)
SVM Binary Classifier	RGB	50.00
Hasan et al. [6]	RGB	50.60
Lu et al. [10]	RGB	65.51
Sultani et al. [17]	RGB	75.41
Zhang et al. [25]	RGB	78.66
Majhi et al. [14]	RGB	78.75*
Zhu et al. [26]	RGB+OF	79.00
Lin et al. [9]	RGB+OF	78.28
Majhi et al. [12]	RGB	79.32*
Zaheer et al. [24]	RGB	79.54
Majhi et al. [11]	RGB	79.71*
Cheng et al. [4]	RGB	77.43
Proposed Method + $L_{Ranking}$ [Eq. 2]	**RGB**	**79.03**
Proposed Method + $L_{Min-Max\ Ranking}$ [Eq. 4]	**RGB**	**80.49**

anomaly classes and gradient is computed through the reverse mode automatic differentiation using TensorFlow.

3.3 Experimental Analysis

Quantitative Analysis. In this paper, two sets of experiments have been carried out for weakly-supervised anomaly detection task in UCF-Crime dataset. At first, experiments are conducted to check the relevance of the inner layer features of C3D architecture followed by a LSTM module. Table 1 and Fig. 3a compares the AUC and ROC performance of the different inner layer features with LSTM. It can be seen from first row of Table 1 that only LEVEL-1 feature results in 72.8% AUC in UCF-Crime dataset. However, only single inner level feature is not sufficient for a robust anomaly detection task. Thus, in subsequent experimentation remaining level features are sequentially concatenated with LEVEL-1 feature followed by LSTM module to draw an inference. When

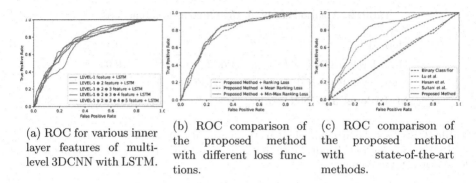

(a) ROC for various inner layer features of multi-level 3DCNN with LSTM.

(b) ROC comparison of the proposed method with different loss functions.

(c) ROC comparison of the proposed method with state-of-the-art methods.

Fig. 3. ROC performance comparison plots on UCF-Crime dataset.

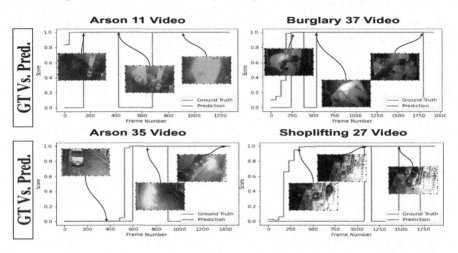

Fig. 4. Visualization of the prediction score w.r.t the ground truth during testing.

LEVEL-1 and 2 features are concatenated ($\oplus$), it results in a marginal improvement (72.8$\longrightarrow$74.82). Further, LEVEL-1, 2 and 3 features are combined which also results in a marginal improvement than that of LEVEL- 1 and 2 features *i.e.* (74.82$\longrightarrow$76.85). With the success of above experimentation, now LEVEL-1, 2, 3 and 4 features are combined which is significantly higher dimension than earlier feature, but results in a marginal performance improvement (76.85$\longrightarrow$78.05). Finally, the proposed method termed as multi-level 3DCNN combines the features from LEVEL-1, 2, 3, 4 and 5 which not only results in a substantial performance improvement (72.8$\longrightarrow$79.03) than that of only LEVEL-1 features but also achieves the state-of-the-art performance for anomaly detection task in UCF-Crime dataset as shown in Table 3.

Secondly, another set of experiments have been carried out to check the implication of different ranking loss functions in training the proposed method. Table 2 and Fig. 3b show the AUC and ROC comparison of the proposed method respectively when trained with different loss functions. The first row of Table 2 shows the AUC performance (79.03) of the proposed method trained with the ranking loss (RL) in (Eq. 2) When the mean-ranking loss in (Eq. 3) is used for training the proposed method there is no substantial improvement in the detection performance (79.03⟶79.14). But, training the proposed multi-level 3DCNN method with the min-max ranking loss in (Eq. 4) not only boosts the detection performance (79.03⟶80.49) substantially but also outperforms the recently reported methods as shown in Table 3 and Fig. 3c.

Qualitative Analysis. To notice the influence of proposed method on anomaly detection task, the prediction scores of the test videos with respect to it's ground truth are visualized as shown in Fig. 4. Interestingly it is found that, the proposed multi-level 3DCNN feature extraction strategy is robust to detect anomalies captured in illumination variations conditions. It is visible from Fig. 4, for the videos *"Arson 11"*, *"Burglary 37"*, *"Arson 35"* the anomaly occurs in inadequate lighting condition and the proposed method is capable of detecting those anomalies accurately. However for the video *"Shoplifting 27"*, the proposed method results in imprecise detection performance. To identify the possible cause of impreciseness the video is analyzed and found that, *a person succeeds to steal a mobile phone in two different attempts which involve multiple long and shot temporal dynamics*. To handle such scenarios effective temporal dependency encoding is required.

4   Conclusion

In this paper, a multi-level 3DCNN framework with a LSTM module and a min-max ranking loss is proposed. The proposed method achieves the competitive performance in UCF-Crime dataset. From the qualitative analysis, the proposed method is seen to be robust in detecting the anomalies even in different illumination conditions. This is due to the multi-level feature extraction scheme and the min-max ranking loss which not only maximizes the margin of separation between normal and anomaly instances but also minimizes the margin among normal instances. Also, it is observed from qualitative analysis that the proposed method still lags in discriminating the anomalies which largely varies in their temporal extent. Thus, in future temporal attention mechanism can be adopted for effective temporal modeling in anomaly detection task.

References

1. Adam, A., Rivlin, E., Shimshoni, I., Reinitz, D.: Robust real-time unusual event detection using multiple fixed-location monitors, vol. 30, pp. 555–560. IEEE (2008)
2. Basharat, A., Gritai, A., Shah, M.: Learning object motion patterns for anomaly detection and improved object detection. In: 2008 IEEE Conference on Computer Vision and Pattern Recognition, pp. 1–8. IEEE (2008)

3. Benezeth, Y., Jodoin, P.M., Saligrama, V., Rosenberger, C.: Abnormal events detection based on spatio-temporal co-occurences. In: 2009 IEEE Conference on Computer Vision and Pattern Recognition, pp. 2458–2465. IEEE (2009)

4. Cheng, J., Zhang, F., Wang, G., Zhang, W.: A multi-stage fusion instance learning method for anomalous event detection in videos. Int. J. Mach. Learn. Cybern. **14**, 445–454 (2022)

5. Cong, Y., Yuan, J., Liu, J.: Abnormal event detection in crowded scenes using sparse representation, vol. 46, pp. 1851–1864. Elsevier (2013)

6. Hasan, M., Choi, J., Neumann, J., Roy-Chowdhury, A.K., Davis, L.S.: Learning temporal regularity in video sequences. In: The IEEE Conference on Computer Vision and Pattern Recognition, June 2016

7. Karpathy, A., Toderici, G., Shetty, S., Leung, T., Sukthankar, R., Fei-Fei, L.: Large-scale video classification with convolutional neural networks. In: CVPR (2014)

8. Krizhevsky, A., Sutskever, I., Hinton, G.E.: ImageNet classification with deep convolutional neural networks. In: Advances in Neural Information Processing Systems, pp. 1097–1105 (2012)

9. Lin, S., Yang, H., Tang, X., Shi, T., Chen, L.: Social MIL: interaction-aware for crowd anomaly detection. In: 2019 16th IEEE International Conference on Advanced Video and Signal Based Surveillance (AVSS), pp. 1–8. IEEE (2019)

10. Lu, C., Shi, J., Jia, J.: Abnormal event detection at 150 FPS in MATLAB. In: Proceedings of the IEEE International Conference on Computer Vision, pp. 2720–2727 (2013)

11. Majhi, S., Das, S., Brémond, F.: DAM: dissimilarity attention module for weakly-supervised video anomaly detection. In: 2021 17th IEEE International Conference on Advanced Video and Signal Based Surveillance (AVSS), pp. 1–8. IEEE (2021)

12. Majhi, S., Das, S., Brémond, F., Dash, R., Sa, P.K.: Weakly-supervised joint anomaly detection and classification. In: 2021 16th IEEE International Conference on Automatic Face and Gesture Recognition (FG 2021), pp. 1–7 (2021). https://doi.org/10.1109/FG52635.2021.9667006

13. Majhi, S., Dash, R., Sa, P.K.: Two-stream CNN architecture for anomalous event detection in real world scenarios. In: Nain, N., Vipparthi, S.K., Raman, B. (eds.) CVIP 2019. CCIS, vol. 1148, pp. 343–353. Springer, Singapore (2020). https://doi.org/10.1007/978-981-15-4018-9_31

14. Majhi, S., Dash, R., Sa, P.K.: Temporal pooling in inflated 3DCNN for weakly-supervised video anomaly detection. In: 2020 11th International Conference on Computing, Communication and Networking Technologies (ICCCNT), pp. 1–6. IEEE (2020)

15. Nazare, T.S., de Mello, R.F., Ponti, M.A.: Are pre-trained CNNs good feature extractors for anomaly detection in surveillance videos? arXiv preprint arXiv:1811.08495 (2018)

16. Ramachandra, B., Jones, M.: Street scene: a new dataset and evaluation protocol for video anomaly detection. In: The IEEE Winter Conference on Applications of Computer Vision, pp. 2569–2578 (2020)

17. Sultani, W., Chen, C., Shah, M.: Real-world anomaly detection in surveillance videos. In: Proceedings of the IEEE Conference on Computer Vision and Pattern Recognition, pp. 6479–6488 (2018)

18. Sun, D., Yang, X., Liu, M.Y., Kautz, J.: PWC-NET: CNNs for optical flow using pyramid, warping, and cost volume. In: Proceedings of the IEEE Conference on Computer Vision and Pattern Recognition, pp. 8934–8943 (2018)

19. Tran, D., Bourdev, L., Fergus, R., Torresani, L., Paluri, M.: Learning spatiotemporal features with 3D convolutional networks. In: The IEEE International Conference on Computer Vision, December 2015
20. Wang, J., Cherian, A.: Gods: generalized one-class discriminative subspaces for anomaly detection. In: Proceedings of the IEEE International Conference on Computer Vision, pp. 8201–8211 (2019)
21. Wu, S., Moore, B.E., Shah, M.: Chaotic invariants of Lagrangian particle trajectories for anomaly detection in crowded scenes. In: 2010 IEEE Computer Society Conference on Computer Vision and Pattern Recognition, pp. 2054–2060. IEEE (2010)
22. Xu, H., Das, A., Saenko, K.: R-C3D: region convolutional 3D network for temporal activity detection. In: Proceedings of the IEEE International Conference on Computer Vision, pp. 5783–5792 (2017)
23. Yim, J., Ju, J., Jung, H., Kim, J.: Image classification using convolutional neural networks with multi-stage feature. In: Kim, J.-H., Yang, W., Jo, J., Sincak, P., Myung, H. (eds.) Robot Intelligence Technology and Applications 3. AISC, vol. 345, pp. 587–594. Springer, Cham (2015). https://doi.org/10.1007/978-3-319-16841-8_52
24. Zaheer, M.Z., Mahmood, A., Shin, H., Lee, S.I.: A self-reasoning framework for anomaly detection using video-level labels. IEEE Signal Process. Lett. **27**, 1705–1709 (2020)
25. Zhang, J., Qing, L., Miao, J.: Temporal convolutional network with complementary inner bag loss for weakly supervised anomaly detection. In: 2019 IEEE International Conference on Image Processing, pp. 4030–4034. IEEE (2019)
26. Zhu, Y., Newsam, S.: Motion-aware feature for improved video anomaly detection. arXiv preprint arXiv:1907.10211 (2019)

Automatically Generating Storylines from Microblogging Platforms

Xujian Zhao[1]([✉]), Junli Wang[1], Peiquan Jin[2], Chongwei Wang[1],
Chunming Yang[1], Bo Li[1], and Hui Zhang[1]

[1] Southwest University of Science and Technology, Mianyang 621010, Sichuan, China
jasonzhaoxj@swust.edu.cn
[2] University of Science and Technology of China, Hefei 230026, Anhui, China

Abstract. Generating storylines from social networks like Twitter and
Sina Weibo provides users with an intuitive way to accurately digest
event information. To automatically generate a storyline from the rich
information hidden in microblogging platforms, in this paper, we present
an effective solution for generating the storyline from microblog posts.
Firstly, primary events are extracted through a social-influence-based
event model with the temporal distribution. Second, an Event Graph
Convolutional Network (E-GCN) model is presented to learn the latent
relationships among events. Such a model helps predict the story branch
of an event and link events. Finally, we conduct experiments on a real
microblog post dataset to measure the effectiveness of our proposal. The
results suggest the effectiveness of our approach.

Keywords: Storyline · Graph convolutional network · Event
extraction

1 Introduction

Microblogs provide valuable data to discover events and their evolution. In the
face of massive and disordered microblog information, how to deeply mine and
analyze the fragmented data to form a storyline reporting an event's development
has been an essential issue for web users. Moreover, storyline generation can benefit several web mining tasks, such as web news retrieval [16], text summarizing,
and public opinion monitoring [14]. Compared to news articles, storyline generation from microblogs is not an easy task. Firstly, there is tremendous homogeneous and useless information in microblogs, which will affect the extraction of
events. Secondly, data sparseness and the lack of context make it challenging to
learn the correlations among events when constructing story branches.

Recently, there have been some studies on storyline generation [3,7,10]. However, most of them employ supervised or semi-supervised models that need
human intervention, or topic clustering approaches based on word significance. In
this paper, we present a new approach for storyline generation from microblogs,
which differs from prior studies in the following points. Firstly, we propose a new

M. Tanveer et al. (Eds.): ICONIP 2022, CCIS 1794, pp. 38–50, 2023.
https://doi.org/10.1007/978-981-99-1648-1_4

social-influence-based model with the temporal distribution to unveil the multi-level event information, which is different from the word significance adopted by previous work. Secondly, we present a new learning model, namely the Event Graph Convolutional Network (E-GCN) model, to learn the latent relationships among representative events. Moreover, our approach does not require human intervention in the learning process and has a stronger learning ability for implicit semantic relations than previous approaches. Briefly, we make the following contributions to this paper.

- We propose a new social-influence-based model with the temporal distribution to extract representative events from microblogs, which is different from the word significance or social contexts adopted by previous work. Our model suggests utilizing the social attribute of microblogs. Specially, we model the representativeness of an event as its social influence and then extract events with significant social-influence as representative events. Further, we propose a temporal distribution-based algorithm to improve the precision of event extraction.
- We present E-GCN, an improved Graph Convolutional Network (GCN) model, to learn the latent relationships among events to link events and predict an event's story branch. We build a heterogeneous event graph and propose a node-category prediction algorithm to predict the story branch of an event rather than just judging whether an event belongs to the topic. Further, we design a divergence-based method to avoid human interference in the storyline's automatic construction.
- We evaluated the proposed approach on two real datasets and compared it with several state-of-the-art methods. The results suggest the effectiveness of our proposal.

The rest of the paper is structured as follows. We first present some related work in Sect. 2. Then, we detail our methodology in Sect. 3 and report the experimental results in Sect. 4. Finally, we conclude the study and discuss future work in Sect. 5.

2   Related Work

In general, the existing related work can be divided into three categories: relevance analysis, feature learning, and tree-based approaches.

The relevance analysis method links events by analyzing the association relationship between events. Nomoto [11] used a two-layer similarity model to determine whether news stories are connected. Liu et al. [8] realized incremental update of the storyline by merging, expanding, and inserting three event operations for new events. Similarly, Cai et al. [1] used four event operations: create, absorb, split, and merge to capture event evolution patterns over time. The feature learning approach uses some learning model for storyline generation. An unsupervised Bayesian model (DSDM) was presented by Zhou et al. [17] to describe the storyline. They modeled the storyline as the joint distribution of document-named entities and topics and inferred the Bayesian model parameters through Gibbs sampling. Then, the documents of the same story branch

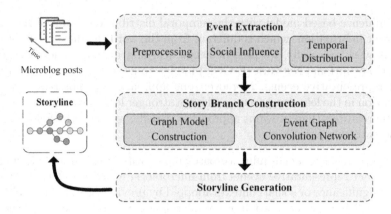

Fig. 1. Architecture for storyline generation

were sorted according to time to obtain the storyline. Mele et al. [9] mapped the news link problem to a Hidden Markov Model (HMM). The tree-based storyline generation aims at solving the problem that the time information in the text cannot determine the sequence of events, Kolomiyets et al. [4] proposed a time-dependent structure to describe the text timeline. All events in the time-dependent structure are connected by a partial order relationship, and each event is a node in the dependency tree. Similarly, Wang et al. [12] considered text and image and combined them with time information to construct a weighted multi-view. In addition, Lin et al. [5] focused on social network data and processed dynamic and sparse social network data to generate a storyline.

3   Methodology

Figure 1 shows the process of storyline generation, which consists of two consecutive tasks: event extraction and story branch construction. First, the microblog posts are processed by a series of machine learning methods. After that, we quantify the representativeness of events as social influence and extract representative events based on the temporal distribution of events. Then, we use heterogeneous graphs to model complex relationships between events. Finally, we utilize the E-GCN model to predict the story branches of events.

The input of system is a set of posts from microblog, $P = \{p_1, p_2, \ldots, p_i, \ldots, p_n\}$, and p_i is a timestamped post, and the output is a time-ordered storyline consisting of representative events.

3.1   Event Extraction

The event extraction includes three modules, namely preprocessing, social influence, and temporal distribution, as shown in Fig. 1.

Preprocessing. For the input, we first perform text preprocessing. Generally, this task has three steps: post-segmentation, temporal expression normalization, and post-filtering. As a complete sentence can express a fully semantic meaning, we can separate posts by punctuation, which indicates a sentence's ending. Further, temporal expressions in the sentence can be regularized by some normalizing algorithm [15]. Finally, after going through the similarity de-duplication module, we get the initial event candidate set.

Social Influence. The storyline aims to show the evolution of related events over time intuitively. Thus, the events used to construct the storyline on different timestamps must broadly represent the corresponding story information. For social networks, opinion leaders are more influential in information diffusion because they usually deliver more critical information than ordinary users. To this end, the microblogs posted by opinion leaders are more likely to be representative events. Therefore, we use a social influence-based model to measure the representativeness of events. The forwarding number, commenting number, and total number of likings are used to calculate an event's representativeness. If a post has many forwards, comments, and likes, we consider that the post contains essential information recognized by many users. As a result, this post will be more likely to discuss representative events than those that forward, comment, and like less. Specifically, the social influence of an event can be represented by Eq. 1.

$$influence(e_i) = log(\alpha \cdot f_n + \beta \cdot c_n + \gamma \cdot l_n + \epsilon) \tag{1}$$

Here, the number of forwards, comments, and likes are denoted as f_n, c_n, and l_n, respectively. The symbols α, β, and γ are the corresponding weights, and ϵ refers to the Euler number.

Temporal Distribution. The storyline consists of many events and reflects the event's evolution with time. For events happening simultaneously, users may have limited attention, which means that users usually focus on events with strong social influence. Thus, extracting representative events requires considering the temporal distribution feature of microblog posts. This paper selects the events with strong social influence based on the events' temporal distribution. Particularly, for an event sequence $E = \{e_1, e_2, \ldots, e_i, \ldots, e_n\}$, we record the events at each timestamp, obtaining the recording series of events. Then, we consider the social influence of an event in timestamp t_i to extract the final events. Finally, we extract representative events to generate the storyline.

3.2   Story Branch Construction

The construction of story branches mainly consists of two modules, Graph Model Construction and E-GCN Construction.

Graph Model Construction. The Graph Convolutional Network (GCN) model [13] is a neural network that operates on graphs and accomplishes semi-supervised learning on graphs. Since a graph can represent much feature information, we model the event features as a graph. More specifically, we build a heterogeneous event graph $G = (V, E)$ to represent the relationship among events. Each node $v \in V$ contains part of the event information. There are mainly two types of nodes: the keyword nodes and the event nodes. We consider nouns, verbs, adjectives, and quantifiers as event keywords. Moreover, each edge $e = (v, v') \in E$ represents a relationship between two nodes. There are three types of edges that are keyword-keyword edges, keyword-event edges, and event-event edges. The degree of correlation between two keyword nodes is calculated by point-wise mutual information, while the TF-IDF value measures the one between keyword nodes and event nodes. Fundamentally, the events in the same story branch occur in a limited time, which means that events with an extensive period are challenging to cluster into a story branch. Thus, we utilize the aging time model to measure the correlation between two events, which is given by Eq. 2. Here, ϵ refers to the Euler number, and t is the factor of the maximum period. t_1 and t_2 are the timestamp of $event_i$ and $event_j$.

$$Edge_{event_i, event_j} = \begin{cases} \epsilon^{-\frac{|t_1-t_2|}{t}} & |t_1 - t_2| > t \\ 1 & otherwise \end{cases} \tag{2}$$

E-GCN (Event Graph Convolutional Network). The GCN is a semi-supervised learning algorithm that requires several nodes with labels. To meet this requirement, we devise a divergence-based method to detect an event in each story branch. Accordingly, we regard the initial story branches as the labeled nodes in GCN. We aim to select the event that is not in the same story branch as the initial story branch to improve the accuracy of subsequent story branch construction. Each initial story branch satisfies the condition indicated by Eq. 3.

$$max_i^n \begin{bmatrix} Sim\left(e_1, E_{initial_{set}}^0\right), ..., \\ Sim\left(e_i, E_{initial_{set}}^{i-1}\right), ..., \\ Sim\left(e_n, E_{initial_{set}}^{n-1}\right), ..., \end{bmatrix} > T \tag{3}$$

Here, $Sim\left(e_i, E_{initial_{set}}^{i-1}\right)$ is the cosine similarity between event e_i and initial story branch set $E_{initial_{set}}^{i-1}$, T refers to the divergence threshold.

The details of initial branch construction are shown in Algorithm 1. First, we utilize the random function to scramble event set E, choosing an event e_1 as the first initial story branch and deleting e_1 from E; Then, we traverse the event set and choose the event e_i that is the most irrelevant to the initial story branch $E_{initial_{set}}^{i-1}$, and deleting e_i from E. This process ensures that the selected events are not in the same story branch as much as possible. We repeat the above steps until the divergence is more significant than the threshold T. Finally, we obtain the initial story branch.

Next, we show how to model the correlations among events through the E-GCN framework. The E-GCN input involves the adjacency matrix and feature matrix, and the feature matrix is calculated by the TF-IDF value. We construct a $N \times N$ weighed adjacency matrix A, where N is the number of events. Moreover, we define a $N \times d$ feature matrix X, where d is the dimension of event features. Consequently, we can use E-GCN to learn implicit semantic relations of events for event linking and predict the story branch to which the event belongs. Specifically, to construct the E-GCN model, we leverage the multi-layer GCN with the following layer-wise propagation rule, as represented by Eq. 4.

Algorithm 1. Story Branch Initialization

Input: event set $E = \{e_1, ..., e_i, ..., e_n\}$
Parameter: maximum event divergence: max_score; divergence threshold: T; similarity between events: $similar$
Output: the initial branch set S

```
 1: S ← ∅;
 2: for i in E.size do
 3:    if S = null then
 4:       S.add(E.get(i));
 5:       E.remove(E.get(i));
 6:    else
 7:       max_score ← 0;
 8:       for j in S.size do
 9:          similar ← cos(E.get(i),S.get(j));
10:          if max_score < similar then
11:             max_score ← similar;
12:          end if
13:       end for
14:       if max_score < T then
15:          S.add(E.get(i));
16:          E.remove(E.get(i));
17:          return S;
18:       end if
19:    end if
20: end for
```

$$H^{(l+1)} = \delta \left(\tilde{D}^{-\frac{1}{2}} \tilde{A} \tilde{D}^{-\frac{1}{2}} H^{(l)} W^{(l)} \right) \tag{4}$$

Here, $\tilde{D}^{-\frac{1}{2}} \tilde{A} \tilde{D}^{-\frac{1}{2}}$ is the symmetric normalized Laplacian matrix, calculating by the adjacency matrix $\tilde{A}$ and diagonal matrix $\tilde{D}$. Meanwhile, W refers to the parameter matrix, and l is the number of layers. In addition, the input layer to E-GCN is denoted as $H^{(0)} = X$. The loss function is defined as cross-entropy error over all labeled event nodes, as shown in Eq. 5, where y_E is the set of event nodes with labels.

$$\min L = - \sum_{e \in y_E} \sum_{f=1}^{F} Y_{ef} \ln Z_{ef} \tag{5}$$

We implement E-GCN by a three-layer GCN, which allows event features to pass among three event nodes. Associated events are clustered into one, and different clusters represent various story branches that each event node belongs to. There is only one node in each branch before training, which is the initial story branch selected by the divergence-based method.

Algorithm 2. Storyline Generation

Input: the story branch set B, the node set N
Output: the storyline tree

```
 1: tree ← ∅;
 2: N.sorted();
 3: B.sorted();
 4: for i in N.size; j in B.size do
 5:    if N.get(i) ≤ B.get(j) then
 6:       tree.add(N.get(i));i ← i + 1;N.remove(N.get(i));
 7:    else
 8:       tree.add(B.get(j));j ← j + 1;B.remove(B.get(j));
 9:    end if
10: end for
11: while N.size ≠ 0 do
12:    tree.add(N.get(0));N.remove(N.get(0));
13: end while
14: while B.size ≠ 0 do
15:    tree.add(B.get(0));B.remove(B.get(0));
16: end while
17: return tree;
```

3.3 Storyline Generation

In the story branch construction module, we predict the story branches to which each event belongs and get the possible links between events. However, the storyline is logical. A complete storyline should not only include story branches, but also transition nodes which refer to the nodes connecting story branches and are highly related to the connected story branches. The reasonable transition nodes make the storyline smooth and the structure integral. Therefore, we need to first identify transition nodes to generate a complete storyline. In the paper, a statistical model represented by Eq. 6 and Eq. 7 is used to define the transition node.

$$branch\_node_i = B_i - \min_{B_i}(num(e_j)) \tag{6}$$

$$transition\_node = \sum B_i - \sum branch\_node_i \tag{7}$$

In the paper, $num(e_j)$ is the number of events that are assigned to the story branch B_i, and the transition node does not belong to the story branch.

The evolution of events in the storyline includes the temporal relationship between events. The development of events in the storyline can only point from previous events to subsequent events. Specifically, the storyline is generated by using the time information in events, story branches, and transition nodes. Algorithm 2 describes the steps of storyline generation.

Table 1. Overview of the datasets

Dataset	Title	Starting and ending time	Number of tweets
Dataset$_1$	Vaccine incident	2018.07.01–2019.09.01	73614
Dataset$_2$	ZTE incident	2018.04.16–2018.07.14	45113

4   Experiment

We collected two real datasets from Sina Weibo[1] to evaluate the performance of our approach. The dataset details are shown in Table 1.

4.1   Performance of Event Extraction

For the evaluation of event extraction, we compare our algorithm with four baseline methods.

(1) **Random**. This method randomly chooses the events.

(2) **TF-IDF** [2]. This method calculates the TF-IDF score and chooses the top-ranked event.

(3) **MWDS** [5]. This method constructs graphs via the similarities between events and uses the Minimum-Weight Dominating Set to select the most representative events.

(4) **DCCI** [14]. Constructing the graph via the similarities between events and selecting the most representative events based on the Degree and Clustering Coefficient Information.

We evaluate our approach on two datasets regarding ROUGE [6] and redundancy. Here, the redundancy of each event is defined as the highest similarity between two events in the set, while the redundancy of the event set is the sum of the redundancy of every event. Table 2 and Table 3 show the results of the event extraction on the two datasets.

Our approach achieves the best performance in terms of ROUGE-1 and ROUGE-L compared with other methods, meaning that our proposal based on the social influence of events can extract the representative event in a story. In addition, our method achieves the second-best performance concerning the redundancy on Dataset$_1$ and the best performance on Dataset$_2$, which implies that most of the detected events by our method contain less redundant information and each detected event only focus on one topic.

4.2   Performance of Story Branch Construction

To evaluate the performance of our proposal in constructing story branches, we compare our algorithm with three baseline methods.

(1) **Story Forest** [7]. It extracts event keywords and calculates the correlation with the Jaccard coefficient, based on which it clusters an event to a story branch.

---

[1] https://weibo.com.

Table 2. Performance of the event extraction on Dataset₁

Methods	ROUGE-1	ROUGE-L	Redundancy
Random	0.68	0.22	28.15
TF-IDF	0.69	0.21	**20.82**
MWDS	0.65	0.32	36.58
DCCI	0.63	0.35	47.95
Ours	**0.82**	**0.51**	23.34

Table 3. Performance of the event extraction on Dataset₂

Methods	ROUGE-1	ROUGE-L	Redundancy
Random	0.73	0.44	31.81
TF-IDF	0.82	0.47	39.20
MWDS	0.68	0.44	41.48
DCCI	0.68	0.43	44.36
Ours	**0.83**	**0.70**	**27.81**

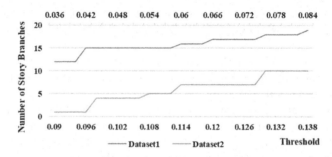

Fig. 2. Number of the initial story branches with different divergence thresholds

(2) **Steiner Tree** [5]. It generates story branches via the Steiner tree algorithm considering the minimum-weight dominating set in approximation.

(3) **Bayesian Model** [3]. This approach models event features and explores the story branch of an event via Gibbs sampling.

To determine the optimal number of story branches, T is optimized by setting the step size to 0.002. Figure 2 shows the number of the initial story branches with different T. The trend of the blue line represents the results on Dataset₁. When the initial layer branch number is 15, the trend is relatively stable. The trend of the red line represents the results on Dataset₂, which shows that the initial layer branch number is more suitable when set to 7. Further, we measure the influence of the maximum period of an event t. As shown in Fig. 3, different t do impact the performance. When t is set to 30, the algorithm gets the best performance in terms of various metrics. For events beyond this period, their correlation will weaken due to time aging.

Table 4. Precision, Recall and F1-score of the story branch construction on Dataset$_1$

Methods	P	R	F1
Bayesian Model	0.75	0.45	0.55
Steiner Tree	0.65	0.66	0.63
Story Forest	0.74	0.51	0.56
Ours	**0.86**	**0.84**	**0.83**

Table 5. Precision, Recall and F1-score of the story branch construction on Dataset$_2$

Methods	P	R	F1
Bayesian Model	0.46	0.57	0.51
Steiner Tree	0.50	**0.68**	0.58
Story Forest	0.41	0.56	0.48
Ours	**0.85**	0.60	**0.70**

Table 4 and Table 5 show the results of story branch construction on the two datasets. Our proposal outperforms the other three approaches in terms of all metrics, although it gets a little lower results than the Steiner Tree on Dataset$_2$. Meanwhile, some unsatisfactory story branch cases are discussed in the paper. Figure 4 shows the evaluation result of generating the individual story branch on Dataset$_1$. It indicates that our method works not better than the comparative approaches in constructing the individual story branch B_4 on Dataset$_1$. The reason is that the two events belonging to the same branch are divided into two independent initial branches in the story branch initialization, which means the performance of the automatic generation of story branches will be highly affected by the story branch initialization.

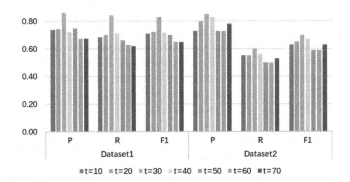

Fig. 3. Precision, Recall and F1-score results for constructing initial story branches with the varying period (t)

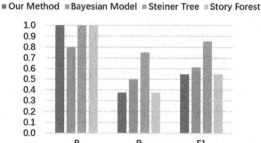

Fig. 4. Precision, Recall and F1-score results for generating the individual story branch B_4 on Dataset$_1$

Table 6. Percentage of the correct linkings

Methods	Dataset$_1$	Dataset$_2$
Story Timeline	0.31	0.30
Steiner Tree	0.41	0.39
Story Forest	0.47	0.33
Ours	**0.64**	**0.42**

4.3   Performance of Storyline Generation

To measure the performance of the storyline generation, we compare our algorithm with three baseline methods.

(1) **Story Timeline.** This method links events according to the timestamp in events.

(2) **Story Forest** [7]. This method links events based on the Jaccard similarity coefficient of event keywords, and proposes several operations such as merge, extend and insert, and use incremental clustering to update the storyline.

(3) **Steiner Tree** [5]. This method builds graphs based on event similarity and generates a storyline based on the minimum weight spanning tree.

Here, we use the percentage of the correct linkings [7] to measure the effectiveness of each method. The results are shown in Table 6. Due to the subjective nature of the criteria used to generate the storyline, the performance of correct edge links is not ideal. For dataset$_1$, the correct linkings percentage given by the Story Timeline algorithm is 0.31, because this method only uses the timestamp of events to generate a storyline, and does not analyze the correlation between events. Both Story Forest and Steiner Tree consider the similarity between the two events, so they have similar performances. In this paper, the event features and relationships are defined as a graph by using the event characteristics, and the implicit semantic association between events is modeled through the event graph convolution network. Compared to the previous works, E-GCN enhances the learning ability to discover implicit semantic relations between events through feature passing, to obtain the best performance.

5   Conclusion

In this paper, we presented a system for generating storylines from microblogs. We detailed two consecutive tasks in storyline generation. First, we extracted representative events by integrating social influence into temporal distribution. Second, we proposed a new ECN model to improve the learning ability of implicit relationships between events. We conducted comparative experiments on a real dataset, and the results suggested the effectiveness of our proposal.

Acknowledgements. This paper is supported by the Humanities and Social Sciences Foundation of the Ministry of Education (17YJCZH260), the National Science Foundation of China (62072419), the Sichuan Science and Technology Program (2020YFS0057).

References

1. Cai, H., Huang, Z., Srivastava, D., Zhang., Q.: Indexing evolving events from tweet streams. In: ICDE, pp. 1538–1539 (2016)
2. Guo, B., et al.: CrowdStory: fine-grained event storyline generation by fusion of multi-modal crowdsourced data. Proc. ACM Interact. Mob. Wearable Ubiquitous Technol. **1**(3), 55:1–55:19 (2017)
3. Hua, T., Zhang, X., Wang, W., Lu, C.T., Ramakrishnan., N.: Automatical storyline generation with help from Twitter. In: CIKM, pp. 2383–2388 (2016)
4. Kolomiyets, O., Bethard, S., Moens, M.F.: Extracting narrative timelines as temporal dependency structures. In: ACL, pp. 88–97 (2012)
5. Lin, C., et al.: Generating event storylines from microblogs. In: CIKM, pp. 175–184 (2012)
6. Lin, C.Y.: ROUGE: a package for automatic evaluation of summaries. In: the Workshop on Text Summarization Branches Out, pp. 74–81 (2004)
7. Liu, B., et al.: Story forest: extracting events and telling stories from breaking news. ACM Trans. Knowl. Discov. Data **14**(3), 31:1–31:28 (2020)
8. Liu, B., Niu, D., Lai, K., Kong, L., Xu., Y.: Growing story forest online from massive breaking news. In: CIKM, pp. 777–785 (2017)
9. Mele, I., Bahrainian, S.A., Crestani., F.: Linking news across multiple streams for timeliness analysis. In: CIKM, pp. 767–776 (2017)
10. Mu, L., Jin, P., Zhao, J., Chen., E.: Detecting evolutionary stages of events on social media: a graph-kernel-based approach. Future Gener. Comput. Syst. **123**, 219–232 (2021)
11. Nomoto., T.: Two-tier similarity model for story link detection. In: CIKM, pp. 789–798 (2010)
12. Wang, D., Li, T., Ogihara, M.: Generating pictorial storylines via minimum-weight connected dominating set approximation in multi-view graphs. In: AAAI (2012)
13. Wu, Z., et al.: A comprehensive survey on graph neural networks. IEEE Trans. Neural Networks Learn. Syst. **32**(1), 4–24 (2021)
14. Yuan, R., Zhou, Q., Zhou., W.: dTexSL: a dynamic disaster textual storyline generating framework. World Wide Web **22**(5), 1913–1933 (2019)
15. Zhao, X., Jin, P., Yue., L.: Discovering topic time from web news. Inf. Process. Manag. **51**(6), 869–890 (2015)

16. Zhao, X., Wang, C., Jin, P., Zhang, H., Yang, C., Li., B.: Post2Story: automatically generating storylines from microblogging platforms. In: ACM MM, pp. 2786–2788 (2021)
17. Zhou, D., Xu, H., He., Y.: An unsupervised Bayesian modelling approach for storyline detection on news articles. In: EMNLP, pp. 1943–1948 (2015)

Improving Document Image Understanding with Reinforcement Finetuning

Bao-Sinh Nguyen[1]([✉]), Dung Tien Le[1], Hieu M. Vu[1], Tuan-Anh D. Nguyen[1], Minh-Tien Nguyen[1,3], and Hung Le[2]

[1] Cinnamon AI, 10th floor, Geleximco building, 36 Hoang Cau,
Dong Da, Hanoi, Vietnam
{simon,nathan,ian,tadashi,ryan.nguyen}@cinnamon.is
[2] Deakin University, Geelong, Australia
thai.le@deakin.edu.au
[3] Hung Yen University of Technology and Education, Hung Yen, Vietnam
tiennm@utehy.edu.vn

Abstract. Successful Artificial Intelligence systems often require numerous labeled data to extract information from document images. In this paper, we investigate the problem of improving the performance of Artificial Intelligence systems in understanding document images, especially in cases where training data is limited. We address the problem by proposing a novel finetuning method using reinforcement learning. Our approach treats the Information Extraction model as a policy network and uses policy gradient training to update the model to maximize combined reward functions that complement the traditional cross-entropy losses. Our experiments on four datasets using labels and expert feedback demonstrate that our finetuning mechanism consistently improves the performance of a state-of-the-art information extractor, especially in the small training data regime.

Keywords: Information Extraction · Reinforcement Learning · Human-In-The-Loop

1 Introduction

Digitizing business documents is crucial for companies and corporations to improve their productivity and efficiency. Although the advent of Document Intelligence brings forth many opportunities to capture the key information of document images, extraction for visually-rich documents such as receipts, invoices, and leaflets remains notoriously challenging due to the spareness of textual information and the variety in layouts and formats. Thus, for an Artificial Intelligence (AI) system to fully understand and extract desired information, it is essential to incorporate the textual, visual, and layout aspects into the model and have it trained in an end-to-end manner.

© The Author(s), under exclusive license to Springer Nature Singapore Pte Ltd. 2023
M. Tanveer et al. (Eds.): ICONIP 2022, CCIS 1794, pp. 51–63, 2023.
https://doi.org/10.1007/978-981-99-1648-1_5

To this end, several approaches have aimed to encode visual and layout information in addition to contextual features to enhance document representations. Earlier approaches focus on improving the performance of document layout analysis and information extraction separately and combining them in a multi-stage pipeline. However, these methods often lead to cascading errors due to the nature of pipeline processing. Recent attempts introduce end-to-end training via Graph Neural Networks [1] and language modeling - LayoutLM [2,3] - for jointly modeling text and layout information.

While the methods above are effective when dealing with benchmark datasets, there exist challenges for practical cases. First, for the model to perform well on a new dataset, a decent amount of labeled training data is required to finetune the model. Benchmark datasets can include up to thousands of samples or even more. However, in reality, only a few labeled samples can be provided for training because data annotation is time-consuming and labor-expensive. Therefore, an open research question still remains: *how do we make the most of these valuable data to enable sample-efficient information extraction?* The second issue is the current training process relies solely on predefined datasets for finetuning in a supervised manner. The supervised training often uses differentiable loss, such as cross-entropy, to predict the locations of the extracted content, which may cause a mismatch between the training objective and the performance metric. More importantly, this opts out the opportunities for domain experts to provide feedback, design the learning criteria, and guide the model to more accurate extraction.

In this paper, we introduce a new fine-tuning method that complements the traditional cross-entropy training with different learning objectives that match better the evaluation criteria. We formulate the information extraction task as a reinforcement learning (RL) problem wherein the information extractor, such as SpanIE-Recur [4], is the policy network, and its output corresponds to actions. We design different reward functions to capture the spatial, categorical, lexical and semantic similarity between the extracted and the ground-truth answers. We then use the proximal policy gradient algorithm (PPO) [5] to learn the optimal policy that maximizes the total rewards. Our approach not only exploits all aspects of training signals from the data but also allows the domain expert to design rewards or provide feedback to improve the system. We evaluate our method on two public and two private visually-rich document datasets and achieve consistent improvement over only using supervised training in terms of F1 scores, especially when the training data is limited. We also conduct a human-in-the-loop experiment where a domain expert provides ranking feedback to finetune the model, showing clear improvement over a few interactions.

Our contributions are three-fold: (i) a novel approach to improve information extraction in business documents using reinforcement learning, (ii) a set of complimentary reward functions to aid the traditional supervised learning (SL), and (iii) extensive experiments on both public (English) and private real-world dataset (Japanese), confirming the benefit of our approach with both limited ground-truth labels and expert feedback.

2   Related Work

Information Extraction (IE) is an increasingly popular task, where the goal is to automatically extract structured information from a given unstructured document. Unlike plain text, visually-rich documents (VRDs) usually contain sparser texts with well-defined layouts and meaningful visual structures, which can previously be addressed using computer vision and graph-based methods [6,7]. With the success of BERT [8] and its derivatives, e.g. LayoutLM [2,3], IE methods for VRDs are seeing a trend of shifting from traditional to NLP techniques, such as sequence labeling and span extraction.

There have been many studies applying span extraction to IE. [9] presented a span-based model for NER, which enables the model to handle the more common sequence labeling approach such as overlapping entities and discontinued entities. One disadvantage of span-based methods is that they usually only extract one answer for one question at a time. To address this issue, [4,10] share the same question-context interaction mechanism which enables simultaneous extraction for multiple questions, but the former employs a recursive linking technique while the latter proposes combining span extraction with sequence labeling to facilitate multi-value extraction. In this paper, we adapt SpanIE-Recur to our task, because it achieves superior performance compared to other sequence labeling approaches on business documents [4], and its architecture also enables RL formulation (see Sect. 4.1). Particularly, we empower SpanIE-Recur by putting it into an RL framework, which allows SpanIE-Recur to take into account the advantage of transfer learning and human feedback for training. Based on that, we can improve the quality of our extraction model.

Reinforcement Learning has been applied to text summarization [11], dialogue generation [12] and machine translation [13]. Most of these methods focus on building an RL agent that generates texts in the forms of summary, dialogue, and different languages based on the reward signal computed directly from the ground truth text and prediction text. The motivation behind applying RL on these works is that RL can directly optimize discrete target evaluation metrics such as ROUGE that are non-differentiable. Recent attempts push the idea further by adding preference learning into the reward model [14–16], thus enhancing the alignment of the metric being optimized with what humans want AI models to do. We extend RL as the technique to our IE task for VRDs. More importantly, to the best of our knowledge, this paper is the very first attempt to apply reinforcement learning for the visually-rich document information extraction task.

3   Background

Information Extraction Backbone. We use SpanIE-Recur [4] as the backbone of our model. SpanIE-Recur addresses the IE problem by the Extractive Question Answering (QA) formulation [8]. Concretely, it replaces the sequence labeling head of the original LayoutLM [2] by a span prediction head to predict the starting and the ending positions of the answers given an input field/tag (hereinafter referred to as a *question*).

In particular, let $D = \{w_0, w_1, ..., w_n\}$ denote the input document context consisting of n input tokens. The pretrained language model converts them into a set of hidden representations $H = \{h_0, h_1, ..., h_n\}$. The t-th question q_t is represented by an embedding vector e_{q_t}. The query-context interaction module g, which is implemented by attention layers, outputs the starting and the ending position of the corresponding answer span: $start_t, end_t = g(H, e_{q_t})$.

Proximal Policy Optimization. Proximal Policy Optimization (PPO) [5] is an on-policy RL algorithm that utilizes the clipped loss function to avoid big changes in the policy update, yet still guarantees improvements. Let s_t and a_t denote the state and action at timestep t respectively, π_θ denote the policy network. The PPO training objective is:

$$J^{PPO}(\theta) = \mathbb{E}[\min\{ra(\theta)\hat{A}_{\theta_{old}}(s_t, a_t), \text{clip}(ra(\theta), 1 - \epsilon, 1 + \epsilon)\hat{A}_{\theta_{old}}(s_t, a_t)\}] \quad (1)$$

where θ is the current policy's parameters, $\hat{A}_{\theta_{old}}(s_t, a_t)$ is the advantage calculated at the old policy parameters θ_{old} before each updated policy iteration, by using any advantage estimation algorithm to transform the rewards [17], and $ra(\theta) = \frac{\pi_\theta(a_t|s_t)}{\pi_{\theta_{old}}(a_t|s_t)}$ is the ratio between the new policy and the old policy. If the ratio ra falls outside the range $1 - \epsilon$ and $1 + \epsilon$, the advantage function will be clipped.

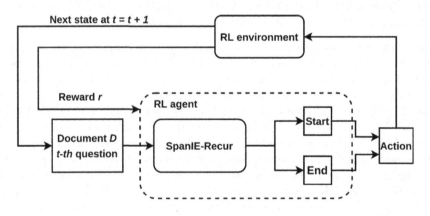

Fig. 1. Reinforcement Learning formulation using SpanIE-Recur backbone.

4   Method

4.1   Problem Formulation for Reinforcement Finetuning

We adapt the original SpanIE-Recur [4] as the policy network $\pi_\theta()$ of the IE agent and finetune it using RL. The only difference is that we replace the learnable question embedding e_{q_t} by the embedding produced from a pretrained multilingual text encoder [18] taking the question text as the input, which can benefit transfer learning settings. We treat the information extraction process as a sequential decision making process so that we can employ RL, where each question to a document corresponds to one timestep in an episode. At each timestep t, the document context D and the t-th question q_t are fed to the model, that is to say, the agent is in the state $s_t = (D, q_t)$. The model predicts the starting position $start_t$ and the ending position end_t of the answer span, thus the agent takes action $a_t = (start_t, end_t)$, which corresponds to extracting the answer string $\hat{y} = D[start_t : end_t + 1]^1$ from the document context. It then receives a reward r based on a reward function (described in Sect. 4.2) and goes to the next timestep $t + 1$ until all questions are traversed by the agent. The RL formulation is shown in Fig. 1.

4.2   Reward Functions

We improve the quality of SpanIE-Recur by defining new reward functions for RL. We argue that the advantage of RL fine-tuning over SL is that RL fine-tuning provides the flexibility in designing the reward that reflects human preferences, which is not available in traditional SL. Moreover, this reward can fully utilize different training signals from the data. Therefore, we introduce a unified reward function, which considers the following criteria of a good answer given an input question.

String Matching Reward. Our string matching reward bases on the Levenshtein distance between the output answer string $\hat{y}$ and the ground truth answer string y. Intuitively, we expect that a higher reward should be given to the output answer that is more similar to the ground truth one and vice versa.

$$r_{string} = 1 - \text{Levenshtein\_distance}(y, \hat{y}) \tag{2}$$

Location Reward. The location reward encourages the location matching between the output answer span and the corresponding ground truth span in the document context. Let $a = (start, end)$ be the predicted starting and ending positions of the span and $a\_gt = (start\_gt, end\_gt)$ be the corresponding ground truth ones. The exact formula for location reward is calculated by intersection over union of two spans:

$$r_{location} = \frac{interArea}{(end - start) + (end\_gt - start\_gt) - interArea} \tag{3}$$

where $interArea$ is the length of the intersection between two spans.

Label Reward. The label reward enforces the correctness of the label (field/tag) of the extracted answer. Particularly, given a question q_t, if the IE

---

[1] Using Python slicing notation.

model extracts the answer $\hat{y} = D[start : end + 1]$, we expect that the actual label of the span $(start, end)$ in the document D matches to q_t, i.e.:

$$r_{label} = \begin{cases} 1 & \text{if } label(\hat{y}) = q_t \\ 0 & \text{if } label(\hat{y}) \neq q_t \text{ and } label(\hat{y}) = other \\ -1 & \text{if } label(\hat{y}) \neq q_t \text{ and } label(\hat{y}) \neq other \end{cases} \quad (4)$$

where $label()$ returns the actual tag of the answer span $\hat{y}$, by obtaining the majority of token's ground truth tags in this span, *other* is a special tag we assign for tokens that do not belong to any targeted field. Intuitively, this reward penalizes more severely if the model mis-recognizes an entity as another targeted field rather than its ground truth field.

Semantic Reward. The semantic reward incentivizes the semantic matching between the output answer and the ground truth one. We utilize the pretrained multilingual sentence encoder [18] to compute the sentence embeddings of the output and the ground truth, and then measure their Cosine similarity in the latent embedding space.

$$r_{semantic} = cosine(enc(y), enc(\hat{y})) \quad (5)$$

where $enc()$ returns the embedding vector of an input sentence by using the sentence encoder.

The final formula for the unified reward.

$$r = \alpha_1 \times r_{string} + \alpha_2 \times r_{location} + \alpha_3 \times r_{label} + \alpha_4 \times r_{semantic} \quad (6)$$

where α_i's are the corresponding weights for each reward component.

4.3   Transfer Learning with Ground-Truth Labels

In this section, we describe the RL fine-tuning procedure based on the following protocol. Starting with a pretrained weight model (e.g. LayoutLM), we finetune the pretrained model on the training set with normal supervised training until convergence. In practice, this training set is divided into smaller subsets with a given size (2%, 5%, 10% or 100% of the entire training data). We finetune the model further with our reinforcement learning for up to $n_{max} = 100000$ iterations. During this process, we utilize the ground truth labels provided with each dataset to compute the aforementioned reward functions. These ground truth labels comprise the actual texts and their corresponding starting and ending positions in the context. The goal is to observe whether our reinforcement finetuning helps to improve the performance of the normal supervised training of the current state-of-the-art model.

4.4   Expert Feedback as Reward

In addition to using ground-truth answers to compute the rewards, we propose to use expert feedback to train the model. In this setting, we mimic the real

---

Algorithm 1. Training protocol

Require: Dataset $\mathbb{D}$, Pretrained SpanIE-Recur $\pi_\theta()$, Maximum number of iterations for RL finetuning n_{max}.

1: Perform traditional supervised training of $\pi_\theta()$ on $\mathbb{D}$ until convergence. $i \leftarrow 0$
2: **while** $i \leq n_{max}$ **do**
3:     Initialize set of trajectories $\mathbb{T} \leftarrow \{\}$. Sample set of documents $\{D_k\}$ from $\mathbb{D}$.
4:     **for** D_k in $\{D_k\}$ **do**
5:         Initialize trajectory $\tau \leftarrow \{\}$, $t \leftarrow 0$.
6:         **for** q_t in all questions **do**
7:             The agent is in state $s_t \leftarrow (D_k, q_t)$.
8:             The agent takes action $a_t \sim \pi_\theta(s_t)$ as described in Section 4.1.
9:             The environment returns corresponding reward r_t calculated by Equation 6.
10:            The environment returns the timestep for the next state $t \leftarrow t+1$.
11:            $\tau \leftarrow \tau \cup \{s_t, a_t, r_t\}$. $i \leftarrow i+1$
12:         **end for**
13:         $\mathbb{T} \leftarrow \mathbb{T} \cup \tau$
14:     **end for**
15:     Given trajectories $\mathbb{T}$, calculate PPO loss function by Equation 1.
16:     Backpropagate the gradients and update the parameters of π_θ.
17: **end while**
18: **return** π_θ

---

environment where a human can give feedback to the model via an interactive interface. The interface for feedback is designed as follows. Given a document and a question, the model outputs softmax distributions over starting and ending positions of the possible answers. We then sample from the distributions to get five pairs of start-end actions, representing the top five answer candidates, which are equivalent to five options/buttons on the screen. To account for cases when the model cannot provide good candidates, we provide a sixth option - a button named No good options available. Experts could select one of the six options that is most appropriate for the question as feedback to the model. The selected candidate is used as ground truth y to compute the reward using Eq. 6 above. Figure 2 (a) shows the interface of our system.

Table 1. Statistic of datasets

Dataset	# of fields	Train	Development	Test
SROIE	4	626	0	347
CORD	30	800	100	100
Inhouse-1	12	481	0	149
Inhouse-2	12	1032	0	433

4.5   Training Algorithm

We describe the detailed protocol to train the information extractor (SpanIE-Recur) with our rewards in Algorithm 1. We sample a document and its set of questions from the training data to form the RL trajectory. For each question, we concatenate the document and question representations to build the current state. Then, we sample one start-end action from the softmax layers of SpanIE-Recur to extract the candidate answer for the question. The reward is computed based on the candidate answer and the ground truth to construct the RL's loss function to optimize SpanIE-Recur.

5   Settings and Evaluation Metrics

Datasets. We use two public and two private datasets in our experiments. The two public datasets are in English: SROIE [19] and CORD [20]. SROIE is a collection of scanned receipt images, where each receipt has four fields to extract: *address, company, date, total.* CORD contains receipts collected from Indonesian shops and restaurants, where there are 30 semantic labels defined under 4 categories, such as *store information, payment information, menu, total.* Compared to SROIE, document images in CORD are captured in the wild, thus the data is more noisy and has lower quality. For private datasets, we collect two in-house datasets: the first one is a collection of Japanese technical document images and the second one is a dataset of Japanese invoices. The statistics of the four datasets are listed in Table 1.

Evaluation Metrics. The results are reported on the test split of the corresponding dataset by evaluating the standard field-level Precision, Recall, and F1 scores (weighted average) as in previous studies [2,3].

Baselines. As far as we know, there is only one prior work [21] which targets the same few-shot learning problem on business documents. However, they only target few simple fields in their experiments and do not cover the broad range of datasets. Thus, we consider the supervised learning (SL) result of SpanIE-Recur [4] (with the LayoutLM backbone) as a competitive baseline, which is also used in [21].

Implementation Detail. Our model uses *LayoutLM-base* with 12 Transformer blocks, the hidden size is 768, the input sequence length is 512 and the total number of parameters is 113M. The question embedding size is also 768. All experiments are conducted on a single Tesla T4 GPU. For all experiments, we use a learning rate of $5e-5$ and the Adam optimizer in the supervised training stage, with the standard cross-entropy loss. The hyper-parameters for PPO training are: the learning rate of $1e-6$, discount factor of 0.95 and clipping rate of 0.2. We set the weights of reward components α_i's to 0.25. These hyper-parameters are manually tuned for the Inhouse-1 dataset and used across experiments. To reduce the effort of tuning in future works, we may use methods that automatically learn hyper-parameter scheduling [22].

Table 2. Results of transfer learning on public datasets.

Dataset		Original SL			+RL			
		Precision	Recall	F1	Precision	Recall	F1	ΔF1
CORD	2%	21.69	2.77	3.04	40.11	15.94	21.23	18.19
	5%	64.33	47.83	51.48	66.39	52.69	57.83	6.35
	10%	79.45	72.98	75.32	80.76	73.05	76.12	0.80
	100%	96.31	94.91	95.39	97.11	95.03	95.71	0.32
SROIE	2%	80.93	78.08	79.46	80.61	79.77	80.16	0.70
	5%	85.94	80.59	83.09	86.07	82.09	83.95	0.86
	10%	88.33	85.27	86.74	89.22	85.37	87.20	0.46
	100%	91.83	91.45	91.61	91.89	91.54	91.68	0.07

Table 3. Results of transfer learning on our in-house datasets. **Pretrained** means the in-house pretrained weight we use to initialize the model before performing transfer learning.

Dataset		Original SL			+RL			
		Precision	Recall	F1	Precision	Recall	F1	ΔF1
Inhouse-1	**Pretrained**	38.24	14.62	18.02	–	–	–	–
	2%	74.44	56.63	62.08	69.39	65.17	66.35	4.27
	5%	86.45	76.64	80.35	84.15	75.60	79.63	−0.72
	10%	89.91	80.29	83.13	89.11	82.92	85.75	2.62
	100%	94.34	94.02	94.03	94.36	94.98	94.37	0.34
Inhouse-2	**Pretrained**	73.83	40.53	48.06	–	–	–	–
	2%	82.18	68.74	73.71	81.18	69.62	74.96	1.25
	5%	85.94	76.32	79.42	83.09	78.95	80.49	1.07
	10%	88.27	81.21	82.81	88.25	82.17	82.91	0.10
	100%	91.42	91.30	91.35	91.42	91.30	91.35	0.00

6   Experimental Results

We confirm the efficiency of our approach in two settings: transfer learning with limited data by using ground-truth labels and learning with human feedback. While the former uses the ground-truth answer to construct different rewards for training the model (Sect. 4.3), the latter uses human feedback (see Sect. 4.4). We also conduct ablation studies to verify the contribution of each reward type.

6.1   Transfer Learning with Limited Data

Training Procedure. We conduct experiments from different subsets of the training data to show the benefit of our proposed reinforcement finetuning

Table 4. Effect of ablating different reward components.

Model	CORD				SROIE			
	Precision	Recall	F1	ΔF1	Precision	Recall	F1	ΔF1
SL model	21.69	2.77	3.04	–	80.93	78.08	79.46	–
w/o string matching	37.87	5.46	7.79	4.75	80.91	78.17	79.67	0.21
w/o location	47.07	5.16	7.82	4.78	80.42	78.85	79.83	0.37
w/o label	31.19	17.51	2.22	19.16	80.52	78.75	79.61	0.15
w/o semantic	2.27	2.54	2.40	−0.64	81.47	77.69	79.52	0.06
Full unified reward	40.11	15.94	21.23	18.19	80.61	79.77	80.16	0.70

mechanism. For the public datasets, we use the pretrained LayoutLM weight *layoutxlm-no-visual*.[2] We use an in-house pretrained weight to initialize the model for the private datasets.

Benchmarking Results. We report the results on CORD and SOIRE datasets in Table 2. Overall, we can observe clearer improvements over the supervised baseline. RL finetuning makes the marginal improvements in the 10% and 100% data scenarios. The contribution is more remarkable in the limited data regimes, where on the CORD dataset, we observe an increase of 18.19% and 6.35% in F1 score for 2% and 5% training data, respectively. On SROIE, the corresponding improvements are 0.70% and 0.86%. We hypothesize that with a large enough amount of data, the backbone model trained with SL receives abundant training signals to become a strong backbone, but in limited data scenarios, RL performs better since it can exploit different aspects of training signals. Since CORD dataset has much more fields than SROIE, it is harder for SL models to learn in limited data scenarios on CORD, thus leaving room for RL contribution. This is the rationale behind the large improvements on CORD compared to SROIE dataset.

Table 3 shows the results on our in-house datasets. We observe similar behaviors of the RL-finetuned models. In most cases, RL finetuning can improve the performances, noticeably when the performances of SL counterparts are humble in 2% data scenarios (4.27% and 1.25% F1 score improvements on Inhouse-1 and Inhouse-2 respectively).

Ablation Study. In this section, we investigate the impact of different reward components in the unified reward function. We use the setting with the 2% training data scenario, but we ablate each single reward component respectively. Table 4 reports the F1 score of each ablated model on CORD and SOIRE data. Without string matching and location rewards, the performances drop significantly, but retain the improvements upon the SL counterpart. We observe the most severe drop when removing the semantic reward component on both datasets, which emphasizes the importance of the semantic matching between

---

[2] https://huggingface.co/taprosoft/layoutxlm-no-visual.

output and ground truth answers. Ablating the label reward on CORD dataset results in comparable performance to that of the full unified reward, but on SROIE dataset, we observe a large drop, thus confirming the helpfulness of the label reward component.

6.2 Learning with Expert Feedback

We conduct an interactive experiment that allows a domain expert to train the system with preference rewards via feedback. For this experiment, we sample five sets with four documents each from the dev set of CORD, use them to get feedback from experts, and evaluate the results on the test set after each interaction. Figure 2(b) shows the F1-score with the mean and standard deviation for five sets, with the result at interaction 0 being from the backbone using only supervised learning on 100% of the training set. After three interactions, the average F1-score of five sets increases marginally at around 0.11%. Yet, considering the small number of documents sampled for feedback and a decent performance of the backbone at the beginning, this increase is notable.

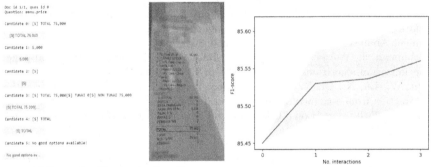

(a) Example of interaction interface

(b) CORD: F1 score with human feedback

Fig. 2. Learning with experts' feedback.

7 Conclusion

This work proposes a novel end-to-end reinforcement learning model with task-focused rewards for the document image information extraction task. Our experiments show that for both English and Japanese documents, our model outputs competitive results with the traditional supervised learning approach when having full access to training data, while performing significantly better when reducing the amount of training data, notably the 18.19% improvement in F1-score for 2% of the CORD training set. In addition, we provide an interactive interface session to get feedback from experts to improve the model's performance. Our results suggest that with as little as two to three interactions, users are able to witness the changes in output for the betterment. Despite this, the feedback interface, along with its connection to the RL model, is still in a preliminary state. For future works, one should consider not only the selected candidate but also the non-selected ones, and how to represent them in the reward model.

References

1. Liu, X., Gao, F., Zhang, Q., Zhao, H.: Graph convolution for multimodal information extraction from visually rich documents. In: Proceedings of the 2019 11 Conference of the North American Chapter of the Association for Computational Linguistics: Human Language Technologies, vol. 2 (Industry Papers), pp. 32–39 (2021)
2. Xu, Y., et al.: LayoutLM: pre-training of text and layout for document image understanding. In: Proceedings of the 26th ACM SIGKDD International Conference on Knowledge Discovery & Data Mining, pp. 1192–1200 (2020)
3. Xu, Y., et al.: LayoutLMv2: multi-modal Pre-training for Visually-rich Document Understanding. In: Proceedings of the 59th Annual Meeting of the Association for Computational Linguistics and the 11th International Joint Conference on Natural Language Processing (Volume 1: Long Papers). Association for Computational Linguistics, pp. 2579–2591, August 2021
4. Nguyen, T.-A.D., Vu, H.M., Son, N.H., Nguyen, M.-T.: A span approach for information extraction on visually-rich documents. In: International Conference on Document Analysis and Recognition, pp. 353–363 (2021)
5. Schulman, J., Wolski, F., Dhariwal, P., Radford, A., Klimov, O.: Proximal policy optimization algorithms. arXiv preprint arXiv:1707.06347 (2017)
6. Yu, W., Lu, N., Qi, X., Gong, P., Xiao, R.: PICK: processing key information extraction from documents using improved graph learning-convolutional networks. In: 2020 25th International Conference on Pattern Recognition (ICPR), pp. 4363–4370 (2021)
7. Davis, B., Morse, B., Price, B., Tensmeyer, C., Wiginton, C.: Visual FUDGE: form understanding via dynamic graph editing. In: Lladós, J., Lopresti, D., Uchida, S. (eds.) ICDAR 2021. LNCS, vol. 12821, pp. 416–431. Springer, Cham (2021). https://doi.org/10.1007/978-3-030-86549-8_27
8. Devlin, J., Chang, M.-W., Lee, K., Toutanova, K.: BERT: pre-training of deep bidirectional transformers for language understanding. In: Proceedings of the 2019 Conference of the North American Chapter of the Association for Computational Linguistics: Human Language Technologies, NAACL-HLT 2019, Minneapolis, MN, USA, 2–7 June 2019, vol. 1 (Long and Short Papers), pp. 4171–4186. Association for Computational Linguistics (2019)
9. Li, F., Lin, Z., Zhang, M., Ji, D.: A span-based model for joint overlapped and discontinuous named entity recognition. In: Proceedings of the 59th Annual Meeting of the Association for Computational Linguistics and the 11th International Joint Conference on Natural Language Processing (Volume 1: Long Papers), pp. 4814-4828. Association for Computational Linguistics, August 2021
10. Son, N.H., Vu, H.M., Nguyen, T.-A.D., Nguyen, M.-T.: Jointly learning span extraction and sequence labeling for information extraction from business documents. arXiv preprint arXiv:2205.13434 (2022)
11. Celikyilmaz, A., Bosselut, A., He, X., Choi, Y.: Deep communicating agents for abstractive summarization. In: Proceedings of the 2018 Conference of the North

American Chapter of the Association for Computational Linguistics: Human Language Technologies, vol. 1 (Long Papers), pp. 1662–1675, June 2018

12. Li, J., et al.: Deep reinforcement learning for dialogue generation. In: Proceedings of the 2016 Conference on Empirical Methods in Natural Language Processing, pp. 1192–1202. Association for Computational Linguistics, November 2016

13. Wu, L., Tian, F., Qin, T., Lai, J., Liu, T.-Y.: A study of reinforcement learning for neural machine translation. In: Proceedings of the 2018 Conference on Empirical Methods in Natural Language Processing, pp. 3612–3621. Association for Computational Linguistics, October 2018

14. Nguyen, D.-H., et al.: Robust deep reinforcement learning for extractive legal summarization. In: Mantoro, T., Lee, M., Ayu, M.A., Wong, K.W., Hidayanto, A.N. (eds.) ICONIP 2021. CCIS, vol. 1517, pp. 597–604. Springer, Cham (2021). https://doi.org/10.1007/978-3-030-92310-5_69

15. Stiennon, N., et al.: Learning to summarize with human feedback. In: Advances in Neural Information Processing Systems, vol. 33, pp. 3008–3021 (2020)

16. Nguyen, D.-H., et al.: Make the most of prior data: a solution for interactive text summarization with preference feedback. In: Findings of the Association for Computational Linguistics: NAACL 2022, pp. 1919–1930. Association for Computational Linguistics, Seattle, July 2022. https://aclanthology.org/2022.findings-naacl.147

17. Schulman, J., Moritz, P., Levine, S., Jordan, M.I., Abbeel, P.: High-dimensional continuous control using generalized advantage estimation. In: 4th International Conference on Learning Representations, ICLR 2016, San Juan, Puerto Rico, 2–4 May 2016, Conference Track Proceedings (2016)

18. Feng, F., Yang, Y., Cer, D., Arivazhagan, N., Wang, W.: Language-agnostic BERT sentence embedding. In: Proceedings of the 60th Annual Meeting of the Association for Computational Linguistics (Volume 1: Long Papers), pp. 878–891. Association for Computational Linguistics, May 2022

19. Huang, Z., et al.: ICDAR 2019 competition on scanned receipt OCR and information extraction. In: 2019 International Conference on Document Analysis and Recognition (ICDAR), pp. 1516–1520 (2019)

20. Park, S., et al.: CORD: a consolidated receipt dataset for post-OCR parsing. In: Workshop on Document Intelligence at NeurIPS 2019 (2019)

21. Wang, Z., Shang, J.: Towards few-shot entity recognition in document images: a label-aware sequence-to-sequence framework. arXiv preprint arXiv:2204.05819 (2022)

22. Le, H., et al.: Episodic policy gradient training. In: Proceedings of the AAAI Conference on Artificial Intelligence, vol. 36, pp. 7317–7325 (2022)

MSK-Net: Multi-source Knowledge Base Enhanced Networks for Script Event Prediction

Shuang Yang[1,2], Daren Zha[1(✉)], and Cong Xue[1]

[1] Institute of Information Engineering, Chinese Academy of Sciences, Beijing, China
{yangshuang,zhadaren,xuecong}@iie.ac.cn
[2] School of Cyber Security, University of Chinese Academy of Sciences, Beijing, China

Abstract. Script event prediction (SEP) aims to choose a correct subsequent event from a candidate list, according to a chain of ordered context events. It is easy for human but difficult for machine to perform such event reasoning. The reason is that human have relevant commonsense knowledge. If we supplement this knowledge from external knowledge bases, machine may be able to improve the reasoning ability. To this end, we introduce a novel approach, named **MSK-Net**, which consists of Question Encoder, Knowledge Searcher, Knowledge Encoder and Result Predictor. As far as we know, this is the first model utilizing multi-source knowledge to solve SEP problem. Specifically, first we use *Question Encoder* to encode the question, including candidate event to be judged and context events, focusing on intra-event contextualization and inter-event order information modelling. Then, we use *Knowledge Searcher* to retrieve relevant knowledge from multi-source knowledge bases (such as ASER and ATOMIC). Third, *Knowledge Encoder* is used to encode the knowledge retrieved in the second step. Last, *Result Predictor* gives the final prediction. Experiments on the widely-used multiple choice narrative cloze (MCNC) task demonstrate our approach achieves state-of-the-art performance compared to other methods. Also, it is worth noting that MSK-Net without external knowledge is still very competitive.

Keywords: Script event prediction · External knowledge · Multi-source knowledge base

1 Introduction

In the field of natural language processing (NLP), there has been a surge of research activities in recent years aimed at improving the ability of machines to perform deep language understanding, which goes beyond what is explicitly stated in the text and relies instead on reasoning and understanding of the world.

Script event prediction (SEP) is one of such research tasks mentioned above. The concept of *script* was first introduced into NLP field by Schank and Abelson [16], which is a structured representation of knowledge capturing the relationship between prototype event sequences and their participants. Then Chambers

© The Author(s), under exclusive license to Springer Nature Singapore Pte Ltd. 2023
M. Tanveer et al. (Eds.): ICONIP 2022, CCIS 1794, pp. 64–76, 2023.
https://doi.org/10.1007/978-981-99-1648-1_6

and Jurafsky [1] first proposed the problem of SEP, and defined it as giving an existing event context to choose the most reasonable subsequent event. Given a snap observation of an event sequence, people can easily predict what will happen next, but it is difficult for machine. Take Fig. 1 as an example, we can easily pick the right answer (*leave*), because it happens in our daily life, maybe just a moment ago. Unfortunately, machines do not have this experience, or we can regard it as commonsense knowledge, which is not explicitly stated in the text, but requires reasoning.

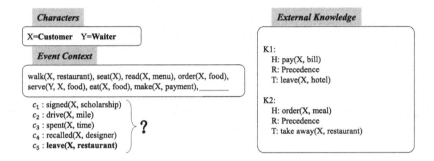

Fig. 1. The left [8] is an example of script event prediction, where correct event is marked in bold, and other four choices are randomly selected; The right is examples of external knowledge.

The previous work of solving SEP problem can be roughly divided into two categories. The first category uses the information contained in event itself, namely *self-contained methods*. Researches [1,5] use count-based approach to learn script knowledge, whose results of the prediction are not ideal. Granroth-Wilding and Clark [4] adopt word embeddings to represent the arguments in an event. Wang et al. [18] propose to integrate chain temporal order information into event relation measuring, achieving good results. Lv et al. [10] and Wang et al. [17] use the attention mechanism to mining multi-level connections between events for prediction. Among them, the more special is work [8], which further overcomes the limitation of information by building a graph structure and integrating the information coming from all of event chains in the training set.

Therefore, a growing number of works focus on how to use more information to improve the prediction accuracy. The second category, represented by works [3,7,11,20], utilizes external knowledge to assist predicting, that is *external knowledge enriched methods*. As shown on the right in Fig. 1, if we supplement this kind of knowledge from external knowledge bases, machine may be able to further improve the reasoning ability. Zhang et al. [20] simultaneously make use of multimodal information including text and image to aid prediction. Ding et al. [3] add the intents and emotions information to embed event. Lee and Goldwasser [7] inject abstract properties (such as sentiment and argument animacy) into the multi-tasking model. Lv et al. [11] integrate external event knowledge of ASER with RoBERTa to make prediction.

The external knowledge used by all these methods is from single source, and the information in one knowledge base is limited. To overcome this problem, we propose a novel approach, named MSK-Net, utilizing multi-source knowledge bases retrieving knowledge to aid prediction. This is a challenging work, because multi-source knowledge bases inevitably bring problems such as noise introduction and data redundancy. MSK-Net consists of four main components, where Knowledge Searcher is used to search event-related external knowledge from multi-source knowledge bases; Question Encoder and Knowledge Encoder are used to encode the question to be judged and relevant external knowledge, respectively; Result Predictor makes the final prediction.

Our contributions can be summarized as follows:

- We utilize multi-source knowledge bases to solve SEP problem, which overcomes the limitation of single one.
- We get accurate representation of events by intra-event contextualization and inter-event order information modelling, which enables MSK-Net to outperform the best self-contained models even without the help of external knowledge.
- MSK-Net can obtain an absolute 3.34% improvement over the best baseline, and it can be easily extended to more and larger knowledge bases.

2   Related Work

Previous works have proposed a variety of event representation forms. Chambers and Jurafsky [1] first represented events as <*verb, dep*> pairs (named *predicate-GR* by [4]), where *verb* refers to the predicate verb describing the event, and *dep* refers to the typed grammatical dependency relationship between the verb and the protagonist. Due to the limited information of 2-tuple, the follow-up works [4,8,10,12,17,18] added multi-argument information to form triple or even quadruple, like <*verb, subj, obj, indirect obj*>. In this paper, we follow the quadruple form.

Recently, more researchers have focused on the construction of event-related knowledge bases, where the knowledge can be used as external knowledge to assist the representation and reasoning of event sequences. Rashkin et al. [14] constructed Event2Mind, a corpus of 25,000 event phrases covering a diverse range of everyday events and people's intents and reactions to them. Later, Sap et al. [15] built a richer 9-dimension commonsense knowledge base organized by *if-then* relationship, namely Atlas of Machine Commonsense for If-Then Reasoning (ATOMIC). In order to scale the data, Zhang et al. [19] developed the knowledge base of Activities, States, Events and their Relations (ASER), where relations are automatically extracted from unstructured text data rather than crowdsourced.

To evaluate the performance of SEP, Chambers and Jurafsky [1] first introduced the narrative cloze (NC) task. In their work, candidate events are all events in the event library, and the evaluation index is the ranking of correct events. However, having no standard dataset makes the comparisons between different models much harder. To remedy it, Pichotta and Mooney [13] used human evaluation to determine the plausibility of chosen candidate, but it is too expensive to do at scale. Then, Granroth-Wilding and Clark [4] modified the NC task to multiple choice narrative cloze (MCNC), which offers a candidate event set to choose. Here, we follow the MCNC setting for evaluating models.

3 Problem Definition

SEP is to predict what will happen next based on a given sequence of context events. Here, an event e_i is defined as (p_i, s_i, o_i, r_i), where p_i is the predicate verb, and s_i, o_i, r_i are the subject, object and indirect object to the verb, respectively. Following previous works [4,8,10,17,18], we also use MCNC task to evaluate all the methods and accuracy as metric. Each instance includes an event chain containing n context events $\{e_1, e_2, \ldots, e_n\}$ and a candidate event set containing k choices $\{e_{c_1}, e_{c_2}, \ldots, e_{c_k}\}$.

For clarity, we summarize important notations and the corresponding definitions throughout this paper in Table 1.

Table 1. Notations and definitions

Notation	Definition	Notation	Definition
$\{e_1, e_2, \ldots, e_n\}$	An event chain containing n context events	e_i	The event at i-th position of an event chain
$\{e_{c_1}, e_{c_2}, \ldots, e_{c_k}\}$	A candidate event set containing k choices	e_{c_j}	The j-th candidate event (for simplicity, sometimes ignoring the subscript and denoting it as e_c)
(p_i, s_i, o_i, r_i)	The predicate verb and subject, object, indirect object to the verb of event e_i	$(e_1, e_2, \ldots, e_n, e_c)$	Obtained by joining the context event chain with each candidate event, which is the question we need to judge whether it conforms to the objective facts (also denoted as q)
<BOS> <EOS>	Used to mark the beginning and end of question q	<SEP>	The separator between the context event and the candidate event in the question q
KB_i	The i-th knowledge base	(h, r, t)	The form of knowledge retrieved from multi-source knowledge bases after processing
p_{ij}, v_{ij}	After processed by the pre-trained tokenizer and pre-trained model, the word pieces and corresponding vector of the predicate p_i. $i \in \{1, \ldots, n, c\}, j \in \{1, 2, \ldots\}$	k_{ij}, u_{ij}	The j-th knowledge from the i-th knowledge base, and its vector. $i \in \{1, \ldots, m\}, j \in \{1, 2, \ldots, q_m\}$
v_i'	The vector after length normalization of v_i, which can be regarded as the updated embedding of e_i. $i \in \{1, \ldots, n, c\}$	u_i'	The fused embedding of u_i by Attention Mechanism (AM). $i \in \{1, \ldots, m\}$
h_i	The output of v_i' after GRU processing. $i \in \{1, \ldots, n, c\}$	h_Q, h_K	The final representation of the question and knowledge, respectively
M_R	A learnable matrix, each row of which represents a kind of relation	M_u, b_u, M_s, b_s	Parameters of the linear layer in Knowledge Encoder and Result Predictor, respectively
s_j	The final score of candidate event e_{c_j}	p_j	The probabilities of e_{c_j} given context event chain
h_{dim}	The size of hidden layer	q_{AS}, q_{AT}	The amount of knowledge selected for each instance in ASER and ATOMIC

4   Methodology

In this section, we introduce our model **MSK-Net**, which is composed of the following four components: (1) Question Encoder, (2) Knowledge Searcher, (3) Knowledge Encoder and (4) Result Predictor. The overall architecture of the proposed model is shown in Fig. 2.

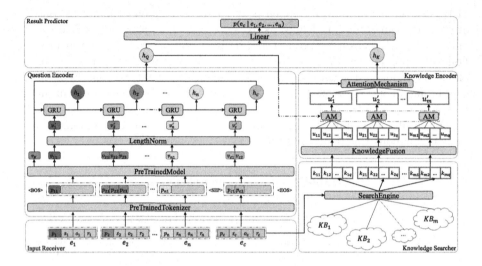

Fig. 2. The overall architecture of MSK-Net, which consists of four main components. Knowledge Searcher is used to search event-related external knowledge; Question Encoder and Knowledge Encoder are used to encode the question to be judged and relevant external knowledge, respectively; Result Predictor makes the final prediction.

4.1   Question Encoder

In our model, the quadruple form of event $e_i = (p_i, s_i, o_i, r_i)$ is taken as input. We combine a sequence of context events and each candidate event as a question $q = (e_1, e_2, \ldots, e_n, e_c)$, where e_c is in candidate event set $\{e_{c_1}, e_{c_2}, \ldots, e_{c_k}\}$. We need to judge which of the k questions is more in line with the law of the objective world. In this section, we introduce how to get the representation of the question.

Recently, transformer-based pre-trained model (e.g., BERT [2], RoBERTa [9] and ALBERT [6]) have performed well in various natural language understanding (NLU) tasks, so we want to use these models to encode the question. Previous work [11] just simply uses the output corresponding to the first token as the representation of the whole event sequence, which ignores a lot of important information. In our work, (1) since predicates have deterministic representative meanings in the four components of an event, we extract the embedding of the corresponding predicate from the output of the pre-trained model. However, most pre-trained models do not embed words but rather tokenized word-pieces (which are often but not always full words), so we take the average over all tokens comprising the lexical entries for each event predicate as the **intra-event** contextualized embeddings of the event. (2) In order to capture the **inter-event** order information, we input the embedding obtained in the previous step into the GRU network to get the final representation of the question. Specifically,

$$
\begin{aligned}
v_i' &= \mathrm{AVG}(v_{i1}, v_{i2}, \dots), \ i \in \{1, \dots, n, c\} \\
h_0 &= v_B \\
h_i &= \mathrm{GRU}(h_{i-1}, v_i'), \ i \in \{1, \dots, n\} \\
h_c &= \mathrm{GRU}(h_n, v_c') \\
h_Q &= v_B + h_c
\end{aligned} \tag{1}
$$

where v_B corresponds to the output of <BOS>; $(v_{i1}, v_{i2}, \dots)$ corresponds to $(p_{i1}, p_{i2}, \dots)$, which are the word pieces of p_i; after length normalization, v_i' can be regarded as the representation of event e_i; h_Q is the final embedding of the question.

4.2   Knowledge Searcher

Knowledge Searcher integrates multi-source knowledge bases, and retrieves relevant knowledge about the given event. Here, we use ASER [19] and ATOMIC [15] as our knowledge sources. ASER is a large-scale eventuality knowledge graph extracted from more than 11-billion-token unstructured textual data, which contains 15 relation types belonging to five categories, 194-million unique eventualities, and 64-million unique edges among them. ATOMIC organizes itself through 877k textual descriptions of inferential knowledge, which includes nine if-then relation types, namely *xIntent, xNeed, xAttribute, xEffect, xWant, xReaction, oReaction, oWant* and *oEffect*. These two knowledge bases both have rich inferential knowledge that is helpful for SEP.

We want to retrieve knowledge relevant to a given event from multi-source knowledge bases, which requires the ability to process massive amounts of information, and Elasticsearch can meet our needs well. Elasticsearch is a distributed search and analytics engine, which can provide near real-time search for all types of data. The biggest advantage is that as our data and query volume grows, the distributed nature of Elasticsearch enables our deployment to grow seamlessly right along with it. This point allows MSK-Net to be easily extended to more and larger knowledge bases.

For ASER data[1], we construct two indexes (similar to the concept of table in relational databases) *core_eventualities* and *core_relations* to store eventualities and relations data respectively. Index *core_eventualities* includes *verbs, skeleton_words_clean, skeleton_words, words, pattern* and *frequency* of an eventuality; Index *core_relations* includes *event1_id, event2_id* and their *relations*. Following

---

[1] https://hkust-knowcomp.github.io/ASER/html/index.html (we use the core version of ASER 1.0).

previous work [11], given a candidate event $e_c = (p_c, s_c, o_c, r_c)$, first we convert it to natural language as "$s_c\ p_c\ o_c\ r_c$", and retrieve the most matching eventuality $\hat{e}_c$ according to the *words* field in the index *core_eventualities*. Then we use $\hat{e}_c$ to retrieve the connected eventuality in index *core_relations*, and select $q_{AS} \times (h, r, t)$ triples among them, where h for *event1.words*, r for *relations* and t for *event2.words*.

For ATOMIC data[2], we import all the data into an index *atomic_all_agg* of Elasticsearch after preprocessing such as deduplication and field segmentation. The index *atomic_all_agg* includes 11 fields, namely *base_event*, *prefix* and the 9 relation types mentioned above. Similarly, given a candidate event "$s_c\ p_c\ o_c\ r_c$", the natural language form of e_c, we choose the entry that best matches it as $\hat{e}_c$ according to the *base_event* field. Then we select 5 (of 9) relationships related to events, which are *oEffect*, *oWant*, *xEffect*, *xNeed* and *xWant*, and choose q_{AT} instances for each relationship. So we get $5 \times q_{AT} \times (h, r, t)$ in total, where h for *base_event*, r for the corresponding relationship and t for the instance.

4.3   Knowledge Encoder

In this section, we use *Knowledge Encoder* to model the knowledge retrieved from multi-source knowledge bases. We encode each knowledge triple with the help of pre-trained model, whose parameter is not shared with the one in *Question Encoder*. First, for a given (h, r, t), we input h and t into the pre-trained model respectively, and get the vector corresponding to the first token of each, denoted as $v_B(h)$ and $v_B(t)$. As for relation r, we utilize a learnable matrix $M_R \in \mathbb{R}^{20 \times h_{dim}}$, each row of which represents a kind of relation[3]. Second, we concatenate three vectors and performed linear transformation to obtain the overall representation of the triplet. Then, we use **Hierarchical Attention Network** (HAN) to fuse the knowledge coming from different knowledge bases. Formulated as follows:

$$u_{i,j} = cat(v_B(h_{i,j}), row\_select(M_R, id(r_{i,j})), v_B(t_{i,j})) \cdot M_u^T + b_u \qquad (2)$$

$$u_i' = Attention(h_Q, u_{i,1}, \dots, u_{i,q_i}) \qquad (3)$$

$$h_K = Attention(h_Q, u_1', \dots, u_i') \qquad (4)$$

where $i \in \{1, 2, \dots, m\}, j \in \{1, 2, \dots, q_i\}$. *cat* denotes the concatenation function, $row\_select(M_R, id(r))$ means to select the corresponding row of matrix M_R according to the relation type of r, M_u and b_u are the parameters of the linear layer. $u_{i,j}$ is the embedding of the j-th knowledge triple of the i-th knowledge base, u_i' is the representation for knowledge in the i-th knowledge base, and h_K is for all knowledge from multi-source knowledge bases.

---

[2] https://homes.cs.washington.edu/~msap/atomic/ (we use the aggregated data v4_atomic_all_agg.csv).

[3] There are 15 relations in ASER data and 5 relation types selected in ATOMIC data.

4.4   Result Predictor

In previous step, we obtain the representation of the question and knowledge for each candidate event. For more clarity, we denote them as h_{Q_j}, h_{K_j} for candidate event e_{c_j}. Here, we use them to predict the probability, and select the candidate event with the highest probability as the final answer.

$$s_j = cat(h_{Q_j}, h_{K_j}) \cdot M_s^T + b_s, \ j \in \{1, 2, \ldots, k\} \tag{5}$$

$$p_j = p(e_{c_j}|e_1, e_2, \ldots, e_n) = \frac{s_j}{\sum_{i=1}^{k} s_i} \tag{6}$$

where s_j is the final score of candidate event e_{c_j}, p_j is corresponding probabilities. M_s and b_s are the parameters of the linear layer.

4.5   Training Object

Given a sequence of context events and a set of candidate event, our goal is to minimize the cross-entropy loss between the right answers and the predicted answers. The loss function of prediction is defined as follows:

$$L(\Theta) = -\frac{1}{N} \sum_{s=1}^{N} log \frac{exp(p_I)}{\sum_{j=1}^{k} exp(p_j)} \tag{7}$$

where p_j is the probability between the context event sequence and the corresponding j-th candidate event. I is the index of the correct subsequent event. Θ is the set of model parameters. N is the number of training instances. k is the number of candidate events in each instance.

5   Experiments

5.1   Dataset

Considering that the extraction quality of the event chains has a great impact on the results of the SEP, in order to exclude other interference factors, we conduct experiments on the widely used dataset provided by [8], which consists of 140,331 training instances, 10,000 development instances and 10,000 instances for test. For each instance, there are 8 context events and 5 candidate events, one of which is correct, others are random selected.

5.2   Baselines

We compare our model with the following two groups of baseline methods.

◇ Self-contained methods:

- **PMI** [1] uses observed verb/dependency counts to calculate the co-occurrence-based Pairwise Mutual Information (PMI).

- **Bigram** [5] proposes n-skip bigrams, calculates event pair relations based on bigram probabilities and trains using maximum likelihood estimation.
- **EventComp** [4] uses a neural network to learn a compositional function for event and a Siamese network to output related score between two events.
- **PairLSTM** [18] uses LSTM hidden states as features for event pair modelling and a dynamic memory network is utilized to automatically induce weights on existing events for inferring a subsequent event.
- **SGNN** [8] constructs narrative event evolutionary graph (NEEG) and uses Scaled Graph Neural Network (SGNN) to represent event and obtain the final results.
- **SAM-Net** [10] combines event-level and chain-level connections to capture richer relationships by attention mechanism.
- **Mcer** [17] enhances the representation learning of events by mining their connections at argument level, event level and chain level.

◇ External knowledge enriched methods:

- **SGNN(MERL)** [20] simultaneously makes use of multimodal information including text and *image* to aid prediction.
- **SGNN+Int+Senti** [3] adds the *intents* and *emotions* information of event participants on the basis of SGNN.
- **FEEL** [7] injects abstract properties (such as *sentiment* and *argument animacy*) into the multi-tasking model.
- **RoBERTa+Representation Fusion** [11] integrates external event knowledge of ASER with RoBERTa to make prediction.

5.3   Experimental Settings

The learning rate is set to 1e−5; the hidden dimension h_{dim} is 768; batch size is 10. We utilize RoBERTa-base as pre-trained model in MSK-Net; the max length of the tokenizer in *Question Encoder* and *Knowledge Encoder* is set to 120 and 10 respectively. We set q_{AS} is 4 for ASER and q_{AT} is 5 for ATOMIC. We adopt the Adam Optimizer and Cross-entropy loss function. We train our model on 2 GPUs in parallel for 2 epoches.

6   Results and Analysis

In this section, we will analysis the experimental results, and give the possible reasons for each model improving the accuracy of SEP.

6.1   Overall Results

Table 2 shows the performance of all compared methods on MCNC task. From the results, we can see that:

(1) MSK-Net achieves the best performance among the compared methods, whether the methods are self-contained or external knowledge enriched. This demonstrates the superiority of our approach.

(2) We can see that MSK-Net outperforms the best self-contained method (i.e. Mcer) by 5.36%, and even the version without external knowledge "MSK-Net (w/o ATOMIC&ASER)" outperforms it by 3.93%. It shows that the improvement of MSK-Net is not only due to the help of external knowledge, but *Question Encoder* also plays an important role in the accurate representation of events, especially on intra-event contextualization and inter-event order information modelling.

(3) The methods in the middle are not all better than the methods in the top, which means that adding external knowledge may not necessarily improve the performance of the model, because it may introduce noise at the same time. However, MSK-Net is able to process it well, which also proves the second conclusion above from another aspect.

(4) As a method that also uses the pre-trained model and ASER data, the accuracy of MSK-Net is still 3.34% higher than that of "RoBERTa+ Representation Fusion". It is worth mentioning that for the version "MSK-Net (w/o ATOMIC)", this increase is 2.92%. This fully proves that MSK-Net is superior in relevant knowledge retrieval and knowledge encoding.

Table 2. Results of script event prediction accuracy (%) on the test set. The top, middle and bottom are the results of self-contained methods, external knowledge enriched methods and variants of MSK-Net, respectively.

Methods	Accuracy (%)
Random	20.00
PMI [1]	30.52
Bigram [5]	29.67
EventComp [4]	49.57
PairLSTM [18]	50.83
SGNN [8]	52.45
SAM-Net [10]	54.48
Mcer [17]	56.64
SGNN (MERL) [20]	53.47
SGNN+Int+Senti [3]	53.88
FEEL [7]	55.03
RoBERTa+Representation Fusion [11]	58.66
MSK-Net (w/o ATOMIC&ASER)	60.57
MSK-Net (w/o ASER)	61.44
MSK-Net (w/o ATOMIC)	61.58
MSK-Net (Complete)	**62.00**

6.2   Comparative Experiments

In this section, we discuss the effects of different knowledge bases and different pre-trained models on our model.

Experiment with Different Knowledge Bases. As shown in Table 3, we take out the bottom row of Table 2 to calculate the differences between different variants of MSK-Net, and discuss the impact of different knowledge bases. We can see that the contribution of ASER is higher than that of ATOMIC, which may be because the data volume of ASER is much larger than that of ATOMIC, so that ASER can provide more useful information. The multi-source knowledge bases complement each other and help the model to improve the accuracy of SEP to the greatest extent.

Table 3. Influence of different knowledge bases.

Methods	Accuracy (%)	△
MSK-Net	**62.00**	–
w/o ATOMIC	61.58	−0.42
w/o ASER	61.44	−0.56
w/o ATOMIC&ASER	60.57	−1.43

Experiment with Different Pre-trained Models. We also conduct experiments to explore the impact of different pre-trained models on MSK-Net. The result is shown in Table 4, and Fig. 3 is the learning curves on development set. We can find that MSK-Net with RoBERTa has obvious advantages compared to ALBERT, cased BERT and uncased BERT, and its accuracy consistently leads throughout training. At the same time, uncased BERT is slightly better than cased BERT, which indicates that the case of tokens is not helpful for the SEP task, and may even introduce interference. As for ALBERT, due to its parameter reduction, its performance during training is not stable, and the accuracy is also the worst among the four models.

Table 4. Influence of different pre-trained models.

Methods	Accuracy (%)
MSK-Net (ALBERT)	54.37
MSK-Net (cased BERT)	60.27
MSK-Net (uncased BERT)	61.34
MSK-Net (RoBERTa)	**62.00**

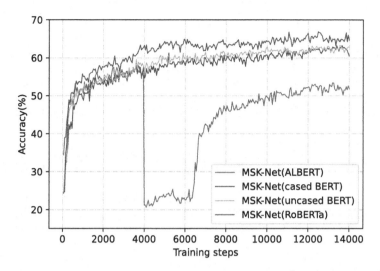

Fig. 3. Learning curves on development set with different pre-trained models.

7 Conclusion and Future Work

In this paper, we propose the MSK-Net model to handle the SEP problem, which consists of Question Encoder, Knowledge Searcher, Knowledge Encoder and Result Predictor. MSK-Net obtains an absolute 3.34% improvement over the best baseline by integrating multi-source external knowledge. Due to the distributed nature of Elasticsearch, MSK-Net can be easily extended to more and larger knowledge bases.

However, various knowledge bases are of different quality, and the introduction of more knowledge bases will inevitably introduce noise at the same time. There is currently no good solution on how to judge the quality of knowledge bases, how to reduce noise, and how to integrate the knowledge bases of different categories or even different modalities. In the future, we will study these problems.

Acknowledgements. We would like to thank Jingqi Suo for supporting our script learning related research, and the anonymous reviewers for their valuable comments and suggestions that help improving the quality of this paper.

References

1. Chambers, N., Jurafsky, D.: Unsupervised learning of narrative event chains. In: ACL 2008, pp. 789–797. The Association for Computer Linguistics (2008)
2. Devlin, J., Chang, M., Lee, K., Toutanova, K.: BERT: pre-training of deep bidirectional transformers for language understanding. In: NAACL-HLT 2019, pp. 4171–4186. Association for Computational Linguistics (2019)

3. Ding, X., Liao, K., Liu, T., Li, Z., Duan, J.: Event representation learning enhanced with external commonsense knowledge. In: EMNLP-IJCNLP 2019, pp. 4893–4902. Association for Computational Linguistics (2019)
4. Granroth-Wilding, M., Clark, S.: What happens next? Event prediction using a compositional neural network model. In: AAAI 2016, pp. 2727–2733. AAAI Press (2016)
5. Jans, B., Bethard, S., Vulic, I., Moens, M.: Skip N-grams and ranking functions for predicting script events. In: EACL 2012, pp. 336–344. The Association for Computer Linguistics (2012)
6. Lan, Z., Chen, M., Goodman, S., Gimpel, K., Sharma, P., Soricut, R.: ALBERT: a lite BERT for self-supervised learning of language representations. In: ICLR 2020 (2020)
7. Lee, I., Goldwasser, D.: FEEL: featured event embedding learning. In: AAAI 2018, pp. 4840–4847. AAAI Press (2018)
8. Li, Z., Ding, X., Liu, T.: Constructing narrative event evolutionary graph for script event prediction. In: IJCAI 2018, pp. 4201–4207. ijcai.org (2018)
9. Liu, Y., et al.: RoBERTa: a robustly optimized BERT pretraining approach. CoRR abs/1907.11692 (2019)
10. Lv, S., Qian, W., Huang, L., Han, J., Hu, S.: SAM-Net: integrating event-level and chain-level attentions to predict what happens next. In: AAAI 2019, pp. 6802–6809. AAAI Press (2019)
11. Lv, S., Zhu, F., Hu, S.: Integrating external event knowledge for script learning. In: COLING 2020, pp. 306–315. International Committee on Computational Linguistics (2020)
12. Pichotta, K., Mooney, R.J.: Statistical script learning with multi-argument events. In: EACL 2014, pp. 220–229. The Association for Computer Linguistics (2014)
13. Pichotta, K., Mooney, R.J.: Learning statistical scripts with LSTM recurrent neural networks. In: AAAI 2016, pp. 2800–2806. AAAI Press (2016)
14. Rashkin, H., Sap, M., Allaway, E., Smith, N.A., Choi, Y.: Event2Mind: Commonsense inference on events, intents, and reactions. In: ACL 2018, pp. 463–473. Association for Computational Linguistics (2018)
15. Sap, M., et al.: ATOMIC: an atlas of machine commonsense for if-then reasoning. In: AAAI 2019, pp. 3027–3035. AAAI Press (2019)
16. Schank, R.C., Abelson, R.P.: Scripts, plans, goals and understanding: an inquiry into human knowledge structures. Technical report (1977)
17. Wang, L., et al.: Multi-level connection enhanced representation learning for script event prediction. In: WWW 2021, pp. 3524–3533. ACM/IW3C2 (2021)
18. Wang, Z., Zhang, Y., Chang, C.: Integrating order information and event relation for script event prediction. In: EMNLP 2017, pp. 57–67. Association for Computational Linguistics (2017)
19. Zhang, H., Liu, X., Pan, H., Song, Y., Leung, C.W.: ASER: a large-scale eventuality knowledge graph. In: WWW 2020, pp. 201–211. ACM/IW3C2 (2020)
20. Zhang, L., Zhou, D., He, Y., Yang, Z.: MERL: multimodal event representation learning in heterogeneous embedding spaces. In: AAAI 2021, pp. 14420–14427. AAAI Press (2021)

Vision Transformer-Based Federated Learning for COVID-19 Detection Using Chest X-Ray

Pranab Sahoo[1]([✉])[iD], Sriparna Saha[1], Samrat Mondal[1], Sujit Chowdhury[1], and Suraj Gowda[2]

[1] Indian Institute of Technology, Patna, India
pranab_2021cs25@iitp.ac.in
[2] Narayana Institute of Cardiac Sciences, Bangalore, India

Abstract. The fast proliferation of the coronavirus around the globe has put several countries' healthcare systems in danger of collapsing. As a result, locating and separating COVID-19-positive patients is a critical task. Deep learning approaches were used in several computer-aided automated systems that utilized chest computed tomography or chest X-ray images to create diagnostic tools. However, current convolutional neural network (CNN) based deep learning algorithms cannot capture the global context because of inherent image-specific inductive bias. These techniques also require large and labeled datasets to train the algorithm, but not many labeled COVID-19 datasets exist publicly. This paper proposes a Federated Learning framework with a Vision Transformer for COVID-19 detection on chest X-ray images to improve training efficiency and accuracy. The transformer architecture can exploit the unlabeled datasets using pre-training, whereas federated learning enables participating clients to jointly train models without disclosing source data outside the originating site. We experimentally establish that our proposed Vision Transformer based Federated Learning architecture outperforms CNN based centralized models. We also provide the characteristics of X-ray images of the COVID-19-affected patients. Our findings show that the proposed model can assist medical professionals in effective COVID-19 screening.

Keywords: COVID-19 · Federated Learning · Vision Transformer · Chest X-ray

1 Introduction

The SARS-CoV-2 virus, which triggered the deadliest COVID-19 epidemic, continues to obliterate the health sector. Public health systems encountered numerous difficulties due to the unprecedented COVID-19 pandemic, including the lack of medical resources that forced healthcare professionals to face the threat of infection. The World Health Organization (WHO) reports that as of June 2022, there

M. Tanveer et al. (Eds.): ICONIP 2022, CCIS 1794, pp. 77–88, 2023.
https://doi.org/10.1007/978-981-99-1648-1_7

were 538,321,874 confirmed COVID-19 cases, including 6,320,599 fatalities. This has brought several countries' health systems dangerously close to disintegrating. Therefore, it is crucial to screen COVID-19-positive patients precisely to make the most use of the scarce resources. Real-time polymerase chain reaction (RT-PCR) is currently regarded as the gold standard in diagnosing COVID-19, however, receiving the test results may take many hours or even days, and it has a low sensitivity of 71%–82.2% [31]. While scientists worldwide have created several vaccines, it will take a long time to immunize everyone on the planet, especially in light of the widespread COVID-19 viral variations due to gene mutations. As a result, faster, more affordable, and user-friendly radiological COVID-19 screening tools are needed. Chest X-rays (CXR) and Computed Tomography (CT) scans have mainly been studied as critical alternatives to RT-PCR testing [32]. Although several studies on CT scans have shown excellent sensitivity and specificity for diagnosing COVID-19, their usage is burdensome due to the high cost and risk of cross-contamination in radiology facilities [25]. Conversely, CXR is a reasonably inexpensive and extensively used method for lung infection detection, and it can also be used for COVID-19 detection [31]. Even though there are several existing works on COVID-19 classification using deep learning approaches, most of them used CNNs for the feature extraction [1,28,31]. Despite its strength, CNNs lack a global understanding of images due to their image-specific inductive biases. CNNs need a large receptive field to capture long-range dependencies, which involve constructing large kernels or extremely deep networks, resulting in a complex model that is difficult to train. Building a robust model with lots of training data is one of the most frequently employed strategies to address this issue. Even though many radiograph images are generated worldwide, the datasets are still restricted due to a lack of expert labels, and the difficulty in sharing patient information outside hospitals owing to privacy concerns. International laws like the General Data Protection Regulation (GDPR) and the Health Insurance Portability and Accountability Act (HIPAA) substantially affect data management policies. It is no longer possible to gather client data without proper consent. The current pandemic condition worsens the problem and makes it difficult for hospitals in many nations to work together. To overcome the above two limitations, we have adapted Vision Transformer (ViT) [7] and Federated Learning (FL) [21] for our proposed work.

ViT has demonstrated state-of-the-art performance in the image classification task by getting over CNN constraints that need to integrate global associations between pixels. ViT provides an alternative framework for learning tasks and circumvents these issues by determining the optimal inductive bias for the task.

Google presented FL as a new paradigm for cooperative network training, allowing participating devices to train models on private data and upload only local training parameters. FL enables multiple healthcare organizations to join and train without disclosing data, which has significant advantages for small organizations with little data. The paper's key contributions include, but are not limited to:

– We proposed and fine-tuned a Vision Transformer-based classifier for COVID-19 screening from CXR images.

- This research also offers an FL-based framework by using a collaborative approach to benefit from the diversified private datasets while keeping the organizations' privacy.
- We have performed extensive experiments on independent and identically distributed (IID), non-IID, and unbalanced data distributions and reported a detailed analysis.

The remaining paper is structured as follows: Section 2 describes the previous related works, followed by Sect. 3, where the characteristics of CXR images of COVID-19 affected patients are discussed. Section 4 gives an overview of the proposed ViT and FL architectures. In Sect. 5, extensive experiments are carried out, followed by a conclusion and future work in Sect. 6.

2 Related Work

The ongoing spread of COVID-19 has significantly affected human life and work around the globe and has presented significant problems for the healthcare system. Computer-aided diagnosis has helped radiologists fight the COVID-19 pandemic from various angles. Success of deep learning motivates researcher to start working on COVID-19 detection [9]. In this regard, several deep learning-based methods have been developed for COVID-19 detection utilizing CXR, CT, and lung ultrasound images [25]. CXR is a reasonably inexpensive and extensively used method for lung infection detection and can also be used for COVID-19 detection [15].

COVID-Net, a CNN-based approach that introduced COVIDx datasets with 358 CXR images, reported an accuracy of 93.3% [31]. COVID-CAPS [1], a capsule-based architecture model for detecting COVID-19, achieved an accuracy of 98.7%. Their architecture consisted of several capsules and convolutional layers. In an another work, Islam et al. [16] used a long short-term memory based CNN to classify COVID-19 from chest X-ray. They have used 1525 COVID-19 samples, 1525 normal images for the experiment and reported an accuracy of 99.4%. In an another work, Turkoglu et al. [29] suggested COVIDetectioNet, a COVID-19 diagnostic technique. This method combined separate datasets to make one large dataset and used 219 COVID-19, 1583 normal, and 4290 pneumonia samples for the experiment and reported an accuracy of 99.18%. All the above works are based on the convolution neural network. ViT-based works are also reported in some literature. For instance, [22] utilized self-attention in local neighborhoods of the query pixels rather than doing calculations globally over the entire image. It shows how local multi-head attention can take the role of convolutions. The authors in [5] extracted small patches of size 2 * 2 and then applied full attention, restricting the architecture to small resolution images only. Many authors have employed self-attention to process CNN outputs for various tasks, such as object identification [2,8,13] and video analysis [27]. In contrast to existing CNN-based approaches, we propose a Vision Transformer [7] based architecture for automated COVID-19 screening from CXR images. Most of the above approaches used minimal data for performing the experiments, raising questions about the model's robustness. Another drawback of these conventional methods is the unwillingness to exchange medical information due to the possibility of compromising doctor-patient confidentiality. Many studies have demonstrated that FL may combines all healthcare organizations and allows them to share their private data while preserving privacy [26]. The vast medical dataset will considerably increase the machine learning model's performance in this scenario. As an example, a privacy-preserving federated patient hashing framework for learning patient similarity across institutions has been presented by Lee et al. [19]. Patients from other hospitals may be located using their model without releasing any patient-level data. In another work, Huang et al. [14] developed a community-based federated learning model to address the problem of obtaining non-IID ICU patient data. They trained one model for each community by clustering the scattered samples into clinically significant groupings that capture comparable diagnoses and geographic locations. Authors in [10] used VGG-16 and ResNet50 as the backbone of their proposed FL model and reported 92% and 92.7% accuracy, respectively. Four prominent pre-trained models, MobileNet, ResNet18, MobileNet-v2, and COVIDNet, were adapted by Boyi Liu et al. [20] for COVID-19 detection. After training, the authors reported ResNet18 model is the quickest and has attained 96.15% accuracy. No large datasets are available for COVID-19 as it is a newly emerging infectious disease, and because of privacy issues, most existing databases are kept private. In this study, we propose to create a collaborative framework using FL with ViT as a base model at each client side. We have adapted the ViT model for better classification and the FL model to benefit from the diversified private datasets while keeping the client's privacy. We show that both approaches have advantages, leading to a robust COVID-19 classification model.

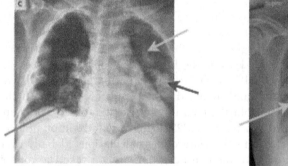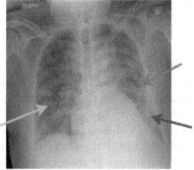

Fig. 1. Red arrows point to the Reticulations, Green arrows point to the GGO, and Blue arrows point to the consolidations. (Color figure online)

3   Chest X-Ray Findings in COVID-19

This section describes the findings in chest X-rays of a COVID-19 patient. COVID-19 patients' chest X-rays show specific abnormalities, including groundglass opacities (GGO), consolidation, and reticulation. In GGO, the opacification of the lung increases without covering blood vessels or airways. Consolidation causes a homogeneous opacification that covers both blood vessels and airways. Reticulation is characterized by numerous tiny opacities in a linear pattern. Peripheral GGO affecting the lower lobes is the most commonly found on chest radiographs. Bronchiectasis, lymphadenopathy, pleural effusion, and cavitation are less commonly seen in COVID-19 patients [24]. These findings are marked by our radiologist and shown in Fig. 1.

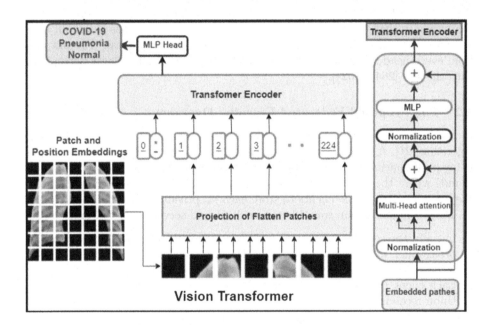

Fig. 2. Overview of the ViT architecture

4   Material and Methods

This section discusses the details of the ViT architecture, followed by our proposed FL framework.

4.1   Overview of ViT Architecture

The Vision Transformer [7] is an attention-based transformer architecture [30] that uses only the encoder part of the original transformer and is suitable for pattern recognition tasks in the image dataset. The workflow of the proposed model is demonstrated in Fig. 2. An Input image $I \in H * W * C$ is divided into a fixed number of patches $[I_1, I_2....I_n] \in I$ of fixed size. These patches are flattened and supplied to the transformer encoder with positional embedding. A learnable embedding is added to the patch embedding sequence, much as the [class] token in BERT [6]. The transformer's encoder layers, including normalization, multi-layer perceptrons, multi-head self-attention, and residual connections, are the same as those used in the regular transformer [30]. Three linear layers comprise the self-attention mechanism, which translates tokens into intermediate representations, keys, queries, and values. The ViT B/16 network is the most appropriate among the assessed options for future testing based on classification performance and computational cost. The ViT-B/16 architecture is set up as follows: Image size = 224 * 224 * 3, Patch size: 16 * 16, Dropout rate: 0.1, and the number of transformer layers employed is 8. The attention layer receives the packages that the transformer encoder puts out and divides the input into numerous heads, each of which learns the self-attention process. The outputs from every head are combined and then transferred to a multi-layer perceptron with the size [2048, 1024].

4.2   The Proposed Federated Learning Overview

In this paper, we have adapted an FL architecture (Fig. 3) using the FedAvg algorithm [21]. A central server hosts the global model while coordinating with many participating clients. The learning phase consists of several communication rounds where the clients asynchronously communicate with the central server. We consider K available clients to store each n_k private data locally.

Each communication round between client and server consist of four steps:

1. Initially, the coordinating server maintains a global ViT model (g) with initial pre-trained weights w and registers the list of willing participants, S_k, to collaboratively train the model.
2. Each client $k \in S_k$, requests for global parameters w to the central server. Upon receiving the global parameters, clients load them into the model and train it locally on a mini-batch b of its local private data. Each client uses mini-batch SGD with a learning rate η_{local} to minimize the local objective, F_k and runs for a pre-defined epoch, E. Clients optimize the model by minimizing the categorical cross-entropy loss.
3. After training the local model for epochs E, the clients send their updated local parameters w_k^t to the server, $k \in s_k$.
4. After receiving updates from all the participating clients, the server updates the global model by aggregating all the clients' local updates using the FedAvg algorithm.

$$w^t \leftarrow \sum_{k=1}^{K} \frac{n_k}{n} w_k^t \qquad (1)$$

Here w^t is the updated parameter at round t, parameters sent by client k at round t are represented by w_k^t, n_k is the number of data points stored on client k, and the total number of data points participated in collaborative training is n. These four steps constitute one round of FL. This process is then repeated many rounds. At each new round t, the client downloads the new global parameters for the next global round. We also notice that a client can be inactive during the training process. The server automatically chooses the set of active clients for the next round.

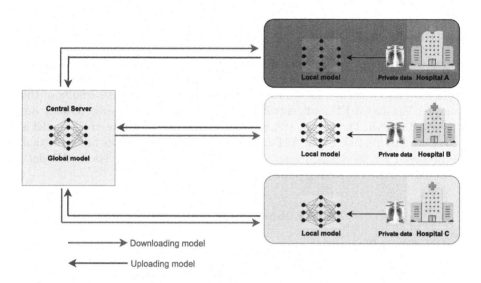

Fig. 3. An overview of federated learning with three hospitals

5   Experimental Result and Analysis

This section discusses the dataset sources and provides analysis of the experimental results. We simulate experiments with 3 hospitals to reduce computational complexity for the proposed work.

5.1   Dataset Preparation

As the COVID-19 outbreak recently, only a few publicly available CXR datasets exist. The dataset used for this work was extracted from various GitHub, Kaggle repositories, and published articles. We have combined and divided them into three different clients. COVID-19 datasets are collected from [11]. It contains 900 COVID-19 samples. Other sets of COVID-19 images are collected from [33]. It contains 243 COVID-19 images. Additional COVID-19 datasets are collected from [23]. It contains 846 COVID-19 images. All the non-COVID images of our experiments are collected from [3,18,23]. The detailed hospital-wise dataset distribution and experimental results are described in next subsections.

5.2 Results

To demonstrate our decentralized and collaborative learning approach's efficiency, we investigated different federated learning settings. In the first step, we examine the results using the IID dataset and then examine how the data distribution of non-IID impacts the model's performance. Finally, we experimented with an unbalanced dataset. The model's performance is assessed using the standard metrics [17].

5.3 Results on IID Data

In this experiment, we have taken the IID data distribution. For this reason, we have taken a single source of a dataset for each class, and we divided the whole data into 3 clients, as shown in Table 1a. The comparative results of the proposed ViT-based FL and centralized ViT model over the same dataset are shown in Table 1b. The overall accuracy of the suggested ViT-based FL model is 97.38% against 98.19% of the ViT-based centralized model. This indicates that the proposed FL model performs similarly to centralized models in IID data distribution while preserving patient privacy.

Table 1. Experiment of IID dataset

(a) Hospital wise IID-dataset

Hospital	Class	Total	Reference
1	COVID-19	300	[11]
	Non-COVID-19	533	[18]
2	COVID-19	300	[11]
	Non-COVID-19	527	[18]
3	COVID-19	300	[11]
	Non-COVID-19	523	[18]

(b) Resuls on IID-dataset

Method	Pre(%)	Sen(%)	Acc(%)
ViT-Centralized	98.7	98.4	98.19
ViT-FL (Proposed)	97.8	98.1	97.38

5.4 Results on Non-IID Data

We consider the non-IID data distribution in this experiment and report the experimental results in Table 2a. For this experiment, we consider different data sources as shown in Table 2b. Despite the non-IID aspect of the data distribution, ViT based FL approach performed well enough to attain 94.4% test accuracy against 95.6% of the centralized model. We notice the slight degradation of accuracy because hospital 2 has significantly less data for training.

5.5 Results on Unbalanced Data

Most clients in the healthcare domain contain unbalanced and non-IID data. For this experiment, we divided the dataset in an unbalanced manner. The data

Table 2. Experiments on Non-IID dataset

(a) Hospital wise non-IID dataset

Hospital	Class	Total	Reference
1	COVID-19	900	[11]
	Non-COVID-19	1050	[3] [23]
2	COVID-19	243	[33]
	Non-COVID-19	390	[3] [23]
3	COVID-19	846	[4]
	Non-COVID-19	1010	[3] [23]

(b) Resuls on Non-IID-dataset

Method	Pre(%)	Sen(%)	Acc(%)
ViT-Centralized	95.4	94.7	95.6
ViT-FL	94.84	92.69	94.4

distributions are shown in Table 3a and results are shown in Table 3b. The proposed model achieves an overall accuracy of 94.4% against 94.2% of the centralized model. The slight degradation of overall accuracy is due to the imbalanced dataset distribution (COVID-19 - 3616, Non-COVID-19 - 10188). However, we noticed a few errors in the form of false positives and false negatives. Both conditions are not desirable in a robust model. When we analyzed the error situations with our radiologists, we found that our model considered some viral pneumonia cases as COVID-19. Some early COVID-19 cases are also considered Non-COVID-19, where there is no significant infection in the CXR.

Table 3. Experiments on unbalanced dataset

(a) Hospital wise unbalanced dataset

Hospital	Class	Total	Reference
1	COVID-19	1205	[3] [23]
	Non-COVID-19	3396	
2	COVID-19	1205	[3] [23]
	Non-COVID-19	3396	
3	COVID-19	1206	[3] [23]
	Non-COVID-19	3396	

(b) Result on unbalanced dataset

Method	Pre(%)	Sen(%)	Acc(%)
ViT-Centralized	85.4	94.0	94.2
ViT-FL	87.4	92.2	94.4

5.6 Comparisons with Existing Methods

There have been several studies on COVID-19 detection, such as [1,12,28,31], but these approaches do not consider data sharing for model training and use CNN as a base model. Data processing is complicated due to the small number of COVID-19 samples and such methodologies are unreliable for medical applications. A large amount of data has been collected and trained to build a better prediction model in the proposed approach. We compare the proposed model with some state-of-the-art traditional deep learning and federated learning techniques. The comparative analysis is represented in Table 4. The results show that the proposed ViT-based FL model's accuracy is comparable to that of centralized models. Our approach also outperforms the CNN-based federated learning approaches proposed by the authors of [10], supporting the employment of an ensemble framework.

Table 4. Comparative analyses of the proposed model with the existing models on the different COVID-19 datasets.

Method	Dataset	Precision (%)	Sensitivity (%)	Accuracy (%)
Toraman et al. [28]	COVID - 1050	91.60	96	97.24
	Non-COVID - 1050			
Wang et al. [31]	COVID - 266	98.9	94	93.3
	Non-COVID - 92			
Feki et al. [10]	COVID - 108	95.89	98.11	97
	Non-COVID - 108			
Proposed Method	COVID-1989	97.8	98.1	97.38
	Non-COVID - 4433			

6   Conclusion and Future Work

In this study, we introduce a ViT-based FL system for improving the classification of COVID-19 CXR images by sharing the data among institutions while maintaining patient privacy. A comparative analysis between the traditional CNN-based centralized learning and the ViT-based FL architecture is presented. Our findings suggest that FL may achieve the same results as centralized learning without requiring private and sensitive data to be shared or centralized. We show that the proposed FL architecture is stable and performs similarly to the centralized learning process despite the non-IID and imbalanced data distribution. FL may link all separate medical institutions, hospitals, and devices, allowing them to exchange and collaborate while retaining their privacy. This collaborative approach will enhance the robustness and trustworthiness of the COVID-19 detection model. We have considered only 3 clients in this work, as adding clients will increase computational power to our limited available resources.

Acknowledgement. Dr. Sriparna Saha gratefully acknowledges the Young Faculty Research Fellowship (YFRF) Award, supported by Visvesvaraya Ph.D. Scheme for Electronics and IT, Ministry of Electronics and Information Technology (MeitY), Government of India, being implemented by Digital India Corporation (formerly Media Lab Asia) for carrying out this research.

References

1. Afshar, P., Heidarian, S., Naderkhani, F., Oikonomou, A., Plataniotis, K.N., Mohammadi, A.: Covid-caps: a capsule network-based framework for identification of covid-19 cases from x-ray images. Pattern Recogn. Lett. **138**, 638–643 (2020)

2. Arya, N., Saha, S.: Multi-modal advanced deep learning architectures for breast cancer survival prediction. Knowl.-Based Syst. **221**, 106965 (2021)
3. Chowdhury, M.E., et al.: Can AI help in screening viral and covid-19 pneumonia? IEEE Access **8**, 132665–132676 (2020)
4. Cohen, J.P., Morrison, P., Dao, L., Roth, K., Duong, T.Q., Ghassemi, M.: Covid-19 image data collection: prospective predictions are the future. arXiv2006.11988 (2020). github.com/ieee8023/covid-chestxray-dataset
5. Cordonnier, J.B., Loukas, A., Jaggi, M.: On the relationship between self-attention and convolutional layers. arXiv preprint arXiv:1911.03584 (2019)
6. Devlin, J., Chang, M.W., Lee, K., Toutanova, K.: BERT: pre-training of deep bidirectional transformers for language understanding. arXiv preprint arXiv:1810.04805 (2018)
7. Dosovitskiy, A., et al.: An image is worth 16x16 words: transformers for image recognition at scale. arXiv preprint arXiv:2010.11929 (2020)
8. Dutta, P., Patra, A.P., Saha, S.: DeePROG: deep attention-based model for diseased gene prognosis by fusing multi-omics data. IEEE/ACM Trans. Comput. Biol. Bioinf. 19, 2770–2781 (2021)
9. Dutta, P., Saha, S., Chopra, S., Miglani, V.: Ensembling of gene clusters utilizing deep learning and protein-protein interaction information. IEEE/ACM Trans. Comput. Biol. Bioinf. **17**(6), 2005–2016 (2019)
10. Feki, I., Ammar, S., Kessentini, Y., Muhammad, K.: Federated learning for covid-19 screening from chest x-ray images. Appl. Soft Comput. **106**, 107330 (2021)
11. figshare: figshare.com, April 2022. http://www.figshare.com/articles/COVID-19_Chest_X-Ray_Image_Repository/12580328/
12. Gupta, A., Gupta, S., Katarya, R., et al.: InstaCovNet-19: a deep learning classification model for the detection of covid-19 patients using chest x-ray. Appl. Soft Comput. **99**, 106859 (2021)
13. Hu, H., Gu, J., Zhang, Z., Dai, J., Wei, Y.: Relation networks for object detection. In: Proceedings of the IEEE Conference on Computer Vision and Pattern Recognition, pp. 3588–3597 (2018)
14. Huang, L., Shea, A.L., Qian, H., Masurkar, A., Deng, H., Liu, D.: Patient clustering improves efficiency of federated machine learning to predict mortality and hospital stay time using distributed electronic medical records. J. Biomed. Inform. **99**, 103291 (2019)
15. Irvin, J., et al.: Chexpert: a large chest radiograph dataset with uncertainty labels and expert comparison. In: Proceedings of the AAAI Conference on Artificial Intelligence, vol. 33, pp. 590–597 (2019)
16. Islam, M.Z., Islam, M.M., Asraf, A.: A combined deep CNN-LSTM network for the detection of novel coronavirus (covid-19) using x-ray images. Inform. Med. Unlocked **20**, 100412 (2020)
17. Japkowicz, N., Shah, M.: Evaluating Learning Algorithms: A Classification Perspective. Cambridge University Press (2011)
18. Kermany, D., Zhang, K., Goldbaum, M., et al.: Labeled optical coherence tomography (OCT) and chest x-ray images for classification. Mendeley Data **2**(2), 651 (2018)
19. Lee, J., Sun, J., Wang, F., Wang, S., Jun, C.H., Jiang, X.: Privacy-preserving patient similarity learning in a federated environment: development and analysis. JMIR Med. Inform. **6**(2), e7744 (2018)
20. Liu, B., Yan, B., Zhou, Y., Yang, Y., Zhang, Y.: Experiments of federated learning for covid-19 chest x-ray images. arXiv preprint arXiv:2007.05592 (2020)

21. McMahan, B., Moore, E., Ramage, D., Hampson, S., y Arcas, B.A.: Communication-efficient learning of deep networks from decentralized data. In: Artificial Intelligence and Statistics, pp. 1273–1282. PMLR (2017)
22. Parmar, N., et al.: Image transformer. In: International Conference on Machine Learning, pp. 4055–4064. PMLR (2018)
23. Rahman, T., et al.: Exploring the effect of image enhancement techniques on covid-19 detection using chest x-ray images. Comput. Biol. Med. **132**, 104319 (2021)
24. Rousan, L.A., Elobeid, E., Karrar, M., Khader, Y.: Chest x-ray findings and temporal lung changes in patients with covid-19 pneumonia. BMC Pulm. Med. **20**(1), 1–9 (2020)
25. Sahoo, P., Saha, S., Mondal, S., Chowdhury, S., Gowda, S.: Computer-aided covid-19 screening from chest CT-scan using a fuzzy ensemble-based technique. In: 2022 International Joint Conference on Neural Networks (IJCNN), pp. 1–8. IEEE (2022)
26. Singh, A., Sen, T., Saha, S., Hasanuzzaman, M.: Federated multi-task learning for complaint identification from social media data. In: Proceedings of the 32nd ACM Conference on Hypertext and Social Media, pp. 201–210 (2021)
27. Sun, C., Myers, A., Vondrick, C., Murphy, K., Schmid, C.: VideoBERT: a joint model for video and language representation learning. In: Proceedings of the IEEE/CVF International Conference on Computer Vision, pp. 7464–7473 (2019)
28. Toraman, S., Alakus, T.B., Turkoglu, I.: Convolutional capsnet: a novel artificial neural network approach to detect covid-19 disease from x-ray images using capsule networks. Chaos Solitons Fractals **140**, 110122 (2020)
29. Turkoglu, M.: Covidetectionet: Covid-19 diagnosis system based on x-ray images using features selected from pre-learned deep features ensemble. Appl. Intell. **51**(3), 1213–1226 (2021)
30. Vaswani, A., et al.: Attention is all you need. In: Advances in Neural Information Processing Systems, vol. 30 (2017)
31. Wang, L., Lin, Z.Q., Wong, A.: Covid-net: a tailored deep convolutional neural network design for detection of covid-19 cases from chest x-ray images. Sci. Rep. **10**(1), 1–12 (2020)
32. Wang, Z., et al.: Automatically discriminating and localizing covid-19 from community-acquired pneumonia on chest x-rays. Pattern Recogn. **110**, 107613 (2021)
33. ML workgroup: github-ml-workgroup (2022). github.com/ml-workgroup/covid-19-image-repository/tree/master/png/

HYCEDIS: HYbrid Confidence Engine for Deep Document Intelligence System

Bao-Sinh Nguyen[1][(✉)], Quang-Bach Tran[1], Tuan-Anh D. Nguyen[1], and Hung Le[2]

[1] Cinnamon AI, 10th floor, Geleximco building, 36 Hoang Cau, Dong Da, Hanoi, Vietnam
{simon,neath,tadashi}@cinnamon.is
[2] Deakin University, Geelong, Australia
thai.le@deakin.edu.au

Abstract. Measuring the confidence of AI models is critical for safely deploying AI in real-world industrial systems. One important application of confidence measurement is information extraction from scanned documents. However, there exists no solution to provide reliable confidence score for current state-of-the-art deep-learning-based information extractors. In this paper, we propose a complete and novel architecture to measure confidence of current deep learning models in document information extraction task. Our architecture consists of a Multi-modal Conformal Predictor and a Variational Cluster-oriented Anomaly Detector, trained to faithfully estimate its confidence on its outputs without the need of host models modification. We evaluate our architecture on real-wold datasets, not only outperforming competing confidence estimators by a huge margin but also demonstrating generalization ability to out-of-distribution data.

Keywords: uncertainty · neural networks · supervised learning · information extraction

1 Introduction

Recent advances in machine learning enables creations of automatic information extractors that can read the input document in image format, locate and understand relevant text lines before organizing the information into computer-readable format for further analysis [1,2]. Despite these successes, in critical domains such as healthcare and banking, humans still have to involve to scrutinize AI outputs as there is no room for AI errors in making important decisions that can affect human life. Confidence score estimation is one critical step towards implementing practical industrial systems wherein AI automates most of the operations yet human will intervene if necessary [3].

Unfortunately, to the best of our knowledge, there exists no holistic solution to reliably estimate the confidence score for the task of document information extraction. Current confidence score approaches are either generic methods verified only for simple image classification tasks [4] or applied only for part of the information extraction process [5].

In this paper, we introduce a novel neural architecture that can judge the result of extracted structured information from documents provided by the information extracting neural networks (hereafter referred to as the IE Networks). Our architecture is hybrid, consisting of two models, which are a Multi-modal Conformal Predictor (MCP) and an Variational Cluster-oriented Anomaly Detector (VCAD). The former aims to combine the neural signals from 3 main stages of information extraction processes including text-box localization, OCR, and key-value recognition to predict the confidence level for each extracted key-value output. The later computes anomaly scores for the raw input document image, providing the MCP with additional features to produce better confidence estimation. The VCAD works on global, low-level features and plays a critical role in lifting the burden of detecting outliers off the MCP, which focuses more on local, high-level features.

We demonstrate the capacity of our proposed architecture on real-world invoice datasets: SROIE [6], CORD [7]) and 2 in-house datasets. The experimental results demonstrate that our method outperforms various confidence estimator baselines (including Droupout [4], temperature scaling [8]). In short, we summarize our contribution as follows:

- We propose a *Multi-modal Conformal Predictor (MCP)* using a Feature Fusion module over 3 Feature Encoders to fuse signals extracted from IE Networks and compute the confidence score of the IE Networks' outputs.
- We provide a *Variational Cluster-oriented Anomaly Detector (VCAD)* to equip the MCP with an ability to handle out-of-distribution data.
- We unify the proposed MCP and VCAD in a single hybrid confidence engine, dubbed as HYCEDIS, that for the first time, can well estimate the confidence of document intelligent system.
- We conduct intensive experiments on 4 datasets with detailed ablation studies to show the effectiveness and generalization of our hybrid architecture on real-world problems.

2   Background

A typical Document Intelligence System consists of multiple smaller steps: text detection, text recognition and information extraction (IE). Given a document image, the usual first step is to detect text lines, using segmentation [9–11] or object detection method [12–14]. The detected text line images can each go through an OCR model to transcribe into text [15]. After all text contents are transcribed, the relevant text entities can be extracted, using entity recognition (sequence tagging) method [16–18], segmentation-based method [1,19], or graph-based method [20–22] which formulates the document layout as a graph of text-lines/words.

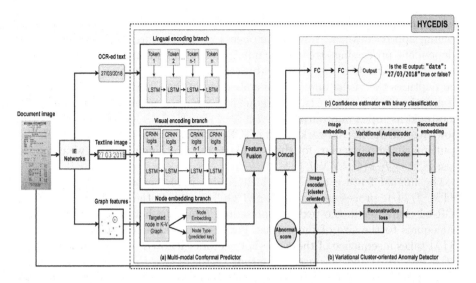

Fig. 1. HYCEDIS architecture. (a) The Multi-modal Conformal Predictor (MCP). (b) The Variational Cluster-oriented Anomaly Detector (VCAD). (c) Confidence estimator (CE). MCP's output vector, plus the VCAD's abnormal score, is fed to fully-connected layers to produce the final output of HYCEDIS, indicating whether the extracted field true or false.

In this paper, we adopt a common IE Network that consisted of 3 main modules: text detection (Layout Analysis), text recognition (CRNN) and graph-based information extraction model (Graph KV). The text detection model shares the same architecture with [9] which utilizes segmentation masks to detect text-lines in the document image. The text recognition (CRNN) uses popular CNN+Bi-LSTM+CTC-loss architecture to transcribe each text-line images into text. Finally, the GCN model [21] performs the node classification tasks from the input document graph constructed from the text-lines' location and text to extract relevant information. Here, for our problems, we classify each node into different key types that represent the categories of the text-line.

3   Methodology

3.1   Multi-modal Conformal Predictor (MCP)

Given extracted intermediate features of IE Networks, our Multi-modal Conformal Predictor aims to estimate the confidence score through predicting whether the final output is *true* or *false*. The MCP architecture (see Fig. 1(a)) contains two main components which are Feature Encoding and Feature Fusion. The Feature Encoding extracts features from different layers of trained IE Networks while the Feature Fusion combine them for predicting the final output.

Feature Encoding. Motivated by designs of late-fusion multi-view sequential learning approaches [23], three components of the Feature Encoding layers are independent processing streams including visual, lingual and structural feature encoders. In particular, the visual feature encoder is a many-to-one LSTM $f_{VF}(\cdot)$ that captures the visual information embedded in the CRNN of the IE Network. It takes the CRNN's logits (whose shape is $T \times F_{in\_vis}$ where T is the number of timesteps) as input and outputs a vector of size $\bar{F}_{out\_vis}$, which represents the knowledge of the IE Networks on its OCR model's neural activations given the input image. In particular, for the i-th extracted text-line image I_i, we compute it as: $E_i^{vis} = f_{VF}(CRNN(I_i))$.

The lingual feature encoder, which is also implemented as a many-to-one LSTM $f_{LF}(\cdot)$, processes the predicted OCR texts of the IE Networks. Each OCR-ed character in the text is represented as an one-hot vector with the size that equals to the size of the corpus. For the i-th extracted OCR-ed text, the LSTM takes a sequence of these one-hot vectors (denoted by $text_i$, whose shape is $T \times F_{in\_OCR}$) and produces an output vector of size F_{out_OCR}, representing the knowledge of the IE Networks on the linguistic meaning and the syntactic pattern of its OCR-ed outputs. We compute it as: $E_i^{OCR} = f_{LF}(text_i)$.

The structural feature encoding $f_{SF}(\cdot)$ is a feed-forward neural network that accesses the information from the final layer of the IE Networks (node classification) – the Graph KV module. Here, the logits before softmax layer of the i-th node in the graph (corresponding to the i-th text box extracted from the document), denoted by $logit_i^{(KV)}$, is the input of the structural feature encoding, and the corresponding output is node embedding vector E_i^{node} representing the knowledge of the IE networks on its final decision (node classification): $E_i^{node} = f_{SF}(logit_i^{(KV)})$.

Feature Fusion. The Feature Fusion network f_{Fusion} takes the three outputs from the Feature Encoding module and produces the ultimate feature vector. We use simple concatenation and Bi-linear pooling [24] as two options for Feature Fusion. Bi-linear pooling use outer-product to combine inputs of different modalities. For simple concatenation, we just concatenate three vectors. For Bi-linear Pooling, we first pool the pair of E_i^{vis} and E_i^{OCR}, and then pool the resulting vector with E_i^{node} to get the pooled output F_i:

$$F_i = f_{Fusion}(E_i^{vis}, E_i^{OCR}, E_i^{node}) \tag{1}$$

3.2   Variational Cluster-Oriented Anomaly Detector (VCAD)

The anomaly detector aims to detect which input image is normal or abnormal, thus bolsters the MCP by a measurement of the normality that the input has. Specifically, the input to the anomaly detector is a compressed representation of the document image, and the output is a score in the range $[0, 1]$ indicating the level of anomaly of the input. This score serves as an additional input to the confidence estimator.

Representing Image Data with Cluster-Oriented Embeddings. In this section, we describe the representation learning of document images. Firstly, the training dataset was classified into some categories based on the appearance and the layout structure of the document image. Then we train a CNN-based image encoder to map each document image into a lower-dimensional vector representation. Here, the CNN architecture is MobileNet [25]. We adopt the triplet loss [26] to learn the compressed representation, wherein the embeddings of images from the same category tend to form a cluster in the embedding space.

Anomaly Detector Training. After constructing embeddings for training images, we build a Variational Auto Encoder (VAE) [27,28] as our anomaly detector (Fig. 1(b)). The VAE outlier detector is first trained on a set of normal (inlier) data to reconstruct the input it receives, with the standard VAE loss function which is the sum of KL term and reconstruction loss:

$$\mathcal{L}_{\text{VAE}}(x;\theta,\phi) = -KL(q_\phi(z|x)\|p_\theta(z)) + \frac{1}{L}\sum_{l=1}^{L} \log p_\theta(x|z^{(l)}) \tag{2}$$

where x, z and L denote the VAE's input, latent variable, and number of samples, respectively. q_ϕ represents the encoder and p_θ the decoder of VAE.

If the input data cannot be reconstructed well, the reconstruction error (implemented as L1 loss between VAE's input and output) is high and the data can be flagged as an outlier. We apply the min-max normalization [29] to the reconstruction losses in order to get the corresponding abnormal scores in the range of $[0, 1]$.

3.3 Hybrid Confidence Estimation

After getting the scalar output from our VCAD, we simply concatenate this scalar with the output of the Feature Fusion module in the MCP. The resulting vector is fed to a confidence estimator (CE), which is implemented as a 2-layer feed-forward neural network. We freeze the VCAD and train the CE and MCP end-to-end on the training data as the set of IE's predictions in the training dataset.

In particular, let x_i denote the input document image, the function $IE(\cdot)$ denote our pipeline of IE networks. The output of IE system is $\hat{v}_i = IE(x_i)$. More specifically, $\hat{v}_i = \{\hat{v}_{ik}\}_{k=1:K_i}$ is the set of K_i predictions where each $\hat{v}_{ik}$ contains location information along with extracted text corresponding to a particular key (e.g: *{'location': [123,234,184,246], 'text': '27/03/2018', 'key': 'date'}*). We also have the ground truth $v_i = \{v_{ij}\}_{j=1:J_i}$ is the set of J_i elements presented in the i−th document.

Let F_{ik} denote the input of our CE corresponding to prediction $\hat{v}_{ik}$, the CE is represented by the function $f_{CE}(\cdot)$ yielding the softmax output $p_{ik} = f_{CE}(F_{ik})$. The label for confidence estimation task is

$$y_{ik} = \mathbb{1}\{\exists j \in \{1:J_i\} \mid v_{ij} \stackrel{\text{match}}{=} \hat{v}_{ik}\} \tag{3}$$

The IE's output is considered to match the ground truth element if both the text contents and the keys match and the locations' IoU is greater than a threshold (0.3 in this paper). y_{ik} is 1 if IE's prediction matches a ground truth element (be correct) and vice versa. Then the loss function is the standard binary cross-entropy loss with label y_{ik} and probability p_{ik}.

4   Experiments

4.1   Datasets and Evaluation Metrics

Datasets. We collect 4 Invoice-like datasets and divide them into 2 tasks, corresponding to English and Japanese language used in the data. For each task, we use the bigger dataset as the main one, and the smaller as the out-of-distribution (OOD) dataset with respect to the main dataset.

We first use pre-trained IE Networks (see Sect. 2) to generate the intermediate features for the MCP as mentioned in Sect. 3.1. The outputs of the IE Networks and the ground-truth IE outputs are used to produce labels for the confidence estimation task (Sect. 3.3).

We only train the confidence models on the training dataset and benchmark them on the testing and corresponding OOD datasets. The evaluation on OOD data is a challenging benchmark since the OOD dataset is totally different from the main one in terms of layout, background and writing styles. Moreover, since the OOD datasets can have different type of keys from those in the main one, we only test the models on fields that share common keys with the main dataset.

(a) Public datasets (*English*)

SROIE - Main dataset. SROIE [6] is a dataset of scanned receipts. There are 4 keys: *address, company, date, total.* The training set has 626 files corresponding to 3859 IE's output key-value fields. We further hold 10% of the training as the validation set. The statistics for the test set are 341 files and 1,640 fields, respectively.

CORD - OOD dataset. CORD [7] contains receipts collected from Indonesian shops and restaurants. Compared to SROIE, CORD document images are captured in the wild, thus the data is noisy and low in quality. CORD field shares only one key with SROIE, which is *total.* We use the CORD-dev set which contains 100 files correspoding to 103 IE's output fields.

(b) In-house datasets (*Japanese*)

In-house 1 - Main dataset. In-house 1 is a dataset containing Japanese invoice documents collected from several vendors. There are 25 keys. Example keys are *issued_ date, total_ amount, tax, item_ name, item_ amount.* The training set has 835 files corresponding to 24,697 IE's output fields, and the test set has 338 files and 10,898 fields.

In-house 2 - OOD dataset. In-house 2 consists of 68 invoice documents from another Japanese company. The document pattern is quite different to the In-house 1 dataset. The two in-house dataset share 4 key types in common, resulting in 3,887 IE's output fields.

Table 1. Ablation study on SROIE dataset

Methods	ECE	AUC
MCP (concatenation)	0.1525	83.75
MCP (bilinear pooling)	0.1175	86.90
MCP (concatenation) + VCAD	0.1385	84.37
MCP (bilinear pooling) + VCAD	**0.1002**	**88.12**

Evaluation Metrics. We use the popular *Area Under the Receiver Operating Characteristic Curve (AUC)* [5,30–32] and *Expected Calibration Error (ECE)* [33] metrics for measuring the performance of confidence predictors.

4.2 Experimental Baselines

Softmax Threshold. Our IE pipeline consists of multiple sequential models, so we adapted [34] by combining both softmax probabilities from OCR and KV models using multiplication (i.e.: $p_{final} = p_{OCR} * p_{KV}$). We then specify a threshold score and considered examples with higher-than-threshold softmax probability as correctly predicted one, and vice versa. The threshold score is tuned on the training dataset.

Temperature Scaling. [8] is a technique that post-processes the neural networks to make them calibrated in term of confidence. Temperature scaling divides the logits (inputs to the softmax function) by a learned scalar parameter T (temperature). We learn this parameter on a validation set, where T is chosen to minimize negative log-likelihood.

Softmax Classifier. Instead of only utilizing the softmax probability of the predicted class as Softmax Threshold, Softmax Classifier is more advanced by making use of the whole softmax vector. Particularly, we build a simple classifier using a feed-forward neural network. The input for the network is the concatenation of the OCR model's softmax vector and the KV model's one.

Monte Carlo Dropout. MC Dropout [4] belongs to the class of Bayesian or variational approaches. By keeping the dropout enabled at test time, we can obtain the variance of the neural network's outputs, and this variance indicates the level of uncertainty. We apply MC Dropout on our KV model, which is the final model in the pipeline.

4.3 Benchmarking Results

Ablation Study. We ablate the effect of VCAD and MCP on the whole hybrid system. Table 1 reports the results on SROIE dataset. Without VCAD, the proposed model achieves best AUC score of 86.90% using bi-linear pooling fusion strategy. Simpler concatenation method underperforms by about 3% demonstrating the importance of using outer-product to retain bit-level relationships among 3 modalities. When the VCAD is integrated, it consistently improves the

Table 2. Performance comparison of baselines and proposed methods on SROIE and CORD datasets

Methods	SROIE		CORD	
	ECE	AUC	ECE	AUC
Softmax threshold	0.1525	83.75	0.1731	66.91
Softmax classifier	0.1400	85.50	0.3289	54.91
MC Dropout	0.1175	86.90	0.5446	43.52
Temperature scaling	0.1385	84.37	0.3787	74.58
MCP	0.1124	86.40	0.1432	75.12
HYCEDIS	**0.1002**	**88.12**	**0.1259**	**77.45**

Table 3. Performance comparison of baselines and proposed methods on In-house datasets

Methods	In-house 1		In-house 2	
	ECE	AUC	ECE	AUC
Softmax threshold	0.1285	68.79	0.5885	53.38
Softmax classifier	0.2810	71.43	0.3945	51.22
MC Dropout	0.3733	66.14	0.3621	48.20
Temperature scaling	0.1728	64.00	0.5879	58.18
MCP	0.0782	86.32	0.3348	60.12
HYCEDIS	**0.0712**	**90.12**	**0.3019**	**61.90**

performance of all fusion methods. Hence, the full hybrid HYCEDIS architecture can reach 88.12% AUC. Similar behaviors can be found with measurement using ECE metric.

Public English Datasets Result. Table 2 shows the performance of all models on public datasets. On both SROIE and its OOD CORD dataset, our full HYCEDIS is consistently the best performer regarding both ECE and AUC scores. Our MCP is the runner-up under ECE metric. The improvements of MCP in AUC and ECE suggests that the signals from intermediate features extracted from text-line images, OCR-ed text and graph structure help improve the accuracy of the softmax-based methods which only rely on some softmax layers of the IE Networks. In addition, when combined with VCAD, the AUC score is further increased and the ECE also downgrades. That manifests the contribution of our VCAD model. We can see a significant performance drop from baselines such as MC-Dropout when being tested on OOD CORD data. Our methods alleviate this issue, maintaining a moderate generalization to strange data.

In-House Japanese Datasets Result. We also benchmark the models on two in-house datasets. In Table 3, our model continues to show the superior performance compared with other baselines. Our MCP model improves about 14.89% and 2% AUC score and reduces 0.0503 and 0.0273 ECE score in In-house 1 and In-house 2 datasets, respectively. When adding VCAD, the performance is improved around 3.82% on In-house 1 dataset and 2.78% on In-house dataset, which again validates our hypothesis on using anomaly detector to enhance conformal predictor.

5 Conclusion

We have introduced a holistic confidence score architecture that aims to verify the result of IE Networks in document understanding tasks. Our architecture takes advantages of a Multi-modal Conformal Predictor and a Variational Cluster-oriented Anomaly Detector to predict whether the IE Networks' output correct or not using features of different granularity. Our hybrid approach surpasses prior confidence estimation methods by a huge margin in benchmarks with invoice datasets. Remarkably, it demonstrates a capability of generalization to out-of-distribution datasets.

References

1. Yang, X., et al.: Learning to extract semantic structure from documents using multimodal fully convolutional neural networks. In: Proceedings of the IEEE Conference on Computer Vision and Pattern Recognition, pp. 5315–5324 (2017)
2. He, T., et al.: An end-to-end textspotter with explicit alignment and attention. In: Proceedings of the IEEE Conference on Computer Vision and Pattern Recognition, pp. 5020–5029 (2018)
3. Zheng, N., et al.: Hybrid-augmented intelligence: collaboration and cognition. Frontiers Inf. Technol. Electron. Eng. **18**(2), 153–179 (2017). https://doi.org/10.1631/FITEE.1700053
4. Gal, Y., Ghahramani, Z.: Dropout as a Bayesian approximation: representing model uncertainty in deep learning. In: International Conference on Machine Learning, pp. 1050–1059 (2016)
5. Mor, N., Wolf, L.: Confidence prediction for lexicon-free OCR. In: 2018 IEEE Winter Conference on Applications of Computer Vision (WACV), pp. 218–225 (2018)
6. Huang, Z., et al.: ICDAR 2019 competition on scanned receipt OCR and information extraction. In: 2019 International Conference on Document Analysis and Recognition (ICDAR), pp. 1516–1520 (2019)
7. Park, S., et al.: CORD: a consolidated receipt dataset for post-OCR parsing (2019)
8. Guo, C., Pleiss, G., Sun, Y., Weinberger, K.Q.: On calibration of modern neural networks. arXiv preprint arXiv:1706.04599 (2017)
9. Baek, Y., Lee, B., Han, D., Yun, S., Lee, H.: Character region awareness for text detection. In: Proceedings of the IEEE/CVF Conference on Computer Vision and Pattern Recognition, pp. 9365–9374 (2019)

10. He, P., et al.: Single shot text detector with regional attention. In: Proceedings of the IEEE International Conference on Computer Vision, pp. 3047–3055 (2017)

11. Long, S., Ruan, J., Zhang, W., He, X., Wu, W., Yao, C.: TextSnake: a flexible representation for detecting text of arbitrary shapes. In: Ferrari, V., Hebert, M., Sminchisescu, C., Weiss, Y. (eds.) ECCV 2018. LNCS, vol. 11206, pp. 19–35. Springer, Cham (2018). https://doi.org/10.1007/978-3-030-01216-8_2

12. Liao, M., Shi, B., Bai, X., Wang, X., Liu, W.: TextBoxes: a fast text detector with a single deep neural network. In: Proceedings of the AAAI Conference on Artificial Intelligence, vol. 31 (2017)

13. Liao, M., Zhu, Z., Shi, B., Xia, G.-S., Bai, X.: Rotation-sensitive regression for oriented scene text detection. In: Proceedings of the IEEE Conference on Computer Vision and Pattern Recognition, pp. 5909–5918 (2018)

14. Liu, Y., Jin, L.: Deep matching prior network: Toward tighter multi oriented text detection. In: Proceedings of the IEEE Conference on Computer Vision and Pattern Recognition, pp. 1962–1969 (2017)

15. Graves, A., Fernández, S., Gomez, F., Schmidhuber, J.: Connectionist temporal classification: labelling unsegmented sequence data with recurrent neural networks. In: Proceedings of the 23rd International Conference on Machine Learning, pp. 369–376 (2006)

16. Yao, L., Mao, C., Luo, Y.: Graph convolutional networks for text classification. In: Proceedings of the AAAI Conference on Artificial Intelligence, vol. 33, pp. 7370–7377 (2019)

17. Liu, X., Gao, F., Zhang, Q., Zhao, H.: Graph convolution for multimodal information extraction from visually rich documents. arXiv preprint arXiv:1903.11279 (2019)

18. Xu, Y., et al.: LayoutLM: pre-training of text and layout for document image understanding. In: Proceedings of the 26th ACM SIGKDD International Conference on Knowledge Discovery & Data Mining, pp. 1192–1200 (2020)

19. Dang, T.A.N., Thanh, D.N.: End-to-end information extraction by character-level embedding and multi-stage attentional U-Net. In: BMVC, p. 96 (2019)

20. Qian, Y., Santus, E., Jin, Z., Guo, J., Barzilay, R.: GraphIE: a graph- based framework for information extraction. arXiv: 1810.13083 (2018)

21. Liu, X., Gao, F., Zhang, Q., Zhao, H.: Graph convolution for multimodal information extraction from visually rich documents. arXiv: 1903.11279

22. Vedova, L.D., Yang, H., Orchard, G.: An invoice reading system using a graph convolutional network **2**, 434–449 (2019)

23. Chung, J.S., Senior, A., Vinyals, O., Zisserman, A.: Lip reading sentences in the wild. In: 2017 IEEE Conference on Computer Vision and Pattern Recognition (CVPR), pp. 3444–3453 (2017)

24. Yu, Z., Yu, J., Fan, J., Tao, D.: Multi-modal factorized bilinear pooling with co-attention learning for visual question answering. In: Proceedings of the IEEE International Conference on Computer Vision, pp. 1821–1830 (2017)

25. Sandler, M., Howard, A., Zhu, M., Zhmoginov, A., Chen, L.-C.: MobileNetV2: inverted residuals and linear bottlenecks. In: Proceedings of the IEEE Conference on Computer Vision and Pattern Recognition, pp. 4510–4520 (2018)

26. Huang, G.B., Kae, A., Doersch, C., Learned-Miller, E.: Bounding the probability of error for high precision optical character recognition. J. Mach. Learn. Res. **13**, 363–387 (2012)

27. Kingma, D.P., Welling, M.: Auto-encoding variational Bayes. arXiv preprint arXiv:1312.6114 (2013)

28. Rezende, D.J., Mohamed, S., Wierstra, D.: Stochastic backpropagation and approximate inference in deep generative models. arXiv preprint arXiv:1401.4082 (2014)
29. Akcay, S., Atapour-Abarghouei, A., Breckon, T.P.: GANomaly: semi-supervised anomaly detection via adversarial training. In: Jawahar, C.V., Li, H., Mori, G., Schindler, K. (eds.) ACCV 2018. LNCS, vol. 11363, pp. 622–637. Springer, Cham (2019). https://doi.org/10.1007/978-3-030-20893-6_39
30. Ayhan, M.S., Berens, P.: Test-time data augmentation for estimation of heteroscedastic aleatoric uncertainty in deep neural networks (2018)
31. Mandelbaum, A., Weinshall, D.: Distance-based confidence score for neural network classifiers. arXiv preprint arXiv:1709.09844 (2017)
32. Hein, M., Andriushchenko, M., Bitterwolf, J.: Why ReLU networks yield high-confidence predictions far away from the training data and how to mitigate the problem. In: Proceedings of the IEEE/CVF Conference on Computer Vision and Pattern Recognition, pp. 41–50 (2019)
33. Naeini, M.P., Cooper, G., Hauskrecht, M.: Obtaining well calibrated probabilities using Bayesian binning. In: Proceedings of the AAAI Conference on Artificial Intelligence, vol. 29 (2015)
34. Hendrycks, D., Gimpel, K.: A baseline for detecting misclassified and out-of-distribution examples in neural networks. arXiv preprint arXiv:1610.02136 (2016)

Multi-level Network Based on Text Attention and Pose-Guided for Person Re-ID

Xi Wang[1], Canlong Zhang[1,2(✉)], Zhixin Li[1,2], and Zhiwen Wang[3]

[1] School of Computer Science and Engineering, Guangxi Normal University,
Guilin 541004, China
[2] Guangxi Key Lab of Multi-source Information Mining and Security,
Guilin 541004, China
zcltyp@163.com
[3] School of Computer Science and Technology, Guangxi University of Science
and Technology, Liuzhou 545006, China

Abstract. Text-based person Re-ID aims to find the target person's image from the image gallery under the condition that the text description about the target person is known. Since there is vast modal difference between the image and text, how to effectively match the semantic features of the image-text is extremely important. Existing schemes mainly consider how to extract more accurate text representation or more complete image representation but ignore multi-granularity feature matching. In this paper, we proposed a Text Attention to Multi-level Network model by Pose and attention-guided for Text-based Person Re-ID(PAMN). Specifically, we firstly design a pose-guided image feature extracting model and an attention-driven text semantics representation model to respectively learn multi-granularity features of image and text, and then employ cross-modal projection matching to align them from different granularities so as to obtain high matching accuracy. Experimental validation is performed on the standard datasets CUHK-pedes and the newly proposed datasets ICFG-pedes, and the experimental results show that the performance of our PAMN is better than other existing methods.

Keywords: person Re-ID · Pose estimation · Multi-level network

1 Introduction

The task of text-based person re-identification (for short:Re-ID) is to find the target person image in a large person image gallery according to the given text

This work is supported by National Natural Science Foundation of China (Nos. 62266009, 61866004, 62276073, 61966004, 61962007), Guangxi Natural Science Foundation (Nos. 2018GXNSFDA281009, 2019GXNSFDA245018, 2018GXNSFDA294001), Guangxi Collaborative Innovation Center of Multi-source Information Integration and Intelligent Processing, and Guangxi "Bagui Scholar" Teams for Innovation and Research Project.

description [9]. Compared with image-based person Re-ID, text-based Re-ID does not require one person's image at least, which to be provided in advance for retrieval. It is not friendly to application in a real-world situation. Text-based people Re-ID is a more challenging task compared with a typical image-text matching task where an image may contain multiple objects because the high-level representation between different pedestrian images is very similar, and there is a small Inter-class between images and text descriptions.

Since the person image contains not only the person itself but also a variety of background and light interference, if the background is completely removed, the confidential information may also be ignored. Previous methods [5,10] have focused on using attention mechanisms for a one-line match, but this largely ignores multi-level interrelationships. [1,7,12,13] Several coarse-grained approaches focus on learning representations on a global scale, i.e., entire images and sentences, but lack fine-grained matching on words and local images. Instead, we use a multi-level network to align image-text features, which preserves the full semantic features of person images and text descriptions at low levels, and more accurately matches the image-text features of pedestrians at both local and global levels. However, different people have different emphases and descriptive habits when describing the same image, which leads to significant differences between different text descriptions. Dissimilar images of the same person will also contain different semantic information due to various viewing angles of the camera or lighting angles, resulting in the images of pedestrians owning different semantic information.

According to the above problems, this paper proposes a multi-level network of pose guidance and adaptive alignment of text attention to solve the problem of text-based person re-identification. The details of the model architecture are shown in Fig. 1. The distinction between the datasets of the text-based person re-identification and image retrieval task is that the former highlights the posture and dress of the person itself. Therefore, this paper uses pose guidance to extract the visual representation of pedestrians so that more accurately obtain the human posture information for pedestrians themselves in-person images. It can avoid the distractions of background information. Specifically, we sent the person image to the resnet 50 network to extract the low-level feature of the person image. At the same time, sent into ImageCNN, the semantic image features are extracted by using the pose estimation image processing branch to obtain more accurate local representation features of the person image. Then the global image features are extracted through the global maximum pooling layer. About text descriptions, although the word order and focus of attention of each text description are many different, the words that precisely describe the appearance and posture of pedestrians are generally a combination of adjectives and nouns. While other word types, such as conjunctions, pronouns, and adverbs, play little role in the search process [9]. Therefore, this paper adds channel attention to the processing TextCNN module and assigns corresponding weights to each channel by calculating the proportion of each channel feature in the overall feature, thereby enhancing the more important text representation features in the text description and weakening the impact of other features. Therefore, we can obtain the low-level feature representation of the text description after the text description enters the BERT pre-trained model and obtain the local features of the text that match the local features of the person image through the TextCNN network similar to the person image processing. The global maximum pooling layer is also used to obtain the global text feature. In addition, in order not to lose the image and text semantic information at various levels, the multi-level network is used to match the image-text representation features from multiple scales. At the same time, we tested our proposed model on the classical datasets CUHK-pedes and the newly proposed datasets ICFG-pedes [3], respectively, and the experiments showed that our method improved in various indicators which also showed the effectiveness of our method.

The main contributions of this article can be summarized as follows:

First, we designed a network of text attention branches that adaptively enhance and suppress text features, thereby reducing the distraction of excess text information.

Secondly, a gesture-guided image branch network is proposed, which can obtain more accurate person image characteristics by extracting the gesture characteristics of pedestrians and fusing them with person images.

Finally, we designed a multi-level matching network that aligns the image-text features under each level from multiple levels of perspective.

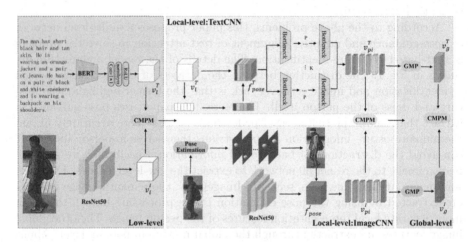

Fig. 1. Text-based person re-identification framework (PAMN). Search for the person image to be found in the image library according to the query statement.

2   Method

2.1   Image Feature Extraction

During the training phase, we assume that the data is $D = \{P_i, T_i\}_{i=1}^{N}$ where N represents the number of image-text pairs in each batch, and each pair of image-text pairs consists of a person image P and the corresponding text description T. In the ImageCNN branch, we use a backbone network (such as ResNet50) to extract the visual features of person images, and the ResNet50 network used is mainly composed of four residual blocks. Different residual blocks can capture semantic information from different levels. For each person image P, we define the feature generated by the third residual block as the low-level semantic feature map of the person image $f_l^P \in R^{H \times W \times C_1}$ and the feature generated by the fourth residual block as the high-level semantic feature map of the person image $f_h^P \in R^{H \times W \times C_2}$. Where H, W, and C_1/C_2 represent the height, width, and channel size of the above feature diagram, respectively. We then obtain a low-level representation of the visual semantic features of the person image $v_l^P \in 5^{C_1}$:

$$v_l^P = GMP\left(f_l^P\right) \tag{1}$$

where GMP represents a global maximum pooling layer that acts as a filter for significant mining information.

We then feed the person image into the CNN branch of the image, where the M key point of the human body in the person image is used to generate M heat maps corresponding to the person image [11], where M = 17. Next, maximize pooling of all feature vectors and connect them to the high-level semantic features of the person image $f_h^P \in R^{H \times W \times C_2}$. Each pose-guided feature map produces an eigenvector through an averaged pooling layer that corresponds to an area containing specific key points. The maximum pooling operation allows feature vectors to fuse information about visible body parts, ignoring occluded parts and redundant information. Enter it into a fully connected layer to obtain person attitude features that represent attitude guidance f_{pose}^P. Since each heat map explicitly encodes information about different areas of the target pedestrian, i.e., occluded areas, the attitude guidance feature map can focus on the unobstructed part of the target pedestrian.

At the same time, we take the PCB [14] strategy to obtain local areas. In particular, the advanced feature map is divided into K horizontal bars, which are recorded as them $\left\{f_{p1}^P, f_{j2}^P, \cdots, f_{pK}^P\right\}$, where $f_{pi}^P \in R^{\frac{H}{W} \times H \times C_2}$. For each bar, similar to equation (1), we still take the global maximum pooling layer to extract the local representation of the visualization $v_{pi}^P \in R^{C_2}$. To fuse all the local representations, we selected the maximum value of each element in the channel dimension and got a global visual representation $v_g^P \in R^{C_2}$:

$$v_g^P = Max\left(v_{p1}^P, v_{p2}^P, \cdots, v_{pK}^P\right) \tag{2}$$

As a result, the visual feature $V^P = \left\{v_l^P, v_{p1}^P, v_{p2}^P, \cdots, v_{pK}^P, v_g^P\right\}$ set contains low-level, local, and global representations.

2.2   Text Feature Extraction

In the TextCNN branch, we use a BERT pre-trained model to decompose each text description T into a list of words and insert two unique markers [CLS] and [SEP] at the beginning and end of this list. This list of words with unique markers added is then embedded in a pre-trained marker. To ensure the consistency of the text length, we set the maximum length of the text to L. The text after each mark describes the input pre-trained model to extract word embedding $t \in R^{L \times D}$, where D represents the dimensions of each word.

In a TextCNN, in order to map the dimensions of the word embedding to the exact channel dimensions as the visual low-level feature mapping, we set the Conv kernel size of the first Conv layer to $1 \times 1 \times D \times C_1$. We can then get a low-level feature map of the text $f_l^T \in R^{1 \times L \times D}$. In order to enhance the more important text words in the text description (such as nouns, adjectives, verbs, etc.) and reduce the impact of other text words (such as conjunctions, pronouns, etc.), we send the processed word embedding into the channel for attention [6] obtain f_{pose}^T and then input it into the text branch network.

The text branch network contains K residual branches, corresponding to the K stripes of the person image. For each branch, it contains P text residual bottlenecks, which is so that the text branch can adaptively learn a text representation that matches the text feature of the local visual feature. The residual text bottleneck has a similar structure to modules in ResNet, consisting of several Conv layers and batch normalization processing layers. It uses a hop-and-drop connection to transmit information from the lower layer to the higher level, effectively suppressing network degradation problems and speeding up model training. Specifically, to keep the text information from being compressed, the stride of all convolutional layers in the bottleneck is set to 1×1. For the first bottleneck of each branch, we changed the channel dimension of the text feature mapping to C_2, which is consistent with the visual advanced feature mapping $f_h^P \in R^{H \times W \times C_2}$, then left the channel dimension unchanged in the remaining bottlenecks. After the multi-branch TextCNN, we get a local feature representation of the text. Similar to the ImageCNN branch, we take the global maximum pooling layer to extract the local representations of the text and select the maximum value of each element in the channel dimension to fuse these local representations. We then get a text semantic feature representation $V^T = \left\{ v_l^T, v_{p1}^T, v_{p2}^T, \cdots, v_{pK}^T, v_g^T \right\}$ that contains low-level, local, and global text features.

2.3   Cross-Modal Projection Matching

In order to eliminate the gap between image modal and text modal features, cross-modal projection matching (CMPM) losses are used at the low, local, and global level representations, and It can correlate representations under different modes by incorporating cross-modal projections into KL divergence[14]. We assume each visual representation v_i^P, $\left\{ \left(v_i^P, v_j^T \right), y_{i,j} = 1 \right\}_{j=1}^{N}$ is an image-text pair $y_{i,j} = 1$ showing the image text corresponds to the same pedestrian, $y_{i,j} = 0$

meaning they are not images and text descriptions from the same person. The probability of v_i^P and v_j^T that the sum is matched can be calculated by:

$$p_{i,j} = \frac{\exp\left(\left(v_i^P\right)^\top \bar{v}_j^T\right)}{\sum_{k=1}^{N} \exp\left(\left(v_i^P\right)^\top \bar{v}_k^T\right)} \tag{3}$$

where $\bar{v}_j^T$ normalized text is represented, represented as $\bar{v}_j^T = \frac{v_j^T}{\|v_j^T\|}$, in CMPM, the scalar projections on top are used as their similarity, and the matching probability $p_{i,j}$ is the ratio of the sum of the similarities of v_i^P and v_j^T the similarities of and. Then the CMPM loss can be calculated as:

$$L_{P2T} = \frac{1}{N} \sum_{i=1}^{N} \sum_{j=1}^{N} p_{i,j} \log\left(\frac{p_{i,j}}{q_{i,j} + \varepsilon}\right) \tag{4}$$

where ε is a small number to avoid number problems $q_{i,j}$ is the probability of a correct match between v_i^P and v_j^T normalization because there may be more than one matching text description in a batch expressed as $q_{i,j} = \frac{y_{i,j}}{\sum_{k=1}^{N} y_{i,k}}$. The above step reduces the distance in a single direction between each visual representation and its matching text representation, and we take a similar step in reverse to match each text representation and its matching visual representation closer together. Therefore, bidirectional CMPM loss is calculated as:

$$L_{CMPM} = L_{P2T} + L_{T2P} \tag{5}$$

The goal in our framework consists of cross-modal representation matching from three levels. CMPM losses in low-level representations are meant to reduce modal gaps at an early stage. CMPM loss in local-level representations enables local alignment between images and text. CMPM loss in the global-level representation ensures more excellent modal compatibility of the final representation of the evaluation. Through the multiple phases of CMPM loss, the degree of matching of the image-text representation can be gradually improved. Finally, based on the sum of the visual and textual representation sets v^P and v^T, the overall objective function evaluates to:

$$L = \lambda_1 L_{CMPM}^l + \lambda_2 \sum_{k=1}^{K} L_{CMPM}^{pK} + \lambda_3 L_{CMPM}^g \tag{6}$$

where λ_1, λ_2, λ_3, is hyperparameters that controls the importance of different CMPM losses. L_{CMPM}^l, $\left\{L_{CMPM}^{pk}\right\}_{k=1}^{K}$, and L_{CMPM}^g are respectively representing the low-level, local-level, and global-level of CMPM losses.

3   Experimental

In this section, we compare the performance of PAMN with advanced text-based person re-identification methods to evaluate our proposed PAMN. In addition, we did ablation studies to demonstrate the proposed method's effectiveness. Finally, the attention graph between the image and the text is visualized to demonstrate PAMN better multi-level matching capabilities.

3.1 Experimental Setup

Datasets and evaluation protocols. We used the CUHK-pedes datasets presented in 2017 and the ICFG-pedes datasets proposed in 2021 to train and evaluate our proposed model. The training set of the CUHK-pedes datasets contains a total of 13,003 person IDs with no duplicates, 34,054 images, and 68,108 text description statements. Each person's ID has four matching images, and each image has two matching text description statements. The test set contained 3074 images corresponding to 1000 person IDs, and the vocabulary of the datasets contained 9408 different words. The ICFG-pedes datasets contain 54,522 person images and 4,102 person IDs. Each image has a text description, and each text description has an average of 37.2 words. Different person IDs have different numbers of corresponding images, and the text descriptions of the datasets contain 5,554 unique words. The training set contains 34674 pairs of image-text pairs with 3102 person IDs, while the test set contains 19848 pairs of image-text pairs corresponding to the remaining 1000 person IDs. Unlike the image size in the CUHK-pedes datasets, the person images in the ICFG-pedes datasets vary in size. Each person's ID has a personal image with different viewing angles and lights.

We use standard top-k accuracy to evaluate the performance of the model. Expressly, given a description of the query text, the images in the test set all match the text. The search is considered successful if any corresponding images of the person are in the first k images. All of our experiments demonstrated the accuracy of the top 1, top 5, and top 10.

3.2 Experimental Details

For the visual feature extraction module, to make a fair comparison with the previous model, we use the resnet50 network as the backbone of the visual processing part. ImageCNN obtains the gesture-guided person image feature map from the person image and then divides the attitude-guided person image feature map into K horizontal bars to obtain K local person image features. We set the output stride of the backbone network to 1. We use horizontal flips (50% probability) to augment the data. All images are normalized and adjusted to 384×128 before being fed into the ImageCNN. We use language representations in the TextCNN module to pre-train the model BERT to contact contextual information to extract word embeddings for text descriptions where the text length is uniformly set to L = 64. The number of local areas in the ImageCNN and TextCNN is set to K = 6. In the TextCNN, the number of bottlenecks in each residual branch is set to P = 3. In image features and text features, some dimension parameters are set to H = 24, W = 8, C_1 = 1024, C2 = 2048, and D = 768, respectively.

When the model was trained, the epoch of the model was 80, and each batch contained N = 64 pairs of image-text pairs. We optimized the model using the Adam [9] optimizer, and the importance hyperparameters of each loss function in λ_1, λ_2, and λ_3 where 1, 1, and 0.1, respectively. In the image and text processing branch, we initialize the learning rate with the first 10 iterations as a warm-up technique, with the base learning rate set to 3×10^{-3}, which is reduced to 0.1 after 50 epochs.

3.3   Comparison with State-of-the-Art Methods

Table 1 shows how our model compares to current advanced methods on the dataset CUHK-pedes, "Baseline-re" is the result of recurrence. PMA [8], ViTAA [15], NAFS [4], TIPCB [2], and our model use ResNet50 as a backbone network for extracting visual features. As seen from the table, our model has achieved good performance on the CUHK-pedes dataset, which verifies the effectiveness of our model. Table 2 shows how our model compares to current advanced methods on the dataset ICFG-pedes. Compared to the most advanced models, our models have improved on the top-1, top-5, and top-10 indicators. This also illustrates the role of the local feature extraction branch of images and texts we designed, validating the importance of introducing local fine-grained image-text matching and multi-level network alignment.

Table 1. Compare with our state-of-the-art methods on CUHK-pedes with the same visual backbone network. The accuracy rate of the top 1, top 5 and top 10 was demonstrated (%).

Method	Backbone	Top@1	Top@5	Top@10
PMA (2020)	ResNet50	53.81	73.54	81.23
ViTAA (2020)	ResNet50	55.97	75.84	83.52
NAFS (2021)	ResNet50	59.94	79.86	86.70
Baseline (2021)	ResNet50	64.26	83.19	89.10
Baseline-re	ResNet50	63.03	82.46	88.5
PAMN (Ours)	ResNet50	**63.94**	**82.97**	**88.87**

3.4   Ablation Studies

Image-text feature alignment. We conducted extensive ablation experiments to demonstrate our proposed gesture-guided ImageCNN and TextCNN methods and the representation of aligned image-text features at different scales. Table 3 shows the detailed comparison of our models on the datasets CUHK-pedes, and Table 4 shows the detailed comparison of our models on the datasets ICFG-pedes. It can be observed that the experimental performance of the baseline model is improved compared with the posture guidance model and the text attention

Table 2. Compare with our state-of-the-art methods on ICFG-pedes with the same visual backbone network. The accuracy rate of the top 1, top 5 and top 10 was demonstrated (%).

Method	Backbone	Top@1	Top@5	Top@10
ViTAA (2020)	ResNet50	50.98	68.79	75.78
SSAN (2021)	ResNet50	54.23	72.63	75.78
Baseline (2021)	ResNet50	54.96	74.72	81.89
Baseline-re	ResNet50	51.10	72.24	80.03
PAMN (Ours)	ResNet50	**52.02**	**73.18**	**80.73**

Table 3. Ablation experiments. The ours_no-att model was compared to the text-only attention model (Ours_no-pose) on CUHK-pedes, and the table showed the accuracy rates (%)of the top 1, top 5, top 10, and map.

Method	Top@1	Top@5	Top@10	mAP
Baseline	63.029	82.466	88.5	53.79
Ours_no-att	63.534	82.87	88.643	53.832
Ours_no-pose	63.256	82.721	88.609	53.817
PAMN	**63.942**	**82.97**	**88.871**	**54.018**

model alone, while the PAMN that combines the gesture guidance model and the text attention model has a more significant improvement compared with the baseline.

Table 4. Ablation experiments. Comparing the ours_no-att model with the text-only attention model (Ours_no-pose) on ICFG-pedes, the table shows the accuracy rates (%)of the top 1, top 5, top 10 and map.

Method	Top@1	Top@5	Top@10	mAP
Baseline	51.108	72.249	80.033	29.313
Ours_no-att	51.637	72.472	80.255	29.647
Ours_no-pose	51.329	72.429	80.212	29.437
PAMN	**52.024**	**73.182**	**80.734**	**29.815**

a) Pose guide model only. This method only extracts the gesture-guided person image features and does not do attention to the text features of the person text description.
b) Text-only attention model. This method only uses the text attention module to extract text description features and does not extract gesture-guided image features from person images. The other components are the same as the

approach we proposed. We chose this method to verify the effectiveness of adding the best images and text representations to text-based people search tasks.

c) PAMN. This is the complete implementation of PAMN that we propose, with images and text representations from three levels, thick to thin. This comparison is made to verify the validity of adding image and text branches to extract feature representations.

3.5 Visual Analysis

To illustrate the reason for the number of local area chunks selected in this article, K = 6, we visualized the experimental results of the number of local locales on different datasets. As shown in Fig. 2 and Fig. 3, the model works best when the number of local areas is set to 6.

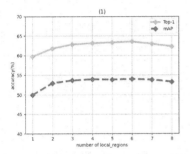

Fig. 2. The effect of local area number K on Top-1 and mAP is shown on the dataset CUHK-pedes.

Fig. 3. The effect of local area number K on Top-1 and mAP is shown on the dataset ICFG-pedes.

We conducted a qualitative assessment of our proposed PAMN. Figure 4 shows our proposed example of PAMN using text to describe the Top-5 results of a search. The two scenarios in line 1 show the success of the corresponding image in the Top-5 search result range. For successful cases, we can observe that

Fig. 4. Visualization of joint alignment between word and image regions at different scales. Red, blue, and yellow highlighted image-text depicts low-level, global, and local-level alignment. (Color figure online)

each text describing the corresponding image has multiple areas that match the partial description. Moreover, line 2 shows the case where the retrieval failed in Top-5. In the case of retrieval failure, we can find that for local details of the text description, such as the "grey bag" in the first query text on line 2, the image retrieval fails because the package shape is not specified in detail. The opposite is another retrieval failure scenario, shown on the left side of line 2 in Fig. 4, where the model failed to retrieve images due to an error in understanding the details of the "light brown purse" in the text description. We visualize the alignment results between text descriptions and image regions at different levels, as shown in Fig. 5. To better visualize our proposed multi-level network, we align the low, global, and local levels of image-text descriptions highlighted in red, blue, and yellow. The visualization results verify the validity of the proposed joint alignment and the necessity of full-scale representation.

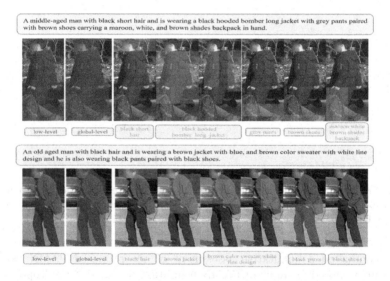

Fig. 5. PAMN uses text to describe an example of a Top-5 result. Retrieve the correct image marked with a green rectangle, the incorrect marked with a red box. (Color figure online)

4   Summary

This paper proposes a multi-level network of pose guidance and adaptive alignment of text attention. In order to pay more attention to the body characteristics of the person itself, we extract the gesture-guided person image features in the ImageCNN and then divide them horizontally into local image features containing the person's posture. At the same time, the TextCNN extraction uses text attention to enhance important text description information, thereby extracting more accurate text description features and then dividing them into text description features corresponding to the local area of the pedestrian. Finally, multi-granular networks align features between different modes at different levels, thereby improving the ability to retrieve person images. Extensive comparative trials and ablation studies on datasets CUHK-pedes and ICFG-pedes demonstrated the validity of our proposed model.

References

1. Antol, S., et al.: VQA: visual question answering. In: Proceedings of the IEEE International Conference on Computer Vision, pp. 2425–2433 (2015)
2. Chen, Y., Zhang, G., Lu, Y., Wang, Z., Zheng, Y.: TIPCB: a simple but effective part-based convolutional baseline for text-based person search. Neurocomputing **494**, 171–181 (2022)
3. Ding, Z., Ding, C., Shao, Z., Tao, D.: Semantically self-aligned network for text-to-image part-aware person re-identification. arXiv preprint arXiv:2107.12666 (2021)
4. Gao, C., et al.: Contextual non-local alignment over full-scale representation for text-based person search. arXiv preprint arXiv:2101.03036 (2021)
5. Gao, P., et al.: Dynamic fusion with intra-and inter-modality attention flow for visual question answering. In: Proceedings of the IEEE/CVF Conference on Computer Vision and Pattern Recognition, pp. 6639–6648 (2019)
6. Hu, J., Shen, L., Sun, G.: Squeeze-and-excitation networks. In: Proceedings of the IEEE Conference on Computer Vision and Pattern Recognition, pp. 7132–7141 (2018)
7. Ji, Z., Wang, H., Han, J., Pang, Y.: Saliency-guided attention network for image-sentence matching. In: Proceedings of the IEEE/CVF International Conference on Computer Vision, pp. 5754–5763 (2019)
8. Jing, Y., Si, C., Wang, J., Wang, W., Wang, L., Tan, T.: Pose-guided multi-granularity attention network for text-based person search. In: Proceedings of the AAAI Conference on Artificial Intelligence, vol. 34, pp. 11189–11196 (2020)
9. Li, S., Xiao, T., Li, H., Zhou, B., Yue, D., Wang, X.: Person search with natural language description. In: Proceedings of the IEEE Conference on Computer Vision and Pattern Recognition, pp. 1970–1979 (2017)
10. Lin, T.-Y., et al.: Microsoft COCO: common objects in context. In: Fleet, D., Pajdla, T., Schiele, B., Tuytelaars, T. (eds.) ECCV 2014. LNCS, vol. 8693, pp. 740–755. Springer, Cham (2014). https://doi.org/10.1007/978-3-319-10602-1_48
11. Miao, J., Wu, Y., Liu, P., Ding, Y., Yang, Y.: Pose-guided feature alignment for occluded person re-identification. In: Proceedings of the IEEE/CVF International Conference on Computer Vision, pp. 542–551 (2019)
12. Nam, H., Ha, J.W., Kim, J.: Dual attention networks for multimodal reasoning and matching. In: Proceedings of the IEEE Conference on Computer Vision and Pattern Recognition, pp. 299–307 (2017)
13. Sarafianos, N., Xu, X., Kakadiaris, I.A.: Adversarial representation learning for text-to-image matching. In: Proceedings of the IEEE/CVF International Conference on Computer Vision, pp. 5814–5824 (2019)
14. Sun, Y., Zheng, L., Yang, Y., Tian, Q., Wang, S.: Beyond part models: person retrieval with refined part pooling (and A strong convolutional baseline). In: Ferrari, V., Hebert, M., Sminchisescu, C., Weiss, Y. (eds.) ECCV 2018. LNCS, vol.

11208, pp. 501–518. Springer, Cham (2018). https://doi.org/10.1007/978-3-030-01225-0_30

15. Wang, Z., Fang, Z., Wang, J., Yang, Y.: *ViTAA*: visual-textual attributes alignment in person search by natural language. In: Vedaldi, A., Bischof, H., Brox, T., Frahm, J.-M. (eds.) ECCV 2020. LNCS, vol. 12357, pp. 402–420. Springer, Cham (2020). https://doi.org/10.1007/978-3-030-58610-2_24

Sketch Image Style Transfer Based on Sketch Density Controlling

Siyuan Yu, Hao Wang, and Anna Zhu$^{(\boxtimes)}$

School of Computer Science and Artificial Intelligence,
Wuhan University of Technology, Wuhan, China
{yusiyuan,283276,annazhu}@whut.edu.cn

Abstract. Sketch Image Style Transfer aims to stylize the sketch images from given art images to make them look like the same artistic styles while still persevering the original sketch contents. Previous methods generally disentangle the content and style of reference image and transfer the style to sketch image. However, the textures or the painting strokes of the reference art image could be a part of content as well as style. It is difficult to decide how much it should be involved for sketch image style transferring. In this paper, we propose a novel sketch image style transfer method to use the sketch density to control it, reaching the common sense that simpler sketch images own richer textures of reference style images after stylization and otherwise the opposite. The proposed model is built upon the general content and style encoding and fused decoding architecture, but adds sketch density extraction to obtain the density level of input sketch image, and uses it to control texture information during transferring. With these special designing, our model is more flexible for inputting multi-density sketch images and reasonable for deciding the degree to transfer the texture styles of reference image. Experimental results on different datasets demonstrate the effectiveness and superiority of our method for sketch image style transfer.

Keywords: Style transfer · Sketch density · Feature disentanglement

1 Introduction

Recent advances in deep learning based algorithms have made it feasible and popular to generate artworks by computers. Image style transfer, as one of the main ways, is to generate the photo-realistic or artistic images from a reference stylized image, given constraint of content images. Sketch Image Style Transfer is a branch of Image style transfer task, which aims to transfer the styles into sketch images. It allows both non-artist users and mature painters to turn simple black and white drawings into more abstract, detailed and fancy artworks.

Most previous sketch style transfer methods have focused on synthesizing face images, or anime images [4] from sketches. They cannot be applied for university sketch style transferring. General style transfer methods [7,9] generate

M. Tanveer et al. (Eds.): ICONIP 2022, CCIS 1794, pp. 113–125, 2023.
https://doi.org/10.1007/978-981-99-1648-1_10

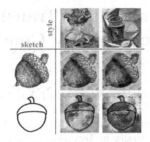

Fig. 1. Different density-level sketch image style transfer results. If the sketch image contains complex line textures, the transferred results should preserve them, otherwise transferring more texture from reference styles.

unsatisfactory results on sketch images due to the lacking of semantic information in the spares sketch lines. Additionally, style encompasses different formal elements of art, such as the color palette, the rendering of the contours, the complex of the brush strokes, etc. Sketch images drawn by different person are also distinguished. If the sketch is drawn with rich lines and complex textures, the transferred results should preserve those characteristics after style transfer. On the contrary, if the sketch is very simple, the transferred results should grab more texture styles from the reference. Considering this common sense as shown in Fig. 1, we propose a novel sketch image style transfer approach, considering the complexity of input sketch image density.

The proposed model is constructed by a content encoder, a style encoder and a density controlled decoder. Instead of taking all the sketch images as the same, we label their levels by the density of sketch lines. The sketch content encoder is built on a variation auto-encoder to output the feature representations of sketch image and its sketch level. To train this encoder, we carefully annotated a multi-density sketch image dataset, which owns 1500 different images with 10 level sketches. The computed sketch level is reused for extracting the content of style images through another style image encoder. It controls how much stroke textures should be extracted from reference image. During decoding stage, a texture controller module is induced to transfer proper degree of texture information from reference image to sketch image. With these designs, our model can generate more texture approximating styles of reference for simple sketch image and preserve more texture details of itself for complex sketch image.

In summary, our contributions in this work are three folds:

- We propose a novel sketch image style transfer approach, which produces adaptive stylized results according to the sketch density of image. It is capable of handling both the real photo-realistic and artistic style-transfer task.
- We design a texture controller module via inducing the sketch density of input image, which could generate better human visual perception matched image texture synthesis performance for both simple line sketches and complex line sketches.
- We introduce a carefully annotated multi-density sketch image dataset. It can benefit the sketch-based style transfer researches.

2 Related Works

Style transfer aims at transferring the style from a reference image to a content image. It needs to integrate the extracted style into the process of image reconstruction, so that the reconstructed image not only retains the high-level semantic information in feature representation, but also conforms to the given style. Neural style transfer proposed by Gatys et al. [7] was the pioneering work to encode the style of an image through a Convolution Neural Network (CNN). The deep learning-based style transfer methods have become popular since then. AdaIN [9] is another classic algorithm of style transfer. The content representation of images and styles in it are all features extracted by VGG network. In the process of image reconstruction, it uses adaptive instance normalisation to integrate styles, which can change the style of the reconstructed image. A lot of subsequent works [10] were proposed based on it.

Sketch to image synthesis is a branch of style transfer. It trends to synthesize real scene objects based on abstract sketches [20] through GANs. SketchyGAN [5] is a typical sketch-to-image synthesis model using GANs, which selectively extracted features by using masking residual units. However, those synthesized real scene objects may only have the same poses, locations or categories with the sketch objects, but not completely preserve the sketch line structures.

The deep learning-based art style transfer work arises from Liu et al. [14], who introduced the double masking mechanism to enforce constraints of content of sketch and used feature map conversion technology to enhance style consistency. Finally, the decoupled style and content information is realized by the inverse process instance normalization. After then, they proposed a self-supervised sketch-to-image synthesis model [2] with a momentum-based mutual information minimization loss to better decouple the content and style information.

3 Method

3.1 Overall Pipeline

Our method is mainly composed of three parts, the sketch content encoding, reference style information extraction and stylized image generation. The overall structure of our framework is shown in Fig. 2.

Given a sketch image $I_{sketch} \in \mathbb{R}^{H \times W \times 3}$ and a style image $I_{style} \in \mathbb{R}^{H \times W \times 3}$, we use an encoder E_c to extract sketch representation Z_c from I_{sketch}, meanwhile predict sketch level s by linear regression, and then extracting corresponding sketch representation Z_t from the reference image I_{style} using encoder E_t according to the sketch level s, making sure that Z_t and Z_c are the presentations in the same sketch density. Both of them are input to a texture controller to transfer the local sketch texture features from I_{style} to I_{sketch}, and then the texture enhanced sketch features are input to generator G. An style encoder E_s is used to extract latent code from I_{style}, and then we use mapping network to obtain the style representation Z_s and input it to generator G for style transfer

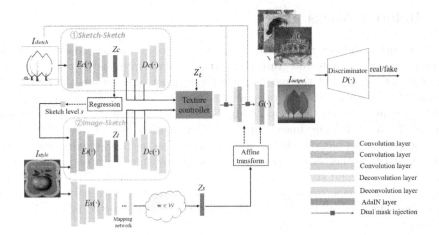

Fig. 2. The overall pipeline of our framework.

on texture enhanced sketch features. Finally, generator G outputs stylized image $I_{output} \in \mathbb{R}^{H \times W \times 3}$, which is used to train discriminator D together with real style image I_{real}.

3.2   Sketch Density Extraction and Encoding

Some lines in the sketch images are simple and some are complex. In this paper, we classify sketch images into 10 levels, from level 0 to level 9, according to the "density" of sketch images as shown in Fig. 4.

We build the encoder-decoder architecture to obtain the sketch image level and its content representation as shown in Fig. 2. It consists of two branches that implement the sketch density extraction and sketch image encoding function.

The first branch is a simple U-Net structure [16] with skip connections that takes I_{sketch} as input to E_c and generate the sketch representation Z_c, and it is then input to D_c and output the reconstruction result I_{rec}. Z_c is also used as input to a linear regression to get a scalar s representing the density level of I_{sketch}. E_c is fixed to the first few layers (up to relu4_1) of a pre-trained VGG-19. The linear regression outputs continuous floating-point numbers between 0 and 9 representing countless sketch levels. So, we adopt VAE [11] by adding several fully connected layers after E_c to get the mean and variance vectors of latent codes, and encoding I_{sketch} as Gaussian distribution.

The second branch is trained after the first branch. We fix the well-trained D_c to train the reference image content encoder E_t. The structure of E_t is similar to E_c, but with an additional input, i.e., the sketch density s of the input sketch image. Similar to CVAE [18], we combine I_{style} with the density level, which is expanded to the same size as I_{style}, and then input them to E_t to get the content representation Z_t. Different sketch level s result in different content representations Z_t for the same image. So, the sketch texture information of style image can be controlled by the density level s. By decoding Z_t through D_c, the final reconstruction result should be consistent with the I_{sketch} of the corresponding level. Since this branch also adopts the structure of VAE [11], it can also overcome the sketch level continuity problem.

The loss functions $\mathcal{L}_{c1}$ for the first branch are:

$$\mathcal{L}_{c1} = \mathcal{L}_{rec} + \mathcal{L}_{kl} + \mathcal{L}_{level} + \mathcal{L}_{gp}, \tag{1}$$

where $\mathcal{L}_{rec}$ is the reconstruction loss for sketch images implemented by L_2. $\mathcal{L}_{kl}$ is the Kullback-Leibler divergence for the latent code in VAE. J is the dimension of the Z_c and Z_t, μ is the mean, and σ is the variance. s is the output of linear regression, and $\bar{s}$ is the ground truth of sketch level.

$$\mathcal{L}_{kl} = -\frac{1}{2} \sum_{j=0}^{J} \left(1 + \log(\sigma_j)^2 - (\mu_j)^2 - (\sigma_j)^2 \right). \tag{2}$$

$$\mathcal{L}_{level} = \|s - \bar{s}\|_2. \tag{3}$$

Additionally, to make the network generates sharper edges, we adopt the $\mathcal{L}_{gp}$ [19] as in Eq. (4), where ∇I_{rec} is the gradient field of I_{rec}, and ∇I_{sketch} is the gradient field of I_{sketch}.

$$\mathcal{L}_{gp} = \|\nabla I_{rec} - \nabla I_{sketch}\|_1. \tag{4}$$

The loss functions $\mathcal{L}_{c2}$ for the second branch are defined similarly in Eq. 5:

$$\mathcal{L}_{c2} = \mathcal{L}_{rec} + \mathcal{L}_{kl} + \mathcal{L}_{gp} + \mathcal{L}_{feat}, \tag{5}$$

where $\mathcal{L}_{feat}$ (as expressed in Eq. (6)) make sure that the features of Z_c and Z_t are consistent when the input to encoder E_c and E_t are the same image. t_l is the decoded feature maps of Z_t in the l_{th} layer of D_c and c_l is the decoded feature maps of Z_c in the l_{th} layer of D_c.

$$\mathcal{L}_{feat} = \sum_{l=0}^{L} \|t_l - c_l\|_1 \tag{6}$$

3.3   Style Encoder

The style representations are achieved through a convolution-based encoder E_s and a mapping network in our method. It is trained together with the generator G. E_s is also fixed to the first few layers (up to relu4_1) of a pre-trained VGG-19 like E_c.

If the style features are controlled only by the output vector of E_s, its ability is very limited because it must follow the probability density of the training data. Similar to StyleGAN2 [10], we use a mapping network that converts the output vector of E_s into a style vector Z_s, so that Z_s can be obtained in no need to follow the distribution of the training data.

3.4   Density Controlled Style Transfer

After acquiring the sketch content Z_c and style representation Z_s, we use two steps to generate the stylized image by the generator G. First, a Texture Controller module is proposed to input content information Z_c, Z_t and $Z_t^{'}$, and output sketch content enhanced representations. $Z_t^{'}$ is the content representation of style image given the highest density level, namely 9 in our paper. As shown in Fig. 2, the first few layers of G are the features from the Texture Controller, aiming at adding texture details to sketch content based on the sketch density. Then, they are further concatenated with transformed style features through AdaIN [9] and Dual Mask Injection (DMI) module [14] to generate the final results.

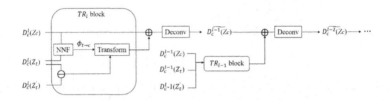

Fig. 3. The process in Texture Controller Module.

The Texture controller adopts the mapping strategy of image analogy [13] to add sketch textures of style image onto sketch image. It is processed as in Fig. 3. In each layer of D_c, we first get the extra detailed textures $\triangle D_c^l(Z_t)$ by subtracting $D_c^l(Z_t)$ from $D_c^l(Z_t^{'})$. Then, Nearest-neighbor Field (NNF) Search is applied on $D_c^l(Z_c)$ and $D_c^l(Z_t)$ to find the mapping $\psi_{t \to c}^l$ from sketch features of I_{style} to that of I_{sketch} by minimizing the following function:

$$\psi_{t \to c}^l = \text{argmin}_q \sum_{x \in N(p), y \in N(q)} \left\| D_{c(x)}^l(Z_t) - D_{c(y)}^l(Z_c) \right\|^2, \qquad (7)$$

where $N(p)$ is the patch around point p in the feature maps of $D_c^l(Z_t^{'})$, and q is its nearest neighbor position in $D_c^l(Z_c^{'})$. We set the patch size to be 3×3. With $\phi_{t \to c}^l$, we warp the texture detail contained feature maps by $\triangle D_c^l(Z_t)(\psi_{t \to c}^l)$. After sum operation as Eq. (8), we can get texture enhanced features $\widetilde{D_c^l(Z_c)}$ of sketch image in l_{th} decoding layer. They further go through the corresponding deconvolution layer of D_c to get the enhanced features in next layer. The same process in the texture controller block is implemented iterative til the setting stopping layers. We use the former three layers of D_c to get the final texture enhanced feature maps.

$$\widetilde{D_c^l(Z_c)} = D_c^l(Z_c) + \triangle D_c^l(Z_t)(\psi_{t \to c}^l). \qquad (8)$$

After then, we implement style transfer in the later few layers of G. First, the style features Z_s is resized to feature maps $f^l(Z_s)$ with the size corresponding to the injection layer of G through affine transformation. Then, AdaIN is applied to transfer the styles onto texture feature enhanced feature maps.

To maintain the contour information of sketch image, the DMI module is used and concatenated with stylization features as shown in Fig. 2. DMI works for value relocation purpose to separately enhance and differentiate the feature maps around contour areas and plain areas. Its output is the sum of the two kinds of transformed feature maps: $f^{'} = f_c + f_p = w_c \times M \times f + w_p \times (1 - M) \times f$. f is the original feature maps processed after AdaIN, and f_c and f_p are separated contour features and plain features, respectively. M is the mask generated by binarizing sketch image, which is used to separate the two kinds of features spatially. w_c and w_p are trainable weights $\in \mathbb{R}^{C \times 1 \times 1}$.

The loss functions $\mathcal{L}_g$ for training the generator G is defined by:

$$\mathcal{L}_g = \mathcal{L}_{rec+s} + \mathcal{L}_s + \mathcal{L}_{pair}. \tag{9}$$

$\mathcal{L}_{rec+s}$ is to constrain the sketch structure of generated image I_{output}. I_{output} is combined with the sketch level s of I_{sketch} and input into E_t, and then decoded by D_c to output the sketch of I_{output}. It should have the same sketch with I_{sketch}.

$$\mathcal{L}_{rect+s} = \|D_c(E_t(I_{output}, s)) - I_{sketch}\|^2. \tag{10}$$

$\mathcal{L}_s$ is to evaluate the consistency of styles features of reference image and generated image. A pre-trained VGG-19 is used to compute this loss as expressed in Eq. (10). Each ϕ_i denotes a layer in VGG-19. In our experiments, we use relu1_1, relu2_1, relu3_1, relu4_1 layers with equal weights. During training, we have two types of inputs, paired data, where I_{sketch} and I_{style} are from the same image, and non-paired data, where I_{sketch} and I_{style} are from different images. For the paired data, an additional $\mathcal{L}_{pair}$ loss implemented in L_2 formulation is used the constrain the generated results. The generator and discriminator plays the minimax game to train the whole model.

$$\mathcal{L}_s = \sum_{i=1}^{L} \|\mu(\phi_i(I_{output})) - \mu(\phi_i(I_{style}))\|_2$$
$$+ \sum_{i=1}^{L} \|\sigma(\phi_i(I_{output})) - \sigma(\phi_i(I_{style}))\|_2. \tag{11}$$

4   Data Construction

Our dataset classifies sketch images into 10 density levels as shown in Fig. 4. For sketch images of the lowest density level 0, it should contain only the basic contour of the object. We apply image segmentation method [15] and edge detection method HED [21] to generate the sketch images in level 0.

For level 1 to 4, we adopt contour detection algorithm CEDN [22], edge detection algorithm Canny, HED and Sketch Simplification [17] to generate the sketch images, respectively. The sketch images extracted by these methods are

Image   0   1   2   3   4   5   6   7   8   9

Fig. 4. Sketch images in different levels.

mainly the contour of the object, and generally do not have particularly obvious texture information. For the rest levels, we expect sketch images having both contour of the object and the specific texture details. Therefore, we use a series of photoshop operations to generate different level sketch images.

To make different level sketches look homologous, we further use sketch simplification to simplify all the sketch images, removing stroke information specific to different methods, and then subtract sketch images of adjacent levels to make sketch images of lower levels do not contain texture details that are not present in sketch images of higher levels.

5   Experiments

5.1   Implementation Details

We collect 1500 images from the Best Artworks of All Time[1]. We split the images into training and testing set with a ratio of 9 : 1. All the comparisons shown in this section were conducted on the testing set, where both the sketches and the art images were unseen to the models. All images are resized to 256×256 regardless of the original aspect ratio. We adopt the Adam optimizer and set the learning rate to 0.0005 with batch size 8, and train our network with 160,000 iterations.

5.2   Ablation Study

The effect of TCM and GAN is tested by removing the corresponding module in the model, respectively. We use FID [8] for the quantitative comparisons. FID is a popular image generation metric that provides a perceptual similarity between two sets of images. The lower the better. For our task, we compute the FID between generated images and style images. Additionally, we also ask two person to vote for their preferred style transfer results. Table 1 shows the statistical result of each model. Some qualitative results are also displayed in Fig. 5.

We found that after removing TCM, the problem of lacking texture details in the background areas of the image sometimes occurs. When the density level

---

[1] https://www.kaggle.com/datasets/ikarus777/best-artworks-of-all-time.

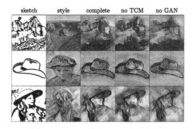

Fig. 5. Qualitative results on evaluating different modules.

of the input sketch image is low, there is often a large blank background on the sketch image, and the network tends to add texture details to the content areas, thus affecting the quality of the generated image. The function of TCM is to control the texture, which can flexibly balance the texture details in the foreground and background areas of the image according to the density level of the sketch image, so that the texture details of the image are evenly distributed. Using the adversarial training, namely the GAN modle, can make the generated images more realistic and reasonable. Therefore, combining both TCM and GAN, the full model can get the best style transfer performance qualitatively and quantitatively.

Table 1. Comparison of the models without TCM, GAN, and the full model.

		no TCM	no GAN	Complete
FID↓	Mean	379.09	337.61	318.78
USER STUDY↑	Overall	11.2%	21.3%	67.5%
	Content	17.6%	18.2%	64.2%
	Style	5.7%	20.2%	74.1%

5.3 Comparison with SOTA Methods

We compare our method with some well-known and state-of-the-art (SOTA) methods. NST [7] and AdaIN [9] are typical image stylization approaches. Art-Flow [1] designs a flow-based network to minimize image reconstruction error and recovery bias. IEST [3] takes advantage of contrast learning and external memory to boost visual quality. StyTR2 [6] implements style transfer using a pure transformer-based architecture. S2Ain [2] raised a novel task of generating artistic images from sketch while conditioned on style images, and subsequently present a self-supervised model to improve the synthesis quality. The quantitative comparison results can be found in Table 2, evaluating by FID and user study. Each vale in user study represents the percentage of votes that the result of the corresponding method is preferred to ours. Our proposed method achieves the best performance on both aspects.

Fig. 6. Style transfer comparison results with other SOTA methods.

Table 2. Quantitative comparison to SOTA models.

		Ours	NST	AdaIN	ArtFlow	IEST	StyTR2	S2A
FID↓	Mean	318.78	408.82	406.25	345.86	403.115	419.95	371.04
USER STUDY↑	Overall	–	5.7%	17.1%	29.4%	35.5%	22.1%	43.2%
	Content	–	8.2%	23.4%	27.6%	24.7%	25.5%	28.9%
	Style	–	6.6%	3.8%	11.5%	34.3%	10.3%	37.6%

Qualitative results are shown in Fig. 6. We can see that the other style transfer methods have difficulty dealing with sketch images consisting of sparse lines, and in severe cases hardly learn any texture information from the style image. However, our method can transfer textures well from reference images when the given sketch image is simple. For example, in the first three rows of Fig. 6, our method can successfully transfer the wave and block textures from given styles. Some of the SOTA methods, e.g., AdaIN and StyTR2, mainly transfer the styles onto contours of the sketch images, without considering the semantic matching. However, our method can infer the semantic information of sketches and transfers styles to corresponding locations and shapes correctly. Additionally, our method has no content constrain about the pair of sketch and style images. So, it is more flexible to transfer styles to different objects, for example, transferring the style of a human image to a bird sketch image as in the fifth row of Fig. 6.

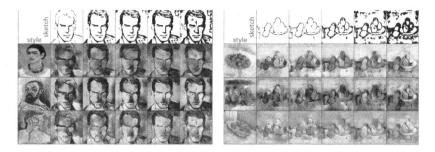

Fig. 7. Multi-level sketch images style transfer results

More qualitative results can be found in Fig. 7. Our model is generic and can be applied to other sketch-to-image tasks. As is shown in Fig. 8, we show the results of our model trained on human face data of CelebA-HQ [12].

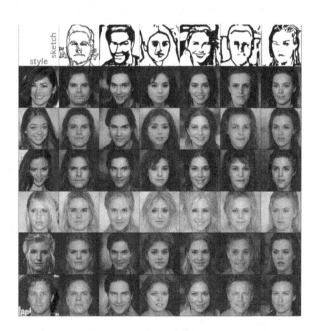

Fig. 8. Qualitative results of our model on human face sketch style transfer.

6   Conclusion

In this work, we presented a novel approach to generate artistic images from sketch while conditioned on style images via sketch density information. The texture controller module in our model allowed flexible controlling over the "texture" element of the style transfer process in different density, and showed its superiority on sketch style transfer task. In addition, We introduced a multi-density sketch dataset to encourage research in this direction.

Acknowledgement. This work was partly supported by the special project of "Tibet Economic and Social Development and Plateau Scientific Research Co-construction Innovation Foundation" of Wuhan University of Technology & Tibet University (No. lzt2021008).

References

1. An, J., Huang, S., et al.: ArtFlow: unbiased image style transfer via reversible neural flows. In: CVPR (2021)
2. Liu, B., Zhu, Y., et al.: A self-supervised sketch-to-image synthesis. In: AAAI (2021)
3. Chen, H., Wang, Z., et al.: Artistic style transfer with internal-external learning and contrastive learning. In: NIPS (2021)
4. Chen, S.Y., Su, W., et al.: Deep generation of face images from sketches. ACM TOG **39**(4) (2020)
5. Chen, W., Hays, J.: SketchyGAN: towards diverse and realistic sketch to image synthesis. In: CVPR (2018)
6. Deng, Y., Tang, F., et al.: Stytr^2: unbiased image style transfer with transformers. In: CVPR (2022)
7. Gatys, L.A., Ecker, A.S., Bethge, M.: Image style transfer using convolutional neural networks. In: CVPR (2016)
8. Heusel, M., Ramsauer, H., Unterthiner, T., Nessler, B., Hochreiter, S.: GANs trained by a two time-scale update rule converge to a local Nash equilibrium. In: NIPS (2017)
9. Huang, X., Belongie, S.: Arbitrary style transfer in real-time with adaptive instance normalization. In: ICCV (2017)
10. Karras, T., Laine, S., Aittala, M., Hellsten, J., Lehtinen, J., Aila, T.: Analyzing and improving the image quality of StyleGAN. In: CVPR (2020)
11. Kingma, D.P., Welling, M.: Auto-encoding variational bayes. In: ICLR (2014)
12. Lee, C.H., Liu, Z., Wu, L., Luo, P.: MaskGAN: towards diverse and interactive facial image manipulation. In: CVPR (2020)
13. Liao, J., Yao, Y., et al.: Visual attribute transfer through deep image analogy. ACM TOG **36**(4), 120 (2017)
14. Liu, B., Song, K., Zhu, Y., Elgammal, A.: Sketch-to-art: synthesizing stylized art images from sketches. In: ACCV (2020)
15. Qin, X., Fan, D.P., et al.: Boundary-aware segmentation network for mobile and web applications. arXiv preprint arXiv:2101.04704 (2021)
16. Ronneberger, O., Fischer, P., Brox, T.: U-net: convolutional networks for biomedical image segmentation. In: Navab, N., Hornegger, J., Wells, W.M., Frangi, A.F. (eds.) MICCAI 2015. LNCS, vol. 9351, pp. 234–241. Springer, Cham (2015). https://doi.org/10.1007/978-3-319-24574-4_28
17. Simo-Serra, E., Iizuka, S., Ishikawa, H.: Mastering sketching: adversarial augmentation for structured prediction. ACM TOG **37**(1), 1–13 (2018)
18. Sohn, K., Lee, H., Yan, X.: Learning structured output representation using deep conditional generative models. In: NIPS (2015)

19. Sun, J., Xu, Z., Shum, H.Y.: Gradient profile prior and its applications in image super-resolution and enhancement. TIP **20**(6), 1529–1542 (2010)
20. Wang, S.Y., Bau, D., Zhu, J.Y.: Sketch your own GAN. In: CVPR (2021)
21. Xie, S., Tu, Z.: Holistically-nested edge detection. In: ICCV (2015)
22. Yang, J., Price, B., Cohen, S., Lee, H., Yang, M.H.: Object contour detection with a fully convolutional encoder-decoder network. In: CVPR (2016)

VAE-AD: Unsupervised Variational Autoencoder for Anomaly Detection in Hyperspectral Images

Nikhil Ojha, Indrajeet Kumar Sinha[✉], and Krishna Pratap Singh

Machine Learning and Optimization Lab, Department of Information Technology,
Indian Institute of Information Technology Allahabad, Prayagraj, UP, India
pcl2016004@iiita.ac.in

Abstract. Anomaly detection in hyperspectral images is an important and challenging problem. Most available data sets are unlabeled, and very few are labelled. In this paper, we proposed a lightweight Variational Autoencoder anomaly detector (VAE-AD) for hyperspectral data. VAE is used to learn the background distribution of the image, and thereafter it is used to construct a background representation for each pixel. Further reconstruction error is calculated between the background reconstructed image and the original image used for anomaly detection. A GMM-based post-processing step is used to construct the final detection map. The comparative analysis with five real-world hyperspectral data sets shows that the proposed model achieves better or comparable results with few learning parameters of the model, and with less time.

Keywords: Anomaly detection · Variational autoencoder · HSI · hyperspectral imaging

1 Introduction

Hyperspectral imaging (HSI) collects and analyzes electromagnetic radiation across a wide spectrum to obtain spectral information about an area. It provides spatial and spectral characteristics of an object for different wavelength ranges, extending beyond visible spectrum [9]. Hyperspectral images (high spectral resolution and plenty of bands) are widely used in many applications such as search and rescue [7], law enforcement [3], military [1,26], geological surveys, mineral exploration [23]. Target detection aims to locate objects of interest spread across a large geographical area; these objects of interest may be the presence of mining fields for search and rescue missions, the location of enemy positions, or bunkers. Spectral matching and anomaly detection are two components of the target detection algorithms. Spectral matching target detection methods discover predetermined objects or materials in an area. These methods require prior knowledge about the spectral signal of the areas of concern, and the method is supervised learning. Algorithms evaluate the similarity between

© The Author(s), under exclusive license to Springer Nature Singapore Pte Ltd. 2023
M. Tanveer et al. (Eds.): ICONIP 2022, CCIS 1794, pp. 126–137, 2023.
https://doi.org/10.1007/978-981-99-1648-1_11

the pixel under test and the known spectral signal for classifying whether the pixel under test belongs to the target or not [19, 29]. Meanwhile, anomaly detection is an unsupervised learning problem and does not require prior knowledge about the target spectrum. Generally, information about the background and anomalies is rarely available, due to which it is used in many military and civilian domain [20]. Anomalies from their surroundings can be distinguished using two important characteristics: 1) the spectral signature of anomalies is quite different from surroundings, and 2) anomalies generally occur in relatively small areas. Methods used to achieve this objective fall under two broad categories: traditional models and deep learning-based methods.

Traditional models use statistical methods to extract background information from the image. The benchmark Reed-Xiaoli detector [24] estimates the background probability density function by computing the covariance and mean vector for background information. Further, Anomaly pixels are obtained by Mahalanobis distance between the test and background pixels. An extended version of RX, called Local RX (LRX) [30] uses a window-based strategy to build a background representation for each pixel and detect anomalies using a square window centred around the pixel under test is squared distance between the mean of processing window pixels and pixel vector is calculated. Additionally, many different variations and improvements to basic RX detector have been developed, such as dual-window-based anomaly detector [14], RX detector for noisy HSI data [25], Kernel-based detector (KRX) [15]. In [22] author has proposed a tensor-based motion descriptor based on incorporating optical flow (OF) with the histogram of oriented gradient (HOG) information on video data to detect anomalous events. Another class of statistical anomaly detection methods is the collaborative representation-based detector (CRD) [18]. The CRD detectors have underline assumptions that a linear combination of neighbouring spatial pixels can approximate each background pixel except anomaly pixels. An extension of the CR detector with inverse distance weight (LSAD-CR-IDW) [27] has been proposed recently, which showed improved performance over the original CR detector.

On the contrary, deep neural networks have shown their advantages in modelling complex datasets. They are being widely used for unsupervised anomaly detection in a variety of fields such as medical images [28], categorical data [11], and time-series data [6] etc. Recently, the usage of deep learning models for anomaly detection in HSI data is gaining popularity as they have shown superior detection performance compared to their statistical counterparts. Generative Adversarial Network (GAN) based model HADGAN [12] achieved a state-of-the-art score on various hyperspectral datasets. Autoencoder (AE) [16], and its variants are also used as the core network for unsupervised anomaly detection in variety of fields [5,10,17]. The major challenge of using deep learning models is their computation time [12]. In this paper, we propose a lightweight hyperspectral anomaly detection method using a variational autoencoder (VAE-AD) [13]. The proposed model uses the reconstruction ability of VAE to generate a reconstructed background image by learning the background distribution of the input image. The anomalies are detected by calculating the error between the reconstructed background image and the original image. After relevant data preprocessing, Gaussian Mixture model (GMM) is used as post-processing creates the final anomaly detection map. Our novel contributions are as follows

- We proposed a novel lightweight generative model, VAE, to reconstruct a background image from a learned background distribution model, and reconstruction error is calculated between them to generate a residual image with suppressed background pixels and anomaly pixels highlighted.
- A PCA, pre-processing, is used to overcomes the curse of dimensionality and to get richer features.
- Further, GMM post-processing creates a detection map by extracting anomaly pixels from the residual image.
- The proposed model's computation time is much less compared to the existing state-of-the-art model.

2 Methodology

A novel variational autoencoder-based anomaly detector (VAE-AD) is proposed for Hyperspectral images (HSI). Its Systematic working process of the proposed model is depicted in Fig. 1. HSI data is used as input to the model, which have a three-dimensional matrix of size $M \times N \times C$ with $M \times N$ is the size of the image, and C is the number of channels or spectral bands.

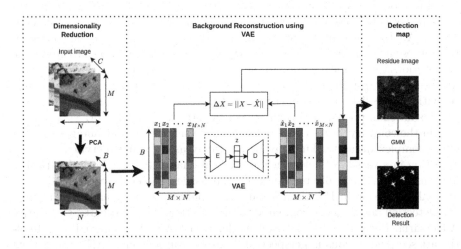

Fig. 1. Proposed VAE-AD model architecture for HSI anomaly detection. First PCA is used to reduce dimension of original HSI data. Then VAE is used to reconstruct background. Finally, GMM is used for getting detection map.

In the proposed VAE-AD model, firstly, the dimension of HSI data is reduced using PCA to a matrix $M \times N \times B$ such that $B < C$. Further, it is converted into a 2D matrix X with $M \times N$ pixel vectors with each vector having B dimensions, i.e., $X = [x_1, x_2, x_3 \ldots x_{M \times N}]$ where $x_i \in \mathbb{R}^{B \times 1}$. Secondly, This 2D matrix is fed to the proposed VAE network. As most of the pixels belong to the background class, the latent feature layer of VAE can learn the image's background distribution. This learned distribution is used to generate a background reconstruction $\hat{x}_i$ of each pixel vector x to produce the background reconstructed image $\hat{X}$. The residual image is obtained by calculating the reconstruction error between X and $\hat{X}$. Finally, a GMM-based method is employed on residual images to obtain the final anomaly detection map.

2.1 Dimensionality Reduction Using PCA

The high correlation among spectral bands allows us to reduce the number of redundant bands (or features) present in the data using the relevant dimensionality algorithm (PCA, in this case).

As anomalies are very low compared to the background, the first principal component does not capture anomaly information and is discarded in the anomaly detection process. However, subsequent B components are retained for the anomaly detection process.

2.2 Background Reconstruction Using VAE

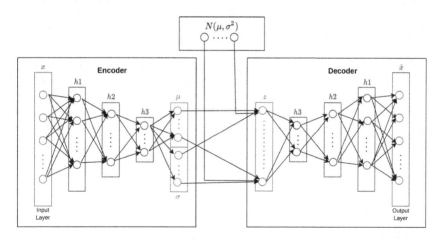

Fig. 2. Variational Autoencoder (VAE) network Architecture. After, feature reduction it is used for background Reconstruction of image.

Variational Autoencoders (VAE) [13] are generative models that learn the input data (x) distribution so that new data can be generated by sampling from the learned distribution. The architecture of the proposed VAE network is shown in Fig. 2. VAE has two parts, an encoder and a decoder. The encoder of VAE is a posterior probabilistic function $q(z|x, \phi)$ and the decoder is $p(x|z, \theta)$, which is the likelihood of x given z. After training, the encoder can approximate the posterior distribution very well and map the input data to the latent space. The latent space in VAE is mapped to a stochastic variable z, which is subject to a Gaussian distribution determined by mean (μ) and variance (σ^2). After the encoding process, $\hat{z}$ is sampled from $N(\mu, \sigma^2)$ which is used to output the reconstructed result $\hat{x}$ by the decoder. Training proceeds by minimizing negative Evidence Lower Bound (ELBO) loss; Kullback-Leibler divergence regularizes the above loss (Eq. 1).

$$ELBO = \mathbb{E}_{q_\phi(z|x)}[\log p_\theta(x|z)] - KL[q_\phi(z|x)\|p(z)] \tag{1}$$

Figure 2 shows the architecture of proposed VAE network. An encoder network is formed by a set of fully connected layers comprising an input layer of size B, 3 hidden layers, and a latent layer. The size of 3 hidden layers is $32, 16, 8$ respectively, and the size of latent layer z was set as $z = \sqrt{B} + 1$, based on work done in [4]. Similarly, the Decoder consists of latent layer z, followed by 3 hidden layer of size $8, 16, 32$, connected to the output layer of size B.

HSI data obtained after PCA-based reduction is used to train the variational autoencoder. Each pixel in the reduced image represents a training sample used for training the VAE. The total number of trainable samples equals the number of pixels in the image. As most of the pixels in the data belong to the background class, VAE can approximately model the background distribution. The idea behind the anomaly detection process using VAE is that when data x_i is passed to the trained model, the model generates a background reconstruction of x_i, i.e., $\hat{x}_i$, if x_i is a background pixel, the network can generate a close reconstruction. In contrast, it will give a large reconstruction error if x_i is anomalous. HSI data X is fed to the network, and a background reconstructed image $\hat{X}$ is obtained. The reconstruction error of the original image (X) and background reconstructed image ($\hat{X}$) is calculated using Eq. 2 to obtain the residual image. The obtained residual image has anomaly pixels highlighted due to their high reconstruction error. This residual image is used to construct the final anomaly detection map.

$$\Delta X = ||X - \hat{X}|| \tag{2}$$

2.3   Anomaly Map Construction

We use GMM [21] to cluster the residual image pixels with high reconstruction error for the purpose of anomaly map construction. Anomaly pixels have high reconstruction error, and so it is used in the final anomaly detection map. Mathematically, the probability density function for GMM is defined as

$$P(x) = \sum_{n=1}^{N} \alpha_n \mathcal{N}(x|\mu_n, \theta_n) \quad \text{s.t.} \quad \sum_{n=1}^{N} \alpha_n = 1 \tag{3}$$

where N is number of mixture components and α_n, the nth distribution in GMM. Gaussian Distribution with μ_n, θ_n as Mean and Variance for n^{th} distribution component is $\mathcal{N}(x|\mu_n, \theta_n)$. The parameters α_n, θ_n and μ_n of GMM are determined by the expectation-maximization (EM) algorithm while the number of mixture components N are provided a-priori [21].

For the final detection map (shown in Fig. 1), residual image data is fed into the GMM model. Further, we use expected maximization (EM) algorithm to calculate the model parameters, which are then used to cluster data points of the same distribution.

3   Experimental Setups

3.1   Dataset

Experiments are conducted on five different datasets, i.e., San Diego Airport, Pavia coast, Texas Urban, Los angles Airport, and Los angles Urban datasets, which are publicly available and provide ground truth values along with the HSI data. The AVIRIS sensor captures the hyperspectral image data of 100×100 pixels for all datasets except for the Pavia coast, which has an image of 110×110 pixels using the ROSIS-03 sensor. The spectral range captured by the AVIRIS sensor is 400–2450 nm, while the ROSIS-03 sensor can capture the spectral range of 440–850 nm. San Diego Airport dataset has HSI images with 224 bands, Pavia coast dataset images have 102 bands, and other datasets have 207 bands. Anomaly pixels in San Diego Airport, Pavia coast, Texas Urban, Los angles Airport, and Los angles Urban datasets are 57, 87, 67, 272, and 68, respectively.

3.2   Evaluation Criteria

We use ROC curve and AUC ([2]) as the evaluation metrics for the proposed model performance. For the ROC curve, a higher detection rate at the same false alarm rate (FAR) indicates a better performance; a value closer to 1 indicates a high degree of separation and shows better performance.

Experiments were performed on Intel©Core^{TM} i3-3220 CPU with 6 GB of RAM running Python 3.7.13, TensorFlow 1.14.0. Evaluation of all compared methods is done on MATLAB R2022a.

4   Results and Discussion

In this section, we elaborate on the performance of the proposed model and also discuss the component-wise analysis of the model to show its effectiveness on various data sets. Further, we compare the results with other existing state-of-the-art models for hyperspectral anomaly detection.

4.1   Analysis of Dimensionality Reduction Process

In this work, two scenarios are considered to verify the effectiveness of PCA on pre-processing for detection. First, the VAE network is trained using the entire HSI data. Next, PCA-based reduction was carried out. AUC score and computation time for both the scenarios are shown in Fig. 3.

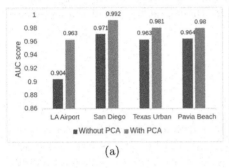
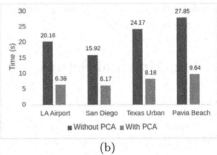

(a)   (b)

Fig. 3. Performance of proposed VAE-AD with and without PCA on 4 datasets. (a) AUC score on four dataset (b) Computation time in second.

Figure 3(a) shows that VAE-AD with PCA as dimension reduction of input images perform better than without feature reduction. In all the datasets AUC score is better with PCA. Also, It is helping VAE-AD to archive better results in less time (Fig. 3(b)). It is observed that PCA-based pre-processing improve AUC score and computation time as PCA creates a richer feature set for the classifier training.

4.2   Analysis of Detection Map Construction Using Gaussian Mixture Model

We use Gaussian mixture model (GMM) foor the final detection map construction. In our experiments, we use Bayesian information criteria (BIC) [8] computes the number of mixture components in an unsupervised manner (3 for all datasets). Two scenarios are studied to find the effectiveness of GMM-based anomaly map construction. First, anomalies were obtained from the residual image using a threshold. As discussed in Sect. 2.2, each pixel value of the residual image indicate the reconstruction error for that pixel. As reconstruction error for anomaly pixels is high, an anomaly detection map is created using a threshold function. For a pixel x_i the anomaly detection result D_r is,

$$D_r = \begin{cases} 0 & \text{if } x_i < \mu + 2\sigma \\ 1 & \text{if } x_i > \mu + 2\sigma \end{cases} \tag{4}$$

where μ is the mean reconstruction error, and σ is the standard deviation of the reconstruction error.

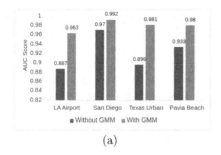
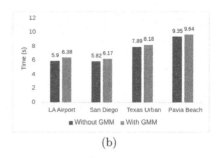

(a)   (b)

Fig. 4. Detection results for GMM-based anomaly map construction on four datasets. (a) AUC score (b) Computation time in second

Later, GMM based technique is used to create the anomaly detection map by clustering the pixels with high reconstruction error. The AUC score and computation time for both the scenarios are shown in Fig. 4. The detection map obtained for the texas image scene in both scenarios is shown in Fig. 5. The experiment using GMM for post-processing shows an increase in anomaly detection scores. The improvement can also be observed from the detection map shown in Fig. 5, as some background pixels are classified as an anomaly when using a simple threshold technique. In contrast, a much cleaner detection map is obtained using GMM for anomaly map construction along with a small computational cost (see Fig. ??).

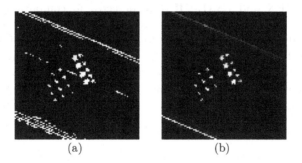

(a)   (b)

Fig. 5. Comparison of detection map for Texas urban image scene: (a) Without using GMM for detection (b) When using GMM for detection

4.3 Comparison with State of the Art Methods

The performance of our proposed VAE-AD model is evaluated against four benchmarks - LRX detector [30], GRX detector [24], LSAD-CR-IDW [27], HADGAN [12]. LSAD-CR-IDW and HADGAN are two state-of-the-art algorithms. GRX, LRX, and LSAD-CR-IDW are statistical anomaly detectors, while HADGAN is the deep learning-based model. The AUC score and computation time for GRX, LRX and LSAD-CR-IDW is recorded for comparison with our model for each of the five datasets. For the LRX detector, window size greatly impacts detection performance. The inner and outer window size for LA airport and San Diego airport is chosen as 11 and 13, and for the beach, the urban scene window size is chosen as 13 and 15. For the LSAD-CR-IDW method, window size and value of parameter λ are chosen as per the original article [27].

Table 1. AUC score comparison with different methods on different datasets

Dataset	GRX	LRX	LSAD-CR-IDW	HADGAN	VAE-AD
LA Airport	0.849	0.944	0.912	0.995	0.963
San Diego	0.830	0.91	0.922	0.990	0.992
Texas Urban	0.992	0.92	0.927	0.997	0.983
LA Urban	0.970	0.90	0.916	0.995	0.982
Pavia beach	0.953	0.854	0.940	0.994	0.980
Average	0.918	0.904	0.923	0.994	0.980

The AUC score and computation time of these algorithm is shown in Table 1 and 2 respectively. We can observe from these tables that the proposed method outperforms the statistical anomaly detection methods such as GRX, LRX and CR detector in terms of AUC score. The model also outperforms the dual-window-based LRX and LSAD-CR-IDW detector in computation time. The reason for the same can be attributed to the fact that both these detectors perform anomaly detection by constructing background representation for each pixel using neighbouring pixels. The state-of-the-art HADGAN model only outperforms the our proposed model in terms of AUC score. However, our proposed model outperformed the HADGAN model in terms of computational time,

Table 2. Computation time in seconds for compared methods on different datasets.

Dataset	GRX	LRX	LSAD-CR-IDW	HADGAN	VAE-AD
LA Airport	0.203	66.61	29.22	180.26	7.25
San Diego	0.221	69.39	22.3	180.24	6.68
Texas Urban	0.248	84.68	32.97	180.27	9.11
LA Urban	0.269	90.96	32.07	180.26	9.9
Pavia Beach	0.227	79.94	51.82	180.43	10.9
Average	0.2336	78.316	33.676	180.292	8.768

as training the HADGAN network on a single dataset can take over three minutes [12]. The lightweight network proposed in this study achieved a near state-of-the-art AUC score and a relatively fast runtime.

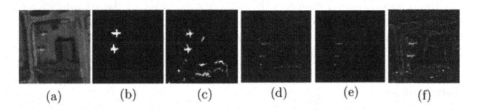

Fig. 6. Detection map for compared methods on Los angles Airport datasets: (a) False colour composite. (b) Ground truth (c) Proposed VAE-AD method (d) GRX (e) LRX (f) LSAD-CR-IDW

The visual detection map for Los angles Airport datasets is shown in Fig. 6. The detection map shows that the proposed VAE-AD method produces visible results quite close to the ground truth compared to other detectors, and it detects anomalies of different shapes and sizes while retaining structural information. The ROC curve obtained for all the datasets is shown in Fig. 7. We observed that the ROC curves obtained, for all scenes, are closed to the ideal curve. So, it indicates that the proposed method meets the detection requirements on various scenes.

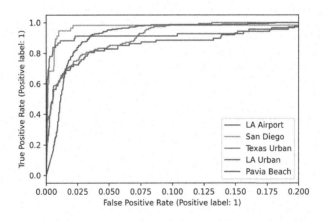

Fig. 7. ROC curve for each dataset obtained using proposed VAE-AD

5   Conclusion

In this paper, we proposed a novel VAE-AD method for HSI anomaly detection. Firstly, the PCA algorithm is used to reduce the dimension of the hyperspectral images. Thereafter, a lightweight VAE network generates a residual image by calculating the reconstruction error between the original image and the background image, and further a Gaussian mixture-based clustering method is used to construct a detection map. The experimental results on various data sets show that the proposed model improves the detection accuracy or the computational time compared to other anomaly detection methods with less number of model parameters. In future, light weight VAE-AD may be deployed on edge computing devices for anomaly detection.

References

1. Ardouin, J.-P., Levesque, J., Rea, T.A.: A demonstration of hyperspectral image exploitation for military applications. In: 2007 10th International Conference on Information Fusion, pp. 1–8 (2007)
2. Bradley, A.P.: The use of the area under the ROC curve in the evaluation of machine learning algorithms. Pattern Recogn. **30**(7), 1145–1159 (1997)
3. Bürsing, H., Gross, W.: Hyperspectral imaging: future applications in security systems. Adv. Opt. Technol. **6**(2) (2017)
4. Cao, V.L., Nicolau, M., McDermott, J.: A hybrid autoencoder and density estimation model for anomaly detection. In: PPSN (2016)
5. Chen, Z., Yeo, C.K., Lee, B.S., Lau, C.T.: Autoencoder-based network anomaly detection. In: 2018 Wireless Telecommunications Symposium (WTS), pp. 1–5 (2018)
6. Choi, K., Yi, J., Park, C., Yoon, S.: Deep learning for anomaly detection in time-series data: review, analysis, and guidelines. IEEE Access **9**, 120043–120065 (2021)
7. Eismann, M.T., Stocker, A.D., Nasrabadi, N.M.: Automated hyperspectral cueing for civilian search and rescue. Proc. IEEE **97**(6), 1031–1055 (2009)
8. Fraley, C., Raftery, A.E.: Model-based clustering, discriminant analysis, and density estimation. J. Am. Stat. Assoc. **97**(458), 611–631 (2002)
9. Goetz, A.F.H., Vane, G., Solomon, J.E., Rock, B.N.: Imaging spectrometry for earth remote sensing. Science **228**(4704), 1147–1153 (1985)
10. Guo, J., Liu, G., Zuo, Y., Wu, J.: An anomaly detection framework based on autoencoder and nearest neighbor. In: 15th International Conference on Service Systems and Service Management (ICSSSM), pp. 1–6 (2018)
11. Ienco, D., Pensa, R.G., Meo, R.: A semi supervised approach to the detection and characterization of outliers in categorical data. IEEE Trans. Neural Netw. Learn. Syst. **28**(5), 1017–1029 (2017)
12. Jiang, T., Li, Y., Xie, W., Qian, D.: Discriminative reconstruction constrained generative adversarial network for hyperspectral anomaly detection. IEEE Trans. Geosci. Remote Sens. **58**(7), 4666–4679 (2020)
13. Kingma, D.P., Welling, M.: Auto-encoding variational Bayes (2013)
14. Kwon, H., Der, S.Z., Nasrabadi, N.M.: Dual-window-based anomaly detection for hyperspectral imagery. In: SPIE Defense + Commercial Sensing (2003)
15. Kwon, H., Nasrabadi, N.M.: Kernel RX-algorithm: a nonlinear anomaly detector for hyperspectral imagery. IEEE Trans. Geosci. Remote Sens. **43**(2), 388–397 (2005)
16. Larochelle, H., Erhan, D., Courville, A.C., Bergstra, J., Bengio, Y.: An empirical evaluation of deep architectures on problems with many factors of variation. In: ICML, pp. 473–480 (2007)

17. Legrand, A., Niepceron, B., Cournier, A., Trannois, H.: Study of autoencoder neural networks for anomaly detection in connected buildings. In: 2018 IEEE Global Conference on Internet of Things (GCIoT), pp. 1–5 (2018)
18. Li, W., Qian, D.: Collaborative representation for hyperspectral anomaly detection. IEEE Trans. Geosci. Remote Sens. **53**(3), 1463–1474 (2015)
19. Manolakis, D., Siracusa, C., Shaw, G.: Hyperspectral subpixel target detection using the linear mixing model. IEEE Trans. Geosci. Remote Sens. **39**(7), 1392–1409 (2001)
20. Manolakis, D., Truslow, E., Pieper, M., Cooley, T., Brueggeman, M.: Detection algorithms in hyperspectral imaging systems: an overview of practical algorithms. IEEE Signal Process. Mag. **31**(1), 24–33 (2014)
21. Bishop, C.M.: Pattern Recognition and Machine Learning. Springer, New York (2006)
22. Mishra, S.R., Mishra, T.K., Sarkar, A., Sanyal, G.: Detection of anomalies in human action using optical flow and gradient tensor. In: Satapathy, S.C., Bhateja, V., Mohanty, J.R., Udgata, S.K. (eds.) Smart Intelligent Computing and Applications. SIST, vol. 159, pp. 561–570. Springer, Singapore (2020). https://doi.org/10.1007/978-981-13-9282-5_53
23. Peyghambari, S., Zhang, Y.: Hyperspectral remote sensing in lithological mapping, mineral exploration, and environmental geology: an updated review. J. Appl. Remote Sens. **15**(03) (2021)
24. Reed, I.S., Yu, X.: Adaptive multiple-band CFAR detection of an optical pattern with unknown spectral distribution. IEEE Trans. Acoust. Speech Signal Process. **38**(10), 1760–1770 (1990)
25. Riley, R.A. Newsom, R.K., Andrews, A.K.: Anomaly detection in noisy hyperspectral imagery. In: Shen, S.S., Lewis, P.E. (eds.) Imaging Spectrometry X, vol. 5546. Society of Photo-Optical Instrumentation Engineers (SPIE) Conference Series, pp. 159–170, October 2004
26. Shimoni, M., Haelterman, R., Perneel, C.: Hypersectral imaging for military and security applications: combining myriad processing and sensing techniques. IEEE Geosci. Remote Sens. Mag. **7**(2), 101–117 (2019)
27. Tan, K., Hou, Z., Fuyu, W., Qian, D., Chen, Yu.: Anomaly detection for hyperspectral imagery based on the regularized subspace method and collaborative representation. Remote Sens. **11**(11), 1318 (2019)
28. Tschuchnig, M.E., Gadermayr, M.: Anomaly detection in medical imaging - a mini review (2021)
29. Zhang, L., Zhang, L., Tao, D., Huang, X.: Sparse transfer manifold embedding for hyperspectral target detection. IEEE Trans. Geosci. Remote Sens. **52**(2), 1030–1043 (2014)
30. Zhao, C., Wang, Y., Qi, B., Wang, J.: Global and local real-time anomaly detectors for hyperspectral remote sensing imagery. Remote Sens. **7**(4), 3966–3985 (2015)

DSE-Net: Deep Semantic Enhanced Network for Mobile Tongue Image Segmentation

Wanqiang Cai and Bin Wang[✉]

Nanjing University of Finance and Economics, Nanjing 210023, China
wangbin@nufe.edu.cn

Abstract. Tongue diagnosis plays an important role in traditional Chinese medicine (TCM) because of noninvasive for health assessment. Taking advantage of the portability of mobile devices to develop a tongue diagnosis system has aroused widespread concern in artificial intelligence community. However, mobile tongue image segmentation is challenging on account of low-quality image and limited computing power. In this paper, we propose a deep semantic enhanced (DSE) network to address these issues. DSE-Net consists of a lightweight feature extraction module, efficient deep semantic enhanced module and the decoder. The encoder adopts shufflenetv2 units as backbone for the reduction of computing pressure from mobile devices and the DSE module with multi-scale feature aggregation is designed to improve the network's recognition of tongue position. In addition, the decoder is designed not only to recover semantics, but also to embed global features from the shallow network for further boosting the retrieval performance. Extensive experiments are conducted on two diverse tongue image benchmarks, including the public tongue dataset collected by special image acquisition device and the lab-made dataset gathered by mobile phones in various uncontrolled environments. The experimental results show the proposed method's efficiency and accuracy which outperforms the state-of-the-art methods for mobile tongue image segmentation.

Keywords: Mobile tongue image segmentation · Deep semantic enhanced network · Multi-scale feature aggregation

1 Introduction

The rich features of tongue image provide significant clues for diagnosis in traditional Chinese medicine (TCM). The early tongue diagnosis mainly depends on the doctor's recognition, which is time-consuming and laborious. With the development of computer vision techniques, more and more researchers are turning

This work was supported in part by the National Natural Science Foundation of China under Grant No. 61876037, the Natural Science Foundation of Jiangsu Province of China under Grant No. BK20221345 and Postgraduate Research & Practice Innovation Program of Jiangsu Province (CWQXW21001).

M. Tanveer et al. (Eds.): ICONIP 2022, CCIS 1794, pp. 138–150, 2023.
https://doi.org/10.1007/978-981-99-1648-1_12

their attention to artificial intelligence. Thus, the question of how to combine artificial intelligence with tongue diagnosis to further improve the efficiency of doctors has been explored.

The appearance of professional tongue image collection device marks that tongue diagnosis has entered a more advanced stage. By designing specific algorithms to process the tongue images collected by the device, the more obvious features of the tongue are highlighted. Such equipment generally appears in hospitals, and the images collected by it have uniform illumination, large tongue coverage area and uniform shooting angle. As a result, tongue image features can be extracted by some classical manual algorithms. However, the equipment is cumbersome and only available in hospitals, which makes it difficult for people to assess their health without leaving home during the sensitive time for COVID-19. As a result, many people are looking forward to tongue diagnosis on mobile devices.

The accuracy of tongue diagnosis depends on the feature extraction algorithm. Arguably, the algorithm that can achieve accurate segmentation on mobile devices is of great significance for efficient tongue diagnosis. In contrast to the tongue images collected by professional equipment, tongue images taken with mobile device are easily affected by the surrounding environments, interference from other parts of the face, the angle of the tongue and the light conditions, which greatly increases the difficulty of the segmentation algorithms, as shown in Fig. 1. Furthermore, segmentation networks suitable for mobile terminals not only face the challenge of low-quality images, but also are strictly limited in the number of network parameters.

Fig. 1. Tongue samples which are affected by low light condition, interference from the noise, different imaging angles and variance of tongue positions.

To address these issues, we propose DSE-Net to achieve the goal of fast and accurate tongue segmentation on mobile devices. DSE-Net is composed of three parts including encoder, DSE module and decoder. The feature extractor is lightweight and can accommodate the memory requirements of mobile devices. The main function of DSE module is to mine the abstract semantics from the encoder and provides details for the decoder. By embedding context, the decoder efficiently fuses the global information from the shallow network with the local information from DSE module. Through the above designs, the proposed network can achieve efficient and accurate segmentation on mobile devices. The remainder of the paper is organized as follows. In Sect. 2, the typical algorithms for tongue image segmentation are reviewed. Section 3 introduces the details of the proposed method. Experimental results are presented and discussed in Sect. 4. Conclusions are drawn in Sect. 5.

2   Relate Work

In the past decades, many methods utilize low-level features of tongue image, such as color and texture, to perform segmentation. They can be classified into four main categories: color thresholding, edge detection, active contour models and graph theory approaches. Zhang et al. [1] proposed a color threshold-based segmentation method with the gray histogram projection and automatic threshold selection. In order to improve the segmentation performance, Zhi et al. [2] manually implanted edge seed points in the image to obtain tongue region edge information by using B-spline method. In addition, a novel automatic tongue image segmentation method [3] based on graph theory was presented and implemented.

Recently, many attempts have been made to apply deep learning techniques to tongue image segmentation. Long et al. [4] firstly designed the end-to-end fully convolutional networks (FCN) for semantic segmentation to extract features. Then DeepLabV2 [5] uses ASPP module to embed contextual information. Deeplabv3 [6] is extended on ASPP to further enhance the ability of the network to capture global context maps. DeepLabV3+ [7] adopts an encoder-decoder structure to recover reduced spatial information as much as possible by upsampling operation. Besides, lightweight networks applied in mobile devices are becoming more popular and MobileNet series [8,9] are very important lightweight network families. Tang et al. [10] proposes a dilated encoder network (DE-Net) to capture more high-level features and get high-resolution output for automated tongue image segmentation.

In this paper, we try to address the challenging issue of low-quality image and limited computing power problems in mobile device segmentation. The contributions of this work are: (1) We propose a novel DSE-Net for tongue segmentation on mobile devices. (2) A multi-scale feature aggregation module (DSE) is designed to accurately identify the tongue region and further improve the performance. (3) Two tongue datasets including the public dataset and the lab-made dataset which are respectively collected by special image acquisition device and mobile phones in various uncontrolled environments are used to evaluate the performance of the proposed method.

3   Proposed Method

The proposed network is made up of three modules: lightweight feature extraction module, deep semantic enhanced module and the decoder (see Fig. 2).

3.1   Lightweight Feature Extraction Module

Considering that mobile devices are limited with computing power and memory space, the feature extraction module should reduce parameters while maintaining accuracy. Shufflenetv2 [11] is not only efficient but also accurate because of the shufflenetv2 units. As a result, we choose shufflenetv2 as backbone and remove

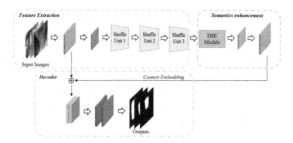

Fig. 2. Workflow diagram of the proposed network. Firstly, images are fed into the feature extraction module. Then DSE module enhances the depth semantics of the extracted features. Finally, the decoder embeds the context and gradually recovers semantic information by up-sampling operations.

the last convolution layer, global pooling layer and full connection layer for subsequent extension.

The feature extraction module is composed of the shufflenetv2 units stacked repeatedly. At the beginning of each unit, feature channels are split into two branches. One branch remains original features to perform identity mapping and the other branch consist of three convolutions to keep the number of output channels the same as the number of input channels. After three convolutions, the two branches are concatenated and the channel shuffle operation is placed at the end of the unit for the purpose of enabling information communication between the two branches. Then the next unit begins. As a result, three successive element-wise operations: channel split, concatenation and channel shuffle operations are merged into a single element-wise operation, as shown in Fig. 3(a). In addition, the unit is slightly modified for spatial down sampling as illustrated in Fig. 3(b).

By adopting the basic shufflenetv2 unit and spatial down sampling unit, proposed network encoder can utilize more feature channels and greater network capacity, which also means that it can reduce computational costs while maintaining accuracy. Thus, the network is very adaptable to mobile device.

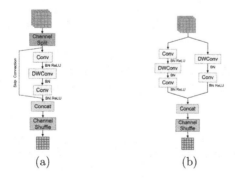

Fig. 3. Illustration of the shuffleNetv2 units: (a) Basic shuffleNetv2 unit. (b) ShuffleNetv2 unit for spatial down sampling.

3.2   Deep Semantic Enhanced Module

Since lightweight feature extraction may cause slight precision loss, we design DSE module to supplement and improve the performance of the encoder.

DSE module plays a key role in improving accuracy. Motivated by [7], we design a parallel structure to aggregate multi-scale feature maps. Different from the pyramid structures, each branch of DSE module is cascaded by dilated convolution with different rates to extract features from different branches. In contrast to standard convolution, dilated convolution can bring about larger receptive fields without additional parameters, which enables more semantic information to be integrated. In addition, the number of parameters introduced by the DSE module is also of concern to us. Inspired by depthwise separable convolution [8], which is to separate the correlation between spatial and channel dimension, the improved dilated separation convolution is divided into two parts: dilated depthwise convolution and pointwise convolution. Dilated separation convolution improves accuracy while pointwise convolution greatly reduces the parameter numbers (see Fig. 4).

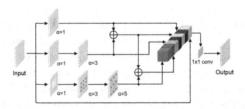

Fig. 4. Illustration of the deep semantic enhanced (DSE) module. The feature maps are parallelly fed into the deep semantic enhanced module. After concatenation, the outputs are obtained by 1×1 convolution.

Formally, we define the feature maps extracted by encoder as X, where $X \in \mathbb{R}^{C \times W \times H}$ (C means the channel numbers of feature map, W and H represents the width and height of the feature map). Then X is sent into four parallel branches $\mathcal{B}_r$, where $r = 0$, 1, 2 and 3. Branch $\mathcal{B}_0$ is equal to skip-connection, which can help recover the full spatial resolution at the network output and Branch $\mathcal{B}_1$ with dilated rate $\alpha = 1$ is essentially standard convolution. By cascading the dilated separation convolution of $\alpha = 1$ and $\alpha = 3$, $\mathcal{B}_2$ expands the receptive field from the original 3×3 to 9×9, which means that the number of pixels can be seen as three times as the original. The last Branch $\mathcal{B}_4$ is cascaded by three dilated separation convolution at $\alpha = 1$, $\alpha = 3$ and $\alpha = 5$, which raises the receptive field to 19×19. Finally, all branches are concatenated and improved feature maps $\tilde{X}$ after deep semantic enhancement are obtained through 1×1 convolution, which is formulated as:

$$\tilde{X} = \mathcal{P}\left(\Theta(\mathcal{B}_0, \mathcal{B}_1, \mathcal{B}_2, \mathcal{B}_3, \sum_0^1 \mathcal{B}_r, \sum_0^2 \mathcal{B}_r, \sum_0^3 \mathcal{B}_r) \right) \qquad (1)$$

where $\mathcal{P}(\cdot)$ represents pointwise convolution and $\Theta(\cdot)$ is the concatenation operation. To summary, DSE module not only has few parameters, but also significantly improves the performance of the network.

3.3 Decoder

After feature extraction and semantic enhancement, the decoder needs to gradually restore the feature maps to its input size. The decoder combines the upsample operation with skip connection to concatenate different level features extracted from the encoder and DSE module. After concatenation, two 3×3 convolutions are used to fine-tune the detail. The module is simple but effective because the context embedding part brings global features, which is beneficial to the restoration of details. The decoder that incorporates context embedding part effectively remedies the information loss and enhances the performance of the network.

3.4 Loss Function

In this paper, we adopt the dice coefficient loss function [12] to deal with the imbalanced data classification of tongue image. As a measure of overlap, the dice coefficient is widely used to assess segmentation performance. It's essentially a binary classification problem which based on pixel-wise. The reason why we choose dice coefficient loss is that the tongue often occupies a small region in the original tongue image. The loss $\mathcal{L}_{dice}$ is defined as follows:

$$\mathcal{L}_{dice} = 1 - \frac{2\sum_{i=1}^{n} f(k,i) g(k,i)}{\sum_{i=1}^{n} f^2(k,i) + \sum_{i=1}^{n} g^2(k,i)}, \ \forall i \in [1, \ n], \ \forall k \in K \tag{2}$$

where n is the number of pixels, i is each pixel of a given image which is classified into a class $k \in K \{tongue, \ background\}$, $f(k,i) \in [0,1]$ and $g(k,i) \in [0,1]$ represent predicted result and ground truth label for class K respectively.

4 Experimental Results

Extensive comparative experiments with the state-of-the-art deep learning methods are conducted on the two benchmark datasets to evaluate the effectiveness of the proposed network.

4.1 Dataset

We use the public dataset BioHit[1] which is collected by professional image acquisition device and the lab-made datasets which is gathered by cellular phone camera in various uncontrolled environments (named CPCA) to evaluate the performance. The examples of tongue images in the BioHit and CPCA are shown in Fig. 5 and 6, respectively.

---

[1] http://github.com/BioHit/TongueImageDat.

BioHit. There are 300 tongue images in public dataset BioHit. Each image is taken by image acquisition device. 200 images are randomly chosen as the training set and 100 images as the test set.

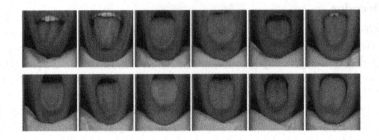

Fig. 5. Examples of tongue images in BioHit.

CPCA. It is composed of 750 tongue images, which are collected from the internet and captured by mobile phones in various environments. These images have a complex background, lighting conditions and tongue position. 503 images are chosen for training and the rest for testing.

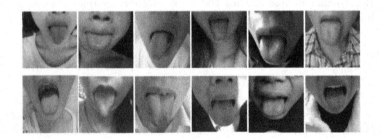

Fig. 6. Examples of tongue images in CPCA.

4.2   Evaluation Metrics

Three standard metrics [13] *Intersection over Union* (*IoU*), *Sensitivity* (*Sen*), and *Accuracy* (*Acc*), are adopted to evaluate the segmentation quality of the proposed network. As the most commonly used indicator *IoU* in segmentation tasks, it represents the intersection and union ratio between the predicted result and the ground truth. The *Sen* means the ability to predict positive pixels and *Acc* defines the ratio of the number of correctly predicted pixels to the total number of predicted pixels. Their definitions are computed as follows:

$$IoU = \frac{TP}{TP + FN + FP} \tag{3}$$

$$Sen = \frac{TP}{TP + FN} \tag{4}$$

$$Acc = \frac{TP + TN}{TP + TN + FP + FN} \tag{5}$$

where TP, TN, FP and FN respectively represent the number of true positive pixels, true negative pixels, false positive pixels, and false negative pixels.

4.3   Implementation Details

We implemented the proposed network on the Keras framework and trained it with the NVIDIA GeForce GTX 1070Ti graphics cards. We set the batch size to be 8 and the images are resized to 256×256. Adam optimizer was adopted to adjust network parameters. The learning rate initially was set to 0.01 and reduced by 10% whenever the training loss stops decreasing until 0.0001.

We also used data augmentation methods like random angle rotation, translation, zooming, shearing and horizontal flipping for data augmentation when training.

4.4   Comparison with the State-of-the-Art

In this section, we conduct extensive experiments on two diverse tongue image datasets and compare with 15 popular deep learning methods which are divided into two categories: accurate networks and real-time networks. On the one hand, accurate networks pay no attention to the number of model parameters and includes FCN-8s [4], U-net [14], SegNet [15], PSPNet [16], DeeplabV2 [5], DeeplabV3 [6] and DeeplabV3+ [7]. On the other hand, real-time networks slightly sacrifice accuracy to reduce the number of parameters and contains MobileNetV2 [8], MobileNetV3 [9], LinkNet [17], BiseNet [18], DFANet [19], ShuffleNetV1 [20], ShuffleNetV2 [11] and GhostNet [21]. Note that all implementations are under the same conditions.

In Table 1, we report the mean ± standard error (SE) of the total IoU, Sen and Acc obtained from the ten runs of fivefold cross-validation, resulting from these methods. We find that the comparison methods generally perform worse on CPCA than on BioHit because the illumination condition of the images in CPCA is poor, the tongue position is tricky and the noise interference is serious. However, the performance of the proposed method across two data sets is stable, and the scores of each index are the highest, which proves that our network is robust and accurate enough for tongue segmentation on mobile devices. In order to intuitively compare the real segmentation performance, we select U-net [14], DeepLabV3+ [7] and MobileNetV3 [9] and proposed network as visual objects from the average performance of the two datasets, as shown in Fig. 7 and 8.

From the segmentation results in Fig. 7 and Fig. 8, we can find that U-net [14] lacks the ability to recognize tongue regions especially in images with small tongue areas. MobileNetV3 [9] could not accurately segment the tongue when processing images with strong light intensity. Moreover, DeepLabV3+ [7] could

Table 1. The scores of Iou, Sen and Acc (mean±SE) for all the competing methods on the two benchmark datasets, BioHit and CPCA.

Method	BioHit			CPCA		
	Iou (%)	Sen (%)	Acc (%)	Iou (%)	Sen (%)	Acc (%)
FCN-8s [4]	84.30±0.53	88.44±0.48	96.42±0.41	73.58±2.56	78.21±2.12	93.57±0.98
U-net [14]	95.29±0.27	97.33±0.21	98.25±0.27	94.25±1.18	97.83±1.19	98.16±0.70
DeepLabV2 [5]	90.87±0.34	95.93±0.26	96.77±0.38	91.10±2.21	92.85±1.67	96.33±0.89
DeepLabV3 [6]	93.12±0.29	97.49±0.22	97.22±0.26	92.41±2.17	94.94±1.22	97.62±0.73
DeepLabV3+ [7]	94.63±0.22	98.27±0.19	98.06±0.16	94.04±0.97	96.10±1.51	98.73±0.29
SegNet [15]	91.72±0.39	93.75±0.34	98.11±0.14	92.92±1.26	97.12±1.14	98.39±0.21
PSPNet [16]	93.07±0.28	97.00±0.27	97.95±0.23	94.97±0.76	97.53±1.28	98.88±0.17
MobileNetV2 [8]	94.48±0.25	96.83±0.20	98.04±0.17	92.29±1.66	96.16±1.20	98.20±0.45
MobileNetV3 [9]	95.37±0.18	97.85±0.12	98.53±0.09	94.31±0.88	98.05±1.03	98.38±0.44
LinkNet [17]	91.03±0.44	95.44±0.36	97.02±0.39	93.54±1.67	97.41±1.63	97.81±1.23
BiseNet [18]	92.92±0.31	97.12±0.15	98.14±0.28	92.90±1.88	97.15±1.51	98.39±0.67
DFANet [19]	69.07±0.87	81.74±1.17	91.95±1.28	55.53±3.06	80.05±2.58	85.40±2.37
ShuffleNetV1 [20]	90.13±0.29	96.26±0.32	97.77±0.34	92.00±2.54	98.05±1.30	98.01±0.59
ShuffleNetV2 [11]	91.07±0.24	98.32±0.15	98.70±0.07	92.66±2.42	98.06±1.38	98.26±0.50
GhostNet [21]	91.33±0.46	97.61±0.33	98.27±0.12	93.59±1.95	97.35±1.62	98.42±0.61
Proposed	**96.55±0.13**	**99.05±0.10**	**99.25±0.05**	**96.48±1.24**	**99.41±0.43**	**99.22±0.55**

not accurately distinguish the pixels around the tongue, which results in a lot of noise at the tongue edge in the segmentation results. Contrarily, the proposed method can not only deal with the change of light intensity effectively, but also show excellent performance in the tricky tongue position and edge pixel discrimination, which also implies that the proposed method can deal with complex images taken by mobile devices.

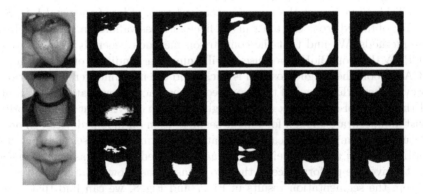

Fig. 7. Visualization of segmentation results on CPCA. From left to right: original tongue images, results obtained by U-net [14], DeepLabV3+ [7], MobileNetV3 [9], proposed method and labels.

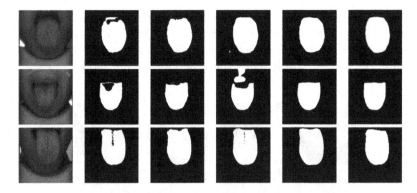

Fig. 8. Visualization of segmentation results on BioHit. From left to right: original tongue images, results obtained by U-net [14], DeepLabV3+ [7], MobileNetV3 [9], proposed method and labels.

In addition, we calculate the size of the model and the segmentation time on CPU, in order to strongly prove that the proposed network can achieve accurate segmentation on mobile devices (see Table 2).

Table 2. The comparison of the proposed network and the state-of-the-art methods on model size and mean segmentation time.

Method	Model size	Segmentation time
FCN-8s [4]	512 MB	81 ms
Unet [14]	355 MB	72 ms
SegNet [15]	224 MB	64 ms
PSPNet [16]	44 MB	36 ms
DeepLabV3+ [7]	20 MB	24 ms
MobileNetV3 [9]	16 MB	20 ms
LinkNet [17]	45 MB	38 ms
BiseNet [18]	87 MB	55 ms
DFANet [19]	86 MB	54 ms
GhostNet [21]	10 MB	18 ms
Proposed	**8 MB**	**15 ms**

Table 2 shows the model size and average segmentation time of all networks. Among the above models, the proposed model has the smallest model size and the least mean segmentation time. In conclusion, the proposed network has high accuracy while occupying less memory space, which means that the proposed model can be well embedded in mobile devices.

Finally, we overlay the segmentation results with the original images as an auxiliary evaluation of the proposed network. From the samples shown in Fig. 9, we can vividly find that the segmentation results can accurately cover the tongue position in the images, which shows the superiority of our model.

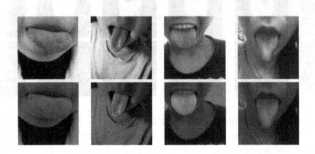

Fig. 9. Visualization of segmentation results.

In summary, the proposed network can quickly segment tongue images while occupying less computing power. Its efficiency and accuracy make it especially suitable for mobile tongue image segmentation.

5   Conclusion

In this paper, we have proposed an DSE-Net to ensure high accuracy while utilizing few parameters for efficient segmentation. The adoption of lightweight feature extraction module provides a prerequisite for mobile deployment. The deep semantic enhancement (DSE) module provides a strong guarantee for accuracy. Moreover, dilated separation convolutions are applied to each branch of DSE module in parallel, which enables the proposed network to accurately identify tongue edge pixels. Different from other decoder, we embed context information, which is very friendly to recover details and improve accuracy. In addition, we adopt the dice coefficient loss function to deal with the problem of unbalanced data distribution in tongue image datasets. Extensive experiments have been conducted on two datasets, including the public dataset BioHit which is collected on specialized device and lab-made dataset CPCA that gathered by mobile devices. Experimental results demonstrate that the proposed method is lightweight, efficient and robust to the changes of illumination condition, imaging angle, low light condition and tongue position, which is suitable for mobile tongue image segmentation task.

References

1. Zhang, L., Qin, J.: Tongue-image segmentation based on gray projection and threshold-adaptive method. Chin. J. Tissue Eng. Res. **14**(9), 1638 (2010)

2. Zhi, L., Yan, J., Zhou, T.: Tongue shape detection based on B-spline. In: International Conference on Machine Learning and Cybernetics, pp. 3829–3832 (2006)

3. Fu, H.G., Wang, W.M., Yang, J.H., Wu, R.Q.: Automatic tongue image segmentation. Inf. Comput. Autom., 790–794 (2008)

4. Long, J., Shelhamer, E., Darrell, T.: Fully convolutional networks for semantic segmentation. In Proceedings of the IEEE Conference on Computer Vision and Pattern Recognition, pp. 3431–3440 (2015)

5. Chen, L.C., Papandreou, G., Kokkinos, I.: DeepLab: semantic image segmentation with deep convolutional nets, atrous convolution, and fully connected CRFs. IEEE Trans. Pattern Anal. Mach. Intell. **40**(4), 834–848 (2017)

6. Chen, L.C., Papandreou, G., Schroff, F., Adam, H.: Rethinking atrous convolution for semantic image segmentation. arXiv preprint arXiv:1706.05587 (2017)

7. Chen, L.-C., Zhu, Y., Papandreou, G., Schroff, F., Adam, H.: Encoder-decoder with atrous separable convolution for semantic image segmentation. In: Ferrari, V., Hebert, M., Sminchisescu, C., Weiss, Y. (eds.) ECCV 2018. LNCS, vol. 11211, pp. 833–851. Springer, Cham (2018). https://doi.org/10.1007/978-3-030-01234-2_49

8. Sandler, M., Howard, A., Zhu, M., Zhmoginov, A., Chen, L. C.: MobileNetV2: inverted residuals and linear bottlenecks. In Proceedings of the IEEE Conference on Computer Vision and Pattern Recognition, pp. 4510–4520 (2018)

9. Howard, A., et al.: Searching for MobileNetV3. In Proceedings of the IEEE/CVF International Conference on Computer Vision, pp. 1314–1324 (2019)

10. Tang, H., Wang, B. et al.: DE-Net: dilated encoder network for automated tongue segmentation. 2020 25th International Conference on Pattern Recognition (ICPR), pp. 2575–2581. IEEE (2021)

11. Ma, N., Zhang, X., Zheng, H.-T., Sun, J.: ShuffleNet V2: practical guidelines for efficient CNN architecture design. In: Ferrari, V., Hebert, M., Sminchisescu, C., Weiss, Y. (eds.) Computer Vision – ECCV 2018. LNCS, vol. 11218, pp. 122–138. Springer, Cham (2018). https://doi.org/10.1007/978-3-030-01264-9_8

12. Gu, Z., Cheng, J., Fu, H.: CE-Net: context encoder network for 2D medical image segmentation. IEEE Trans. Med. Imaging **38**(10), 2281–2292 (2019)

13. Rezatofighi, H., Tsoi, N., Gwak, J.: Generalized intersection over union: a metric and a loss for bounding box regression. In: Proceedings of the IEEE/CVF Conference on Computer Vision and Pattern Recognition, pp. 658–666 (2019)

14. Ronneberger, O., Fischer, P., Brox, T.: U-Net: convolutional networks for biomedical image segmentation. In: International Conference on Medical Image Computing and Computer-Assisted Intervention, pp. 234–241 (2015)

15. Badrinarayanan, V., Kendall, A., Cipolla, R.: SegNet: a deep convolutional encoder-decoder architecture for image segmentation. IEEE Trans. Pattern Anal. Mach. Intell. **39**(12), 2481–2495 (2017)

16. Zhao, H., et al.: Pyramid scene parsing network. In: Proceedings of the IEEE Conference on Computer Vision and Pattern Recognition, pp. 2881–2890 (2017)

17. Chaurasia, A., Culurciello, E.: LinkNet: exploiting encoder representations for efficient semantic segmentation. In: 2017 IEEE Visual Communications and Image Processing (VCIP), pp. 1–4 (2017)

18. Yu, C., Wang, J., Peng, C., Gao, C., Yu, G., Sang, N.: BiSeNet: bilateral segmentation network for real-time semantic segmentation. In: Ferrari, V., Hebert, M., Sminchisescu, C., Weiss, Y. (eds.) ECCV 2018. LNCS, vol. 11217, pp. 334–349. Springer, Cham (2018). https://doi.org/10.1007/978-3-030-01261-8_20

19. Li, H., Xiong, P., Fan, H., Sun, J.: DFANet: deep feature aggregation for real-time semantic segmentation. In: Proceedings of the IEEE/CVF Conference on Computer Vision and Pattern Recognition, pp. 9522–9531 (2019)

20. Zhang, X., Zhou, X., Lin, M., Sun, J.: ShuffleNet: an extremely efficient convolutional neural network for mobile devices. In: Proceedings of the IEEE Conference on Computer Vision and Pattern Recognition, pp. 6848–6856 (2018)
21. Han, K., Wang, Y., Tian, Q., et al.: GhostNet: more features from cheap operations. In: Proceedings of the IEEE/CVF Conference on Computer Vision and Pattern Recognition, pp. 1580–1589 (2020)

Efficient-Nets and Their Fuzzy Ensemble: An Approach for Skin Cancer Classification

Dibyendu Das[1], Nikhilanand Arya[2]([✉]) [iD], and Sriparna Saha[2] [iD]

[1] Ramakrishna Mission Vivekananda Educational and Research Institute Belur, Howrah, India

[2] Indian Institute of Technology Patna, Bihar, India
{nikhilanand_1921cs24,sriparna}@iitp.ac.in

Abstract. Skin cancer is common and deadly among all cancer types, and its increasing cases in the last decade have put tremendous stress on dermatologists. With the advancement in medical imaging techniques, dermoscopic visual inspection with proper training of dermatologists can achieve approximately 80% diagnostic accuracy. However, in real-life scenarios, most dermatologists ignore the procedural algorithms (3-point checklist, ABCD rule, Menzies method, 7-point checklist) and follow their experience-based instincts. It raises the need for automated dermoscopy diagnosis, and this paper proposes a novel Choquet Fuzzy Ensemble of reward penalized Efficient-Nets for multi-class skin cancer classification. The base classifiers of the architecture are trained with the novel macro F1_score-based rewarding technique to handle the class imbalance of International Skin Imaging Collaboration (ISIC) data. After that, we combine the prediction probabilities of base classifiers using Choquet fuzzy integral to get the final predicted labels. The proposed architecture is evaluated based on ISIC multi-class skin cancer classification. The rewarded cross-entropy loss-based training regime showcased its superiority over weighted cross entropy loss training by attaining 2.61%, 3.06%, and 2.65% improvements in balanced accuracies of base classifiers. The proposed ensemble also outperforms the existing state-of-the-arts in terms of performance. Our model's highest balanced accuracy (88.15%) over its base classifiers and the state-of-the-art makes our model efficient and trustworthy in the classification goal.

Keywords: Skin cancer · Ensemble learning · Choquet fuzzy integrals · Reward function

1 Introduction

A study on skin cancer by the American Cancer Society (ACS) [1] suggests an enormous increase in skin cancer cases globally. If we see the figures, non-melanoma skin cancer contributes to 2–3 million and melanoma skin cancer

D. Das and N. Arya—Equal contribution.

© The Author(s), under exclusive license to Springer Nature Singapore Pte Ltd. 2023
M. Tanveer et al. (Eds.): ICONIP 2022, CCIS 1794, pp. 151–162, 2023.
https://doi.org/10.1007/978-981-99-1648-1_13

accounts for 132,000 cases globally each year. The ACS has an estimated 97,220 situ (noninvasive) melanoma, confined to the epidermis, and 99,780 invasive melanoma, spread to the dermis, resulting in 197,700 cases of melanoma in the U.S. only. The past decade (2012–2022) has observed a 31% shoot up in new invasive melanoma cases diagnosed annually. The occurrence of skin cancer is perturbing, as every three cancer diagnoses have one skin cancer. Americans are very susceptible to it because one in five Americans will have skin cancer at some point in their lives. If we analyze the statistics of melanoma deaths, 7,650 people will die of melanoma in 2022, which is an increase of 6.5% from last year. Although melanomas occurrences are low (<5%) among all skin cancers in the United States, 75% of all skin cancer-related deaths correspond to melanomas. The sharp decline in the 5-year survival rate from 99% to 14% between early and late detection of melanoma shows the criticality of early-stage detection. Shifting our view from uncommon but more catastrophic melanoma [13] to common and less fatal keratinocyte cancer such as squamous cell carcinomas (including actinic keratoses and Bowen's disease) and basal cell carcinomas shows the highest economic burden for Medicare patients [1].

The surge in skin cancer cases and shortage of dermatologists per capita [10] establishes the fact that there is a dire need for automated dermatology to eliminate the human intervention for the assessment of dermoscopic images [3]. Medical practitioners and patients can proactively track skin lesions and detect cancer earlier. It may benefit the patients by reducing economic expenses and can be a life savior with early-stage detection. The automated system may be helpful for the clinician as well by reducing the manual overhead.

2 Related Works

An artificial intelligence (AI) based automated system requires a plethora of data for learning, and from a data perspective, an earlier effort to create a public archive of very few images was made [3,12]. Too small dataset lacks the incorporation of multi-class classification tasks and compromises the generalization ability of the AI architectures. In recent years, the ISIC[1] has begun to aggregate a large-scale publicly accessible dataset of more than 33,000 dermoscopic images from leading clinical centers internationally. A look into the past literature on automated skin cancer classification using dermoscopic images shows several works. *Codella et al.* [5] have used 5248 dermoscopy images of melanoma (334), atypical nevi (144), and benign lesions (2146) by combining deep learning, sparse coding, and support vector machine (SVM) learning algorithms for melanoma vs. non-melanoma lesions, and melanoma vs. atypical lesions identification. Previous studies of image analysis using deep learning in skin cancer detection have been drawn to dermatologists' attention [8,9,11]. In the work of *Dascalu and David* [8], dermoscopy images acquired from a skin magnifier with polarized light were sonified to audio outputs by a deep learning (DL) algorithm, and the audios were further analyzed by a secondary DL for benign and malignant classification of

---

[1] https://challenge.isic-archive.com/data/.

skin lesions. The convolutional neural network (CNN) is one of the deep learning methods with the potential to analyze general and highly variable tasks in dermoscopic images. *Li and Shen* [11] used the ISIC2017 dataset [6] and proposed a deep learning framework consisting of two fully convolutional residual networks (FCRN) and a straight-forward CNN for lesion segmentation, lesion classification, and lesion dermoscopic feature extraction tasks, respectively. *Kassani and Kassani* [9] have used the ISIC2018 dataset [6,20] to analyze the performance of several state-of-the-art convolutional neural networks and selected ResNet50 as the best CNN in dermoscopic images classification.

The efficacy of CNNs in recent research motivated us to design our novel architecture for eight-class skin cancer classification tasks using ISIC2018 [6,20], ISIC2019 [6,7,20], and ISIC2020 [15] data. The proposed work is also inspired by the success of classifier ensembling techniques to improve the classification accuracy over individual classifiers [2,14]. The proposed architecture uses ensemble of three Efficient-Nets (B4, B5 and B6) motivated by the top performing architecture of ISIC2019 challenge's leader-board. The existing state-of-the-art architecture is the ensemble of all Efficient-Nets (B0 to B6) where B4, B5 and B6 are the best performing models in terms of balanced accuracies. The contributions of this study are as follows:

– We propose the new Macro-F1 Score-based reward function algorithm for training base classifiers (specifically, Efficient-Nets). It makes the model more robust for the class imbalance data.
– We propose a Choquet Fuzzy Integral based ensemble of base classifiers, which utilizes the probabilistic outcomes of each classifier to get the final prediction.

3   Dataset

The dataset used in this study is sourced from ISIC Archive, but we have downloaded it from Kaggle (SIIM-ISIC Melanoma Classification)[2]. The Kaggle repository consists of dermoscopy images from ISIC2018, ISIC2019, and ISIC2020 resulting in a total of 57964 images, out of which 25272 belong to ISIC2018-19 and 32692 belong to ISIC2020. We have utilized the JPEG version of these images with uniform sizes 512×512 for our study. The dataset is categorized into eight different types of skin cancers as Melanoma (MEL), Melanocytic Nevus (NV), Basal cell carcinoma (BCC), Actinic Keratoses (AK), Benign Keratosis (BKL), Dermatofibroma (DF), Vascular Lesion (VASC), and Squamous cell carcinoma (SCC). These target classes are directly available for ISIC2018-19 data, but for the categorization of ISIC2020 data, we have used the diagnosis column from the metadata file. The un-categorized samples from the dataset are mapped to separate unknown (UNK) classes, and we have discarded these samples from our study along with the redundant instances, resulting in 31265 images as a final dataset. The classwise distribution of the data is depicted in Fig. 1.

---

[2] https://www.kaggle.com/c/siim-isic-melanoma-classification.

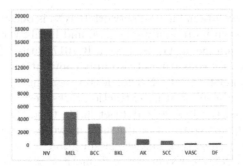

Fig. 1. Class-wise data distribution of ISIC (2018, 2019, 2020) skin cancer training data where x and y axes represents eight different types of skin cancers and respective image counts in the dataset, respectively.

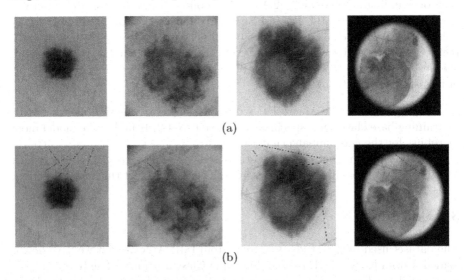

Fig. 2. (a) Some original dermoscopic images of skin cancer without hair insertion and (b) Skin cancer dermoscopic images with hair insertion using Buffon's needle concept.

The data is further divided into a train-test (80:20) set for training and testing the model, and 15% of the training set is selected as validation data. Most of the dermoscopic lesion images in the data portray overlapping body hair with the lesion region, and several hair-removal techniques have been suggested. Some issues, such as how to interpolate overlapping parts, remained, nevertheless. We thus use a different strategy by enhancing the fake body hairs to images using Buffon's needle [4] as the foundation. A sample representation of artificial hair insertion can be visualized from Fig. 2a and 2b.

The generalization and robustness are the primary traits of any AI architecture. We have incorporated some pre-processing steps to the train data during training to maintain these traits. It includes random application of various image transformation techniques such as transpose, flip, rotate, random brightness, random contrast, motion blur/ median blur/Gaussian blur/Gauss noise, Optical distortion/grid distortion/elastic transform, CLAHE, hue saturation value, shift scale rotate, cutout, and normalize.

4   Methods

The proposed architecture is the Choquet fuzzy integral [16] ensemble of three different EfficientNets (B4, B5, and B6) [18] with a reward function penalization for miss-classifications, and it is depicted in Fig. 3 and 4, respectively.

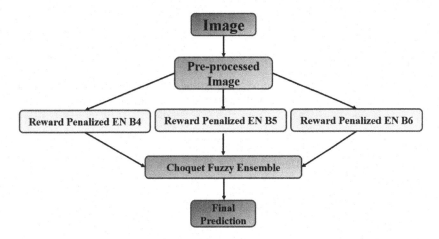

Fig. 3. The proposed architecture: Choquet Fuzzy Ensemble of Reward Penalized Efficient-Nets (EN) B4, B5 and B6.

The data is highly class imbalanced and can be seen from Fig. 1. So, we have performed weighted random sampling in each training batch to over-sample the minority classes. The best three EfficientNets (B4, B5, and B6) are selected after training and evaluating the balanced test accuracy of all possible EfficientNets on the final test data. The training of Efficient-Nets is performed separately in a five-fold stratified cross-validation framework with the proposed reward function and the best model from each fold is selected. We have averaged the performance of best models from each fold to get the final evaluation measure over test data. The average softmax outcomes from each Efficient-Net, representing the class probabilities of eight different skin cancer classes, are ensemble with Choquet fuzzy integral for final classification results. The reward function and Choquet fuzzy integral are further explained in Subsects. 4.1 and 4.2.

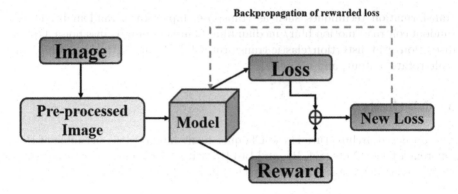

Fig. 4. The reward function workflow for the base classifier.

4.1 Reward Function

In this section, we propose a novel rewarding algorithm to handle the class imbalance of the ISIC skin cancer dataset being used in this study.

Algorithm 1. Algorithm for Reward Function

Input: Batches from Train Dataloader
Output: Penalized Loss

    Setting :
    Class $= \{c_1, c_2, \cdots, c_T\}$, Batch_size $= l$, loss_fun $=$ loss()
    Training_Data $= \{(x_i, y_i) : i = 1(1)n, \ y_i \in Class\}$
    Batch $= \{\{(x^{(j)}, y^{(j)}) : j = 1(1)l\}_k : k = 1(1)[n/l]\}$
    model $=$ model()
1: **for** item in Batch **do**
2:     input $= \{x^{(j)} : j = 1(1)l\}$
3:     label $= \{y^{(j)} : j = 1(1)l, \ y^j \in Class\}$
4:     $\{\hat{y}^{(j)} : j = 1(1)l\} =$ model(input)
5:     calculate Precison P_t, and Recall R_t for each $t \in Class$
6:     Macro-F1_Score $= \frac{1}{|Class|} \sum \frac{2 P_t R_t}{P_t + R_t}$
7:     Reward $= \frac{1}{Macro-F1\_Score + \epsilon}$
8:     loss $=$ loss _fun (output, label)
9:     Penalized_loss $=$ loss $+$ Reward
10: **end for**

To handle the class imbalance, we have used the concept of reinforcement learning [19] which suggests that whenever a model makes any mistake, it learns from it. We know that the Macro-F1_score measures the class-wise importance. For that reason, we have introduced a reward function as inverse of Macro-F1_score. We have calculated Macro-F1_score for each batch. For some batches, it could be zero, in that case, an epsilon is added. The reward is then incorporated with the loss function of the model to penalize or reward the incorrect and correct classifications, respectively. The detailed implementation is presented in Algorithm 1. The rewarding technique is not an overhead in terms of complexity as the reward penalization is performed for each item present in the train batch during training with batch size l, as given in the algorithm. It adds up only linear complexity for the calculation of Macro-F1_score and respective rewarded loss if compared to the complexity of non-rewarded loss calculation.

4.2   Ensemble: Choquet Fuzzy Integral

In this research, we suggest an integration of several classifiers using fuzzy fusion to make use of the ascendancy of separate Efficient-Net classifiers rather than a single one. The input of the fuzzy fusion is directly regarded as the confidence ratings from several classifiers. The uncertainty of the decision scores is a piece of extra information from a classifier harnessed by the fusion strategy. For our work, we formulated the problem as follows.

Problem Formulation:

- Let C_j denotes the j_{th} model, where j=1,2,$\cdots$,M.
- acc_j be the test accuracy for the j_{th} model.
- Test set
  $(D_{Test}) = \{(x^{(i)}, y^{(i)}) \; : \; x^{(i)} \in \mathbf{R}^{C \times W \times H}, y^{(i)} \in \mathbf{R}^d, i = 1(1)n\}$.
  Here C, W and H represents the Channel, Width and Height of the input image, $x^{(i)}$, d is the number of classes.
- $V(.)$ = Measure of consistency of a classifier $\in [0,1]$ and calculated as:
  $V(C_i) = (acc_i)/(\sum_{i=1}^{M} acc_i)$. If S is the set of all classifiers, then V(S) = 1 indicates that the classifier can be trusted and that its findings are consistent, but $V(\phi) = 0$ indicates that the classifier cannot be trusted.
- Here, we assume that for any two classifiers they are capturing different views of a dataset, so if C_1 and C_2 are two classifiers then in mathematical form $C_1 \cap C_2 = \phi$ and from theory of fuzzy integral [17] we can find a Fuzzy measure, $\lambda > -1$ in such a way that we can estimate the importance of two models together in following way:

$$V(C_1 \cup C_2) = V(C_1) + V(C_2) + \lambda V(C_1)V(C_2) \qquad (1)$$

- **Definition of Choquet Fuzzy Integral :** Suppose μ is the fuzzy measure on $\mathcal{F}$, a collection of subsets of S. The Choquet fuzzy integral of the function mapping: $h : \mathcal{F} \to \mathcal{R}$ with relation to μ is explained by:

$$Ch_\mu(h) = \sum_{i=1}^{M} h_{(i)}[\mu(A_{(i)}) - \mu(A_{(i+1)})] \qquad (2)$$

Here, i is the subset size, $h_{(1)} \leq h_{(2)} \leq \cdots \leq h_{(M)}$. Moreover $A_{(i)} = i, \cdots, M, A(M+1) = \phi$

Now, we have to calculate the λ using the following equation:

$$1 + \lambda = \prod_{i=1}^{M}(\lambda V(C_i) + 1) \tag{3}$$

For each input image $x^{(i)}$ corresponding to model C_j, we have the prediction for d different classes as $\hat{Y}_i^j = (\hat{y}_{i,1}^j, \hat{y}_{i,2}^j, \cdots, \hat{y}_{i,d}^j)$. We combine these outputs from each model with corresponding model importance and define $X = (X_1, X_2, \cdots, X_d)$, where $X_k = (\hat{y}_{i,k}^j, V(C_j))$ for all $j = 1, 2, \cdots, M$.

Further, we reorder each X_k in descending order based on $\hat{y}_{i,k}^j$ values. Let, $\hat{Y}_i = (y_1, y_2, \cdots, y_d)$ be the ensemble output with respect to $x^{(i)}$. After finding X_k, we need to find the ensemble output $y_k \in \hat{Y}_i$ with the help of Algorithm 2.

Algorithm 2. Algorithm for construction of final Prediction

Input: $X = (X_1, X_2, \cdots, X_d)$
Output: Final Prediction
    Setting : $X_k = (\hat{y}_{i,k}^j, V(C_j)) \ \forall \ j = 1, \cdots, M$ & $x^{(i)}$.
1: **for** *Each* X_k **do**
2:    **for** $j = 1, 2, \cdots, M$ **do**
3:       $f_{cur} = f_{prev} + X_k[j][1] + \lambda f_{prev} X_k[j][1]$
4:       $pred = pred + X_k[j][0](f_{cur} - f_{prev})$
5:       $f_{prev} = f_{cur}$
6:    **end for**
7:    $y_k = pred \in \hat{Y}_i$
8: **end for**
9: $\hat{y}_i \leftarrow \text{argmax}(\hat{Y}_i)$

Thus through fuzzy integrals, the robustness is experimentally found to be higher as compared to the previously obtained normalized softmax probabilities. From the Algorithm 2, it is clear that the final prediction of any given input $x^{(i)}$ is calculated with the help of softmax probabilities of all possible, d classes obtained by each of the M different base classifiers. Hence, the proposed choquet fuzzy ensemble has the complexity of $\mathcal{O}(d \times M)$.

5   Results

This section establishes the efficacy of the proposed reward function and Choquet Fuzzy ensemble.

Table 1. Comparative results of Efficient-Nets (ENs) in different training setups.

Model	Balanced accuracy (%)		
	Rewarded loss	Non-rewarded loss	Weighted loss
EN B4	**87.37**	84.76	86.64
EN B5	**87.51**	84.45	86.88
EN B6	**86.62**	83.97	85.53

From Table 1, we can observe that the proposed reward function is superior over non-rewarded loss and weighted loss. The weighted cross entropy loss is the popular state-of-the art to tackle the class imbalance and it has been frequently used in top architectures of ISIC-2019 challenge. Inclusion of our proposed reward function in the training of Efficient-Nets shows 2.61%, 3.06%, and 2.65% improved balanced accuracies over non-rewarded loss; 0.73%, 0.63%, and 1.29% improvement over weighted loss for Efficient-Nets B4, B5 and B6, respectively. Following the efficacy of "with reward function training", we select these models as base classifier for our final ensemble.

Table 2. Comparative results of our proposed ensemble with state-of-the-art for skin cancer classification.

Model	Balanced accuracy (%)	
	Rewarded loss	Non-rewarded loss
Choquet Fuzzy Ensemble	**88.15**	85.17
Average Ensemble	87.80	85.02
ISIC-2019 Leaderboard: Rank 1	87.68	

To showcase the efficacy of our proposed Choquet Fuzzy Ensemble over a simple (average) ensemble and existing state-of-the-art (Top performer of ISIC-2019 Challenge Leaderboard titled "Skin Lesion Classification Using Loss Balancing and Ensembles of Multi-Resolution EfficientNets")[3], we analyze the results of these two using the same training strategies mentioned earlier. From Table 2, it is evident that the Choquet Fuzzy ensemble outperforms the average ensemble and existing state-of-the-art results in multi-class skin cancer classification. The proposed ensemble outperforms the average ensemble and ISIC-2019 Leaderboard: Rank 1 by 0.35% and 0.47% for "with reward function training" setup. If we further compare the balanced accuracies of Choquet fuzzy ensemble from Table 2 and base classifier Efficient-Nets (B4, B5, and B6) from Table 1 in reward function training setup, then there is performance improvement of 0.78%, 0.64%, and 1.53%, respectively. Our proposed model achieves better performance than

---

[3] https://challenge.isic-archive.com/leaderboards/2019/.

the existing techniques because of its two main components: (1) rewarding process, which improves the model's generalization capability by penalizing in case of wrong predictions and rewarding in case of correct predictions. It stops our models from being biased towards the majority classes. (2) the Choquet Fuzzy ensemble of these rewarded/penalized base classifiers does not give equal importance to all the classifiers. Instead, it prioritizes them based on their membership value derived using Choquet Fuzzy integral.

6   Conclusion and Future Work

We conclude this study with the novel Choquet Fuzzy ensemble of Efficient-Nets in a reward function training setup. The proposed architecture showcases its superiority over the base classifiers and simple ensemble technique in multi-class skin-cancer classification. The inclusion of reward function in the training regime has helped the model learn better about the minority class and handled the critical class imbalance issue of the data. The Choquet Fuzzy ensemble of EfficientNets and its proven efficacy over a simple ensemble for dermoscopic diagnostic can be helpful for dermatologists and patients in the early detection of skin cancer. It may help reducing the burden of increasing skin-cancer cases by rapid diagnosis and also reduce the economic burden of the patients.

In the future, researchers can use additional sources of information coming from clinical investigations and demographic details of the patients to develop multi-modal architectures for skin cancer classification. Further, deep learning-based architectures can be developed to predict the type of skin cancer using mobile camera images instead of dermoscopic images to ease the diagnosis for patients and dermatologists.

Acknowledgments. Dr. Sriparna Saha gratefully acknowledges the Young Faculty Research Fellowship (YFRF) Award, supported by Visvesvaraya Ph.D. Scheme for Electronics and IT, Ministry of Electronics and Information Technology (MeitY), Government of India, being implemented by Digital India Corporation (formerly Media Lab Asia) for carrying out this research.

References

1. Cancer facts and figures 2022: American cancer society. https://www.cancer.org/content/dam/cancer-org/research/cancer-facts-and-statistics/annual-cancer-facts-and-figures/2022/2022-cancer-facts-and-figures.pdf
2. Arya, N., Saha, S.: Multi-modal classification for human breast cancer prognosis prediction: proposal of deep-learning based stacked ensemble model. IEEE/ACM Trans. Comput. Biol. Bioinf. **19**(2), 1032–1041 (2022). https://doi.org/10.1109/TCBB.2020.3018467
3. Barata, C., Ruela, M., Francisco, M., Mendonca, T., Marques, J.S.: Two systems for the detection of melanomas in dermoscopy images using texture and color features. IEEE Syst. J. **8**(3), 965–979 (2014). https://doi.org/10.1109/JSYST.2013.2271540. http://ieeexplore.ieee.org/document/6570764/

4. Buffon, G.: Essai d'arithm'etique morale (1777)
5. Codella, N., Cai, J., Abedini, M., Garnavi, R., Halpern, A., Smith, J.R.: Deep Learning, sparse coding, and SVM for melanoma recognition in dermoscopy images. In: Zhou, L., Wang, L., Wang, Q., Shi, Y. (eds.) MLMI 2015. LNCS, vol. 9352, pp. 118–126. Springer, Cham (2015). https://doi.org/10.1007/978-3-319-24888-2_15
6. Codella, N.C.F., et al.: Skin lesion analysis toward melanoma detection: a challenge at the 2017 International symposium on biomedical imaging (ISBI), hosted by the international skin imaging collaboration (ISIC). In: 2018 IEEE 15th International Symposium on Biomedical Imaging (ISBI 2018), pp. 168–172. IEEE, Washington, DC, April 2018. https://doi.org/10.1109/ISBI.2018.8363547. https://ieeexplore.ieee.org/document/8363547/
7. Combalia, M., et al.: BCN20000: dermoscopic lesions in the wild. arXiv e-prints arXiv:1908.02288, August 2019
8. Dascalu, A., David, E.O.: Skin cancer detection by deep learning and sound analysis algorithms: a prospective clinical study of an elementary dermoscope. EBioMedicine **43**, 107–113 (2019). https://doi.org/10.1016/j.ebiom.2019.04.055
9. Hosseinzadeh Kassani, S., Hosseinzadeh Kassani, P.: A comparative study of deep learning architectures on melanoma detection. Tissue Cell **58**, 76–83 (2019). https://doi.org/10.1016/j.tice.2019.04.009. https://linkinghub.elsevier.com/retrieve/pii/S0040816619300904
10. Kimball, A.B., Resneck, J.S.: The US dermatology workforce: a specialty remains in shortage. J. Am. Acad. Dermatol. **59**(5), 741–745 (2008). https://doi.org/10.1016/j.jaad.2008.06.037
11. Li, Y., Shen, L.: Skin lesion analysis towards melanoma detection using deep learning network. Sens. (Basel, Switzerland) **18**(2), E556 (2018). https://doi.org/10.3390/s18020556
12. Mendonca, T., Ferreira, P.M., Marques, J.S., Marcal, A.R.S., Rozeira, J.: PH^2 - a dermoscopic image database for research and benchmarking. In: 2013 35th Annual International Conference of the IEEE Engineering in Medicine and Biology Society (EMBC), pp. 5437–5440. IEEE, Osaka, July 2013. https://doi.org/10.1109/EMBC.2013.6610779. http://ieeexplore.ieee.org/document/6610779/
13. Meyskens, F.L., et al.: Cancer prevention: obstacles, challenges, and the road ahead. JNCI J. Nat. Cancer Inst. **108**(2) (2016). https://doi.org/10.1093/jnci/djv309. https://academic.oup.com/jnci/article-lookup/doi/10.1093/jnci/djv309
14. Paul, S., Saha, S., Singh, J.P.: COVID-19 and cyberbullying: deep ensemble model to identify cyberbullying from code-switched languages during the pandemic. Multimedia Tools Appl., 1–17 (2021). https://doi.org/10.1007/s11042-021-11601-9
15. Rotemberg, V., et al.: Publisher correction: author correction: a patient-centric dataset of images and metadata for identifying melanomas using clinical context. Sci. Data **8**(1), 88 (2021). https://doi.org/10.1038/s41597-021-00879-x. http://www.nature.com/articles/s41597-021-00879-x
16. Sugeno, M., Murofushi, T.: Pseudo-additive measures and integrals. J. Math. Anal. Appl. **122**(1), 197–222 (1987). https://doi.org/10.1016/0022-247X(87)90354-4. https://linkinghub.elsevier.com/retrieve/pii/0022247X87903544
17. Tahani, H., Keller, J.: Information fusion in computer vision using the fuzzy integral. IEEE Trans. Syst. Man Cybern. **20**(3), 733–741 (1990). https://doi.org/10.1109/21.57289. http://ieeexplore.ieee.org/document/57289/
18. Tan, M., Le, Q.: EfficientNet: rethinking model scaling for convolutional neural networks. In: Chaudhuri, K., Salakhutdinov, R. (eds.) Proceedings of the 36th International Conference on Machine Learning. Proceedings of Machine Learning

Research, vol. 97, pp. 6105–6114. PMLR, 09–15 June 2019. https://proceedings. mlr.press/v97/tan19a.html

19. Tiwari, A., Saha, S., Bhattacharyya, P.: A knowledge infused context driven dialogue agent for disease diagnosis using hierarchical reinforcement learning. Knowl. Based Syst. **242**, 108292 (2022). https://doi.org/10.1016/j.knosys.2022.108292. https://www.sciencedirect.com/science/article/pii/S0950705122000971

20. Tschandl, P., Rosendahl, C., Kittler, H.: The HAM10000 dataset, a large collection of multi-source dermatoscopic images of common pigmented skin lesions. Sci. Data **5**(1), 180161 (2018). https://doi.org/10.1038/sdata.2018.161. http://www.nature. com/articles/sdata2018161

A Framework for Software Defect Prediction Using Optimal Hyper-Parameters of Deep Neural Network

Rakesh Kumar$^{(\boxtimes)}$ and Amrita Chaturvedi

Department of Computer Science and Engineering, Indian Institute of Technology (BHU), Varanasi, India
{rakeshkumar.rs.cse18,amrita.cse}@iitbhu.ac.in

Abstract. Software defect prediction (SDP) models are widely used to identify the defect-prone modules in the software system. SDP model can help to reduce the testing cost, resource allocation, and improve the quality of software. We propose a specific framework of optimized deep neural network (ODNN) to develop a SDP system. The best hyper-parameters of ODNN are selected using the stage-wise grid search-based optimization technique. ODNN involves feature scaling, oversampling, and configuring the base DNN model. The performance of the ODNN model on 16 datasets is compared with the standard machine learning algorithms viz. Naïve Bayes, Support Vector Machine, Random Forest, Ada Boost, and base DNN model in terms of Accuracy, F-measure, and Area Under Curve (AUC). Experimental results show that the ODNN framework outperforms base DNN (BDNN) with 11.90% (accuracy), 0.26 (f-measure), and 0.13 (AUC). The statistical analysis using Wilcoxon signed-rank test and Nemenyi test show that the proposed framework is more effective than state-of-the-art models.

Keywords: Deep neural network · Software defect prediction · Machine learning · Grid search based optimization · Nemenyi test

1 Introduction

Software defect prediction (SDP) is an essential topic for researchers in software engineering. The primary goal of SDP is to find defective software modules before they are tested by a software tester [1]. It is crucial to detect faults early in the software development process to provide a cost-effective and high-quality software product [2]. Identifying defects in software costs almost 50% of software development costs [3]. Identifying defects at an early stage of the software development life cycle can prevent spreading defects from one stage to later stages. In later stages, they may become more complex and expensive to fix [3].

Supported by organization IIT (BHU) Varanasi India.

Previously, many researchers have developed SDP models using standard machine learning algorithms, ensemble techniques, and deep learning [4]. The SDP model is trained to learn the relation between software metrics and output labels so that it can be used to predict defect-prone and non-defect-prone modules on the current software version [5]. This SDP task is performed with the help of machine learning algorithms like Support Vector Machine [6], Random Forest [7], Naive Bayes [8], Ada Boost [9], Ensemble learning [10], Deep learning models [11], etc.

Deep learning models have recently received a lot of attention due to their better performance in various fields [4]. The use of a Deep Neural network for SDP has already been investigated in [11], where the results showed minor improvements over other machine learning models in most of the datasets. So, in this study, a novel framework ODNN has been proposed to extend the base DNN model. ODNN model involves data imbalance handling, feature scaling, and grid search-based optimization to improve performance significantly. The finding of the optimal values of hyper-parameters help us to achieve better performance measures as compared to other standard machine learning algorithms, viz. Naïve Bayes (NB), Support vector machine (SVM), Random Forest (RF), AdaBoost (AdaBoost), and base DNN.

The available software defect datasets are imbalanced. Therefore, addressing the data imbalance problem in SDP is a crucial step in the proposed framework. Addressing this issue is the primary step in our approach. Thereafter, we applied the metric scaling techniques to map the metrics values in a specific range. Then we used the ODNN model to achieve promising results. The contribution of the paper are as follows:

- Proposed a specific SDP framework, ODNN using optimal hyper-parameters of deep neural network. The hyper-parameters tuning is performed using a grid search-based optimization technique in three stages to get better results. Such type of framework for SDP is the first work to the best of our knowledge.
- Performed comparative analysis of the SDP models using three performance measures. Performed statistical tests to show that the proposed framework, ODNN is a significantly effective model for predicting defects in software defect datasets.

The rest of the paper is structured as follows, Sect. 2 discusses the related research, and Sect. 3 explains the proposed approach. Experimental setup is described in Sect. 4. Section 5 presents the results and discussion, and finally, the conclusion and future work is discussed in Sect. 6.

2   Related Research

In this section, we discuss related research about SDP models. Recently, SDP has become an active area of research in software engineering [2,12,13]. Set of software metrics proposed by McCabe, Halstead, CK metrics, or object-oriented metrics play a crucial role in building the SDP models [11]. Artificial intelligence-based standard machine learning algorithms have been increasingly used to develop SDP models over the last ten years. These algorithms have achieved the bottleneck performance (80–85% accuracy) [2,12]. Matloob et al. presented a literature study and concluded that Bagging, Boosting, and Random forest are the most frequently used algorithms; PROMISE and NASA datasets are mostly used by the researchers; accuracy, f-measure, ROC–AUC and MCC are the preferable performance parameters. They further concluded that, the 10-fold cross-validation technique is the most reliable validation technique, and Synthetic minority oversampling techniques (SMOTE) are the most common sampling techniques to handle data imbalance [10].

After that, deep learning models attracted the researchers to enhance the performance of standard machine learning algorithms [4]. A basic DNN model consists input layer, a number of hidden layers, size of each hidden layer, weight vector, activation function, and output layer. The most popular approach for tuning and constructing neural network design is the empirical search optimization (trial and error) method. More than 40% of the papers used a trial and error approach to define the deep neural network topology [14]. Only 10% of the articles provided evident optimization efforts. The trial and error approach is a time-consuming technique and also results in poor performance. The grid search-based optimization technique is used to estimate the optimal values of hyper-parameters.

Deep learning is an advanced learning technique based on the human brain's functions. Deep learning is a branch of machine learning consisting of several layers, and each layer produces some simplified output that is fed to the next layer. The popular deep learning models are deep neural network (DNN), Convolutional Neural Network (CNN), Recurrent Neural Network (RNN), and Long Short Term Memory (LSTM) Networks [4]. The deep neural network is the most utilized model in recent studies. AUC is the most frequently used performance parameter of deep learning models [3]. Deep learning-based models can provide more accurate results for complex and big projects. But, these models are complicated to understand the function of inner layers. These models take much more time than machine learning models.

3 Proposed Approach

Our proposed approach, optimized deep neural network (ODNN), is an extension of the base DNN model [11]. The proposed method improves the performance of the base model DNN in terms of Accuracy, F-measure, and AUC. Samir et al. [11] used the hit and trial-error approach to identify the number of the hidden layers and hidden layer size to predict the best results. The hit and trial-error method is a heuristic-based approach that is a complex task and does not produce effective results. So, we have improved this hit and trial-error method by automated hyper-parameter selection using a grid search-based technique.

ODNN is based on the basic DNN model (BDNN). Figure 1 shows the step-by-step process to develop the ODNN model. We have split the datasets into training and testing datasets using a 10-fold cross-validation method. We observed that the selected datasets are imbalanced (2.1% to 63.6% defects), so we addressed the data imbalance issue. After that, we scaled the datasets and built a basic DNN model. After building a basic DNN, the grid search-based optimization technique was applied to handle the hyper-parameter configuration using three stages. The step-by-step process to implement the proposed ODNN is discussed in the following subsections.

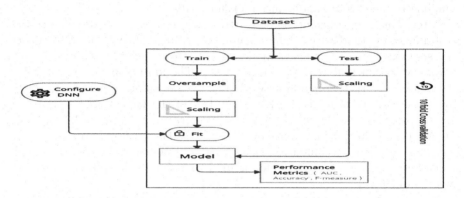

Fig. 1. Framework for ODNN model using hyper-parameter configuration

3.1 Dataset Imbalance Handling and Scaling

Previous studies on SDP [15] have shown that 80% of defects occur only from 20% of modules, which results in an imbalanced dataset. A study by Malhotra and Kamal [16] shows that oversampling technique helps to enhance the state-of-the-art results. The selected 16 datasets[1] are highly imbalanced (2.1% to 63.6% defects). To overcome this issue, we have used synthetic minority oversampling techniques (SMOTE) on the datasets.

When the values in different columns are spread over a large range, it becomes a significant obstacle for many machine learning algorithms. So, we used the standardization scaling technique based on standard deviation and mean to scale the datasets. Standardization is defined in Equation (1), where μ represents the mean of the software metrics m, σ is the standard deviation of the metrics, X is the metric vector, and X' is the scaled metric vector.

$$X' = (X - \mu)/\sigma \quad \forall \quad X \in m \tag{1}$$

---

[1] https://github.com/klainfo/DefectData.

3.2 Grid Search Based Hyper-Parameter Optimization Technique (GSBO)

The key idea in ODNN is to configure the hyper-parameters of the DNN to select the optimal values using the grid search-based hyper-parameter optimization technique. Let DNN have k number of hyper-parameters denoted as $\eta_1, \eta_2, ..., \eta_k$. Let the respective domain values for each hyper-parameter be $\alpha_1, \alpha_2, ...\alpha_n$. Our main objective is to find a set of optimal hyper-parameters (δ^*) so that we can maximize the validation accuracy (val acc) α of the ODNN. The val acc α of ODNN model is defined as function $\alpha(\eta, D_{train}, D_{val})$, where, η is the set of hyper-parameters, D_{train} and D_{val} are the training and validation samples.

We have randomly assigned the hyper-parameter value to a small subset of the dataset to find the initial set of effective hyper-parameters values. These initial hyper-parameters values are used in later stages for grid search-based optimization. Algorithm 1 demonstrates the concept of grid search-based optimization (GSBO).

Algorithm 1: To implement grid search based optimization algorithm (GSBO)

Input: A set of hyper-parameters $\eta = \eta_1, \eta_2, .., \eta_k$ // k is total number of
      hyper-parameters

Total no. of stages=Z, z=1,2,..,Z

Input training data for each stage $D_{train} = D_{train}^1, D_{train}^2, .., D_{train}^z$,

Validation dataset D_{val}

Output: A set of optimal hyper-parameters δ^* // Optimal
      hyper-parameters obtained after all the stages

Algorithmic Steps:

for *stage z= 1 to Z* **do**

    for *i= 1 to l* **do**

        | α_i=compute $\alpha(\eta_i, D_{train}^z, D_{val})$

    end

    for *j=l+1 to Z* **do**

        | g=grid_search$(\eta_i, \alpha_i)_{i=1}^{j-i}$

        η_j=max args$_{\eta \in a} a(\eta, g)$

        α_i=compute $\alpha(\eta_i, D_{train}^z, D_{val})$

    end

    Reset $\eta_{1:k}$=best k configs $\in (\eta_1, ..., \eta_z$// obtained based on val acc α

end

Return $\delta^* = \max \arg_{h \in (\eta^1, ..., \eta^z)} \alpha_j$

Stage 1: Number of Layers, Layers Size, and Activation Function Optimization Using GSBO: In the first stage, the basic architecture of neural network will be optimized. In the basic architecture, the parameters are the number of layers, the size of hidden layers, and the type of activation function for each layer. At the output layer, the sigmoid function and one neuron are fixed. To speed up the grid search optimization, we keep the number of neurons at the current hidden layer less than the previous layer. It drastically decreases the number of operations ($O(n^2)$). Accuracy metrics and loss functions are used for optimization. Algorithm 2 is used to explain Stage 1 of grid search-based hyper-parameter optimization. In Algorithm 2, set of activation functions η_1^1={Tanh, Relu, Softmax, Linear, Softplus, Sigmoid, hard_sigmoid, softsign}, set of number of layers η_2^1={2,3,4,5,6,8,10,11}, and set of size of first hidden layer (no. of neurons) η_3^1={5,10,15,20,40,60,80,100} are evaluated while keeping other remaining parameter values fixed. The output of the Algorithm 2 is the set of optimized hyper-parameters δ^1.

Algorithm 2: To implement grid search based optimization algorithm at stage 1

Input: A dataset DS[X,Y], A set of neurons, set of number of hidden layers, set of different activation functions, Training dataset D_{train} and Validation dataset D_{val}

Output: A set of optimal hyper-parameters δ^1 // Optimal hyper-parameter obtained after first Stage

Algorithmic Steps:

Step 1: Create a Sequential Deep Learning Model (SDLM) with the basic hyper-parameters

Step 2:Define the grid search parameters, param = dict(layers, neuron, activation function)

SDLM.add(input dimension, layers, neuron, activation function)

Step 3: GS=GridSearchCV(estimator = SDLM, param_grid=param)

Step 4: grid_output = grid.fit(X, Y)

Step 5: print("Best: hidden layer, number of neuron, activation function") // (grid_output.best_score, grid_output.best_params))

Stage 2: Learning Rate and Optimizer Optimization Using GSBO: We have obtained three basic optimal hyper-parameters of the deep learning model from Stage 1 (δ^1). Now, we will tune the learning rate and optimizer (optimization algorithm) hyper-parameters of the DNN in Stage 2. Tuning the learning rate is an important consideration. When the learning rate is too low, the convergence of algorithm and network becomes very slow; while if the learning rate is too large, then the convergence of algorithm and network fails. Algorithm 3 is used to explain Stage 2 of grid search-based optimization in which input parameters are δ^1 (optimal number of layers, size of layers, activation function) obtained from stage 1, set of learning rate η_1^2={0.0001, 0.001, 0.01, 0.1, 0.2} and set of optimization algorithms η_2^2={Adam, SGD, Adagrad, Nadam, RMSprop, Adamax, Adadelta} and remaining parameters are kept the same. The output of the Algorithm 3 is the set of optimized hyper-parameters δ^2.

Stage 3: Epoch and Batch Size Values Optimization Using GSBO: In this Stage 3, the epoch and batch size values are optimized based on the hyper-parameters obtained from Stage 1 (δ^1), and Stage 2 (δ^2). Algorithm 4 is used to describe the grid search-based optimization at Stage 3. The input parameters

---

Algorithm 3: To implement grid search based optimization algorithm at Stage 2

Input: A dataset DS[X,Y], Set of optimal values obtained from the Stage 1 δ^1, set of the learning rate η_1^2, set of optimizers η_2^2, Training dataset D_{train} and Validation dataset D_{val}

Output: A set of optimal hyper-parameters δ^2 // Optimal hyper-parameters obtained after second stage

Algorithmic Steps:

Step 1: Create a sequential deep learning model SDLM with the set of optimized hyper-parameters δ^1

Step 2: Define the grid search parameters, param = dict(set of learning rate, set of optimizers)

SDLM.add(input dimension, layers, neuron, activation function)

SDLM.add(learning rate, optimizer)

Step 3: GS=GridSearchCV(estimator=SDLM, param_grid=param)

Step 4: grid_output = grid.fit(X, Y)

Step 5: print("Best: learning rate, optimizers) // (grid_output.best_score, grid_output.best_params))

---

are the set of batch size η_1^3={10, 20, 40, 60, 80, 100} and set of epochs η_2^3={10, 50, 100, 150, 200}. The output of Algorithm 4 is the set of optimized hyper-parameters δ^3.

4 Experimental Setup

The proposed approach ODNN has been implemented using Python ver 2.7.12. Keras library with Theano was used at the backend. The proposed framework was implemented on 16 datasets (8 datasets from the PROMISE repository and eight datasets from the NASA repository) to validate the effectiveness of the model [11]. The description of the dataset is given in Table 1. The datasets were collected from the GitHub repository[2]. Two-way statistical analysis is performed to evaluate the significance of the ODNN. We have used three performance measures viz. Accuracy, F-measure, and Receiver Operator Characteristic Area Under Curve (ROC-AUC) to compare the performance of the proposed model.

4.1 Research Questions

RQ1: Is the proposed ODNN model performs better than standard machine learning algorithms?

To compare our proposed approach ODNN and answer the research question (RQ1) effectively, we have implemented two machine learning algorithms i.e. Naive Bayes (NB) and Support Vector Machine (SVM), one bagging technique i.e. Random Forest (RF), and one booting technique i.e. AdaBoost.

RQ2: Is the proposed ODNN model performs better than BDNN model ?

---

[2] https://github.com/klainfo/DefectData.

Algorithm 4: To implement grid search based optimization algorithm at stage 3

Input: A dataset DS[X,Y], Set of optimal values obtained from Stage 1 δ^1, Set of optimal values obtained from Stage 2 δ^2, set of batch sizes η_1^3, set of epochs η_2^3, Training dataset D_{train} and Validation dataset D_{val}

Output: A set of optimal hyper-parameters δ^3 // Optimal hyper-parameters obtained after third stage

Algorithmic Steps:

Step 1: Create a sequential deep learning model SDLM with the set of optimized hyper-parameters δ^1 and δ^2

Step 2: Define the grid search parameters, param = dict(set of batch sizes, set of epochs)

SDLM.add(input dimension, layers, neuron, activation function)

SDLM.add(learning rate, optimizer)

SDLM.add(set of batch sizes, set of epochs)

Step 3: GS=GridSearchCV(estimator=SDLM, param_grid=param)

Step 4: grid_output = grid.fit(X, Y)

Step 4: print("Best: batch size, epoch) // (grid_output.best_score, grid_output.best_params))

Table 1. Description of software projects used in this study

Dataset	Tera Promise								NASA							
Projects	Ant 1.7	Jedit 4.0	Log4j 1.0	Lucene 2.4	Poi 3.0	Prop 1.0	Prop 5.0	Xalan 2.6	CM1	JM1	KC1	KC2	KC3	PC1	PC2	MC2
#Metrics	20	20	20	20	20	20	20	20	37	21	94	21	39	37	36	39
#Module	745	306	135	340	442	18471	8516	885	327	7782	145	522	194	705	745	126
%Defects	22.3	24.5	25.2	59.7	63.6	14.8	15.3	46.4	12.8	21.5	41.4	20.5	18.6	8.7	2.1	35.2

To answer research question 2, we have compared the results of the base deep learning model BDNN [11] with the proposed approach on the same datasets.

5   Results and Discussion

ODNN model has used 10-fold cross-validation techniques to split the dataset into training and testing datasets. Each experiment is repeated ten times with the same dataset to overcome variation in results. The average of performance measures over all the ten experiments is the final value of that measure. The performance of the proposed model, optimized deep learning model (ODNN), and machine learning models are presented in Table 2. The boxplot representation for each performance measure of different models is shown in Fig. 2.

Statistical Evaluation: The two non-parametric statistical tests Wilcoxon signed-rank test [17] and the Nemenyi test [18] suggested by Demsar [19] are performed on the results of six prediction models over 16 datasets. In Table 3, the mean difference between the performance of different models is shown in the right upper triangle. The p-values less than 0.05 obtained between two models using Wilcoxon signed-rank test show that the models are significantly different

Table 2. Performance of different algorithms in terms of accuracy, F-measure, and ROC AUC

Accuracy (%)						F-measure						ROC-AUC					
Projects	NB	SVM	RF	AB	BDNN	ODNN	NB	SVM	RF	AB	BDNN	ODNN	NB	SVM	RF	AB	BDNN	ODNN
Ant 1.7	78.57	75.85	81.81	77.45	82.93	95.41	0.55	0.54	0.58	0.51	0.61	0.90	0.80	0.79	0.83	0.79	0.82	0.97
Jedit 4.0	77.06	75.57	78.97	74.12	81.23	96.22	0.49	0.54	0.53	0.48	0.59	0.89	0.75	0.76	0.79	0.72	0.79	0.98
Log4j 1.0	83.67	79.50	78.67	76.19	80.56	95.98	0.61	0.55	0.55	0.49	0.58	0.89	0.82	0.79	0.78	0.71	0.80	0.95
Lucene 2.4	60.00	69.38	72.06	69.62	70.28	95.35	0.54	0.72	0.76	0.73	0.65	0.96	0.73	0.78	0.79	0.75	0.66	0.97
Poi 3.0	52.46	76.29	80.56	78.22	67.45	92.39	0.46	0.80	0.84	0.83	0.75	0.93	0.79	0.83	0.89	0.84	0.78	0.96
Prop 1.0	80.11	72.94	83.24	74.16	80.36	82.67	0.34	0.41	0.45	0.40	0.43	0.52	0.69	0.76	0.81	0.75	0.86	0.85
Prop 5.0	81.49	67.17	76.20	70.06	72.12	76.52	0.26	0.39	0.24	0.37	0.41	0.37	0.69	0.73	0.73	0.72	0.85	0.78
Xalan 2.6	71.21	74.08	76.78	73.73	77.27	93.58	0.60	0.69	0.74	0.70	0.64	0.92	0.78	0.82	0.85	0.82	0.74	0.96
CM1	78.19	73.28	82.76	80.63	83.45	97.73	0.30	0.31	0.27	0.29	0.39	0.85	0.69	0.69	0.75	0.73	0.87	0.97
JM1	78.79	71.35	78.15	73.77	79.27	84.71	0.30	0.43	0.40	0.40	0.45	0.67	0.66	0.70	0.72	0.68	0.79	0.87
KC1	73.17	69.83	74.86	69.31	76.46	87.59	0.41	0.47	0.47	0.44	0.51	0.76	0.69	0.69	0.73	0.69	0.75	0.90
KC2	83.41	78.16	81.44	79.77	83.24	92.89	0.51	0.59	0.55	0.56	0.62	0.83	0.84	0.83	0.84	0.81	0.84	0.92
KC3	76.74	72.59	78.71	72.74	84.95	94.11	0.37	0.32	0.39	0.35	0.52	0.83	0.66	0.66	0.74	0.62	0.81	0.96
PC1	87.31	79.44	90.63	86.13	93.89	97.06	0.32	0.31	0.35	0.31	0.59	0.81	0.81	0.83	0.88	0.82	0.92	0.97
PC2	83.30	89.40	96.38	93.83	96.79	98.85	0.09	0.06	0.07	0.07	0.32	0.59	0.59	0.66	0.75	0.62	0.98	0.98
MC2	71.40	68.01	68.18	66.53	75.98	95.47	0.44	0.47	0.47	0.50	0.48	0.92	0.77	0.72	0.75	0.69	0.70	0.98
Median	78.38	73.68	78.84	74.14	80.46	**94.73**	0.43	0.47	0.47	0.46	0.55	**0.84**	0.74	0.76	0.78	0.73	0.81	**0.96**

(left bottom triangle of Table 3). The mean score and critical diagram obtained using Nemenyi test show the clear performance of each model over 16 datasets (Fig. 3).

Results From Table 2: We can see that the performance of ODNN is superior to other models with 94.73% (accuracy), 0.84 (f-measure), and 0.96 (AUC). We can clearly see that the performance of the ODNN model is lesser on the three larger datasets Prop 1.0, Prop 5.0, and JM1. Hence, we can conclude that the ODNN is performing better than all the models over all datasets but producing reduced performance (<90% accuracy, <0.7 f-measure, <0.9 AUC) on larger datasets.

Results From Fig. 2a,b,c: It can be seen that the boxplot performance of ODNN is visualized as the best performance among all the models.

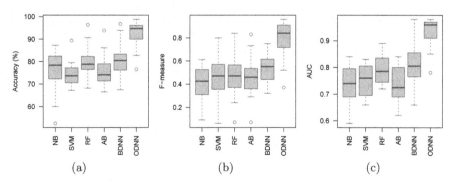

Fig. 2. Boxplot performance of different approaches in term of (a) Accuracy, (b) F-measure, and (c) AUC

Table 3. Wilcoxon signed-rank test analysis (p<0.05): Mean difference and p-value among the performance of different models

(a) Accuracy (%)						(b) F-measure						(c) AUC					
Mean difference (Coloumn-Row)(Shown in Right upper triangle), and p-value (Shown in Left bottom triangle)																	
	NB	SVM	RF	AB	BDNN	ODNN	NB	SVM	RF	AB	BDNN	ODNN	NB	SVM	RF	AB	BDNN	ODNN
NB	0.00	−1.50	3.91	-0.04	4.33	**16.23**	0.00	0.06	0.07	0.05	0.12	**0.38**	0.00	0.02	0.05	0.00	0.08	**0.20**
SVM	0.50	0.00	5.41	1.46	5.84	**17.73**	0.02	0.00	0.00	-0.01	0.06	**0.32**	0.06	0.00	0.04	−0.02	0.06	**0.18**
RF	0.08	0.00	0.00	-3.95	0.43	**12.32**	0.03	0.78	0.00	-0.01	0.06	**0.31**	0.00	0.00	0.00	−0.05	0.02	**0.15**
AB	0.99	0.06	0.00	0.00	4.37	**16.27**	0.08	0.17	0.25	0.00	0.07	**0.33**	1.00	0.02	0.00	0.00	0.08	**0.20**
BDNN	0.01	0.00	0.72	0.00	0.00	**11.90**	0.00	0.04	0.06	0.02	0.00	**0.26**	0.03	0.05	0.40	0.02	0.00	**0.13**
ODNN	0.00	0.00	0.00	0.00	0.00	0.00	0.00	0.00	0.00	0.00	0.00	0.00	0.00	0.00	0.00	0.00	0.00	0.00

Results From Table 3: The mean difference between all the models are shown. The bold font shown in the table shows the maximum difference of the ODNN model with other models. A mean difference of 17.73% accuracy, 0.38 f-measure, and 0.20 AUC is the highest gain by the ODNN model as compared to other models. The p-value among the models is less than 0.05 which shows that the models are significantly different. E.g., the p-values of 0.72 (> 0.05) between BDNN and RF show that they are not significantly different models despite of the fact that the mean difference between RF and BDNN is 0.43%.

Results From Fig. 3a,b,c: ODNN with the mean score of 5.88 (accuracy), 5.84 (F-measure), and 5.84 (AUC) is the best performing model as compared to other models. SVM (1.69 accuracy) and AB (2.06 accuracy) belong to the statistically low-performing group (shaded part). RF (3.94 accuracy), BDNN(4.44 accuracy), and ODNN (5.89 accuracy) belong to a statistically high-performing group (Non-shaded part) in terms of accuracy score. NB with a 3.00 mean score (accuracy) is at the borderline, which means that it cannot be categorized into a group clearly. Similarly, the critical diagrams of f-measure and AUC can be analysed.

From the Above Results: , we can conclude that the DNN model developed using the proposed approach has outperformed (14 out of 16 datasets) the BDNN model [11] and other popular machine learning algorithms. We can also conclude that our approach has the highest average AUC ROC, accuracy, and F-measure as compared to other models. Our approach has shown a 11.90% accuracy, 0.26 F-measure, and 0.13 increase in average AUC ROC measure than the BDNN model proposed in [11]. Our proposed model's performance values are quite fluctuating and sometimes low, especially in the case of relatively large datasets like prop-1, prop-5, JM1, etc.

5.1   Answers of RQs

Answer of RQ1: From Tables 2, 3 and Fig. 2,3, we can conclude that the proposed ODNN model performs better than standard machine learning models.

Answer of RQ2: From Tables 2, 3 and Fig. 2,3, we can conclude that the proposed ODNN model performs better than BDNN models.

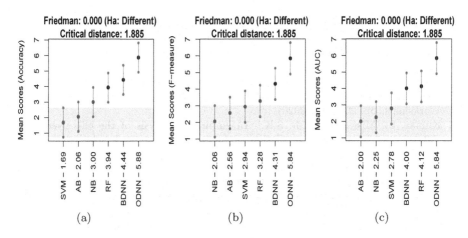

Fig. 3. Critical diagram performance analysis of proposed approach and other approaches using Nemenyi Test conducted on 16 datasets in terms of (a) Accuracy, (b) F-measure, and (c) AUC

6   Conclusion and Future Scope

In this study, we tried to find a more efficient solution to detect the defects in the software modules to increase their reliability and thus reduce the cost of software maintenance. With deep learning models gaining immense significance due to their superior performance in many areas, we explored deep learning and a unique framework to improve its performance in this task of SDP. Our experimental results prove that our proposed approach outperforms the base DNN model by 11.90% accuracy, 0.26 F-measure, and 0.13 increase in average AUC ROC measure. ODNN produces high performance at least in 14 out of 16 datasets than other models in terms of ROC AUC, Accuracy, and F-measure performance metrics. But the performance of the model in the case of relatively big datasets like prop-1, prop-5, etc. is not that satisfying, which we intend to improve in the future work of this study

In the future, we intend to use various feature extraction techniques with deep learning model to increase its performance. We also intend to study the performance of different deep learning algorithms like CNN, LSTM, RNN, etc. The exploration can also be extended to study the effect of various feature selection techniques on Deep learning models.

References

1. Thota, M.K., Francis, H., Shajin, Rajesh, P., et al.: Survey on software defect prediction techniques. Int. J. Appli. Sci. Eng. **17**(4), 331–344 (2020)
2. Rathore, S.S., Kumar, S.: A study on software fault prediction techniques. Artif. Intell. Rev. **51**(2), 255–327 (2019)

3. Pachouly, J., Ahirrao, S., Kotecha, K., Selvachandran, G., Abraham, A.: A systematic literature review on software defect prediction using artificial intelligence: Datasets, data validation methods, approaches, and tools. Eng. Appl. Artif. Intell. **111**, 104773 (2022)

4. Omri, S., Sinz, C.: Deep learning for software defect prediction: a survey. In: Proceedings of the IEEE/ACM 42nd International Conference on Software Engineering Workshops, pp. 209–214 (2020)

5. Kumar, L., Misra, S., Rath, S.K.: An empirical analysis of the effectiveness of software metrics and fault prediction model for identifying faulty classes. Comput. Standards Interfaces **53**,1–32 (2017)

6. Corinna, C., Vladimir, V.: Support-vector networks. Mach. Learn. **20**, 273–297 (1995). https://doi.org/10.1007/bf00994018

7. Breiman, L.: Random forests. Mach. Learn. **45**(1), 5–32 (2001)

8. Murphy, K.P.: Naive bayes classifiers, university of british columbia (2006)

9. Freund, Y., Schapire, R.E.: A decision-theoretic generalization of on-line learning and an application to boosting. J. Comput. Syst. Sci., **55**(1), 119–139 (1997)

10. Matloob, F.: A systematic literature review. IEEE Access, Software defect prediction using ensemble learning (2021)

11. Samir, M., El-Ramly, M., Kamel, A.: Investigating the use of deep neural networks for software defect prediction. In: 2019 IEEE/ACS 16th International Conference on Computer Systems and Applications (AICCSA), pp. 1–6 (2019)

12. Chatterjee, S., Maji, B.: A bayesian belief network based model for predicting software faults in early phase of software development process. Appl. Intell. **48**(8), 2214–2228 (2018)

13. Kumar, R., Chaturvedi, A., Kailasam, L.: An unsupervised software fault prediction approach using threshold derivation. IEEE Trans. Reliab. **71**(2), 911–932 (2022)

14. Pontes, F.J., Amorim, G.F., Balestrassi, P.P., Paiva, A.P., Ferreira, J.R.: Design of experiments and focused grid search for neural network parameter optimization. Neurocomput., **186**, 22–34 (2016)

15. Zimmermann, T., Nagappan, N., Zeller, A.: Predicting bugs from history. In: Softw. Evol., pp. 69–88. Springer, Heidelberg (2008). https://doi.org/10.1007/978-3-540-76440-3_4

16. Malhotra, R., Kamal, S.: An empirical study to investigate oversampling methods for improving software defect prediction using imbalanced data. Neurocomputing **343**, 120–140 (2019)

17. Wilcoxon, F.: Individual comparisons by ranking methods. Int. Biometric Society **1**(3), 80–83 (1945)

18. Nemenyi, P.B.: Distribution-free multiple comparisons. Nemenyi 1963, Princeton University (1963)

19. Demšar, J.: Statistical comparisons of classifiers over multiple data sets. J. Mach. Learn. Res. **7**, 1–30 (2006)

Improved Feature Fusion by Branched 1-D CNN for Speech Emotion Recognition

Medha[1]($\boxtimes$), Jitender Kumar Chhabra[2], and Dinesh Kumar[3]

[1] Indraprastha Institute of Information Technology Delhi, Delhi, India
medha130101@gmail.com
[2] Computer Engineering Department, National Institute of Technology,
Kurukshetra, Haryana, India
[3] Electronics and Communication Engineering Department,
Delhi Technological University, Delhi, India

Abstract. With the expeditious growth in web-based technologies for interaction amongst human beings, a massive amount of audial data is produced, transferred, consumed, and processed. The demand to automate the process to acquire the sentiments conveyed for a continuous stream of large audio files, necessitates efficient analysis and prediction through robust scientific techniques. A diverse range of the concepts as reported in the literature under the domain of Speech Emotion Recognition (SER) have proved pivotal for the recent advancements in voice recognition applications, as the services are inclusive of predicting emotion for real time audial input. The proposed 1-D Convolutional Neural Network (CNN) architecture assimilates the features extracted from the branched network design to improve the accuracy for the datasets under consideration with 1-D handcrafted features for each audio sample as input to the proposed model. The performance of the model is evaluated on the basis of accuracy, loss, precision, recall, and F-1 score. The accuracies achieved on the validation data for Emo-DB and TESS datasets are 83.33% and 99% respectively. Highly encouraging metric-based evaluation attained through the proposed pipeline surpasses the literature reviewed and hence is a reliable and competent technique to approach SER.

Keywords: Speech Emotion Recognition (SER) · Deep Learning · Convolutional Neural Network (CNN) · 1-D CNN

1 Introduction

The unceasing research in and around the procedure to estimate the underlying sentiment through visual, audial and textual data generated on the web is evident of the constant demand for development of efficacious techniques. The initial research methods revolved around specific feature engineering and preprocessing of audio signals, minimizing the aspect of generalisation of the complex process as the research methodologies were quite restricted to researchers

M. Tanveer et al. (Eds.): ICONIP 2022, CCIS 1794, pp. 175–186, 2023.
https://doi.org/10.1007/978-981-99-1648-1_15

possessing in-depth knowledge and a broader view to signal processing as an essential pre-requisite. With limited availability of relevant data and instability in natural forms of audio due to variation in age and gender amongst speakers, sarcastic and ambiguous statements, varying pronunciations, distinct languages and cultures across nationalities, SER remains complicated yet broad as a problem to be resolved. The initial success in the field was marked by application of Machine Learning (ML) for SER. Non-Linear ML classifiers as Hidden Markov Models (HMMs) [1–3], Support Vector Machines (SVMs) [4–6] and Gaussian Mixture Models (GMMs) [7] demonstrated appreciable accuracy after implementing complex pre-processing techniques and mathematical derivations on the raw data. Networks(ANN) [8] and Deep Neural Networks (DNNs) [9] as well as enhancement of openly accessible corpus. Deep Learning (DL) eliminated the need for comprehensive feature engineering. The ability of DNNs to identify and process the most relevant features for identification of each class label declares it to be best suited for multi-class classification for SER.

The contemporary research revolves around utilising simulated datasets and automated feature extraction through CNNs and Recurrent Neural Networks (RNNs) [10]. The design adopted in the experiments performed as a part of the proposed research work involves identifying and extracting physical features for each audio input, contrary to recent research which is extensively based on exploiting the ability of CNNs to learn from high dimensional input as Mel-Spectrogram images. The intent to select handcrafted features over spectrogram images is to test the competency of energy and cepstral features, reducing the space required to cache original as well as augmented audio samples without affecting the efficacy of the overall result for SER.

2   Related Work

The features derived through speech hold a profound application in sculpting appropriate input for training traditional ML model designs for SER. The appropriate choice of set of features directly influences the performance of the model and requires an exhaustive knowledge of speech signal processing [30]. With further growth and deployment of advanced procedures, as for Genetic Algorithms(GA) [13], Generalized Discriminant Analysis(GerDA) [14], DNN and Extreme Learning Machine (ELM) [15], Restricted Boltzmann Machine (RBM) [16], Generative Adversarial Networks (GANs) [17], Transfer Learning for Human-Computer Interaction (HCI) [31], the input feature set proved to be a highly critical aspect and hence was modified quite frequently across diverse published research for SER.

The introduction of RNNs, LSTMs [10] and emerging use of CNNs along with Long Short-Term Memory (LSTM) [19], across domains, led a perceptible change in the approach towards SER as research works focused to inflate architecture design rather than feature extraction as CNNs were designed to self-drive the process to learn best features for multi-class classification. Introduction and successful implementation of 1-D and 2-D CNN LSTM Networks delivered benchmark results by presenting a Deep CNN (DCNN) architecture, consisting of four consecutive Local Feature Learning Blocks (LFLBs) with Log-Mel Spectrogram to learn high level features from a 2-D grid, visualized as a 2-D image patch, followed by LSTM and Dense Layers [20]. The individual architectures proposed were further fused together to develop a merged deep 1-D and 2-D CNN [21]. The benchmark methodology [20,21] inspired new techniques incorporating modifications to popular CNN architectures with Log-Mel Spectrograms as input. The performance for modified CNN was evaluated on Emo-DB Dataset and the accuracy of the model was restricted to 65% even after extensive training [22]. Lack of 1-D features and shallow 1-D CNNs failed to generate satisfactory results on specific datasets even when there was ample data available as the problem statement had been reduced to predicting only positive and negative emotions [23]. One of the most recent works displays the procedure of two-way feature extraction with distinct DNNs and the corresponding results are highly effective [25,26]. As observed through the review, the application of CNNs for analysing audial input is highly inspired by a commendable performance of CNNs for image recognition and the progress for techniques devised in SER surfaced to be extremely aligned with the techniques used for Visual Emotion Recognition (VER) as LSTMs, Autoencoders [27] and pre-trained models as ResNet50, VGG16 etc. for input as visual representation of audio in the form of Log-Mel Spectrograms. For a 1-D feature vector, several CNN architectures are being explored to surpass the accuracy for Spectrogram as input to CNNs with an intention to preserve the space during processing of augmented as well as original data.

3 Motivation

The proposed research methodology continues to add to studies, aiming at developing the most accurate as well as efficient, additionally,rather an uncomplicated network design, easier to understand and modify, to further facilitate SER. The final task in hand is to predict one of the seven emotions as the strongest emoted sentiment for the input voice signal with optimum time and space consumption, viable use of resources and acceptable performance, evaluated by defined metrics. The accuracy is expected to be at par with several benchmark techniques, improving the results of related works, forming the basis of comparison amongst system designs and procedures.Also, it has been concluded strongly through the results achieved in recent work that an efficient 1-D CNN architecture with highly suited hand-crafted features is a well-equipped system for SER [24] and hence forms the basis of motivation for the proposed research with an aim to overcome the shortcomings and improve accuracy of branched CNNs for SER across all distinct categories.

4 Methodology

4.1 Proposed Improved Method

Thorough observation of the results received for Emo-DB induces the conclusion that the evaluated performance on the standard dataset is not reliable enough for practical applications. To supply for the need of an improved CNN architecture, a 1-D CNN, inspired from the model design for fusion of deep and shallow features [22], is being proposed. Deep Convolutional Neural Networks (DCNNs) are exposed to a high risk of losing global information whereas the fact that a set of global features is insufficient to classify input successfully also holds true. Hence, a relatively efficient approach is to fuse the output feature maps through a deep and a shallow sub-network. The improved 1-D CNN architecture, as shown in Fig. 1, is based on feature fusion but modifies the input to 1-D acoustic and spectral features rather than a 2-D Log-Mel Spectrogram as the input to the CNN. As the input is 1-D feature vector rather than a Log-Mel Spectrogram, the CNN architecture utilizes 1-D convolution layers to eliminate the need to reshape the input by expanding dimensions to suit traditional 2-D CNN. The deeper sub-network architecture design has a number of layers arranged for successive convolution and pooling operations as compared to the shallower branch. Batch Normalisation Layer is embedded to stabilize the training process and enhance generalisation which helps coordinate the continuous adjustment of varying weights. It is followed by ReLu activation for branched sub-networks. The outputs from two distinct sub-branches are fused before flattening. The model consists of two fully connected layers with two dropout layers before the final activation layer.

4.2 Data Augmentation

Data Augmentation is an important technique to increase the generalisation performance as it supplies for lack of appropriate data for small but well-simulated datasets by adding random but relevant variations to existing data [28]. Appropriate augmentation eliminates the probability of poor predictions due to background noise, necessitating its utilization to serve predictions on real-time input as general audial input is extremely prone to environmental sound [29].

The adopted approach to augment audio involves addition of Additive White Gaussian Noise (Appropriate). AWGN is sampled from a Gaussian Distribution with a mean value of zero and hence is easier to add and visualise. Other techniques adopted involve modifying the audio stream by stretching with respect to duration of the audio sample as well as varying pitch simultaneously for each audio sample.

4.3 Feature Extraction

Techniques and procedures extracted traditionally [30], have been explored to add best suited features for training the model. The proposed work utilizes a set of 162 feature values, each value extracted through one of the 5 key characteristic features of audio, for each audio sample which is supplied as input to 1-D CNN. Only five features are used to fasten the process of extraction and the categorical details for each feature as explained next.

1. Zero Crossing Rate (ZCR) - The procedure for evaluation of ZCR is the relative comparison of change of sign for the amplitude value for consecutive samples as specified in Eq. 1

$$ZCR_t = \frac{1}{2N} \sum_{k=t.N}^{(t+1).N-1} |sign(s(k)) - sign(s(k+1))| \qquad (1)$$

$$where, sign(s(k)) = \begin{cases} 1 & s(k) > 0 \\ -1 & s(k) < 0 \\ 0 & s(k) = 0 \end{cases}$$

ZCR_t is ZCR for frame t where size of each frame is N, $s(k)$ represents k^{th} sample, and tN and $(t+1)(N-1)$ stand for the first and last sample frames respectively. ZCR is indicative of the noisiness of the signal. A frame with considerable noise contributes immensely to the final value for ZCR.

2. Root Mean Square Energy (RMS) - As represented through Eq. 2, RMS_t is the root of average energy of all samples in a frame t. The RMS value is representative of the loudness of the audio signal.

$$RMS_t = \sqrt{\frac{1}{N} \sum_{k=t.N}^{(t+1).N-1} s(k)^2} \qquad (2)$$

3. Chroma-based Feature or Pitch Class Profiles - It adds to 12 feature values, each for twelve chroma values represented by the set, C, C , D, D , E, F, F , G, G , A, A , B, consisting of twelve pitch spelling attributes as used in Western music notation. It accounts for capturing the varying pitch across successive frames. It is evaluated using logarithmic value of Short-Time Fourier Transform(STFT).

4. Spectrogram-based Feature - The extracted Log Mel Spectrograms, pictorially representing power distribution over time along with frequency, are reduced to a single dimension. After evaluating the mean over each column, a 2-D matrix is essentially reduced to a 1-D feature vector with 128 feature values.

5. Cepstral-based Features - The features used for the proposed work are Mel-Frequency Cepstrum Coefficients (MFCC), adding 20 feature values to set of 1-D input features. Mel-Frequency Cepstrum is the representation of the short term power spectrum for each frame utilizing linear cosine transform of log power spectrum on a non-linear mel frequency scale [39]. The conversion from general frequency, let f to mel frequency m, is given by the Eq. 3

$$m = 2595(log_{10}((f/700) + 1)) \qquad (3)$$

The feature set is a combination of local as well as global features. The output dimension of features extracted for the case of chromagram, MFCC, and Spectrograms is a 2-D matrix for each audio frame. However, to create a 1-D input vector for each audial input, the values across the time domain in the matrix are averaged to acquire a 1-D feature vector for each feature.

4.4   1-D CNN Architecture

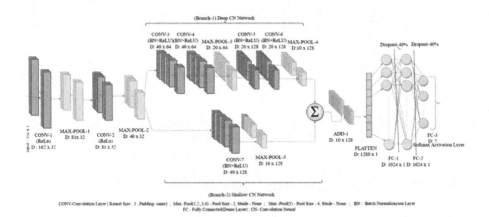

Fig. 1. Proposed Improved 1-D CNN Architecture

The CNN architecture contains seven Convolution Layers (CONV), five Pooling Layers (MAX-POOL) and three Fully Connected Layers (FC) where the last FC layer consists of seven neurons to serve a prediction for multi-class classification. The input is fed to CONV1 with 32 filters to add depth to the output and the output dimension after first convolution operation is 162×32. The activation function used with convolution is Rectified Linear Unit (ReLu). To further reduce the spatial dimension of the output, convolution is followed by a procedure to select the maximum value for the given input window by MAX-POOL1. The pool size for pooling operation is 2 and hence the dimensions of the input window is 2 across each of the 32 feature maps with 162 feature values, which, as a result, is reduced to 81 feature values. After the intermediate output with dimensions 81×32 is processed through successive layers of CONV2 and MAX-POOL2, the output is served as input to branched sub-networks. Before fusing the output delivered by the branched networks, the output through each individual branch is restricted to have similar output dimensions. The deeper branch follows successive convolutions (CONV3, CONV4), batch normalization, activation and pooling (MAX-POOL3) with 64 filters for each convolution layer. The same arrangement of layers is repeated with consecutive convolutions (CONV5, CONV6) with filter size as 128. For the shallower branch (Branch-2), CONV7 has 128 filters, followed by batch normalization and activation. MAX-POOL5 has been set to evaluate maximum value over an input window of size 4. The kernel size is set as 3×3 for each CONV layer. The output from the two sub-networks is fused before flattening to form a layer with final dimensions as 128×10. Three FC layers are appended where the last FC layer implements Softmax Activation with 40% dropout in between FC layers to reduce overfitting.

4.5   Model Evaluation

The overall model accuracy is evaluated using two parameters, *Loss* and *Accuracy*. The efficiency of prediction for each individual class for the data in the dataset is evaluated on the basis of *precision, recall* and *F-1 Score* as specified by the following equations.

$$Precision = \frac{TP}{TP + FP} \tag{4}$$

$$Recall = \frac{TP}{TP + FN} \tag{5}$$

$$F1 = \frac{2 * Precision * Recall}{Precision + Recall} = \frac{2 * TP}{2 * TP + FP + FN} \tag{6}$$

where *TP, TN, FP, and FN* have the value for the count for True Positive, True Negative, False Positive and False Negative for each class respectively.

5   Datasets

The datasets used to train and test the model for SER are the Berlin Database of Emotional Speech (Emo-DB) [11] and Toronto Emotional Speech Set (TESS) [12]. Both the datasets discussed are simulated, easily accessible and supply for discrete and separable emotions providing ease of modelling. The datasets are distinct considering gender dependency in audio utterances which tests the ability of model to adapt well to speaker dependent as well as speaker independent data through Emo-DB and TESS respectively.

6   Results and Discussions

6.1   Environment and Implementation Details

The research work utilizes Python and its built-in libraries. Tensorflow is used to model DNNs with Keras. The hardware details include 12th Gen Intel(R) Core(TM) i7-12700H CPU and 16 GB Memory support. The model is compiled with Stochastic Gradient Descent (SGD) as optimizer with learning rate as 0.01 for 100 epochs with batch size of 64 for both of the datasets. SGD parameters as decay and momentum are set to values 10^{-6} and 0.8 respectively. The loss function being used is Categorical Cross-Entropy and the metric for evaluation is accuracy. The dataset is split into train set and test set following the split ratio 80:20.

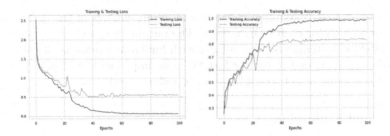

Fig. 2. Loss and Accuracy plot for Training and Testing Data for Emo-DB Dataset

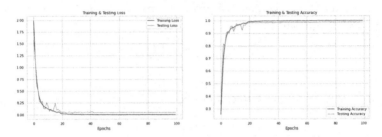

Fig. 3. Loss and Accuracy plot for Training and Testing Data for TESS Dataset

6.2   Loss and Accuracy Curves for Emo-DB and TESS

After the final iteration of optimization, the values for loss and accuracy over test set for Emo-DB are 0.55 and 83.33% and for TESS are 0.04 and 98.67% respectively.The plots for loss and accuracy, as represented in figs. 2 and 3, are descriptive of the model's ability to learn and adapt well.

6.3   Classification Report for Emo-DB and TESS

For speaker independent classification over the test set for Emo-DB, the data for actual labels as *Happy* and *Neutral* have been predicted incorrectly for *Anger* and *Boredom* respectively due to similar characteristics of audio input which also accounts for low recall values for the two classes as presented in Table 2. The model performs fairly well on the test set for TESS as inferred from Table 2 as the audio samples in the test set are not gender differentiated.

6.4   Comparative Analysis for Emo-DB and TESS

Accuracy has been selected as the primary basis of comparison. The presented work performs relatively better than a number of distinct techniques deployed in recent work as shown in Figs. 4 and 5. For Emo-DB, the accuracy is improved over the results for deep and shallow feature fusion with input as Log-Mel Spectrogram [22], Generative Noise Sampling with 1-D features and DNNs [28],3-D Scalogram as input to concatenated CNNs and RNNs [37], clustering based

Table 1. Classification Report for Emo-DB Dataset

Emotion	Precision	Recall	F-1 Score
Angry	0.83	0.96	0.89
Boredom	0.77	0.84	0.80
Disgust	0.89	0.94	0.91
Fear	0.89	0.87	0.88
Happy	0.80	0.65	0.72
Neutral	0.79	0.71	0.75
Sad	0.91	0.84	0.87
Average	0.84	0.83	0.83

Table 2. Classification Report for TESS Dataset

Emotion	Precision	Recall	F-1 Score
Angry	0.99	0.98	0.99
Disgust	0.99	0.99	0.99
Fear	0.98	1.00	0.99
Happy	0.99	0.99	0.98
Neutral	0.99	1.00	1.00
Sad	0.99	0.99	0.99
Surprise	0.99	0.97	0.98
Average	0.98	0.98	0.98

Genetic Algorithm for feature optimization [35] and metaheuristic algorithms as NSGA-II and Cuckoo Search for feature selection [34] with SVM as classifier. For TESS, the accuracy is considerably better than a shallow 1-D CNN architecture with MFCC as input [23] and has also improved over pre-trained models with Spectrograms as input [26].

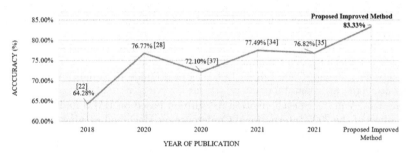

Fig. 4. Comparative Analysis for Emo-DB

Fig. 5. Comparative Analysis for TESS

7   Conclusion

The discussed approach and presented results for SER prove the ability of a simple 1-D CNN design over complex methodologies to predict emotion. The process of feature selection, even though costs expensive on time relative to a black box approach supported by CNNs for a visual input, reduces the space complexity to a significant extent. The process of selection, combination and derivation of 1-D feature vectors provides great flexibility and control to learn and develop the best suited input for faster processing and optimum space utilization. Further, merging of deep and shallow convolution layers contributes immensely to maximize the probability of a successful prediction. The performance of model on other open accessible databases can be tested and improved accordingly, supporting and enhancing the proposed design. As the proposed approach is optimised on space, it can be implemented economically to serve the purpose of SER on the data being put up continuously on web and serve emotion based results.

References

1. Rabiner, L.R.: A tutorial on hidden Markov models and selected applications in speech recognition. Proc. IEEE **77**, 257–286 (1989)
2. Nogueiras, A.; Moreno, A.; Bonafonte, A.; Mariño, J.B. Speech emotion recognition using hidden Markov models. In: Proceedingsof the Seventh European Conference on Speech Communication and Technology, Aalborg, Denmark, 3–7 September (2001)
3. Nwe, T.L., Foo, S.W., De Silva, L.C.: Speech emotion recognition using hidden Markov models. Speech Commun. **41**, 603–623 (2003)
4. Hsu, C.W.; Chang, C.C.; Lin, C.J. A Practical Guide to Support Vector Classification. 2003; pp. 1396–1400
5. Lin, Y.L.; Wei, G. Speech emotion recognition based on HMM and SVM. In Proceedings of the 2005 International Conference on Machine Learning and Cybernetics, Guangzhou, China, 18–21 August 2005; Volume 8, pp. 4898–4901
6. Chavhan, Y., Dhore, M., Pallavi, Y.: Speech Emotion Recognition Using Support Vector Machines. Int. J. Comput. Appl. **1**, 86–91 (2010)
7. Erden, M., Arslan, L.M.: Automatic detection of anger in human-human call center dialogs. In Proceedings of the Twelfth Annual Conference of the International Speech Communication Association, Florence, Italy, 27–31 August (2011)
8. Amir, N., Kerret, O., Karlinski, D.: Classifying emotions in speech: A comparison of methods. In: Proceedings of the Seventh European Conference on Speech Communication and Technology, Aalborg, Denmark, 3–7 September (2001)
9. Amer, M., Siddiquie, B., Richey, C., Divakaran, A.: Emotion Detection in Speech Using Deep Networks. In: Proceedings of the 2014 IEEE International Conference on Acoustics, Speech and Signal Processing (ICASSP), Florence, Italy, 4–9 May (2014)
10. Khalil, R.A., Jones, E., Babar, M.I., Jan, T., Zafar, M.H., Alhussain, T.: Speech emotion recognition using deep learning techniques: a review. IEEE Access **7**, 117327–117345 (2019)
11. Burkhardt, F., Paeschke, A., Rolfes, M., Sendlmeier, W.F., Weiss, B.: A database of German emotional speech. In: Proceedings of the Ninth European Conference on Speech Communication and Technology, Lisboa, Portugal, 4–8 September (2005)

12. Dupuis, K., Pichora-Fuller, M.K.: Recognition of emotional speech for younger and older talkers: Behavioural findings from the toronto emotional speech set. Can. Acoust. Acoust. Can. **39**, 182–183 (2011)
13. Philippou-Hübner, D., Vlasenko, B., Grosser, T., Wendemuth, A.: Determining optimal features for emotion recognition from speech by applying an evolutionary algorithm. In: Proceedings of the Eleventh Annual Conference of the International Speech Communication Association, Chiba, Japan 26–30, pp. 2358–2361 (2010)
14. Stuhlsatz, A., Meyer, C., Eyben, F., Zielke, T., Meier, H.G., Schüller, B.: Deep neural networks for acoustic emotion recognition: Raising the benchmarks. In: Proceedings of the 2011 IEEE international conference on acoustics, speech and signal processing (ICASSP), Prague, Czech Republic, 22–27 May (2011)
15. Han, K., Yu, D., Tashev, I.: Speech Emotion Recognition Using Deep Neural Network and Extreme Learning Machine. In: Proceed-ings of the Fifteenth Annual Conference of the International Speech Communication Association, Singapore, 14–18 September (2014)
16. Sánchez-Gutiérrez, M.E., Albornoz, E.M., Martinez-Licona, F., Rufiner, H.L., Goddard, J.: Deep Learning for Emotional Speech Recognition. In: Martínez-Trinidad, J.F., Carrasco-Ochoa, J.A., Olvera-Lopez, J.A., Salas-Rodríguez, J., Suen, C.Y. (eds) Pattern Recognition. MCPR 2014. Lecture Notes in Computer Science, vol 8495. Springer, Cham (2014)
17. Latif, S., Rana, R., Qadir, J.: Adversarial Machine Learning Additionally, Speech Emotion Recognition: Utilizing Generative Adversarial Networks For Robustness. arXiv (2018) arXiv:1811.11402
18. Wöllmer, M., Kaiser, M., Eyben, F., Schüller, B., Rigoll, G.: LSTM-Modeling of continuous emotions in an audiovisual affect recognition framework. Image Vis. Comput. **31**, 153–163 (2013)
19. Trigeorgis, G., et al.: Adieu Features? End-To-End Speech Emotion Recognition Using A Deep Convolutional Recurrent Network. In: Proceedings of the IEEE International Conference on Acoustics, Speech and Signal Processing (ICASSP), Shanghai, China, 20–25 March (2016)
20. Zhao, J., Mao, X., Chen, L.: Speech emotion recognition using deep 1D and 2D CNN LSTM networks. Elsevier Biomed. Signal Process. Contr. **47**, 312–323 (2019)
21. Zhao, J., Mao, X., Chen, L.: Learning Deep Features to Recognize Speech Emotion using Merged Deep CNN. IET Signal Processing. 12. (2018). https://doi.org/10.1049/iet-spr.2017.0320
22. Sun, L., Chen, J., Xie, K., Gu, T.: Deep and shallow features fusion based on deep convolutional neural network for speech emotion recognition. Int. J. Speech Technol. **21**(4), 931–940 (2018). https://doi.org/10.1007/s10772-018-9551-4
23. Mekruksavanich, S., Jitpattanakul, A., Hnoohom, N.: Negative Emotion Recognition using Deep Learning for Thai Language, 2020 Joint International Conference on Digital Arts, Media and Technology with ECTI Northern Section Conference on Electrical, Electronics, Computer and Telecommunications Engineering (ECTI DAMT & NCON), pp. 71–74, (2020)
24. Li, Y., Baidoo, C., Cai, T., Kusi, G.A.: Speech Emotion Recognition Using 1D CNN with No Attention. In: 2019 23rd International Computer Science and Engineering Conference (ICSEC), 2019, pp. 351–356 (2019)
25. Alnuaim, A.A., et al.: Human-computer interaction with detection of speaker emotions using convolution neural networks. Intell. Neurosci. **2022**, 1–16 (2022)
26. Aggarwal, A., et al.: Two-way feature extraction for speech emotion recognition using deep learning. Sensors **22**, 2378 (2022)

27. Patel, N., Patel, S., Mankad, S.H.: Impact of autoencoder based compact representation on emotion detection from audio. J Ambient Intell. Human Comput. **13**, 867–885 (2022)
28. Tiwari, U., Soni, M., Chakraborty, R., Panda, A., Kumar Kopparapu, S.: Multi-Conditioning and Data Augmentation using Generative Noise Model for Speech Emotion Recognition in Noisy Conditions. In: Proceedings of the ICASSP 2020–2020 IEEE International Conference on Acoustics, Speech and Signal Processing (ICASSP), Barcelona, Spain, 4–8 May (2020)
29. Salamon, J., Bello, J.P.: Deep convolutional neural networks and data augmentation for environmental sound classification. IEEE Signal Process. Lett. **24**(3), 279–283 (2017)
30. El Ayadi, M., Kamel, M.S., Karray, F.: Survey on speech emotion recognition: Features, classification schemes, and databases. Pattern Recogn. **44**(3), 572–587 (2011)
31. Song, P., Jin, Y., Zhao, L., Xin, M.: Speech emotion recognition using transfer learning. IEICE Trans. Inf. Syst. **97**, 2530–2532 (2014)
32. Chatterjee, R., Mazumdar, S., Sherratt, R.S., Halder, R., Maitra, T., Giri, D.: Real-time speech emotion analysis for smart home assistants. IEEE Trans. Consum. Electron. **67**(1), 68–76 (2021)
33. Badshah, A.M., Ahmad, J., Rahim, N., Baik, S.W.: Speech emotion recognition from spectrograms with deep convolutional neural network. Int. Conf. Platform Technol. Serv. (PlatCon) **2017**, 1–5 (2017)
34. Kanwal, S., Asghar, S.: Speech emotion recognition using clustering based GA-optimized feature set. IEEE Access **9**, 125830–125842 (2021)
35. Yildirim, S., Kaya, Y., Kılıç, F.: A modified feature selection method based on metaheuristic algorithms for speech emotion recognition. Appl. Acoust. **173**, 107721 (2021) ISSN 0003–682X
36. Chen, M., He, X., Yang, J., Zhang, H.: 3-D convolutional recurrent neural networks with attention model for speech emotion recognition. IEEE Signal Process. Lett. **25**(10), 1440–1444 (2018)
37. Aghajani, K., Esmaili Paeen Afrakoti, I.: Speech emotion recognition using scalogram based deep structure. Int. J. Eng. **33.2**, 285–292 (2020)
38. Choudhary, R.R., Meena, G., Mohbey., K.K.: Speech Emotion Based Sentiment Recognition using Deep Neural Networks. J. Phys.: Conf. Series. Vol. 2236. No. 1. IOP Publishing (2022)
39. Koolagudi, S.G., Rastogi, D., Rao, K.S.: Identification of Language using Mel-Frequency Cepstral Coefficients (MFCC), Procedia Eng. **38** 3391–3398 (2012) , ISSN 1877-7058

A Multi-modal Graph Convolutional Network for Predicting Human Breast Cancer Prognosis

Susmita Palmal[(✉)], Nikhilanand Arya, Sriparna Saha, and Somanath Tripathy

Indian Institute of Technology, Patna, India
{susmita_2121cs34,nikhilanand_1921cs24,sriparna,som}@iitp.ac.in

Abstract. Breast cancer is one of the most often found malignancies in women. For more focused treatment and disease management, a better prognosis for breast cancer is crucial. If breast cancer prognosis predictions were correct, a substantial number of people may be spared from unnecessary adjuvant systemic treatment and the enormous medical costs. Several studies have already been conducted to accomplish this. But, most studies employ specific gene expression data to create a predictive model. However, multi-modal cancer data sets have become accessible recently (gene expression, copy number alteration, and clinical). The introduction of multi-modal data presents possibilities for a more thorough investigation of the molecular aspects of breast cancer and, consequently, can enhance diagnosis. To incorporate multi-modal cancer data sets and to create a computational model for the prognosis of breast cancer, we proposed a novel classification model in this study, that is based on multi-modal graph convolutional networks (MGCN). To extract features, we first build a graph convolutional network (GCN) for individual modalities. And then, we feed the concatenated features generated by GCN into the stack-based ensemble model. The GCN model explores the underlying non-regular structural information from the data and learns the nodes' (or samples') hidden representation based on its properties and those of its surrounding nodes. This model outperforms currently used methods, according to the predictive performance assessed using various performance indicators. The precision, balanced accuracy, and Matthew's correlation coefficient values produced by this model are 0.869, 0.740, and 0.498, respectively.

Keywords: Graph Convolutional Network (GCN) · Stack-based ensemble model · Multi-modal learning · Breast Cancer

1 Introduction

By the end of 2020, 7.8 million women had been diagnosed with breast cancer, making it the most prevalent cancer in the world[1]. Additionally, it is becoming

---

[1] https://www.who.int/news-room/fact-sheets/detail/breast-cancer.

M. Tanveer et al. (Eds.): ICONIP 2022, CCIS 1794, pp. 187–198, 2023.
https://doi.org/10.1007/978-981-99-1648-1_16

increasingly clear that breast cancers are much more heterogeneous diseases than what the clinical subtypes indicate, and therefore earlier prognostic prediction is required for more specialized treatment and management [1]. A major issue with cancer prognosis prediction is the estimation of cancer patients' chances of survival [2]. In order to estimate whether and when an event (such as patient death) will occur within a specified time frame [3], cancer survival prediction can be expressed as a censored survival analysis issue. The five-year survival rate is a widely used statistic for cancer prognosis in the field of medical information retrieval [4]. By forecasting survival rates, a more accurate prediction model may be able to assist patients with breast cancer. It could also aid medical professionals in making accurate diagnoses for their patients.

The issue of predicting a cancer patient's prognosis has been addressed in earlier studies. On the basis of gene expression data, a prognosis prediction method based on support vector machines with a recursive feature elimination approach has been developed [5]. Concerning multi-modality, a model has been proposed by *Sun et el.* that uses hybrid signature consisting of two clinical markers and three gene markers made up from both the seventy gene expression data and clinical markers for the prediction of breast cancer prognosis [6]. *Gevaert et al.* also suggested a Bayesian Network-based probabilistic model that used genetic and clinical data [7], for the prognosis of breast cancer of type negative-lymph-node. Recent progress in deep learning techniques demonstrates that a model with several modalities of data sources performs better than a model with a single data source. To establish this fact *Sun et. al.* conducted interdisciplinary research work for predicting the prognosis of human breast cancer. They proposed an unique multimodal deep neural network by incorporating multidimensional data [8]. By combining genomic data and pathological pictures, *Sun et al.* have also proposed the GPMKL model for detecting the prognosis of breast cancer [9]. Similar to this, *Zhang et al.* introduced a unique Multiple Kernel Learning model (HI-MKL) for predicting the prognosis of Glioblastoma Multiforme by combining histopathological imaging and multi-omics data [10]. In the recent work done by Li-Hsin Cheng, Te-Cheng Hsu, and Che Lin, they integrated systems biology feature selection with ensemble learning. They selected genes with strong prognostic predictive potential [11]. *Ariya et al.* also introduced some deep learning based models for this prediction study [20–22].

Although the aforementioned deep learning-based approaches to cancer survival prediction have reached acceptable results, there are still a lot of prospects for development in the subsequent area. Previous research effort did not address how to use the underlying relationships of structural information between samples. In order to address this issue, we suggest a novel Multimodal Graph Convolutional Network (MGCN) for cancer patients survival prediction in this study. We first constructed two graphs utilizing the gene expression profile and the DNA copy number alteration (CNA) profile. The graph explores the inherent relationships among samples (patients) [12]. Based on the graphs, we suggest a graph convolutional network to get the embedding representation of each sample. Finally, the classification of long-term survival or short-term survival is made based on a given threshold (the community often adopts a 5-year survival rate for breast cancer) by utilizing embedded feature representation of individual samples. In brief, the following contributions are made by this paper:

- A graph is built for each particular modality (gene expression profile, CNA profile), with each node representing a sample. In order to study the intrinsic relationship between nodes, edges connecting any two nodes have been built based on the underlying correlation between nodes (samples).
- Graph Convolutional Network (GCN) is used to create a model that reflects the node embedding and learns the samples' connections in addition to their own attributes. The GCN model learns the nodes' hidden representations using both its own characteristics and the features of the nodes that are nearby.
- Using the final feature embedding produced by GCN, stacking of features or embeddings from individual modalities is applied. To highlight the crucial significance of the multimodal data, a random-forest classifier [14] is utilised to classify the stacked patients' data based on short-time and long-time survivors. More than 5-year survivors are considered long-time survivors and less than 5-year survivors are considered short-time survivors. The entire experiment uses ten-fold cross validation.

The rest of the paper is organized as follows. We outline the proposed work in Sect. 2. Section 3 discusses experimental results. Section 4 presents the paper's conclusion.

2   Proposed Work

In our proposed work (Fig. 1), we have developed GCN based feature extraction with a Random forest classifier for the classification of breast cancer patients as long-time and short-time survivors. To capture the structural relations among samples, a graph is formed by using the samples as nodes and the correlation existing between any two nodes as edges. A unique graph has been created for each modality (Gene expression or Copy Number Alteration). In order to establish an edge between any two nodes, a certain correlation threshold is chosen based on experimental results. Pearson correlation [18] has been used here. After forming the graph, convolution is applied to learn the irregular or non-Euclidean structured data which exists among connecting nodes [13]. After the GCN-based model training is finished, the final node embedding is recovered and the feature vector is extracted. The final feature vector is then created by concatenating or stacking the feature vectors from the individual modalities. The final classification is then carried out via the Random Forest classifier [14]. Here, due to a significantly less number of features existing in Clinical Data, GCN does not perform well in generating informative node embedding. So, clinical data is directly concatenated with the extracted features from other modalities to create the stacked feature set.

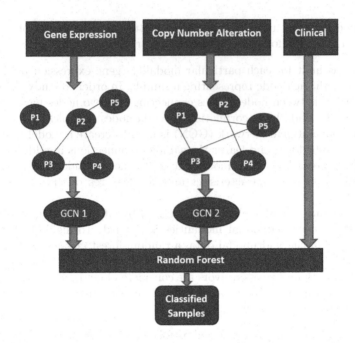

Fig. 1. MGCN model architecture

2.1   Data Set

The dataset that is accessible on Github[2] has been utilised here. The pre-processed version of METABRIC[3] dataset is available in this Github page. The METABRIC dataset contains roughly 24000, 26000, and 27 features for the gene expression data, Copy Number Alteration(CNA) profile, and clinical data, respectively. Clinical features include lymph nodes positive, age at diagnosis, grade etc. There are 1980 samples. Among which there are 1489 long-time survivors and 491 short-time survivors. More than 5 years survivors are considered as long-time survivors and less than 5 years survivors are considered as short-time survivors. To deal with short sample size and high dimensional data, *Sun et al.* [8] reduced the number of dimensions by using the well-known feature selection technique, mRMR [15]. Using mRMR, the 200 top-ranked genes are selected from CNA data (see table 4). Similarly, 400 top-ranked genes from gene expression data are selected and from Clinical data, only 25 features are selected. These are the all selected features that have been used for the breast cancer prognosis prediction for the existing MDNNMD [8] model. The same feature set is also utilized in our proposed model.

---

[2] https://github.com/USTC-HIlab/MDNNMD.
[3] https://www.cbioportal.org/study/summary?id=brcametabric.

Table 1. Selected features for the experiment

Dataset	Total Features	Selected Features
Clinical	27	25
Gene Expression	24368	400
CNA	26298	200

2.2   Graph Convolutional Network(GCN)

In a convolutional neural network (CNN), the input neurons are multiplied by a set of weights, also referred to as filters or kernels. The kernels allow CNNs to learn the features from nearby cells by acting as a sliding window across the entire data set. Similar operations are carried out using the semi-supervised Graph Convolutional Networks (GCN), where the model learns the features by looking at neighbouring nodes considering non-Euclidean structured data or irregular data:

Consider a graph G, having V and E as the set of nodes and edges, respectively. Here, the adjacency matrix is denoted as A, which represents the edge connection between nodes. The forward pass equation (Eq. 1) for the hidden layer of GCN is:

$$H^{[i+1]} = \sigma(W^{[i]} H^{[i]} A^*) \tag{1}$$

Here A^* is the normalized version [13] of A, $W^{[i]}$ is the weight matrix, $H^{[i]}$ is the $i^t h$ hidden layer, σ is the activation function and X is the node feature matrix. The dot product of A and X represents the sum of connected or neighboring nodes' features. The outcome of this dot product operation will be referred to as AX in this study.

In order to the model convergence, the features must be normalised to prevent vanishing/exploding gradients. By computing the Degree Matrix (D) and conducting the dot product operation of the inverse of D with AX, data is normalized (Eq. 2) in GCNs.

$$Normalized\,features = D^{-1}AX \tag{2}$$

The term "degree" is the number of connected edges of a particular node. Further the normalization equation is modified to symmetric normalization [13] (Eq. 3) as:

$$Normalized\,features = D^{-1/2}AD^{-1/2}X \tag{3}$$

So, the forward pass equation (eq. 4) for the hidden layer of GCN is:

$$H^{[i+1]} = \sigma(W^{[i]} H^{[i]} D^{-1/2}AD^{-1/2}X) \tag{4}$$

The Loss function is calculated by the cross-entropy error over all labeled examples.

2.3   Steps of Proposed Technique (MGCN)

Complete workflow of the proposed method is depicted in the following steps.

1. Individual Graphs are constructed for Gene expression and CNA modality, where samples are considered as nodes. Between any two nodes, the edge is established if the Pearson Correlation [18] between node features is more than experimentally obtained threshold (0.1 for Gene expression and 0.2 for CNA).
2. The 1980 samples in our data set are randomly split into 10 subgroups, of which 9 are combined and used as the training set, while the last subset is used as the testing set consecutively.
3. The additional training set is split into a training set that comprises 80% of the data and a validation set that comprises 20%. In order to determine the best settings, we first train each individual GCN independently for the CNA modality and gene expression.
4. GCN is applied to extract the features from final node embedding of Gene expression and CNA modality, separately. GCN is not applied on clinical data because it has very less number of features, which lacks to build the graph for structural information sharing.
5. All the clinical features along with extracted features from the final layer of trained GCN of gene expression and CNA are considered and concatenated together.
6. Standardisation is applied on stacked data. Further up-sampling is performed on Random Forest [14] to handle imbalance dataset.
7. Finally classification is performed using Random Forest classifier.

2.4   Experimental Setup

The proposed method is implemented in Python (version 3.7). We have used GCN for feature extraction and Random forest for class label prediction. In this experiment, GCN model is built and trained using Spektral API that is built on Tensorflow 2. To construct the graph for Gene expression data and CNA data the correlation threshold are chosen as 0.1 and 0.2, respectively. The proposed model is trained with 10 fold cross-validation. GCN model description is given in Table 2.

2.5   Objective Function

Our model is refined using a supervised environment. Here, overfitting of the model is addressed using the L2 regularisation [19] approach. The loss function utilised in this case is the cross-entropy loss (Eq. 5) defined below:

$$L(y_p, \hat{y}_p) = -\frac{1}{N} \sum_{i=0}^{N} [y_p i log \hat{y}_{pi} - (1 - y_{pi}) log(1 - \hat{y}_{pi})] + \frac{1}{\lambda} \sum_{l=1}^{L} \sum_{t=1}^{T} w_t^{l^2} \quad (5)$$

Table 2. Description of GCN model

# hidden layer of GCN	3
# First hidden layer units	500
#Second hidden layer units	200
#Third hidden layer units	100
# Activation function in hidden layers	ReLU
# Activation function in output layer	softmax
Training Epoch	80
Learning rate	0.001
Optimizer	SGD
Loss function	binary cross-entropy
	+ L2 regularization

Here the original class label is y_{p_i} whereas $\hat{y}_{p_i}$ is the predictive score. The batch size is N. L is the number of embedding layers and T is the number of trainable weight metrics. W is the weight matrics. W_t^l is the tth weight matrix in the lth layer.

3 Experimental Results

In this section, we have reported different experimental results obtained.

3.1 Evaluation Measures

As the evaluation measures, Accuracy(Acc), Precision(Pre), Matthews correlation coefficient (Mcc), Sensitivity(Sn), Specificity(Sp) and Balanced Accuracy values are considered. These metrices are defined below:

$$Accuracy = \frac{TP + TN}{TP + TN + FP + FN} \qquad Pre = \frac{TP}{TP + FP}$$

$$Mcc = \frac{TP \times TN - FP \times FN}{\sqrt{(TP + TN) \times (TP + FP) \times (TN + FN) \times (TN + FP)}}$$

$$Sensitivity = \frac{TP}{TP + FN}, \qquad Specificity = \frac{TN}{TN + FP}$$

$$BalancedAccuracy = \frac{Sensitivity + Specificity}{2}$$

Here TP, TN, FP, and FN denote the numbers of true positives, true negatives, false positives, and false negatives, respectively. A more trustworthy statistical measure is the Matthews correlation coefficient (MCC). It only generates a high score if the prediction generates good results in terms of all true positives, false negatives, true negatives, and false positives values. We have reported Balanced Accuracy because this metric is helpful when there is an imbalance between the two classes, meaning that one class appears substantially more frequently than the other. It is the arithmetic mean of sensitivity and specificity.

3.2 Results Using 10 Fold Cross-Validation Setting

Ten fold cross-validation result for the prediction of breast cancer survival using MGCN based stacked ensemble is depicted in Table 3. The experimental results are reported for all possible combinations of different modalities. In terms of Acc, Mcc, Pre, Sn, and Balanced Acc, we can see in the last column of Table 3, that all three combined modalities consistently outperform any two combined modalities.

Table 3. 10 fold cross validation results of MGCN

Metrics	Gene Exp+ CNA	Gene Exp+ Clinical	CNA+ Clinical	Gene Exp+ CNA+Clinical
Acc	0.674	0.814	0.805	**0.817**
Mcc	0.115	0.491	0.452	**0.498**
Pre	0.780	**0.869**	0.855	**0.869**
Sn	0.790	0.887	0.893	**0.891**
Sp	0.324	**0.593**	0.536	0.591
balanced Acc	0.557	0.740	0.714	**0.741**

3.3 Comparison with Other Prediction Methods

We have compared the proposed model with three widely used methods for prognosis of breast cancer: Logistic regression(LR) [17], Random Forest(RF) [14], Support Vector Machine(SVM) [16]. Table 4 presents the results in detail. It can be seen that the proposed work consistently produces the best outcomes. MGCN outperforms the Logistic regression and Support Vector Machine classifiers in terms of Acc, Mcc, Pre and Balanced Acc whereas it outperforms Random Forest classifiers in terms of Mcc, Pre and Balanced Acc respectively. Here, the gene expression, CNA, and clinical modalities are concatenated, standardized, and then used with LR, RF, and SVM for further classification. 10-fold cross-validation is used here.

Table 4. Comparison of performance metrics of LR, RF, SVM and proposed work

Metrices	LR [17]	RF [14]	SVM [16]	MGCN
Acc	0.82	**0.822**	0.778	0.817
Mcc	0.459	0.462	0.420	**0.498**
Pre	0.753	0.791	0.550	**0.869**
Sn	0.956	**0.966**	0.840	0.891
Sp	0.405	0.383	0.589	**0.591**
balanced Acc	0.680	0.674	0.714	**0.741**

In Table 5, the existing state-of-the-art MDNNMD [8] is considered for the performance comparison. As per the results published by the MDNNMD's work, two different stringency levels were considered: Sp = 99% and Sp = 95%. In order to get better predictive performance, they have considered manual selection of threshold values to maintain Specificity 99% and 95%, respectively, However, the standard threshold value for binary classification is 0.5 (i.e., if prediction ≥ 0.5 then predicted class is 1 otherwise 0). In our proposed method, common classification threshold (0.5) is giving good performance. So, we have not further manually set any classification threshold value. Although the specificity values of MDMMMD are 0.99 and 0.95, the sensitivity values are very poor, 0.20 and 0.45, respectively. Sensitivity of our model is 0.891, which is 69.1% and 44.1% better than sensitivity of MDNNMD with sp = 99% and sp = 95%, respectively. For performance comparison, we have considered the balanced accuracy metric, which is the average of sensitivity and specificity. Both sensitivity and specificity must be improved in order to get any improvement in balanced accuracy. Here, the balanced Acc of our method is 0.741%, which is 14.6% and 4.1% better than balanced Acc of MDNNMD with sp = 99% and sp = 95%, respectively. Mcc value (0.498) of our method also shows improvement by 1.2%, with respect to MDNNMD.

Table 5. 10 fold cross validation results with state of the art

Metrics	MDNNMD [8] (Sp = 0.99)	MDNNMD [8] (Sp = 0.95)	MGCN
Mcc	0.356	0.486	**0.498**
Pre	**0.875**	0.749	0.869
Sn	0.200	0.450	**0.891**
Sp	**0.990**	0.950	0.591
balanced Acc	0.595	0.700	**0.741**

3.4   Discussion

Based on the observed results, it is established that the MGCN for the breast cancer prognosis prediction is performing better with respect to state of the art [8] technique as well as other well known classification techniques like LR [17], RF [14] and SVM [16]. The extensive study has been done by combining different modalities using MGCN, and it is observed that after combining all three modalities, the model's performance has been improved and better results have been attained in terms of different metrics (see Table 3). This observation reveals that the underlying structural information sharing between the samples using Graph Convolution improves the predictive performance. It also reveals that the correlated samples' feature vector is improved with the information gained from the nearby samples, which was unexplored in the earlier studies.

4   Conclusion

In the current paper, we have proposed a multi-modal graph convolutional network (MGCN) for the correct prediction of breast cancer prognosis. Our dataset includes 1980 samples and feature sets with three modalities-Gene expression, Copy number alteration, and Clinical data. The Gene expression, Copy number alteration, and Clinical data contain 400, 200 and 25 pre-processed features respectively. Using experimentally determined threshold correlation values, edges connecting the samples are established to construct individual graphs for gene expression and CNA modalities. Further, the Graph convolution has been used to extract highly informative features from individual modality by structural information sharing among correlated samples. Extracted features from distinct modality are stacked and fed to Random Forest [14] classifier for correct class prediction of the samples. The precision, balanced accuracy, and Matthew's correlation coefficient values produced by this model are 0.869, 0.74, and 0.491, respectively. In our model, as the Mcc and Balanced Acc values are better than the state of art and the other prediction methods, it can be concluded that our propose model can handle well the imbalanced data set. The underlying structural information sharing among the samples allows for the construction of more enriched features and improves prediction performance. Also, its efficacy in predicting both true positive and true negative outcomes is good. In future work, we will apply this model for other disease prediction having imbalanced data set. In order to improve the model, we will also use an attention-based strategy by prioritizing the feature sets.

Acknowledgment. Dr. Sriparna Saha gratefully acknowledges the Young Faculty Research Fellowship (YFRF) Award, supported by Visvesvaraya Ph.D. Scheme for Electronics and IT, Ministry of Electronics and Information Technology (MeitY), Government of India, being implemented by Digital India Corporation (formerly Media Lab Asia) for carrying out this research.

References

1. Yersal, O., Barutca, S.: Biological subtypes of breast cancer: Prognostic and therapeutic implications. World J. Clin. Oncol. **5**(3), 412–424 (2014). https://doi.org/10.5306/wjco.v5.i3.412
2. Xiao, Y., Jun, W., Lin, Z., Zhao, X.: A deep learning-based multi-model ensemble method for cancer prediction. Comput. Methods Programs Biomed. **153**, 1–9 (2018)
3. Cheerla, A., Gevaert, O.: Deep learning with multimodal representation for pancancer prognosis prediction. Bioinformatics **35**(14), i446–i454 (2019)
4. Kim, D.W., Lee, S., Kwon, S., Nam, W.: Deep learningbased survival prediction of oral cancer patients. Sci. Reports **9**(1), 1–10 (2019)
5. Xu, X., Ya, Z., Liang, Z., Wang, M., Li, A.: A gene signature for breast cancer prognosis using support vector machine. In: International Conference on BioMedical Engineering and Informatics, pp. 928–931 (2012)

6. Sun, Y., Goodison, S., Li, J., Liu, L., Farmerie, W.: Improved breast cancer prognosis through the combination of clinical and genetic markers. Bioinformatics **23**(1), 30–37 (2006)
7. Gevaert, O., Smet, F.D., Timmerman, D., Moreau, Y., Moor, B.D.: Predicting the prognosis of breast cancer by integrating clinical and microarray data with bayesian networks. Bioinformatics **22**(14), e184–e190 (2006)
8. Sun, D., Wang, M., Li, A.: A multimodal deep neural network for human breast cancer prognosis prediction by integrating multi-dimensional data. IEEE/ACM Trans. Comput. Biol. Bioinf. **16**(3), 841–850 (2019)
9. Sun, D., Li, A., Tang, B., Wang, M.: Integrating genomic data and pathological images to effectively predict breast cancer clinical outcome. Comput. Methods Programs Biomed. **161**, 45–63 (2018)
10. Zhang, Y., Li, A., He, J., Wang, M.: A novel MKL method for GBM prognosis prediction by integrating histopathological image and multi-omics data. IEEE J. Biomed. Health Inform. **24**(1), 171–179 (2020)
11. Cheng, L.H., Hsu, T.C., Lin, C.: Integrating ensemble systems biology feature selection and bimodal deep neural network for breast cancer prognosis prediction. Sci Rep. 2021 Jul 21;11(1):14914. PMID: 34290286; PMCID: PMC8295302. https://doi.org/10.1038/s41598-021-92864-y
12. Zhang, S., Tong, H., Xu, J., Maciejewski, R.: Graph convolutional networks: a comprehensive review. Comput. Social Netw. **6**(1), 1–23 (2019). https://doi.org/10.1186/s40649-019-0069-y
13. Kipf, T., Welling, M.: Semi-Supervised Classification with Graph Convolutional Networks (2017). arXiv preprint arXiv:1609.02907. ICLR 2017
14. Breiman, L.: Random Forests. Mach. Learn. **45**, 5–32 (2001). https://doi.org/10.1023/A:1010933404324
15. Peng, H., Long, F., Ding, C.: Feature selection based on mutual information criteria of max-dependency, max-relevance, and minredundancy. IEEE Trans. Pattern Anal. Mach. Intell. **27**(8), 1226–1238 (2005)
16. Xu, X., Zhang, Y., Zou, L., Wang, M., Li, A.: A gene signature for breast cancer prognosis using support vector machine. In: Biomedical Engineering and Informatics (BMEI), 2012 5th International Conference on IEEE, pp. 928–931 (2012)
17. Jefferson, M., Pendleton, N., Lucas, S., Horan, M.:MComparison of a genetic algorithm neural network with logistic regression for predicting outcome after surgery for patients with nonsmall cell lung carcinoma Cancer, **79**(7), 1338–1342 (1997)
18. Immink, K.A.S., Weber, J.H.: Minimum pearson distance detection for multilevel channels with gain and/or offset mismatch. IEEE Trans. Inf. Theor. **60**(10), 5966–5974 (2014). https://doi.org/10.1109/TIT.2014.2342744
19. Phaisangittisagul, E.: An Analysis of the Regularization Between L2 and Dropout in Single Hidden Layer Neural Network. In: 2016 7th International Conference on Intelligent Systems, Modelling and Simulation (ISMS), 2016, pp. 174–179, https://doi.org/10.1109/ISMS.2016.14
20. Arya, N., Saha, S.: Multi-modal advanced deep learning architectures for breast cancer survival prediction, Knowledge-Based Systems, Volume 221, 2021, 106965, ISSN 0950-7051. https://doi.org/10.1016/j.knosys.2021.106965.
21. Arya, N., Saha, S.: Multi-Modal Classification for Human Breast Cancer Prognosis Prediction: Proposal of Deep-Learning Based Stacked Ensemble Model. In: IEEE/ACM Transactions on Computational Biology and Bioinformatics, vol. 19, no. 2, pp. 1032–1041, 1 March-April 2022, https://doi.org/10.1109/TCBB.2020.3018467

22. Arya, N., Saha, S.: Generative incomplete multi-view prognosis predictor for breast cancer: GIMPP. IEEE/ACM Trans. Comput. Biol. Bioinform. **9**(4), 2252–2263. Epub 2022 Aug 8. PMID: 34143737. https://doi.org/10.1109/TCBB.2021.3090458

Anomaly Detection in Surveillance Videos Using Transformer Based Attention Model

Kapil Deshpande[1], Narinder Singh Punn[1(✉)] , Sanjay Kumar Sonbhadra[2] ,
and Sonali Agarwal[1]

[1] Indian Institute of Information Technology Allahabad,
Jhalwa, Prayagraj, Uttar Pradesh, India
{mit2020040,pse2017002,sonali}@iiita.ac.in
[2] Department of CSE, ITER, Siksha 'O' Anusandhan, Bhubaneswar, Odisha, India
sanjaykumarsonbhadra@soa.ac.in

Abstract. Surveillance footage can catch a wide range of realistic anomalies. This research suggests using a weakly supervised strategy to avoid annotating anomalous segments in training videos, which is time consuming. In this approach only video level labels are used to obtain frame level anomaly scores. Weakly supervised video anomaly detection (WSVAD) suffers from the wrong identification of abnormal and normal instances during the training process. Therefore it is important to extract better quality features from the available videos. With this motivation, the present paper uses better quality transformer-based features named Videoswin Features followed by the attention layer based on dilated convolution and self attention to capture long and short range dependencies in temporal domain. This gives us a better understanding of available videos. The proposed framework is validated on real-world dataset i.e. ShanghaiTech Campus dataset which results in competitive performance than current state-of-the-art methods. The model and the code are available at https://github.com/kapildeshpande/Anomaly-Detection-in-Surveillance-Videos.

Keywords: Video anomaly detection · Weakly supervised · Videoswin features · Attention layer

1 Introduction

Video anomaly detection has gained a lot of attention due to its applications in surveillance systems. The cost of deploying surveillance systems has reduced significantly in recent years but it still requires human intervention in detecting anomalous events like fighting, abusing, stealing, etc. Considering the additional cost of human labor and the loss of productive time, the development of intelligent algorithms for video anomaly detection is required. The vague nature of

---

All authors contributed equally.

© The Author(s), under exclusive license to Springer Nature Singapore Pte Ltd. 2023
M. Tanveer et al. (Eds.): ICONIP 2022, CCIS 1794, pp. 199–211, 2023.
https://doi.org/10.1007/978-981-99-1648-1_17

anomaly and the unavailability of annotated data makes anomaly detection difficult. There are various unsupervised [1,2] and weakly supervised [3–5] solutions present. Generally, unsupervised anomaly detection tries to learn the distribution of normal events and mark outliers as anomalies. Since it is impossible to learn all possible normal events distribution therefore this model is highly biased and fails in the case of real-world events. It tries to combat the above problem by using both normal and anomalous events while training.

Weakly supervised approaches require significantly less effort as compared to supervised learning because it requires only video-level labels instead of frame-level. However the major challenge of weakly supervised approaches is in identifying the abnormal snippets from the anomalous videos, this is because: the abnormal videos contain a large number of normal snippets and the abnormal events can have only slight differences from normal events. All these above issues can be resolved by using multiple instance learning (MIL) [6] where the training set is divided into the same numbers of abnormal and normal snippets. Two bags are created i.e. a normal bag which contains snippets from a normal video and an abnormal bag that contains snippets from an abnormal video. The snippet with the maximum anomaly score is selected from each bag and the loss is back propagated. Although this method partially addresses the previous issues but it also introduces the following problems: The highest anomaly score can be from normal bag instead of abnormal bag and when anomaly videos have multiple anomaly in the single video it fails to leverage additional anomalies because it only take the snippet with highest anomaly score from the abnormal bag.

To address all these issues the proposed solution used the Robust Temporal Feature Magnitude (RTFM) learning model inspired by Tian et al. [7]. This model relies on the temporal feature magnitude i.e. l2 norm of features for anomaly detection, where normal snippets are represented by low magnitude features, while abnormal snippets are represented by high magnitude features. This model try to maximize δ_{score} which denotes the difference between the mean of l2 norm of top K features from the abnormal and normal bag where K is the number of abnormal snippets in an abnormal video. This solves the previously discussed problem because: It's more likely to choose anomalous snippets from abnormal videos instead of normal videos. It can utilize multiple anomalies in the anomaly videos which will result in better utilization of training data.

It is important to extract better features from the available videos to avoid the wrong identification of abnormal and normal instances during the training process. Researchers have been inspired to employ video transformers as feature extractors to handle anomaly detection tasks as a result of their recent success with video classification tasks. Therefore the proposed model uses a transformer based features named Videoswin Features [8] which have consistently outperformed the CNN based models like I3D [9], C3D [10], etc. The feature extraction is followed by an attention layer based on dilated convolution to capture most relevant long and short range dependencies [11–14]. The proposed solution is validated on a real-world dataset i.e. ShanghaiTech Campus dataset which results in competitive performance than current state-of-the-art methods. The major contribution of the present research work are described below:

- To improve the understanding of given videos, a newer transformer based feature extraction model is used named videoswin transformer.
- To highlight relevant features an attention layer based on dilated convolution and self attention that captures long and short range temporal dependencies.
- A comparative study with current state-of-the-art approaches is conducted to examine the effects of the proposed model on the open source ShanghaiTech dataset. The proposed model achieved competitive performance (AUC score) than current state-of-the-art methods.

The rest of the paper is divided into various sections, where Sect. 2 covers the prevailing work in anomaly detection, followed by proposed methodology in Sect. 3. Section 4 presents the experimental analysis and finally concluding remarks are presented in Sect. 5.

2   Related Work

Traditional video anomaly detection uses unsupervised learning [15,16] algorithms where it tries to learn the distribution of normal events and mark outliers as anomalies. Since it is impossible to learn all possible normal events distribution therefore this model is highly biased and fails in the case of real-world events. Other methods use one-class classification [1,2] assuming only normal labeled data is available. Some approaches rely on tracking [1,17] to model people's regular movement and identify deviations as anomalies. Since it is tough to acquire accurate information of tracks, numerous strategies for avoiding tracking and learning global motion patterns, such as topic modeling [18], have been used, context-driven method [19] social force models [20], histogram-based methods [21], motion patterns [22], Hidden Markov Model (HMM) on local spatiotemporal volumes[23], and mixtures of dynamic textures model [19]. These techniques learn distributions of normal motion patterns from training videos of normal behaviors and discover low likely patterns as anomalies. After the initial success of the sparse representation and dictionary learning methodologies, researchers employed sparse representation [15,16] to learn the dictionary of patterns. Where anomalous patterns have high reconstruction errors during testing. After the initial success of deep learning in image classification, many techniques for video action classification [24,25] have been developed.

Alternatively, some approaches rely on data reconstruction utilizing generative models to learn normal sample representations by (adversarial) reducing the reconstruction error [26–28]. These methods presume that undetected abnormal videos/images can often be poorly reconstructed, and samples with large reconstruction errors are considered anomalies. These techniques may overfit the training data and fail to distinguish abnormal from normal events due to a lack of prior knowledge about anomaly.

To solve the above problems Sultani et al. [6] introduced a weakly supervised solution that can learn anomaly patterns by using both normal and anomaly videos using MIL-based models with CNN as the backbone for feature extraction. However, it fails to separate noise present in the positive bag and this can lead to normal snippets being mistaken as abnormal. In this context, to clear the noise present in the positive bag Zhong et al. [29] proposed to use a graph convolution neural network. Although it partially solved the problem, it was computationally heavy. The RTFM model [7] which solves the above problem by using the l2 norm-based ranking loss function. Although it still uses CNN as the backbone for feature extraction.

To capture consistency between successive frames, traditional attention approaches employ consecutive frames and transform them into handcrafted motion trajectories. Other methods such as stacked RNN [30], LSTM [3], convolutional LSTM [3], and GCN-based [29] can capture short-range fixed-order temporal dependencies but they either fail to capture long-range dependencies or they are computationally expensive. Following this context, the proposed attention layer uses dilated convolution based attention mechanism which captures short and long-range temporal dependencies and is computationally inexpensive as compared to other methods. The proposed method uses a more effective transformer-based model for feature extraction and a temporal attention layer for necessary feature enhancement, thus improving the model's overall performance.

3   Proposed Method

The proposed framework is divided into 3 stages as given in Fig. 1. As the exact location or frame-level labels are not provided for learning, the proposed solution follows a weakly supervised learning where the videos of different duration are divided into a fixed number of snippets containing the same number of frames. The proposed solution assumed that snippets obtained from an anomaly video contain at least one anomaly snippet, but the snippets from normal videos contain all normal snippets. In stage 1, A pre-trained videoswin model for feature extraction of the snippets. In stage 2 an attention layer is applied to the feature to capture relevant long and short range dependencies in the temporal domain. At last in stage 3 RTFM model is used for anomaly detection on the features obtained from stage 3.

3.1   Stage 1 (Feature Extraction)

To extract features this paper uses videoswin transformer model which is trained on large-scale datasets like Kinetics [31] and ImageNet [32]. The use of a pre-trained model allows us to extract better quality features. Traditional transformer models calculate self-attention with respect to all the elements present but in the case of images, it is computationally expensive to perform. To solve this issue, the swin transformer divides images into windows and calculates self-attention inside this window only. Now it slides the window on the images to get the self-attention value of the whole set of images more efficiently.

To begin the feature extraction process, the first step is to divide the videos into frames (of size let's say H × W). Now the set of these frames (T) makes the

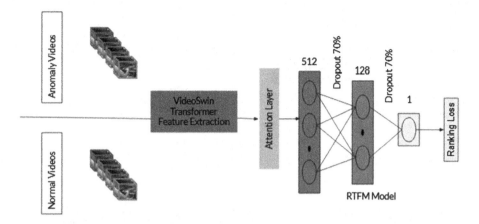

Fig. 1. The proposed model architecture.

video for feature extraction where each video has RGB channels. This gives us the input dimension as N × C × T × H × W, where N is the batch size and C is the number of channels.

3.2   Stage 2 (Attention Layer)

The main objective of this stage is to learn the discriminative representation of normal and abnormal snippets by improving the quality of the feature map obtained from stage 1. This objective is achieved using an attention layer that can encode the long and short range dependencies in temporal domain on the feature map while drawing focus of the model towards most relevant features.

The proposed attention layer is shown in Fig. 2. Given an input feature map $F \in \mathbb{R}^{T \times D}$, it produces the output attention feature maps $F' \in \mathbb{R}^{T \times D}$. It consists of two modules, the one on the left is a short range module, it is used to capture short-term temporal dependencies and the one on the right is a long range module it is used to compute global temporal context.

To calculate the global temporal context, the pairwise temporal self attention is calculated which produces the feature map $M \in \mathbb{R}^{T \times T}$. It first applies the conv1D layer to reduce information to $F^c \in \mathbb{R}^{T \times D/4}$ where $F^c = \text{conv1D}(F)$, then it applies 3 conv1d layers separately. $F^{c1} = \text{conv1D}(F^c)$, $F^{c2} = \text{conv1D}(F^c)$, $F^{c3} = \text{conv1D}(F^c)$. It will combine these 3 conv1D layers with $F^{c4} = \text{conv1D}((F^{c1} * (F^{c2})^T) * F^{c3})$. A residual is added, which gives the final output, $M = F^{c4} + F^c$, where $M \in \mathbb{R}^{T \times T}$.

To calculate the short term temporal dependencies it applies the conv1D layer which gives it the output, $K = \text{conv1D}(F)$, where $F \in \mathbb{R}^{T \times D}$. The output M from the long range module is concatenated with the output K from the short range module and a residual connection is added to give us the final output, $F' = \text{concat}(M, K) + F^c$, where $F \in \mathbb{R}^{T \times D}$.

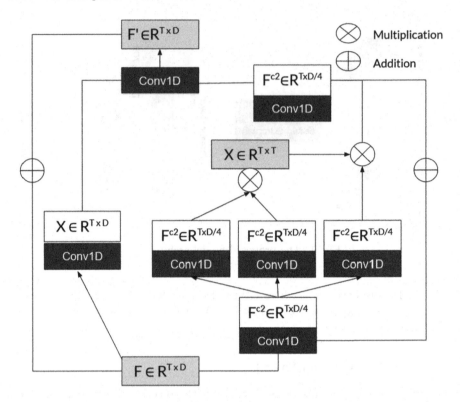

Fig. 2. The proposed attention layer architecture

3.3   Stage 3 (Anomaly Detection)

The proposed anomaly detection model uses Robust Temporal Feature Magnitude Learning (RTFM) model, in which temporal feature magnitude i.e. l2 norm of video snippets are used for anomaly detection where normal snippets are represented by low magnitude features, while abnormal snippets are represented by high magnitude features. The proposed model assumes that anomalous snippets have a larger mean feature magnitude than normal snippets.

Let $\|x\|$ be the feature magnitude of snippets where x^+ means abnormal snippet and x^- means normal snippet, which are obtained by normal (X^+) and abnormal (X^-) videos. Model learns by trying to maximize the $\delta_{\text{score}}(X^+, X^-)$ which denotes the difference between the mean of l2 norm of topK features from the abnormal and normal bag where k is the number of abnormal snippets in abnormal video. To maximize the $\delta_{\text{score}}(X^+, X^-)$, the loss function (shown in 1) is optimized during backpropagation.

$$L(X^+, X^-) = max(0, m - mean(topK(\|X^+\|))$$
$$+ mean(topK(\|X^-\|)) \tag{1}$$

where m is a constant predefined margin.

A binary cross-entropy based loss function is applied to learn the snippet classifier as shown in 2. It trains a snippet classifier with 0 and 1 class labels indicating normal and abnormal snippets respectively.

$$loss = -ylog(x) + (1 - y)log(1 - x) \tag{2}$$

where x is the mean of l2 norm of topK features, $x = mean(topK(\|X^+\|))$, and y is the binary value indicating actual class labels as normal or abnormal.

$$Smoothness = \Sigma f(v^i) - f(v^{i+1})^2 \tag{3}$$

Temporal smoothness is used between consecutive video snippets to vary anomaly score smoothly between video snippets.

$$Sparsity = \Sigma f(v_i) \tag{4}$$

Anomaly frequently happens over a brief period of time in real-world circumstances which leads to sparse anomaly scores of segments in the anomalous bag. To avoid this issue, a sparsity term is used.

$$Finalloss = \lambda 1 * Eq.1 + \lambda 2 * Eq.2 +$$
$$\lambda 3 * Eq.3 + \lambda 4 * Eq.4 \tag{5}$$

where λ's are the respective learning rates for the Eq.s.

4 Experiments

4.1 Dataset Description

This paper uses a large-scale video anomaly detection dataset called the ShanghaiTech Campus dataset [33]. It includes video from fixed angle street surveillance cameras. It has 437 videos from 12 different backgrounds, with 130 anomalous and 307 normal videos. This is a popular benchmark dataset for anomaly detection tasks that uses both anomalous and normal data. To restructure the dataset into a weakly supervised training set, Zhong et al. [29] picked a sample of anomalous testing videos and turned them into training videos so that all 13 background scenes are covered by the training and testing set. To convert the dataset into weekly supervised, this paper used the same approach as used by Zhong et al. [29] and Tian et al. [7]. Figure 3 shows the sample normal and abnormal clips from the dataset.

ShanghaiTech

Normal

Abnormal

Fig. 3. ShanghaiTech dataset normal and abnormal clips

4.2 Evaluation Metric

To measure the model's performance, this paper used frame-level receiver operating characteristics (ROC) as well as its area under the curve (AUC) score, following the previous methods [6, 7, 29]. AUC score is a measure of separability. It represents the model's ability to discriminate between classes. An AUC score of 1 means the model can separate both classes perfectly. AUC score of 0 means the model is reciprocating the results means it predicts positive class as negative and vice-versa. AUC score of 0.5 means the model has no class separation capacity. The ROC curve is plotted at all possible classification thresholds by calculating the values of TPR and FPR at every threshold from 0 to 1.

4.3 Implementation Details

For feature extraction from pre-trained videoswin transformer model on Kinetics dataset, each video is divided into frames of size 224×224, for video is divided into T = 32 temporal segments where each segment is 16 frames long, this gives us ten crop features of dimensions 32×1024. Cropping snippets into the four corners, center and their flipped form is referred as ten cropping.

In Eq. 1 the margin, $m = 100$ and the value of $k = 3$. The 3 fully connected (FC) layers in the RTFM model have 512, 128 and 1 nodes respectively where 1st and 2nd FC layer is followed by a ReLU activation function and the last layer is followed by sigmoid function. A dropout function is added after every layer with rate = 0.7. The model is trained using adam optimizer with weight decay of 0.005 and learning rate of 0.001 with batch size = 32 for 500 epochs. Each mini batch has 32 samples chosen at random from normal and abnormal videos. For fare comparison, this paper used the same benchmark setup used by Sultani et al. [6], Zhong et al. [29] and Tian et al. [7].

4.4 Result Analysis

The results are reported on the ShanghaiTech Campus dataset [33]. Where two backbone models for feature extraction are used namely I3D [9] and videoswin [8]. Comparisons with the previous weakly supervised solutions are given in Table 1 and visually presented in Fig. 4. Furthermore, the inference drawn is analysed with the help of ROC curves as given in Fig. 5.

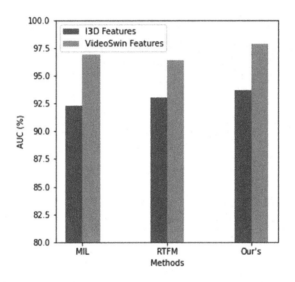

Fig. 4. Comparison I3D vs Videoswin Features

Table 1. The comparative analysis of video anomaly detection models. The best outcomes are shown in bold font.

Method	Feature	AUC
MIL	I3D	92.3
MIL	Videoswin	96.9
RTFM	I3D	93.0
RTFM	Videoswin	96.4
Proposed model	I3D	93.7
Proposed model	**Videoswin**	**97.9**

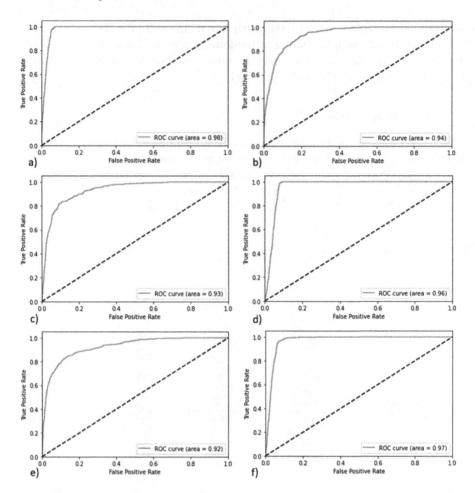

Fig. 5. ROC curves of the a) proposed model using videoswin backbone, b) proposed model using I3D backbone, c) RTFM model using I3D backbone, d) RTFM model using videoswin backbone, e) MIL model using I3D backbone, and f) MIL model using videoswin backbone

The usage of videoswin features leads to better performance than I3D features because of improved video understanding. MIL model specially performed better with videoswin features, it even outperformed the RTFM model which was previously performing better than MIL with I3D features. To compare the attention layer introduced, this paper added a different attention layer to previous methods namely LSTM, CBAM [34], RTFM's Attention Layer [7]. The results obtained are given in Table 2. With the introduction of the proposed attention layer a better AUC score of around 1% is acquired. The usage of LSTM and CBAM results in decreased performance because the models fail when high dimensional feature maps are given as input [35].

Table 2. The comparative analysis of various attention layers on the video anomaly detection models. The best outcomes are shown in bold font.

Method	Feature	AUC
MIL + LSTM	I3D	89.0
MIL + LSTM	Videoswin	96.6
RTFM + LSTM	I3D	89.0
RTFM + LSTM	Videoswin	96.6
MIL + CBAM	I3D	88.0
MIL + CBAM	Videoswin	96.9
RTFM + CBAM	I3D	87.5
RTFM + CBAM	Videoswin	96.2
RTFM + No attention	I3D	91.0
RTFM + No attention	Videoswin	97.1
Proposed model	**Videoswin**	**97.9**

5   Conclusion

In this research work, a weakly supervised strategy is proposed. It uses better quality features extracted from videoswin transformer model, followed by an attention layer to encode the long and short range dependencies in the temporal domain. The use of the robust temporal feature magnitude (RTFM) model makes this approach better than multiple instance learning (MIL) based techniques because it learns more discriminative features than the MIL model and it exploits abnormal data more easily. It is found from experiments that the use of better quality features and an improved attention layer resulted in improved performance of the model. In future, more experiments can be performed by exploring different strategies to minimize the noise present in the positive bag.

References

1. Basharat, A., Gritai, A., Shah, M.: Learning object motion patterns for anomaly detection and improved object detection. In: 2008 IEEE Conference On Computer Vision and Pattern Recognition, pp. 1–8. IEEE (2008)
2. Wang, J., et al.: Learning fine-grained image similarity with deep ranking. In: Proceedings of the IEEE Conference on Computer Vision and Pattern Recognition, pp. 1386–1393 (2014)
3. Liu, W., Luo, W., Li, Z., Zhao, P., Gao, S., et al.: Margin learning embedded prediction for video anomaly detection with a few anomalies. In: IJCAI, pp. 3023–3030 (2019)
4. Pang, G., Cao, L., Chen, L., Liu, H.: Learning representations of ultrahigh-dimensional data for random distance-based outlier detection. In: Proceedings of the 24th ACM SIGKDD International Conference on Knowledge Discovery & Data Mining, pp. 2041–2050 (2018)

5. Pang, G., Shen, C., van den Hengel, A.: Deep anomaly detection with deviation networks. In: Proceedings of the 25th ACM SIGKDD International Conference On Knowledge Discovery & Data Mining, pp. 353–362 (2019)
6. Sultani, W., Chen, C., Shah, M.: Real-world anomaly detection in surveillance videos. In: Proceedings of the IEEE Conference on Computer Vision and Pattern Recognition, pp. 6479–6488 (2018)
7. Tian, Y., Pang, G., Chen, Y., Singh, R., Verjans, J.W., Carneiro, G.: Weakly-supervised video anomaly detection with contrastive learning of long and short-range temporal features (2021)
8. Liu, Z., et al.: Video swin transformer. arXiv preprint arXiv:2106.13230 (2021)
9. Carreira, J., Zisserman, A.: Quo vadis, action recognition? a new model and the kinetics dataset. In: proceedings of the IEEE Conference on Computer Vision and Pattern Recognition, pp. 6299–6308 (2017)
10. Tran, D., Bourdev, L.D., Fergus, R., Torresani, L., Paluri, M.: C3d: generic features for video analysis, vol. 2(7), p. 8. CoRR, abs/ arXiv: 1412.0767 (2014)
11. Punn, N.S., Agarwal, S.: Chs-net: A deep learning approach for hierarchical segmentation of covid-19 via ct images. Neural Proces. Lett. 1–22 (2022)
12. Punn, N.S., Agarwal, S.: Rca-iunet: a residual cross-spatial attention-guided inception u-net model for tumor segmentation in breast ultrasound imaging. Mach. Vis. Appl. 33(2), 1–10 (2022)
13. Agrawal, P., Punn, N.S., Sonbhadra, S.K., Agarwal, S.: Impact of attention on adversarial robustness of image classification models. In: 2021 IEEE International Conference on Big Data (Big Data), pp. 3013–3019. IEEE (2021)
14. Agarwal, S., Pandey, G.: Svm based context awareness using body area sensor network for pervasive healthcare monitoring. In: Proceedings of the First International Conference on Intelligent Interactive Technologies and Multimedia, pp. 271–278 (2010)
15. Lu, C., Shi, J., Jia, J.: Abnormal event detection at 150 fps in matlab. In: Proceedings of the IEEE International Conference on Computer Vision, pp. 2720–2727 (2013)
16. Zhao, B., Fei-Fei, L., Xing, E.P.: Online detection of unusual events in videos via dynamic sparse coding. CVPR **2011**, 3313–3320 (2011)
17. Wu, S., Moore, B.E., Shah, M.: Chaotic invariants of lagrangian particle trajectories for anomaly detection in crowded scenes. In: 2010 IEEE Computer Society Conference on Computer Vision and Pattern Recognition, pp. 2054–2060 (2010)
18. Hospedales, T., Gong, S., Xiang, T.: A markov clustering topic model for mining behaviour in video. In: 2009 IEEE 12th International Conference on Computer Vision, pp. 1165–1172. IEEE (2009)
19. Li, W., Mahadevan, V., Vasconcelos, N.: Anomaly detection and localization in crowded scenes. IEEE Trans. Pattern Anal. Mach. Intell. 36(1), 18–32 (2014). https://doi.org/10.1109/TPAMI.2013.111
20. Mehran, R., Oyama, A., Shah, M.: Abnormal crowd behavior detection using social force model. In: 2009 IEEE Conference on Computer Vision and Pattern Recognition, pp. 935–942 (2009). https://doi.org/10.1109/CVPR.2009.5206641
21. Cui, X., Liu, Q., Gao, M., Metaxas, D.N.: Abnormal detection using interaction energy potentials. In: CVPR 2011, pp. 3161–3167. IEEE (2011)
22. Saleemi, I., Shafique, K., Shah, M.: Probabilistic modeling of scene dynamics for applications in visual surveillance. IEEE Trans. Pattern Anal. Mach. Intell. 31(8), 1472–1485 (2008)

23. Kratz, L., Nishino, K.: Anomaly detection in extremely crowded scenes using spatio-temporal motion pattern models. In: 2009 IEEE Conference on Computer Vision and Pattern Recognition, pp. 1446–1453 (2009). https://doi.org/10.1109/CVPR.2009.5206771

24. Karpathy, A., Toderici, G., Shetty, S., Leung, T., Sukthankar, R., Fei-Fei, L.: Large-scale video classification with convolutional neural networks. In: Proceedings of the IEEE conference on Computer Vision and Pattern Recognition, pp. 1725–1732 (2014)

25. Tran, D., Bourdev, L., Fergus, R., Torresani, L., Paluri, M.: Learning spatiotemporal features with 3d convolutional networks. In: Proceedings of the IEEE International Conference on Computer Vision, pp. 4489–4497 (2015)

26. Venkataramanan, S., Peng, K.C., Singh, R.V., Mahalanobis, A.: Attention guided anomaly detection and localization in images. arXiv preprint arXiv:1911.08616 (2019)

27. Xu, D., Ricci, E., Yan, Y., Song, J., Sebe, N.: Learning deep representations of appearance and motion for anomalous event detection. arXiv preprint arXiv:1510.01553 (2015)

28. Zong, B., et al.: Deep autoencoding gaussian mixture model for unsupervised anomaly detection. In: ICLR (2018)

29. Zhong, J.X., Li, N., Kong, W., Liu, S., Li, T.H., Li, G.: Graph convolutional label noise cleaner: Train a plug-and-play action classifier for anomaly detection. In: Proceedings of the IEEE/CVF Conference on Computer Vision and Pattern Recognition, pp. 1237–1246 (2019)

30. Luo, W., Liu, W., Gao, S.: A revisit of sparse coding based anomaly detection in stacked rnn framework. In: Proceedings of the IEEE International Conference on Computer Vision, pp. 341–349 (2017)

31. Carreira, J., Noland, E., Hillier, C., Zisserman, A.: A short note on the kinetics-700 human action dataset. arXiv preprint arXiv:1907.06987 (2019)

32. Deng, J., Dong, W., Socher, R., Li, L.J., Li, K., Fei-Fei, L.: Imagenet: A large-scale hierarchical image database. In: 2009 IEEE Conference on Computer Vision and Pattern Recognition, pp. 248–255. IEEE (2009)

33. Liu, W., Luo, W., Lian, D., Gao, S.: Future frame prediction for anomaly detection-a new baseline. In: Proceedings of the IEEE Conference on Computer Vision and Pattern Recognition, pp. 6536–6545 (2018)

34. Woo, S., Park, J., Lee, J.-Y., Kweon, I.S.: CBAM: convolutional block attention module. In: Ferrari, V., Hebert, M., Sminchisescu, C., Weiss, Y. (eds.) ECCV 2018. LNCS, vol. 11211, pp. 3–19. Springer, Cham (2018). https://doi.org/10.1007/978-3-030-01234-2_1

35. Majhi, S., Dash, R., Sa, P.K.: Temporal pooling in inflated 3dcnn for weakly-supervised video anomaly detection. In: 2020 11th International Conference on Computing, Communication and Networking Technologies (ICCCNT), pp. 1–6. IEEE (2020)

Change Detection in Hyperspectral Images Using Deep Feature Extraction and Active Learning

Debasrita Chakraborty[1] , Susmita Ghosh[2] , Ashish Ghosh[1(✉)] ,
and Emmett J. Ientilucci[3]

[1] Indian Statistical Institute, Kolkata, India
ash@isical.ac.in
[2] Jadavpur University, Kolkata, India
[3] Rochester Institute of Technology, New York, USA
emmett@cis.rit.edu

Abstract. Manual labelling of changes present in a pair of remotely sensed hyperspectral images is costly and time-consuming. As the label information is less, one might take an active learning approach where the machine learning model can learn with smart human supervision. However, there is a lack of research in the literature around change detection in partially labelled hyperspectral images. This article proposes a convolutional autoencoder-based model for detecting changes in hyperspectral images, which would reduce the data's dimensionality and learn from unlabelled samples. The final classifier model has been re-trained using active learning. After each epoch, the model builds a decision boundary and automatically picks samples for manual labelling based on an uncertainty parameter modelled using the beta distribution function. The selected pixels' label information is fed into the model to improve the accuracy of change detection, and the model is iterated a number of times by adding the labelled examples to the training set. Starting with a small and non-optimal training set, the model is permitted to query for the labels of k most uncertain samples at each iteration to build the updated decision boundary. It has been seen that the optimal decision boundary could be constructed by fewer labelled samples only and thus eliminating the requirement for a huge training set. According to the results, the suggested model needs extremely minimal training data (only 17.14 % and 18.57 % of training data for Bay Area and Santa Barbara images respectively) to obtain a comparatively higher level of performance.

Keywords: Hyperspectral Images · Change Detection · Active Learning · Convolutional Neural Network

1 Introduction

Change detection [19] in a pair of co-registered [16] remotely sensed images is a relatively complex task. The problem becomes even more challenging when

M. Tanveer et al. (Eds.): ICONIP 2022, CCIS 1794, pp. 212–223, 2023.
https://doi.org/10.1007/978-981-99-1648-1_18

the dimensionality of the images is high as seen for hyperspectral image pairs [2]. These images [7] provide information of a location through many bands involving wavelengths outside the visible spectrum. Each pixel, thus contains immense information about a sizeable region of the place. Thus, a pixel captures both spatial and spectral information simultaneously. As manually labelling each pixel is very difficult and expensive, the challenge of detecting changes using supervision methods becomes even more unfavourable.

The classification performance is often influenced by the quality of labelled samples used during training. Manual generation of training set is often accomplished by visual assessment of a scene and sequential labelling of each pixel. This step is time intensive, tedious, costly and redundant. In reality, a training set includes numerous neighborhood pixels with the same information. Although such redundancy is not hazardous to the quality of the outcomes if handled appropriately, it significantly slows down the training process. To make the models as efficient as feasible, the training set should be kept as small as possible and concentrated on the pixels that truly contribute to decision boundary thereby increasing the model's performance. Algorithms [8], involving active learning [15] can assist in overcoming the paucity of training data.

This manuscript presents an active learning [5] based strategy for semi-automatic change detection in hyperspectral images. A convolutional autoencoder (CAE) [12] based model is used which would reduce the dimensionality of the pixels. The autoencoder based model is particularly suited in this context as it can learn features from unlabelled data as well. In such case, re-training with labelled samples would help in fine-tuning. The proposed classifier uses a twin encoder and scores the unlabeled pixels with an uncertainty value. At each epoch, the model automatically selects the top k samples deemed most informative as per the calculated uncertainty score and queries the human annotator for their labels. The label information of the selected pixels is provided to the model for improving the existing decision boundary, and the procedure is thus repeated by continuously adding the labelled samples to the training set. As mentioned, starting with a small and non-optimal training set, the model constructs the ideal collection of labelled samples to minimise classification error. This reduces the need for a large training set. The outcomes of experiments confirm the consistency of the procedures.

2 Related Research

Active learning algorithms [8,15] actively seek labels from the user or the expert annotator. At each iteration the model itself chooses a few uncertain samples and queries the user about the label information. The model selects the instances it considers important for constructing the decision boundary. It is seen that in active learning based training of models, the number of examples necessary to train the model is substantially smaller than the number required in traditional supervised learning. Such algorithms are widely used in environmental monitoring [11] and classification [4], species classification [9], multi-label classification [21], classification of hyperspectral images [6], etc. Recently, active learning has been adopted in change detection [13] too. Complexity of labelling each pixel (as changed or unchanged) in a pair of hyperspectral images demands for active learning framework requiring comparatively lesser labelled samples. The high dimensionality of these images, on the other hand, is another interesting property which is both useful as well as a challenge.

Deep learning [17,18] has emerged as a relatively impressive technique for dimensionality reduction. In recent years, they have been notably used for analysing remotely sensed satellite images [10], change detection [8], etc. Deep learning has been integrated with active learning for change detection in areal images [14]. However, literature on change detection in hyperspectral images with active learning is poor. This is mainly because of lack of labelled data as well as high dimensionality. Unsupervised methods [3] are elegant alternatives but lack the knowledge from an expert annotator. These methods often include finding a difference image and thresholding technique. Change vector analysis using spectral angle mapping was carried out by reserachers [3] and the difference image was analysed using Otsu's thresholding. A spatial processing has also been done by averaging the pixels of the input image pair in a watershed-based segmentation map that correspond to the same geographical area. Finally, the change map is spatially regularised to eliminate the occurrence of disconnected pixels. Although this method gives good performance, it doesn't fully utilise the potential of the partially annotated data. Researchers have also proposed semi-supervised methods [22] which involves distance metric learning for change detection on hyperspectral images. However, it lacks the benefit of spatial information in the images. Hence, it would be useful if the change detection can utilise the partial labelled data, unlabelled data, spectral information and spatial information simultaneously.

In this context, it may be noted that use of abundance of unlabelled data may lead to improved performance if done in a strategic manner. Autoencoder (AE) based feature extraction [1,17,18], could be a potential modification in this regard. An AE can be used to learn repeated patterns [20] because it maps similar values to similar ranges. So, pixels which are similar in nature will be efficiently mapped to similar range in the reduced dimension too. Convolutional networks are structurally much more suitable for images. Thus, we may use a convolutional autoencoder (CAE) for the present problem. Borrowing this idea, this article proposes a CAE based model which would reduce the dimensionality of the pixels. The model is then fine-tuned by stacking the encoder of the CAE on a classification layer which is trained through active learning.

3   Proposed Method

As mentioned, the proposed method exploits the efficacy of active learning to train a model which would detect changes present in a hyperspectral image pair in a semi-automated manner. The model is built by the encoders of CAEs pre-trained on the existing (labelled or unlabelled) samples. The following subsection describes the proposed method in detail.

3.1 Unsupervised Pre-training of Sliding Convolutional Autoencoder

The proposed method uses two identical CAEs for feature extraction which slide over the two images of the same region captured at different time instants. The network architecture of each CAE is shown in Fig. 1. The two networks slide across the images by a fixed stride of one. To avoid boundary issues, the images are suitably padded with zeros. The network takes a 9 × 9 neighborhood of pixels and tries to reconstruct it back at the output. This is chosen so that the computational complexity does not increase a lot and at the same time the effects of noisy pixels may be avoided. The CAE is trained for 50 epochs with Adam optimiser to minimise the mean square error of reconstruction.

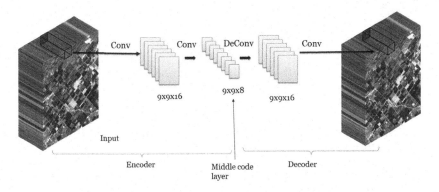

Fig. 1. Architecture of the CAE network.

The input to the network is, therefore, 9 × 9 × 224. The CAE network learns the spatial as well as spectral features and reduces the dimensionality of the input space while trying to reconstruct it back. Since an AE maps different input values to different ranges [20], the CAE will learn to map the unchanged pixels from both the images into the same range as both the images would have similar intensity values for those pixels. On the other hand, if the pixels represent a changed region, the corresponding intensity values will be different, and hence the CAE will map the pixel values for the two images to different ranges. The network will, in a way, learn to distinguish between the changed and unchanged pixels. The CAE is useful because it can also make use of samples which are unlabelled. Using active learning based re-training, the network can be fine-tuned further with very few labelled data.

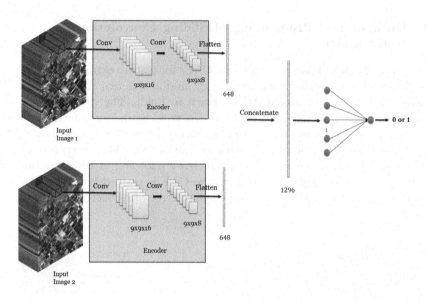

Fig. 2. Architecture of the twin encoder change detector (TECD) model used.

3.2 Active Re-training of Twin Encoder Change Detector (TECD) Model

Once the CAE is trained, the encoders of the two CAE networks are taken and the decoders are discarded. The output at the middle layer of the CAEs represents the extracted features of each 9×9 input neighborhood of the images. The extracted features from the two encoders of the CAEs are flattened and concatenated to act as input to a fully connected classification layer. It is an obvious question as to why the two features were not subtracted from each other to find the difference. This is because the difference between the extracted features is not always as pronounced as the difference between the actual pixel intensities. Moreover, noise and other false factors like artifacts and outliers impact the information about change in the difference value. Thus, it would make more sense to learn the weights of the classification layer for aggregation or difference of the extracted features to generate the change map. The label information of a pixel at the final layer corresponds to the central pixel of the 9×9 input neighborhood. The labelled samples in the dataset are divided into training and testing set in a 70% and 30% proportion respectively. At the first epoch, the network [Fig. 1] is provided with a random percentage (between 10–20%) of the training labels for forming the initial decision boundary. This is the initial tiny training set for the model assumed to be marked by the experts. After each epoch, the network would score the unlabelled pixels with a pseudo class score based on the current decision boundary. This pseudo class score (output of the classifier) would be used to determine the uncertainty of each pixel. The pseudo class score is the probability of the pixel belonging to the changed class. If the pseudo class score is 0, then the probability of the pixel belonging to the changed class is 0 and hence depending on the existing decision boundary it is pseudo-marked as an unchanged pixel. Similarly, if the pseudo class score is 1, then the probability of the pixel belonging to the changed class is 1 and hence depending on the existing decision boundary it is pseudo-marked as a changed pixel. However, if the pseudo class score is 0.5, then the pixel can be pseudo marked as either changed or unchanged with equal probabilities. The uncertainty of the pixels depend on how close they are to the decision boundary which is characterised by the output (O) of 0.5 (suggesting a mid point between the classes represented by 0 and 1 at the output). The uncertainty is modelled as a beta distribution function given by,

$$U = \frac{O^{\alpha-1}(1-O)^{\beta-1}}{\mathbf{B}(\alpha,\beta)}, \tag{1}$$

where α and β are the shape parameters. The beta function $\mathbf{B}$ is usually represented in terms of gamma functions (Γ) as,

$$\mathbf{B}(\alpha,\beta) = \frac{\Gamma(\alpha+\beta)}{\Gamma(\alpha)\Gamma(\beta)}, \tag{2}$$

for normalisation purposes. In this case, the values of α and β are chosen to be 2. This indicates that if the output O is close to 0 or 1 (which implies that the sample belongs to unchanged or changed class respectively), it will not be treated as an uncertain sample as the value of U would be close to zero. However, a point lying close to the decision boundary will generate output O close to 0.5 and the value of U would be close to 1. If the samples are ranked in decreasing order by U, the most uncertain samples will be the ones on the top. At each epoch the model is allowed to choose only the top k of these uncertain samples (or pixels in this case). The actual labels of these chosen pixels are queried by the model to the annotator. The annotator labels the said samples and they are included in the training set for training the model in the next epoch. The model is trained in this manner for 100 epochs with Adam optimiser to minimise the cross-entropy loss.

4   Results

In this study, two pairs of hyperspectral images are considered for experimentation. These two datasets have incomplete ground truth information i.e. they have abundant unknown pixels along with a few labelled (change and unchanged) pixels. The following section describes the dataset on which the experiments have been performed to carry out the said task.

4.1 Dataset Description

The first dataset is Bay Area [3] which was captured on 2013 and 2015 with the AVIRIS sensor surrounding the city of Patterson (California). There are 224 spectral bands and the image size is 600 × 500. In the ground truth data, there are 39,270 pixels labelled as changed, 34,211 pixels labelled as unchanged and 2,26,519 pixels unlabelled. There is a similar scenario with the second dataset Santa Barbara [3] which was taken on 2013 and 2014 with the AVIRIS sensor over the Santa Barbara region (California). There are 224 spectral bands and the size of the image is 984 × 740. In ground truth, there are 52,134 changed pixels, 80,418 unchanged pixels and 5,95,608 pixels are unlabelled or unknown (Fig. 3).

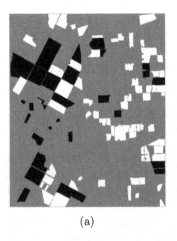 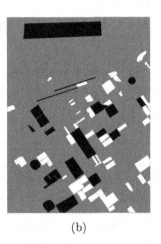

(a)   (b)

Fig. 3. Ground Truth for (a) Bay Area and (b) Santa Barbara dataset. (Black-Unchanged, White- Changed, Gray- Unknown).

4.2 Experiments

The model is compared with an existing unsupervised [3] (denoted as Method 1) and a semi-supervised [22] (denoted as Method 2) methods. Due to scarcity of literature on change detection methods for hyperspectral images involving active learning, comparative analysis with any active learning based models could not be done. However, the model is compared with a case where the same proposed model is trained with full training set (70% of the labelled samples) (called as Method 3). The results reported in Table 1 are shown for the testing sets.

In order to decide on the value of k, we used 10-fold cross validation on the initial smaller training set. It has been observed that the optimal value of k for the Bay Area and Santa Barbara images were 12 and 24 respectively. After 100 epochs, the model needed only 8817 and 17231 training samples for the Bay Area and Santa Barbara images and these numbers constitute only 17.14% and 18.57% of the training samples. The variation of F-Score with the percentage of samples used for training from the train sets (70% of the data) is provided in Fig. 4. It can be seen that after a certain amount of training samples, the performance of the model does not increase any further. Rather, if the entire train set is used to train the model, the performance is slightly degraded.

Table 1. Comparison of the results obtained on the two datasets by various models.

	Bay Area			Santa Barbara		
	ROC-AUC	Accuracy	F-Score	ROC-AUC	Accuracy	F-Score
Proposed	**0.9979**	**0.9843**	**0.9843**	**0.9983**	**0.9851**	**0.9844**
Method 1	0.9915	0.9646	0.9649	0.9915	0.9694	0.9679
Method 2	0.9870	0.9559	0.9560	0.9879	0.9647	0.9630
Method 3	0.9923	0.9645	0.9649	0.9868	0.9647	0.9629

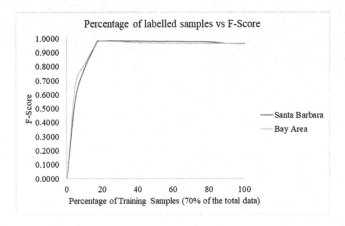

Fig. 4. Variation of F-Score with the percentage of training samples

The change maps generated by the various models are provided in Figs. 5 and 6. For most of the pixels, the labels are unknown. Hence the change map may be used as a supplementary specimen for the human annotator.

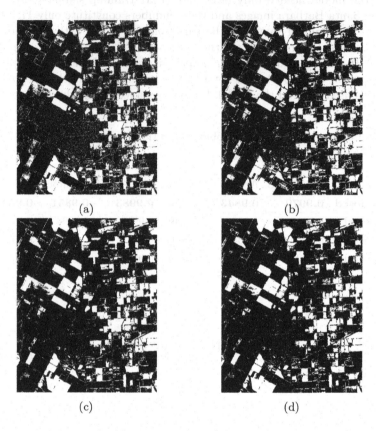

(a)   (b)

(c)   (d)

Fig. 5. Change map (Black- Unchanged, White- Changed) obtained for Bay Area dataset by the (a) Proposed model, (b) Method 1, (c) Method 2 and (d) Method 3.

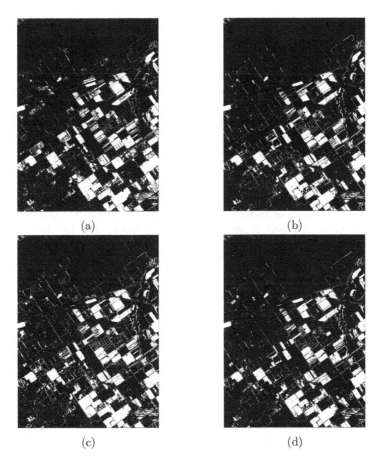

(a)   (b)

(c)   (d)

Fig. 6. Change map (Black- Unchanged, White- Changed) obtained for Santa Barbara dataset by the (a) Proposed model, (b) Method 1, (c) Method 2 and (d) Method 3.

5   Conclusion

As observed from the experiments, the proposed model used very little (only 17.14% and 18.57% for Bay Area and Santa Barbara images respectively) of the train set (70% of the existing labelled data) to achieve an elevated accuracy. The proposed model could achieve better accuracy than the supervised model (which used the entire train set i.e. 70% of the existing labelled data) even after using a comparatively lesser amount of training data. Fully supervised methods consider all samples equally and disregard the location of the samples with respect to the decision boundary. Few pixels may be found distant from the decision boundary (for example, pixels depicting major prominent changes), whilst others may be found close to the boundary (for example, pixels depicting slight subtle changes). Active learning takes this concept into account and does a smart selection of labelled samples as compared to random selection as it is done in supervised learning. Since the datasets are incompletely labelled, the proposed model can also be used as a complementary option for finding the labels of the pixels. It is also observed [Fig. 5 and 6] that many tiny localised regions of changes are predicted by the proposed model. Such minute changes can be seen in the slightly lower central region of the change map obtained for Bay Area dataset. For the Santa Barbara dataset, the upper left quadrant show some minute changes. The other models either brought out many noisy pixels as changes or suppressed the minute information completely. The true information about these unlabelled pixels (actual changes or simply noise) can only be judged once they are validated by a domain expert.

Acknowledgement. We would like to thank Department of Science and Tech- nology, Ministry of Science and Technology (Grant Number- DST/ICPS/CLUSTER/Data Science/2018/General dated 7 January 2019). We would also like to thank Indo-U.S. Science and Technology Forum (IUSSTF) for funding the project titled Indo-US Joint Center on Distributed Deep Learning Framework for Classification (Ref. No.: IUSSTF/AUG/JC/024/2018).

References

1. Chakraborty, D., Narayanan, V., Ghosh, A.: Integration of deep feature extraction and ensemble learning for outlier detection. Pattern Recogn. **89**, 161–171 (2019)
2. Datta, A., Ghosh, S., Ghosh, A.: Supervised feature extraction of hyperspectral images using partitioned maximum margin criterion. IEEE Geosci. Remote Sensing Lett. **14**(1), 82–86 (2016)
3. Fandino, J.L., Heras, D.B., Argüello, F., Mura, M.D.: GPU Framework for Change Detection in Multitemporal Hyperspectral Images. In: 10th International Symposium on High-Level Parallel Programming and Applications, pp. 115–132 (2017)
4. Geiß, C., Thoma, M., Taubenböck, H.: Cost-sensitive multitask active learning for characterization of urban environments with remote sensing. IEEE Geosci. Remote Sensing Lett. **15**(6), 922–926 (2018)
5. Ghosh, S., Roy, M., Ghosh, A.: Semi-supervised change detection using modified self-organizing feature map neural network. Appl. Soft Comput. **15**, 1–20 (2014)
6. Haut, J.M., Paoletti, M.E., Plaza, J., Li, J., Plaza, A.: Active learning with convolutional neural networks for hyperspectral image classification using a new bayesian approach. IEEE Trans. Geosci. Remote Sensing **56**(11), 6440–6461 (2018)
7. Jin, X., Gu, Y., Liu, T.: Intrinsic image recovery from remote sensing hyperspectral images. IEEE Trans. Geosci. Remote Sensing **57**(1), 224–238 (2018)
8. Li, Y., Peng, C., Chen, Y., Jiao, L., Zhou, L., Shang, R.: A deep learning method for change detection in synthetic aperture radar images. IEEE Trans. Geosci. Remote Sensing **57**(8), 5751–5763 (2019)
9. Luo, T., et al.: Active learning to recognize multiple types of plankton. J. Mach. Learn. Res. **6**(4), 589–613 (2005)
10. Piramanayagam, S., Saber, E., Schwartzkopf, W., Koehler, F.W.: Supervised classification of multisensor remotely sensed images using a deep learning framework. Remote Sensing **10**(9), 1429 (2018)
11. Pozdnoukhov, A., Kanevski, M.: Monitoring network optimisation for spatial data classification using support vector machines. Int. J. Environ. Pollut. **28**(3–4), 465–484 (2006)

12. Romero, A., Gatta, C., Camps-Valls, G.: Unsupervised deep feature extraction for remote sensing image classification. IEEE Trans. Geosci. Remote Sensing **54**(3), 1349–1362 (2016)
13. Roy, M., Ghosh, S., Ghosh, A.: A neural approach under active learning mode for change detection in remotely sensed images. IEEE J. Selected Topics Appl. Observ. Remote Sensing **7**(4), 1200–1206 (2013)
14. Ruzicka, V., D'Aronco, S., Wegner, J.D., Schindler, K.: Deep Active Learning in Remote Sensing for Data Efficient Change Detection. In: Proceedings of MACLEAN: MAChine Learning for EArth ObservatioN Workshop. vol. 2766, pp. 1–11. RWTH Aachen University (2020)
15. Schohn, G., Cohn, D.: Less is More: Active Learning with Support Vector Machines. In: International Conference on Machine Learning. vol. 2, pp. 839–846. Citeseer (2000)
16. Vakalopoulou, M., Karantzalos, K.: Automatic Descriptor-based Co-registration of Frame Hyperspectral Data. Remote Sensing **6**(4), 3409–3426 (2014)
17. Vincent, P., Larochelle, H., Bengio, Y., Manzagol, P.: Extracting and Composing Robust Features with Denoising Autoencoders. In: Proceedings of the 25th International Conference on Machine Learning, pp. 1096–1103. ACM (2008)
18. Vincent, P., Larochelle, H., Lajoie, I., Bengio, Y., Manzagol, P.A.: Stacked Denoising Autoencoders: Learning Useful Representations in a Deep Network with a Local Denoising Criterion. J. Mach. Learn. Res. **11**, 3371–3408 (2010)
19. Wang, Q., Yuan, Z., Du, Q., Li, X.: GETNET: a general end-to-end 2-d CNN framework for hyperspectral image change detection. IEEE Trans. Geosci. Remote Sensing **57**(1), 3–13 (2018)
20. Wang, Y., Yao, H., Zhao, S.: Auto-encoder based dimensionality reduction. Neurocomput. **184**, 232–242 (2016)
21. Wu, J., et al.: Multi-label active learning algorithms for image classification: overview and future promise. ACM Comput. Surv. **53**(2), 1–35 (2020)
22. Yuan, Y., Lv, H., Lu, X.: Semi-supervised change detection method for multi-temporal hyperspectral images. Neurocomputing **148**, 363–375 (2015)

TeethU²Net: A Deep Learning-Based Approach for Tooth Saliency Detection in Dental Panoramic Radiographs

Nripendra Kumar Singh🆔 and Khalid Raza$^{(\boxtimes)}$🆔

Department of Computer Science, Jamia Millia Islamia, New Delhi 110025, India
nripendra1900555@st.jmi.ac.in, kraza@jmi.ac.in

Abstract. Detection of tooth saliency is an open problem in the complex dental radiograph. In this work, a new architecture of the deep learning model, TeethU²Net, is proposed for state-of-the-art tooth saliency detection in dental panoramic radiograph (DPR) images. We optimized the original U²-Net in terms of custom loss function and training scheme for the challenging tasks of segmenting each tooth boundary, which improves the result of contour detection over all previous deep learning-based approaches. In this experiment, we utilized a dataset of 1500 challenging dental panoramic radiographs grouped into 10 different categories. We trained the network from scratch. The dataset was divided into 1224 and 276 data samples across all the categories for training and testing, respectively. The proposed TeethU²Net model achieves an accuracy of 0.9740, specificity of 0.9969, precision of 0.9880, recall of 0.8707, and an F1-score of 0.9047, which is better than the previously reported results.

Keywords: Deep learning · dental image segmentation · panoramic radiographs · saliency detection

1 Introduction

Dental radiography is a specialty in the field of dentistry that helps in the diagnosis of oral disease and routine appointments. Broadly, dental radiographs are acquired in two ways: intraoral and extraoral. In an intraoral, a film or sensor is placed inside the mouth, for example, peri-apical radiographs. extraoral film or sensors placed in the outer region of the mouth, for example, panoramic radiographs, cone beam computed tomography (CBCT), etc. [1]. Panoramic radiographs are popular in dentistry because of their wider field of view, economical, faster acquisition, and least motion artifact. However, it has a few limitations, such as lower resolution and a more complex structure [2]. Panoramic radiographs are widely used in the examination of periodontal tooth conditions, bone anomalies, periapical caries/lesions, and routine check-ups to diagnose in the initial stage.

M. Tanveer et al. (Eds.): ICONIP 2022, CCIS 1794, pp. 224–234, 2023.
https://doi.org/10.1007/978-981-99-1648-1_19

While supervised and unsupervised deep learning-based interpretation achieved promising results in other medical domains [3,4], deep learning in dental image analysis achieved significant growth after the first notable work published by Ronneberger and collaborators [5] on dental bitewing x-ray segmentation. There is current literature reporting the progress of deep learning in the interpretation of various modalities of the dental domain [6–9].

Literature suggests that the majority of tooth segmentation tasks in dental panoramic radiographs use a deep learning model or a combination of statistical models to segment and classify the tooth boundary [9]. For instance, the work of [10] forwarded a hybrid approach, a statistical model top-up on the neural network to provide initial segmentation of the teeth region and scaling of the position at the same time. This work is evaluated with 14 dental panoramic images with an average accuracy, recall, and dice overlap of 0.790, 0.827, and 0.7440, respectively. Study in the [11] led a writing survey on segmentation techniques applied to dental images. In the review, they found a gap in the all-encompassing radiograph images and, to fill this gap, they introduced a new dataset containing 1500 dental panoramic radiographs and proposed a deep learning model for segmentation of teeth with an initial result of 0.98 of accuracy, 0.84 of precision, and 0.76 of recall. The studies in [12] proposed a mask-based R-CNN network for the segmentation of individual teeth in dental panoramic radiographs. The training of the network was performed with 846 dental annotations from 30 panoramic radiographs and 20 radiograph images used for validation and testing. The proposed method achieved 0.858 of accuracy, 0.893 of recall, and 0.877 of an average intersection-over-union (IoU). Subsequently, in the work [13], the authors proposed TSASNet, an attention-based two-stage network for tooth segmentation, and employed the same dataset used in [14] and evaluated the network on the metrics for accuracy, precision, recall, and dice of 0.969, 0.9497, 0.937, and 0.927, respectively.

Our main contributions to this paper are as follows:

– We proposed a custom loss function for training the proposed deep learning network.
– The TeethU^{2}Net architecture achieved the drawing of all teeth contours in the complex panoramic images to count all visible teeth efficiently and will potentially aid in accurate computational interpretation. Also, we train our model with a full scan of a panoramic image while, as per our knowledge, all previously reported work in this domain was performed on a random patch or individual tooth patch scheme for training the model.

2 Methods

2.1 Network Architecture

We proposed a TeethU^{2}Net architecture based on a two-level nested U-Net model for tooth saliency detection. We modified and optimized the state-of-the-art saliency object detection architecture U2-Net [15] in many ways. Firstly, we introduced a custom loss function BCEDice, l_{BCED} loss instead of the standard BCE (Binary Cross Entropy). This provides better tooth edge visibility compared to the default U^2-Net and other previous approaches. Secondly, we introduced cosine schedular in the training process, which started with a large learning rate and rapidly dropped to a minimum. The literature suggests that the cosine scheduler improves the model convergence in a short span of time [16]. The architecture of the proposed TeethU^{2}Net is illustrated in Fig. 1. The TeethU2Net is the stacking of different sizes of U-Net modules in a U-shape structure rather than a cascading style. Usually, sequential stacking of U-Net is represented as "(U×n-Net)" where n is the number of U-Net blocks, and has been employed in DocUNet [17] and CU-Net [18] for different applications. The problem with sequential stacking (cascade models) is that it increases the computation cost by a multiple of n. We inherited the U^2-Net [15] philosophy in our TeethU^{2}Net architecture, which adopted exponential notation for nested U-structures as "Un-Net", where n is 2 for a two-level nested U-structure. TeethU^{2}Net consists of 11 stages (cubical blocks in Fig. 1), all stages divided into three parts: *(i)* There are six encoder stages containing residual U-blocks, which are configured to capture large-scale information to the low resolution of the input feature map; *(ii)* There are five decoder blocks placed in symmetry with the corresponding encoder block. At each stage, the decoder concatenates the up-sampled feature map from the symmetric encoder, and *(iii)* result of the saliency probability map from each decoder, fused with a result of the last encoder to generate a final saliency probability map.

2.2 Loss Function

In the training of most convolutional neural networks (CNN), cross-entropy (CE) is used as the default loss function. However, the original U^2-Net model used binary cross-entropy (BCE) to calculate the loss of each term and finally calculate the overall loss L_T in the training process, as represented by equation (1). In our case, when we look across the training dataset, we found that the ground truth is largely inconsistent in two ways: first, some of the annotations leave sharp visible corners and sometimes rectangular boxes against the tooth, and second, the annotation has been performed by using certain anchor points for marking the tooth boundary, which creates a fusion of edges in the adjacent tooth, which creates a mask of multiple teeth clubbed together in ground truth annotation. Boundary segmentation learned by the standard BCE loss from inconsistent annotation affected by class imbalance. To reduce the class imbalance effect, we proposed a modified loss function $l_B CED$ in Eq. (2), to improve the edge visibility for each tooth object, as recent literature suggests that dice loss and Tversky loss [19] performed better in the highly imbalanced dataset.

$$L_T = \sum_{n=1}^{n} w_{side}^{(n)}(l_{BCD})_{(side)}^{(n)} + w_{fuse}(l_{BCD})_{fuse} \tag{1}$$

where l_{BCED} (n = 1 to 6) is the loss of each side output, w_{side}^{n} and w_{fuse} are the weight of each loss term, and the proposed loss l_{BCED} is calculated as:

$$l_{BCED} = \alpha * l_{BCE} + l_{Dice} \tag{2}$$

where $\alpha = 0.5$ is taken to balance the loss, l_{BCE} is the standard binary cross-entropy represented by Eq. (3) and l_{Dice} is the dice loss represented by Eq. (4).

$$l_{BCE} = - \sum_{(i,j)}^{H,W} [P_{g(i,j)} \log P_{s(i,j)} + (1 - P_{g(i,j)}) \log(1 - P_{s(i,j)})] \tag{3}$$

$$l_{Dice} = 1 - \frac{2 * \sum_{(i,j)}^{H,W} P_{g(i,j)} P_{s(i,j)} + \epsilon}{\sum_{(i,j)}^{H,W} P_{g(i,j)}^2 + \sum_{(i,j)}^{H,W} P_{s(i,j)}^2 + \epsilon} \tag{4}$$

where (i,j) are the coordinates of each pixel in the image space, (H,W) is the input image size and ϵ is the smoothness factor set to 1, to ensure that the function is not in an undefined state. $P_{g(i,j)}$ denotes ground truth pixel values and $P_{s(i,j)}$ denote predicted saliency map. During the training process model tries to minimize the resulting loss L_T in Eq. (1). In the testing, we use $(l_{BCD})_{fuse}$ to produce a final saliency map.

2.3   Implementation Details

In the training of dental panoramic images of size 1127×1991, initially resized to 512×512 using bilinear interpolation for preserving information. First, we did not use any pre-trained backbone network. Hence, we trained our network from scratch and initialized the weight of all convolutional layers using uniform Xavier initialization [20]. Next, we trained our network using the Adam optimizer [21] with the cosine scheduler along with default hyperparameters (initial learning rate lr = 1e−3, weight decay = 0, eps =1e−8, betas = (0.9, 0.999)). Our network performed the training of up to 1000 epochs with a batch size of 2 until the training loss converges without a validation set. Our complete network is implemented on Pytorch version 1.10.0 using the Python programming language. Both training and testing were executed on a 32-core Dell workstation with an Intel Xeon silver 4110 × 2.10 GHz CPU (64 GB RAM) and an NVIDIA Quadro P5000 GPU (16 GB VRAM).

2.4 Dataset

A dataset of 1500 dental panoramic radiographs used in this work was created by Gil Silva et al., [14] and is now freely available on the Web. We received a pre-annotated dataset for academic research work by Gil Silva et al., all 1500 images divided into 10 separate categories, described in Table 1. The category size varies from 45 to 457 image samples based on less or more than 32 teeth, restorations, and prostheses present in the image. The size of all the panoramic images in the dataset is 1127 × 1991. We trained our network on 1224 images and tested it on 276 unseen images. We augment the training data by horizontal flipping to increase the training instances for better generalization.

Table 1. Description of the dataset.

Category	1	2	3	4	5	6	7	8	9	10
Avg, No of 32 Teeth	Yes	Yes	Yes	Yes	No	No	No	No	No	No
Restoration	Yes	Yes	No	No	No	Yes	Yes	Yes	No	No
Appliance OR Implants	Yes	No	Yes	No	Yes	Yes	Yes	No	Yes	No

2.5 Evaluation Metrics

The output of our tooth saliency network is the probability map of the input images with the same spatial resolution. To evaluate the performance of our network against the ground truth image, looking at previous work [11,14,22] for proper comparison, we consider the same evaluation measures, described as follows:

$$Accuracy = \frac{(T_P + T_N)}{(T_P + F_N + F_P + T_N)} \tag{5}$$

$$Specificity = \frac{T_N}{(F_P + T_N)} \tag{6}$$

$$Precision = \frac{T_P}{(T_P + F_P)} \tag{7}$$

$$Recall = \frac{T_P}{(T_P + F_N)} \tag{8}$$

$$F1 - score = \frac{2 * Recall * Precision}{(Recal + Precision)} \tag{9}$$

where T_P, F_N, F_P, T_N represent true positive, false negative, false positive, and true negative, respectively.

3   Results

3.1   Quantitative Analysis

The performance of our proposed TeethU²Net model is presented in Table 2. It summarises overall quantitative results across the category of test data. When we interpret the test results of individual categories for the statistical analysis, we see that some of the results are unsatisfactory, perhaps due to rough ground truth annotation, while the predicted mask is quite smooth and realistic. We removed those outliers and calculated the standard deviation among the remaining data points, category-wise. The range of the standard deviation is 0.002–0.08, which demonstrates that our network is quite stable with consistent generalization in

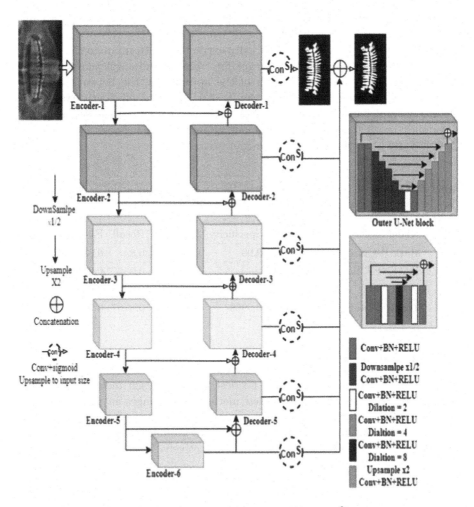

Fig. 1. Architecture of the proposed TeethU²Net.

the results. We also compared our results with other recent state-of-the-art methods, namely Mask R-CNN [14], U-Net* [22], and TSASNET [13]. Table 3 demonstrates a comparison between TeethU^{2}Net and another competing network on a similar dataset. Table 3 also compares the saliency segmentation performance of our proposed methods and other networks on five evaluation metrics. We see that TeethU^{2}Net outperformed U-Net* in terms of accuracy, specificity, and precision with a significant difference, while U-Net* achieved higher recall and F1-score compared to our network. This is due to multiple augmentation and ensemble during the training process. When we compared with another deep learning approach Mask R-CNN and TSASNet, our network performed better result on most of the metrics, except accuracy is better when compared to Mask R-CNN [14]. However, TSASNet [13] performed pretty balanced and had significantly better results on recall and F1-score. Although, a direct comparison of results may not be fair, as every method has a different training data size and training scheme. Mask R-CNN [14] used only 193 images from a few categories of the dataset for training the network, and individually extracted tooth input to the network training. U-Net* [22] used 80 of images for training and employed a patching scheme for training images. In both of the approaches, the network does not train on full-size images. However, the TeethU^{2}Net was efficiently trained on full-size natural panoramic images. Now when we compared the segmentation of complex tooth regions in the previous approach, the network failed to find difficult parts of teeth, like the tooth-root area.

Table 2. Comparison of results of TeethU^{2}Net with previous architectures Mask R-CNN, U-Net ensembles configuration (U-Net*), and TSASNet.

Model	Accuracy	Specificity	Precision	Recall	F1-score
Mask R-CNN [14]	0.98	0.99	0.94	0.84	0.88
TSASNET [13]	0.9694	—	0.9497	0.9377	0.9272
U-Net* [22]	0.9521	0.9636	0.9357	0.9430	0.9342
TeethU^{2}Net	0.9740	0.9969	0.9880	0.8707	0.9047

3.2 Qualitative Analysis

Figure 2 depicts the integration of the best result on each metric used in the performance analysis of our proposed method. All images in the collage are comprised of the original dental panoramic image, ground truth segmentation, predicted segmentation mask, and superimposed ground truth vs predicted contours arranged from left to right column, respectively.

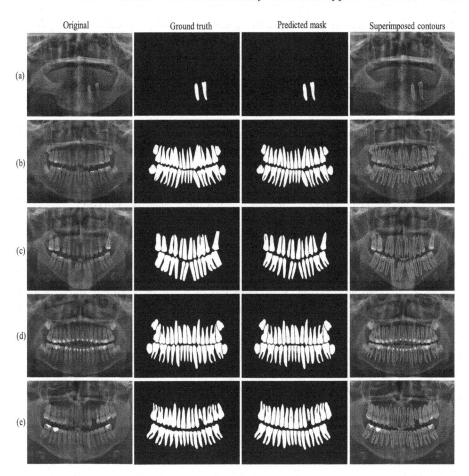

Fig. 2. Illustration of the best results for saliency mask prediction and tooth segmentation according to metric employed for the model performance analysis as (a) Accuracy (b) Specificity (c) Precision (d) Recall (e) F1-Score. To visualize segmentation contour drawn over ground truth (green color) and TeethU^{2}Net segmentation (light orange color).

Here, we visualize that higher recall presents good segmentation results as compared to other metrics and even poor results in overall recall against accuracy and specificity. This is because better segmentation demands a balanced relation between precision and recall. However, our main objective is to detection of contour over each tooth across the panoramic image. After visual analysis we saw that our model is free from learning of any artifacts learning, presence of dental prosthesis like crown, implant, bridge and dental arch (see Fig. 2(d)). Overall our model produces the state-of-art segmentation in all the conditions (see Fig. 2(a) to (e)). Every tooth object is detected separately in all our predicted tooth contours, even ground truth contours failed to achieve similar results

Table 3. Performance of the TeethU^{2}Net among all the ten categories of the dataset.

Category	Accuracy	Specificity	Precision	Recall	F1-score
Cat-1	0.9621	0.9908	0.9668	0.8670	0.9124
Cat-2	0.9652	0.9961	0.9812	0.8638	0.9085
Cat-3	0.9719	0.9970	0.9972	**0.9085**	0.9125
Cat-4	0.9656	0.9980	0.9917	0.8378	0.8999
Cat-5	0.9833	0.9959	0.9908	0.8379	0.9031
Cat-6	0.9626	0.9980	0.9909	0.8688	0.8964
Cat-7	0.9653	0.9947	0.9798	0.9037	0.8915
Cat-8	0.9742	0.9973	0.9969	0.8870	**0.9139**
Cat-9	0.9620	0.9977	**0.9889**	0.8258	0.8969
Cat-10	**0.9974**	**0.9999**	0.9963	0.9066	0.9125

due to poor edge annotation. Segmentation of teeth in a similar dataset done by [10] was largely affected by bridge and missing teeth using a neural network-based approach, while work performed by [14] & [22] achieved somehow better segmentation results compared to the previous one by applying deep learning-based approach but it is unable to detect unique contours along teeth. Thus, our approach outperformed in drawing unique teeth contours. All of these would help in the automatic generation of accurate medical reports and computational diagnoses.

4   Conclusion and Future Work

Over the last decade, many approaches were made using supervised and unsupervised techniques for saliency segmentation and detection of tooth or tooth region. Segmentation of teeth in the panoramic radiograph is essential to extract actual boundaries to automate various clinical interpretations and computational diagnoses. However, with the advent of artificial intelligence, a lot of possibilities to increase the accuracy in the segmenting of the tooth and other lesion objects across the various modality. Segmenting anterior and posterior surfaces accurately in the dental panoramic image is essential for the interpretation of complex tasks in an automated decision support system. Our proposed system effectively performed the detection of broken tooth conditions and even detected complete teeth in the presence of dental prosthesis. The majority of earlier findings [10,14,22] reported that broken teeth, missing teeth, and prosthesis conditions are the bottleneck in the tooth segmentation task. Thus, considering our proposed work, demonstrated promising results even with inconsistent annotated data.

Future work could be aimed at standardizing the dataset annotation on the larger data volume to get better accuracy even with complex tooth anatomical structure. To reduce the dataset size problem researchers may utilize the potential of artificially generated image using generative adversarial network (GANs) based augmentation for better generalization [23], as it performed well in other medical image analysis domains to achieve a better result for semantic segmentation of tooth and other areas of dental application. Besides of intact tooth segmentation, other dental treatments, lesions and disorders can be studied using different segmentation and detection approach to differentiate the normal and abnormal objects in dental panoramic x-ray. For further studies, our framework can be utilized by more advanced dental modality like Cone beam computed tomography.

References

1. Woodward, T.M.: Dental Radiology. Topics Companion Animal Med. **24**(1), 20–36 (2009)
2. Reddy, M.S., Mayfield-donahoo, T., Vanderven, F.J.J., Jeffcoat, M.K.: A comparison of the diagnostic advantages of panoramic radiography and computed tomography scanning for placement of root form dental implants. Clin. Oral Implants Res. **5**(4), 229–238 (1994)
3. Wani, N., Raza, K.: Integrative approaches to reconstruct regulatory networks from multi-omics data: A review of state-of-the-art methods. In: Computational Biology and Chemistry (2019)
4. Raza, K., Singh, N.K.: A tour of unsupervised deep learning for medical image analysis. Current Med. Imaging **17**(9), 1059–1077 (2021)
5. Ronneberger, O., Fischer, P., Brox, T.: U-net: Convolutional networks for biomedical image segmentation. In: Lecture Notes in Computer Science (including subseries Lecture Notes in Artificial Intelligence and Lecture Notes in Bioinformatics) (2015)
6. Babu, A., Onesimu, A., Martin Sagayam, K.: Artificial Intelligence in dentistry: Concepts, Applications and Research Challenges. In: E3S Web of Conferences, p. 297 (2021)
7. Heo, M.-S., et al.: Artificial intelligence in oral and maxillofacial radiology: what is currently possible? Dentomaxillofacial Radiol. **50**(3), 20200375 (2021)
8. Kumar, A., Bhadauria, H.S., Singh, A.: Descriptive analysis of dental X-ray images using various practical methods: A review. PeerJ Comput. Sci. **7**, e620 (2021)
9. Singh, N.K., Raza, K.: Progress in deep learning-based dental and maxillofacial image analysis: a systematic review. Expert Syst. Appl. **199**, 116968 (2022)
10. Wirtz, A., Mirashi, S.G., Wesarg, S.: Automatic Teeth Segmentation in Panoramic X-Ray Images Using a Coupled Shape Model in Combination with a Neural Network. In: Lecture Notes in Computer Science (including subseries Lecture Notes in Artificial Intelligence and Lecture Notes in Bioinformatics) (2018)
11. Silva, G., Oliveira, L., Pithon, M.: Automatic segmenting teeth in X-ray images: trends, a novel data set, benchmarking and future perspectives. Expert Syst. Appl. **107**, 15–31 (2018)
12. Lee, J.H., Han, S.S., Kim, Y.H., Lee, C., Kim, I.: Application of a fully deep convolutional neural network to the automation of tooth segmentation on panoramic radiographs. Oral Surg., Oral Med., Oral Pathol. Oral Radiol. **129**(6), 635–642 (2020)

13. Zhao, Y., et al.: TSASNet: Tooth segmentation on dental panoramic X-ray images by two-stage attention segmentation network. Knowl. Based Syst. **206**, 106338 (2020)
14. Jader, G., Fontineli, J., Ruiz, M., Abdalla, K., Pithon, M., Oliveira, L.: Deep instance segmentation of teeth in panoramic x-ray images. In: Proceedings - 31st Conference on Graphics, Patterns and Images, SIBGRAPI 2018, pp. 400–407 (2019)
15. Qin, X., Zhang, Z., Huang, C., Dehghan, M., Zaiane, O.R., Jagersand, M.: U2-Net: Going deeper with nested U-structure for salient object detection. Pattern Recogn. **106**, 107404 (2020)
16. Loshchilov, I., Hutter, F.:. SGDR: Stochastic gradient descent with warm restarts. In: 5th International Conference on Learning Representations, ICLR 2017 - Conference Track Proceedings (2017)
17. Ma, K., Shu, Z., Bai, X., Wang, J., Samaras, D.: Docunet: Document image unwarping via a stacked u-net. In: Proceedings of the IEEE Conference on Computer Vision and Pattern Recognition, pp. 4700–4709 (2018)
18. Tang, Z., Peng, X., Geng, S., Zhu, Y., Metaxas, D.N.: Cu-Net: Coupled U-nets. In: British Machine Vision Conference 2018, BMVC 2018 (2019)
19. Jadon, S.: A survey of loss functions for semantic segmentation. In: 2020 IEEE Conference on Computational Intelligence in Bioinformatics and Computational Biology, CIBCB 2020 (2020)
20. Glorot, X., Bengio, Y.: Understanding the difficulty of training deep feedforward neural networks. J. Mach. Learn. Res. **9**, 249–256 (2010)
21. Kingma, D.P., Ba, J.L.: Adam: A method for stochastic optimization. In: 3rd International Conference on Learning Representations, ICLR 2015 - Conference Track Proceedings (2015)
22. Koch, T.L., Perslev, M., Igel, C., Brandt, S.S.: Accurate segmentation of dental panoramic radiographs with u-nets. In: 2019 IEEE 16th International Symposium on Biomedical Imaging (ISBI 2019), pp. 15–19 IEEE (2019)
23. Singh, N.K., Raza, K.: Medical image generation using generative adversarial networks: A review. Health informatics: A computational perspective in healthcare, pp. 77–96 (2021)

The `EsnTorch` Library: Efficient Implementation of Transformer-Based Echo State Networks

Jérémie Cabessa[1,2,3]([✉]), Hugo Hernault[1], Yves Lamonato[1], Mathieu Rochat[1,4], and Yariv Z. Levy[1]

[1] Playtika Ltd., 1003 Lausanne, Switzerland
{hugoh,yvesl,yarivl}@playtika.com
[2] Laboratory DAVID, UVSQ – Université Paris-Saclay, 78000 Versailles, France
jeremie.cabessa@uvsq.fr
[3] Institute of Computer Science of the Czech Academy of Sciences, 8207 Prague 8, Czech Republic
[4] Mathematics Section (SMA), EPFL, 1015 Lausanne, Switzerland
mathieu.rochat@epfl.ch

Abstract. Transformer-based models have revolutionized NLP. But in general, these models are highly resource consuming. Based on this consideration, several reservoir computing approaches to NLP have shown promising results. In this context, we propose `EsnTorch`, a library that implements echo state networks (ESNs) with transformer-based embeddings for text classification. `EsnTorch` is developed in `PyTorch`, optimized to work on GPU, and compatible with the **transformers** and **datasets** libraries from Hugging Face: the major data science platform for NLP. Accordingly, our library can make use of all the models and datasets available from Hugging Face. A transformer-based ESN implemented in `EsnTorch` consists of four building blocks: (1) An embedding layer, which uses a transformer-based model to embed the input texts; (2) A reservoir layer, which can implements three kinds of reservoirs: recurrent, linear or null; (3) A pooling layer, which offers three kinds of pooling strategies: mean, last, or None; (4) And a learning algorithm block, which provides six different supervised learning algorithms. Overall, this work falls within the context of sustainable models for NLP.

Keywords: reservoir computing · echo state networks · natural language processing (NLP) · text classification · transformers · BERT · python library · Hugging Face

1 Introduction

In 2017, the *transformer* model opened the way for a new generation of language models [29]. A transformer consists of encoder-decoder blocks augmented with a self-attention mechanism. This architecture solves parallelization and

M. Tanveer et al. (Eds.): ICONIP 2022, CCIS 1794, pp. 235–246, 2023.
https://doi.org/10.1007/978-981-99-1648-1_20

long-term dependency issues encountered by classical recurrent neural networks (like LSTMs, GRUs, etc.). The transformer gave rise to a multitude of models that broke the barriers of NLP. In particular, the BERT model, which is composed of several encoder blocks, achieves impressive performance on most common NLP tasks [3]. In its pre-trained form, BERT can be used as a powerful word or sentence dynamic embedding, taking over several previous pre-trained embeddings, like word2vec, GloVe, FastText, and ELMo.

But the transformer-based models are highly resource consuming. For instance, BERT contains from 110M to 340M parameters. And while the pre-trained model is available off-the-shelf, the fine-tuning process remains computationally expensive. In an effort to address these drawbacks, lighter and faster versions of BERT have been proposed [20,26].

The issues of high model complexity and expensive fine-tuning process have been addressed from the perspective of *reservoir computing (RC)*, and more particularly, using *echo state networks (ESNs)* [12–15]. An ESN is composed of an inputs layer, a random recurrent reservoir on neurons, and a output layer. During training, the input and reservoir weights are kept fixed, and only the output weights are learned, usually via simple regression methods. The recurrent architecture of the reservoir provides the memory necessary to the handling of textual data. Their fast and light training process counterbalances the high computational cost of transformer-based models. ESNs have been applied successfully to a large variety of machine learning problems [17,18]. Recently, deep ESNs have been introduced [6].

In the context of NLP, several studies based on echo state networks have already been conducted (see [1] for further details on these related works). For instance, a biologically inspired reservoir computing approach to grammatical inference, semantic representation, and language acquisition with applications in human-robot interaction has been proposed [5,8–11,27]. On the machine learning side, ESNs have been considered for automatic speech recognition, showing that decoders can be replaced by ESNs without performance drop [24]. ESNs have also been applied to named entity recognition (NER) [19] and authorship attribution [22]. Attention-based ESNs with FastText embedding as inputs have been proposed and successfully applied to question classification [4]. ESNs have also been considered in the general context of text classification, using either static GloVe or dynamic BERT embedding as inputs [1,2]. These ESNs achieve good accuracy with particularly fast training times. Besides, ESNs have been considered as one among other fast methods for computing sentence representations, using the pre-trained word embeddings FastText and GloVe as inputs [30]. This work shows that the quality of the pre-trained word embedding plays a crucial role in the performance of the subsequent encoder that builds upon it. Finally, a different reservoir computing approach to transformers has also been proposed [23]. In this work, the so-called reservoir transformers achieve better performance-efficiency trade-offs than classical transformers.

Based on these considerations as well as on recent studies from ours [1,2], we propose `EsnTorch`, a library that implements echo state networks (ESNs) with transformer-based embeddings as inputs, in the context of text classification. `EsnTorch` is developed in `PyTorch` and optimized to work on GPU in a parallelized way. `EsnTorch` operates in conjunction with the `transformers` and `datasets` libraries from Hugging Face: the major data science platform for NLP. Accordingly, it can make use of the 60K models and 7K datasets available from this platform. A transformer-based ESN implemented in `EsnTorch` consists of four building blocks: (1) An embedding layer which uses a transformer-based model to embed the input texts; (2) A reservoir layer which implements three kinds of reservoirs: recurrent, linear or null; (3) A pooling layer which offers three kinds of pooling strategies: mean, last, or None; (4) And a learning algorithm block which provides six different supervised learning algorithms. We believe that the combined transformer-ESN approach to NLP proposed in this work offers major advantages in terms of computational efficiency. Overall, this study falls within the context of sustainable models for NLP. `EsnTorch` is available on GitHub at the following address: https://github.com/PlaytikaResearch/esntorch.

2   Related Works

Several Python libraries targeted to the implementation of ESNs already exist, but to the best of our knowledge, none of them possess the combined features of being implemented in `PyTorch`, optimized to operate on GPU, specifically targeted for NLP, and compatible with Hugging Face.

In particular, ReservoirPy is a complete, well designed and user-friendly library for reservoir computing implemented in `numpy` [28]. The library contains several attractive features: offline and online training, parallel implementation, sparse matrix computation, advanced learning rules, and compatibility with `hyperopt` for hyperparameter tuning. DeepESN, PyRCN and easyesn are three libraries for deep ESNs and ESNs, respectively, also implemented in `numpy`. The two last ones are compatible with `scikit-learn` [25]. In addition, EchoTorch is a very complete library for ESNs implemented in `PyTorch` [21]. It has been used for an NLP application [22]. PyTorch-ESN is a well-designed `PyTorch` module implementing Echo State Networks. The readout is trainable by ridge regression or by PyTorch's optimizers. Implementation of deep ESNs is also possible.

3   ESNs for Text Classification

Echo state networks. An *leaky integrator echo state network (ESN)* is a recurrent neural network composed of N_u input units, N_x hidden units referred to as the *reservoir*, and N_y output units. The input units are linked to the reservoir (weights $\mathbf{W}_{\text{in}}$), the reservoir is recurrently connected (weights $\mathbf{W}_{\text{res}}$ and bias $\mathbf{b}_{\text{res}}$), and projects onto the output units (weights $\mathbf{W}_{\text{out}}$ and bias $\mathbf{b}_{\text{out}}$).

The input, reservoir and output states of the network at time $t > 0$ are denoted by $\mathbf{u}(t) \in \mathbb{R}^{N_u}$, $\mathbf{x}(t) \in \mathbb{R}^{N_x}$ and $\mathbf{y}(t) \in \mathbb{R}^{N_y}$, respectively. The state $\mathbf{x}(0)$ is the *initial state*. The dynamics of the network is governed by the following equations:

$$\tilde{\mathbf{x}}(t + 1) = f_{\text{res}}\big(\mathbf{W}_{\text{in}}\mathbf{u}(t + 1) + \mathbf{W}_{\text{res}}\mathbf{x}(t) + \mathbf{b}_{\text{res}}\big) \tag{1}$$

$$\mathbf{x}(t + 1) = (1 - \alpha)\mathbf{x}(t) + \alpha\tilde{\mathbf{x}}(t + 1) \tag{2}$$

$$\mathbf{y}(t + 1) = f_{\text{out}}\big(\mathbf{W}_{\text{out}}\mathbf{x}(t + 1) + \mathbf{b}_{\text{out}}\big) \tag{3}$$

where f_{res} and f_{out} are the *activation functions* of the reservoir and output units (applied component-wise), and α is the *leaking rate* ($0 \leq \alpha \leq 1$).

The leaking rate α modulates the updating speed of the reservoir dynamics (cf. Eq. (2)) [17]. The input weights $\mathbf{W}_{\text{in}}$ as well as the biases $\mathbf{b}_{\text{res}}$ and $\mathbf{b}_{\text{out}}$ are initialized randomly from uniform distributions $\mathcal{U}(-a, a)$ and $\mathcal{U}(-b, b)$, respectively, where a is the *input scaling* and b is the *bias scaling*. The input scaling affects the non-linearity of the reservoir dynamics [17]. The reservoir weights $\mathbf{W}_{\text{res}}$ are also initialized randomly from a uniform or a Gaussian distribution, then modified to have a given *sparsity* r, and finally rescaled such that the *spectral radius*[1] of the matrix $\mathbf{W} := (1 - \alpha)\mathbf{I} + \alpha\mathbf{W}_{\text{res}}$ is equal to some given value ρ. In practice, taking $\rho < 1$ ensures that the *echo state property* – an asymptotic stability condition ensuring that a consistent learning can be achieved – is satisfied in most situations [7,14,17,18,32]. The spectral radius ρ regulates the effect of past inputs on the reservoir states: larger spectral radii being associated with longer input memories [17].

In an ESN, the input and reservoir weights $\mathbf{W}_{\text{in}}$ and $\mathbf{W}_{\text{res}}$ are kept fixed, and only the output weights $\mathbf{W}_{\text{out}}$ are trained. This feature render ESNs particularly computationally efficient. Notice that an ESN with N_x reservoir units contains only $|\mathbf{W}_{\text{out}}| + |\mathbf{b}_{\text{out}}| = N_y \times (N_x + 1)$ learning parameters (e.g., 2002 parameters for an ESN with 1000 reservoir units and 2 output units). Usually, the output weights $\mathbf{W}_{\text{out}}$ are computed by minimizing a loss function of the predictions and labels by means of a Ridge regression. However, any other supervised learning algorithm can be envisioned. In general, some initial transient of the ESN dynamics is used to *warm up* the reservoir, and the initial state of the reservoir modified accordingly [17].

Training paradigm. ESNs have been successfully applied to text classification tasks [1,2]. In this framework, a *transformer-based ESN* consists of a 4-block model of the form:

$$\text{EMBEDDING} + \text{RESERVOIR} + \text{POOLING} + \text{LEARNING ALGO.}$$

More specifically, the model takes a tokenized text as input. The EMBEDDING layer embeds the successive tokens into corresponding input vectors. The RESERVOIR layer then passes the embedded inputs into a reservoir, producing

---

[1] The spectral radius of a matrix $\mathbf{W}$, denoted by $\rho(\mathbf{W})$, is the largest absolute value of the eigenvalues of $\mathbf{W}$.

a sequence of reservoir states (cf. Eq. (1)-(2)). The POOLING layer merges the reservoir states into a single vector, which constitutes the *text embedding* per se. After all texts have been processed in this way, the LEARNING ALGO block takes all *text embeddings* together with their corresponding *labels* and fed them to a supervised learning algorithm, in order to learn the association between them. The whole process is illustrated in Fig. 1.

The `EsnTorch` library implements the above mentioned model and training paradigm in an optimized way.

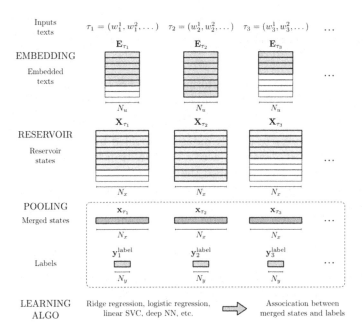

Fig. 1. Custom training paradigm of an ESN for a text classification task. Horizontal rectangles represent vectors. Empty rectangles represent null padding vectors used for batch parallelization. The ESN is composed of 4 blocks. **EMBEDDING:** each raw input text is tokenized and embedded into a sequence of input vectors (green rectangles). **RESERVOIR:** the input vectors (green rectangles) are passed through the ESN with "warm" initial state (yellow rectangle), yielding corresponding reservoir states (blue rectangles). **POOLING:** the reservoir states are merged into a single merged state (blue rectangle). The process is repeated for all input texts. **LEARNING ALGO:** a supervised learning algorithm is trained to learn the association between the merged states (blue rectangles) and their corresponding labels (red rectangles).

4   EsnTorch

The **EsnTorch** library is developed in **PyTorch**, optimized to work on GPU in a parallelized way, and operates in conjunction with the **transformers** and **datasets** libraries from Hugging Face [16,31]. The required imports are the following:

```
import torch

from datasets import load_dataset, Dataset, concatenate_datasets
from transformers import AutoTokenizer
from transformers.data.data_collator import DataCollatorWithPadding

import esntorch.esn as esn
import esntorch.learning_algo as la
```

As described in Sect. 3, a transformer-based ESN for text classification consists of a 4-block model. **EsnTorch** implements each of these blocks (see Sects. 4.1-4.4 below). In particular:

- **EsnTorch** has access to the 7K datasets provided by Hugging Face.
- The EMBEDDING layer can access the 60K transformer-based models provided by Hugging Face to embed the input texts.
- The RESERVOIR layer can implements three kinds of reservoirs: recurrent, linear or null.
- The POOLING layer offers three types of pooling strategies: mean, last, or None.
- The LEARNING ALGO block provides six different learning algorithms.

The next sections describe the dataset creation, as well as the instantiation, training and evaluation of a model in more details.

4.1   Dataset

The creation or download, tokenization, and preparation of a dataset and its dataloaders are achieved by means of the **datasets** library [16]. The code below illustrates the preparation of the TREC dataset (question classification). Here, the **bert-base-uncased** tokenizer is used. For compatibility purposes with our library, the **label** and **length** columns should be renamed by **labels** and **lengths**, respectively. Sorting the data by length significantly increases their processing speed. The batch size should be determined by the available memory.

```
# Load, tokenize and prepare dataset and dataloaders
tokenizer = AutoTokenizer.from_pretrained('bert-base-uncased')

def tokenize(sample):
    sample = tokenizer(sample['text'], truncation=True,
                       padding=False,
                       return_length=True)
    return sample

dataset = load_dataset('trec', split=None)
dataset = dataset.map(tokenize, batched=True)
dataset = dataset.rename_column('label-coarse', 'labels')
```

```
dataset = dataset.rename_column('length', 'lengths')
dataset = dataset.sort('lengths')
dataset.set_format(type='torch', columns=['input_ids', 'attention_mask',
                                          'labels', 'lengths'])

dataloader_d = {}

for k, v in dataset.items():
    dataloader_d[k] = torch.utils.data.DataLoader(v, batch_size=256,
        collate_fn=DataCollatorWithPadding(tokenizer))
```

4.2   Model

The instantiation of a model is achieved in four steps:

1. Set the parameters of the model;
2. Define a pooling strategy;
3. Define a learning algorithm;
4. Warm up the model, if needed.

The code below provides an example of instantiation of an ESN.

```
# ESN parameters
device = torch.device('cuda' if torch.cuda.is_available() else 'cpu')

esn_params = {
              'embedding': 'bert-base-uncased',  # model name
              'input_dim': 768,                   # embedding dim
              'distribution': 'uniform'           # 'uniform', 'gaussian'
              'dim': 1000,
              'sparsity': 0.9,
              'spectral_radius': 0.9,
              'leaking_rate': 0.5,
              'activation_function': 'tanh',      # 'tanh', 'relu'
              'input_scaling': 0.1,
              'bias_scaling': 0.1,
              'mean': 0.0,
              'std': 1.0,
              'pooling_strategy': 'mean',         # 'mean', 'last', None
              'learning_algo': None,              # initialized below
              'criterion': None,                  # initialized below
              'optimizer': None,                  # initialized below
              'bidirectional': False,             # True, False
              'mode' : 'recurrent_layer',         # 'no_layer',
                                                  # 'linear_layer',
                                                  # 'recurrent_layer'
              'deep' : False,                     # for deep esn
              'nb_layers' : None,                 # if deep, nb of reservoirs
              'device': device,
              'seed': 42
              }
# Step 1: Instantiate the ESN
ESN = esn.EchoStateNetwork(**esn_params)

# Step 2: Instantiate the learning algo
ESN.learning_algo = la.RidgeRegression(alpha=10.0)

ESN = ESN.to(esn_params['device']) # put model on device

# Step 3: Warm up the ESN on 20 sentences
ESN.warm_up(dataset['train'].select(range(20)))
```

Regarding step 1, most parameters are self-explanatory and more details can be found in the documentation of the library. In particular, The `embedding` parameter is the name of the Hugging Face model used to embed the input texts (the list of all models can be found here). The `input_dim` should correspond to the dimension of this embedding. The next 10 parameters specify the reservoir characteristics: size, distribution, weights, etc. The `mean` and `std` parameters are only considered if `distribution` =`"gaussian"`. The `bidirection` parameter specifies whether the input texts are processed in a bidirectional way or not.

The `mode` parameter can take three different values

`"recurrent_layer"`, `"no_layer"` or `"linear_layer"`

which specifies the kind of reservoir to be considered. In the `"recurrent_layer"` mode, a recurrent reservoir is defined according to the previous parameters. In this case, a "classical" ESN is implemented, as described in Sect. 3. In the `"no_layer"` mode, no reservoir is considered, meaning that the input layer is directly fed to the learning algorithm. This feature allows to assess the proper contribution of the reservoir to the results, by shutting down the whole reservoir. In the `"linear_layer"` mode, a linear (i.e., non-recurrent) reservoir is implemented. This feature enables to evaluate the contribution of the recurrence of the reservoir, by removing this characteristics.

For step 2, the `pooling_strategy` parameter can take the three values

`"mean"`, `"last"`, or `None`

which correspond to three kinds of pooling layers. The `"mean"` and `"last"` pooling define the merged state as the mean and last of the reservoir states, respectively. The `None` pooling leaves the reservoir states unmerged (cf. [1,2,22] for further details). In general, the `"mean"` pooling performs significantly better than the others. Finally, the `deep` parameter implements a deep ESN and is discussed in further details in Sect. 4.5.

Regarding step 3, six learning algorithms divided two families can be considered:

(i) The ones for which there exists a closed-form solution (e.g. Ridge regression), or which are adapted from the `scikit-learn` library (e.g. Linear SVC):

`RidgeRegression(...)`, `RidgeRegression_skl(...)`, `LinearSVC(...)` and
`LogisticRegression_skl(...)`.

In this case, only the algorithm is to be specified.

(ii) The ones that are trained via a gradient descent method implemented inside the library (e.g. logistic regression):

`LogisticRegression(...)` and `DeepNN(...)`.

In this case, in addition to the learning algorithm itself, a `pytorch` criterion and optimizer need to be given.

Example of a learning algorithms of type (i) and (ii) are given in the code snippet below. Custom learning algorithms can be added to the file `learning_alog.py`.

```
# Type (i) learning algo
ESN.learning_algo = la.LinearSVC(C=1.0)

# Type (ii) learning algo
ESN.learning_algo = la.LogisticRegression(input_dim=768, output_dim=6)
ESN.criterion = torch.nn.CrossEntropyLoss()
ESN.optimizer = torch.optim.Adam(ESN.learning_algo.parameters(),lr=0.01)
```

Once instantiated, the model is put on the required device (CPU or GPU) by means of the .to(device) method.

In step 4, the model is warmed up by passing a certain number of texts from the train set, and its initial state is modified accordingly. This is done by means of the warm_up() method.

4.3 Training

The training of the model is achieved via the fit() method. For training algorithms of type (i), no additional parameter is required. For training algorithms of type (ii), the number of epochs and number of steps after which the loss is printed can be specified (otherwise default values are used). The training process is illustrated in the code snippet below.

```
# For learning algo of type (i):
ESN.fit(dataloader_d["train"])

# For learning algo of type (ii):
ESN.fit(dataloader_d["train"], epochs=10, iter_steps=50)
```

4.4 Evaluation

After training, the predictions and accuracy on the train and test sets can be obtained by means of the **predict()** method. The predictions can further be used to compute the classification table of the model. These features are illustrated in the following code snippet.

```
# Train predictions and accuracy
train_pred, train_acc = ESN.predict(dataloader_d["train"])
train_pred, train_acc

(array([0, 3, 0, ..., 1, 1, 0]), 92.49816581071167)

# Test predictions and accuracy
test_pred, test_acc = ESN.predict(dataloader_d["test"])
test_pred, test_acc

(array([0, 0, 0, ..., 3, 1, 1]), 93.2)

# Classification report
from sklearn.metrics import classification_report

test_truth = dataset_d['test']['labels']
print(classification_report(test_pred.tolist(), test_truth.tolist()))

              precision    recall  f1-score   support
```

0	0.99	0.91	0.95	151
1	0.79	0.93	0.85	80
2	0.78	1.00	0.88	7
3	0.95	0.94	0.95	66
4	0.98	0.97	0.97	115
5	0.93	0.93	0.93	81
accuracy			0.93	500
macro avg	0.90	0.94	0.92	500
weighted avg	0.94	0.93	0.93	500

4.5 Deep ESNs

Deep ESNs can also be implemented. The instatiation, training and evaluation of a deep ESN is similar to what has been described for a regular ESN (see Sects. 4.2–4.4). The only difference relies in the instantiation part, where a group of reservoirs instead of a single one is instantiated. Towards this purpose, the "deep" parameter is set to True and the "nb_layers" to some integer $P \in \mathbb{N}$ that represents the desired number of reservoirs. Each other parameter related to the reservoir characteristics (like "dim", "sparsity", "spectral_radius", etc.) is given either as a list of values [v1,...,vP] or as a single value v. In the former case, the successive reservoirs $R_1,...,R_P$ of the deep ESN are built on the basis of the successive parameter values of [v1,...,vP], respectively. In the latter case, all reservoirs $R_1,...,R_P$ are constructed with respect to the same parameter value v.

5   Conclusion

We introduced EsnTorch, a user-friendly library that implements echo state networks with transformer-based embeddings for NLP applications. EsnTorch is developed in PyTorch, optimized to work on GPU, and operates in conjunction with the transformers and datasets libraries from Hugging Face: the major data science platform for NLP. The transformer-ESN model described in Sect. 3 has already been implemented with a previous version of this library, and shown promising results [1,2].

We believe that the combined transformer-ESN approach to NLP proposed in this work offers major advantages in terms of computational efficiency. Overall, this study falls within the context of sustainable models for NLP.

Acknowledgment. The authors are grateful to Playtika Ltd. for contributing to an inspiring R&D environment. The research was partially done with institutional support RVO: 67985807 and partially supported by the grant of the Czech Science Foundation AppNeCo No. GA22-02067S.

References

1. Cabessa, J., Hernault, H., Kim, H., Lamonato, Y., Levy, Y.Z.: Efficient text classification with echo state networks. In: International Joint Conference on Neural Networks, IJCNN 2021, pp. 1–8. IEEE (2021)

2. Cabessa, J., Lamonato, H.H.Y., Levy, Y.Z.: Combining bert and echo state networks for efficient text classification. Applied Intelligence (Submitted 2022)
3. Devlin, J., Chang, M., Lee, K., Toutanova, K.: BERT: pre-training of deep bidirectional transformers for language understanding. In: Burstein, J., Doran, C., Solorio, T. (eds.) Proceedings of the 2019 Conference of the North American Chapter of the Association for Computational Linguistics: Human Language Technologies, NAACL-HLT, Volume 1, 2019. pp. 4171–4186. ACL (2019)
4. Di Sarli, D., Gallicchio, C., Micheli, A.: Question classification with untrained recurrent embeddings. In: Alviano, M., Greco, G., Scarcello, F. (eds.) AI*IA 2019. LNCS (LNAI), vol. 11946, pp. 362–375. Springer, Cham (2019). https://doi.org/10.1007/978-3-030-35166-3_26
5. Dominey, P.F., Hoen, M., Inui, T.: A neurolinguistic model of grammatical construction processing. J. Cogn. Neurosci. **18**(12), 2088–2107 (2006)
6. Gallicchio, C., Micheli, A., Pedrelli, L.: Design of deep echo state networks. Neural Netw. **108**, 33–47 (2018)
7. Gandhi, M., Jaeger, H.: Echo state property linked to an input: Exploring a fundamental characteristic of recurrent neural networks. Neural Comput. **25**(3), 671–696 (2013)
8. Hinaut, X., Dominey, P.F.: Real-time parallel processing of grammatical structure in the fronto-striatal system: A recurrent network simulation study using reservoir computing. PLOS ONE **8**(2), 1–18 (2013)
9. Hinaut, X., Lance, F., Droin, C., Petit, M., Pointeau, G., Dominey, P.F.: Corticostriatal response selection in sentence production: Insights from neural network simulation with reservoir computing. Brain Lang. **150**, 54–68 (2015)
10. Hinaut, X., Petit, M., Pointeau, G., Dominey, P.F.: Exploring the acquisition and production of grammatical constructions through human-robot interaction with echo state networks. Front. Neurorobot. **8**, 16 (2014)
11. Hinaut, X., Twiefel, J.: Teach your robot your language! trainable neural parser for modeling human sentence processing: Examples for 15 languages. IEEE Trans. Cogn. Dev. Syst. **12**(2), 179–188 (2020)
12. Jaeger, H.: Short term memory in echo state networks. GMD-Report 152, GMD - German National Research Institute for Computer Science (2002)
13. Jaeger, H.: Echo state network. Scholarpedia **2**(9), 2330 (2007)
14. Jaeger, H.: The "echo state" approach to analysing and training recurrent neural networks. GMD Report 148, GMD - German National Research Institute for Computer Science (2001)
15. Jaeger, H., Haas, H.: Harnessing nonlinearity: predicting chaotic systems and saving energy in wireless communication. Science **304**(5667), 78–80 (2004)
16. Lhoest, Q., et al.: Datasets: A community library for natural language processing. In: Proceedings of the 2021 Conference on Empirical Methods in Natural Language Processing: System Demonstrations, pp. 175–184. ACL (2021)
17. Lukoševičius, M.: A practical guide to applying echo state networks. In: Montavon, G., Orr, G.B., Müller, K.-R. (eds.) Neural Networks: Tricks of the Trade. LNCS, vol. 7700, pp. 659–686. Springer, Heidelberg (2012). https://doi.org/10.1007/978-3-642-35289-8_36
18. Lukoševičius, M., Jaeger, H.: Reservoir computing approaches to recurrent neural network training. Comput. Sci. Rev. **3**(3), 127–149 (2009)
19. Ramamurthy, R., Stenzel, R., Sifa, R., Ladi, A., Bauckhage, C.: Echo state networks for named entity recognition. In: Tetko, I.V., Kůrková, V., Karpov, P., Theis, F. (eds.) ICANN 2019. LNCS, vol. 11731, pp. 110–120. Springer, Cham (2019). https://doi.org/10.1007/978-3-030-30493-5_11

20. Sanh, V., Debut, L., Chaumond, J., Wolf, T.: Distilbert, a distilled version of BERT: smaller, faster, cheaper and lighter. CoRR abs/1910.01108 (2019)
21. Schaetti, N.: Echotorch: Reservoir computing with pytorch. https://github.com/nschaetti/EchoTorch (2018)
22. Schaetti, N.: Behaviors of reservoir computing models for textual documents classification. In: International Joint Conference on Neural Networks, IJCNN 2019 Budapest, Hungary, July 14–19, 2019, pp. 1–7. IEEE (2019)
23. Shen, S., Baevski, A., Morcos, A., Keutzer, K., Auli, M., Kiela, D.: Reservoir transformers. In: Proceedings of the 59th Annual Meeting of the Association for Computational Linguistics and the 11th International Joint Conference on Natural Language Processing (Volume 1: Long Papers), pp. 4294–4309. ACL, Online (2021)
24. Shrivastava, H., Garg, A., Cao, Y., Zhang, Y., Sainath, T.N.: Echo state speech recognition. In: IEEE International Conference on Acoustics, Speech and Signal Processing, ICASSP 2021, pp. 5669–5673. IEEE (2021)
25. Steiner, P., Jalalvand, A., Stone, S., Birkholz, P.: Pyrcn: A toolbox for exploration and application of reservoir computing networks (2021)
26. Sun, Z., Yu, H., Song, X., Liu, R., Yang, Y., Zhou, D.: Mobilebert: a compact task-agnostic BERT for resource-limited devices. In: Jurafsky, D., Chai, J., Schluter, N., Tetreault, J.R. (eds.) Proceedings of the 58th Annual Meeting of the Association for Computational Linguistics, ACL 2020, pp. 2158–2170. ACL (2020)
27. Tong, M.H., Bickett, A.D., Christiansen, E.M., Cottrell, G.W.: Learning grammatical structure with echo state networks. Neural Netw. **20**(3), 424–432 (2007)
28. Trouvain, N., Pedrelli, L., Dinh, T.T., Hinaut, X.: *ReservoirPy*: an efficient and user-friendly library to design echo state networks. In: Farkaš, I., Masulli, P., Wermter, S. (eds.) ICANN 2020. LNCS, vol. 12397, pp. 494–505. Springer, Cham (2020). https://doi.org/10.1007/978-3-030-61616-8_40
29. Vaswani, A., et al: Attention is all you need. In: Guyon, I., von Luxburg, U., Bengio, S., Wallach, H.M., Fergus, R., Vishwanathan, S.V.N., Garnett, R. (eds.) Advances in Neural Information Processing Systems 30: Annual Conference on Neural Information Processing Systems 2017, pp. 5998–6008 (2017)
30. Wieting, J., Kiela, D.: No training required: Exploring random encoders for sentence classification. In: 7th International Conference on Learning Representations, ICLR 2019, New Orleans, LA, USA, May 6–9, 2019. OpenReview.net (2019)
31. Wolf, T., et al.: Transformers: State-of-the-art natural language processing. In: Proceedings of the 2020 Conference on Empirical Methods in Natural Language Processing: System Demonstrations, pp. 38–45. ACL, Online (202,
32. Yildiz, I.B., Jaeger, H., Kiebel, S.J.: Re-visiting the echo state property. Neural Netw. **35**, 1–9 (2012)

Wine Characterisation with Spectral Information and Predictive Artificial Intelligence

Jianping Yao[1], Son N. Tran[1(✉)], Hieu Nguyen[1], Samantha Sawyer[2], and Rocco Longo[2,3]

[1] School of Information and Technology, University of Tasmania, 7249 Hobart, Australia
{jianping.yao,sn.tran,hieu.nguyen}@utas.edu.au
[2] Tasmania Institute of Agriculture. Mt Pleasant, 7250 Hobart, Australia
samantha.sawyer@utas.edu.au
[3] Winequip, Dudley Park, 5008 Adelaide, Australia
rocco@winequip.com.au

Abstract. The purpose of this paper is to use absorbance data obtained by human tasting and an ultraviolet-visible (UV-Vis) scanning spectrophotometer to predict the attributes of grape juice (GJ) and to classify the wine's origin, respectively. The approach combined machine learning (ML) techniques with spectroscopy to find a relatively simple way to apply them in two stages of winemaking and help improve the traditional wine analysis methods regarding sensory data and wine's origins. This new technique has overcome the disadvantages of the complex sensors by taking advantage of spectral fingerprinting technology and forming a comprehensive study of the employment of AI in the wine analysis domain. In the results, Support Vector Machine (SVM) was the most efficient and robust in both attributes and origin prediction tasks. Both the accuracy and F1 score of the origin prediction exceed 91%. The feature ranking approach found that the more influential wavelengths usually appear at the lower end of the scan range, 250 nm (nanometers) to 420 nm, which is believed to be of great help for selecting appropriate validation methods and sensors to extract wine data in future research. The knowledge of this research provides new ideas and early solutions for the wine industry or other beverage industries to integrate big data and IoT in the future, which significantly promotes the development of 'Smart Wineries'.

Keywords: Smart agriculture · Machine learning · Wine characterisation

1 Introduction

With the increasing demand for smart agriculture and production, wine analysis and new technologies for rapid analysis are developed. Due to wine containing multiple chemical components [5], manually executed analyses still take a

© The Author(s), under exclusive license to Springer Nature Singapore Pte Ltd. 2023
M. Tanveer et al. (Eds.): ICONIP 2022, CCIS 1794, pp. 247–259, 2023.
https://doi.org/10.1007/978-981-99-1648-1_21

large proportion of the wine production time. The concept of Smart Winery was introduced into the winemaking industry to reduce the costs associated with labour, uncertainty and errors, simplify and stabilize the winemaking process [7–9,11,18]. For example, Longo et al. explained the possibility and method of timely and objectively monitoring the grape juice to better control, monitor and optimize the winemaking process [20]. As illustrated by Fig. 1, The chemical composition during the process between grapes are harvested and crushed to make grape juice (GJ) will impact the final wine quality and flavor. For example, phenolics impact wine color, and palate attributes [4]. During this step, human tasting can be used to collect wine sensory data in different winemaking stages before bottling to label the samples' attributes. Sensory data is popular to be used as the attributes to analyze the wine's chemical composition as their representation.

The traditional wine attributes analysis relies primarily on wine experts' tasting, which is very time-consuming and expensive. In addition, many factors, including physical conditions and residues in the mouth, affect human tastes, causing analysis results sometimes to be inaccurate. Therefore, the wine industry is always searching for a more automated, less costly, and accurate way to extract the sensory data of wine, which triggers the combination of IoT and AI in this field to offer a better solution.

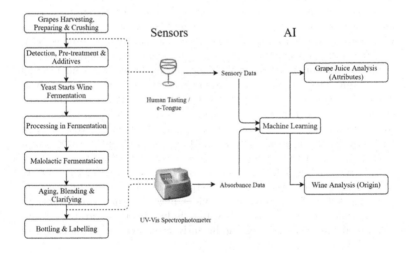

Fig. 1. Wine process

Some sensors have been employed to automate the wine attributes collection process. For example, the electronic nose (E-nose) can monitor the evolution of desirable chemicals in place of human tasters. However, the data collected by these sensors is yet to be commercialized [5] because complex sensors like E-nose require preprocessing the raw data to digitalize them for analysis. Therefore, the collected data can only be analyzed by professionals and objective mechanisms to effectively determine and identify the composition and quality of wine products. Compared with E-nose, ultraviolet-visible (UV-Vis) spectroscopy is a more standard method to assess parameters throughout the winemaking process with a UV-Vis scanning spectrophotometer. On the other hand, the development of artificial intelligence (AI), especially machine learning (ML), has been successfully applied in most aspects of wine research and winemaking [3,6,18,25,28]. However, most of the research is not comprehensive enough to combine with sensors to identify the particular attributes of the wine.

This paper comprehends two tasks, with both datasets provided by the Tasmanian Institute of Agriculture (TIA), Launceston, Tasmania (Australia). Task I investigates the relationship between UV-Vis and grape juice's key sensory features (astringency, bitterness, and herbaceous). In task I (i.e., regression task), we aimed to predict the data of the astringency, bitterness, and herbaceous characteristics of grape juice with different treatment through UV-Vis absorbance unit values, which were collected by UV-Vis scanning spectrophotometer. The astringency, bitterness, and herbaceous labels for each sample were collected by human tasting. Tasters are constituted by a number of panelists who received professional tasting training. The purpose of task II (i.e., classification task) is to classify the region and vineyard of the grape juice samples through basic juice parameters such as pH, total soluble solids (TSS), total acidity (TA), harvest type, and UV-Vis absorbance unit values. Both Tasks adopt the same set of ML algorithms - Random Forest (RF), Support Vector Machine (SVM), Deep Neural Networks (DNN, 1-3 layers), Convolutional Neural Network (CNN, 1 dimensional), Long Short-Term Memory (LSTM) and Bidirectional LSTM. However, the evaluation metrics for algorithms are different for two tasks - Task I as the regression task uses Mean Absolute Error (MAE), Root Mean Square Error (RMSE), and Explained Variance Score (EVS); Task II as the classification task uses Accuracy and F1 scores and tests them by the leave-one-out method.

This paper finds an efficient method that combines with ML approaches to identify grape juice's sensory characteristics by establishing the links between them and Spectroscopy. The sensory characteristics of grape juice under process are one of the keys that decide the wine's quality and category. The automation of sensory characteristics promotes the development of the smart winery industry by significantly saving time and cost. Spectral data combined with some basic chemical parameters are also adopted by the ML method to identify the wine's geographical origin, which is significant for its pricing and grading, to detect its authenticity. The wine industry welcomes new explorations and technologies that bring efficiency and reliability to production and quality.

2   Related Work

Sensory data is previously collected from human tasting and electronic sensors. In human tasting, a number of volunteers are recruited and offered a training. During this period, they acquire the ability to taste and score wine samples' quality and various sensory parameters [7,11,24]. Some researchers make efforts to replace human taste with machines [18,23]. For example, [18] used a bionic electronic nose (E-Nose) to collect the sensory data. Their results gained support and confidence in the reliability of machine sensors relative to human tasting. [23] introduced a series of E-Noses and Tongues for the wine tasting to be developed as the trends. For origin prediction, [8] used chemical elements to identify wines' origin. They determined 13 elements (e.g., Al, Cd & Co), which effectively distinguish origin and authenticity. The study of [9] aimed to use spectroscopy in the visible and wavelength near-infrared (NIR) regions to do the non-destructive measurement of wines and predict the chemical compositions (e.g., ethanol, Free/Total SO_2 & pH). Their research proved that spectroscopy is feasible and effective to predict the basic chemical composition of wine.

Thousands of companies and organisations take advantage of ML's ability to help with decision-making and prediction to save the labour, time, and cost of analysis [6,28]. In past years, SVM has proved its good robustness and performance for high-dimensional space cases [24], and it is widely used to deal with the classification or regression problem of wine quality prediction [3,18,25]. [22] tried to adopt SVM to process quality and price prediction, but they failed to achieve an ideal result. The main goal of [1]'s team was to compare two feature selection methods, Simulated Annealing (SA) and Genetic Algorithm (GA). In [18], SVM was shown to achieve the best performance in vintages and fermentation processes prediction while Neural Networks was the best in production areas and varietals predictionBackpropagation. RF has also been commonly used and achieved good results in various studies [10,18,25]. For example, [10] stated that RF is better than K-nearest Neighbourhood and SVM in their wine quality prediction. [26] relabelled the Red Wine Dataset (UCI) data to make it a binary classification problem (good/bad) and compared Logistic Regression, and RF's effect combined with 10-fold cross-validation. The RF improved the classification by 8% to 85% compared to Logistic Regression's 77%. In addition, [16]'s team used the same dataset to compare the performance of SVM, RF and Naïve Bayes, and the experimental results obtained were 67.25%, 65.83% and 55.91% respectively. However, compared to SVM and RF, [15] stated Artificial Neural Networks (ANN), after appropriate tuning, can get a better prediction accuracy than SVM in small datasets. [11] established three ANN regression models. Model 1 used 100 wavelength's raw absorbance values (1596–2396 nm) to predict the sensory data of Pinot Noir. Model 2 and 3 used weather and water balance data to predict sensory data and wine colour (CIELab, RGB with CMYK), respectively.

Although machine learning has been applied to wine data in several applications, this paper is the first work to comprehensively study different ML models, including shallow learning and deep learning approaches, for different tasks (regression and classification). The use of spectral information extracted from wine and grape juices for prediction is promising for real-life applications.

3   The Color of GJ/WINE

Colour that developed in the pressing process (pressing of the grapes to get juice) is one of the essential factors for grape juice and wine, not only because it influences the customer's purchase decision, but also because it can be used to identify varieties [12], estimate the phenolic content in wine [2], judge wine quality [14], and detect adulteration and frauds [13].

Monitoring of colour development is vital to winemakers to assist in controlling the consistency and quality of wine during production. Typically, winemakers may establish control or reference value by archiving their product data into a database that can be readily compared between different batches of products. Then in production, real-time comparison of the wine colour conducted by analysts may grasp the process of wine manufacturing and ensure the normal fermentation of wine products.

Figure 2 shows the contrast spectrogram of the irradiation wavelength from 200 nm to 600 nm. Generally, the light below 380nm is ultraviolet light and cannot be seen by human eyes, so we used grey and white stripes instead. From 380 to 600 nm, we can see violet, blue, green, yellow, and orange from left to right.

Spectroscopy or spectral fingerprinting technology has been used widely in the wine industry because it is a mature, accessible, and reliable technology to analyse wine quality through its colour. UV-Vis spectroscopy (the ultraviolet region is 180–390 nm and visible region is 390–780 nm) is one of the most commonly used branches in this technology. Other types of spectral fingerprinting technology include near-infrared (NIR), infrared (IR), mid-infrared (MIR), nuclear magnetic resonance (NMR), and mass (MS) [14]. UV-Vis spectroscopy has been used to quantify compounds in the food and beverage industries, such as polyphenolics in red wine products [21]. The most significant advantage of this technology is that it is fast and straightforward to apply and requires less technical training [27]. The spectral fingerprint relates to the light absorbance in the UV-Vis range of the electromagnetic spectrum according to Beer-Lambert law formula:

$$A = \epsilon l c \tag{1}$$

Because the molar attenuation coefficient (ϵ) of the solution is the same, when the concentration of the solution (c) and the optical path length (l) is fixed, the absorbance (A) of the same solution's samples should be close or the same. Therefore, if we measure the absorbance of wine in different process steps beforehand and record these data into a table, then we can determine the quality of GJ / wine through the absorbance. Considering the reliability and effectiveness of spec-

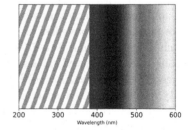

Fig. 2. Absorbance Spectrum

troscopy, some wine analysis professionals believed that more spectral databases of a variety of wines should be developed [12]. We choose to train the ML models on absorbance data of GJ for the same reason.

4   Grape Juice Tasting

4.1   Data Collection

The absorbance data of grape Juice is used to train the regression model to predict the values of three sensory attributes (Astringency, Bitterness, and Herbaceous), and its collecting process will be explained in the next section - Juice (or Grape) Origin Prediction. This section mainly introduces the process we collected the labeling data (the three sensory attributes) of each sample. A panel of 11 panelists (six males, five females; 23–59 years), the post-graduate students or staff of TIA, was convened. Each panelist had completed a minimum of five training sessions over the two weeks prior to the formal sensory analysis. The protocols and training for the descriptive analysis (DA) that we adopt are based on a research paper published in the journal "Food Research International" [19]. Briefly, a generic DA protocol was applied [17], with one-hour training sessions for all descriptors: 'sweetness', 'astringency', 'bitterness', 'acidity', and 'herbaceous'. A sample of each grape juice treatment (n = 7) was provided during the training sessions. Panelists practiced the evaluation of intensity rating for all attributes. 'High' and 'low' intensity standards were obtained using different concentrations of reference standards in water or juice (i.e., 15 and 150 g/L fructose for 'sweetness,' 0.1 and 1 g/L quinine sulfate for 'bitterness,' 1.5 and 15 g/L tartaric acids for 'acidity,' 0.1 and 1 g/L tannin for 'astringency,' one-quarter or one cup of fresh grass for 'herbaceous'). While we were mainly interested in the 'astringency' and 'bitterness' descriptors for the Chardonnay grape juice, as associated with the presence of phenolics, other taste and flavor attributes were included to avoid a 'dumping' effect (i.e., dumping occurs when panelists are limited to responding to only one attribute at the time). As per standard formal DA, panelists were seated and served seven pre-poured covered glasses containing juice samples in randomized order (Williams block design), with each glass was assigned with a 3-digit code. Individual spittoons, citric acid-pectin solution, and unsalted crackers were also served for a mouth rinse and to reduce palate fatigue. The panelists used ballot charts and pencils to rate the intensity of each descriptor from 0 to 9 (0 = absent; 9 = very intense). Three formal DA sessions were conducted to assess each treatment three times formally. Social science ethics approval for collecting tasting data was obtained from the University of Tasmania's Research Integrity and Ethics Unit (Ref No: H0018377). The 11 judges scored each GJ replicate. Total phenolic content and the UV-Vis absorbance were measured (from 200 to 600 nm) for each replicate.

For evaluation, we use Mean Absolute Error (MSE) and Root Mean Square Error (RMS). In addition, Explained Variance Score (EVS) should also be applied to measure the model's total variance. Its formula is as follow:

$$explained\_variance(y, \hat{y}) = 1 - \frac{Var\{y - \hat{y}\}}{Var\{y\}} \tag{2}$$

y is the correct (true) label value, $\hat{y}$ is the predicted value of the model, and Var is the Variance. The best EVS can be 1.0, while the low value represents poor performance.

4.2   Prediction Results

In Task 1, eight ML models have been tested on the attributes of the grape juice samples, which are Astringency (Table 1: Astringency Est.), Bitterness (Table 1: Bitterness Est.) and Herbaceous (Table 1: Herbaceous Est.). For astringency estimation, SVR had the highest performance in the prediction of astringency - the scores of MAE and RMSE were the smallest, and the EVS score was the largest. DNN (1 layer) and LSTM were the second and third best models. (SVR) also had the best performance in Bitterness prediction - achieved the best scores in all three evaluation metrics. DNN (1 layer) and bi-LSTM followed. In Herbaceous prediction (Table 1: Herbaceous Est.), the best model rankings were SVR, DNN (1 layer), and LSTM. The gap between LSTM and bi-LSTM was not obvious because the latter's MAE score was slightly better than the former. Overall, SVR (linear kernel) had the best performance in attributes prediction tasks. Compared with other tested models, it shows certain robustness. The second-best algorithm identified is DNN (1 layer). However, it should be noted that the size of the dataset limited the prediction performance of each model, making prediction tasks difficult. The more detailed and more extensive datasets will be more helpful for robust prediction.

Table 1. Astringency, Bitterness, and Herbaceous estimation using Machine Learning models.

Model	Astringency Est.			Bitterness Est.			Herbaceous Est.		
	MAE↓	RMSE↓	EVS↑	MAE↓	RMSE↓	EVS↑	MAE↓	RMSE↓	EVS↑
SVR	1.287	1.759	0.336	0.792	1.250	0.526	1.402	1.769	0.356
RF	1.671	2.062	0.086	1.180	1.533	0.268	1.658	2.019	0.149
DNN.1	1.518	1.900	0.226	0.992	1.400	0.390	1.506	1.836	0.296
DNN.2	1.660	2.037	0.109	1.206	1.564	0.239	1.621	1.998	0.166
DNN.3	1.687	2.052	0.095	1.272	1.646	0.157	1.650	2.048	0.124
1D-CNN	1.787	2.167	−0.009	1.433	1.800	−0.009	1.767	2.198	−0.009
LSTM	1.565	1.951	0.182	1.104	1.480	0.318	1.546	1.893	0.251
bi-LSTM	1.607	1.977	0.160	1.036	1.437	0.357	1.543	1.932	0.220

5   Juice (or Grape) Origin Prediction

5.1   Data Collection

In this task, juice samples from Chardonnay and Pinot noir grapes were kept at 4°C overnight. Then, they were centrifuged using a 5804 Eppendorf (Hamburg, Germany) for 15 min (at 3350 radial centrifugal force), diluted at a ratio of 1 to 5 with 1 M HCl (Merck, Darmstadt, Germany), and incubated in darkness at an ambient temperature (22°C) for 1 h. Next, we scan the samples with a Genesys 10S UV-Vis spectrophotometer (Thermo Scientific, Waltham, MA, USA) and record the absorbance unit values (contained the spectral phenolic fingerprint) every 2 nm from 200 to 600 nm. Because the samples were placed in disposable 10 mm quartz cuvettes (Brand-GMHB, Wetheim, Germany), specific wavelengths (below 250 nm) were discounted. In the dataset, each sample has the following categories: variety, vineyard, region, the block of its region, harvest type (e.g., by hand or by machine), the replicate number, TSS, pH value, and TA and absorbance unit values (from 200 to 600 nm, in 2 nm increments). We visualize the data to show the details of the absorbance data. We can see that, in Fig. 3a, the absorbance units status of two Chardonnay grape juice samples are from different regions, which are Tamar Valley and Pipers Brook (Tasmania, Australia), with peaks at around 220 nm. Figure 3b shows two Chardonnay samples from different vineyards (we called them A and B) in the same region (Tamar Valley). We can see from the absorbance unit values of the Chardonnay sample from A (black line) that almost all its values are higher than the sample from B. Figure 3c shows two Grape juice samples from different points during the grape pressing process, Free Run and Hard Pressing. We can see they are very different in UV-Vis absorbance unit values. The black one (Free Run)'s values are much higher than the Hard Pressing sample. In terms of attributes, their bitterness scores are similar (Free Run is 2 and Hard Pressing is 3); their Astringency and Herbaceous values are very different (Free Run has 3, 4 respectively, and both values of Hard Pressing are 9). Figure 3d shows the details about all treatments of the grape juice, the black line (Hard Pressing) on the top; Free run (blue), and Cycle 1 (Orange) at the bottom of all lines. The details of their related attributes are shown in the upper right corner, among which 'A' represents Astringency, 'B' represents Bitterness, and 'H' represents Herbaceous.

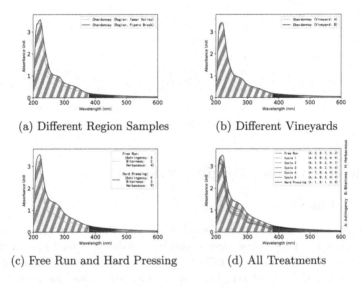

(a) Different Region Samples

(b) Different Vineyards

(c) Free Run and Hard Pressing

(d) All Treatments

Fig. 3. the Absorbance Data of Samples

5.2 Prediction Results

Table 2 is the results of task II. In leave-one-juice-out, we can see that all models have similar performance. DNN (1-layer) is relatively better than other models in terms of Region prediction. LSTM has relatively better performance in terms of Vineyard prediction, but their advantage is not significant because based on the leave-one-juice-out method (It classified the group by the type of samples, and the dataset is divided into 31 parts in total), the types of samples are relatively rare. Especially in vineyard prediction, because the number of the vineyard class is more than others, The problem that there is no group class in the training set corresponding to the test set also appears. Therefore, the result of vineyard prediction through leave-one-juice-out is not good and effective. Through leave-one-juice-out, the model is difficult to be trained enough. In contrast, leave-one-sample-out method is more effective and accurate. In this method, the dataset was divided into 93 parts, using one part as the test set each time. Most algorithms have ideal results around 80%, among which SVM (linear kernel) has the best performance (more than 90%). It has the highest accuracy and F1 score in both Region and Vineyard predictions. Compared with other algorithms, all the DNN methods do not provide satisfactory results, which may be due to the small size of the dataset impacting on performance. As in Table 2, SVM shows the strongest performance. Especially through the leave-one-sample-out method, which can be used to predict both Region and Vineyard.

Table 2. Region and Vineyard Prediction

| Model | Leave-one-juice-out | | | | Leave-one-sample-out | | | |
| | Region | | Vineyard | | Region | | Vineyard | |
	Accuracy	F1	Accuracy	F1	Accuracy	F1	Accuracy	F1
SVM	0.559	0.556	0.172	0.144	0.914	0.913	0.925	0.926
RF	0.624	0.618	0.161	0.139	0.796	0.785	0.710	0.704
DNN.1	0.677	0.673	0.108	0.100	0.742	0.733	0.613	0.594
DNN.2	0.602	0.591	0.129	0.118	0.796	0.791	0.699	0.695
DNN.3	0.591	0.591	0.118	0.118	0.785	0.769	0.667	0.655
1D-CNN	0.430	0.431	0.065	0.058	0.828	0.826	0.796	0.778
LSTM	0.581	0.586	0.172	0.166	0.806	0.800	0.860	0.861
bi-LSTM	0.505	0.504	0.108	0.096	0.839	0.837	0.849	0.848

Table 3. Wavelength Importance Ranking

No.	Astringency		Bitterness		Herbaceous		Region		Vineyard	
	RF	SVR	RF	SVR	RF	SVR	RF	SVC	RF	SVC
1	210	204	204	204	216	204	402	232	206	206
2	348	220	206	206	222	206	206	230	204	260
3	350	200	244	220	204	212	420	210	218	262
4	204	208	330	222	206	222	414	228	212	264
5	208	216	238	218	322	220	202	246	208	266

6   Wavelength Importance

Table 3 is the wavelength importance ranking of GJ attributes and origin prediction through RF and SVM (linear kernel). We selected the top 5 most important wavelengths of each object. To better show the importance of each wavelength, we visualized their scores in RF (Fig. 4a) and SVM (Fig. 4b). The peak of each line is the most important wavelength of the object. In RF, the value of the Y-axis is the feature importance score, which is similar to the absolute coefficients scores that also represent the importance as the Y-axis value in SVM. The two groups of importance values were normalized (from 0 to 1). For example, the wavelength of attribute bitterness in both RF and SVM reaches the peak (the most important) at 204nm. According to the results (Table 3), in RF, the relatively more important wavelengths for attribute prediction are 204 and 222nm. In SVM, 216, 220, 204, and 222nm are more important. Thus, 204 and 222nm are the top two wavelengths to predict the sensory data. RF selected 200, 202, 206, and 208 nm for GJ origin prediction, while SVM selected 210nm as the most important in both region and vineyard prediction. From Table 3, we can

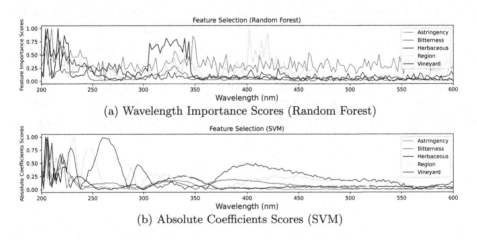

(a) Wavelength Importance Scores (Random Forest)

(b) Absolute Coefficients Scores (SVM)

Fig. 4. The Visualization of Wavelength importance

see that the highest-scoring wavelengths are from 200 to 400 nm, with a small part being outside 400 nm. Thus the most important wavelengths are from 200 to 420 nm will be helpful for the GJ/wine analysis (attributes and origin prediction). In Fig. 4a and Fig. 4b, from 200 to 250 nm, at the front of the wavelength range, the peaks and troughs show that prediction of this range will be unstable so that we would choose the more stable and relatively high range (250–420 nm).

7   Conclusions

This paper effectively combined ML with IoT technique using UV-Vis spectroscopy to predict GJ's sensory attributes and the origin of grapes (region and vineyard). The experimental results can provide guidance and reference for industrial production regarding wine analysis. Based on the results, SVM has the best efficiency among serval algorithms in these tasks, whether attributes prediction or origin prediction. Especially in origin prediction, it achieved more than 91% in accuracy and F1 score, proving its' practical value in production or quality inspection. By analyzing the important wavelengths, SVM has also provided a particular wavelength range that could be used for validation or select sensors. Therefore, this paper brings new ideas to wine producers and other beverage or food production areas by providing solutions to automatically obtain the wine's sensory and origins data for wine quality, categories, or authenticity analysis. In the future, we will look for further integration of ML technology and wine analysis to assist with winemaking, such as vineyard weather prediction or wine variety prediction. We believe that smart wineries that combine machine learning, IoT, and big data will be the future trend in the wine production industry because they will further improve the quality of wine and reduce costs and risks for wineries.

References

1. Aich, S., Al-Absi, A.A., Lee Hui, K., Sain, M.: Prediction of quality for different type of wine based on different feature sets using supervised machine learning techniques. In: 2019 21st International Conference on Advanced Communication Technology (ICACT), pp. 1122–1127 (2019)
2. Beaver, C., Collins, T.S., Harbertson, J.: Model optimization for the prediction of red wine phenolic compounds using ultraviolet-visible spectra. Molecules (Basel, Switzerland) 25(7) (2020)
3. Beltrán, N., Duarte-Mermoud, M., Soto Vicencio, V., Salah, S., Bustos, M.: Chilean wine classification using volatile organic compounds data obtained with a fast gc analyzer. IEEE Trans. Instrum. Meas 57(11), 2421–2436 (2008)
4. Blanco, V.Z., Auw, J.M., Sims, C.A., O'Keefe, S.F.: Effect of Processing on Phenolics of Wines, pp. 327–340. Springer, US, Boston, MA (1998). https://doi.org/10.1007/978-1-4899-1925-0_27
5. Castillo-Valero, J.S., Villanueva, E.C., García-Cortijo, M.C.: Regional reputation as the price premium: estimation of a hedonic model for the wines of castile-la mancha. Revista de la Facultad de Ciencias Agrarias 50(2), 293–310 (2018)
6. Chase, J., Charles, W.: Machine learning is changing demand forecasting. J. Bus. Forecasting 35(4), 43–45 (2016)

7. Costa, N.L., Llobodanin, L.A.G., Castro, I.A., Barbosa, R.: Finding the most important sensory descriptors to differentiate some vitis vinifera l. south american wines using support vector machines. European Food Res. Technol. 245(6), 1207 (2019)

8. Costa, N.L.d., Ximenez, J.P.B., Rodrigues, J.L., Barbosa, Jr., F., Barbosa, R.: Characterization of cabernet sauvignon wines from california: determination of origin based on icp-ms analysis and machine learning techniques. European Food Res. Technol. 246(6), 1193 (2020)

9. Cozzolino, D., Kwiatkowski, M., Waters, E., Gishen, M.: A feasibility study on the use of visible and short wavelengths in the near-infrared region for the non-destructive measurement of wine composition. Anal. Bioanal. Chem. 387(6), 2289 (2007)

10. Er, Y., Atasoy, A.: The classification of white wine and red wine according to their physicochemical qualities. Int. J. Intell. Syst. Appli. Eng. 4, 23–23 (2016). https://doi.org/10.18201/ijisae.265954

11. Fuentes, S., Tongson, E., Viejo, C., Torrico, D.: Machine learning modeling of wine sensory profiles and color of vertical vintages of pinot noir based on chemical fingerprinting, weather and management data. Sensors (Switzerland) 20(13) (2020)

12. Geană, E.I., Ciucure, C.T., Apetrei, C., Artem, V.: Application of spectroscopic uv-vis and ft-ir screening techniques coupled with multivariate statistical analysis for red wine authentication: Varietal and vintage year discrimination. Molecules 24(22) (2019)

13. Hinojosa-Nogueira, D., Pérez-Burillo, S., Ángel Rufián-Henares, J., Pastoriza de la Cueva, S.: Characterization of rums sold in spain through their absorption spectra, furans, phenolic compounds and total antioxidant capacity. Food Chemistry 323 (2020)

14. Kerslake, F., Longo, R., Dambergs, R.: Discrimination of juice press fractions for sparkling base wines by a UV-Vis spectral phenolic fingerprint and chemometrics. In: MDPIAG (2018)

15. Kumar, S., Kraeva, Y., Kraleva, R., Zymbler, M.: A deep neural network approach to predict the wine taste preferences. In: Solanki, V.K., Hoang, M.K., Lu, Z.J., Pattnaik, P.K. (eds.) Intelligent Computing in Engineering. AISC, vol. 1125, pp. 1165–1173. Springer, Singapore (2020). https://doi.org/10.1007/978-981-15-2780-7_120

16. Kumar, S., Agrawal, K., Mandan, N.: Red wine quality prediction using machine learning techniques. In: 2020 International Conference on Computer Communication and Informatics (ICCCI), pp. 1–6 (2020)

17. Lawless, H.T., Heymann, H.: Sensory Evaluation of Food. FSTS, Springer, New York (2010). https://doi.org/10.1007/978-1-4419-6488-5

18. Liu, H., Li, Q., Yan, B., Zhang, L., Gu, Y.: Bionic electronic nose based on mos sensors array and machine learning algorithms used for wine properties detection. Sensors (Switzerland) 19(1) (2019)

19. Longo, R., Blackman, J.W., Antalick, G., Torley, P.J., Rogiers, S.Y., Schmidtke, L.M.: Volatile and sensory profiling of shiraz wine in response to alcohol management: comparison of harvest timing versus technological approaches. Food Res. Int. 109, 561–571 (2018)

20. Longo, R., Dambergs, R.G., Westmore, H., Nichols, D.S., Kerslake, F.L.: A feasibility study on monitoring total phenolic content in sparkling wine press juice fractions using a new in-line system and predictive models. Food Control 123, 106810 (2021). https://doi.org/10.1016/j.foodcont.2019.106810

21. Martelo-Vidal, M., Vázquez, M.: Determination of polyphenolic compounds of red wines by uv-vis-nir spectroscopy and chemometrics tools. Food Chem. **158**, 28–34 (2014)
22. Palmer, J., Chen, B.: Wineinformatics: Regression on the grade and price of wines through their sensory attributes. Fermentation **4**(4), 84 (2018)
23. Rodríguez-Méndez, M., et al.: Electronic noses and tongues in wine industry. Front. Bioeng, Biotechnol. **4** (2016)
24. Sáenz-Navajas, M.P., et al.: Modelling wine astringency from its chemical composition using machine learning algorithms: Special macrowine 2018 (sarragosse). OENO One **53** (2019)
25. Thakkar, K., Shah, J., Prabhakar, R., Narayan, A., Joshi, A.: Ahp and machine learning techniques for wine recommendation (2016)
26. Trivedi, A., Sehrawat, R.: Wine quality detection through machine learning algorithms. In: ICRIEECE, pp. 1756–1760 (2018)
27. Urbano, M., Luque de Castro, M.D., Pérez, P.M., García-Olmo, J., Gómez-Nieto, M.A.: Ultraviolet-visible spectroscopy and pattern recognition methods for differentiation and classification of wines. Food Chem. **97**(1), 166–175 (2006)
28. Viejo, C., Torrico, D., Dunshea, F., Fuentes, S.: Emerging technologies based on artificial intelligence to assess the quality and consumer preference of beverages. Beverages **5**(4), 62 (2019)

MRCE: A Multi-Representation Collaborative Enhancement Model for Aspect-Opinion Pair Extraction

Yaxin Liu[1,2], Yan Zhou[1,2(✉)], Ziming Li[1,2], Dongjun Wei[3], Wei Zhou[2], and Songlin Hu[1,2]

[1] School of Cyber Security, University of Chinese Academy of Sciences, Beijing, China
[2] Institute of Information Engineering, Chinese Academy of Sciences, Beijing, China
{liuyaxin,zhouyan,liziming,zhouwei,husonglin}@iie.ac.cn
[3] HKU Business School, The University of Hong Kong, Hong Kong, China
dongjun@connect.hku.hk

Abstract. Aspect-Opinion Pair Extraction (AOPE) is an emerging combination task of fine-grained sentiment analysis. Traditional works devise pipeline frameworks for AOPE, which potentially suffer from error propagation. To solve this problem, numerous joint methods have been proposed recently. However, these joint methods have not simultaneously considered the following three points: (1) hierarchically linguistic information captured by pre-trained language models (PLMs), (2) comprehensive word-level semantic relation learning, (3) explicit and overall subtask interaction modeling. In this paper, we propose a Multi-Representation Collaborative Enhancement (MRCE) model, which can address the above three issues with a joint framework. Extensive experiments on three widely used datasets demonstrate that our model outperforms the state-of-the-art methods.

Keywords: Fine-grained sentiment analysis · Pre-trained language models · Representation enhancement

1 Introduction

Aspect-Opinion Pair Extraction (AOPE) [2], a combination task of fine-grained sentiment analysis, targets to jointly extract the aspect terms and pair-wise opinion terms from review sentences. With the help of AOPE, people can obtain a glimpse of the pros and cons of a product or service. The complete AOPE task generally involves three subtasks, including Aspect Term Extraction (ATE), Opinion Term Extraction (OTE)[1], and Aspect-Opinion Pair Recognition (AOPR). For instance, given the sentence *"The scenery is beautiful"*, AOPE will extract the aspect term *"scenery"* and the corresponding opinion term *"beautiful"* in the form of an aspect-opinion pair (*"scenery"*, *"beautiful"*).

---

[1] For brevity, we refer to ATE and OTE as term extraction.

© The Author(s), under exclusive license to Springer Nature Singapore Pte Ltd. 2023
M. Tanveer et al. (Eds.): ICONIP 2022, CCIS 1794, pp. 260–271, 2023.
https://doi.org/10.1007/978-981-99-1648-1_22

Traditional works mainly design pipeline frameworks to conduct AOPE [9, 17]. Regardless of their intuition, they are easily trapped in error propagation. To tackle this issue, researchers have proposed various joint frameworks. Several methods adopt the grid tagging scheme and solve all subtasks by a single module [4, 21]. Most joint methods couple aspect and opinion co-extraction with a module for AOPR [2, 3, 23]. However, there are three practical difficulties to be resolved. **Firstly**, existing works employ various pre-trained language models (PLMs) without fully exploiting the representative abilities of PLMs. It has been validated that BERT captures a rich hierarchy regarding linguistic information in its all-layer outputs [15]. **Secondly**, the task-specific representations for AOPR need to be improved. To capture complex word-level relations for AOPR, existing works adopt either the self-attention or biaffine mechanisms, of which the complementary benefits are unexplored. In addition, none of works consider relative position information into AOPR. **Thirdly**, existing works lack explicit and overall subtask interaction learning. Though SDRN [5] explicitly models interactions between term extraction and pair recognition, it requires hand-designed hyper-parameters for interaction modeling. Besides, it cannot capture explicit interactions between ATE and OTE.

In this paper, we intend to work on AOPE and accordingly propose a Multi-Representation Collaborative Enhancement (MRCE) model. Specifically, we first fully utilize the rich hierarchy of BERT. All-layer outputs of BERT are incorporated to enhance the representative power of our model. Then, we integrate a position-aware self-attention mechanism with a term-aware relation classifier, so as to enhance the representations of AOPR. Finally, concerning explicit and overall subtask interaction modeling, we develop two interactive units to capture interactive information among ATE, OTE, and AOPR. On the basis, our MRCE collaborates the above three perspectives of representation enhancement and implements AOPE in an end-to-end manner. We conduct extensive experiments on three public datasets. The results demonstrate that our proposed model outperforms the state-of-the-art methods.

2   Related Works

Aspect-Opinion Pair Extraction is a fundamental combination task of fine-grained sentiment analysis. Conventional works mainly devised pipeline frameworks to fulfill AOPE. Hu et al. [13] employed association mining to extract aspect terms and took the closest adjective to aspect terms as related opinion terms. Zhuang et al. [27] utilized the dependency relation templates to recognize aspect-opinion pairs. Although these pipeline methods have achieved satisfied results, they easily get trapped in error propagation.

To alleviate error propagation, recent efforts focus on the joint frameworks with deep learning techniques. Zhao et al. [25] performed ATE and OTE using span category classification, and recognized aspect-opinion pairs via span-span relation classification. Zhang et al. [23] separately extracted aspect terms and opinion terms, and modeled aspect- and opinion-aware sentiment dependency to determine aspect-opinion pairs. Chen et al. [2] adopted the sequence tagging method to co-extract aspect and opinion terms, and designed a supervised self-attention mechanism for pair recognition. Besides, Wu et al. [21] proposed the Grid Tagging Scheme (GTS) so as to conduct the complete AOPE task with a single module. Wu et al. [20] improved GTS with more syntactic knowledge. Interestingly, Chen et al. [3] formulated AOPE as an MRC problem and Yan et al. [22] converted AOPE into an index generation problem. These two kinds of approaches to AOPE are teacher-forced, which suffer from exposure bias [24].

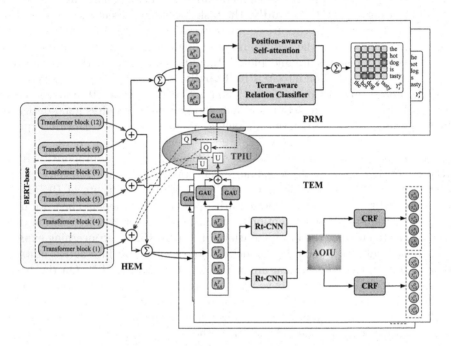

Fig. 1. The architecture of our MRCE model.

3   Our Approach

3.1   Task Definition

Given a review sentence $\mathbf{S}$, we use a and o to represent the aspect term and opinion term, respectively. Moreover, we use the superscripts ^{s} and ^{e} to denote the start position and end position of an aspect or opinion term. Accordingly, for the sentence $\mathbf{S}$, AOPE extracts a set of all the aspect terms $AT = \{(a^s, a^e)_{i=1}^{|A|}\}$, a set of all the opinion terms $OT = \{(o^s, o^e)_{j=1}^{|O|}\}$, and a set of all the aspect-opinion pairs $AOP = \{(a^s, a^e, o^s, o^e)_{p=1}^{|P|}\}$.

3.2   Network Architecture

Hierarchical Encoding Module. Due to the remarkable success achieved by PLMs, we opt for the BERT$_{BASE}$ model as our base encoder. Given a review sentence with N tokens, we can obtain all-layer hidden states $H = \{H_1, H_2, ..., H_L\}$, where $H_l \in \mathbb{R}^{N \times d_e}$ denotes the output of the l-th Transformer block of BERT.

As Jawahar et al. [15] proved, BERT$_{BASE}$ has a rich hierarchy regarding semantics. Thus, we fully utilize all-layer outputs of BERT$_{BASE}$ as follows,

$$H^{shared} = \frac{1}{4} \sum_{l=9}^{12} H_l, \ H^{pair} = \frac{1}{4} \sum_{l=5}^{8} H_l, \ H^{term} = \frac{1}{4} \sum_{l=1}^{4} H_l, \qquad (1)$$

where H^{pair} and H^{term} are used for pair recognition and term extraction, respectively. To allow H^{pair} and H^{term} to be distinguishable and meanwhile learn shared knowledge across all subtasks [7], we take H^{shared} as the sharing information and compute the inputs of PRM and TEM at the 1-th step by:

$$H_1^P = H^{shared}W_0 + H^{pair}W_1, \ H_1^T = H^{shared}W_2 + H^{term}W_3, \qquad (2)$$

where $W_i \in \mathbb{R}^{d_e \times d_h}$ ($i \in [0,3]$) is a trainable parameter. From the 2-th step, H_s^{pair} and H_s^{term} are updated with interactive features produced by TPIU. The details will be described in Sect. 3.3. After that, we can obtain the input representations $H_s^P \in \mathbb{R}^{N \times d_h}$ for PRM and $H_s^T \in \mathbb{R}^{N \times d_h}$ for TEM.

Pair Recognition Module. Prior works capture word-level semantic relations mainly by either the self-attention mechanism [2] or the biaffine classifier [23]. In our work, we make them complement each other to benefit AOPR.

Zhou et al. [26] stated that the opinion words closer to an aspect term might have a greater impact on it. Thus, we advance self-attention [1] with a relative position bias *pos* [14], to construct our position-aware self-attention mechanism. On the basis, the word-pair attention score $c_{s,i,j} \in C_s$ is computed by:

$$c_{s,i,j} = \text{softmax}(\tanh(h_{s,i}^{\prime P}W_4 + h_{s,j}^{\prime P}W_5)W_6 + pos_{i,j}), \ h_{s,i}^{\prime P} = \tanh(h_{s,i}^P). \qquad (3)$$

Recently, Biaffine [8] is popular as a relation classifier. Hence, we adopt the biaffine classifier to construct our term-aware relation classifier. Given the representation H_s^P, Biaffine calculates the term-aware relation score $b_{s,i,j} \in B_s$ between a pair of aspect and opinion tokens. For final prediction of AOPR, we combine the above two word-pair relation distributions by $V_s = \lambda B_s + (1-\lambda)C_s$, where λ is a hyper-parameter.

Term Extraction Module. An aspect term or opinion term generally contains multiple words [26]. To enable parallel multi-gram information learning, we adapt the LR-CNN model [10] into a rethinking convolutional neural network (Rt-CNN). Our Rt-CNN simply stacks multiple CNN layers with a rethinking mechanism[2]. With two individual Rt-CNNs, we can obtain contextual representations $H_s^A \in \mathbb{R}^{N \times d_c}$ for ATE and $H_s^O \in \mathbb{R}^{N \times d_c}$ for OTE.

Then, we feed H_s^A and H_s^O into AOIU, resulting enhanced aspect-oriented hidden representation T_s^A and opinion-oriented hidden representation T_s^O. The details will be described in Sect. 3.3. After that, two Conditional Random Field (CRF) networks separately predict two sequences of label probabilities $p(Y_s^A \mid X)$ and $p(Y_s^O \mid X)$ for ATE and OTE, respectively.

3.3   Recurrent Interactive Units

To model explicit and overall subtask interactions without manually designed parameters, we devise two interactive units: Aspect-Opinion Interactive Unit (AOIU) and Term-Pair Interactive Unit (TPIU). As Fig. 1 shows, AOIU and TPIU are recurrently performed S steps to produce high-level linguistic features.

Aspect-Opinion Interactive Unit: We employ pair attention [5] to exchange interactive features between ATE and OTE. Thus, the useful clues $H_s^{A \leftarrow O}$ and $H_s^{O \leftarrow A}$ can be generated. We then concatenate H_s^A and $H_s^{A \leftarrow O}$ to produce our final aspect-oriented representation $T_s^A \in \mathbb{R}^{N \times 2d_c}$. Similarly, we can also acquire the opinion-oriented representation $T_s^O \in \mathbb{R}^{N \times 2d_c}$.

Term-Pair Interactive Unit: We devise TPIU to enable information interactions between term extraction and pair recognition. Our TPIU is mainly based on the Gated Attention Unit (GAU) [14], which has excellent performance on capturing token-to-token relationships. Concretely, at the s-th recurrent step, TPIU calculates two token-to-token score matrices to respectively reflect term-aware and pair-aware relations at the token level. One is $U_s = \mathrm{GAU}^A(H_s^T) + \mathrm{GAU}^O(H_s^T)$, of which $u_{s,i,j}$ aims to measure the probability that the i-th and j-th tokens belong to the same term. The other is $Q_s = \mathrm{GAU}^P(H_s^P)$, where $Q_{s,i,j} \in Q_s$ implies the degree to which the i-th and j-th tokens are pair-wise. Thus, from the 2-th step, the task-specific representations H^{pair} and H^{term} in Eq. (2) will be linearly transformed with mutual clues U_s and V_s.

3.4   Joint Training

Given the training dataset $\mathcal{D}$, we optimize TEM by minimizing the negative log likelihood loss of sequence labeling: $L^T = -\sum_{\mathcal{D}}(\sum_{i=1}^N log(p(Y_{S,i}^A \mid X_i)) + \sum_{i=1}^N log(p(Y_{S,i}^O \mid X_i)))$. For training PRM, we utilize the cross-entropy loss to calculate the loss L^P. Besides, we find that the gold label grid $\tilde{Y}^P$ is symmetrical. To simulate this observation, we define a symmetrical loss for regularization:

$$L^R = \frac{1}{D \times N \times N} \sum_{\mathcal{D}} \sum_{i=1}^N \sum_{j=1}^N \mid v_{d,i,j} - v_{d,j,i} \mid, \qquad (4)$$

where $\mid \cdot \mid$ refers to the absolute value operation.

---

[2] More details can be can be referred to https://github.com/guitaowufeng/LR-CNN.

In order to train our model in an end-to-end manner, we combine the losses of TEM and PRM. The final loss of our model is defined as $L(\Theta) = L^T + L^P + \alpha L^R + \beta\|\Theta\|_2$, where α and β are trade-off factors. Besides, Θ represents all trainable parameters of our whole model.

3.5 Inference Layer

For a review sentence $\mathbf{S}$, we can obtain the $AT = \{(a_i^s, a_i^e)_{i=1}^{|A|}\}$ and $OT = \{(o_j^s, o_j^e)_{j=1}^{|O|}\}$ sets. Given an aspect term (a_i^s, a_i^e) and an opinion term (o_j^s, o_j^e), the probability that they are pair-wise is computed by:

$$\gamma = \frac{1}{2}\Big(\frac{1}{\mid a_i^e - a_i^s \mid}\sum_{m=a_i^s}^{a_i^e}\sum_{n=o_j^s}^{o_j^e} v_{m,n} + \frac{1}{\mid o_j^e - o_j^s \mid}\sum_{n=o_j^s}^{o_j^e}\sum_{m=a_i^s}^{a_i^e} v_{n,m}\Big), \tag{5}$$

where $v_{m,n}$ and $v_{n,m}$ are from V_S. By comparing γ with a pre-defined threshold $\hat{\gamma}$, we can determine if $(a_i^s, a_i^e, o_j^s, o_j^e)$ can be added into the AOP set.

4 Experiments

4.1 Datasets and Experimental Settings

We evaluate our proposed model on three public aspect-level sentiment analysis datasets from SemEval 2014 [19] and SemEval 2015 [18], including reviews from restaurant and laptop. The statistics of our used datasets can be found in [2].

We adopt BERT$_{\text{BASE}}$[3] as our base encoder. Thus, we set d_e, d_h, and d_c to 768, 256, and 256, respectively. The parameters used in Rt-CNN are set the same with [10]. Besides, we set S to 2, which is the best choice by experimental validation. For training, the AdamW optimizer with a warmup rate of 0.1 is used, and the learning rate of it is set to 2e-5 for fine-tuning BERT. As for training our model, we set the learning rate to 1e-3. The coefficients α and β in our loss function are set to 1e-3 and 1e-5. The batch size is set to 10 and the dropout rate is set to 0.5. During inference, the threshold $\hat{\gamma}$ is set to 0.5. To evaluate the performance of our model, we use the F1-score as our main metric.

4.2 Baselines

For fair comparisons, we select two categories of baseline methods: (1) pipeline methods, such as HAST [16], IMN [11], and SPAN [12]; (2) joint methods, such as SpanMlt [25], GTS [21], OTE-MTL [23], BMRC [3], and SDRN [2]. Notice that the pipeline methods are simply used for ATE and OTE. Following the work of SDRN, we equip a relation detection (RD) module with them for AOPR.

---

[3] https://github.com/huggingface/transformers.

Table 1. The comparison F1-score (%) of baseline methods and our model on AOPR. Baseline methods with the superscript * are cited from the original paper [2]. Besides, baseline methods with the superscript † are reproduced by us.

Models		14Res	14Lap	15Res
Pipeline	HAST+RD* [16]	73.55	64.05	65.20
	IMN+RD* [11]	73.69	62.98	65.56
	SPAN+RD* [12]	74.17	65.99	67.55
Joint	SpanMlt† [25]	75.65	68.69	67.02
	GTS† [21]	76.69	68.20	66.24
	OTE-MTL† [23]	76.29	63.15	66.67
	BMRC† [3]	75.37	68.29	66.81
	SDRN† [2]	76.33	67.63	70.62
	MRCE(ours)	**77.73**	**69.85**	**71.08**

4.3   Main Results

The comparison results of all the baseline methods and our model on the AOPR task are shown in Table 1. We consistently boost the F1-score across our used three datasets. For example, our MRCE model surpasses the SOTAs (i.e., 76.69, 68.69, 70.62) of previous joint methods by 1.04, 1.16, and 0.46 absolute F1-score on three datasets. We also present F1 results on ATE and OTE of our model and the baseline joint approaches. Our MRCE model sustains universal superior performance for these two tasks on all datasets. As shown in Table 2, when comparing with the previous best F1-score of ATE and OTE, our model achieves 0.22 and 0.98 improvements on 14Res, 1.06 and 0.35 improvements on 14Lap, as well as 0.79 and 0.2 improvements on 15Res.

In summary, compared with pipeline methods, our MRCE model outperforming them on AOPR across all datasets signifies that our approach has the ability to alleviate error propagation. Moreover, we collaborate three perspectives of representation enhancement, which enables our MRCE model to perform better for the complete AOPE task. Evidently, our work provides AOPE with a more desirable solution with marginal performance gains.

4.4   Model Analysis

The Effect of Input Representation Enhancement. We simply take the last hidden state of BERT to produce inputs for TEM and PRM. This adaptation without input representation enhancement is termed 'w/o IREH'. From Table 3, we notice that the 'w/o IREH' method drops the performances by significant margins on three subtasks, especially on AOPR. Typically, the F1 results decrease by 9.23, 16.84, and 8.74 on 14Res, 14Lap, and 15Res, respectively. Such remarkable decline demonstrates that (1) simply employing the last-layer output of BERT as the base input representation is extremely insufficient for AOPE,

Table 2. The F1-score (%) of joint methods and our model on ATE and OTE.

Models	14Res		14Lap		15Res	
	ATE	OTE	ATE	OTE	ATE	OTE
SpanMlt[†]	81.28	84.05	76.14	75.71	72.36	76.69
GTS[†]	86.59	87.44	80.13	80.49	68.98	76.92
OTE-MTL[†]	88.25	87.71	82.86	81.38	73.59	78.32
BMRC[†]	85.82	86.83	80.23	82.69	70.79	78.49
SDRN[†]	89.10	87.41	82.51	81.37	72.79	79.96
MRCE (ours)	**89.32**	**88.69**	**83.92**	**83.04**	**74.38**	**80.16**

and (2) full usage of all-layer outputs of BERT is quite pivotal to advance the representative power of our MRCE model.

To further validate the critical role of our hierarchical idea to enhance task-specific representations, we replace H^{pair} and H^{term} in Eq. (2) with H^{avg}, which is the average of all-layer outputs of $BERT_{BASE}$. There have no shared features to model subtask correlations at the representation level anymore. The experimental F1 results are reported in Table 3, from which we can observe that 'w/o hier' produces more undesirable F1 results on all subtasks than MRCE does. This proves that employing all-layer outputs of BERT without considering its rich hierarchy hurts the performance of AOPE.

Table 3. The F1-score (%) of removing different components in our MRCE model.

Models	14Res			14Lap			15Res		
	AOPR	ATE	OTE	AOPR	ATE	OTE	AOPR	ATE	OTE
MRCE	77.73	89.32	88.69	69.85	83.92	83.04	71.08	74.38	80.16
w/o IREH	68.50	83.58	85.20	53.01	76.15	77.27	62.34	67.83	74.42
w/o hier	76.52	88.44	87.78	68.04	82.22	81.72	70.95	72.82	79.88
w/o AOIU	76.99	89.18	87.88	67.80	82.62	81.58	70.65	73.07	79.76
w/o TPIU	76.98	88.94	88.23	66.35	82.38	81.81	70.23	73.71	79.60
w/o PASA	74.72	88.60	87.86	63.69	83.40	82.40	68.21	71.99	79.44
w/o TARC	76.64	88.05	87.95	68.00	82.91	81.72	69.99	73.73	79.84
w/o *pos*	77.39	88.94	87.36	67.51	83.71	81.58	70.42	73.77	79.09
w/o L^R	76.57	88.72	88.13	67.39	82.89	82.42	70.24	72.93	78.93

The Effect of AOPR-Specific Representation Enhancement. To investigate the effect of comprehensively enhancing task-specific representation of AOPR, we build up the following adaptations: 'w/o PASA', 'w/o TARC', and 'w/o *pos*'. The results in Table 3 show that 'w/o PASA' performs the worst on AOPR. For the 14Res, 14Lap, and 15Res datasets, the F1 results drop by

3.01, 6.16, and 2.87, respectively. This presents the vital importance of our pair-aware self-attention mechanism. After we omit the relative position bias from the pair-aware self-attention mechanism, the 'w/o *pos*' method also weakens the performance of MRCE on AOPR to some extent. Such a decline conveys to us that integrating relative position information provides slight promotion to AOPR, thus potentially benefiting ATE and OTE. All the above three adaptive methods perform worse overall than MRCE. Therefore, we can determine that each semantic factor (i.e., term-aware semantic relations, word-pair semantic relations, relative position information) has its own positive effect on enhancing representations for AOPR.

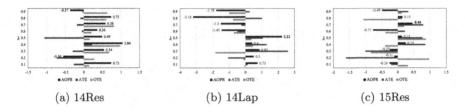

(a) 14Res   (b) 14Lap   (c) 15Res

Fig. 2. The F1-score (%) with different values of λ.

To further demonstrate the effect of our auxiliary constraint for PRM training, we remove L^R from our total loss, yielding the 'w/o L^R' method. The F1 results produced by 'w/o L^R' decrease, which reveals that leaving out the symmetrical constraint about PRM learning devastates the performance of MRCE. Furthermore, to choose the optimal value of λ for our model, we primarily concern the superior F1 results on all subtasks. After this condition is met, we then decide λ according to the F1-score on AOPR. As shown in Fig. 2, only when the values of λ are 0.4, 0.5, and 0.7 respectively on 14Res, 14Lap, and 15Res, can our above two requirements be meanwhile satisfied.

The Effect of Interaction Modeling. Our work develops two interactive units to model explicit and overall subtask interactions. To investigate their influences, we separately omit them and construct two adaptations, i.e., 'w/o AOIU' and 'w/o TPIU'. As shown in Table 3, we can figure out that 'w/o AOIU' performs worse than MRCE, especially on term extraction. Even worse, the F1-score on ATE dramatically reduces on 15Res, i.e., 74.38→73.07. The above two results prove that explicitly modeling interactions between ATE and OTE is helpful to each other. About the 'w/o TPIU' method, from the 2-*th* recurrent step, the input representations of TEM and PRM are updated without integration of interactive information between term extraction and pair recognition. As we can see in Table 3, the F1 results obtained by 'w/o TPIU' are unsatisfactory on all subtasks. This indicates that the complete AOPE task can benefit from explicit interaction modeling between term extraction and pair recognition.

In addition, 'w/o TPIU' performs even worse on AOPR than 'w/o AOIU', which supports that identifying aspect terms and opinion terms can assist pair recognition. Combing the performances achieved by 'w/o AOIU' and 'w/o TPIU', we can also observe that better term extraction (i.e., ATE, OTE) brings better pair recognition. This result is an evidence that recognizing term pairs can refine term extraction. All these observations show us that explicit and overall interaction modeling among all subtasks plays an important role in AOPE.

4.5 Case Study

To clearly show the effectiveness of our proposed model, we pick some examples from testing datasets and present the predicted results of SDRN and our MRCE model in Table 4. As illustrated from the first and third cases, MRCE extracts more precise aspect terms, thus making MRCE do better in recognizing aspect-opinion pairs. However, SDRN predicts less precise aspect terms than our MRCE model does. We think the reason is that SDRN thoroughly shares the term representation to jointly extract aspect terms and opinion terms. This is likely to bring conflicts between aspect-oriented representation learning and opinion-oriented representation learning. Moreover, by observing the second and third cases, we figure out that our model is also competent to deal with complex pair-wise relations, even for the long and complicated review sentence (the 3rd case). In general, taking all cases together, we can suggest that AOPE benefits from our proposed collaborative representation enhancement.

Table 4. Case study. The gold aspect terms and opinion terms in the sentences are colored as red and blue, respectively.

Sentence	SDRN	MRCE
The omlette for brunch$_1$ is great$_1$.	(omlette, great)	(omlette for brunch, great)✓
The atmosphere$_{1,2}$ was pretty nice$_1$ but had a bit lacking$_2$, which it tries to make up for with a crazy$_3$ scheme of mirrors$_3$.	(atmosphere, nice) ✓ (atmosphere, lacking)✓	(atmosphere, nice)✓ (atmosphere, lacking)✓ (scheme of mirrors, crazy)✓
I love$_1$ their chicken pasta$_{1,2}$ can't remember the name but is sooo good$_2$.	(chicken, love) (chicken, good)	(chicken pasta, love)✓ (chicken pasta, good)✓

5 Conclusion

In this paper, we study Aspect-Opinion Pair Extraction (AOPE) task and propose the MRCE model. Specifically, we collaborate representations enhanced from three perspectives. Firstly, the rich hierarchy of BERT is fully used to improve the input representative power of MRCE. Secondly, we enhance context representation of pair recognition by (1) complementary benefits of self-attention and biaffine mechanisms, and (2) relative position information. Thirdly, we devise two interactive units, i.e., AOIU and TPIU, to model explicit and overall interactions for AOPE. Experimental results on three public datasets demonstrate the effectiveness of our proposed method.

Acknowledgment. This research is supported by the National Natural Science Foundation of China under grant No. 61702500.

References

1. Bahdanau, D., Cho, K.H., Bengio, Y.: Neural machine translation by jointly learning to align and translate. In: 3rd International Conference on Learning Representations, ICLR 2015 (2015)
2. Chen, S., Liu, J., Wang, Y., Zhang, W., Chi, Z.: Synchronous double-channel recurrent network for aspect-opinion pair extraction. In: Proceedings of the 58th Annual Meeting Of The Association For Computational Linguistics, pp. 6515–6524 (2020)
3. Chen, S., Wang, Y., Liu, J., Wang, Y.: Bidirectional machine reading comprehension for aspect sentiment triplet extraction. In: Proceedings of the AAAI Conference on Artificial Intelligence, vol. 35, pp. 12666–12674 (2021)
4. Chen, Z., Huang, H., Liu, B., Shi, X., Jin, H.: Semantic and syntactic enhanced aspect sentiment triplet extraction. In: Findings of the Association for Computational Linguistics: ACL-IJCNLP 2021, pp. 1474–1483 (2021)
5. Chen, Z., Qian, T.: Relation-aware collaborative learning for unified aspect-based sentiment analysis. In: Proceedings of the 58th Annual Meeting of the Association for Computational Linguistics, pp. 3685–3694 (2020)
6. Devlin, J., Chang, M.W., Lee, K., Toutanova, K.: Bert: Pre-training of deep bidirectional transformers for language understanding. In: Proceedings of the 2019 Conference of the North American Chapter of the Association for Computational Linguistics: Human Language Technologies, vol. 1 (Long and Short Papers), pp. 4171–4186 (2019)
7. Ding, K., et al.: Mssm: a multiple-level sparse sharing model for efficient multi-task learning. In: Proceedings of the 44th International ACM SIGIR Conference on Research and Development in Information Retrieval, pp. 2237–2241 (2021)
8. Dozat, T., Manning, C.D.: Deep biaffine attention for neural dependency parsing. In: 5th International Conference on Learning Representations, ICLR 2017, Toulon, France, 24–26 April 2017, Conference Track Proceedings (2017). https://openreview.net/forum?id=Hk95PK9le
9. Fan, Z., Wu, Z., Dai, X., Huang, S., Chen, J.: Target-oriented opinion words extraction with target-fused neural sequence labeling. In: NAACL, pp. 2509–2518 (2019)
10. Gui, T., Ma, R., Zhang, Q., Zhao, L., Jiang, Y.G., Huang, X.: Cnn-based chinese ner with lexicon rethinking. In: IJCAI, pp. 4982–4988 (2019)
11. He, R., Lee, W.S., Ng, H.T., Dahlmeier, D.: An interactive multi-task learning network for end-to-end aspect-based sentiment analysis. In: ACL, pp. 504–515 (2019)
12. Hu, M., Peng, Y., Huang, Z., Li, D., Lv, Y.: Open-domain targeted sentiment analysis via span-based extraction and classification. In: Proceedings of the 57th Annual Meeting of the Association for Computational Linguistics, pp. 537–546. Association for Computational Linguistics, Florence, Italy (July 2019)
13. Hu, M., Liu, B.: Mining and summarizing customer reviews. In: Proceedings of the tenth ACM SIGKDD International Conference on Knowledge Discovery and Data Mining, pp. 168–177 (2004)
14. Hua, W., Dai, Z., Liu, H., Le, Q.: Transformer quality in linear time. In: International Conference on Machine Learning, pp. 9099–9117. PMLR (2022)

15. Jawahar, G., Sagot, B., Seddah, D.: What does bert learn about the structure of language? In: Proceedings of the 57th Annual Meeting of the Association for Computational Linguistics, pp. 3651–3657 (2019)
16. Li, X., Bing, L., Li, P., Lam, W., Yang, Z.: Aspect term extraction with history attention and selective transformation. In: IJCAI (2018)
17. Peng, H., Xu, L., Bing, L., Huang, F., Lu, W., Si, L.: Knowing what, how and why: A near complete solution for aspect-based sentiment analysis. In: Proceedings of the AAAI Conference on Artificial Intelligence, vol. 34, pp. 8600–8607 (2020)
18. Pontiki, M., Galanis, D., Papageorgiou, H., Manandhar, S., Androutsopoulos, I.: Semeval-2015 task 12: Aspect based sentiment analysis. In: Proceedings of the 9th International Workshop on Semantic Evaluation (SemEval 2015), pp. 486–495 (2015)
19. Pontiki, M., Galanis, D., Pavlopoulos, J., Papageorgiou, H., Androutsopoulos, I., Manandhar, S.: Semeval-2014 task 4: Aspect based sentiment analysis. In: Proceedings of the 8th International Workshop on Semantic Evaluation (SemEval 2014), pp. 27–35. Association for Computational Linguistics, Dublin, Ireland (Aug 2014)
20. Wu, S., Fei, H., Ren, Y., Ji, D., Li, J.: Learn from syntax: Improving pair-wise aspect and opinion terms extractionwith rich syntactic knowledge. In: IJCAI, pp. 3597–3963 (2021)
21. Wu, Z., Ying, C., Zhao, F., Fan, Z., Dai, X., Xia, R.: Grid tagging scheme for aspect-oriented fine-grained opinion extraction. In: Findings of the Association for Computational Linguistics: EMNLP 2020, pp. 2576–2585 (2020)
22. Yan, H., Dai, J., Ji, T., Qiu, X., Zhang, Z.: A unified generative framework for aspect-based sentiment analysis. In: Proceedings of the 59th Annual Meeting of the Association for Computational Linguistics and the 11th International Joint Conference on Natural Language Processing (Vol. 1: Long Papers), pp. 2416–2429 (2021)
23. Zhang, C., Li, Q., Song, D., Wang, B.: A multi-task learning framework for opinion triplet extraction. In: Findings of the Association for Computational Linguistics: EMNLP 2020, pp. 819–828 (2020)
24. Zhang, W., Feng, Y., Meng, F., You, D., Liu, Q.: Bridging the gap between training and inference for neural machine translation. In: Proceedings of the 57th Annual Meeting of the Association for Computational Linguistics, pp. 4334–4343 (2019)
25. Zhao, H., Huang, L., Zhang, R., Lu, Q., et al.: Spanmlt: A span-based multi-task learning framework for pair-wise aspect and opinion terms extraction. In: Proceedings of the 58th Annual Meeting of the Association for Computational Linguistics, pp. 3239–3248 (2020)
26. Zhou, Y., Huang, L., Guo, T., Han, J., Hu, S.: A span-based joint model for opinion target extraction and target sentiment classification. In: IJCAI, pp. 5485–5491 (2019)
27. Zhuang, L., Jing, F., Zhu, X.Y.: Movie review mining and summarization. In: Proceedings of the 15th ACM International Conference on Information and Knowledge Management, pp. 43–50 (2006)

Diverse and High-Quality Data Augmentation Using GPT for Named Entity Recognition

Huanlei Chen, Weiwen Zhang[✉], Lianglun Cheng, and Haiming Ye

School of Computer Science and Technology, Guangdong University of Technology,
Guangzhou, China
{zhangww,llcheng}@gdut.edu.cn

Abstract. Data augmentation technology has been widely used in computer vision and speech with good results. In computer vision and speech, simple manipulation of gold data can achieve great data augmentation effects. However, in NLP (natural language processing), simple operations on data, such as "randomly delete words", "swap word positions", can have a huge impact on the semantics of sentences. This impact on semantics can be devastating for fine-grained tasks like NER (named entity recognition). In this work, we propose a novel model to generate diverse and high-quality data for NER, which is called DHQDA (**D**iverse and **H**igh-**Q**uality **D**ata **A**ugmentation). Our model outputs the data by using a small-scale neural network to prompt the key and value in the transformer block of the PLM (pre-trained language model). Our experimental results demonstrate that DHQDA performs more stable and better than baseline methods on both Chinese and English datasets, whether in rich or low-resource situations.

Keywords: Data augmentation · Named entity recognition ·
Pre-trained language models · Prompt learning

1 Introduction

Deep learning has shown its excellent performance in a variety of high-resource scenarios. In the high-resource scenario, it allows the large number of parameters of the deep learning model to be trained well, thus bringing out its powerful performance. However, many applications lack training data in practice, such as ship information, biomedicine, and other scenarios. With the limited data, deep learning models are prone to overfitting in low-resource scenarios.

Data augmentation is an effective approach to tackle the low-resource problem for deep learning. It is widely used in the field of computer vision such as cropping, rotating, or flipping images [3,14]. In the field of speech, researchers performed data augmentation by changing the speed or intonation of speech [13,22]. In NLP, data augmentation methods include random deletion/swap/insertion [28], synonym replacement [28,31], back translation [12,29], language generation models [7,12], etc.

© The Author(s), under exclusive license to Springer Nature Singapore Pte Ltd. 2023
M. Tanveer et al. (Eds.): ICONIP 2022, CCIS 1794, pp. 272–283, 2023.
https://doi.org/10.1007/978-981-99-1648-1_23

As a sub-task in NLP and an important part of knowledge graph construction [15, 30], NER relies on context when working, and requires high-quality data during training. However, existing methods [7, 12, 28, 29, 31] do not work very well to generate diverse and high-quality data or are not suitable for NER task. The common issue is that the information contained in the text is fragile, and a little change may cause damage to the information in the text and generate a large amount of noise. Random deletion/swap/insertion of gold data tends to destroy the semantic information in the sentences, and the noise generated is unstable for the enhancement of the NER model. Synonym replacement relies on external knowledge, which is lacking in many domains. DAGA [7] is a language generation model for NER data augmentation. In the case of few-shot, the generated sentences are not flexible enough and the noise contained in its generated data has a greater impact on the final performance of the NER model, due to poor data quality. Therefore, a diverse and high-quality data augmentation is desired to address the issue.

In this work, we propose a novel data augmentation method called DHQDA (**D**iverse and **H**igh-**Q**uality **D**ata **A**ugmentation) for NER. Our model outputs the data by prompting PLM (pre-trained language model). We adopt the GPT as our pre-trained model, by using a small-scale neural network for prompting the key and value in the transformer block. We flatten the original training data in BIO format or other labeling methods into sentences as training data for our model. We construct a ship information NER dataset named SIND (in Chinese) to verify the effectiveness of DHQDA. In addition, we also conduct a series of experiments on MIT-Restaurant dataset (in English) [17] and Conll2003 (in English) [26]. From the experimental results, it can be observed that the performance of DHQDA is more stable and robust compared to DAGA [7] and Random Delete/Swap/Insertion [28]. We average the improvement in F1 scores of the NER model for each of the four cases on the three datasets and find that our model outperforms the best baseline method by 1.66%, 1.19% and 1.48% in term of F1 scores on Conll2003, MIT-Restaurant and SIND, respectively.

We summarize the contributions of this work as follows:

- To address the diversity and quality of the augmented data generated, we propose a novel model (DHQDA) for NER data augmentation.
- To evaluate the effectiveness of DHQDA, we construct a ship information NER dataset.
- We explore the effectiveness of DHQDA in both English and Chinese datasets.

The remaining sections of the paper are organized as follows. In Sect. 2, we present an overview of related work on data augmentation and prompt learning. We describe our model and illustrate some preprocessing operations in Sect. 3. In Sect. 4, we verify the effectiveness of DHQDA with experimental results. In Sect. 5, we explore why the data generated by our model is effective for the enhancement of the NER model. Finally, we conclude and share our future plans in Sect. 6.

2   Related Work

2.1   Data Augmentation

DA (data augmentation) refers to generating more data to expand the training set to improve the robustness of the model without collecting additional data [10, 25]. Data augmentation is more widely used in computer vision and speech than in NLP. In computer vision, researchers performed DA by simply rotating, cropping, or flipping images [3, 14]. In speech, researchers achieved great improvement by DA with changing the intonation or speed of speech [13, 22]. In this case, it is not easy to destroy the information presented in images and speech.

Ding et al. [7] proposed a language model called DAGA, which is based on LSTM for generating labeled sequences. In the case of few-shot, the sentences generated by DAGA are not flexible enough. Wei et al. [28] proposed the operations of synonym replacement, random insertion, random deletion, and random exchange of sentences for DA on text classification tasks. şahin and Steedman [23] generated additional training data on downstream tasks of POS (part-of-speech) tagging via dependency tree morphing. Dai and Adel [5] used a binomial distribution to randomly decide whether the token should be replaced or the segment should be shuffled. In a sentence, a slight change can cause a big difference in semantics. These simple operations on sentences have great randomness and can easily destroy the semantics of sentences. The semantic change is fatal for fine-grained tasks, for instance NER. NER has higher requirements for the quality of data. Fabbri et al. [9] employed data augmentation via round-trip translation for few-shot abstractive summarization. However, that translation method is not suitable for NER tasks.

To solve the above problems, we propose a novel model to generate diverse and high-quality training examples for NER.

2.2   Prompt Learning

Since the publication of GPT3 [1], prompt learning has received a lot of attention and has performed well in NLP downstream tasks. The purpose of prompt learning is to change the downstream task to a text generation task by adding "prompt information" to the input without significantly changing the structure and parameters of the pre-trained language model.

Many researchers have proposed methods to manually construct prompt templates for prompt learning. Ding et al. [8] formalized NER task as cloze-style tasks to utilize the knowledge of BERT [6] by manually constructing prompt templates (In this sentence, [Entity] is a [MASK]) for solving zero-shot scenarios. Cui et al. [4] also used the method of constructing a cloze-style template ([Candidate span] is a [Entity type] entity) to put the candidate entities in the sentence into the template to complete the sequence labeling. Schick and Schütze [24] solved the problem of text classification and natural language inference in few-shot scenarios by constructing a cloze problem (It was ___. [Input text]). Manually constructing prompt templates is labor-intensive and it can be difficult to determine the most appropriate template.

Chen et al. [2] utilized the knowledge of BART [16] by automatically generating prompt information, and then determining the entity location through a pointer network. Ma et al. [18] proposed a template-free method to convert the NER problem into an Entity-oriented LM problem. During training, the position of the entity predicts the label words, and the position of the non-entity predicts the original word. Gao et al. [11] proposed a method to generate discrete templates based on the T5 [21] model. In this work, we utilize the knowledge of GPT [1,19,20] using prompt information generated through a small neural network. Through the method of prompt learning, we can make more full use of the knowledge learned by GPT in the pre-training stage to generate diverse and high-quality data.

3   Our Method

In this section, we introduce the proposed model (DHQDA). DHQDA generates diverse and high-quality sentences by using pre-trained models with prompt tuning.

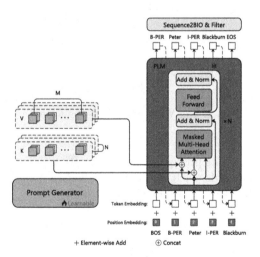

Fig. 1. Overview of DHQDA. K and V are respectively used to prompt the key and value in the attention mechanism, M represents the length of the prompt and N represents the number of layers of the Transformer decoder.

The overview of DHQDA is shown in Fig. 1. After the initial token is given, it is transformed into model input by Token Embedding and Position Embedding, and the pre-trained models generate the augmented data prompted by the Prompt Generator, where K and V are respectively used to prompt the key and value in the attention mechanism, and M represents the length of the prompt, and N represents the number of layers of the Transformer decoder. Finally, the generated data is filtered by Filter and converted to the specified format by Sequence2BIO.

In Sect. 3.1, we introduce preprocessing operations on training data. In Sect. 3.2, we describe the overall architecture of our model. We explain our model in three parts, including Language Modeling, Prompt Generator & Prompt-guided Attention and Squence2BIO & Filter.

3.1 Data Preprocessing

First of all, we need to preprocess our training set to convert BIO, BIOSE or BIOS format (NER labeling methods) data into Tag-Word or Word-Tag sentences, as shown in Fig. 2. We have two ways to flatten labeled data. One is to put the word in front of the label (Word-Tag), and the other is to put the label in front of the word (Tag-Word). During the flattening process, we ignore the non-entity "O". Finally, the flattened data is used as the training data for our model.

Fig. 2. Tag-Word and Word-Tag format.

During the pre-training process, there are no "BIOSE-Tag" words, so we need to add these special words, such as "B-PER", "I-PER", etc., to the vocabulary and tokenizer of the pre-trained model.

3.2 Data Generation

After data preprocessing, we adapt the output of the pretrained model to the Tag-Word or Word-Tag distribution by prompting the attention layer of the pretrained model. We adopt the GPT series model [1,19,20] as our pre-trained model. GPT model has powerful language generation ability.

Language Modeling. Through data preprocessing, we convert NER data in BIO and other formats into sequences $S_1 = \{tag_1, word_1, tag_2, word_2, ...tag_n, word_n\}$ or $S_2 = \{word_1, tag_1, word_2, tag_2, ..., word_n, tag_n\}$, where n is the length of the original sentence. During the transformation, we will ignore the non-entity "O". We convert these sequences into tokens $U = \{u_1, ..., u_m\}$, where m represents the length of the tokens.

Multiple layers of Transformer decoders compose the GPT architecture [27]. First, we compute the tokens mapping to the trained word vector matrix and mark the position of each token with a position embedding matrix. We express the above steps as Eq. (1):

$$h_0 = U_i W_e + W_p \tag{1}$$

where h_0 is the result of tokens computed by the word embedding matrix and the position embedding matrix. $U_i = \{u_{i-k}, ..., u_{i-1}\}$, k is the context window size, $W_e \in R^{v \times d_{model}}$ is the word embedding matrix, $W_p \in R^{pos \times d_{model}}$ is the position embedding matrix, v represents the size of the vocabulary, and pos is the longest sentence length.

The i-th token is calculated by the Transformer block with the first k tokens determined, formalizing this step as Eqs. (2)–(3):

$$h_l = \text{TransformerBlock}(h_{l-1}), \forall l \in [1, N] \tag{2}$$

$$P(u_i|u_{i-k}, ..., u_{i-1}) = \text{softmax}(h_N^i W_e^T) \tag{3}$$

where h_l represents the output of the Transformer at layer l, and N is the total number of layers of the Transformer.

And our training objective can be expressed as Eq. (4):

$$P(U) = \prod_{i=1}^{m} P(u_i|u_{i-k}, ..., u_{i-1}) \tag{4}$$

Prompt Generator and Prompt-guided Attention. In this subsection, we describe the generation of prompt information and the role of prompt information in our model.

In our model, we freeze the pre-trained model and maximize our training objective by prompting the key and value of the attention layer. We generate the prompt information by training a small-scale neural network. The training of the small-scale network of the Prompt Generator requires only a negligible quantity of data, which enables DHQDA to show strong performance in low-resource scenarios. The generator is defined as follows:

$$P_e = E_M W_{pe} \tag{5}$$

$$\theta = \tanh(P_e W_1 + b_1) W_2 + b_2 \tag{6}$$

where E_M is the identity matrix of length M, M is the length of the prompt, $W_{pe} \in R^{M \times d_{model}}$, $W_1 \in R^{d_{model} \times d_{model}}$, $W_2 \in R^{d_{model} \times d_\theta}$, b_1, b_2 are trainable parameters, d_{model} represents the dimensionality of input and output of transformer block, $d_\theta = 2 \times N \times d_{model}$. We divide θ into two parts according to the first dimension, which are used to prompt key and value respectively, formalized as $\theta_k = \{\theta_k^1, \theta_k^2, ..., \theta_k^N\}$ and $\theta_v = \{\theta_v^1, \theta_v^2, ..., \theta_v^N\}$.

In layer l, given the input sequence $X^l = \{x_1, ..., x_m\}^T$, we first calculate the query/key/value:

$$Q^l = X^l W_Q^l, K^l = X^l W_K^l, V^l = X^l W_V^l \tag{7}$$

where $W_Q^l, W_K^l, W_V^l \in R^{d_{model} \times d_{model}}$. Then, we concatenate the prompt parameters generated by the prompt generator with the keys and values of the pretrained model:

$$Attention^l = \text{softmax}(\frac{Q^l[K^l; \theta_k^l]^T}{\sqrt{d}})[V; \theta_v^l] \tag{8}$$

Through the guidance of attention, we can adapt the output distribution of the frozen pretrained model to our training objective.

Squence2BIO and Filter. In the end, we need to convert the generated data to a specified format such as BIO and filter out some illegal data from the final generated data to improve the quality of the final generated data.

Similar to DAGA [7], we have the procedure as follows: 1) delete sentences with all "O" tags 2) delete sentences with unknown token 3) delete sentences that do not meet the tagging rules 4) delete the exact same sentences but different tags sentence. In addition to the above mentioned, we also need to delete sentences containing words like "B-word", "I-word", where "word" is not in the label set, due to the powerful and flexible language generation capability of the GPT model.

4 Experiments

In this section, we undertake a series of experiments using English and Chinese NER datasets in order to demonstrate the effectiveness of DHQDA and to find a suitable flattening format.

4.1 Dataset

To demonstrate the effectiveness of DHQDA, we conduct experiments on three datasets.

Table 1. The statistical details of SIND.

Train	Dev.	Test
1.2 K	0.2 K	0.4 K

We verify the stability of the data generated by our model with the NER model improvement in English on Conll2003 [26] and MIT-Restaurant [17]. In the above two datasets, we set MIT-Restaurant [17] to the 100-shot case to simulate the low-resource case.

In order to verify the effectiveness of the data generated by DHQDA in improving the NER model in the Chinese specific domain, we created a ship information dataset named SIND. We crawled data from some ship information websites[1] and annotated them. The dataset contains information on important transactions in the shipping sector, ship shipping, shipyard activities, etc. The statistical details of SIND are shown in Table 1.

4.2 Evaluation

We use BiLSTM+Linear softmax as the architecture of the NER model. The data generated by the methods is evaluated by the F1 score obtained by the final result of the NER model. During the experiment, we keep the hyperparameters of the NER model unchanged, and only add data generated by various methods to the training data.

4.3 Main Result

In this subsection, we demonstrate the effectiveness of DHQDA through experimental results and explore the impact of two forms of Word-Tag and Tag-Word on the model.

Effectiveness of Our Model. In this experiment, we choose DAGA [7] and RD/RS/RI (Random Delete/Swap/Insertion) [28] as the baseline methods. In the RD method, we remove the words and the corresponding tags from the sentence with 5% probability. In the RS method, we swap the positions of the words and the corresponding tags in the sentence with 5% probability. In the RI method, we select the words and corresponding tags in the sentence with 5% probability, and then insert them randomly into the original sentence.

We divide the experiment into several cases {0, 1, 6, 12, 16}, which respectively represent the number of generated data in every 64 pieces of NER training data (includes gold data and generated data). The quality of the data is judged by observing the effect on the performance of the NER model as the amount of generated data increases.

The experimental results are shown in Table 2. From the experimental results, it can be found that our model DHQDA is effective and stable. By adding the data generated by our model, the performance of the NER model can be improved relative to not adding any generated data. DHQDA has excellent performance in all three datasets. Compared with DAGA [7] and RD/RS/RI [28], DHQDA is more stable and outperformed on both Chinese and English datasets, whether in rich or low-resource situations. It indicates that DHQDA generates higher quality data and less noise.

---

[1] http://www.eworldship.com/, http://news.sol.com.cn/.

Table 2. Results of model effectiveness evaluation (F1 score).

Dataset	Method	Number of generated data(/64)				
		0	1	6	12	16
Conll2003	DAGA	77.40	76.27	78.10	77.70	77.31
	RD		77.16	77.65	73.61	77.54
	RS		78.64	76.39	75.36	78.45
	RI		76.25	78.10	75.44	78.21
	DHQDA		**78.97**	**78.23**	**79.91**	**78.92**
MIT-Restaurant	DAGA	53.77	52.70	**56.04**	54.86	54.59
	RD		54.40	53.03	53.50	54.90
	RS		54.20	53.96	54.62	54.87
	RI		54.67	52.49	52.59	54.04
	DHQDA		**54.75**	55.26	**56.04**	**56.89**
SIND	DAGA	60.52	59.17	59.68	60.79	64.17
	RD		61.20	60.45	61.41	65.20
	RS		61.53	61.13	61.98	62.87
	RI		60.50	61.16	62.60	61.79
	DHQDA		**61.82**	**62.70**	**64.31**	**65.35**

Word-Tag vs. Tag-Word. We train our model with data in Word-Tag and Tag-Word formats to explore the impact on the performance of the NER model, respectively.

The performance of the two formats on the three datasets is shown in Table 3. From the experimental results, we can find that although the model trained with data in Tag-Word format does not show better performance than the model trained with data in Word-Tag format in all cases, in most cases, the model trained with data in Tag-Word format performs better. Therefore, we generally adopt Tag-Word format data for training and generation.

Table 3. Word-Tag vs. Tag-Word (F1 score).

Dataset	Format	Number of generated data(/64)				
		0	1	6	12	16
Conll2003	Word-tag	77.40	**79.11**	**80.17**	79.57	77.45
	Tag-Word		78.97	78.23	**79.91**	**78.92**
MIT-restaurant	Word-tag	53.77	53.13	55.08	54.92	55.21
	Tag-Word		**54.75**	**55.26**	**56.04**	**56.89**
SIND	Word-tag	60.52	**62.22**	60.75	62.14	63.76
	Tag-word		61.82	**62.70**	**64.31**	**65.35**

5   Analysis

In this section, we will explore why the data generated by DHQDA is effective in improving the performance of the NER models.

Diversity of Expression. Figure 3 shows some examples of data generated by our model. By learning from the training data, our model can generate diverse data.

In the same sentence starting with "Teenager", different character entities can be matched, such as "Dann Lehman", "Andrew Melanson" and other different names, and appear in different contexts. Moreover, the same entity appears multiple times in different contexts. This kind of changeable data allows the NER model to learn the situation of the same type of entities in different contexts, thereby improving the robustness of the NER model.

Fig. 3. Diversity of generated data. From top to bottom are examples on Conll2003, MIT-Restaurant and SIND.

More Annotated Entities. From the data generated by our model, we find that some entities that never appeared in the gold data can be annotated.

For example, in the generated sentences, some locations that have never appeared in the training corpus, such as "Appalachia", "Pyongyang", and "Kendal" are annotated with the "B-LOC" label. This indicates that our prompt information can well transform our task into the generation task of GPT. By this way, our model can reduce the noise in the generated data while utilizing the powerful generation ability of GPT [1,19,20], making our model more stable in improving the performance of the NER model. This is also the reason why our model is more powerful than previous data augmentation methods.

6   Conclusion and Future Work

In this paper, we proposed a novel model (DHQDA) for NER data augmentation to reduce noise in generated data and generate diverse data. DHQDA improves the robustness of NER models by generating more diverse and higher quality data. Experimental results demonstrate that DHQDA performs more stable and better than baseline methods on both Chinese and English datasets, whether in rich or low-resource situations. We average the improvement in F1 scores of the NER model for each of the four cases on the three datasets and obtain F1 scores for our model that are 1.66%, 1.19%, and 1.48% higher than the best performing baseline method on each dataset (Conll2003, MIT-Restaurant, and SIND). In addition, we find that our model performs better when trained with flattened data in Tag-Word format.

In the future, we will try to apply our method to other sequence labeling tasks. In addition, we will explore data augmentation for other subtasks of knowledge graph construction to make our knowledge graph construction system perform better.

Acknowledgements. This research is supported by Key-Area Research and Development Program of Guangdong Province under Grant 2019B010153002, Key Program of NSFC-Guangdong Joint Funds under Grant U1801263, Science and Technology Projects of Guangzhou under Grant 202007040006, Program of Marine Economy Development (Six Marine Industries) Special Foundation of Department of Natural Resources of Guangdong Province under Grant GDNRC [2020]056, Top Youth Talent Project of Zhujiang Talent Program under Grant 2019QN01X516, and Guangdong Provincial Key Laboratory of Cyber-Physical System under Grant 2020B1212060069.

References

1. Brown, T., Mann, B., Ryder, N., et al.: Language models are few-shot learners. In: NeurIPS (2020)
2. Chen, X., et al.: Lightner: A lightweight generative framework with prompt-guided attention for low-resource NER. arXiv preprint arXiv:2109.00720 (2021)
3. Ciregan, D., Meier, U., Schmidhuber, J.: Multi-column deep neural networks for image classification. In: 2012 IEEE Conference on Computer Vision and Pattern Recognition (2012)
4. Cui, L., Wu, Y., Liu, J., Yang, S., Zhang, Y.: Template-based named entity recognition using BART. In: Findings of the Association for Computational Linguistics: ACL-IJCNLP (2021)
5. Dai, X., Adel, H.: An analysis of simple data augmentation for named entity recognition. In: COLING (2020)
6. Devlin, J., Chang, M.W., Lee, K., Toutanova, K.: BERT: Pre-training of deep bidirectional transformers for language understanding. In: NAACL-HLT (2019)
7. Ding, B., et al.: DAGA: Data augmentation with a generation approach for low-resource tagging tasks. In: EMNLP (2020)
8. Ding, N., Chen, Y., Han, X., et al.: Prompt-learning for fine-grained entity typing. arXiv preprint arXiv:2108.10604 (2021)
9. Fabbri, A., Han, S., et al.: Improving zero and few-shot abstractive summarization with intermediate fine-tuning and data augmentation. In: NAACL-HLT (2021)
10. Feng, S.Y., Gangal, V., Wei, J., et al.: A survey of data augmentation approaches for NLP. In: ACL/IJCNLP (Findings) (2021)

11. Gao, T., Fisch, A., Chen, D.: Making pre-trained language models better few-shot learners. In: ACL/IJCNLP (2021)
12. Iyyer, M., Wieting, J., Gimpel, K., Zettlemoyer, L.: Adversarial example generation with syntactically controlled paraphrase networks. In: NAACL-HLT (2018)
13. Ko, T., Peddinti, V., Povey, D., Khudanpur, S.: Audio augmentation for speech recognition. In: INTERSPEECH (2015)
14. Krizhevsky, A., Sutskever, I., Hinton, G.E.: Imagenet classification with deep convolutional neural networks. In: NIPS (2012)
15. Lai, T., Cheng, L., Wang, D., Ye, H., Zhang, W.: RMAN: relational multi-head attention neural network for joint extraction of entities and relations. Appl. Intell. (2022)
16. Lewis, M., Liu, Y., et al.: BART: Denoising sequence-to-sequence pre-training for natural language generation, translation, and comprehension. In: ACL (2020)
17. Liu, J., Pasupat, P., Cyphers, S., Glass, J.: Asgard: A portable architecture for multilingual dialogue systems. In: ICASSP (2013)
18. Ma, R., Zhou, X., Gui, T., Tan, Y., Zhang, Q., Huang, X.: Template-free prompt tuning for few-shot NER. arXiv preprint arXiv:2109.13532 (2021)
19. Radford, A., Narasimhan, K.: Improving language understanding by generative pre-training (2018). https://cdn.openai.com/research-covers/language-unsupervised/language_understanding_paper.pdf
20. Radford, A., Wu, J., Child, R., Luan, D., Amodei, D., Sutskever, I.: Language models are unsupervised multitask learners. OpenAI Blog $1(8)$, 9 (2019)
21. Raffel, C., et al.: Exploring the limits of transfer learning with a unified text-to-text transformer. J. Mach. Learn. Res. (2020)
22. Ragni, A., Knill, K.M., Rath, S.P., Gales, M.J.F.: Data augmentation for low resource languages. In: INTERSPEECH (2014)
23. Şahin, G.G., Steedman, M.: Data augmentation via dependency tree morphing for low-resource languages. In: EMNLP (2018)
24. Schick, T., Schütze, H.: Exploiting cloze-questions for few-shot text classification and natural language inference. In: EACL (2021)
25. Shorten, C., Khoshgoftaar, T.M., Furht, B.: Text data augmentation for deep learning. J. Big Data (2021)
26. Tjong Kim Sang, E.F., De Meulder, F.: Introduction to the CoNLL-2003 shared task: Language-independent named entity recognition. In: Proceedings of the Seventh Conference on Natural Language Learning at HLT-NAACL (2003)
27. Vaswani, A., Shazeer, N., et al.: Attention is all you need. In: Advances in Neural Information Processing Systems (2017)
28. Wei, J., Zou, K.: EDA: Easy data augmentation techniques for boosting performance on text classification tasks. In: EMNLP-IJCNLP (2019)
29. Yu, A.W., Dohan, D., Le, Q., Luong, T., Zhao, R., Chen, K.: Fast and accurate reading comprehension by combining self-attention and convolution. In: International Conference on Learning Representations (2018)
30. Zhang, H., Chen, Q., Zhang, W.: Improving entity linking with two adaptive features. In: Frontiers of Information Technology & Electronic Engineering (2022)
31. Zhang, X., Zhao, J., LeCun, Y.: Character-level convolutional networks for text classification. In: Advances in Neural Information Processing Systems (2015)

Transformer-Based Original Content Recovery from Obfuscated PowerShell Scripts

Michal Dedek[iD] and Rafał Scherer[(✉)][iD]

Czestochowa University of Technology, Czestochowa, Poland
{michal.dedek,rafal.scherer}@pcz.pl

Abstract. Microsoft PowerShell is a scripting language and a command-line utility, widely used by professionals to automate tasks and to manage system services. Due to the fact of its prevalence, it was recently seen abused by malicious parties in their offensive operations. Unfortunately, antimalware software is often helpless with PowerShell scripts, as each copy of the script can be unique thanks to obfuscation techniques. Obfuscation is a process of altering the source code through various transformations so that the syntax changes, but the program's operation is unaffected. The technique is nowadays mostly used by attackers to prevent their code from being flagged as malicious and to impede its analysis. Most of the current solutions to recover the original content from obfuscated scripts are based on human-written algorithms, which make them difficult to maintain and prone to errors.

We present a solution to deal with obfuscated code by a Transformer-based model operating on a character level to reverse the obfuscation process. We do it on the example of obfuscated PowerShell commands, but the method is generic so that it can be used for other scripting languages as well. We were able to successfully recover full content in 92% cases and recover at least 90% of the content in 100% cases. The most important aspect of our approach is the ability to almost fully automate the process of creating a deobfuscator.

Keywords: PowerShell · deobfuscation · Obfuscation detection · Transformer · Machine learning

1 Introduction

We live in times of omnipresent security threats. Every day, new malware strains are developed and the control over thousands of computers is taken over by cybercriminals. Antivirus software is successful nowadays in detecting known external malicious binaries, but at the same time, not very effective in detecting attacks abusing system utilities, already installed on the computer.

The project financed under the program of the Polish Minister of Science and Higher Education under the name "Regional Initiative of Excellence" in the years 2019-2023 project number 020/RID/2018/19 the amount of financing PLN 12,000,000.

One of the most known utility software is Microsoft Powershell. Preinstalled in Windows operating system, it consists of a scripting language and an interactive command-line shell. Its aim is to provide a simple interface over system internals to automate tasks such as executing programs, modifying the configuration, accessing system services, working with files, etc.

Unfortunately, PowerShell's versatility and the fact it is "already there" on Windows machines, made it a favorite tool for malicious actors. According to McAfee's report for 2020, there was a high increase in attacks conducted with its usage [5]. Symantec corporation also made a very thorough analysis of malicious usage of PowerShell, describing techniques used to drop and execute the malware on the host, bypass detection systems and perform lateral movement afterwards [8].

Malware creators have two goals: to avoid detection and to make the analysis difficult for security experts. That is why they willingly employ obfuscation, as it accomplishes both of these tasks by ensuring the uniqueness of the script each time it is used and making the code incomprehensible.

Obfuscation is a collection of techniques to alter source code so that the program behavior is preserved, but the syntax is modified in different ways (example in Fig. 1). This is mostly done automatically, using tools called obfuscators. Many techniques are based on randomization and various transformations or encoding, all of which not only confuse the reader but also decrease similarity between copies.

PowerShell supports a variety of ways a simple instruction can be written. That opens a door to potential abuse, motivated by a desire to hide from malware detection mechanisms.

Some obfuscation methods modify the program's execution flow, for example by encoding commands, splitting data into pieces, rebranching statements, adding new instructions or replacing existing. The rest of the techniques just alter how the code "looks". Depending on what is allowed in the language, they may introduce new characters, alter the case of the letters or change variable and function names, but they won't affect the execution flow.

String manipulation is an umbrella term for methods like splitting, reordering and reversing the string. All mentioned techniques can be applied separately, but more commonly are used together.

The randomization technique is about changing variable, function and token names as well as other user-definable fields to random ones. Its purpose is to make each copy of the script unique, as the technique is built upon the assumption that most antimalware programs work by matching known fragments of a code block to samples in their database.

Having a method to simplify overly-complicated expressions would be beneficial not only in threat discovery. The ability to reverse the obfuscation process and make otherwise incomprehensible scripts intelligible would be exceedingly important for malware analysis done by researchers. Such a tool would be priceless also in forensics to prove the malicious intentions of the attacker or after

```
1    $client = New-Object System.Net.Sockets.TCPClient('192.168.1.17',4444);
2    $stream = $client.GetStream();
3
4    [byte[]]$bytes = 0..65535|%{0};
5  ⊟while(($count = $stream.Read($bytes, 0, $bytes.Length)) -ne 0){
6        $recvstr = [System.Text.Encoding]::ASCII.GetString($bytes, 0, $count);
7        $stdout = (Invoke-Expression $recvstr -ErrorVariable stderr | Out-String);
8        $sendback = $stderr + [Environment]::NewLine + $stdout ;
9        $sendbyte = ([text.encoding]::ASCII).GetBytes($sendback);
10       $stream.Write($sendbyte, 0, $sendbyte.Length);
11       $stream.Flush();
12  };
13   $client.Close();
```

```
1  ⊟ &( $ShELlID[1]+$SHeLlid[13]+'x') ( ( [REGEX]::maTcHES("')''NiOJ-'X'+]3,1[)
2    (gnIRtSot.ECNErEFerpesOBrEv$ (& |)421]RaHC[,'YBO'  ecalper- 63]RaHC[,'xTZ'
3    ecalper-93]RaHC[,)97]RaHC[+65]RaHC[+911]RaHC[(ecalper-)'
4    '+')'+'(e'+'so'+'lc'+'.tneilcXT'+'z'+';'+'};'+')(hsul'+'F.ma'+'e'+'rtsX'+'TZ
5    ;)ht'+'gneL.etybdnes'+'xTZ'+'  ,0  ,etybdnesxTZ(et'+'irw.mae'+'r'+'tsxTZ
6    ;)k'+'c'+'ab'+'d'+'n'+'esxTZ('+'s'+'e'+'tyBteG.)I'+'ICSA'+'::]gnidoc'+'n'+'e'+
7    '.txe'+'t['+'( ='+' etybd'+'nesxTZ  ; tu'+'odts'+'xTZ'+'  eniL'+'w'+'eN::'+']
8    tn'+'emnor'+'ivnE[ '+'+ rr'+'edt'+'sxTZ'+' = k'+'c'+'abdne'+'s'+'xT'+'Z
9    ;'+')gnir'+'tS-tuO YBO r'+'re'+'d'+'t'+'s e'+'lbaira'+'Vror'+'rE'+'- rtsv'+'ce'
10   '+'rXT'+'z'+' nois'+'se'+'r'+'pxE-ek'+'ovn'+'I( ='+' t'+'u'+'odtsxTZ
11   '+';)tn'+'uo'+'cXTZ'+'  ,'+'O'+'  '+'se'+'tybXT'+'Z(gnirtS'+'t'+'e'+'G.IICSA::]g'
12   +'nido'+'cn'+'E.t'+'x'+'eT'+'.met'+'s'+'yS[ = '+'rts'+'vcer'+'xTZ  '+'
13   {)0'+' e'+'n- '+'))htgn'+'eL.sety'+'bxTZ'+'  ,0  ,s'+'et'+'yb'+'xT'+'Z(dae'
14   +'R.maer'+'tsxTZ = tnuo'+'cXTZ(('+'elih'+'w;}0{'+'%YBO53556..O ='+' set'+'
15   'ybxTZ]'+'][' +'ety'+'b['+';)'+'('+'m'+'aert'+'St'+'e'+'G.tneil'+'cXT'+'
16   'Z = maertsxTZ;)4444,pB8w1'+'0'+'1.1.86'+'1.29108w(tneilc'+'PCT.s'+'t'+'ekc'+'
17   'oS.teN.'+'metsyS tcej'+'bO-weN'+' ='+' tneilcXTZ'(('"  , '.','rig'+'
18   'hTto'+'L'+'eFT') -joIN'' ) )
```

Fig. 1. A PowerShell script creating a reverse shell and its obfuscated version.

a security breach, where a team of security experts needs to investigate what happened on the compromised machines.

This paper solves the problem of reversing the obfuscation. To this end, we use a Transformer-based model working on a character-level, unlike in the default Transformer application in NLP, where each word is a single token. To train the model, we develop a custom generator of synthetic training data, which is also one of the key elements of our approach.

2   Related Works

There are a number of studies related to detecting malicious or obfuscated scripts written in interpreted languages like PowerShell or JavaScript. The number of works focused on deobfuscation is significantly less. In 2018, Liu et al. proposed a method called PSDEM, which was designed to work with malicious Microsoft Word documents, capturing PowerShell code at the moment of its execution and then performing deobfuscation on the collected snippet [4]. The deobfuscation consisted of several stacked algorithms to consecutively extract Base64-encoded commands, decode them if ASCII encoding was used, join split strings, remove insignificant characters and reverse data manipulations such as reordering. All these operations were done using human-crafted algorithms, with heavy use of regular expressions. Although being potentially accurate, the method was complicated and hard to maintain. If the obfuscation tool introduced new ways to encode a script, this method would become useless until its authors accordingly adapt it to support new transformations. Maintaining the method would mean not only being up-to-date with obfuscators' releases, but also the frustrating obligation to manually implement deobfuscation algorithms, which is a difficult task.

A similar study was conducted by Ugarte et al., whose effort resulted in the creation of PowerDrive, a multi-stage deobfuscator [6]. Their approach was to progressively process obfuscated scripts, cleaning them up using regular expressions, removing any anti-debugging checks, overriding some built-in PowerShell methods, and finally executing suspicious scripts to obtain information about the contacted URLs.

Another research group, Li et al., proposed an AST-based method of PowerShell script deobfuscation [3]. They start by employing subtrees to identify obfuscated yet recoverable script pieces, which are then deobfuscated in the emulation phase. The obfuscation detection is done by first selecting features such as the entropy of script pieces, length of tokens, distribution of AST types, or the depth of ASTs and then passing the feature vector to the classifier (logistic regression with gradient descent). After successful detection, an obfuscated script piece is processed using an emulation-based recovery, which means a sandboxed PowerShell session is spawned to run a questionable script. Despite promising results, this method has a few major drawbacks. The deobfuscation is performed dynamically by creating a sandboxed interpreter session, which creates a small, but present security risk and definitely slows down the whole process. Another disadvantage is related to the fact that deobfuscation done this way does not simplify all the expressions. If the code contains pointless instructions, they still will be logged as long as they are executed.

It is difficult to compare the results of our deobfuscator with related works because the datasets used by other researchers were not disclosed. Moreover, proposed deobfuscation approaches were so different from each other that their authors often proposed their own evaluation methods. A fair, number-based comparison is almost impossible at this stage of global research as there is no common, established evaluation scheme. With all that in mind, instead of using numbers to compare our work with others, we focus on the undisputed advantages of our solution, using reasonable metrics and suitable criteria for deobfuscation quality assessment.

Our approach has several significant benefits that all mentioned methods lack: it is fully automated, generic, and flexible. Thanks to the use of a state-of-the-art machine learning model, it relieves software developers from the necessity of manually tweaking deobfuscation algorithms to keep them up to date with the latest obfuscation techniques. Its versatility makes our solution a fit for dealing with obfuscation in different scripting languages without unnecessary adjustments.

3   Deobfuscation

A process reverse to obfuscation would take an obfuscated script and return a raw, original version, ideally the same script which was used by an attacker to create the obfuscated copy. We will call such a process a deobfuscation, while a deobfuscator would be a tool to carry it out. Building it without any help from machine learning models would be a torment because of the variety of obfuscators used in the wild and multiple configurable options they come with, complemented by the fact that generated code is heavily based on randomization.

Manually programming a deobfuscation algorithm would require us to know all these details about the obfuscator and its execution configuration, which was used to produce an obfuscated script copy. However, this information is known only to the attacker. The defense teams only have a suspicious script they want to analyze without any metadata about it.

There were several attempts to solve the task of deobfuscation using, e.g., regular expressions, simplifying ASTs, or running the obfuscated code in a sandbox, but they all were very limited in their capabilities and had severe drawbacks mentioned earlier.

We suspected that NLP methods handling sequences could be leveraged to translate obfuscated code back into the original one. At the same time, the use of machine learning would solve many problems present in manual solutions. The definitive advantage of our approach would be bypassing the need to know exact obfuscator details and having to implement the algorithm manually.

There are many sequence-oriented machine learning algorithms, including recurrent neural networks, LSTMs, GRUs and models derived from the Transformer family. All of these have been successfully used in the language translation task, but at the moment of writing this paper, the state-of-the-art approach is to use Transformers [7]. Transformer model immediately gained popularity because of its excellent results in machine translation. It was designed to work with sentences; however, almost any sequence of data can be encoded and processed by this type of network. The Transformer model heavily relies on the attention mechanism presented by Bahdanau et al. in 2015 [1], which works a bit like the attention in the human mind.

When we answer a question (or translate a sentence), for each individual word in our answer, we focus on different words in the question. Similarly, the Transformer model has an internal matrix of attention weights between input and output sequences, which are gradually adjusted in the learning process by the backpropagation mechanism. In other words, attention can be seen as a relationship between tokens in input and output sequences.

The Transformer model consists of two cooperating parts: an encoder and a decoder. The former takes an input sequence and translates it into an internal, hidden vector representation in the latent space, which retains its meaning, whereas the latter takes that representation (sometimes called "the code") and translates it to an output sequence. The mechanism capable of drawing a connection between the two is nothing more than the mentioned attention.

Just as Transformer learns to "understand" source and target languages during incremental training using pairs of translated sentences, it can also learn to build a mapping between any two interdependent sequences, at least theoretically. Since programming languages, just like natural languages, have their grammar and vocabulary, it was reasonable to examine if there was any possibility of employing this model in transforming data from one form (obfuscated) to another (original).

The idea was to teach the encoder how to understand the "true meaning" of obfuscated scripts and to teach the decoder how to generate simple, not obfuscated PowerShell code with the same meaning - perfectly the same scripts that were used to generate their obfuscated versions.

The model has three different attention blocks: self-attention in the encoder, self-attention in the decoder, and encoder-decoder attention. They allow forming relationships within the input sequence, within the output sequence, and between the input and the output. Despite serving disparate purposes, their build is quite similar—with a small exception in the decoder, where additional masking is necessary to hide tokens that are not known yet. The model's capability of focusing on several, even unrelated, aspects of the same token at the same time is called Multi-Head Attention.

As machine learning algorithms are primarily non-deterministic and are just an approximation of a difficult, complicated process, we did not aim for the complete strictness of the code outputted by the network. It does not have to be synthetically correct, as there is absolutely no need to execute it. The leading purpose of our work was to create a deobfuscator that helps security specialists and researchers get an insight or a clue about what the code actually does. We also see its usefulness as an internal part of anti-malware software: when passing a suspicious, obfuscated script to a classifier, additional information from a deobfuscator would be a great help in discovering malicious intents.

4   Dataset

We needed plenty of high-quality data: both normal PowerShell commands and their obfuscated copies. We could not find any ready-made collection, so we needed to build it on our own. Before deciding for a fully synthetic dataset, we tried several different approaches, but none of them gave us quality results like the final one.

Apart from its difficulty, obtaining data from public sources comes with a significant drawback: the snippets are usually in an unstructured form, with a lot of rubbish. With that in mind, we finally decided to take the synthetic approach by creating a PowerShell commands generator, which could provide a countless number of unique learning examples. The whole process of creating fully synthetic training data, illustrated by Fig. 2, consisted of two stages—generation followed by obfuscation. The generation stage's purpose was to obtain a large number of PowerShell commands showing a variety of options, arguments, parameters and expressions supported by language. For that task, we designed a special generator, which example output we present in Table 1.

The obfuscation stage was designed to acquire obfuscated counterparts of code snippets generated in the previous phase. For this part we used the Invoke-Obfuscation toolkit, along with our own-made scripts to automate the whole

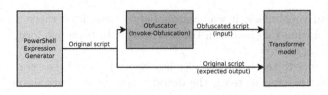

Fig. 2. Overview of the dataset generation environment.

Table 1. Example output from the generator

```
vmzoe-xjgoykfbvqbxxrh -woggulmjsepimed "$vbwzhmO.yfamjkm" -b $hnfho
-eaymluxffmhcfgi $ukslk2.qmkfz -yfkvasgjyl C:\jrxe.vjf
```

```
Ngtid -S "21tyP" -W "cWQdeSIu" -Q "jYQDbnpoVDM" "Bw7_g" |
Jpuk-IxvbbMaczqFvhqe {$_.Txozd -O 'SwOQUyy'}
```

```
Yfea-NtsywDcxnbAphmk -D 1 -O $jhhqg6.Ujwxj -A "yxRqM" jdvybezgyjptp.lhf
| Xcryw-Oampfj Gepxi, Tdijm, Sbett
```

process. Another advantage of a fully synthetic approach was having a total control over data. If a certain language construct was still unrecognized by the network, we could generate more examples with it. The same would be very difficult with data obtained from third parties.

The synthetic dataset consisted of 30 000 samples used for training and 8 000 samples for testing – 38 000 samples in total, split with a ratio close to 0.8. The average length of raw (original) and obfuscated commands were respectively 69 and 227 characters, which we illustrate in Fig. 3.

5   Model

There are several machine learning algorithms to deal with sequences. We used a state-of-the-art Transformer model, which is mostly used in natural language processing. One of its main features is the attention mechanism.

The default usage of sequential models used in natural language processing is to take a sentence, split it into words, encode them as numbers (tokens) and pass such vector to the network. With a regular (unobfuscated) PowerShell code, it would be sensible to do a similar thing, breaking commands and expressions into tokens—the equivalent of words in a sentence. The flat sequence of tokens would actually consist of concrete leaves in the code's Abstract Syntax Tree, namely command names, flags, parameters, variables, strings, numbers, etc. However, this form of tokenization would become problematic with obfuscated code because of its structure and use of special syntax tricks. Obfuscated code is often so overly complicated that even the PowerShell Integrated Script Environment's parser is lost. This is the reason why we chose the character-level

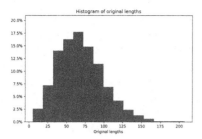 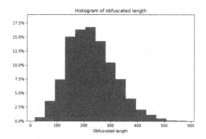

Fig. 3. (a) Histogram of original command lengths (b) Histogram of obfuscated command lengths

encoding. Each subsequent character in a snippet was treated as a single token for the input sequence to the model. This means the whole model's vocabulary was about a hundred elements long because that was the total number of distinct characters used in the dataset. Despite its disadvantages, a character-level encoding, primarily being slower and using more memory, has significant benefits: it is more accurate and dramatically simplifies the model. Having a token-level encoding would require a script to be preprocessed by a PowerShell parser, not only during training but, more importantly, also in the final application, which would notably slow down the deobfuscation process.

For the Transformer model hyperparameters, at the beginning, we used the defaults proposed in [7], which turned out to be sufficient for our proof-of-concept without introducing too much overload on our development environment. Later, we slightly tuned the parameters to achieve better results. The final size characteristics were as follows: there were both three encoder and three decoder layers, ten attention heads, and each feed-forward layer consisted of 640 (512+128) hidden neurons. For our case, it was sufficient and gave us good results; however, for more difficult problems, there is always an option to scale the network up.

The vocabulary used to map input characters to their corresponding token representation contained 104 elements: both lowercase and uppercase English letters, digits, whitespace, special characters such as dot, comma, etc.

6   Training

The weights of neurons were initialized using the Xavier uniform distribution, a method described in [2]. To optimize them during training, we used the Adam algorithm, with a learning rate of 0.0001. For betas, coefficients used for computing running averages of gradient and its square, we used 0.9 and 0.98, respectively. The epsilon value, used to improve numerical stability, was equal to 1-9.

There were 167 epochs needed to train the model up to a point there was no significant loss reduction in the validation set. To prevent neurons from co-adaptation and thus model overfitting, we used a dropout layer, which is an effective regularization technique. Its value was set at 0.1.

The Transformer model, like most sequential models, is not a fast learner. Our approach, where every character of a script is encoded as a separate token, despite its certain advantages, slows down the learning process even more. However, thanks to the faster and faster computer equipment, and the ability to put samples in batches (in our case, each batch contained 64 samples), the amount of time needed to obtain a working deobfuscator is not appalling either, especially as the process usually takes place on the mainframe computers or in the cloud. In our case, the training took 2 h, 19 min, and 50 s on four NVidia Tesla V100 SXM3 32 GB GPUs, which is an acceptable duration given the fact it is not meant to be repeated very often.

7 Results

The created deobfuscator outperformed our expectations. The simple idea of treating original and obfuscated PowerShell code just as two languages, and translating one to another was proved to be working. We were able to recover 100% of the scripts in 92% cases and at least 90% of the content of the original scripts in 100% cases[1].

Although the model is still not perfect and can have problems with some more complicated scripts, the concept is proven to be correct. The quality of deobfuscation can still be improved by obtaining a better dataset (for example, by further developing the expression generator) and scaling the network up. As we can see in Table 2, the network is capable of not only cleaning the obfuscated command from unnecessary characters and joining strings together but also of restoring the replaced or encoded fragments.

Table 2. Comparison between obfuscated, deobfuscated and original commands

Obfuscated	`(('Copy-Ite'+'m '+'-Filter'+' *.'+'t'+'xt'+' -'+'P'+'ath {'+'1}D:{'+'0}t'+'e'+'mp{0}'+'T'+'es'+'t_Folder{1} -Recur' +'se'+' -Dest'+'inat'+'ion'+' {1'+'}D:{0}tem'+'p{0}Tes'+'t_' +'F'+'older1{'+'1'+'}')-f[char]92,[char]39)	. ($pshoME[4]+$psHomE[30]+'X')`
Deobfuscated	`Copy-Item -Filter *.txt -Path 'D:\temp\Test_Folder' -Recurse -Destination 'D:\temp\Test_Folder1'`
Original	`Copy-Item -Filter *.txt -Path 'D:\temp\Test_Folder' -Recurse -Destination 'D:\temp\Test_Folder1'`

The task of properly evaluating the efficiency of our model in deobfuscation is difficult in a similar way to translation quality evaluation in natural language processing. The metrics used for that are not perfect in the situation when there is no single correct answer. For a single obfuscated command, there are often several "correct" deobfuscated versions. This is because, during the obfuscation

---

[1] For all of the scripts, Jaro-Winkler distance was above 0.9 and for 92% of the scripts, the distance was equal to 1.0, which means the original and deobfuscated versions were identical.

phase, some information is lost, for example, the original case of the letters in a command's name. The obfuscator often diversifies them to make the code more random and unique. The analogous situation is with additional or missing whitespace, but caveats like this are prevalent. For a security researcher, who just wants to reduce the complexity of obfuscated code, such small differences are irrelevant.

Due to these factors, models are often prone to underestimation, which means they are actually better than the results say. Despite these inconveniences, we employ some metrics to evaluate our solution while reminding that we supplied just a single "correct" version for a command, being it the original one, before the obfuscation. There is no common, well-established approach to evaluate deobfuscation quality. For that task, we utilize metrics used typically in NLP and statistics. When it comes to comparing sequences of characters, there are metrics to calculate similarity or distance between strings. One of them is Jaro-Winkler distance.

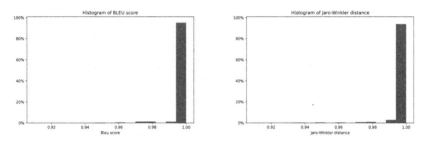

Fig. 4. (a) Histogram of BLEU score (b) Histogram of Jaro-Winkler distance

In Fig. 4, we present histograms of the Jaro-Winkler distance and BLEU score computed over the validation set. The average for both metrics was equal to 0.998. As far as model usage is concerned, it can be used even on ordinary machines. A 100-character code snippet takes about 0.3 s to deobfuscate on a dual-core 3.5 GHz CPU.

It is important to note that the relationship between the input script length and the processing time is not direct. Of course, deobfuscation time depends on the length of the input (obfuscated) script, but primarily it depends on the output (deobfuscated) sequence length. There is almost a linear relationship between the deobfuscated (and original, as they should be almost the same) script length and the deobfuscation time.

The relationship between obfuscated script length and deobfuscation time at first glance seems more chaotic; however, there is a simple explanation for this behavior.

The obfuscated copies of the same length can take different amounts of time to deobfuscate, and conversely, the obfuscated copies of the very same original script can differ in length, but the network will still process them in the same amount of time. This is caused by the structure of obfuscated code and Transformer model characteristics. First, the relationship between the original

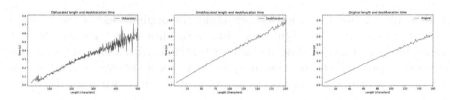

Fig. 5. (a) Obfuscated length and deobfuscation time (b) deobfuscated length and deobfuscation time (c) original length and deobfuscation time

(and consequently deobfuscated) script length and obfuscated copy length is not exactly linear. The obfuscator heavily relies on randomness, and it introduces varying amounts of "junk" to the obfuscated scripts. This junk will be later cut out by the deobfuscator.

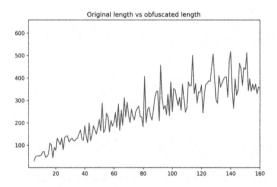

Fig. 6. Original command length and obfuscated command length

The other aspect is how the Transformer model transforms a sequence: it outputs a vector of probabilities only for a single token at a time. In other words, it generates only the next token, and to generate the full output sequence, it needs to be repeatedly fed with its own output until the EOS token ("end of sentence") is reached. This recurring process has a more significant impact on deobfuscation time than the length of the input sequence. If our model spots a pattern of junk in the input, regardless of its length, it omits it—that is why a more obfuscated and longer script will not necessarily be processed longer.

8   Conclusion

For a couple of years, PowerShell has been employed by malware groups in their offensive operations. It allows attackers to leverage the system's built-in automation and management utilities for their own profit, and its usage does not leave traces on the hard disc drive. Malicious PowerShell scripts are often transformed by so-called obfuscators to avoid alerting the antimalware software and to frustrate security analysts. This makes detecting obfuscation and recovering the original content of the scripts a substantial challenge. There were several attempts to achieve these goals, both together and separately. Most of the current deobfuscation solutions are manually crafted, using regular expressions and human-written algorithms, which makes them hard to maintain in the world of constantly changing malware.

We proposed a fully automated, generic approach to deobfuscation. Our bundled solution recovers the original content of obfuscated scripts, revealing the code true operation to security analysts and antimalware software. The most significant advantage of our method is its reliance on one of the state-of-the-art machine learning models instead of human-crafted algorithms, making it easy to maintain its supremacy against the latest obfuscation techniques. The deobfuscation is implemented using a character-level Transformer model, trained in a specific way so that it actually understands the PowerShell language and the concept of obfuscation. As the results show, our model is fully capable of completing its job in a fast, accurate way. It correctly restores the full original content of 92% of them.

References

1. Bahdanau, D., Cho, K., Bengio, Y.: Neural machine translation by jointly learning to align and translate **1409**, 09 (2014)
2. Glorot, X., Bengio, Y.: Understanding the difficulty of training deep feedforward neural networks. J. Mach. Learn. Res. - Proc. Track **9**, 249–256 (2010)
3. Li, Z., Chen, Q.A., Xiong, C., Chen, Y., Zhu, T., Yang, H.: Effective and light-weight deobfuscation and semantic-aware attack detection for powershell scripts. In: Proceedings of the 2019 ACM SIGSAC Conference on Computer and Communications Security, CCS 2019, page 1831–1847. Association for Computing Machinery, New York (2019)
4. Liu, C., Xia, B., Yu, M., Liu, Y.: Psdem: A feasible de-obfuscation method for malicious powershell detection. In: 2018 IEEE Symposium on Computers and Communications (ISCC), pages 825–831 (2018)
5. McAfee. Mcafee labs threat report 11.20 (2020)
6. Ugarte, D., Maiorca, D., Cara, F., Giacinto, G.: PowerDrive: accurate de-obfuscation and analysis of powershell malware. In: Perdisci, R., Maurice, C., Giacinto, G., Almgren, M. (eds.) DIMVA 2019. LNCS, vol. 11543, pp. 240–259. Springer, Cham (2019). https://doi.org/10.1007/978-3-030-22038-9_12
7. Vaswani, A.: Attention is all you need (2017)
8. Wueest, C., Stephen, D.: The increased use of powershell in attacks. In Proceedings CA, Symantec Corporation World Headquarters, pp. 1–18 (2016)

A Generic Enhancer for Backdoor Attacks on Deep Neural Networks

Bilal Hussain Abbasi, Qi Zhong, Leo Yu Zhang[(✉)], Shang Gao, Antonio Robles-Kelly, and Robin Doss

School of Information Technology, Deakin University, VIC 3216, Australia
leo.zhang@deakin.edu.au

Abstract. Backdoor attack, which attempts to manipulate model prediction on specific poisoned inputs, poses a serious threat to deep neural networks. It mainly utilizes poisoned datasets to inject backdoor(s) into a model through training or fine-tuning. The backdoor will be activated by attacker specified triggers that are included in the datasets and associated with the pre-defined target classes. To achieve a better trade-off between attack effectiveness and stealthiness, many studies focus on more complex designs like using natural-appearing poisoned samples with smaller poisoning rates. Effective as they are, the results of the heuristic studies can still be readily identified or invalidated by existing defenses. It is mainly because the backdoored model is often overconfident in predicting poisoned inputs, also its neurons exhibit significantly different behaviour on benign and poisoned inputs. In this paper, we propose a generic backdoor enhancer based on label smoothing and activation suppression to mitigate these two problems. The intuition behind our backdoor enhancer is two-fold: label smoothing reduces the confidence level of the backdoored model over poisoned inputs, while activation suppression entangles the behaviour of neurons on benign/poisoned samples. In this way, the model is backdoored gently. Extensive experiments are conducted to assess the proposed enhancer, including using three different network architectures and three different poisoning mechanisms on three common datasets. Results validate that the enhancer can enhance various backdoor attacks, even the most rudimentary ones, to the level of state-of-the-art attacks in terms of effectiveness and bypassing detection.

Keywords: Backdoor Attacks · Backdoor Enhancer · Label Smoothing

1 Introduction

Deep learning has gained hype based on its outstanding performance and is being implemented in many highly sensitive areas, such as medical sciences, military, autonomous vehicles, and space technologies [1–3,10]. Unfortunately, based on recent studies, it has been discovered that deep learning models are

---

B. H. Abbasi and Q. Zhong—These authors contributed equally to this work.

© The Author(s), under exclusive license to Springer Nature Singapore Pte Ltd. 2023
M. Tanveer et al. (Eds.): ICONIP 2022, CCIS 1794, pp. 296–307, 2023.
https://doi.org/10.1007/978-981-99-1648-1_25

prone to backdoor attacks [7,11,17]. Such attacks aimed at controlling the model to predict a specific output for a specific input are often deadly, as they can be implemented at any stage of the deep learning life cycle and in almost all deep learning domains (like natural language processing, speech recognition, video recognition) and many alike applications [6,30,32].

In the literature, poisoning a small proportion of training samples is one of the most popular ways that adversaries employ to achieve backdoor attacks. More precisely, adversaries insert a specifically crafted trigger into this selected subset of data and assign attacker-specified target label(s) to the poisoned samples. Then a model trained/fine-tuned using poisoned samples will inevitably have the backdoor injected. During inference, the backdoored model still behaves normally on benign inputs but returns the target label on poisoned inputs that contain the trigger.

On the other hand, MLaaS (Machine Learning as a Service) platforms [23] launched by various cloud service providers enable customers to outsource their deep neural network (DNN) model training tasks. The unprotected open channel and unreliable model training process increase the risk of the DNN models being compromised since the adversaries (e.g., unreliable MLaaS providers) have complete control of the model training process. In some security-sensitive areas like facial recognition, autonomous vehicles and the health sector, such arbitrary control of DNNs can result in dire consequences. As a concrete example, [16] discovered that some pre-trained models obtained from an online open-source model platform (Caffe model zoo) were backdoored.

Moreover, to increase backdoor stealthiness and bypass backdoor countermeasures, a surplus amount of sophisticatedly designed backdoor attacks have been proposed in the past few years. For example, to generate natural-appearing poisoning samples, Zhao et al. [31] employed natural raindrops as triggers, and Liu et al. suggested using natural light reflection as a trigger for computer vision tasks [18]. Lin et al. proposed to composite multiple existing benign features as triggers [14]. Whereas, Li et al. took advantage of steganography to hide triggers within clean samples [11]. It was also reported by [28] that, instead of using one static trigger and one target label, using multiple target labels simultaneously could also increase attack stealthiness.

From the defenders' view, backdoored models usually exhibit overconfidence in poisoned inputs and their intermediate neurons' behaviour on benign and poisoned inputs are different. Based on this observation, various backdoor defenses have been proposed. Typical examples include offline backdoor detection and removal methods like Neural Cleanse (NC) [26] and Artificial Brain Stimulation (ABS) [16], as well as online detection methods like STRong Intentional Perturbation (STRIP) [8]. Most backdoor attacks, including the ones with improved or optimized stealthiness mentioned above, can be detected by one or a few of these defenses [8,16,26]. Such observation drives the arm-race of defense/attack further and leads to the philosophy of designing even more elaborated trigger/poison sample generation methods. For example, recent studies in [20,21,24] advocated generating input-specific triggers, with the help of a generative network or autoencoder, to bypass defense. Clearly, such attacks rely on stronger assumptions, since training a separate model for trigger generation is not only costly but also requires access to the whole clean dataset. And the poisoning rate needs to be adjusted to ensure attack effectiveness.

In this paper, we propose a generic backdoor enhancer framework that aims to improve backdoor sustainability without relying on strong assumptions about the adversary. Two strategies, label smoothing and activation suppression, are employed to achieve this goal. Our intuition is simple, direct yet effective. Similar to the classic backdoor attacks [7, 9, 14], we only need to poison a small part of the training dataset with smoothed target labels. This will reduce the prediction overconfidence and partially invalidate backdoor defenses. Similarly, to entangle the behaviour of benign and poisoned inputs at the intermediate layers of DNN, we employ a novel loss function to suppress the poisoned samples' irregular activation during the backdoor injection. Without resorting to stronger assumptions and sophisticated neural-based solutions, the resultant backdoor attack invalidates existing state-of-the-art (SOTA) defenses.

In summary, the main contributions of this paper are as follows:

1. We propose a generic backdoor enhancer framework using label smoothing and activation suppression techniques.
2. The proposed enhancer can be applied to various types of backdoor attacks to strengthen their attack effectiveness without changing the adversary's assumptions.
3. Extensive experiments validate the proposed enhancer can enhance various backdoor attacks, even the most rudimentary ones, to the level of SOTA attacks in terms of effectiveness and bypassing detection.

2   Preliminaries

This section discusses basic working principle of backdoor attacks and SOTA backdoor defenses such as NC [26], STRIP [8] and ABS [16].

2.1   Backdoor Attacks

BadNets, introduced by [9] in 2017, is the first work that reveals backdoor threats in DNN models. It is a naive backdoor attack where the trigger is sample-agnostic and the target label is static, i.e., different poisoned samples are injected with the same trigger type, trigger position and target labels. Another example of naive backdoor attacks is [7], in which the authors blend triggers into benign samples to generate poisoned samples. Such attacks are effective but are not stealthy as they can be easily detected or mitigated by some SOTA defenses, e.g., NC [26], STRIP [8] and ABS [16], etc.

To make attacks more stealthy, researchers have proposed steganography-inspired methods such as invisible backdoor [13] and natural backdoor [18,31], as well as multi-target backdoor [28], dynamic backdoor [24], and other methods that attempt to build complex mappings between triggers and target labels.

Most advanced backdoor methods have been proven to bypass some defense mechanisms like NC and STRIP successfully, however, it is still unclear if these advanced backdoor methods can evade ABS.

2.2   Backdoor Defenses

In the literature, various backdoor defenses [4, 5, 8, 12, 15, 16, 22, 25–27] have been proposed to mitigate the backdoor threat. Among all these existing defenses, NC, ABS, and STRIP are deemed as benchmark defenses because, in various cases, these defenses could not be bypassed easily due to their coherent methodologies. Ergo, we briefly discuss these defenses below.

NC [26]. This is the first work in which backdoor models can be detected by reverse-engineering the triggers. NC is built on two assumptions, namely that the trigger is static and that it is the smallest external perturbation or feature that can cause any benign sample to be misclassified as a target label.

STRIP [8]. It is one of the popular online backdoor detection methods based on the observation that benign and poisoned samples exhibit different entropy (or randomness). The intuition behind the different entropy is due to the fact that once deliberate perturbations are applied to benign inputs, resulting predictions exhibit high randomness.

ABS [16]. It is regarded to be an improved version of NC, which can identify compromised neurons by scanning the model and analyzing the internal neurons' behaviour. Moreover, the triggers can be reverse-engineered and the target labels can be identified as well. It is based on the assumption that certain intermediate neurons get highly excited in the presence of backdoor triggers, while they show less excitation in case of benign inputs. Additionally, it also assumes that the target label output activation is activated by only one compromised neuron.

In a nutshell, to the best of our knowledge, very few, if it is not none, existing backdoor attacks are able to completely resist all three aforementioned defenses simultaneously. It is mainly because the intuitions of the three defenses are compensation for each other. In this work, we focus on proposing a generic backdoor enhancer by invalidating the assumptions of these defenses.

3   Methodology

This section presents details of the proposed backdoor enhancer. Before delving into the details, we first discuss the threat model and the rationale of our method.

3.1   Threat Model

The adversary is assumed to have access to and can manipulate the training data, as well as the parameters, structure and training process of the victim model. He aims to enhance the backdoor robustness while maintaining the backdoors of the victim model without modifying the adversary's assumptions (e.g., trigger/poisoned samples generation and poisoning rate). To meet the expectations, the proposed backdoor enhancer should have the following properties:

(1) Fidelity: It does not degrade the backdoor success rate as well as the model accuracy on benign inputs.
(2) Sustainability: It is able to sustain SOTA defenses such as NC, STRIP and ABS. i.e., the backdoor must still be active/undetectable after applying these defenses.

3.2 Intuition

As analyzed in Sect. 2.2, the methodologies of most existing backdoor defenses are based on the assumptions that (1) backdoored models exhibit overfitting on poisoned samples and (2) their intermediate neurons exhibit higher activation on poisoned inputs as compared to that on benign inputs. Our backdoor enhancer is designed with the idea that these assumptions no longer hold.

We utilize the label smoothing technique to address the overfitting issue instead of the conventional hard-labeling method on the poisoned samples. The label smoothing technique provides some flexibility in class predictions by encouraging incorrect classes to have some weight instead of zeroing them out. It has proven to be able to well tackle the overfitting issue within neural networks [19].

To address the abnormal neuron activation behaviour, taking inspiration from convolutional network visualization [29], we utilize the activation suppression technique in the last convolution layer of the backdoor model. Specifically, in a convolutional neural network, the deeper layers tend to learn more abstract and meaningful representations that contribute more towards the classification tasks [29]. Suppressing the activation of the poisoned samples in the last convolution layer of the backdoor model during the training phase can effectively entangle the intermediate neurons' behaviour on benign inputs and poisoned inputs.

3.3 Proposed Backdoor Enhancer

For better illustration, we divide the proposed backdoor enhancer framework into two parts: poisoned dataset crafting and backdoor injection.

Poisoned Dataset Crafting. Without loss of generality, we consider a naive label poisoning DNN backdooring problem on a C-classes image classification task. Suppose $D = \{x_i, y_i\}_{i=1}^{N}$ indicates the original benign dataset containing N samples, f is a convolutional neural network selected by experts that can achieve SOTA performance on an image classification task, where $x_i \in \{0, \ldots, 255\}^{w \times h \times c}$ is a benign sample and $y_i \in \{0, \ldots, C-1\}$ is its corresponding label. We follow the definition used by [26] to define naive poisoned samples generation method:

$$x_i^p \leftarrow \mathsf{Poi}(x_i, m, \Delta), \tag{1}$$

where $x_i \in D_1$ is the original benign image, D_1 is a subset of D, x_i^p is the poisoned sample, Δ is the trigger, m is a two-dimension matrix called *mask*. Let $y_t \in \{0, \ldots, C-1\}$ be the target label specified by the adversary. We first convert the target label y_t into a one-hot encoded label vector $(v_1, \ldots, v_C)$, where $v_t = 1$ $(t = y_t+1)$ and $v_i = 0$ $(i \neq t)$. Then, we apply the label smoothing method on it to get a smoothed label $y_t^* = (v_1^*, \ldots, v_C^*)$, where

$$v_i^* = (1 - \alpha)v_i + \alpha/C, \ i \in \{1, \ldots, C\}, \tag{2}$$

Here, $\sum_{i=1}^{C} v_i^* = 1$, $\alpha \in [0, 1]$ is the smoothing factor that controls the label smoothing effect. If $\alpha = 0$, we obtain the original hard label y_t. If $\alpha = 1$, we obtain the uniformly distributed smooth label. Finally, we can get the poisoned dataset as $D_P = \{x_i^p, y_t^*\}_{i=1}^{M}$, the updated benign dataset $D_B = D \backslash D_1$, and $\rho = \frac{M}{N}$ indicates poisoning rate.

Backdoor Injection. Once the poisoned dataset is generated using the aforementioned method, a backdoor can be injected to a DNN model by minimizing the customized model training process as follows:

$$-\frac{1}{|D_B|} \sum_{x \in D_B} \sum_{i=1}^{C} v_i \log(p_i(x, \theta)) - \frac{1}{|D_P|} \sum_{x \in D_P} \sum_{i=1}^{C} v_i^* \log(p_i(x, \theta)) + \frac{\lambda}{|D_P|} \sum_{x \in D_P} \|F^{(j)}(\theta, x)\|_2,$$

$$\tag{3}$$

where v_i/v_i^* is the i-th value of the ground-truth label of x, p_i is the i-th output of the softmax of CNN f, and θ is the trainable model weight set. Furthermore, $F^{(j)} : \mathbb{R}^{w \times h \times c} \to \mathbb{R}^{w_j \times h_j \times c_j}$ denotes the mapping function that propagates an input x through the network f to the j-th $(j \in [1, 2, \cdots, L])$ layer. λ is a parameter that controls the importance of the activation suppression term.

As mentioned in Sect. 3.2, we select the last convolution layer to construct the mapping function.

4   Experiments

4.1   Experiment Setting

In this section, we evaluate the performance of our proposed backdoor enhancer against three SOTA defenses: ABS [16], NC [26] and STRIP [8]. We conduct all the experiments on three different image classification benchmark datasets

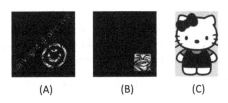

(A)   (B)   (C)

Fig. 1. Different backdoor triggers used in our experiments.

(CIFAR-10, SVHN and Fashion-MNIST (FMNIST)), three different trigger patterns (as shown in Fig. 1), and three network architectures (ResNet-20, VGG-16, and CNN). For better illustration, we refer to the trigger patterns in Fig. 1 as 'Trigger A', 'Trigger B' and 'Trigger C', respectively. 'Benign model' refers to the model that does not incorporate any backdoor (namely clean model). Models trained with the classic backdooring techniques (with hard labels) are referred to as 'Hard Label' whereas models trained with our technique are referred to as 'LSAS'.

Evaluation Metrics. We measure the backdoor success as the percentage of benign inputs stamped with the trigger that get predicted as the target label by the backdoor model and refer it to as 'BSR' Moreover, the clean samples accuracy is simply labeled as 'CA'. Ideally, our goal is to maintain both BSR and CA (the higher the better). For defense evaluation, STRIP uses FAR (False Acceptance Rate) as a measure to differentiate between clean and infected models. Ideally, for an adversary to achieve his backdooring goal, he will expect the FAR to be higher. Whereas, NC uses the anomaly index as a measure to identify if any given model is backdoored. For any benign model, the anomaly index should be less than 2 which is also the ideal scenario for the attacker. Similarly, ABS uses REASR (Reverse Engineer Attack Success Rate) which is defined as the percentage of benign inputs that get subverted by reverse engineered trigger to the target label. Identical to NC, ABS also outputs the target label and its corresponding REASR.

4.2 Results and Analysis

In this section, we evaluate the performance of our backdoor enhancer in terms of fidelity and sustainability. It is important to mention here that, we only report the results where the label smoothing factor (α) is 0.6 and the activation suppression factor (λ) is 0.1.

Fidelity. As discussed earlier, the fidelity property of the backdoor enhancer contains two goals, i.e., to enable a backdoor model to achieve high BSR and CA simultaneously. Backdoor models trained by our proposed technique satisfy both goals. We show the BSR and CA in Table 1. Here we only report results of backdoor models trained using trigger Fig. 1 (B). As it can be seen, our proposed technique achieves high attack success rates and simultaneously maintains the clean sample accuracy. In some instances, it can also be observed that our proposed method also enhances the clean accuracy. For example, in SVHN model trained using VGG-16 architecture, we can observe that clean accuracy of our proposed method is greater than that of backdoor model trained with hard labels. Whereas, the backdoor success rate of our proposed method is almost same as that of models trained with hard labels. This shows that our proposed method successfully fulfills the fidelity property of backdoor attacks.

Sustainability. The sustainability property refers to the defense-evading capabilities of backdoor models. As mentioned previously, we evaluate our methodology against three SOTA backdoor defenses. By Recalling the evaluation metrics,

Table 1. Comparison of CA and BSR of different models trained with different architectures and datasets.

Model Type	CIFAR-10		SVHN		FMNIST	
	CA	BSR	CA	BSR	CA	BSR
Benign	84.66%	–	96.05%	–	91.39%	–
Hard labels	86.66%	99.75%	95.15%	100%	93.93%	99.99%
LSAS	86.21%	98.75%	96.18%	99.94%	93.73%	96.81%

Table 2. Comparison of stealthiness measure. We report anomaly indices of models under column 'NC', FAR under 'STRIP' and REASR under 'ABS' columns.

Model Type	CIFAR-10			SVHN			FMNIST		
	NC	STRIP	ABS	NC	STRIP	ABS	NC	STRIP	ABS
Benign Model	1.32	100%	0.94 (L1)	1.68	100%	0	0.97	99.70%	1.0 (L1)
Hard Label	2.17 (L7)	0%	1.0 (L7)	4.78 (L7)	0%	1.0 (L7)	2.67 (L7,8)	0.05%	0.8 (L7)
LSAS (Trig. A)	1.17	100%	0	1.63	100%	0.88 (L1)	1.77	100%	1.0 (L8)
LSAS (Trig. B)	1.57	100%	0.94 (L1)	1.56	100%	0	1.03	100%	1.0 (L8)
LSAS (Trig. C)	0.89	100%	0	1.61	100%	0.86 (L2)	1.75	100%	1.0 (L8)

already discussed in Sect. 4.1, for an attack to be successful it should achieve high FAR to evade STRIP, low anomaly index, and REASR to evade NC and ABS respectively. These results are presented in Table 2. As we can see, in all cases our methodology achieves a higher False Acceptance Rate for STRIP, and a low Anomaly Index for NC. However, in ABS high REASR is observed in many cases but the target labels flagged by ABS are incorrect. For instance, with the backdoor model trained on CIFAR-10 and trigger B, it can be seen that although anomaly index and FAR are completely favorable (to evade respective defenses), REASR in ABS is high. However, the infected label flagged by ABS is wrong. i.e., label 1. Similar cases can be observed in other instances. Interestingly, we can also observe that even for some clean models ABS returns high REASR although the models are completely benign and are trained from scratch. For instance, the CIFAR-10 model. Whereas for all backdoor models trained with hard labels, ABS and NC are able to detect the correct target label (label 7) and STRIP exhibits extremely low FAR. Moreover, this behaviour is also observed in the ABS original paper, where authors observed high REASR values for a number of clean models. We believe, this reasoning can justify the instances where high REASR in LSAS models is observed but ultimately, the flagged infected label is wrong (not the target label) which implies that our methodology results in behaviour that is close to benign models.

5   Ablation Studies

In this section, we conduct experiments to further investigate the effects of varying different parameters on the CIFAR-10 dataset using VGG-16 architecture.

5.1   Effect on STRIP FAR by Varying FRR

Firstly we observe the changes in FAR for STRIP detection by changing the FRR (False Rejection Rate) values. Note that authors in [8] mention that they get the best results when the FRR value was set to 1%. Hence, the results reported in Table 2 are calculated with preset FRR value of 1%. Furthermore, in this section, we conduct some additional experiments by varying the FRR values from 0.5% to 3% as mentioned in the original paper. Note that according to the authors, there is a trade-off between FAR and FRR. i.e., by increasing the FRR value one may get lower FAR values and vice-versa. In order to observe changes by varying the FRR values, we conduct these experiments and report the results in Table 3. We can see from the results that backdoor models trained with hard labels exhibit low FAR even when FRR is increased. However, in the case of trigger C (blended trigger), we get a comparatively high FAR. But by increasing the FRR values, we can observe a decrease in overall FAR values. On the other hand, models trained by our method (LSAS) consistently exhibit high FAR values, which means that irrespective of the trigger type, our methodology is able to bypass STRIP detection even when FRR values are changed.

Table 3. Comparison of STRIP FAR by varying FRR between ordinary backdoor models and LSAS.

Model Type	Trigger A		Trigger B		Trigger C	
	FRR	FAR	FRR	FAR	FRR	FAR
Hard Label	0.5%	5%	0.5%	0%	0.5%	66.5%
	1%	0%	1%	0%	1%	45.5%
	2%	0%	2%	0%	2%	32.5%
	3%	0%	3%	0%	3%	25.6%
LSAS	0.5%	100%	0.5%	100%	0.5%	100%
	1%	100%	1%	100%	1%	100%
	2%	100%	2%	100%	2%	100%
	3%	100%	3%	100%	3%	100%

Table 4. Effect of varying α.

α	NC	STRIP	ABS
0.5	1.37	100%	1.0 (L7)
0.6	2.24 (L9)	100%	1.0 (L7)
0.7	1.37	100%	0.1 (L3)
0.8	1.03	100%	0.7 (L7)
0.9	1.04	100%	0.3 (L3)

Table 5. Effect of varying λ.

λ	NC	STRIP	ABS
0.1	1.18	100%	1.0 (L2)
0.2	6.02 (L5, L4, L3, L2)	100%	0.94 (L1)
0.3	1.73	100%	0.98 (L1)
0.4	Runtime error	100%	1.0 (L5)

5.2   Effect of Varying Label Smoothing Factor

As discussed previously, our proposed method utilizes a combination of label smoothing and activation suppression. Therefore, one might wonder what happens if we only apply label smoothing and train the backdoor models. Will this still be sufficient to evade the aforementioned defense mechanisms? In order to answer these questions, we further move forward and conduct some additional experiments in which we train the backdoor models only with label smoothing. For these experiments, we use Trigger B and change the label smoothing factor (α) from 0.5 to 0.9. We further evaluate these models on NC, STRIP, and ABS to see if the models are still able to evade these defenses. Results can be seen in Table 4. From these results, it is clear that by only applying label smoothing we can easily bypass NC and STRIP defenses. However, we are not able to evade ABS even with high values of α (except when α is 0.7 and 0.9 where REASR is very low). However, as per the results mentioned in Table 2, this is not the case. It is due to the fact that ABS utilizes inner neuron activations to highlight anomalies and consequently detect backdoors within models. In this regard, although label smoothing does help to twist the decision boundaries in some cases it can not provide the level of stealthiness needed to avoid ABS detection. Whereas, activation suppression can easily help achieve this goal by suppressing inner neuron activations. This means that the activation suppression technique along with label smoothing is vital to evade all defense mechanisms at the same time, hence making our proposed technique generic.

5.3   Effect of Varying Activation Suppression Factor

Next, we conduct further experiments to observe the effects of varying activation suppression values (λ). Recall that our original experiments are conducted by selecting α as 0.6 and the activation suppression value as 0.1. Even though λ we choose for our experiments is very small, it is able to evade tested defenses. In these experiments, we train backdoor models with λ values from 0.1 to 0.4 to observe the changes and to see if the resulting backdoor models are still able to maintain the required level of stealthiness. For these experiments, we use the same settings for the dataset, architecture, and trigger as used in Sect. 5.2. We report the results in Table 5. Based on these results we can observe that these models are still able to evade all three defenses since NC exhibits a high anomaly index but flags the incorrect labels as infectious when λ is 0.2, whereas it exhibits a low anomaly index when λ is further increased to 0.3. Similarly, we achieve high FAR values (100%) for all four λ values and ABS also flags wrong labels as infectious. It is important to note here, when we train the backdoor model with $\lambda = 0.4$, the model accuracy is severely declined (10%) which is why NC could not complete the reverse engineering process. Therefore, we can say that λ value above 0.3 is not feasible. Because in that case, the backdoor model is not capable of maintaining acceptable CA due to high neuron activation suppression.

6   Conclusion

In this work, we proposed a simple but effective generic backdoor enhancer, which we believe can make existing backdoor methodologies stronger and stealthier at the same time. Extensive experiments were conducted to validate it. Furthermore, we analyzed the effect of varying different parameters on the effectiveness of our method. The results prove our method is more effective than SOTA methods. The goal of this work is to encourage the research community to take simple regularization techniques like label smoothing into consideration while designing backdoor defense mechanisms so that innovative methods can be designed against such drastic attacks.

References

1. Aggarwal, R., et al.: Diagnostic accuracy of deep learning in medical imaging: A systematic review and meta-analysis. NPJ Digital Med. **4**(1), 1–23 (2021)
2. Bistron, M., Piotrowski, Z.: Artificial intelligence applications in military systems and their influence on sense of security of citizens. Electronics **10**(7), 871 (2021)
3. Brunton, S.L.: Data-driven aerospace engineering: Reframing the industry with machine learning. AIAA J. **59**(8), 2820–2847 (2021)
4. Chen, B., et al.: Detecting backdoor attacks on deep neural networks by activation clustering. arXiv preprint arXiv:1811.03728 (2018)
5. Chen, H., Fu, C., Zhao, J., Koushanfar, F.: DeepInspect: A black-box trojan detection and mitigation framework for deep neural networks. In: IJCAI, vol. 2, p. 8 (2019)
6. Chen, X., Salem, A., Backes, M., Ma, S., Zhang, Y.: BadNL: Backdoor attacks against NLP models. In: ICML 2021 Workshop on Adversarial Machine Learning (2021)
7. Chen, X., Liu, C., Li, B., Lu, K., Song, D.: Targeted backdoor attacks on deep learning systems using data poisoning. arXiv preprint arXiv:1712.05526 (2017)
8. Gao, Y., Xu, C., Wang, D., Chen, S., Ranasinghe, D.C., Nepal, S.: Strip: A defence against trojan attacks on deep neural networks. In: Proceedings of the 35th Annual Computer Security Applications Conference, pp. 113–125 (2019)
9. Gu, T., Dolan-Gavitt, B., Garg, S.: Badnets: Identifying vulnerabilities in the machine learning model supply chain. arXiv preprint arXiv:1708.06733 (2017)
10. Li, G., Yang, Y., Qu, X., Cao, D., Li, K.: A deep learning based image enhancement approach for autonomous driving at night. Knowl.-Based Syst. **213**, 106617 (2021)
11. Li, S., Xue, M., Zhao, B.Z.H., Zhu, H., Zhang, X.: Invisible backdoor attacks on deep neural networks via steganography and regularization. IEEE Trans. Dependable Secure Comput. **18**(5), 2088–2105 (2020)
12. Li, Y., Lyu, X., Koren, N., Lyu, L., Li, B., Ma, X.: Neural attention distillation: Erasing backdoor triggers from deep neural networks. In: ICLR (2021)
13. Li, Y., Li, Y., Wu, B., Li, L., He, R., Lyu, S.: Invisible backdoor attack with sample-specific triggers. In: Proceedings of the IEEE/CVF International Conference on Computer Vision, pp. 16463–16472 (2021)
14. Lin, J., Xu, L., Liu, Y., Zhang, X.: Composite backdoor attack for deep neural network by mixing existing benign features. In: Proceedings of the 2020 ACM SIGSAC Conference on Computer and Communications Security, pp. 113–131 (2020)

15. Liu, K., Dolan-Gavitt, B., Garg, S.: Fine-pruning: Defending against backdooring attacks on deep neural networks. In: RAID (2018)
16. Liu, Y., Lee, W.C., Tao, G., Ma, S., Aafer, Y., Zhang, X.: Abs: Scanning neural networks for back-doors by artificial brain stimulation. In: Proceedings of the 2019 ACM SIGSAC Conference on Computer and Communications Security, pp. 1265–1282 (2019)
17. Liu, Y., et al.: Trojaning attack on neural networks (2017)
18. Liu, Y., Ma, X., Bailey, J., Lu, F.: Reflection backdoor: a natural backdoor attack on deep neural networks. In: Vedaldi, A., Bischof, H., Brox, T., Frahm, J.-M. (eds.) ECCV 2020. LNCS, vol. 12355, pp. 182–199. Springer, Cham (2020). https://doi.org/10.1007/978-3-030-58607-2_11
19. Müller, R., Kornblith, S., Hinton, G.E.: When does label smoothing help? In: Advances in Neural Information Processing Systems, vol. 32 (2019)
20. Nguyen, A., Tran, A.: Input-aware dynamic backdoor attack (2020)
21. Nguyen, T.A., Tran, A.T.: WaNet-Imperceptible warping-based backdoor attack. In: International Conference on Learning Representations (2021)
22. Qiao, X., Yang, Y., Li, H.: Defending neural backdoors via generative distribution modeling. In: Advances in Neural Information Processing Systems 32 (2019)
23. Ribeiro, M., Grolinger, K., Capretz, M.A.: Mlaas: Machine learning as a service. In: 2015 IEEE 14th International Conference on Machine Learning and Applications (ICMLA), pp. 896–902. IEEE (2015)
24. Salem, A., Wen, R., Backes, M., Ma, S., Zhang, Y.: Dynamic backdoor attacks against machine learning models. arXiv preprint arXiv:2003.03675 (2020)
25. Shen, Y., Sanghavi, S.: Learning with bad training data via iterative trimmed loss minimization. In: International Conference on Machine Learning, pp. 5739–5748. PMLR (2019)
26. Wang, B., et al.: Neural cleanse: Identifying and mitigating backdoor attacks in neural networks. In: 2019 IEEE Symposium on Security and Privacy (SP), pp. 707–723. IEEE (2019)
27. Xu, X., Wang, Q., Li, H., Borisov, N., Gunter, C.A., Li, B.: Detecting AI trojans using meta neural analysis. In: 2021 IEEE Symposium on Security and Privacy (SP), pp. 103–120. IEEE (2021)
28. Xue, M., He, C., Wang, J., Liu, W.: One-to-n & n-to-one: Two advanced backdoor attacks against deep learning models. IEEE Trans. Dependable Secure Comput. (2020)
29. Zeiler, M.D., Fergus, R.: Visualizing and understanding convolutional networks. In: Fleet, D., Pajdla, T., Schiele, B., Tuytelaars, T. (eds.) ECCV 2014. LNCS, vol. 8689, pp. 818–833. Springer, Cham (2014). https://doi.org/10.1007/978-3-319-10590-1_53
30. Zhai, T., Li, Y., Zhang, Z., Wu, B., Jiang, Y., Xia, S.T.: Backdoor attack against speaker verification. In: ICASSP 2021–2021 IEEE International Conference on Acoustics, Speech and Signal Processing (ICASSP), pp. 2560–2564. IEEE (2021)
31. Zhao, F., Zhou, L., Zhong, Q., Lan, R., Zhang, L.Y.: Natural backdoor attacks on deep neural networks via raindrops. In: Security and Communication Networks 2022 (2022)
32. Zhao, S., Ma, X., Zheng, X., Bailey, J., Chen, J., Jiang, Y.G.: Clean-label backdoor attacks on video recognition models. In: Proceedings of the IEEE/CVF Conference on Computer Vision and Pattern Recognition, pp. 14443–14452 (2020)

Attention Based Twin Convolutional Neural Network with Inception Blocks for Plant Disease Detection Using Wavelet Transform

Poornima Singh Thakur⬛, Pritee Khanna(✉)⬛, Tanuja Sheorey⬛, and Aparajita Ojha⬛

PDPM Indian Institute of Information Technology, Design and Manufacturing, Jabalpur 482005, India
{poornima,pkhanna,tanush,aojha}@iiitdmj.ac.in

Abstract. Plant disease detection using computer vision techniques may provide better solutions for disease control in the agriculture field. Most of the initial machine learning and deep learning models were trained on datasets with plant disease images captured in controlled conditions. For real-time in-field disease detection, the models must be exposed to in-field conditions for a better learning experience. In some recent studies, deep learning models have been developed using in-field datasets. But these models perform well only for a limited number of crops and plant diseases. The models that have been developed to cover a large number of plant diseases are mostly heavyweights with high computational and memory demands. A lightweight plant disease detection model proposed in this work is trained to detect a large number of disease varieties of different crops. The proposed Wavelet-based Inception Network (WINet), is a parallel attention-based convolutional neural network with inception blocks for plant disease identification. The twin networks of the model are independently trained using RGB images and their discrete wavelet transforms. The twins consist of Inception v7 blocks that help in extracting multi-level features and the squeeze-and-excitation attention mechanism that helps in fetching salient regions from the input. The model attains high accuracy on the PlantVillage and three other in-field datasets. A comparison with five recent models demonstrates that the model outperforms existing models. The proposed model has a lightweight structure with around one million trainable parameters, which makes it suitable for IoT-based smart agriculture solutions.

Keywords: Convolutional Neural Network · Wavelet Transform · Plant Disease Detection · Attention Mechanism · Image Classification

1 Introduction

There has been a significant increase in food production demand due to a rapidly growing population worldwide, but the agriculture industry faces a serious crisis

M. Tanveer et al. (Eds.): ICONIP 2022, CCIS 1794, pp. 308–319, 2023.
https://doi.org/10.1007/978-981-99-1648-1_26

in maintaining the quantum of the crop yield due to heavy losses on account of plant diseases [8]. In developing countries, crop monitoring is more challenging due to limited resources. To control diseases, farmers depend on traditional disease control methods like the spraying of pesticides that have adverse effects on the health conditions of humans as well as soil nutrients.

The opinion of experts is important for disease identification and treatment. However, this can only be given by visiting the cropland and inspecting the entire farm, which is an expensive and time-consuming task. Typically, farmers treat diseases based on the suggestions of pesticide suppliers. To mitigate the gap between farmers and experts, many researchers are working on efficient and accurate automated systems for early-stage disease identification. Globally, smart agriculture solutions that integrate the Internet of Things (IoT) and machine learning (ML) based techniques for early disease diagnosis and control are being investigated to address these issues. As a result, there have been considerable advancements made in the field of vision-based technologies for diagnosing and detecting plant diseases in the real-time.

Due to the accessibility of massive data and effective training methods combined with the availability of powerful computing, many automatic methods based on deep learning (DL) algorithms have been introduced for disease identification. Convolutional neural network (CNN) architectures have demonstrated outstanding results in the diagnosis of plant diseases due to their powerful feature learning capabilities [3,15]. In addition to standard designs like AlexNet, GoogleNet, VGG16, and ResNet with transfer learning methodologies [1,18], customized CNN architectures have also been developed for plant disease detection [11,26]. More recently, CNN models with attention mechanisms have been developed that perform exceptionally well in detecting plant diseases [4–7,13,28]. Most of the studies used publicly available datasets, which are either captured in laboratory conditions or background segmented. As real-time disease detection on the test dataset is quite complicated, Chen et al. [24], Liu et al. [3], Thapa et al. [15] introduced some in-field crop disease detection datasets to tackle testing accuracy on field datasets. As a leaf in these datasets contains a single disease, another dataset [24] is developed where a single leaf suffers from multiple diseases.

Despite these developments, plant disease detection remains a challenge due to the variety of disease types for different crops, the evolution of new diseases, and the unavailability of in-field data for most crops. The existing methods are either for single crops or focused on the complex deployment of mobile devices for in-field testing. The size of the models is generally quite large to be deployed on mobile devices. While DL models are data-hungry, lightweight CNN models do not generalize well for all types of crops. Therefore, research continues to identify approaches for accurate and early-stage disease diagnosis while maintaining the model size.

The work introduced in this paper is a lightweight in-field disease detection method based on attention with wavelet CNNs. As a mathematical tool, wavelets are known to extract information from images. The attention mechanism has been used to improve the model's performance. The proposed work aims to examine the potential of wavelet transform with an attention mechanism for in-field disease detection. In this work, the input images are transformed using Haar-based wavelet transforms and fed into an attention-based CNN with inception modules for plant disease identification. Parallelly, the original image is also fed to the twin CNN and the features obtained through the twins are combined to predict the disease classes with higher accuracy. The main contributions of the work are summarized as:

- A parallel attention-based CNN model WINet with twin networks is introduced that combines the spatial and wavelet domain features for plant disease detection and identification
- The model is trained and tested on three in-field datasets and the benchmark dataset PlantVillage
- The model outperforms five recent plant disease detection methods with higher accuracy, precision, recall, F1 score, and better kappa score.

The paper is organized as follows. Section 2 describes the related work in the area of plant disease identification. Section 3 introduces the approach for wavelet-based CNN. Datasets used in the model building, evaluation measures, experimental settings, and results are discussed Sect. in 4. Section 5 concludes the work with future directions.

2   Related Work

With the release of PlantVillage dataset [12], many researchers have made great progress in plant disease detection and various models have been proposed [13,25]. Mohanty et al. [18] introduced the PlantVillage dataset [12] and compared the performances of the AlexNet and GoogleNet based on training from scratch, transfer learning, and fine-tuning. Ferentinos [10] compared the performances of ResNet50, DenseNet121, and VGG16 on the extended PlantVillage dataset with 87,848 images. Too et al. [25] fine-tuned the performance of different ResNet models upto 152 layers, DenseNets with 121 layers, VGG16 and Inception V4. The DenseNet model achieved 99.75% accuracy on the PlantVillage dataset. ResNet-based image feature extraction and parallel model creation to pass image meta-data in parallel have been used in Picon et al. [19]. However, the PlantVillage dataset is captured in laboratory conditions with a fixed background, so the performance of most of the methods developed using the dataset faces issues when they are tested in outdoor in-field conditions [18]. In plant pathology, a large annotated dataset with real-time capturing conditions is an open challenge.

Two shallow networks have been introduced in Li et al. [14] where the initial four layers of the VGG-16 model are used for image feature extraction, and classification is performed by using Kernel SVM and Random Forest methods. Kernel SVM showed a high precision of 0.94 on the maize, apple, and grape diseases. Karthik et al. [13] have introduced a residual attention network for plant disease identification and have reported 98.6% accuracy on the PlantVillage dataset. Chen et al. [4] have used depth-wise separable convolution with dense blocks and an attention mechanism. Their model performed well on maize species. Chen et al. [6] have used the MobileNet v2 model with an attention mechanism for rice disease detection. They have reported 99.67% accuracy on 10 classes from PlantVillage and 98.48% accuracy on a rice dataset. In a work by present authors [23], a combination of VGG16 and inception modules is used to obtain a lightweight and high-performing plant disease detection model. The authors have reported a high misclassification rate in the case of multiple diseases in a single image of the apple dataset. Chen et al. [5] also presented a modified MobileNet v2 model that included depth-wise separable convolution. Both spatial and channel attention were used in this model. This modified model achieved 99.71% accuracy on a portion of the PlantVillage dataset and 99.13% accuracy on a custom dataset. Recently, residual and inception blocks have been utilized in Zhao et al. [28] to develop a CNN network. In the network, they also used a modified convolutional block attention module (CBAM). The model achieved 99.55% average accuracy on the tomato, potato, and corn datasets.

The wavelet-based methods have been incorporated into various applications, including image classification [22], segmentation [20], and compression [17]. For plant disease detection, Deshapande et al. [9] applied histogram and Haar wavelet features as an input to the k-NN and SVM classifiers for maize disease detection. Their model is shown to achieve 88% accuracy with the SVM classifier. Wavelet-based CNNs for disease detection task have been incorporated in [2,16]. The Wavelet transform has been used to extract image features for disease detection in banana trees Bernardes et al. [2] and cotton disease detection Mathew et al. [16]. In another work by Zhao et al. [27], continuous wavelet transform has been used for image feature extraction with hyperspectral imaging-based plant disease segmentation. However, not much has been explored by researchers for plant disease detection using CNN with wavelet transform.

It is observed that most of the recent works are either based on attention mechanisms [4–7,13,28] or shallow CNN models [4,6] for plant disease classification with single species and only a small number of disease classes. Thapa et al. [24] developed an apple dataset with four classes. One of the classes contains images with multiple diseases in a single image. In order to develop a plant disease detection model that can detect a large number of diseases with high precision over many different plant species in field conditions, a twin attention-based network with image input in spatial and wavelet domains is proposed in the present work. In spite widely used in research, the combination of CNN and attention mechanisms with spatial and frequency domains has rarely been explored in the area of plant disease detection.

3 Proposed Work

The proposed plant disease detection and classification model, named WINet, consists of two identical parallel CNNs. Each CNN twin independently processes an image in two different forms: the original RGB image and its wavelet transform. The CNNs are composed of inception blocks with attention mechanisms. As depicted in Fig. 1, initially an image of size $224 \times 224 \times 3$ is subjected to the discrete wavelet transform (DWT) using the Haar wavelet. The DWT is considered an efficient operator and is widely used for image analysis. In the basic 2D DWT, the image is first passed through low-pass and high-pass filters, then it is column-wise half downsampled. Again, the output is passed through the low-pass and high-pass filters, and row-wise half downsampled. In this way, the input image is decomposed into high-frequency (HF) and low-frequency (LF) bands with approximate, vertical, horizontal, and diagonal features.

The obtained results of the four sub-band images are concatenated to generate a single image of size $112 \times 112 \times 4$ that is used as an input to one of the twin CNNs. The original image in the RGB form is also fed as the parallel input to the second CNN, as shown in Fig. 1. The main idea behind using wavelet transform is that for in-field images, frequency domain analysis combined with spatial analysis can help in learning a better representation of different plant diseases.

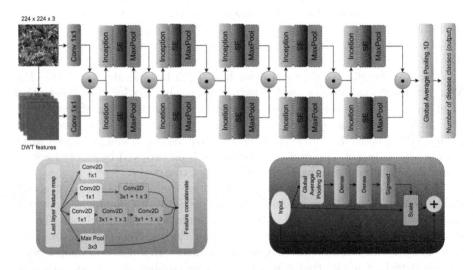

Fig. 1. Proposed attention-based twin CNN with inception v7 blocks for plant disease identification using wavelet transform named as WINet

Each of the twin networks of WINet starts with a convolution layer containing 32 filters. The filter size of this layer with DWT of the image is 1×1, and that with RGB input is of the size 5×5. The basic building blocks of the proposed model are modules consisting of Inception v7 blocks followed by squeeze-and-excitation (SE) blocks and max pooling layers. There are five such modules in each of the networks. Feature maps obtained from each of the parallel modules in the same position are concatenated and fed into the next modules of both networks.

At the end, a global average pooling (GAP) layer is added, followed by the output layer for classification. In this model, the LeakyReLU activation function is used throughout the layers except in the classification layer, where softmax function is used depending on the labels of the datasets.

The model was trained and tested on three in-field datasets and a dataset having a large number of plant species and diseases with images captured in laboratory conditions. Details of model building and its evaluation are presented in the next section.

4   Results and Discussion

The proposed plant disease detection model, WINet, was built by performing different experiments with the well-known public dataset PlantVillage [12]. This dataset was created in a laboratory with controlled background conditions, and each image contains only one type of disease. To train the model in the field conditions, three datasets are also used in which images are captured in the field conditions. Details of the datasets used in the study are given below.

1. Apple Dataset: A challenge was introduced during CVPR 2020 for plant disease detection on a dataset with 3651 leaf images of apple leaves having diseases in four categories. This contains 1821 labelled images in 4 classes [24]. Figure 2(a) presents one sample image from the dataset
2. Maize Dataset: This public dataset is created by Fujian Institute of Subtropical Botany, Xiamen, China. A total of 481 leaf images from the maize field are captured in four classes [3]. Fig. 2(c) presents one sample image from the dataset
3. PlantVillage Dataset: It is one of the most frequently used disease detection datasets, consisting of 54,305 images in 38 disease categories [12] of 14 plant species. The images are of plant leaves captured after plucking them from plants and placing them in a laboratory environment with a fixed background. Figure 2(c) presents one sample image from the dataset
4. Rice Dataset: This rice dataset is introduced by the Fujian Institute of Subtropical Botany, Xiamen, China. It contains 560 images of various types of rice diseases in five categories [3]. It contains in-field as well as laboratory condition images. Figure 2(d) presents one sample image from the dataset.

The architecture of WINet was finalized after extensive experiments with different components. Additionally, the model's performance was compared with five CNN models recently developed for plant disease detection [4–6,13,28]. These include lightweight models that have made use of various attention mechanisms. The following sections provide information on the evaluation measures used to assess the model's performance, experimental design, and findings.

The datasets were divided into training, validation, and test sets with a ratio of 64:16:20, respectively. The proposed model and existing models were trained using the training subsets from the datasets after scaling images to $224 \times 224 \times 3$. On each dataset, the model was trained using the cross-entropy loss function

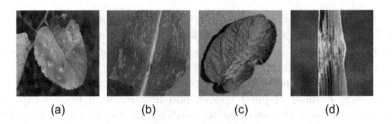

Fig. 2. Sample image from each dataset (a) Apple, (b) Maize, (c) PlantVillage, and (d) Rice datasets.

and the Adam optimizer. The batch size was set to 16, and the learning rate was set to 0.0001. The validation dataset was utilized to evaluate the model's performance at the end of each epoch. The model was evaluated on the test dataset after achieving the desired level of classification accuracy on the training and validation subsets.

All the experiments were performed on an NVIDIA DGX A100 160 GB station with four GPU A100 cards, each with 40 GB of memory. It has the Ubuntu 18.04 LTS operating system on the machine, with an AMD 7742 processor at 2.25–3.4 GHz and 512 GB of RAM. The proposed model and other selected models for comparison were implemented using the Keras framework with NVIDIA CUDA v11.5 and cuDNN v8.3 libraries.

4.1 Performance Evaluation

The performance of the proposed model is evaluated on all the datasets mentioned above and compared with other state-of-the-art methods. The results are summarized in Table 1. For comparing the model's performance, five recently introduced CNN-based plant disease classification models are chosen [4–6,13,28]. These are the models with attention mechanisms and lightweight structures. Each model represents a unique technique for disease detection. Table 1 shows the quantitative results of the different CNN models on all the datasets. The proposed model has an accuracy of 99.45% on the PlantVillage dataset. Table 1 illustrates that the WINet achieves the best performance in all metrics. It is indeed remarkable that the model performs significantly better for the in-field datasets.

The Grad-CAM results have been generated using activation maps of the last feature fusion layer of the network. Grad-CAM helps to visualize areas where attention has been given while classification. Gradient-weighted class activation maps (Grad-CAM) [21] for some sample images from the four datasets obtained with the WINet model and other competing models are displayed in Fig. 3. With an improved knowledge of the texture and structure of the disease, WINet better emphasizes the affected area. From the figure, it is clear that the proposed model better focuses on the disease when compared with other works.

Table 1. Comparison of the work with other state-of-the-art methods

Approach	Loss	Accuracy	Precision	Recall	F1 score	AUC	Kappa
Apple							
Karthik et al. [13]	1.56	62.37	62.84	61.83	62.35	83.53	0.45
Chen et al. [4]	1.96	55.91	56.35	54.84	55.58	78.32	0.36
Chen et al. [5]	0.79	83.33	83.7	82.8	83.25	94.1	0.76
Chen et al. [6]	0.63	83.33	85.47	82.26	83.83	95.59	0.76
Zhao et al. [28]	0.58	88.71	**89.62**	88.17	88.89	95.81	**0.84**
WINet	**0.34**	**88.93**	88.93	**88.93**	**88.93**	**97.19**	**0.84**
Maize							
Karthik et al. [13]	1.17	54.32	59.72	53.09	56.21	83.19	0.39
Chen et al. [4]	1.26	49.38	50.85	37.04	42.86	76.16	0.33
Chen et al. [5]	0.6	87.65	87.65	87.65	87.65	96.03	0.84
Chen et al. [6]	0.5	**88.89**	**91.03**	87.65	89.31	96.78	0.85
Zhao et al. [28]	1.4	77.78	78.75	77.78	78.26	94.55	0.7
WINet	**0.42**	**88.89**	88.75	**87.65**	88.19	**96.99**	**0.85**
PlantVillage							
Karthik et al. [13]	0.16	95.83	96.2	95.6	95.89	99.7	0.96
Chen et al. [4]	0.4	87.94	89.59	86.71	88.07	99.14	0.85
Chen et al. [5]	1.07	74.63	80.92	69.64	75.03	98.18	0.74
Chen et al. [6]	0.17	96.68	97.49	95.83	96.64	99.26	0.97
Zhao et al. [28]	0.12	97.28	97.49	97.06	97.27	99.78	0.97
WINet	**0.03**	**99.45**	**99.49**	**99.45**	**99.47**	**99.97**	**0.99**
Rice							
Karthik et al. [13]	0.99	71.67	79.55	58.33	69.31	88.26	0.64
Chen et al. [4]	0.75	76.67	83.02	73.33	77.87	92.93	0.71
Chen et al. [5]	0.3	**96.67**	**96.67**	**96.67**	**96.67**	98.97	**0.95**
Chen et al. [6]	**0.25**	95	96.61	96.61	96.61	**99.72**	0.94
Zhao et al. [28]	0.41	91.67	91.67	91.67	91.67	98.55	89.27
WINet	0.4	**96.67**	**96.67**	**96.67**	**96.67**	99.01	0.94

4.2 Ablation Study

An ablation study was performed on the PlantVillage dataset to identify the contribution of various components. Initially, only one network was used with RGB images. Then only the DWT input-based single network was used to study the effect of changing the network input type. In the third setting, the parallel CNN was developed without the SE block. Finally, the proposed parallel network was also tested with the SE block. Results of the ablation study are presented in Table 2 that illustrates the proposed model is more effective than other models.

The applicability of a model in IoT-based agriculture systems is strongly influenced by its memory and computation requirements. To make the model suitable for mobile/handheld devices like drones and smartphones, it is important that the model has a small memory requirement and fewer floating-point operations (FLOPs). Table 3 presents the overall parameter count, trainable parameter count, and GegaFLOPs (GFLPOs). As per the table, WINet has a

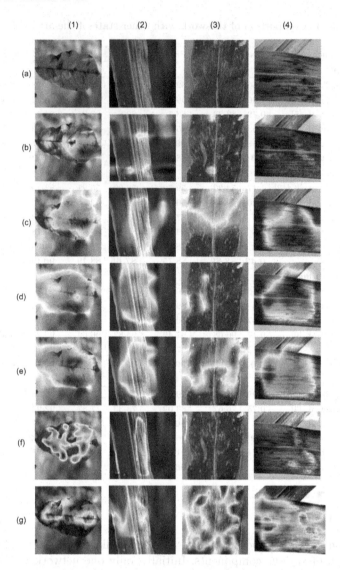

Fig. 3. Grad-CAMs for (1) Apple, (2) Maize, (3) PlantVillage, and (4) Rice datasets. (a) input image, (b) Karthik et al. [13], (c) Chen et al. [4], (d) Chen et al. [5], (e) Chen et al. [6], (f) Zhao et al. [28], and (g) WINet

comparable number of parameters count while it maintains better performance. Although the models by Karthik et al. [13] and Chen et al. [4] have fewer trainable parameters, their performance is not that impressive on the two datasets. Similarly, in the case of FLOPs Chen et al. [5] model has the least count. In a way, the proposed model lies in the middle of memory requirements and FLOPS counts, keeping its classification performance much better than other models.

Table 2. Ablation study of the proposed WINet model on the PlantVillage dataset

Approach	Loss	Accuracy	Precision	Recall	F1-score	AUC	Kappa
PlantVillage							
RGB CNN	0.04	99.08	99.13	98.99	99.06	99.94	0.99
RGB CNN with SE	0.04	99.34	99.37	99.3	99.33	99.92	0.99
Wavelet CNN	0.06	98.49	98.6	98.44	98.52	99.9	0.98
Wavelet CNN with SE	0.04	99.21	99.25	99.17	99.21	99.9	0.99
WINet	**0.03**	**99.45**	**99.49**	**99.45**	**99.47**	**99.97**	**0.99**

Table 3. Comparison of the trainable parameters and FLOPs

Approach	Total parameters (M)	Trainable parameters (M)	GFLOPs	Memory (MB)
Karthik et al. [13]	**0.72**	**0.72**	3.59	2.8
Chen et al. [4]	0.82	0.82	3.4	**0.76**
Chen et al. [5]	4.32	2.06	**0.78**	16.8
Chen et al. [6]	4.32	2.06	0.83	16.9
Zhao et al. [28]	6.71	6.71	11.9	25.8
WINet	1.04	1.04	2.67	4.7

5 Conclusions and Future Work

Accurate in-field plant disease detection is a challenging task. The automation of the process with the help of deep learning models has gained significance in recent years due to the improved performance of deep learning models. With the aim of developing an in-field plant disease detection system, a parallel attention-based CNN model has been introduced in the present work to deal with a large number of plant diseases on a variety of plants. The model takes inputs in the RGB and DWT domains and processes them through Inception and SE blocks to extract relevant features for improved classification. To develop the model, three in-field datasets of different crops were also used to train and validate the models. The results of experiments show that the proposed model outperforms five recent attention-based CNN models on all the datasets. t is planned to expand work for disease detection and localization tasks in the future.

References

1. Barbedo, J.G.A.: Impact of dataset size and variety on the effectiveness of deep learning and transfer learning for plant disease classification. Comput. Electron. Agric. **153**, 46–53 (2018)
2. Bernardes, A.A., et al.: Identification of foliar diseases in cotton crop. In: Topics in Medical Image Processing and Computational Vision, pp. 67–85. Springer (2013). https://doi.org/10.1007/978-94-007-0726-9_4

3. Chen, J., Chen, J., Zhang, D., Sun, Y., Nanehkaran, Y.A.: Using deep transfer learning for image-based plant disease identification. Comput. Electronics Agricul. **173**, 105393 (2020)
4. Chen, J., Wang, W., Zhang, D., Zeb, A., Nanehkaran, Y.A.: Attention embedded lightweight network for maize disease recognition. Plant Pathology (2020)
5. Chen, J., Zhang, D., Suzauddola, M., Zeb, A.: Identifying crop diseases using attention embedded mobilenet-v2 model. Appli. Soft Comput. **113**, 107901 (2021)
6. Chen, J., Zhang, D., Zeb, A., Nanehkaran, Y.A.: Identification of rice plant diseases using lightweight attention networks. Expert Syst. Appli. **169**, 114514 (2021)
7. Chen, X., Zhou, G., Chen, A., Yi, J., Zhang, W., Yahui, H.: Identification of tomato leaf diseases based on combination of abck-bwtr and b-arnet. Comput. Electron. Agric. **178**, 105730 (2020)
8. DESA. World population prospects (2019). www.un.org/development/desa/publications/world-population-prospects-2019-highlights.html. (Accessed 30 May 2020)
9. Deshapande, Anupama S.., Giraddi, Shantala G.., Karibasappa, K.. G.., Desai, Shrinivas D..: Fungal disease detection in maize leaves using haar wavelet features. In: Satapathy, Suresh Chandra, Joshi, Amit (eds.) Information and Communication Technology for Intelligent Systems. SIST, vol. 106, pp. 275–286. Springer, Singapore (2019). https://doi.org/10.1007/978-981-13-1742-2_27
10. Ferentinos, K.P.: Deep learning models for plant disease detection and diagnosis. Comput. Electron. Agricul. **145**, 311–318 (2018)
11. Huang, S., Zhou, G., He, M., Chen, A., Zhang, W., Yahui, H.: Detection of peach disease image based on asymptotic non-local means and pcnn-ipelm. IEEE Access **8**, 136421–136433 (2020)
12. Hughes, D., Salathé, M., et al.: An open access repository of images on plant health to enable the development of mobile disease diagnostics. arXiv preprint arXiv:1511.08060 (2015)
13. Karthik, R., Hariharan, M., Anand, S., Mathikshara, P., Johnson, A., Menaka, R.: Attention embedded residual cnn for disease detection in tomato leaves. Appli. Soft Comput. **86**, 105933 (2020)
14. Li, Y., Nie, J., Chao, X.: Do we really need deep cnn for plant diseases identification? Comput. Electron. Agric. **178**, 105803 (2020)
15. Liu, X., Min, W., Mei, S., Wang, L., Jiang, S.: Plant disease recognition: A large-scale benchmark dataset and a visual region and loss reweighting approach. IEEE Trans. Image Process. **30**, 2003–2015 (2021)
16. Mathew, D., Kumar, C.S., Cherian, K.A.: Foliar fungal disease classification in banana plants using elliptical local binary pattern on multiresolution dual tree complex wavelet transform domain. In: Information Processing in Agriculture (2020)
17. Mishra, D., Singh, S.K., Singh, R.K.: Wavelet-based deep auto encoder-decoder (wdaed)-based image compression. IEEE Trans. Circ. Syst. Video Technol. **31**(4), 1452–1462 (2020)
18. Mohanty, S.P., Hughes, D.P., Salathé, M.: Using deep learning for image-based plant disease detection. Front. Plant Sci. **7**, 1419 (2016)
19. Picon, A., Seitz, M., Alvarez-Gila, A., Mohnke, P., Ortiz-Barredo, A., Echazarra, J.: Crop conditional convolutional neural networks for massive multi-crop plant disease classification over cell phone acquired images taken on real field conditions. Comput. Electron. Agric. **167**, 105093 (2019)
20. Preethi, S., Aishwarya, P.: An efficient wavelet-based image fusion for brain tumor detection and segmentation over pet and mri image. Multimedia Tools Appli. **80**(10), 14789–14806 (2021)

21. Selvaraju, R.R., Cogswell, M., Das, A., Vedantam, R., Parikh, D., Batra, D.: Grad-cam: Visual explanations from deep networks via gradient-based localization. In: Proceedings of the IEEE International Conference on Computer Vision, pp. 618–626 (2017)
22. Serte, S., Demirel, H.: Gabor wavelet-based deep learning for skin lesion classification. Comput. Biol. Med. **113**, 103423 (2019)
23. Thakur, P.S., Sheorey, T., Ojha, A.: Vgg-icnn: A lightweight cnn model for crop disease identification. Multimedia Tools Appli., 1–24 (2022)
24. Thapa, R., Snavely, N., Belongie, S., Khan, A.: The plant pathology 2020 challenge dataset to classify foliar disease of apples. arXiv preprint arXiv:2004.11958 (2020)
25. Too, E.C., Yujian, L., Njuki, S., Yingchun, L.: A comparative study of fine-tuning deep learning models for plant disease identification. Comput. Electron. Agricul. **161**, 272–279 (2019)
26. Yadav, S., Sengar, N., Singh, A., Singh, A., Dutta, M.K.: Identification of disease using deep learning and evaluation of bacteriosis in peach leaf. Ecological Informat. 101247 (2021)
27. Zhao, X., Zhang, J., Huang, Y., Tian, Y., Yuan, L.: Detection and discrimination of disease and insect stress of tea plants using hyperspectral imaging combined with wavelet analysis. Comput. Electron. Agric. **193**, 106717 (2022)
28. Zhao, Y., Sun, C., Xing, X., Chen, J.: Ric-net: A plant disease classification model based on the fusion of inception and residual structure and embedded attention mechanism. Comput. Electron. Agric. **193**, 106644 (2022)

A Medical Image Steganography Scheme with High Embedding Capacity to Solve Falling-Off Boundary Problem Using Pixel Value Difference Method

Nagaraj V. Dharwadkar[1]([✉]), Mufti Mahmud[2,3,4]([✉]), Ashutosh A. Lonikar[1], and David J. Brown[2,3,4]

[1] Department of Computer Science, Rajarambapu Institute of Technology, Islampur, Maharashtra, India
nagaraj.dharwadkar@ritindia.edu
[2] Department of Computer Science, Nottingham Trent University, Nottingham NG11 8NS, UK
{Mufti.mahmud,David.brown}@ntu.ac.uk
[3] CIRC, Nottingham Trent University, Nottingham NG11 8NS, UK
[4] MTIF, Nottingham Trent University, Nottingham NG11 8NS, UK

Abstract. Medical images have a vital role in the healthcare industry. The medical sector uses the internet to facilitate the distant sharing of medical information among hospitals and clinics and provide patients with e-health services. We must share a patient's report secretly so that the intruders can't steal the patient's data. The pixel value differencing technique is utilised in this study to store a patient's medical information report in various medical imaging, such as ultrasound images, computed tomography scans, X-rays, magnetic resonance images, electrocardiographs, and microscopic images. The fundamental objective is to maintain the visual appearance of the medical images so that physicians can analyse and give accurate results and extract information reports precisely. This PVD scheme works on different types of image formats such as Portable Network Graphics (PNG), Joint Photographic Experts Group (JPG or JPEG), BitMaP (BMP), and Tag Image File Format (TIFF). Measurement metrics such as embedding capacity, the difference in histograms between the stego and the cover image, and the peak signal-to-noise ratio (PSNR) are employed to evaluate the effectiveness of the suggested method. On a series of medical images, we have tested this new PVD approach and found that it provides significant payload capacity with the high visual quality of the stego image. The majority of PVD techniques described in the literature only apply to grayscale images, and those that apply to RGB images have falling off boundary problem. RGB images have pixel values that span from 0 to 255, but when the pixels are modified using the PVD technique, sometimes these pixel values fall outside of this range, which causes erroneous results to be obtained during extraction. Additionally, utilising a difference in the histograms of the stego and the cover image, the attacker in a typical PVD technique can disclose the existence and length of the secret message. This novel PVD methodology tackles the classic PVD technique's falling-off boundary issue and provides some security to the secret message from the histogram quantisation attack.

Keywords: Steganography · PSNR · PVD · RGB · LSB

© The Author(s), under exclusive license to Springer Nature Singapore Pte Ltd. 2023
M. Tanveer et al. (Eds.): ICONIP 2022, CCIS 1794, pp. 320–332, 2023.
https://doi.org/10.1007/978-981-99-1648-1_27

1 Introduction

In the medical field, an ethical code requires all medical observations and analyses to be kept confidential. A large amount of sensitive data is shared between the hospitals over the internet to study and analyse the patient reports. The advancement of internet technology has enabled the procedure of treatment and remote medical inspection, often known as telemedicine, where patients and medical specialists are not in the exact location. So, one of the major concerns is providing security to this data. Apart from that, storing patient information in the hospital database consumes storage. Cryptography and steganography are both used to provide security for secret information. In cryptography, we convert the sensitive data into an unknown format that the attacker could not identify. In steganography, confidential information is hidden in some media such as audio, images, videos, etc. Steganography is the best strategy we can apply to enhance the security of medical images because it does not catch the attacker's attention.

In the literature, many authors have suggested various steganographic to secure the data over the internet. Some of the authors used steganography and cryptography together to provide increased security. "One of the most often used steganography algorithms is LSB (Least Significant Bit). This technique replaces the least significant bits of each pixel with the secret message bits" [1]. Many writers changed this technique to enhance payload capacity and improve security, but the scheme was still susceptible to steganalysis and was insecure. Apart from LSB substitution, in 2003, Wu and Tsai suggested a new secured approach known as pixel value differencing, or PVD [2]. However, the drawbacks of this method were that we could only use this PVD on grayscale images, and this method could induce significant distortion, lowering image quality. Several studies have been proposed to increase this algorithm's embedding capacity and visual quality. However, each technique has its own set of strengths and weaknesses. Most of the approaches were based on grayscale images, and many have pixel fall-off boundary issues.

Abnormal steps in the pixel difference histogram imply the attendance of concealed information. The histogram can also be used to compute the length of concealed bits [3]. PVD has a high capacity, but many steganalysis attacks have doubted its usefulness. These algorithms utilise difference histogram quantisation to reveal the appearance of a secret message in a stego image [4].

Using the steganography techniques some authors have proposed ways to transmit patients' information over the internet securely. Shabir A. and colleagues suggested, "a method for concealing electronic patient records (EPRs) in medical images" [5]. For e-healthcare applications, it was a computationally efficient technique. This method, however, may only be used with grayscale images. After that, Budi Santoso [6] suggested a colour image steganography system for microscopic images. The PVD approach was used to suggest this solution. They mainly discussed about microscopic images in this work. They discovered that the PVD strategy creates stego images with higher PSNR values than the LSB substitution method. Then Shivani Jain [7] reviewed how to secure patient information encoded in medical images using steganography techniques. Roseline et al. proposed a modified least significant bit (LSB) technique capable of protecting and hiding medical data to solve the crucial authentication issue [8].

Mohammed et al. suggested "a pixel contrast based medical image steganography to ensure and secure patient data" [9]. The Huffman coding technique changes confidential message before it is hidden, which will help improve security and capacity. Nasir et al. published an e-healthcare watermarking method to secure information in medical images [12]. This method uses encryption techniques to increase the watermark's security before the information is inserted into a medical image.

We discovered from the literature that PVD is one of the well-known steganography techniques for embedding a huge quantity of data in the cover image while ensuring optimum visual quality. As a result of the fact that a colour pixel is made up of three different colours—red, green, and blue—and that PVD primarily operates on two consecutive non-overlapping components, a colour pixel cannot be embedded with secret message bits using the simple traditional PVD process. So, we want to alter the pixel value algorithm, which works on the colour medical images and solves the fall boundary problem. We have discovered in the literature that the PVD technique is vulnerable to the histogram quantisation attack. We want to ensure that the approach we're proposing isn't susceptible to the histogram quantisation attack. In this paper, we want to provide security to the medical information report of a patient using the pixel value differencing method. We also want to reduce the healthcare industry's storage cost by storing the patient information in the medical images.

The remaining paper is divided into the following sections: Sect. 2 describes the conventional pixel differencing method proposed by Wu and Tsai in 2003. The extraction and embedding methods employed in the suggested strategy will be examined in Sect. 3 of the paper. Section 4 presents the experimentation's findings. After we compare our proposed strategy to some of the most popular approaches in the literature in Sect. 5, the paper ends in Sect. 6.

2 PVD Method

Wu and Tsai [2] proposed the PVD algorithm in 2003, using a 256 grey-valued image as the cover image. The difference d is determined from two sequential pixels of non-overlapping blocks. The image is partitioned into two-pixel blocks in a zigzag pattern throughout all rows of the image, as seen in Fig. 1. The difference is calculated as $|g_{i+1} - g_i|$ if the value of two consecutive pixels P_i and P_{i+1} are g_i and g_{i+1}. The difference can lie between -255 and 255 but consider only absolute value. After that, check the range $R_k = [l_k, u_k]$ of d in the quantisation range Table 1. Where the lower and the upper bound of R_k are represented as l_k and u_k. After getting the R_k calculate the width of subrange w_k as $u_k - l_k + 1$. Each range's width is assumed to be a power of two in the traditional PVD method. The count of bits $'n'$ that may be inserted between two-pixel blocks is of the cover image is calculated using $n = \lfloor w_k \rfloor$. Then using Eq. 1, compute the novel difference d'.

$$d' = \{l_k + b \ for \ d \geq \ 0; \ -(l_k + b) \ for \ d < 0; \tag{1}$$

where b represents the secret message's decimal value, which lies in the range 0 to $u_k - l_k$, so the range of d' will be from l_k to u_k. The changes that occur when we substitute d

with d' are probably invisible to the viewer. After that, perform an inverse calculation using Eq. 2 to calculate the modified pixel values g_i' and g_{i+1}'.

$$(g_i', g_{i+1}') = \begin{cases} \left(g_i + \lceil \frac{m}{2} \rceil, g_{i+1} - \lfloor \frac{m}{2} \rfloor\right) & if \ \ dmod2 = 1; \\ \left(g_i - \lfloor \frac{m}{2} \rfloor, g_{i+1} + \lceil \frac{m}{2} \rceil\right) & if \ \ dmod2 = 0; \end{cases} \tag{2}$$

where $m = \left| d_i' - d_i \right|$. If the modified values of the pixel fall in the range from 0 to 255, then embedding is performed; otherwise, the block is excluded from embedding.

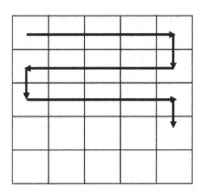

Fig. 1. Reading the image to create a two-pixel block

First, the modified pixel difference $\left| g_i' - g_{i+1}' \right|$ is calculated during the extraction procedure. After finding the range $R_k=[l_k, u_k]$ in which this difference lies, calculate the width w_k of the subrange and compute the count of bits inserted into two successive pixels as $n = \lfloor w_k \rfloor$. Find the decimal value of the secret message b using $d' - l_k$. Convert this decimal value to binary bits, the message embedded between two consecutive pixels.

Table 1. Pixel value differencing

Range	R1	R2	R3	R4	R5	R6
Upper bound	0	8	16	32	64	128
Lower bound	7	15	31	63	127	255

3 Proposed Methodology

The suggested technique is broken down into two components in this section: extraction and embedding procedure.

4 Embedding Algorithm

Input: RGB medical image 'I', Secret Message 'M'
Output: Stego medical image 'S'

1. Split 'I' into r, g, and b channels.
2. Pick a channel and repeat steps 3–13 for all consecutive pixels of the channel.
3. Let $e = 1$
4. $d_i = |P_{i+1} - P_i|$ // absolute difference
5. Find $R_i = [l_i, u_i]$ using Table 1 such that $d_i \geq l_i$ & $d_i \leq u_i$.
6. Calculate pixels values by taking $m = |u_i - d_i|$ in Eq. (3)

$$(P_i', P_{i+1}') = \left\{ \left(P_i + \left\lceil \frac{m}{2} \right\rceil, P_{i+1} - \left\lfloor \frac{m}{2} \right\rfloor \right) \text{ if } d_i mod2 = 1; \right.$$

$$\left(P_i - \left\lfloor \frac{m}{2} \right\rfloor, P_{i+1} + \left\lceil \frac{m}{2} \right\rceil \right) \text{ if } d_i mod2 = 0; \tag{3}$$

7. IF $P_i < 0$ OR $P_i > 255$ OR $P_{i+1} < 0$ OR $P_{i+1} > 255$ THEN
   $e = 0$
   GO TO STEP 2
   ELSE GO TO STEP 8
8. $w_i = u_i - l_i + 1$ //quantisation width of the range
9. $t = \lfloor w_i \rfloor$ // number of bits to be included in two pixels
10. Convert 'M' to the decimal value $'b'$ by reading $'t'$ bits from 'M'.
11. $d_i' = \{ l_i + b \text{ for } d_i \geq 0; \quad -(l_i + b) \text{ for } d_i < 0; \quad$ //new difference value
12. Change the pixel values by taking $m = |d_i' - d_i|$ in Eq. (3).
13. Repeat steps 2-12 until all channels are done embedding of 'M'.
14. Concatenate r, g, and b channels to get 'S'

Many pixel value differencing technique modifications suffer from the falling off boundary problem. We modify the pixel values according to Eq. (2) in the traditional approach. But during modifications, sometimes the pixels may fall off the boundaries of the range. Sometimes, the estimated pixels' value may be less than 0 or larger than 255. The extracted data will be inaccurate, and the generated image will be erroneous. So, to get precise results, it is essential to address this issue in the proposed scheme. To solve this issue in the proposed method, first, we perform fall-off boundary checking as suggested in [2] by calculating the modified pixels using Eq. (3) and taking the value of m as $|u_i - d_i|$. As u_i is the highest value in the range l_i to u_i, pixel pair $\left(P_i', P_{i+1}' \right)$ created by using u_i will have the greatest difference. The maximum range $\left(P_{i+1}' - P_{i+1}' \right)$ covers all the ranges produced by $\left(P_i', P_{i+1}' \right)$. As a result, by examining the values $\left(P_i', P_{i+1}' \right)$ that are obtained by employing u_i, the block's falling-off boundary can be checked. If any of the pixels P_i' or P_{i+1}' fall off the boundary, then we discard that block for hiding the secret message and start from the new block. The proposed technique addresses the falling-off boundary problem in this way.

5 Extraction Algorithm

Input: Stego medical image 'S'
Output: Secret Message' M'

1. Split 'S' into r, g, and b channels.
2. Pick a channel and repeat steps 3–11 for all consecutive pixels of the channel.
3. Let $e = 1$
4. $d_i' = |P_{i+1}' - P_i'|$ // absolute difference
5. Find $R_i=[l_i, u_i]$ using Table 1 such that $d_i' \geq l_i$ & $d_i' \leq u_i$.
6. Modify the pixels by taking $m = |u_i - d_i|$ using Eq. (3)
7. IF $P_i < 0\ OR\ \ P_i > 255\ OR\ \ P_{i+1} < 0\ OR\ P_{i+1} > 255$ THEN
      $e = 0$
      GO TO STEP 1
      ELSE GO TO STEP 7
8. $w_i = u_i - l_i + 1$ //Quantisation width of the range
9. $t = \lfloor w_i \rfloor$ // Number of bits present in two pixels
10. $b = d_i' - l_i$ // Secret message in decimal notation
11. Convert $'b'$ to $'t'$ number of binary bits, which is a secret message hidden in (P_i, P_{i+1}).

5.1 Experimental Results

The experimental findings of the suggested approach are presented in this section. We tested our proposed technique on many medical images from the "National Library of Medicine's Open Access Biomedical Images Search Engine" [10, 11] with diverse image features. However, the results of only six images are shown in this paper (see Fig. 2). We first split the medical image into three channels during the embedding procedure since PVD can work only on two non-consecutive overlapping components colour components we can't apply the PVD algorithm on all colour components simultaneously. Then we read the medical information report from the text file to hide in all three channels. For this experiment, we have taken the patient information from the same text file to hide in all the RGB channels. Still, we can also take three different text files containing various information related to the patient. We combine the RGB channels to create the stego medical image after incorporating the patient's medical information report in the image pixels. After that, during the extraction of patient data from the medical photograph, we again split the stego image into blue, red, and green channels and employ the extraction algorithm to it, and we get the embedded patient information in three different files corresponding to the red, blue, and green channel.

Figure 3 shows the original and stego images of the CT scan, and Fig. 4 shows their histograms which indicate the similarity between the cover and stego image. We can observe that the stego and the original images have a similar visual appearance. The histograms of the original and stego images are shown in Fig. 5, and we can see that there is very little change between the histograms of the cover image and the stego image. So, the proposed scheme is also robust to histogram quantisation as there is a

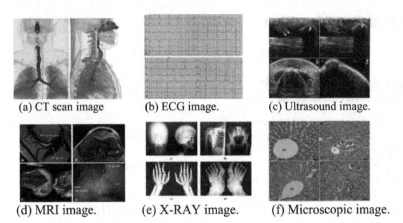

(a) CT scan image   (b) ECG image.   (c) Ultrasound image.

(d) MRI image.   (e) X-RAY image.   (f) Microscopic image.

Fig. 2. Medical images used to test the proposed scheme

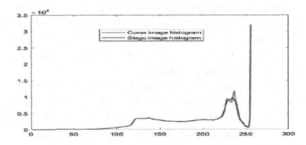

(a)   (b)

Fig. 3. (a) CT scan cover image. (b) CT scan stego image

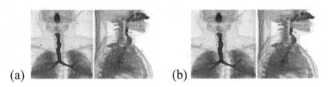

(a)   (b)

Fig. 4. (a) CT scan cover image histogram. (b) CT scan stego image histogram

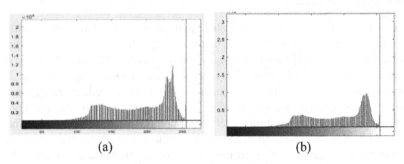

Fig. 5. Histogram difference of CT scan cover and stego image

minor difference in the stego and cover image histograms. So, the intruders can't find the presence of the medical information report of a patient in the stego medical images using histogram difference.

6 Comparison

The hiding capacity of the medical images depends upon the visual quality and size ($h \times w$) of the images used as the cover image. As a result, if we choose a higher-quality image, the hiding capacity will be increased. The embedding capacities of the selected medical images with the size variation are shown in Table 3. In our experiment, we used a patient's medical report kept in a text file to secretly insert into the pixels of medical images. PSNR is the parameter used to measure the visual appearance of medical images. The value of the PSNR varies according to the size of the text file. So, we have taken text files of different sizes, such as 10 KB, 20 KB, and 30 KB, and compared the results. We used an online tool to compare a patient's embedded medical information report in medical pictures with the extracted one. We have taken the results of six medical images CT scan, ECG, Ultrasound, MRI, X-ray, and microscopic image for comparison. After that, we will compare the results of the suggested method with techniques found in the published writings (Table 2).

Table 2. Embedding capacity of the medical images with differences in size

Cover image	Size	Capacity	Size	Capacity
Image Name	$h \times w$	bits	$h \times w$	bits
CT Scan image	512×381	797844	512×512	1303677
ECG image	512×378	946089	512×512	1280731
Ultrasound image	512×341	800723	512×512	1199728
MRI image	512×486	999377	512×512	1053927
X-ray image	512×361	686413	512×512	977931
Microscopic image	512×383	980115	512×512	1303677
Average		868426.83		118611.83

Figure 6 depicts a bar graph comparing the embedding capacity variation of different medical images with an increase in size. From the graph, we can say that the embedding capacity of the image will rise as its size does, whereas Fig. 7 represents a graph comparing PSNR values of files of sizes 10 KB, 20 KB, and 30 KB. A high PSNR value indicates better image quality. From Fig. 7, we can say that the image's visual quality decreases as the text file size increases.

We have used an online tool to check if extracted patient information is identical to the embedding. Character by character checking is performed by that tool, and similarity and difference percentages are shown. The outcomes of this procedure are depicted in the Table. 4. These results will differ from the text we hide in the medical image. The

Table 3. PSNR value of the medical images with 10KB, 20KB, and 30KB text file

Cover image		PSNR		
	Size $h \times w$	Text (10 KB)	Text (20 KB)	Text (30 KB)
CT Scan image	512 × 381	47.8573	44.5368	42.7892
ECG image	512 × 378	45.6454	42.4303	40.7091
Ultrasound image	512 × 341	45.5398	43.2665	41.5305
MRI image	512 × 486	46.7170	43.1794	41.5624
X-ray image	512 × 361	46.0373	42.9253	40.5773
Microscopic image	512 × 383	45.3255	42.5396	40.2072
Average		46.1870	43.1463	41.2292

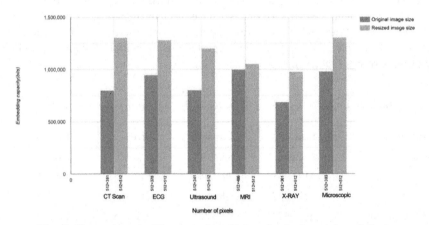

Fig. 6. Change in embedding capacity with increase in the number of pixels

outcomes in Table 4 show that we have the same information in the extracted text file which was there in the embedded one. There is some change in the embedded and extraction text, but it is acceptable.

We will compare the proposed scheme's results with Nasir et al. [12]. For comparison, we used 3-channel grayscale images from the MediPix online medical image library, which is free and available to the public [11]. The imperceptibility of the stego image produced by the suggested technique has been assessed using the SSIM and PSNR parameters. The similarity between two images is evaluated using SSIM (structural similarity measure). If the value of SSIM is 1, then it indicates that both the images are the same. To determine how similar (or different) two comparable photographs are from one another, normalised cross-correlation (NCC) is used. We have taken a text file of size 5 KB for comparison. The images which we have used are displayed in Fig. 2.

The Fig. 8 shows the medical images which we have used to compare proposed scheme with Nasir et al. [12] scheme. According to the experimental findings in Table 5,

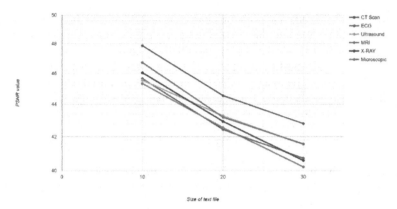

Fig. 7. Change in PSNR value with increasing size of the text file

Table 4. Comparison of embedded and extracted data

Cover image	Red Channel		Green Channel		Blue Channel	
	Similarity (%)	Difference (%)	Similarity (%)	Difference (%)	Capacity (%)	Difference (%)
CT Scan image	100	0	99.99	0.01	99.99	0.01
ECG image	99.99	0.01	100	0	100	0
Ultrasound image	100	0	99.99	0.01	99.99	0.01
MRI image	100	0	100	0	99.99	0.01
X-ray image	99.99	0.01	99.99	0.01	99.99	0.01
Microscopic image	99.99	0.01	99.99	0.01	99.99	0.01
Average	99.99	0.01	99.99	0.01	99.99	0.01

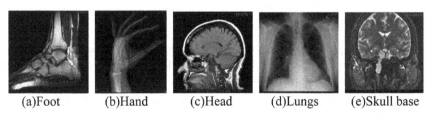

| (a)Foot | (b)Hand | (c)Head | (d)Lungs | (e)Skull base |

Fig. 8. Medical images used to compare with Nasir et al. [12] scheme

the suggested method has a greater PSNR and SSIM value than Nasir's scheme, and the NCC value is obtained as unity. The SSIM value near one show that the stego and the cover image are structurally similar, and the higher PSNR value indicates better visual quality. As a result, the suggested system is imperceptible and applicable to numerous applications.

Roseline et al. [8] took text with 5,8 characters and calculated the PSNR and MSE after embedding that text into the medical images using the improved LSB technique. Setyono and Setiadi [15] calculated MSE and PSNR by embedding 5 bits in the images. Hashim et al. [14] and Abd-El-Atty et al. [13] did the same thing, but they haven't used the MSE as a measuring parameter. Table 6 compares the proposed scheme results with these researchers by embedding five characters in the medical image.

Table 5. Experimental results of Nasir et al. [12] scheme and proposed scheme

Cover image	Nasir et al. [12]			Proposed scheme		
512 × 512	PSNR	NCC	SSIM	PSNR	NCC	SSIM
Foot	42.601	1.0	0.9821	51.4432	1.0	0.995710
Hand	40.8921	1.0	0.95123	51.9443	1.0	0.994618
Head	42.8909	1.0	0.98547	49.0833	1.0	0.998665
Lungs	42.6007	1.0	0.97456	52.0307	1.0	0.996374
Skull base	42.601	1.0	0.9821	50.2823	1.0	0.998054
Average	42.3171	1.0	0.97509	50.9567	1.0	0.996684

Table 6. Comparison of the PSNR and MSE of the proposed scheme with the literature

Author	PSNR	MSE
Hashim et al. [14]	72.29	-
Abd-El-Atty et al. [13]	73.27	-
Setyono and Setiadi [15]	63.52	0.0289
Roseline et al. [8]	80.364	0.00060
Proposed scheme	81.7092	0.00043869

Comparing the proposed system to existing strategies found in the literature, Table 6 and the graph in Fig. 9 show that it has a large PSNR value and a lower MSE. So, the proposed method is high imperceptibility.

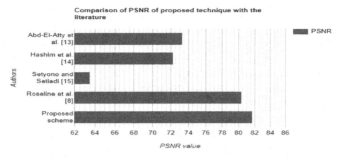

Fig. 9. Comparison of PSNR value of proposed technique with the literature

7 Conclusion

An efficient RGB medical image steganography technique has been proposed using a pixel value differencing methodology. The proposed scheme can be applied to various colour medical photographs such as ultrasound, CT scans, X-rays, MRIs, ECG, and microscopic images. It works on different image types such as PNG, JPG(JPEG), TIFF, and BMP. The experimental findings demonstrate that the suggested approach maintains the visual quality of the medical pictures so that the physician can analyse and give accurate results and extract medical information reports accurately. The proposed method has good embedding capacity and doesn't have the falling-off boundary problem. Apart from that, the technique is somewhat robust to histogram quantisation attacks. In the future, we can research on more steganographic attacks of PVD and improve the scheme's security against them.

References

1. Chan, C.K., Cheng, L.M.: Hiding data in images by simple LSB substitution. Pattern Recognit. **37**, 469–474 (2004)
2. Wu, D.-C., Tsai, W.-H.: A steganographic method for images by pixel value differencing. Pattern Recognit. Lett. **24**, 1613–1626 (2003)
3. Zhang, X., Wang, S.: Vulnerability of pixel-value differencing steganography to histogram analysis and modification for enhanced security. Pattern Recogn. Lett. **25**(3), 331–339 (2004)
4. Zaker, N., Hamzeh, A., Katebi, S., Samavi, S.: Improving security of pixel value differencing steganographic method. In: NTMS 2009, 3rd International Conference on New Technologies, Mobility and Security, Cairo, Egypt, 20–23 December 2009 (2009)
5. Loan, N.A., Parah, S.A., Sheikh, J.A., Akhoon, J.A., Bhat, G.M.: Hiding Electronic Patient Record (EPR) in medical images: a high capacity and computationally efficient technique for e-healthcare applications. J. Biomed. Inf. **73**, 125–136 (2017)
6. Santoso, B.: Color-based microscopic image steganography for telemedicine applications using pixel value differencing algorithm. J. Phys.: Conf. Ser. **1175**, 012057 (2019)
7. Jain, S., Dubey, S., Singhal, V.: Review of steganography techniques for securing patient information embedded in medical image. Int. J. Sci. Res. Comput. Sci. Appl. Manag. Stud. **9**(2), 1–3 (2020)
8. Ogundokun, R.O., Abikoye, O.C.: A safe and secured medical textual information using an improved LSB image steganography. Int. J. Digital Multimedia Broadcast. **2021**, 8827055 (2021)

9. Hashim, M.M., Mahmood, A.A., Mohammed, M.Q.: A pixel contrast based medical image steganography to ensure and secure patient data. Int. J. Nonlinear Anal. Appl. **12**, 1885–1904 (2021)

10. National Library of Medicine's Open Access Biomedical Images Search Engine. https://openi.nlm.nih.gov. Accessed 13 June 2022

11. MedPix™ Medical Image Database, available at: https://medpix.nlm.nih.gov/home. Accessed 22 June 2022

12. Hurrah, N.N., Parah, S.A., Sheikh, J.A.: A secure medical image watermarking technique for e-healthcare applications. In: Handbook of Multimedia Information Security: Techniques and Applications, vol. 6, pp. 119–141 (2019)

13. Abd-El-Atty, B., Abd El-Latif, A.A., Amin, M.: New quantum image steganography scheme with hadamard transformation. In: Hassanien, A.E., Shaalan, K., Gaber, T., Azar, A.T., Tolba, M.F. (eds.) AISI 2016. AISC, vol. 533, pp. 342–352. Springer, Cham (2017). https://doi.org/10.1007/978-3-319-48308-5_33

14. Hashim, M.M., Taha, M.S., Aman, A.H.M., Hashim, A.H.A., Rahim, M.S.M., Islam, S.: Securing medical data transmission systems based on integrating algorithm of encryption and steganography. In: 7th International Conference on Mechatronics Engineering (ICOM), Putrajaya, Malaysia, pp. 1–6 (2019)

15. Setyono, A., Setiadi, D.R.I.M.: Securing and hiding secret message in image using XOR transposition encryption and LSB method. J. Phys.: Conf. Ser. **1196**, 012039 (2019)

Deep Ensemble Architecture: A Region Mapping for Chest Abnormalities

Ashok Ajad$^{(\boxtimes)}$(iD), Taniya Saini$^{(\boxtimes)}$(iD), M. Kumar Niranjan$^{(\boxtimes)}$(iD),
Ansuj Joshi$^{(\boxtimes)}$(iD), and M. L. Kumar Swaroop$^{(\boxtimes)}$(iD)

AI CoE, L&T Technology Services, Bengaluru, India
{ashok.ajad,taniya.saini,niranjankumar.m,ansuj.joshi,
swaroopkumar.ml}@ltts.com,
{cse.aa9,tania.gagiyan1,niranjankumarm12,ansujj,swaroopkml96}@gmail.com

Abstract. Chronic respiratory diseases are very prominent now a days, these lung diseases become severe if not treated on time and may lead to lung cancer. National Cancer Registry Programme, India reported that 49.2% of males and 55.2% of females had been diagnosed with lung cancer in the year 2021. Considering lung abnormalities as a serious problem, In the proposed paper, we come up with a deep ensemble architecture as well as the approach for the data creation. An artificial intelligence (AI) based deep ensembled model is developed which identifies the abnormalities like Cardiomegaly, Collapse, Reticulonodular Pattern, Consolidation, Calcification, Bronchitis, Nodule, Osseous Lesions, Support devices and Pleural Effusion etc. The model also localizes the accurate position where the problem occurs. The mAP values obtained from the localization model on supervised and weakly supervised data are 0.323 and 0.376 respectively.

Keywords: Region Mapping · Localization · mAP · IOU · POI · Yolo · transformers

1 Introduction

In the field of the radiological Imaging, chest x-ray (CXR) has played a tremendous role in finding the lung-based abnormalities. X-ray is the initial view of any lung abnormality up to a certain extent, mostly it is used in the field of radiological imaging as it costs less as compared to CT and MRI scans. To detect the abnormalities with localization in an x-ray with the limited set of labelled data.

The most common and severe diseases usually occur in the lung part of the human body and these diseases must be detected as early as possible otherwise it can be transformed to severe lung diseases such as covid-19, pneumonia, tuberculosis, asthma, lung cancer etc.

Major diseases that could occur from the lung abnormalities are Pneumonia (Possibly that can occur when Pleural Effusion, Consolidation and Reticulonodular Pattern are found), Tuberculosis (Possibly occurs when Pleural Effusion, Consolidation, Nodule and Calcification are found), Lung Cancer (Possibly

Supported by organization L&T Technology Services.

occurs when Pleural Effusion, Collapse, Nodule and Reticulonodular Pattern). In recent times, the most dangerous virus which is spreading all over the world and leading to the substantial number of deaths is Corona Virus (COVID-19) which can also be detected with the help of abnormality like Consolidation. Also, to detect these kinds of diseases the radiologist may take some time (depends on the experience) and effort to find the problem.

There are various algorithms like R-CNN, Fast R-CNN, Faster R-CNN, SSD and YOLO which performs [7] which performs very well on object detection task. R-CNN detects the objects by dividing image into several regions and then it applies the selective search algorithm over those regions, After selecting considerable regions it shortlists 2000 regions out of it. Those regions are passed into the CNN(VGG, AlexNet) and finally using SVM and bounding box regressor it detects the object. The disadvantage of the R-CNN takes quite more time for execution due to which the updated version as Fast R-CNN. In Fast R-CNN [14] the image divided into several regions and pass through CNN, further the obtained feature map are passed into the ROI pooling layer, beside the SVM this algorithm uses softmax and linear regression as its output layer. Faster R-CNN [12,13] replaces the selective search algorithm with a new neural network which ultimately increases the accuracy and reduces the over all time [1,4].

By dividing the image into several regions and then passing into CNN one by one takes a lot of time and memory for evaluation. YOLO [6,19] over passes these demerits and passes the whole image at once to the CNN by dividing the image into grids, the classification and object detection task are done simultaneously in this algorithm. The newer versions of this algorithm makes it more faster by introducing non-max suppression and anchor box.

A deep ensembled architecture has been introduced which helps us to label the data-set and identify the abnormalities that usually occurs in lung with their localization and which reduces the time and effort of radiologists. Once you pass the input x-ray image through the model, model divides the input x-ray image into several regions and passes the whole image to Neural Network (NN). As a final output the localization algorithm gives us the localization in terms of Bounding box (four Coordinates). An output of this is passed Transformation such that it provides us the region with respect to localization. The algorithm focuses on the following abnormalities i.e., Cardiomegaly, Collapse, Reticulonodular Pattern, Consolidation, Calcification, Bronchitis, Nodule, Osseous Lesions, Support devices and Pleural Effusion , Lung Opacity etc.

2   Related Work

In [1,15], an approach of weakly supervised learning model (U-Net model) for detection and drawing a bounding box is used, based on the lung zones. Here in this paper, they have segmented lungs into 6 main parts based on the U-Net model. With the help of reports they have drawn the bounding box for lung opacity detection. As an output of U-Net model a dataset has been created called silver dataset, RetinaNet Model takes silver dataset as its input for detection of lung opacity and as a result 95% of accuracy has been obtained.

The approach given in [2] for classification of x-ray abnormalities used VGG16 as a Pre-trained model. They have achieved the AUC (area under curve) scores of 0.89, 0.84, and 0.82 for the Pneumothorax, Pneumonia and Pulmonary Edema. For better interpretation of feature map an weakly supervised technique(Class activation Map Grad-CAM) has been used, the output obtained from Grad-CAM is divided into certain instances that passed through a localization model.

In [3], the detection of 7 lung abnormalities (consolidation, effusion, fibrosis, infiltration, mass, nodule and pleural thickening) and diagnosis of TB is done using various combinations of pre-trained convolutional neural networks (CNN). The high performed CNNs used for TB detection includes VGG16, VGG19, Inception V3, ResNet34, ResNet50 and ResNet101[20] which is evaluated using specificity, recall, F1 score and AUC.

The best accuracy obtained is 98.46%, a specificity of 100%, F1 score of 0.986 and AUC of 0.999 with train-validation ratio is of 9:1. After the classification, a localization approach is being followed by taking feature maps from the final convolutional layers and global average pooling layer together. The generated attention map identifies the abnormal regions in the lung x-ray.

One of the essential part of x-ray analysis is identifying and localizing the main "region of interest (ROI)". The paper[4] represents the review of all techniques for lung boundary detection [13–15]. It works on different kinds of x-ray studies like- pa view, ap view and lateral view, also worked on deformed lungs. It uses various categories of algorithms- based on rule, pixel classification, model, hybrid, deep learning and concluded that "Hybrid" and "Deep learning based" algorithms surpass all other algorithms.

[5], The paper localize the abnormalities in chest x-ray using unsupervised Fuzzy C-Means(FCM) and K-Means(KM) Clustering methods. The x-ray images are first segmented and then divided into non-overlapping images with different pixels size(16 to 128) based on the patches and these patches then applied on clusters for classification of extracted features. Accuracy of models of different pixel sizes are from 92.1% to 88.7% for FCM and 92.2% to 88.8% for KM models respectively.

For weakly-supervised classification and localisation of the thorax diseases and to create the new radiological reports [6] have used Deep Convolutional Neural Network(DCNN) and natural language processing(NLP) respectively. Observation and Impressions has got around more than 90% in all three aspect like recall, f1-score and precision. For the classification and Localization of x-ray images, an approach of weakly supervised model are used with the pre-trained ImageNet model like AlexNet, GoogleNet, VGGNet-16 and ResNet-50[20]. In this model they have implemented the multi-label classification and bounding box are generated with help of heat map for localization of an abnormality. The comparison has been made on this models where ResNet-50 has got the better accuracy for Atelectasis, Cardiomegaly, Effusion, Infiltration, Nodule, Pneumonia and Pneumothorax [10,11] whereas for the Mass abnormality AlexNet has shown better accuracy compared to others. All the object detection techniques are evaluated and compared in [7]. The paper categories the object detection technique into two parts generic and salient, Generic method further categories as "Region Proposal Based Frameworks" and "Regression/Classification Based Frameworks". Region based consists of R-CNN (Region based CNN), SPP-net (Spatial Pyramid Pooling) [17], Fast R-CNN [14], Faster R-CNN [13], R-FCN, FPN (Feature Pyramid Network) and Mask R-CNN, while Regression/Classification based consists of YOLO [18,19] (You Only Look Once) and SSD (single-shot detector). Salient object detection focuses more on objects rather than the surroundings and thus works on "bottom-up and "top-down" approach.

They have displayed the comparative results on VOC-2007 as follows-SSD512 with mAP 81.6, Faster R-CNN with mAP 78.8, Fast R-CNN with mAP 70.0, SPP with mAP 60.9, R-CNN(VGG) with mAP 66.0, R-CNN (Alex Net) with mAP 58.5. The results based on COCO are as follows- R-FCN (ResNet) with mAP 85.0, SSD with mAP 82.2, YOLOv2 with mAP 78.2, Faster R-CNN[12][13] with mAP 75.9, Fast R-CNN[14] with mAP 68.4, R-CNN(VGG) with mAP 62.4, R-CNN (Alex Net) with mAP 53.3.

As medical images have different characterization than normal images [10] hence, they are treated differently via DL also. CLU-CNNs (Clustering CNN) is unique architecture proposed in [8] which is specially designed for medical domain related data, it is constructed using "Agglomerative Nesting Clustering Filtering" ANCF (helps for adapting the domain) and BN-IN (gives more stability to the network). CLU-CNN works well with small dataset and can also be easily expanded further also it gives high positioning accuracy and has fast speed. For medical domain adaptation they concluded that CLAHE performed tremendously, as a base object detection algorithm Faster R-CNN performs better than SSD and FCN.

For the lung segmentation of x-ray images, [9] have used the UNet model with the help of efficient Net architecture. Where the model trained and tested on the two public dataset called RSNA Pneumonia and JSRT dataset and dataset is divided into 60% as training, 20% as validation and 20% as testing. To ensure the model performs more accurate so, they have used five different UNet models and ensembled all the models in single model and verified on the above-mentioned dataset and the model was able to predict the lungs and two parts as right and left lung. Where they were able to achieve the F1 score (dice Score) more than 90%.

3   Data Exploration

3.1   Weakly Supervised Dataset

The dataset is divided into two parts- supervised and weakly supervised, where supervised data is consists of one in-house data and one open source data (VinBig from Kaggle) and weakly supervised data consists of one in-house data and one open source data (PAD Chest). Where this one in-house data called as "in-data1" and PAD chest data is called as "in-data2". For supervised data the marking of abnormalities is done by a radiologist. We considered 17 output classes for supervised data and 13 output classes for weakly supervised data. Around 7,000 training data-points were taken for model training and around 300 data-points were there for validation and testing part in supervised case. After getting the trained model from supervised data, the weakly supervised data is inferred from it and weakly-labels are generated. Around 50,000 data-points are available for training and 22,00 data-points for validation and testing in case of weakly labels.

The proposed architecture has taken 10% from the overall data distribution in supervised case and for weakly supervised case for the testing marked data. So that it can be correctly validated.

3.2   Database of Region Mapping

For every abnormalities there are some different regions where the diseases are present. So, for identifying the specific regions in x-ray image, a database is created by annotating the single x-ray image (as a reference image) with the help of LabelMe [21] annotation tool. All regions of the each and every abnormality is annotated separately and saved in JSON format, where, this JSON contains the contours of the regions in abnormality.

4   Deep Ensemble Architecture

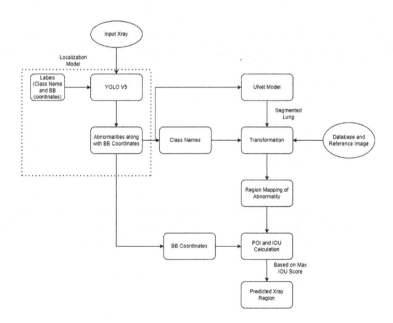

Fig. 1. Deep Ensembled Model.

An approach of deep ensemble architecture is majorly divided as two parts.(1) Localization (2) Region Mapping. where, approach helps us to identify the chest abnormalities and classify them with their regions (Fig. 1).

Pre-processing steps for (1) Localization includes the image normalization and resize into 512×512 and then passed into the YOLOv5 model [19,22] with annotation of abnormality in form of bounding box as $x, y \in x_{min}, y_{min}, x_{max}, y_{max}$, also the class names are converted into the class id $id \in class$ and stored in text format(as labels) $\{id_1, id_2, id_3 \ldots id_n\}$ where id's are the class-ids defined based on classes,along with box coordinates $x_{min}, y_{min}, x_{max}, y_{max}$ which is simultaneously passed to the model. Lung segmentation plays an important role in localization and region mapping for our approach. As a pre-processing step for (2) Region Mapping, UNet [9] Model is used as segmentation model, which consists of five different models of efficient net architecture and these models are ensembled and post-proceessed to produce lung segmentation as shown in Fig. 2(b). The reason behind using five different models and ensembling them is to get efficient segmented lung and these segmented lungs are passed to region mapping approach for regional mapping on bounding box.

4.1   Localization

YOLOv5 architecture [19,22] has shown in Fig. 2 is trained using a object detection objective. As a pre-processed x-ray image is passed through model, which is able to classify the abnormality on input image. The YOLOv5 comes under the four different models as such YOLOv5s, YOLOv5m, YOLOv5l, YOLOv5x (small, medium, large and extra-large models). Here, an YOLOv5x(extra-large) model has been used in our approach. The x-ray image and label of abnormality in form of annotations has been passed through YOLO model. The YOLO model consists of three major parts as architecture: (1) Backbone: CSPDarknet, (2) Neck: PANet, and (3) Head: Yolo Layer. The pre-processed image first passed into CSPDarknet for feature extraction, and then fed to PANet for feature fusion. Finally, Yolo Layer outputs detection results (class, score, location, size). YOLO is a single-stage object detector model which uses Leaky ReLU in its middle and hidden layers and sigmoid in its final layer as its activation function. For optimization of function the model has 2 options of SGD (Stochastic Gradient Descent) and adam, while experimenting we have used both and got better results with the default SGD optimizer. This model produces the output in the form of Bounding Boxes of an specific abnormality.

During identification of abnormality, pre-processed image is converted into input tensor is divided into S × S grid and this is responsible for identification of abnormality if it lies in center of grid. The model uses the Binary Cross-Entropy with Logits Loss function for calculating loss and object score from PyTorch, it also gives the option for choosing Focal loss as a loss function.

$$loss = l_{box} + l_{cls} + l_{obj} \tag{1}$$

where the l_{box}, l_{cls}, l_{obj} are the loss function of regression Bounding box, classification and confidence respectively.

$$l_{box} = \lambda_{coord} \sum_{i=0}^{S^2} \sum_{j=0}^{B} I_{i,j}^{ojb} b_j (2 - w_i x h_i)$$

$$[(x_i - \hat{x}_i^j)^2 + (y_i - \hat{y}_i^j)^2 + (w_i - \hat{w}_i^j)^2 + (h_i - \hat{h}_i^j)^2]$$

$$(2)$$

$$l_{cls} = \lambda_{class} \sum_{i=0}^{S^2} \sum_{j=0}^{B} I_{i,j}^{ojb} \sum_{C \in classes} p_i(c) \log(\hat{p}_l(c)) \tag{3}$$

$$l_{obj} = \lambda_{noobj} \sum_{i=0}^{S^2} \sum_{j=0}^{B} I_{i,j}^{noobj} (c_i - \hat{c}_l)^2 +$$

$$\lambda_{obj} \sum_{i=0}^{S^2} \sum_{j=0}^{B} I_{i,j}^{obj} (c_i - \hat{c}_l)^2 \tag{4}$$

where λ is loss coefficient, $\hat{x}, \hat{y}$ are the coordinates of grids and $\hat{w}, \hat{h}$ are the width and height of grid. If the target contains grid at (i, j). Then 1 is the value for $I_{i,j}^{obj}$ or 0 for $I_{i,j}^{obj}$ The target probability of the category is represented as $p_i(c)$ and the true value of the category is $\hat{p}_l(c)$. The length of the total number of categories is exactly equal to two If the grid at (i, j) contains targets, then the value $I_{i,j}^{obj}$ is 1; otherwise, the value is 0. represents the category probability of the target, and $\hat{p}_l(c)$ is the true value of the category. The length of the two is equal to the total number of categories C. [22]

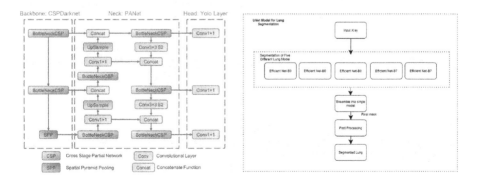

Fig. 2. Localisation and Segmentation Architecture.

4.2   Region Mapping

The output of YOLOv5 is dividied into classnames and bounding box coordinates, where classnames$\{id_1, id_2, id_3 \ldots id_n\}$ is passed to transformation along with Segmented Lungs from UNet model. This classnames import the specific region of abnormality from the database of region mapping. The minimum rectangles is calculated from the segmented lung from UNet model, the lung from the reference image(region mapping database) and separated into two different lungs, where the coordinates of this rectangles $x_{minrR}, y_{minrR}, x_{maxrR}, y_{maxrR}$ $x_{minlR}, y_{minlR}, x_{maxlR}, y_{maxlR}$ $x_{minrI}, y_{minrI}, x_{maxrI}, y_{maxrI}$

$x_{minlI}, y_{minlI}, x_{maxlI}, y_{maxlI}$ where, $r \in rightlung$, $l \in Leftlung$ and $R \in ReferenceImage$, $I \in InputImages$ The Transformation is used to identify the specific region of abnormality, where $d_r, d_l \in D$, where D is absolute distance between the points is calculated based on the reference and input image lungs which is also known as POI(Point of Intersection).

$$D = abs(Point(x_{minR}, y_{minR}) - Point(x_{minI}, y_{minI})) \tag{5}$$

The height and width ratio is calculated from reference and input images which were in PASCAL format $H_R, H_I \in H$ $W_R, W_I \in W$, where $H \in Height$ and $W \in Width$.

$$H = H_R/H_I \tag{6}$$

$$W = W_R/W_I \tag{7}$$

with the help of distance, height ratio and width ratio regions of reference is normalized on input images. Then the bounding box coordinates of YOLOv5 output is passed and region is calculated based on the specific abnormality.

Table 1. On the task of the Localization Supervised and Weakly Supervised Technique - combination of the Open-Source and in-house data-set.

Tags	Supervised Technique			Weakly Supervised		
	Images	mAP@0.5	mAP@0.5:0.95	Images	mAP@0.5	mAP@0.5:0.95
All	203	0.323	0.148	1196	0.376	0.162
Calcification	203	0.291	0.081	1196	0.318	0.0901
Pleural Effusion	203	0.385	0.137	1196	0.427	0.136
Fibrosis	203	0.284	0.0899	1196	0.318	0.103
Consolidation	203	0.333	0.089	1196	0.392	0.148
Hilar Enlargement	203	0.373	0.169	1196	0.458	0.192
Cardiomegaly	203	0.575	0.361	1196	0.644	0.382
Nodule	203	0.575	0.361	1196	0.267	0.12
Surgery	203	0.745	0.422	1196	0.751	0.354
Diaphragmatic Abnormalities	203	0.502	0.231	1196	0.576	0.204
Mediastinal Widening	203	0.659	0.351	1196	0.677	0.355
Pneumothorax	203	0.502	0.173	1196	0.238	0.101

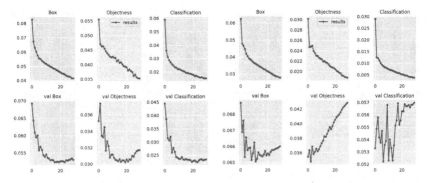

Fig. 3. Loss graphs of Deep Ensemble Model. (a). Results of Supervised (b) Results of weakly Supervised.

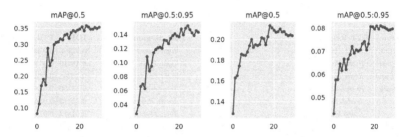

Fig. 4. mAP graphs of Deep Ensemble Model. (a). Results of Supervised (b) Results of weakly Supervised.

5   Experiments and Results

Mainly two different experiments were conducted for the data-sets preparations:(1) Based on **supervised technique**, where this part of data is composed of images along with their labels and bounding box coordinates. (2) Based on **weakly supervised technique**, where this part of data is composed of images along with their labels. The main purpose is to identify the coordinates of this part of data, for that the data is inferred on trained model of supervised technique has been used and inferred labels of supervised models are verified with ground truth of this data and generated labels and coordinates were called as "weakly labels". An localized model has been trained for the identification of bounding boxes and its labels.

The metrics like precision, recall, mean average precision(mAP@0.5) with threshold of 0.5 and mean average precision(mAP@0.5:0.95) with threshold value between 0.5 to 0.95. The mean average precision(mAP) is considered as best performance evaluation metric for localization model. The mAP resultant of **supervised technique** and **weakly supervised technique** for multi-class is given in Table 1 and overall mAP resultant for both **supervised** and **weakly supervised** is shown in Fig. 4. The losses like bounding box, objectness, classification and accuracy like precision, recall graph for both **supervised** and

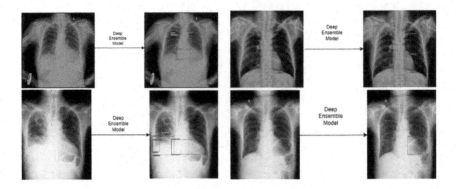

Fig. 5. Output of Model.

Table 2. Results based on the Region Mapping Technique.

Class Name	GT Region	ML Region	IOU	POI	1-POI
Consolidation	Right Upper Lobe	Right Upper Lobe	0.32785	0.050931	0.9491
Pleural Effusion	Right Basal	Right Basal	0.44210	0.01562	0.98428
Pleural Effusion	Right Lower Lobe	Right Lower Lobe	0.32058	0.08212	0.91788
Cardiomegaly	Retrocardiac Region	Retrocardiac Region	0.13356	0.05859	0.094141
Calcification	Aortic Region	Aortic Region	0.23115	0.01953	0.98047
Nodule	Right Middle Lobe	Right Middle Lobe	0.01523	0.07812	0.92188
Cardiomegaly	Retrocardiac Region	Retrocardiac Region	0.14488	0.03149	0.96851
Collapse	Right Upper Lobe	Right Upper Lobe	0.64219	0.02470	0.9753
Calcification	Left Middle Lobe	Left Middle Lobe	0.34639	0.07370	0.9263
Nodule	Right Upper Lobe	Right Upper Lobe	0.02664	0.05426	0.94574
Cardiomegaly	Azygo-esophageal Recess and Retrocardiac Region	Azygo-esophageal Recess	0.10530	0.09959	0.90041
Nodule	Right Lower Lobe	Right Lower Lobe	0.00448	0.15625	0.84375
Nodule	Right Upper Lobe	Right Upper Lobe	0.02421	0.09285	0.90715
Osseous Lesions	Right Lung	Right Lung	0.13893	0.09447	0.90553
Osseous Lesions	Left Lung	Left Lung	0.33818	0.14405	0.85595

weakly supervised models is shown in Fig. 3 respectively. The precision, recall and mAP obtained from the localization models of supervised data and weakly supervised data are 0.421,0.325, 0.323 and 0.57, 0.374, 0.376 respectively.

On the second part of result, the regional identification of bounding boxes on X-rays are done on in-houses images with multi-classes abnormalities and verified with ground-truth of images. For the resultant visual representation, four different images of in-house data-set with multi-classes abnormalities are chosen and shown in Fig. 5 maximum Intersection of Union(IoU) score and minimum Point of Intersection(PoI) distance of region of an specific class and (1-PoI) are the evaluation metrics were used and resultant of regional localization(region mapping) are shown in Table 2. Also, metric called IoU(Intersection of Union) additionally used for comparison of **supervised** model result is given in Table 3. Approximate execution time for images is around **5.96 ms**.

Table 3. Comparison of our results to the other previous results.

IOU Score

Model	Dataset	Collapse	Consolidation	Cardiomegaly	Nodule	Pleural Effusion
SOTA Model [23]	NIH Chest X-ray	0.488	0.715	0.989	0.081	0.693
ResNet-50 [24]	NIH Chest X-ray	0.818	0.918	1	0.404	0.882
Our Model	Vinbig Data	0.782	0.856	0.971	0.704	0.861
Our Model	PAD Chest	0.801	0.847	0.954	0.745	0.831
Our Model	In-house Dataset	0.821	0.881	0.981	0.767	0.898

6   Conclusion

The research has shown the localization and region mapping helps the radiologist to specify the diseases based on the abnormality and their region produced by the ensemble model, which also reduces efforts and time to be spent on the medical images and also quality of report can be enhanced. The two-phase deep ensemble architecture(localization and region mapping) has been proposed and implemented in this paper.

Due to limited annotated data-set and region information available on the different abnormalities of lung and proposed methodology can only predict the insights of specific diseases based on the abnormalities classified in this paper.

Finally, the proposed work provides initial identification on classification of abnormalities. Method further provides the annotation towards the medical images like in-house data-set. The deep ensemble model is able to classify the specific abnormalities with their regions accurately.

References

1. Wu, J., et al.: Automatic bounding box annotation of chest x-ray data for localization of abnormalities. In: 2020 IEEE 17th International Symposium on Biomedical Imaging (ISBI). IEEE (2020)
2. Schwab, E., et al.: Localization of critical findings in chest X-ray without local annotations using multi-instance learning. In: 2020 IEEE 17th International Symposium on Biomedical Imaging (ISBI). IEEE (2020)
3. Guo, R., Passi, K., Jain, C.K.: Tuberculosis diagnostics and localization in chest X-Rays via deep learning models. Front. Artif. Intell. **3**, 74 (2020)
4. Candemir, S., Antani, S.: A review on lung boundary detection in chest X-rays. Int. J. Comput. Assist. Radiol. Surg. **14**(4), 563–576 (2019). https://doi.org/10.1007/s11548-019-01917-1
5. Chandra, T.B., et al.: Localization of the suspected abnormal region in chest radiograph images. In: 2020 First International Conference on Power, Control and Computing Technologies (ICPC2T). IEEE (2020)
6. Wang, X., et al.: Chestx-ray8: Hospital-scale chest x-ray database and benchmarks on weakly-supervised classification and localization of common thorax diseases. In: Proceedings of the IEEE Conference on Computer Vision and Pattern Recognition (2017)

7. Zhao, Z.Q., et al.: Object detection with deep learning: a review. IEEE Trans. Neural Netw. Learn. Syst. **30**(11), 3212–3232 (2019)
8. Li, Z., et al.: CLU-CNNs: object detection for medical images. Neurocomputing **350**, 53–59 (2019)
9. Kim, Y.-G., et al.: Deep Learning-based Four-region Lung Segmentation in Chest Radiography for COVID-19 Diagnosis. arXiv preprint arXiv:2009.12610 (2020)
10. Ajad, A., Gupta, S., Sadhwani, K.J.: CARES: knowledge infused chest X-ray report generation scheme. In: RSNA 2020–106th Annual Meeting (2020)
11. Pradhan, J., Ajad, A., Pal, A.K., Banka, H.: Multi-level colored directional motif histograms for content-based image retrieval. Visual Comput. J. **36**(9), 1847–1868 (2020)
12. Chen, X., Gupta, A.: An implementation of faster rcnn with study for region sampling. arXiv preprint arXiv:1702.02138 (2017)
13. Cheng, B., et al.: Revisiting rcnn: on awakening the classification power of faster rcnn. In: Proceedings of the European Conference on Computer Vision (ECCV) (2018)
14. Girshick, R.: Fast r-cnn. In: Proceedings of the IEEE International Conference on Computer Vision (2015)
15. Li, X., et al.: H-DenseUNet: hybrid densely connected UNet for liver and tumor segmentation from CT volumes. IEEE Trans. Med. Imaging **37**(12), 2663–2674 (2018)
16. Akcay, S., Breckon, T.P.: An evaluation of region based object detection strategies within x-ray baggage security imagery. In: 2017 IEEE International Conference on Image Processing (ICIP). IEEE (2017)
17. Purkait, P., Zhao, C., Zach, C.: SPP-net: deep absolute pose regression with synthetic views. arXiv preprint arXiv:1712.03452 (2017)
18. Wang, X., et al.: Data-driven based tiny-YOLOv3 method for front vehicle detection inducing SPP-net. IEEE Access **8**, 110227–110236 (2020)
19. Fang, Y., et al.: Accurate and automated detection of surface knots on sawn timbers using YOLO-V5 model. BioResources **16**(3), 5390–5406 (2021)
20. Wen, L., Li, X., Gao, L.: A transfer convolutional neural network for fault diagnosis based on ResNet-50. Neural Comput. Appl. **32**(10), 6111–6124 (2020)
21. Torralba, A., Russell, B.C., Yuen, J.: Labelme: online image annotation and applications. Proc. IEEE **98**(8), 1467–1484 (2010)
22. Xu, Q., et al.: Effective face detector based on YOLOv5 and superresolution reconstruction. Comput. Math. Methods Med. **2021** (2021)
23. Wang, X., et al.: Hospital-scale chest x-ray database and benchmarks on weakly-supervised classification and localization of common thorax diseases. In: IEEE CVPR, vol. 7 (2017)
24. Rozenberg, E., Freedman, D., Bronstein, A.: Localization with limited annotation for chest x-rays. Machine Learning for Health Workshop. PMLR (2020)

Privacy-Preserving Federated Learning for Pneumonia Diagnosis

Sagnik Sarkar[1], Shaashwat Agrawal[1], Thippa Reddy Gadekallu[2,6], Mufti Mahmud[3,4,5(✉)] (iD), and David J. Brown[3,4] (iD)

[1] School of Computer Science and Engineering, Vellore Institute of Technology, Vellore, Tamil Nadu, India
{sagnik.sarkar2018,shaashwat.agrawal2018}@vitstudent.ac.in
[2] School of Information Technology and Engineering, Vellore Institute of Technology, Vellore 632014, India
thippareddy.g@vit.ac.in
[3] Department of Computer Science, Nottingham Trent University, Nottingham NG11 8NS, UK
{mufti.mahmud,david.brown}@ntu.ac.uk
[4] Computing and Informatics Research Centre, Nottingham Trent University, Nottingham NG11 8NS, UK
[5] Medical Technologies Innovation Facility, Nottingham Trent University, Nottingham NG11 8NS, UK
[6] Department of Electrical and Computer Engineering, Lebanese American University, Byblos, Lebanon

Abstract. Early diagnosis of diseases has become the major focus of researchers today. Machine Learning (ML) and Deep Learning (DL) algorithms have provided a much-needed boost to this field to make early diagnosis possible. With the help of sufficient data and computation, DL algorithms can be developed to detect diseases with high precision. Even with this uplift, gathering high-quality and quantity data for medical studies is very difficult. Although implementing Federated Learning (FL) solves data availability issues, its high variance makes it incompatible with Medical Diagnosis. In this paper, we present an FL approach for diagnosing pneumonia in patients that is easy to use and provides state-of-the-art results. Before training, a combination of pre-processing steps is performed that significantly increase the performance of the FL architecture.

Keywords: Federated Learning · Image Processing · Medical Diagnosis

1 Introduction

Pneumonia is a major disease that affects millions of people every year. According to the World Health Organisation (WHO), it was the leading cause of death in children below the age of 5 with approximately 700,000. It fills the air sacs in our lungs with fluids causing irritation, fever, coughing and several other symptoms. Early detection of such a disease is pertinent for preventing further

M. Tanveer et al. (Eds.): ICONIP 2022, CCIS 1794, pp. 345–356, 2023.
https://doi.org/10.1007/978-981-99-1648-1_29

casualties. Since the infection is from a bacteria, fungi or virus and is localised in the lungs, an X-ray image of the chest has been used to study and diagnose pneumonia.

Early Diagnosis of diseases has seen a shift from traditional methods to automated algorithms that perform the task more efficiently and easily. Machine Learning (ML) has been the leading technology in this space providing high-performance algorithms for different use cases. Deep Learning (DL) algorithms, especially Convolution Neural Networks (CNN) work well with image datasets. Standardised architectures such as VGG, ResNet [20] have provided state-of-the-art results in the medical field [27]. Perfecting a model, especially complex ones such as ResNet demands a lot of computation power, time as well as centrally located data. Considering that the computation power can be consolidated, gathering enough medical data that is generally private is very tough. Medical studies often fail due to the lack of such data. Even if one does have the data, containing private information in a huge quantity can often lead to hacking attempts and privacy breaches [46].

To overcome data availability and privacy concerns, Federated Learning (FL) has been extensively researched [9]. FL provides a distributed computing framework where client edge devices train on a DL model in their local system with their private data which then aggregates to form a central server model. The server model becomes a single representation of all the client data making it perfect for diagnosing purposes. Its architecture keeps every client's identity anonymous, all the while providing an all-round algorithm [2,49].

In this paper, we implement the Optical Coherence Tomography and Chest X-ray image dataset [25] taken from Kaggle using Federated Learning. The emphasis in this paper is laid on the preprocessing steps followed by Convolutional Neural Network (CNN) that is suited to the FL system. An ablation study is performed considering various parameters to provide the best possible outcome for this dataset. The main contributions of the paper are:

- Benchmarking the Optical Coherence Tomography and Chest X-ray image dataset for pneumonia detection using Federated Learning.
- Experimentation and exploration of the dataset with various factors such as hyperparameters, image processing filters, etc.

The paper division is done as follows. Section 2 presents a state-of-the-art literature review of current developments in disease diagnosis using ML and FL. Section 3 explains the proposed methodology and architecture of the algorithm followed by Sect. 4 that analyses the results obtained. Finally, the conclusion is present in Sect. 5.

2   Literature Survey

In recent years artificial intelligence (AI) has been applied in diverse problem domains to solve various challenging problems including student engagement [44], virtual reality exposure therapy [45], text classification [1,36,42,43], cyber security [4,17,21,52], neurological disease detection [11,19,38] and management [3,5,6,23,33,48], elderly care [13,35], biological data mining [31,32], fighting pandemic [7,10,28,30,40,41,47], and healthcare service delivery [12,16,24]. In particular, machine learning has been extensively used to develop medicine and medical diagnosis. Deep Learning algorithms have been applied to cases of pneumonia, tumour, skin diseases, etc. detection by providing image samples of the respective diseases and classifying the sample as benign or otherwise. [22] explored the various Deep Learning strategies used for pneumonia detection. Especially today, with the COVID-19 pandemic, pneumonia diagnosis has been treated with utmost importance. Many approaches have been applied for example ensemble learning [29], transfer learning [34], and more. Several Convolutional Neural Network (CNN) architectures like VGG [15], ResNet [50] and AlexNet [39] have also been applied for the same.

Although applying DL algorithms provide high performance, their real-life feasibility seems to be low. FL on the other hand, is more suited to handle large, private data. Figure 1 shows an example of a centralised Federated Learning architecture.

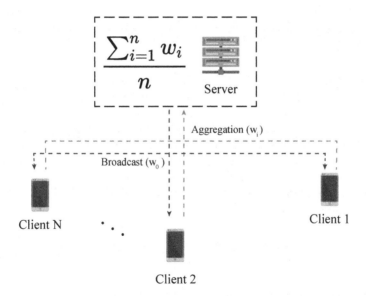

Fig. 1. Generic architecture of a Federated Learning system.

In terms of research for pneumonia detection using Federated Learning some work has been done using other publicly available and private X-ray image datasets, but most of the work has focused on COVID-19 and not pneumonia in general. On the one hand, works like [18,37] survey and analyse the use of FL in COVID-19 cases while on the other hand, few works including [26] focus on pneumonia as a whole. The work considers data from different hospitals, preprocess them, trains the local clients using those non-IID data and then aggregates the weights to obtain the final global model.

From the literature review, we can infer that the research on pneumonia detection, especially using FL has been lagging and most of the focus has shifted to COVID-19. Among the multiple publicly available pneumonia datasets, hardly any of them have been tested and experimented on.

3   Methodology

In this section, an overview of the Federated Learning Architecture is provided. The deep learning model architecture and the dataset used in this work have been elaborated upon.

3.1   Federated Learning

A centralised Federated learning architecture has been utilized for the current application, with a single global server and several client devices. For the first round, the server (w_0) and client weights (w_i) are initialised. And in each subsequent round, the server broadcasts the weights to each available client as Eq. 1.

$$w_i \leftarrow w_0, i \in clients \tag{1}$$

The clients train their models on their local dataset and resend the trained models to the server. Finally, aggregation of model weights is performed on the server side to form the global model as depicted in Eq. 2. The experimental setup ensures that the data distribution is of a non-Identically and Independently Distributed (IID) nature. Each client has a different size of randomized data available to them. In each round, the clients train for 2 epochs to prevent underfitting after aggregation. Experiments have been conducted using 20–30 clients and 10–20 training rounds.

$$w_0 \leftarrow \frac{1}{n} \sum_{i \in clients} w_i \tag{2}$$

3.2   Model Architecture

The Federated Learning System primarily operates on a parameterised prediction function to perform distributed training and server generalisation. The chest X-Ray dataset and the expected binary output require a prediction function to extract vital features in the two-dimensional image matrix and predict based on information obtained from these features. A convolutional neural network (CNN) is therefore employed for this task. However, due to the communication overhead and the low computing capabilities of edge devices in the FL architecture, the model must be lightweight and robust. With this in view, the model contains several convolution blocks and a final inference block. The convolution block consists of two convolution layers each with the same number of output features and a kernel size of 3. The output features of the convolution layers are passed through a ReLU activation.

Furthermore, at the end of this set of convolution layers, batch normalisation is performed and max-pooled with a stride and kernel size of 2. The number of output features starts from 16 in the first convolution block and increases by a factor of 2 in every successive block. There are 5 convolution blocks making the final number of output features to 256. The final three-dimensional vector is flattened and passed through the inference block which consists of 3 ReLU activated linear layers. The output however is sigmoid activated to ensure that the binary output is in the range [0, 1].

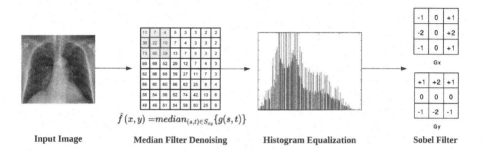

$$\hat{f}(x, y) = median_{(s,t) \in S_{xy}}\{g(s, t)\}$$

Input Image   **Median Filter Denoising**   **Histogram Equalization**   **Sobel Filter**

Fig. 2. Image Preprocessing steps for feature enhancement

3.3 Dataset Preprocessing

The chest X-Ray dataset is a subset of the dataset in [25] which contains Optical Coherence Tomography and Chest X-Ray images. The Chest X-Ray image section of the dataset contains 3883 pneumonia-labelled images and 1349 normal-labelled images. The X-Ray images yield decent performance in prediction, further processing improves the presentation of decisive features and the ease of processing. Figure 2 depicts the processing steps utilised. The main processing steps include - Median Filtering, Histogram Equalization, and Sobel Filter for edge extraction. The Median filter constitutes an essential step to smoothen the pixels corresponding to noise. This facilitates the upcoming steps and removes anomalous features in the image. The X-Ray images tend to be characterised by an abnormal amount of exposure thus creating unwanted spikes of illumination for undesirable features while the important features get subdued. Histogram equalisation creates an even distribution of illumination across all features providing prominence to crucial features that were otherwise overpowered. Due to the single channel of colour in x-ray images, the gradients and edges in the image constitute vital features for prediction. Using the Sobel filter to extract these features provides an opportunity to reduce the compute capability of the prediction function.

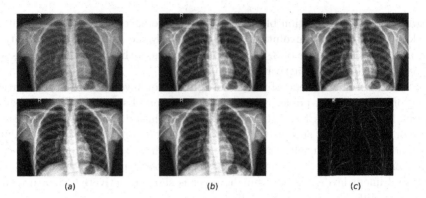

Fig. 3. (a) Histogram Equalization (b) Median Filter (c) Sobel filter

4   Results and Discussion

In this section, the impact of applying the filter pipeline and the results obtained are broadly discussed. The Data Analysis section elaborates upon the processed images and the features highlighted. While the performance analysis section provides information on results obtained while training, performance metrics of the federated system on the processed pneumonia dataset and the inference from the trends.

4.1   Data Analysis

The raw x-ray images available in the dataset even though suitable as inputs for neural networks, need to be processed to obtain optimal and practical results. The preprocessing pipeline as mentioned in the previous section encompasses three stages - equalisation of feature prominence, denoising and feature extraction. Figure 3 depicts the effects of the filters used in the three mentioned stages. Upon histogram equalisation, the features become more notable and a sharp contrast between dominant features can be ascertained. Furthermore, in case of anomalous exposure or illumination, histogram equalisation can re-illuminate the grayscale image to improve feature representation and improve prediction performance. The median filter uses a kernel size of 7 to denoise the image. This is a necessary step to avoid noisy pixels contributing to illegitimate features. Additionally, the median filter maintains the sharpness of the dominant features thus not contributing to feature degradation as is common with other kinds of denoising filters. Finally, the Sobel filter extracts the edges of the features reducing complexity and increasing the density of relevant information for the model to process.

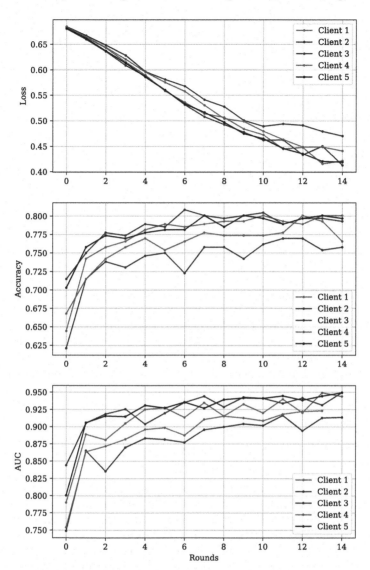

Fig. 4. Performance of 5 clients based on AUC, Accuracy and loss.

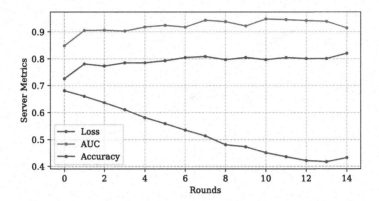

Fig. 5. Overall Server Model Performance

4.2 Performance Analysis

The Federated Learning system with a uniquely distributed preprocessed dataset is trained and simulated on an Ubuntu 20.04 local system accelerated by an Nvidia RTX 3060 Mobile GPU. The overall training of the FL system has been characterised by the combination of metrics from the server model and the client model. The server and the client models have been tested on random subsets of the preprocessed dataset and evaluated based on Binary Cross-entropy Error (3), Area under the Receiver Operating Characteristic (ROC) curve and mean accuracy. For the simulation, the FL system has been trained for 15 rounds with 20 clients with each client training for 2 epochs per round.

$$H(p, q) = -\sum_i p_i \, log(q_i) \tag{3}$$

Since the subset of the data for each client in the Federated System has been randomly assigned, the data from one client to another varies in size, selection, order and other regularising factors. This ensures that each client is distinct and the training characteristics are diverse. Figure 4 represents the trends in the performance metrics of 5 random clients from the client pool. Even though there is a discernible difference in individual client performance, the final binary cross-entropy loss tends to settle at around 0.43 and the trends in test accuracy and AUC scores follow a healthy training curve and settle at around 0.777 and 0.926 respectively.

The server performance plotted in Fig. 5 highlights a gradual increase in the accuracy and AUC score, while there is a characteristic concave drop in the binary cross-entropy loss indicating that there are general features that the entire system is learning as a whole. There is a noticeable drop in performance in the server as compared to the clients at the end of every round. This behaviour can be attributed to global information generalisation in the server as compared to the client that personalises the local data to a high degree with higher performance as a goal.

The CNN architecture used in the application to train on the dataset has 7,676,465 parameters. Observing the client and server graphs, we can infer that the training curve is smooth and the trend fluctuation with respect to the accuracy and AUC values is minimal.

The images available in the dataset have minimal feature clarity and unclear edges. These have been overcome using the preprocessing steps supported by the CNN model.

5 Conclusion and Future Scope

In this paper, we have successfully benchmarked the Optical Coherence Tomography and Chest X-ray image dataset for pneumonia detection using Federated Learning. The server and client models both are able to reach an approximate accuracy score of 0.8 and an AUC score of 0.93. The proposed architecture is built to provide straightforward processing and development steps with the much-required in-depth analysis of a pneumonia dataset. The FL architecture helps broaden the scope of the algorithm as well as secure the private data of patients or hospitals.

Although the work implements pneumonia detection in an FL setup, more experimentation can be done with a much higher number of clients, other state-of-the-art architectures such as VGG or ResNet, and even image processing filters. The number of training rounds can be increased on further research with a larger dataset. Since the algorithm performs similarly for client and server models, the efficiency of client training can be improved upon. Other federated aggregation algorithms can be tested on the dataset too. The researchers can also explore integrating FL with explainable artificial intelligence and also digital, twins [8,14,51].

References

1. Adiba, F.I., et al.: Effect of corpora on classification of fake news using naive bayes classifier. Int. J. Autom. Artif. Intell. Mach. Learn. **1**(1), 80–92 (2020)
2. Agrawal, S., et al.: Federated learning for intrusion detection system: concepts, challenges and future directions. Comput. Commun. **195**, 346–361 (2022)
3. Ahmed, S., Hossain, M., Nur, S.B., Shamim Kaiser, M., Mahmud, M., et al.: Toward machine learning-based psychological assessment of autism spectrum disorders in school and community. In: Proceedings of TEHI, pp. 139–149 (2022)
4. Ahmed, S., et al.: Artificial intelligence and machine learning for ensuring security in smart cities. In: Data-Driven Mining, Learning and Analytics for Secured Smart Cities, pp. 23–47 (2021)
5. Akhund, N.U., et al.: Adeptness: Alzheimer's disease patient management system using pervasive sensors-early prototype and preliminary results. In: Proceedings of Brain Information, pp. 413–422 (2018)
6. Al Banna, M., Ghosh, T., Taher, K.A., Kaiser, M.S., Mahmud, M., et al.: A monitoring system for patients of autism spectrum disorder using artificial intelligence. In: Proceedings of Brain Informatics, pp. 251–262 (2020)

7. AlArjani, A., et al.: Application of mathematical modeling in prediction of covid-19 transmission dynamics. Arab. J. Sci. Eng. **47**, 1–24 (2022)
8. Alazab, M., et al.: Digital twins for healthcare 4.0-recent advances, architecture, and open challenges. IEEE Cons. Electron. Maga. (2022)
9. Antunes, R.S., André da Costa, C., Küderle, A., Yari, I.A., Eskofier, B.: Federated learning for healthcare: systematic review and architecture proposal. ACM Trans. Intell. Syst. Technol. (TIST) **13**(4), 1–23 (2022)
10. Bhapkar, H.R., et al.: Rough sets in covid-19 to predict symptomatic cases. In: COVID-19: Prediction, Decision-Making, and its Impacts, pp. 57–68 (2021)
11. Biswas, M., Kaiser, M.S., Mahmud, M., Al Mamun, S., Hossain, M., Rahman, M.A., et al.: An xai based autism detection: the context behind the detection. In: Proceedings of Brain Informatics, pp. 448–459 (2021)
12. Biswas, M., et al.: Accu3rate: a mobile health application rating scale based on user reviews. PloS one **16**(12), e0258050 (2021)
13. Biswas, M., et al.: Indoor navigation support system for patients with neurodegenerative diseases. In: Proceedings of Brain Informatics, pp. 411–422 (2021)
14. Chengoden, R., et al.: Metaverse for healthcare: a survey on potential applications, challenges and future directions. arXiv preprint arXiv:2209.04160 (2022)
15. Dey, N., Zhang, Y.D., Rajinikanth, V., Pugalenthi, R., Raja, N.S.M.: Customized vgg19 architecture for pneumonia detection in chest x-rays. Pattern Recogn. Lett. **143**, 67–74 (2021)
16. Farhin, F., Kaiser, M.S., Mahmud, M.: Towards secured service provisioning for the internet of healthcare things. In: Proceedings of AICT, pp. 1–6 (2020)
17. Farhin, F., Kaiser, M.S., Mahmud, M.: Secured smart healthcare system: blockchain and bayesian inference based approach. In: Proceedinsg of TCCE, pp. 455–465 (2021)
18. Feki, I., Ammar, S., Kessentini, Y., Muhammad, K.: Federated learning for covid-19 screening from chest x-ray images. Appl. Soft Comput. **106**, 107330 (2021)
19. Ghosh, T., et al.: Artificial intelligence and internet of things in screening and management of autism spectrum disorder. Sustain. Cities Soc. **74**, 103189 (2021)
20. Ikechukwu, A.V., Murali, S., Deepu, R., Shivamurthy, R.: Resnet-50 vs vgg-19 vs training from scratch: a comparative analysis of the segmentation and classification of pneumonia from chest x-ray images. Glob. Transit. Proc. **2**(2), 375–381 (2021)
21. Islam, N., et al.: Towards machine learning based intrusion detection in iot networks. Comput. Mater. Contin **69**(2), 1801–1821 (2021)
22. Jaiswal, A.K., Tiwari, P., Kumar, S., Gupta, D., Khanna, A., Rodrigues, J.J.: Identifying pneumonia in chest x-rays: a deep learning approach. Measurement **145**, 511–518 (2019)
23. Jesmin, S., Kaiser, M.S., Mahmud, M.: Artificial and internet of healthcare things based alzheimer care during covid 19. In: Proceedings of Brain Information, pp. 263–274 (2020)
24. Kaiser, M.S., et al.: 6g access network for intelligent internet of healthcare things: opportunity, challenges, and research directions. In: Proceedings of TCCE, pp. 317–328 (2021)
25. Kermany, D., Zhang, K., Goldbaum, M., et al.: Labeled optical coherence tomography (oct) and chest x-ray images for classification. Mendeley Data **2**(2), 651 (2018)
26. Khan, S.H., Alam, M.G.R.: A federated learning approach to pneumonia detection. In: 2021 International Conference on Engineering and Emerging Technologies (ICEET), pp. 1–6. IEEE (2021)

27. Khan, W., Zaki, N., Ali, L.: Intelligent pneumonia identification from chest x-rays: a systematic literature review. IEEE Access **9**, 51747–51771 (2021)
28. Kumar, S., et al.: Forecasting major impacts of covid-19 pandemic on country-driven sectors: challenges, lessons, and future roadmap. Pers. Ubiquitous Comput., 1–24 (2021)
29. Kundu, R., Das, R., Geem, Z.W., Han, G.T., Sarkar, R.: Pneumonia detection in chest x-ray images using an ensemble of deep learning models. Plos One **16**(9), e0256630 (2021)
30. Mahmud, M., Kaiser, M.S.: Machine learning in fighting pandemics: a covid-19 case study. In: COVID-19: Prediction, Decision-Making, and its Impacts, pp. 77–81 (2021)
31. Mahmud, M., Kaiser, M.S., McGinnity, T.M., Hussain, A.: Deep learning in mining biological data. Cogn. Comput. **13**(1), 1–33 (2021)
32. Mahmud, M., Kaiser, M.S., Hussain, A., Vassanelli, S.: Applications of deep learning and reinforcement learning to biological data. IEEE Trans. Neural Netw. Learn. Syst. **29**(6), 2063–2079 (2018)
33. Mahmud, M., et al.: Towards explainable and privacy-preserving artificial intelligence for personalisation in autism spectrum disorder. In: Proceedings of HCII, pp. 356–370 (2022)
34. Manickam, A., Jiang, J., Zhou, Y., Sagar, A., Soundrapandiyan, R., Samuel, R.D.J.: Automated pneumonia detection on chest x-ray images: a deep learning approach with different optimizers and transfer learning architectures. Measurement **184**, 109953 (2021)
35. Nahiduzzaman, M., et al.: Machine learning based early fall detection for elderly people with neurological disorder using multimodal data fusion. In: Proceedings of Brain Information, pp. 204–214 (2020)
36. Nawar, A., et al.: Cross-content recommendation between movie and book using machine learning. In: Proceedings of AICT, pp. 1–6 (2021)
37. Naz, S., Phan, K.T., Chen, Y.P.P.: A comprehensive review of federated learning for covid-19 detection. Int. J. Intell. Syst. **37**(3), 2371–2392 (2022)
38. Noor, M.B.T., Zenia, N.Z., Kaiser, M.S., Mamun, S.A., Mahmud, M.: Application of deep learning in detecting neurological disorders from magnetic resonance images: a survey on the detection of alzheimer's disease, parkinson's disease and schizophrenia. Brain Inf. **7**(1), 1–21 (2020)
39. Özsoy, Y., Taşkin, D.: Comparison of deep learning models alexnet and googlenet in detection of pneumonia and covid19. In: 2021 International Conference on Engineering and Emerging Technologies (ICEET), pp. 1–3. IEEE (2021)
40. Paul, A., et al.: Inverted bell-curve-based ensemble of deep learning models for detection of covid-19 from chest x-rays. Neural Comput. Appl., 1–15 (2022)
41. Prakash, N., et al.: Deep transfer learning for covid-19 detection and infection localization with superpixel based segmentation. Sustain. Cities Soc. **75**, 103252 (2021)
42. Rabby, G., Azad, S., Mahmud, M., Zamli, K.Z., Rahman, M.M.: Teket: a tree-based unsupervised keyphrase extraction technique. Cogn. Comput. **12**(4), 811–833 (2020)
43. Rabby, G., et al.: A flexible keyphrase extraction technique for academic literature. Procedia Comput. Sci. **135**, 553–563 (2018)
44. Rahman, M.A., Brown, D.J., Shopland, N., Burton, A., Mahmud, M.: Explainable multimodal machine learning for engagement analysis by continuous performance test. In: Proceedings of HCII, pp. 386–399 (2022)

45. Rahman, M.A., et al.: Towards machine learning driven self-guided virtual reality exposure therapy based on arousal state detection from multimodal data. In: Proceedings of Brain Informations, pp. 195–209 (2022)
46. Rehman, M.U., et al.: A novel chaos-based privacy-preserving deep learning model for cancer diagnosis. IEEE Trans. Netw. Sci. Eng. **9**, 4322–4337 (2022)
47. Satu, M.S., et al.: Short-term prediction of covid-19 cases using machine learning models. Appl. Sci. **11**(9), 4266 (2021)
48. Sumi, A.I., et al.: fassert: a fuzzy assistive system for children with autism using internet of things. In: Proceedings of Brain Information, pp. 403–412 (2018)
49. Taheri, R., Shojafar, M., Alazab, M., Tafazolli, R.: Fed-iiot: a robust federated malware detection architecture in industrial iot. IEEE Trans. Ind. Inf. **17**(12), 8442–8452 (2020)
50. Talo, M.: Pneumonia detection from radiography images using convolutional neural networks. In: Proceedings of SIU, pp. 1–4 (2019)
51. Wang, S., Qureshi, M.A., Miralles-Pechuaán, L., Huynh-The, T., Gadekallu, T.R., Liyanage, M.: Explainable AI for b5g/6g: technical aspects, use cases, and research challenges. arXiv preprint arXiv:2112.04698 (2021)
52. Zaman, S., et al.: Security threats and artificial intelligence based countermeasures for internet of things networks: a comprehensive survey. IEEE Access **9**, 94668–94690 (2021)

Towards Automated Segmentation of Human Abdominal Aorta and Its Branches Using a Hybrid Feature Extraction Module with LSTM

Bo Zhang[1], Shiqi Liu[2], Xiaoliang Xie[2], Xiaohu Zhou[2],
Zengguang Hou[1,2,3]✉, Meng Song[2,3], Xiyao Ma[2,3], and Linsen Zhang[1,2]

[1] University of Science and Technology Beijing, Beijing 100083, China
[2] State Key Laboratory of Management and Control for Complex Systems,
Institute of Automation, Chinese Academy of Sciences, Beijing 100190, China
zengguang.hou@ia.ac.cn
[3] University of Chinese Academy of Sciences, Beijing 100049, China

Abstract. Abdominal aortic aneurysm (AAA) is a disease with high rates of morbidity and mortality. For AAA treatment, appropriately covered stents are placed to prevent blood from entering the aneurysm. Before the interventional procedure, the morphology of the abdominal arteries (the aorta and its branches) is of the utmost importance to formulate surgical plans and prepare surgical instruments. Due to accurate vessel measurements, in particular, custom-made fenestrated stent grafts and chimney stent grafts are widely used for complicated AAAs. Therefore, rapid and accurate reconstruction of the vascular from CTA images is necessary. In this study, we proposed a novel network for automated segmentation of the human abdominal aorta and its branches. The hybrid feature extraction module, which combines convolution and transformer, represents intra-frame vessel feature information well. And the inter-frame vessel structure information is extracted by a special attention mechanism that includes the LSTM module. The results of 38 patients' CTA image sequences show that the proposed network achieves state-of-the-art performance. The proposed method can assist physicians with preoperative diagnosis.

Keywords: Abdominal Aortic Aneurysm · Segmentation · Computed Tomography Angiography

1 Introduction

Computed tomography angiography (CTA) is one of the most commonly used imaging techniques for vascular evaluation [1–3]. Obtaining morphological information and the location of vascular openings from CTA images is a critical step for successful abdominal aortic aneurysm (AAA) repair surgery [4]. Preoperative CTA information can assist doctors in planning the surgical path and selecting

M. Tanveer et al. (Eds.): ICONIP 2022, CCIS 1794, pp. 357–368, 2023.
https://doi.org/10.1007/978-981-99-1648-1_30

appropriate surgical instruments to prevent blood from entering the aneurysm. The size of the stent used for AAAs determines whether there will be type I or type II endoleak after surgery, which has a significant impact on the prognosis of the surgery [4,5]. Therefore, the premise for AAA treatment is the rapid and accurate assessment of vessel morphology in CTA images.

Currently, some commercial medical imaging software provides the function of image editing, segmentation, and modeling by manual or interactive methods. However, the problem is that it's time-consuming and laborious to use. In order to solve this problem, Kosasih et al. proposed an automatic aortic segmentation method using active contour models [6]. Siriapisith et al. proposed a 3D segmentation method that exploits the concept of variable neighborhood search based on voxel intensities and gradients [7]. According to the CT value(HU), Caradu et al. used a semi-automatic segmentation method for AAA [8]. There is a growing interest in applications of deep learning in medical image analysis. Some groups used a 3D convolutional neural network(CNN) to realize the segmentation of abdominal aortic vessels [9,10]. Fantazzini et al. and Habijan et al. proposed three single-view CNNs to effectively segment the aortic lumen from axial, sagittal, and coronal planes [11,12]. Based on CNN, the novel networks were proposed by introducing attention-gating or other advantages of modules [13,14]. Moreover, by combining deep learning and traditional image analysis, higher accuracy of the automatic segmentation also has been achieved [1,15].

Despite the fact that many methods achieve vessel segmentation, there are still numerous challenges. (1) The CTA image sequence is volumetric data. The majority of segmentation methods only used 2D convolutional segmentation network, resulting in a significant loss of information on the 3D structure of blood vessels. (2) The branches of the abdominal aorta, such as renal arteries and the celiac artery, deliver oxygenated blood to the human vital organs. The stent reserves appropriate fenestrations (holes) or a chimney configuration in abdominal aorta surgery, which significantly improves the success rate [16]. Existing segmentation methods can only extract the aorta and cannot accurately extract important branches, which may lead to insufficient surgical planning information and surgical failure. (3) Blood vessels are a small fraction of the volumetric data. The large variation in cross-sectional size of blood vessels and background remains an issue in CTA images.

To address the issues raised above, we present an automated abdominal artery vessels segmentation network based on CTA images. In this study, convolution and transformer are combined in the hybrid feature extraction module to increase the receptive field size and learn more information about discrete aortic branches. Furthermore, in order to extract inter-frame information from the CTA series, a special attention mechanism with the LSTM module is used. It can fully utilize 3D spatial information. Gradient Harmonizing Mechanism (GHM) loss is used to correct the imbalance between vessel and background. Finally, the images of the abdominal aorta and its branches are accurately segmented.

Contributions and Novelties. (1) The vessels of the abdominal artery are precisely segmented, including not only the aorta but also its branches such as the renal arteries and the celiac artery. (2) The problem of 3D information loss caused by 2D convolution is solved, and inter-frame information fusion improves segmentation accuracy even further. (3) Using a hybrid structure based on convolution and transformer, better feature representation and receptive field are learned, which further achieves the segmentation results of branch vessels.

2   Method

The overview of the proposed network is shown in Fig. 1. The novel network has an encoder-decoder architecture in which the green region is the encoder and the blue region is the decoder. The input(the shape is H × W) is processed in two parallel branches. In the one branch, the image is split into a series of patches(patches size is 4 × 4). And in the other branch, the image shape is downsampled to H/4 × W/4 by convolution and max-pooling in the downsampling module. Then, the two parts are concatenated together and fed into hybrid feature extraction module. Furthermore, in the first hybrid module, the LSTM module participates in the calculation for getting inter-frame information. In the decoder part, the convolution and upsampling layer are used, and expand the low-resolution feature and the high-resolution feature into the same size (H/4 × W/4). Then, these features are sent into the channel attention module, the expanding layer, and the liner projection. Finally, the vessels are segmented from the original CTA images.

2.1   Patch Embedding and Downsampling Module

As the input of the network, all the CTA series were exported to H×W pixel size(512×512). In this part, the images are processed in two parallel branches. In the one branch, as the preprocess of the transformer, one frame is split into a series of patches with 4×4 size. In the other branch, for the same shape of the output, the same operation is used twice including convolution, max-pooling, batch normal, and ReLU activation function. The output shape is B×H/4×W/4×2C (B is the batch size, C is the embedding dimension).

2.2   Hybrid Feature Module

As the popular segmentation methods currently, many researchers used convolution and attention modules in their works. But the two methods are different. Convolution is a local operation that only models the relationship between neighboring pixels. However, the transformer is a global operation modeling the relationship among all pixels. Since they can complement each other, we adopted those two operations to obtain thorough information in this part. In order to utilize the vascular structure information between frames, the LSTM module is used. In Fig. 2, the structure of the hybrid feature layer is shown in detail.

In every hybrid feature module, the input is sent to Trans-block branch and Conv-block branch separately. In the first hybrid module, the input of the Trans-block branch comes from a part of the patch embedding module(the shape is

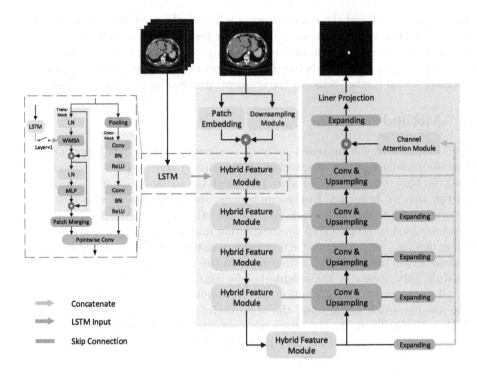

Fig. 1. The novel net for CTA image segmentation.

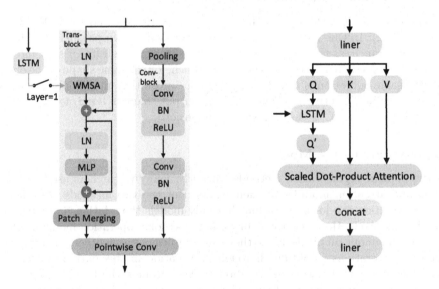

Fig. 2. The structure of the hybrid feature module.

Fig. 3. The flow work of WMSA with LSTM.

B×H/4×W/4×C) and the input of Conv-block branch is from the other part of the downsampling module(the shape is B×H/4×W/4×C). The other hybrid modules' input is the output of the up layer.

In Trans-block, the multi-head attention mechanism module is used to obtain the target and global image relationship, including liner, window based self-attention(WMSA), and multilayer perceptron(MLP) module with the residual connection. Especially, a novel part is used to improve network performance in the Trans-block of the first hybrid feature module. In CTA series, the previous frame is similar to the next. We used LSTM to realize information extraction between adjacent frames in our net. The detailed flow work is shown in Fig. 3.

Compared with the general WMSA, the Q values of the adjacent eight frames are processed in the LSTM module. When a weight information Q is put into the module, the output Q' combines the current frame's information with the near frames' information.

In Conv-block, local features are extracted by max-pooling layer and the same operation twice(including convolution, batch normal, and ReLu activation function). In the end, the pointwise convolution is used to generate a new feature map.

2.3 Decoder Part

In the decoder, we put both the output of the deeper layer and the feature map of the same layer from the encoder into every convolution and upsampling layer. The detailed flow work is shown in Fig. 4. The module includes the same operation twice(including convolution, batch normal, and ReLU activation function) and one upsampling layer(bilinear upsampling).

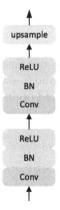

Fig. 4. The detail flow work of the convolution and upsampling layer.

After four calculations in upsampling layers, the four results are obtained. The results and the deepest layer's output are expanded to the same size respectively (the size is H/4×W/4 and the number of channels does not change).

And then, a channel attention module is used. In the module, the more crucial information about channels can be given higher weights among feature maps with different depths. In the end, the expanding and liner layer is used to restore to H×W size and get the vessel image.

2.4 Loss

In CTA images, the target area is imbalanced from the non-target area. The abdominal aortic vessels only comprise a small part of the overall image. The narrow blood vessels are more severe. In this part, Gradient Harmonizing Mechanism loss function (L_{GHM}) is used to solve the problem.

$$L_{GHM} = \sum_{i=1}^{N} \frac{CE\left(p_i, p_i^*\right)}{GD\left(g_i\right)} \tag{1}$$

where $CE\left(p_i, p_i^*\right)$ represents the cross-entropy loss of the i_{th} sample and $GD\left(g_i\right)$ represents the gradient density of the i_{th} sample as:

$$GD(g) = \frac{1}{l(g)} \sum_{k=1}^{N} \delta\left(g_k, g\right) \tag{2}$$

$$g = |p - p^*| = \begin{cases} 1 - p, \text{ if } p^* = 1 \\ p, \text{ if } p^* = 0 \end{cases} \tag{3}$$

where $GD(g)$ is the gradient density at the g gradient position, $l(g)$ is the length in $\left[g - \frac{\varepsilon}{2}, g + \frac{\varepsilon}{2}\right]$, and $\delta\left(g_k, g\right)$ is the gradient g_k in $\left[g - \frac{\varepsilon}{2}, g + \frac{\varepsilon}{2}\right]$ or not.

2.5   Performance Evaluation Metrics

We evaluated our model by using two metrics: mean dice and mean HD95. The dice coefficient is the most frequently used metric in medical image competitions. It is an ensemble similarity measure and is usually used to calculate the similarity between two samples, with a threshold of $[0, 1]$. The best result of segmentation is 1, and the worst is 0. In this paper, the mean dice is as follows:

$$dice = \frac{2|X \cap Y|}{|X| + |Y|} \tag{4}$$

$$mean \; dice = \frac{1}{n} \sum dice \tag{5}$$

where X is the collection of predictive values, Y is the collection of the ground truth, and n is the number of samples.

Dice is more sensitive to the inner filling of the mask, while Hausdorff distance (HD) is more sensitive to the segmented boundary. The HD is

$$d_H(X, Y) = \max\left\{d_{XY}, d_{YX}\right\} = \max\left\{\max_{x \in X} \min_{y \in Y} d(x, y), \max_{y \in Y} \min_{x \in X} d(x, y)\right\} \quad (6)$$

where 95%HD (HD95) is similar to maximum HD. However, it is based on the calculation of the 95th percentile of the distances between boundary points in X and Y. And the mean HD95 is

$$mean\ HD95 = \frac{1}{n}\sum HD95 \quad (7)$$

where n is the number of samples.

3   Results and Discussion

3.1   Clinical Data and Hardware

The clinical CTA data were collected from the department of radiology, Peking Union Medical College Hospital. The study protocol was approved by the Ethics Committee of the hospital. The methods were carried out in accordance with the approved guidelines and regulations. All the images are real abdominal CTA data from 38 patients. CTA examinations were performed on two CT scanners (made by Philips and Siemens). The age of patients is from 47 to 87, including 23 males and 15 females.

Among the collected 38 cases, 36 patients' data is randomly divided into the training set and the remaining 2 patients' are testing set. All the patients' CTA data is exported to images with the size of 512×512. The training set includes 8769 images, and the testing set includes 520 images. The proposed net is achieved based on Python 3.8.12. All experiments were conducted under the Pytorch frameworks using an NVIDIA V100 TENSOR CORE GPU.

3.2   Experiment Results and Discussion

The proposed net is trained using GHM loss with the Adam optimizer and a batch size of 8. The learning rate was set to 0.001. The network was trained for a total of 100 epochs. Compared with the existing approaches, the proposed method has a better segmentation result in CTA image (Table 1). Ours gets the best result in mean dice and the second-best result in mean HD95. The results of the Swin-Unet are far worse than other methods, probably because the images are downscaled and upscaled. We can not get any result if the input size is modified to 512 in the net.

As illustrated in Fig. 5, it shows the results of using different segmentation methods and ours is better than others intuitively for the same CTA image. Besides, we used the VTK software to reconstruct the 3D model by segmentation results. The 3D models show the overall results of different methods in Fig. 6. For most of these methods, the abdominal aorta and common iliac artery can be segmented clearly. For The celiac artery and its branches, our method is as good as Swin-Unet and much better than others. On the renal artery, the method

Table 1. The results of ours and existing approaches.

Methods	Mean dice	Mean HD95
U-Net [17]	0.8537	16.83
U-Net++ [18]	0.8345	**16.34**
TransUNet [19]	0.9038	17.97
Swin-Unet [20]*	0.8041	31.76
Ours	**0.9109**	16.65

*: The images were resized to 224 for training and testing, and expanded the results to 512 for calculating mean dice and mean HD95.

of U-Net++ and TransUNet is difficult to get the vessel. From the second and third columns in Fig. 5, our segmentation results are the best. Furthermore, for this patient, there are two left renal arteries and one is much thinner than the other in Fig. 6 A. Only our proposed method achieves a good result. In Fig. 6 E, there are more error results on small vessels around the abdominal aorta. Our proposed method outperforms other methods in vascular structure and small vessel segmentation.

We designed ablation experiments to validate the main parts of the network in Table 2. Compared B with A and C, LSTM plays an important role in segmentation. Some vessels are not segmented if not using the LSTM module. For the channel attention module in B and E, the mean dice score increased by 3 points and the mean HD95 of E is much better. It shows that there are more advantages to segmentation details. Besides, in D and E, we changed the number of Trans-block in every layer. Using two blocks (including shift window which is similar to Swin-Unet) in the net, the score is lower than using one block. The reason is LSTM module may be affected by the shift window.

Table 2. The ablation experiments.

Group	LSTM	channel attention	Trans-block number	mean dice	mean HD95
A*			1	0.7275	20.25
B	✓		1	0.8747	24.36
C*		✓	1	0.7579	20.36
D	✓	✓	2	0.8988	18.48
E	✓	✓	1	0.9109	16.65

*: Some images are not segmented

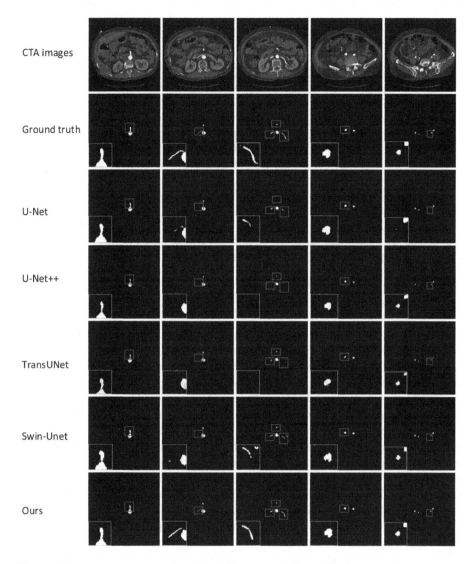

Fig. 5. The segmentation results with different methods on CTA images and the parts in green are zoomed in. (Color figure online)

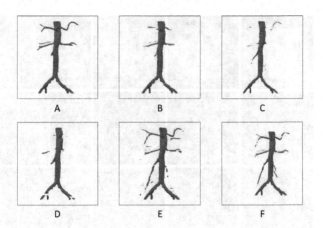

Fig. 6. The 3D models reconstructed by different segmentation results on one patient. A: Ground truth; B: U-Net; C: U-Net++; D: TransUNet; E: Swin-Unet; F: Ours.

4   Conclusion

The study proposed a novel segmentation network to achieve automated abdominal arteries segmentation in CTA images. By utilizing 3D structural information, the network can achieve accurate extraction of the aorta and its branches in CTA images. The LSTM module is used in conjunction with a special attention mechanism to obtain inter-frame information on vessel construction in series images, resulting in more accurate vessel segmentation. To improve the segmentation performance of branching blood vessels, the hybrid feature extraction module(convolution combined with a transformer module) can extract more feature information and a better receptive field. In this study, validation was performed on a physician-annotated dataset and the best results were obtained. In ablation experiments, it also confirmed the advanced nature of each part in the network. The key information of AAA surgery can be quickly extracted using this method, which can help doctors make accurate planning, select appropriate surgical instruments, and improve surgery success rates. In the future, we will investigate the relationship between vessel morphology and stents in order to directly select stents, reduce the difficulty of preoperative planning, and improve success rates even further.

Acknowledgements. This work was supported in part by the National Natural Science Foundation of China under Grant 62073325, and Grant U1913210; in part by the National Key Research and Development Program of China under Grant 2019YFB1311700; in part by the Youth Innovation Promotion Association of CAS under Grant 2020140; in part by the National Natural Science Foundation of China under Grant 62003343; in part by the Beijing Natural Science Foundation under Grant M22008.

References

1. Lareyre, F., Adam, C., Carrier, M., Raffort, J.: Automated segmentation of the human abdominal vascular system using a hybrid approach combining expert system and supervised deep learning. J. Clin. Med. **10**(15), 3347 (2021)
2. Moccia, S., De Momi, E., El Hadji, S., Mattos, L.S.: Blood vessel segmentation algorithms-review of methods, datasets and evaluation metrics. Comput. Methods Prog. Biomed. **158**, 71–91 (2018)
3. Wanhainen, A., et al.: Editor's choice-european society for vascular surgery (esvs) 2019 clinical practice guidelines on the management of abdominal aorto-iliac artery aneurysms. Eur. J. Vasc. Endovasc. Surg. **57**(1), 8–93 (2019)
4. Chaikof, E.L., et al.: The society for vascular surgery practice guidelines on the care of patients with an abdominal aortic aneurysm. J. Vasc. Surg. **67**(1), 2–77 (2018)
5. Sénémaud, J.N., et al.: Intraoperative adverse events and early outcomes of custom-made fenestrated stent grafts and physician-modified stent grafts for complex aortic aneurysms. J. Vasc. Surg. **71**(6), 1834–1842 (2020)
6. Kosasih, R.: Automatic segmentation of abdominal aortic aneurism (aaa) by using active contour models. Sci. J. Inf. **7**(1), 66–74 (2020)
7. Siriapisith, T., Kusakunniran, W., Haddawy, P.: 3d segmentation of exterior wall surface of abdominal aortic aneurysm from ct images using variable neighborhood search. Comput. Biol. Med. **107**, 73–85 (2019)
8. Caradu, C., Spampinato, B., Vrancianu, A.M., B'erard, X., Ducasse, E.: Fully automatic volume segmentation of infrarenal abdominal aortic aneurysm computed tomography images with deep learning approaches versus physician controlled manual segmentation. J. Vasc. Surg. **74**(1), 246–256 (2021)
9. López-Linares, K., García, I., García-Familiar, A., Macía, I., Ballester, M.A.G.: 3d convolutional neural network for abdominal aortic aneurysm segmentation. arXiv preprint arXiv:1903.00879 (2019)
10. Fedotova, Y., Epifanov, R.U., Karpenko, A., Mullyadzhanov, R.: Automatically hemodynamic analysis of aaa from ct images based on deep learning and cfd approaches. In: Journal of Physics: Conference Series, vol 2119, p. 012069. IOP Publishing (2021)
11. Fantazzini, A., et al.: 3d automatic segmentation of aortic computed tomography angiography combining multi-view 2d convolutional neural networks. Cardiovasc. Eng. Technol. **11**(5), 576–586 (2020)
12. Habijan, M., Gali'c, I., Leventi'c, H., Romi'c, K., Babin, D.: Abdominal aortic aneurysm segmentation from ct images using modified 3d u-net with deep supervision. In: 2020 International Symposium ELMAR, pp. 123–128. IEEE (2020)
13. Chandrashekar, A., et al.: A deep learning pipeline to automate high-resolution arterial segmentation with or without intravenous contrast. Ann. Surg. **276**, e1017–e1027 (2020)
14. Dziubich, T., Białas, P., Znaniecki, Ł, Halman, J., Brzeziński, J.: Abdominal aortic aneurysm segmentation from contrast-enhanced computed tomography angiography using deep convolutional networks. In: Bellatreche, L., et al. (eds.) TPDL/ADBIS/EDA -2020. CCIS, vol. 1260, pp. 158–168. Springer, Cham (2020). https://doi.org/10.1007/978-3-030-55814-7_13
15. Mohammadi, S., Mohammadi, M., Dehlaghi, V., Ahmadi, A.: Automatic segmentation, detection, and diagnosis of abdominal aortic aneurysm (aaa) using convolutional neural networks and hough circles algorithm. Cardiovasc. Eng. Technol. **10**(3), 490–499 (2019)

16. Anders, W., Fabio, V., Van Herzeele, I., et al.: European society for vascular surgery(esvs) 2019 clinical practice guidelines on the management of abdominal aortoiliac artery aneurysms. Eur. J. Vasc. Endovasc. Surg. **57**, 1–97 (2018)
17. Ronneberger, O., Fischer, P., Brox, T.: U-Net: convolutional networks for biomedical image segmentation. In: Navab, N., Hornegger, J., Wells, W.M., Frangi, A.F. (eds.) MICCAI 2015. LNCS, vol. 9351, pp. 234–241. Springer, Cham (2015). https://doi.org/10.1007/978-3-319-24574-4_28
18. Zhou, Z., Rahman Siddiquee, M.M., Tajbakhsh, N., Liang, J.: UNet++: a nested u-net architecture for medical image segmentation. In: Stoyanov, D., et al. (eds.) DLMIA/ML-CDS -2018. LNCS, vol. 11045, pp. 3–11. Springer, Cham (2018). https://doi.org/10.1007/978-3-030-00889-5_1
19. Chen, J., et al.: Transunet: transformers make strong encoders for medical image segmentation.arXiv preprint arXiv:2102.04306 (2021)
20. Cao, H., et al.: Swin-unet: Unet-like pure transformer for medical image segmentation. arXiv preprint arXiv:2105.05537 (2021)

P-LSTM: A Novel LSTM Architecture for Glucose Level Prediction Problem

Abhijeet Swain[1], Vaibhav Ganatra[1], Snehanshu Saha[2], Archana Mathur[3]($\boxtimes$), and Rekha Phadke[3]

[1] Department of Computer Science and Information Systems, BITS Pilani, K. K. Birla Goa Campus, India
{f20180540,f20190010}@goa.bits-pilani.ac.in
[2] Department of Computer Science and Information Systems and APPCAIR, BITS Pilani, K. K. Birla Goa Campus, India
snehanshu.saha@ieee.org
[3] Nitte Meenakshi Institute of Technology, Bangalore, India
{archana.mathur,rekha.phadke}@nmit.ac.in

Abstract. We introduce a novel LSTM architecture, parameterized LSTM (p-LSTM) which utilizes parameterized Elliott (p-Elliott) activation at the gates. The advantages of parameterization is evident in better generalization ability of the network to predict blood glucose levels of patients from a real, vetted data set. The parameter of the Elliott activation is learned from the backpropagation steps of the LSTM which reaps the benefits of learning flexible patterns from data using all features and causal features, as the parameter values change in training phase of p-LSTM. The learning of the parameter is also facilitated by fixed point methods on p-Elliott. This leads to better fit and adds explainability in prediction (due to causal features) to the blood glucose fluctuation patterns over time. The coupling of LSTM architecture with p-Elliott leads to superior prediction of glucose levels. It also provides an excellent technique to fit highly nonlinear temporal data, in comparison to the performance of state-of-the-art methods.

Keywords: p-LSTM · p-Elliott · Blood Glucose prediction · Fixed point · Prediction horizon · Causality

1 Introduction

Diabetes is a disease that potentially impedes a healthy life and causes permanent damages. About 422 million people worldwide have been detected with diabetes and possibly many more remain undetected. According to a report from WHO, 1.5 million deaths are directly attributed to diabetes each year [12]. Common symptoms of diabetes include strong feelings of hunger, feeling of thirst, frequent urination, signs of fatigue, blurry vision and delayed healing of wounds. People with Type-1 diabetes may also experience weight loss. The speed with which symptoms develop in Type-1 and Type-2 diabetes is different,

M. Tanveer et al. (Eds.): ICONIP 2022, CCIS 1794, pp. 369–380, 2023.
https://doi.org/10.1007/978-981-99-1648-1_31

where symptoms develop rapidly in Type-1 diabetes but they develop slowly in Type-2. Symptoms in Type-1 diabetes are mild enough to escape attention and if not detected and treated in time, could lead to life-threatening complications such as ketoacidosis and hypoglycemia resulting in seizures and coma. If the sugar level is not controlled and continues to remain high, long-term health problems can occur including heart and blood vessel diseases, stroke, blindness, nerve damage, kidney disease or even amputation of a foot or leg. A system with the ability to predict the glucose level in blood, especially in diabetic patients may go a long way in preventing such complications. Glucose variations in Type-1 diabetes patients occur due to various parameters such as insulin dosage, diet, lifestyle, sleep quality, stress etc. An accurate blood glucose prediction model must take such variables into account in order to predict the glucose level effectively. Hence, instead of relying on traditional Time Series Modeling Algorithms, use of novel Machine Learning and Deep Learning techniques allows for greater precision in diagnosis, delivery, and treatment.

2 Related Work

Multiple studies have been conducted in healthcare, centered around blood glucose by utilizing Machine Learning techniques. [9] uses Auto-Regressive Integrated Moving Average (ARIMA) and Support Vector Regression (SVR) models for hypoglycemia prediction. Moving Average (MA), SES and Support Vector Machine (SVM) models have been used in [11] with the models being trained on the data from the initial 7 d, and tested on data from the next 3 d. Neural Network based approaches for predicting glucose level are employed in [8,14]. In [12], the authors use a recurrent neural network model consisting of LSTM cells to predict the blood glucose levels with a prediction horizon of 30 and 60 min. The authors of [13] suggest a deep learning paradigm to predict blood glucose level upto 30 min in the future based on continuous blood glucose monitoring system data. They validate their results using Prediction Error-Grid Analysis (PRED-EGA), designed especially for glucose predictors. A shortcoming in both these models is that these are not multivariate, i.e. they use only the blood glucose history to predict the future glucose levels, and do not consider other physiological parameters (as mentioned earlier) involved in glucose dynamics. A hybrid model comprising multi-layered CNN with a modified RNN containing GRU cell and a fully-connected layer has been shown to be effective in predicting blood glucose level [17]. The model was trained on Type-1 Diabetes patient data, consisting of continuous glucose monitoring entries, carbohydrate intake and insulin information. Although the achieved results are promising, the combined use of CNN and GRU makes the model computationally intensive.

The authors of [2] tested 12 different machine learning algorithms over 13 different feature sets to predict blood-glucose levels. They suggest that diabetes diary data collected from patients is not sufficient and data should instead be collected more frequently through sensors to help improve predictions. Therefore, we use the Ohio T1DM dataset [10], which consists glucose level data collected from periodic self-monitoring as well as physiological data from a band. We use this data to train LSTM-based models to predict the blood glucose level from the physiological history of the diabetes patient. [1,3,19] show how modifications to the LSTM architecture may improve its performance. Inspired from such precedence, we modify the LSTM activation function in an attempt to achieve better performance on the problem of blood glucose level prediction.

Another common shortcoming across all the multivariate techniques described earlier is that the use of multiple physiological features in predicting the blood glucose level inevitably incorporates more noise in the training data, due to intrinsic variations in the variables. This may hinder the model efficacy, and might necessitate the use of complicated architectures for effective prediction. In order to overcome this problem and to offer explainability of the models, we use the *causal* features, a subset of the set of all features to train the LSTM model (thereby reducing the noise affecting the model performance) and compare its performance with the models trained on all features. Our contributions in this paper can be summarized as follows:

1. We introduce the novel parameterised Eliott activation function, which is the parameterised version of the Elliott activation function. We show, theoretically and experimentally, the suitability of parameterized Elliott function as an adaptive activation function, when compared with existing activation functions such as the tanh function.
2. We modify the LSTM architecture, where we replace the activation function of the LSTM gates (input, forget and output) with the Elliott and parameterized Elliott activation functions and compare their performance against their tanh counterparts (tanh and parametric-tanh). We save 'parameter-tuning' efforts by learning it from backpropagation and fixed point theory.
3. We identify the causal features in the training data and demonstrate their utility by comparing the performance of the same model architecture when trained on all the features to that trained on only the causal features.

3 Methodology

3.1 A Novel Activation Function: Motivation

Current approaches of choosing a suitable Activation Function (AF) for classification task do not derive from data patterns i.e. it is still a brute-force procedure where past evidence of well-performing activation functions are tried. Since activation functions are supposed to be universal approximators over a single hidden layer or multi-hidden layer neural networks, RelU, sigmoid or tanh are popular choices as they are known to approximate unknown non-linearities well. If this approach somehow fails, a different AF is tested on the network, till the network learns to approximate the ideal function. Another approach is to investigate several activation functions together on the data and pick the one which performs best. To the best of our knowledge, insights on 'learning' the best-performing AF is not available in literature, except for the standard smoothness or saturation properties AFs are supposed to possess. It is therefore worthwhile to investigate possibilities of learning an AF within a framework or architecture which uses the inherent patterns and variances from data. The possibilities of such an approach could save significant time and effort for tuning the model and also opens up avenues for discovering essential features of not-so-popular AFs. The inherent idea is to consider a 'fixed-form' activation and parameterize it. *The parameter is 'learned' via the backpropagation step of the LSTM network such that the shape of the activation, determined by the parameter, is learned from data. Thus, if the dataset changes, so does the final form of the activation.*

This approach is seldom explored in literature. The more common approach is the use of several activation functions. Authors of [4] studied the performance of 23 different Activation Functions using them in LSTM models. The performance was evaluated by testing the model on IMDB, Movie Review and MNIST classification datasets. They found that the Elliott Activation Function performed the best among the 23 functions tested. In [15], the authors study the effect of different activation functions and optimizers on predicting stock prices. They used Linear Regression, Support Vector Regression and LSTM to predict stock prices. They observed that LSTM performed better compared to the other models, and changing activation function from the standard tanh seemed to improve the results. However, in our approach, since the activation function is determined from data, it is intrinsically designed to accommodate variances in data which leads to better fitting and stability in training. This is exactly what we observe in the empirical investigation. We call this activation function as parameterized Elliott (p-Elliott).

3.2   Structure of P-LSTM

LSTM is widely applied on multiple domains, and the major difference with the recurrent neural network is that LSTM has a complex memory cell in the hidden layer. A single LSTM block is composed of four major components: an input gate, a forget gate, an output gate, and a cell state. We have applied the Elliott function as activation and recurrent activation function. The below equation represents the Elliott function

$$f(x) = \frac{0.5x}{1 + |x|} + 0.5 \tag{1}$$

and the first order derivative of the Elliott function is

$$f'(x) = \frac{0.5}{(|x| + 1)^2} \tag{2}$$

There are multiple reasons to implement the Elliott function instead of other activation functions. Some of the reasons and salient features of the Elliott activation function are (A) The function's derivative saturates as the $|x|$ increases. However, the saturation rate is less than other activation functions, such as tanh and (B) Elliott function requires less computation in comparison to tanh function. Let us discuss on the major components and the relevant forward propagation equation.

– Forget gate: A forget gate is responsible for how much information should be kept from the previous step. The outcome of the forget gate is represented as f_t, $f_t = Elliott(W_f * [h_{t-1}, x_t] + b_f)$. The forget gate based on x_t (current input) and h_{t-1} decides how much information should be considered from the previous state c_{t-1} using the equation $f_t * c_{t-1}$

– Input gate: This gate determines what new information it is going to store in the cell state. The output of the input gate is $i_t = Elliott(W_i * [h_{t-1}, x_t] + b_i)$. Next an Elliott layer which creates a vector $\hat{c}_t$ is combined with i_t to decide the information to store in cell. $\hat{c}_t$ is represented by the equation: $\hat{c}_t = Elliott(W_c * [h_{t-1}, x_t] + b_c)$.

– Cell state: It is the memory of the LSTM. The cell state is updated by the following equation: $C_t = f_t * C_{t-1} + i_t * \hat{c}_t$

– The outcome of this gate is o_t. The output gate state is described by the following equation: $o_t = Elliott(W_o * [h_{t-1}, x_t] + b_o)$. The cell state is passed through the Elliott function and combined with the output o_t to produce the h_t. The final output h_t is $o_t * Elliott(C_t)$.

For backward propagation, it is required to compute the derivatives for all major components of the LSTM. J is the cost function and the relationship between v_t and hidden state h_t is $v_t = w_v * h_t + b_v$. The predicted value $y' = softmax(v_t)$. The derivative of the hidden state can be shown as:

$$\frac{\partial J}{\partial h_t} = \frac{\partial J}{\partial v_t} \frac{\partial v_t}{\partial h_t}, \frac{\partial J}{\partial h_t} = \frac{\partial J}{\partial v_t} \frac{\partial(w_v * h_t + b_v)}{\partial h_t}, \frac{\partial J}{\partial h_t} = \frac{\partial J}{\partial v_t} w_v$$

The variable involved in the output gate is o_t.

$$\frac{\partial J}{\partial o_t} = \frac{\partial J}{\partial v_t} \frac{\partial v_t}{\partial h_t} \frac{\partial h_t}{\partial o_t}, \frac{\partial J}{\partial o_t} = \frac{\partial J}{\partial h_t} \frac{\partial h_t}{\partial o_t}, \frac{\partial J}{\partial o_t} = \frac{\partial J}{\partial h_t} \frac{\partial(o_t * Elliott(C_t))}{\partial o_t}, \frac{\partial J}{\partial o_t} = \frac{\partial J}{\partial h_t} Elliott(C_t)$$

C_t is the cell state and the chain rule for cell state can be written as

$$\frac{\partial J}{\partial C_t} = \frac{\partial J}{\partial v_t} \frac{\partial v_t}{\partial h_t} \frac{\partial h_t}{\partial C_t} \tag{3}$$

$$\frac{\partial J}{\partial C_t} = \frac{\partial J}{\partial h_t} \frac{\partial h_t}{\partial C_t} \tag{4}$$

$\frac{\partial J}{\partial h_t}$ value already we have calculated as part of hidden state equation, $\frac{\partial h_t}{\partial C_t} = \frac{\partial(o_t * Elliott(c_t))}{\partial c_t} = \frac{0.5 o_t}{(|c_t| + 1)^2}$. After setting the value of $\frac{\partial h_t}{\partial C_t}$ in Eq. 4, we obtain: $\frac{\partial J}{\partial C_t} = \frac{\partial J}{\partial h_t} \frac{0.5 o_t}{(|c_t| + 1)^2}$. The chain rule for $\hat{c}_t$ is: $\frac{\partial J}{\partial \hat{c}_t} = \frac{\partial J}{\partial h_t} \frac{\partial h_t}{\partial C_t} \frac{\partial C_t}{\partial \hat{c}_t}, \frac{\partial J}{\partial \hat{c}_t} = \frac{\partial J}{\partial C_t} \frac{\partial C_t}{\partial \hat{c}_t}$. We need to derive only $\frac{\partial C_t}{\partial \hat{c}_t}$ since $\frac{\partial J}{C_t}: \frac{\partial C_t}{\partial \hat{c}_t} = \frac{\partial(f_t * C_{t-1} + \hat{c}_t * i_t)}{\partial \hat{c}_t} = i_t$. After replacing the value of $\frac{\partial C_t}{\partial \hat{c}_t}$, we arrive at: $\frac{\partial J}{\partial \hat{c}_t} = \frac{\partial J}{\partial C_t} * i_t$. Similarly, $\frac{\partial J}{\partial a_c} = \frac{\partial J}{\partial \hat{c}_t} * \frac{0.5}{(|a_c| + 1)^2}$. The following derivatives for input gate

$$\frac{\partial J}{\partial i_t} = \frac{\partial J}{\partial C_t} \hat{c}_t, \frac{\partial J}{\partial a_i} = \frac{\partial J}{\partial C_t} \hat{c}_t \frac{0.5}{(|a_i| + 1)^2}$$

For forget gate, the derivatives are: $\frac{\partial J}{\partial f_t} = \frac{\partial J}{\partial C_t}C_{t-1}$, $\frac{\partial J}{\partial a_f} = \frac{\partial J}{\partial C_t}C_{t-1}\frac{0.5}{(|a_f|+1)^2}$ where Z_t is the concatenation of the h_{t-1}, x_t. The derivatives of the weights are: $\frac{\partial J}{\partial w_f} = \frac{\partial J}{\partial a_f}Z_t$, $\frac{\partial J}{\partial w_i} = \frac{\partial J}{\partial a_i}Z_t$, $\frac{\partial J}{\partial w_v} = \frac{\partial J}{\partial v_t}h_t$, $\frac{\partial J}{\partial w_o} = \frac{\partial J}{\partial a_o}Z_t$.

3.3   Handling the Parameter of the Elliott Activation

We propose two ways to learn the parameter of the Elliot activation, instead of the grid-search or heuristics/metaheuristics. we show that both ways lead to similar, efficient inferences.

p-Elliott Function: One of the major benefits of the parameterized Elliott function is that it further decreases the rate of saturation in comparison to the non-parameterized Elliott function. We have applied one parameter α, which controls the shape of the Elliott function. There will be different derivatives if we apply parameterized Elliott function in LSTM. The PEF (Parameterized Elliott Function): $PEF = \frac{0.5\alpha x}{1+|\alpha x|} + 0.5$. After the introduction of the PEF, the hidden state equation turns out to be: $h_t = O_t\alpha_c Elliott(C_t)$. As per the chain rule, the derivative for α_c will be written as: $\frac{\partial J}{\partial \alpha_c} = \frac{\partial J}{\partial v_t}\frac{\partial v_t}{\partial h_t}\frac{\partial h_t}{\partial \alpha_c}$, $\frac{\partial J}{\partial \alpha_c} = \frac{\partial J}{\partial h_t}\frac{O_t\alpha_c Elliott(C_t)}{\partial \alpha_c}$, $\frac{\partial J}{\partial \alpha_c} = \frac{\partial J}{\partial h_t}O_t * Elliott(C_t)$. After each iteration, the α_c is updated as per Eq. 5.

$$\alpha_c\mathrel{+}= \delta * \frac{\partial J}{\partial \alpha_c} \tag{5}$$

For α_o, which is parameter for output gate Elliott function, the derivative can be derived according to the equations: $\frac{\partial J}{\partial \alpha_o} = \frac{\partial J}{\partial v_t}\frac{\partial v_t}{\partial h_t}\frac{\partial h_t}{\partial O_t}\frac{\partial O_t}{\partial \alpha_o}$, $\frac{\partial J}{\partial \alpha_o} = \frac{\partial J}{\partial O_t}\frac{\alpha_o Elliott(a_o)}{\partial \alpha_o}$, $\frac{\partial J}{\partial \alpha_o} = \frac{\partial J}{\partial O_t}Elliott(a_o)$. The α_o is updated as per Eq. 6.

$$\alpha_o\mathrel{+}= \delta * \frac{\partial J}{\partial \alpha_o} \tag{6}$$

Similarly, we can derive α_i, α_f and $\hat{\alpha_c}$ and update the parameters.

The Alternative–Fixed Point Analysis of p-Elliott: Suitable value of the parameter can also be found by Fixed point theory. We follow the procedure laid down by Saha et al. [16] to compute fixed points of the p-Elliott for stable training and to arrive at suitable values of the parameter, depending on the initialization scheme followed above. We proceed to find the fixed points in the following manner. Writing the p-Elliott as, $f(x) = \frac{0.5x\alpha}{1+|x\alpha|} + 0.5$ and using the definition of fixed point i.e. $f(x) = x$, we obtain $0.5x\alpha+0.5\left(1 + |x\alpha|\right) = x(1+|x\alpha|)$. Assuming $|x\alpha| > 0$ i.e. $x > 0, \alpha > 0$, we get $\alpha = \frac{0.5-x}{x^2-x}$ or alternatively, by assuming $x < 0$ or $\alpha < 0$, $\alpha = \frac{x-0.5}{x^2}$. For a constant value of α, if we begin from any initial x_0, p-Elliott converges to a stable fixed point. We experimentally demonstrate the stability of fixed point of p-Elliott by assuming $\alpha = 0.32$ for one of the patients (id 563). By running python script to generate iterates for p-Elliott at $x_0 = 0.9$, the fixed point was found at $\alpha = 0.580$. To investigate its stability, we started again from $x_0 = 0.1$, $x_0 = 0.4$ and $x_0 = 0.8$ (keeping α same) and it reached to the same fixed point. To validate the observation, we experimented from different starting points, and reached at the same fixed point. The values of these iterates can be fetched from the GitHub repository we created [5]. This is another way of obtaining a suitable α value which can be used instead of finding it through back-propagation within LSTM yielding comparable MAPE since the fixed point corresponds to minima in the loss landscape, proved by [16].

3.4   Causality Analysis

The available literature lacks the causal analysis of physiological feature data on the blood glucose level of patients. In order to identify the causal features among the features present in the dataset, we have used Granger Causality [7] along with Transfer Entropy [18]. Only those features were considered causal which were Granger Causing glucose levels with a confidence of 90% and had a positive local Transfer Entropy value.

4   Dataset and Experiment

In order to validate the proposed theory, we modify the architecture of the LSTM Cell as stated earlier and use it to predict the blood glucose levels in 5 patients of the OhioT1DM dataset. In the following subsections, we provide details about the data (and its pre-processing), network architecture, evaluation methods and the performance of the models.

4.1   Dataset

From the OhioT1DM dataset, we have captured the data from five people with Type-1 diabetes, aged between 40 to 60 years. They were subjected to insulin pump therapy and were using Continuous Glucose Monitoring (CGM) throughout the eight-week duration of the data collection. The patients continuously wore Medtronic 530G insulin pumps, and Medtronic Enlite CGM sensors to capture different physiological values for monitoring. The life-events of the patients were recorded through a smartphone app while Basis Peak fitness tracker was worn to capture the physiological values. The features captured from the five patients comprises of - a CGM blood glucose level recorded every 5 min; blood glucose levels from periodic self-monitoring of blood glucose (finger sticks); insulin doses - both bolus and basal; self-reported mealtimes with carbohydrate estimates; self-reported times of exercise, sleep, work, stress, and illness; and 5-minute aggregations of heart rate, galvanic skin response (GSR), skin temperature, air temperature, and step count. But these had many instances of missing data value. Hence, the dataset was sampled to record data in 15-minute intervals to reduce the percentage of missing data with interpolation method.

The various attributes, namely sleep-quality, basal_insulin, temp_basal, bolus_insulin, carb, meal, work intensity, stress, illness, exercise, hypo-events from Ohio T1DM Dataset, which are self-reported life event attributes, are considered as categorical variables. Also, the dataset is divided into Time buckets based on perception. In this step, the 24-hour time slots are divided into 7 different Time flag buckets [6]. This has been done to track activities of patients for better regulation. It also helps in more reliable and accurate prediction of blood glucose value.

4.2 LSTM Model and Evaluation

The model architecture consists of an LSTM layer, which processes the incoming sequence, followed by a fully-connected layer and an output layer. We train models for each of the 4 modifications to the LSTM architecture, i.e. usage of the tanh, parametric-tanh, Elliott and the parametric-Elliott activation functions within the LSTM. In an attempt to bisect the explainability of the model, we repeat the experiment twice for each patient, once using all features in the dataset, and once using only the causal features identified using Granger Causality and Transfer Entropy. Any Granger Causal feature with a positive local transfer entropy for any of the 5 patients was included in the set of causal features. The trained models are then used to predict the blood glucose level in the 5 patients. We train models to predict the glucose level for the next 15, 30 and 45 min using the 6 h glucose history as input to the model. The hyperparameters such as learning rate and the LSTM hidden size have been fine-tuned and are common across all variants. The performance of the models are evaluated using the mean absolute percentage error (MAPE) between the predicted glucose level and the actual glucose level in the test set. All the models have been trained using the Root Mean Squared Error Loss, and optimized using the Adam Optimizer. The parameter values for the parametric activation functions have been initialized from a standard normal distribution. All the models were trained 3 times and the average value of the MAPE is reported along with the variations.

4.3 Results

The results from our experiments can be summarized as:

1. Causal features are more effective in summarizing the blood glucose variations than all features. Irrespective of the LSTM architecture, models trained only on causal features have lower MAPE values.
2. The Elliott and parametric Elliott activation functions are better suited as activation functions within the LSTM than the tanh and the parametric tanh activations as the former leads to lower MAPEs in glucose prediction, irrespective of the features used for training.
3. The parametric Elliott activation within the LSTM results in more stable training when compared to the parametric tanh as it leads to lower standard deviation in the MAPE across multiple trials.

Table 1 shows the performance of the models using different activation functions for predicting the glucose level for the 15 min prediction horizon using all/causal features. It can be clearly seen that the MAPE values for the causal

Table 1. MAPE values for glucose level prediction for 15 min horizon using all/causal features. p-Elliott is the best performing AF. The biggest difference in the MAPE values between all/causal features is italicized in the table.

MAPE (%)	559	563	570	575	588
tanh	14.563±3.131 / 9.572 ± 1.694	*23.679 ± 5.279/ 8.55 ± 0.585*	16.598 ± 2.399 / 7.049 ± 1.16	15.353 ± 7.91/ 9.446 ± 2.16	21.137 ± 5.069/ 9.706 ± 2.327
p-tanh	14.397 ± 2.646/ 7.681 ± 1.65	15.372 ± 0.505/ 6.902 ± 0.279	*16.399 ± 2.878/ 3.85 ± 0.302*	11.201 ± 1.774/ 13.094 ± 1.955	12.107 ± 2.808/ 10.785 ± 1.959
Elliott	7.414 ± 0.725/ 7.031 ± 0.054	7.392 ± 0.477/ 5.664 ± 0.257	*7.634 ± 1.103/ 4.179 ± 0.621*	9.162 ± 0.653/ 8.866 ± 2.119	6.505 ± 0.332/ 6.515 ± 0.373
p-Elliott	**7.385 ± 0.906/ 6.606 ± 0.824**	**6.384 ± 0.557/ 5.669 ± 0.303**	**5.823 ± 0.667/ 3.718 ± 0.053**	*11.191 ± 0.932/ 7.975 ± 1.069*	**6.796 ± 0.706/ 6.231 ± 0.459**

Table 2. MAPE values for glucose level prediction for 30 min horizon using all/causal features. p-Elliott has a superior performance compared to other AFs. The biggest difference in the MAPE values between all/causal features is italicized in the table.

MAPE(%)	559	563	570	575	588
tanh	18.237 ± 1.421/ 10.985 ± 0.652	20.474 ± 3.332/ 9.621 ± 0.354	16.408 ± 2.773/ 6.114 ± 0.153	20.465 ± 2.048/ 16.618 ± 2.628	*32.145 ± 4.894/ 13.537 ± 2.591*
p-tanh	13.104 ± 1.465/ 9.934 ± 0.482	19.284 ± 2.942/ 9.183 ± 0.361	*16.476 ± 2.61/ 5.985 ± 0.072*	22.533 ± 5.971/ 18.429 ± 3.597	18.482 ± 1.61/ 12.592 ± 3.083
Elliott	*18.859 ± 1.541/ 10.157 ± 0.269*	11.719 ± 0.072/ 9.546 ± 0.169	9.391 ± 0.433/ 6.396 ± 0.124	16.499 ± 1.374/ 13.432 ± 0.406	13.452 ± 0.985/ 8.314 ± 0.033
p-Elliott	*13.337 ± 1.843/ 9.122 ± 0.198*	**10.838 ± 0.272/ 8.837 ± 0.047**	**8.759 ± 0.62/ 6.284 ± 0.107**	**15.371 ± 1.141/ 13.569 ± 0.635**	**10.632 ± 0.342/ 7.688 ± 0.098**

Table 3. MAPE values for glucose level prediction for 45 min horizon using all/causal features. p-Elliott has a superior performance compared to other AFs. The biggest difference in the MAPE values between all/causal features is italicized in the table.

MAPE(%)	559	563	570	575	588
tanh	23.081 ± 0.625/ 13.741 ± 0.713	24.534 ± 4.576/ 12.981 ± 0.485	21.519 ± 3.981/ 8.940 ± 0.409	*34.573 ± 7.318/ 20.819 ± 1.198*	16.060 ± 1.712/ 17.517 ± 3.717
p-tanh	15.985 ± 0.338/ 14.168 ± 0.153	*24.273 ± 1.794/ 13.187 ± 0.884*	18.809 ± 2.797/ 9.096 ± 0.385	25.209 ± 4.055/ 25.633 ± 1.551	18.793 ± 1.460/ 16.997 ± 1.238
Elliott	*22.116 ± 1.656/ 13.126 ± 0.108*	14.226 ± 0.505/ 12.423 ± 0.069	14.203 ± 0.698/ 9.679 ± 0.53/	26.766 ± 2.917/ 21.982 ± 1.530	14.829 ± 0.771/ 11.142 ± 0.277
p-Elliott	**15.317 ± 0.063/ 12.648 ± 0.180**	**14.300 ± 0.906/ 12.105 ± 0.053**	**12.114 ± 0.349/ 8.462 ± 0.075**	*29.561 ± 4.323/ 22.027 ± 0.822*	**15.906 ± 0.449/ 10.499 ± 0.217**

features are lower than that of all features. In fact, for Patient-563, there is a difference of 15% in the error between causal and all features in the 15 min predictions. Table 2 shows the results for the 30 min prediction horizon and Table. 3 for the 45 min prediction horizon. From the tables, it can also be seen that the MAPE values for the Elliott and parametric Elliott activations are lesser than that of the tanh and parametric tanh functions. The difference in performance on all features is >18% for Patient-588 in the 30 min prediction horizon. The difference in variability of the parameterized tanh and parameterized Elliott is 5% for Patient-563 in the 45 min prediction horizon indicating the instability of the p-tanh and the corresponding stability of the p-Elliott activation. It is clear that p-LSTM with parameterized Elliott activation trained on causal features

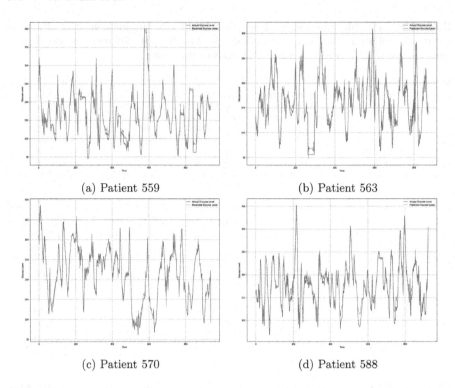

(a) Patient 559

(b) Patient 563

(c) Patient 570

(d) Patient 588

Fig. 1. The predicted glucose levels (orange) and the actual glucose levels (blue) for the 15 min prediction horizon using p-LSTM for four patients. (Color figure online)

performs the best. Its performance is much better when compared to existing time-series forecasting methods such as vanilla LSTMs (9–18% MAPE for 15 min, 15–21% for 30 min and 14–26% for 45 min), moving average (∼12% for 15 min, ∼16% for 30 min and ∼21% for 45 min) and ARIMA (∼22% for 15 min, ∼28–30% for 30 min and ∼33% for 45 min). All contributions combined, a MAPE of 16.598% for Patient-570 in the 15 min prediction using tanh activation, reduces to a MAPE of 3.718% by the use of p-Elliott activation and causal features. This is a remarkable difference achieved through the clever choice of training features and some modification of the existing architecture!

5   Conclusion

Our investigation is motivated by the search for an explainable neural network architecture which has reasonable grounds for efficient prediction in time series data. Consequently, using causal features, a subset of the set of all features, to train the LSTM model (thereby reducing the noise affecting the model performance) and accomplishing meaningful inference on the blood glucose prediction task is of utmost importance. As demonstrated by empirical results, we were successful in this endeavour where predictions using causal features only, generally yielded superior inference compared to the model performance trained on all features. Along the way, we proposed an efficient design of p-LSTM architecture which extends beyond the standard Vanilla-LSTM and the use of standard 'tanh' activation in such designs. The introduction of the novel architecture is grounded on firm theoretical arguments of learning from data, reflecting in superior generalization over available benchmarks. This is done by allowing the parameter in p-Elliott to be learned via backpropagation. The novel architecture is interlaced with techniques bypassing 'parameter-tuning' overheads. The p-LSTM results are compared with that of state-of-the-art time series forecasting methods. We observe that the average MAPE for p-LSTM is 6.0398%, 9.1% & 13.1482% for prediction horizon of 15, 30 & 45 min, which is about 2–2.5 times better than the existing methods. The result of our investigation is a State-of-the-Art method that may be extended to inferences on other time series forecasting tasks such as stock price prediction, anomaly detection etc. Another future direction for this research is to test the generalization ability and effectiveness of p-LSTM on longer time-frames ($\sim$1 day or longer).

References

1. Arpit, D., Kanuparthi, B., Kerg, G., Ke, N.R., Mitliagkas, I., Bengio, Y.: h-detach: Modifying the lstm gradient towards better optimization (2018). https://doi.org/ 10.48550/ARXIV.1810.03023, https://arxiv.org/abs/1810.03023
2. Borle, N.C., Ryan, E.A., Greiner, R.: The challenge of predicting blood glucose concentration changes in patients with type i diabetes. Health Informatics J. **27**(1), 1460458220977584 (2021) , https://doi.org/10.1177/1460458220977584, pMID: 33504254
3. Du, M.: Improving lstm neural networks for better short-term wind power predictions. In: 2019 IEEE 2nd International Conference on Renewable Energy and Power Engineering (REPE), pp. 105–109 (2019). https://doi.org/10.1109/REPE48501. 2019.9025143
4. Farzad, A., Mashayekhi, H., Hassanpour, H.: A comparative performance analysis of different activation functions in LSTM networks for classification. Neural Comput. Appl. **31**(7), 2507–2521 (2017). https://doi.org/10.1007/s00521-017-3210-6
5. Ganatra, V., Swain, A., Saha, S., Mathur, A.: p-LSTM (June 2022). https://github. com/Vaibhav-Ganatra/p-LSTM
6. Gould, P.G., Koehler, A.B., Ord, J.K., Snyder, R.D., Hyndman, R.J., Vahid-Araghi, F.: Forecasting time series with multiple seasonal patterns. European J. Operational Res. **191**(1), 207–222 (2008). https://doi.org/10.1016/j.ejor.2007.08. 024, https://www.sciencedirect.com/science/article/pii/S0377221707008740
7. Granger, C.W.J.: Investigating causal relations by econometric models and cross-spectral methods. Econometrica **37**(3), 424–438 (1969). https://www.jstor.org/ stable/1912791
8. Hamdi, T., et al.: Artificial neural network for blood glucose level prediction. In: 2017 International Conference on Smart, Monitored and Controlled Cities (SM2C), pp. 91–95 (2017). https://doi.org/10.1109/SM2C.2017.8071825

9. Jensen, M.H., Christensen, T.F., Tarnow, L., Seto, E., Dencker Johansen, M., Hejlesen, O.K.: Real-time hypoglycemia detection from continuous glucose monitoring data of subjects with type 1 diabetes. Diabetes Technol. Therapeutics **15**(7), 538–543 (2013). https://doi.org/10.1089/dia.2013.0069, https://doi.org/10.1089/dia.2013.0069, pMID: 23631608

10. Marling, C., Bunescu, R.: The ohiot1dm dataset for blood glucose level prediction: Update 2020. In: CEUR Workshop Proceedings, vol. 2675, pp. 71–74 (09 2020)

11. Marling, C., Wiley, M., Bunescu, R., Shubrook, J., Schwartz, F.: Emerging applications for intelligent diabetes management. AI Magazine **33**(2), 67 (2012). https://doi.org/10.1609/aimag.v33i2.2410, https://ojs.aaai.org/index.php/aimagazine/article/view/2410

12. Martinsson, J., Schliep, A., Eliasson, B., Mogren, O.: Blood glucose prediction with variance estimation using recurrent neural networks. J. Heal. Informatics Res. **4**(1), 1–18 (2020). https://doi.org/10.1007/s41666-019-00059-y, https://doi.org/10.1007/s41666-019-00059-y

13. Mhaskar, H.N., Pereverzyev, S.V., van der Walt, M.D.: A deep learning approach to diabetic blood glucose prediction. Front. Appli. Mathem. Stat. **3** (2017). https://doi.org/10.3389/fams.2017.00014, https://www.frontiersin.org/article/10.3389/fams.2017.00014

14. Pappada, S., et al.: Neural network-based real-time prediction of glucose in patients with insulin-dependent diabetes. Diabetes Technol. Therapeutics **13**, 135–41 (2011). https://doi.org/10.1089/dia.2010.0104

15. Rana, M., Uddin, M.M., Hoque, M.M.: Effects of activation functions and optimizers on stock price prediction using lstm recurrent networks. In: Proceedings of the 2019 3rd International Conference on Computer Science and Artificial Intelligence, CSAI 2019, pp. 354–358. Association for Computing Machinery, New York (2019). https://doi.org/10.1145/3374587.3374622, https://doi.org/10.1145/3374587.3374622

16. Saha, S., Nagaraj, N., Mathur, A., Yedida, R., H R, S.: Evolution of novel activation functions in neural network training for astronomy data: habitability classification of exoplanets. Euro. Phys. J. Special Topics **229**(16), 2629–2738 (2020). https://doi.org/10.1140/epjst/e2020-000098-9

17. Shahid, S., Hussain, S., Khan, W.A.: Predicting continuous blood glucose level using deep learning. In: Proceedings of the 14th IEEE/ACM International Conference on Utility and Cloud Computing Companion, UCC 2021, Association for Computing Machinery, New York (2021). https://doi.org/10.1145/3492323.3495598, https://doi.org/10.1145/3492323.3495598

18. Vicente, R., Wibral, M., Lindner, M., Pipa, G.: Transfer entropy-a model-free measure of effective connectivity for the neurosciences. J. Computat. Neurosci. **30**, 45–67 (2011). https://doi.org/10.1007/s10827-010-0262-3

19. Xu, H., et al.: Modified lstm with memory layer for power grid signal classification. In: 2020 IEEE 4th Conference on Energy Internet and Energy System Integration (EI2), pp. 3693–3697 (2020). https://doi.org/10.1109/EI250167.2020.9347143

Wide Ensemble of Interpretable TSK Fuzzy Classifiers with Application to Smartphone Sensor-Based Human Activity Recognition

Runshan Xie[1,2] and Shitong Wang[1,2(✉)]

[1] School of AI and Computer Science, Jiangnan University, Wuxi 214122, China
wxwangst@aliyun.com
[2] Taihu Jiangsu Key Construction Lab. of IoT Application Technologies, Wuxi, Jiangsu, China

Abstract. In this study, by a wide ensemble of Takagi-Sugeno-Kang (TSK) fuzzy sub-classifiers without an individual aggregation step, an interpretable fuzzy classifier (WEIFC) is developed from a novel perspective. WEIFC has two merits: (1) the antecedent parts of fuzzy rules in each sub-classifier of WEIFC are built on a different bootstrapped data subspace, which guarantees both the diversity among the sub-classifiers and the avoidance of the curse of dimensionality caused by the multi-dimensional and even high-dimensional input data. (2) all sub-classifiers on their respective bootstrapped data subspaces can be trained in parallel without an individual aggregation step, which guarantees both the fast training procedure and good interpretability. According to the novel ensemble structure of WEIFC, it becomes very suitable for applications where the classification testing accuracy and interpretability should be well balanced. As a result, WEIFC is applied to the smartphone sensor-based human activity recognition (SSHAR) task to evaluate its practicability. Compared with the thirteen state-of-the-art classification methods for SSHAR, the experimental results on the benchmarking dataset human activity recognition (HAR) show that WEIFC has better classification testing accuracy than most of them.

Keywords: TSK fuzzy classifiers · single structure · interpretability · generalization

1 Introduction

Over the past decades, Takagi-Sugeno-Kang (TSK) fuzzy classifiers [1–3] have earned great success in many application fields, including image processing [4, 5], financial prediction [6], and industrial control [7]. Owing to both universal approximation and

This work was supported in part by the National Natural Science Foundation of China under Grants U20A20228, 61772198, 61972181, by the Natural Science Foundation of Jiangsu Province under Grant BK20191331, and by National First-class Discipline Program of Light Industry and Engineering (LITE2018), and by Postgraduate Research & Practice Innovation Program of Jiangsu Province KYCX22_2315 .

M. Tanveer et al. (Eds.): ICONIP 2022, CCIS 1794, pp. 381–394, 2023.
https://doi.org/10.1007/978-981-99-1648-1_32

high interpretability, TSK fuzzy classifiers become preferable when classification accuracy and interpretability should be balanced in many real-life applications like medical informatics. Various optimization methods have been developed to construct an individual TSK fuzzy classifier for various practical demands. Such typical fuzzy classifiers include the well-known ANFIS [8], genetic algorithm (GA)-based TSK classifiers [9], neural-fuzzy hybridization-based TSK fuzzy classifiers [10], collaborative TSK fuzzy systems [11], multitask TSK classifiers [12], interval Type 2 fuzzy systems [13, 14] and transfer-learning-based TSK fuzzy classifiers [15] for leveraging the knowledge gained from the related scenes [16]. Often, TSK fuzzy classifiers are combined to seek improved classification performance [17–19] and/or avoidance of the curse of dimensionality [20]. Below we briefly summarize three existing combination structures of TSK fuzzy classifiers.

1) Hierarchical structures: Hierarchical TSK fuzzy classifiers organize several and even many low-dimensional TSK fuzzy sub-classifiers in three hierarchical ways, namely, cascaded, aggregated and incremental [21–24]. Typical works include an extended fuzzy system framework which considers a prioritization of the fuzzy rules by using the hierarchical representation [21], an adaptive hierarchical fuzzy system that facilitates the tuning of some parameters of some controllers and simultaneously reducing the number of both input variable and fuzzy rules in each processor [22], a hierarchical fuzzy classifier which is built in a block-by-block way to achieve both improved accuracy and concise interpretability by negative correlation learning [23]. Because intermediate variables between such hierarchical structures are always not explainable, the whole hierarchical fuzzy classifier becomes not fully interpretable.

2) Bagging and boosting structure: TSK fuzzy sub-classifiers [25] can also be combined in bagging [26] and/or boosting [27] ways. Bagging reduces the correlation of TSK fuzzy sub-classifiers by randomly sampling the original training dataset as new training datasets for each TSK fuzzy sub-classifier. As such, enhanced diversity between TSK fuzzy sub-classifiers can be expected. Different from bagging, boosting has to add a new TSK fuzzy sub-classifier after training the previous TSK fuzzy sub-classifiers. Though bagging and boosting has satisfactory learning capability, they still have the following drawbacks. Firstly, since bagging and boosting select all the features to generate fuzzy rules, they inevitably suffer from the curse of dimensionality when facing multidimensional and even high dimensional data. Secondly, boosting must train each TSK fuzzy sub-classifier separately, so its training time will be very consuming. Thirdly, while majority-voting or especially weighting strategies are carried out on the outputs of all the sub-classifiers, bagging and boosting are generally not well interpretable.

3) Deep/wide structures: Different from the above TSK fuzzy classifiers, deep networks together with fuzzy learning or stacked structures of fuzzy classifiers [28–31] were proposed to pursue better classification performance and/or better uncertainty-handling capability. For example, in [28], a hierarchical deep neural network is created to acquire fuzzy and neural representation for effective uncertainty-handling capability and promising performance. In [29], a fused model based on type-2 fuzzy

learning and residual U-net and SegNet is proposed to obtain satisfactory performance and simultaneously tackle the problem of poor interpretability in breast cancer diagnosis. In [30], a fuzzy deep belief net based on fuzzy restricted Boltzmann machines is established to improve a deep belief net in the sense of both classification accuracy and robustness. In our recent researches [32–35], with the use of interpretable zero-order TSK fuzzy rules, four stacked structures of deep TSK fuzzy classifiers were proposed to share both the stacked generalized principle [36] and promising classification performance of TSK fuzzy classifiers so as to guarantee enhanced testing accuracies and high interpretability. Except for deep structures of TSK fuzzy classifiers, several wide ensemble structures [37, 38] have been recently endeavored to provide a new wide learning method of TSK fuzzy classifiers. By analogizing the knowledge dropout of human beings, the fuzzy-knowledge-out concept [37] was invented to earn extra generalization capability, and accordingly a wide ensemble WL-TSK [37] of TSK fuzzy classifiers based on this concept is devised to achieve satisfactory classification performance with high interpretability after the explicit use of the commonly-used aggregation strategies like averaging, weighting and majority-voting [25] on all the obtained sub-classifiers. More notoriously, our recent work—WIG-TSK [39] advances the above wide structure in [37] to avoid an individual commonly-used aggregation step and simultaneously acquire more generalization capability.

However, as pointed out in [40], classification testing accuracy and interpretability should be well balanced when designing a fuzzy classifier. In order to achieve such a goal, in this study, we propose a wide ensemble of interpretable TSK fuzzy classifiers WEFC, which is a single rather than a combination structure without an individual aggregation step. Its basic idea is to develop a wide structure by exerting double randomness to generate all fuzzy TSK sub-classifiers on their respective bootstrapped data subspaces and then training them in parallel for only once. The first randomness for each sub-classifier is to form the corresponding bootstrapped data subspace of the original features randomly in a bootstrapped way [41, 42]. The second randomness is to adopt the random selection method [23, 34, 37, 40, 43] to generate the antecedent parts of fuzzy rules in all the sub-classifiers of WEIFC. In this way, the antecedent parts of all the sub-classifiers are determined on their respective bootstrapped data subspaces. After encapsulating the antecedent parts of all the sub-classifiers into a single structure that actually avoids the use of an individual aggregation step, the consequent parts of all fuzzy rules will be determined in parallel for only once on their respective data subspaces.

Based on the above, WEIFC becomes very suitable for the applications where the classification testing accuracy and interpretability should be well balanced. As we all know, smartphone sensor-based human activity recognition (SSHAR) [44–46] is often used in high-risk applications such as healthcare services. Concretely, smartphone sensors have recently become an effective and inexpensive means of monitoring real-time patient activities for clinicians to make medical recommendations [44]. An example is [42], where smartphone sensors are used to monitor real-time human sleep positions to detect a dangerous sleep disorder—positional obstructive sleep apnea. In addition, smartphone sensors can also monitor Parkinson's disease [47]. Since the classification methods play an important role in SSHAR, and the signals from smartphone sensors are often very noisy, this requires the classification methods to achieve a good trade-off between classification testing accuracy and interpretability. As a result, WEIFC is applied for SSHAR to evaluate its practicability.

The contributions of this study can be summarized as follows.

1) We propose a wide ensemble of interpretable TSK fuzzy classifiers WEIFC to achieve a good tradeoff between classification testing accuracy and interpretability and then apply WEIFC to the practical scenario SSHAR.

2) We divide the original input features into several overlapping subspaces in a boot-strapped manner, which can guarantee the diversity among the sub-classifier and simultaneously avoid the curse of dimensionality caused by the multi-dimensional and even high-dimensional input data. In addition, after the antecedent parts of fuzzy rules in all the sub-classifier of WEIFC are built, we train the corresponding conse-quents of fuzzy rules in all the sub-classifier for only once without any individual aggregation step, which guarantees fast training procedure and good interpretability of WEIFC.

3) Compared with thirteen advanced and even state-of-the-art classification methods for SSHAR, the experimental results on the well-known human activity recognition dataset HAR show that WEIFC has better classification testing accuracy than most of them.

The remainder of this paper is organized as follows. In Sect. 2, a brief introduction of zero-order TSK fuzzy classifier is given. In Sect. 3, the fuzzy classifier WEIFC is proposed. The experimental results obtained by WEIFC and the comparative methods on the well-known human activity recognition dataset HAR are reported in Sect. 4. The final section concludes this paper.

2   On Interpretable Zero-Order TSK Fuzzy Classifiers

Since zero-order TSK fuzzy classifiers are basic components (*i.e.*, sub-classifiers) of the proposed WEIFC, we will briefly introduce the concept of zero-order TSK fuzzy classifiers and their interpretability (*i.e.*, linguistically interpretable fuzzy rules).

As for a multi-class classification task, a zero-order TSK fuzzy classifier consists of the total K fuzzy rules in which the kth ($1 \leq k \leq K$) fuzzy rule can be expressed as

IF x_1 is A_{k1} and x_2 is A_{k2} and $\cdots$ and x_d is A_{kd} THEN a_k, $k = 1, 2, \cdots, K$ (1)

where *'and'* is a fuzzy conjunction operator, x_j is the jth feature of a sample $x \in \mathbb{R}^d$ which has a total of d features, A_{kj} is the antecedent part fuzzy set on the jth ($1 \leq j \leq d$) feature of the kth fuzzy rule, the consequent vector $a_k \in \mathbb{R}^C$ denotes the output of the kth fuzzy rule, for $j = 1,2,...,d$. With a simple defuzzification [48], the actual output y of such a fuzzy classifier can be expressed as follows

$$Y = \sum_{k=1}^{K} \frac{\phi^k(x)}{\sum\limits_{l=1}^{K} \phi^l(x)} a_k = \sum_{k=1}^{K} \tilde{\phi}^k(x) a_k \qquad (2)$$

where

$$\phi_k(\boldsymbol{x}) = \prod_{j=1}^{d} \phi_{kj}(x_j) \tag{3}$$

in which $\phi_{kj}(x_j)$ is taken as the commonly-used Gaussian fuzzy membership functions [3, 28, 32, 33] in this study:

$$\phi_{kj}(x_j) = exp(\frac{-(x_j - c_{kj})^2}{\delta_{kj}}) \tag{4}$$

where c_{kj} and δ_{kj} denote the corresponding center and width of Gaussian fuzzy membership function, which can be obtained by some clustering algorithm (such as fuzzy c-means clustering method, FCM [49]) or other methods. For example, according to the random selection method [23, 34, 37, 40, 43], the value of Gaussian center c_{kj} and width δ_{kj} can be quickly yet effectively determined as follows. Firstly, each feature is artificially partitioned into five equal partitions like {0, 0.25, 0.5, 0.75, 1} which have clear linguistic values, *e,g.*, {*very low (VL)*, *low (L)*, *medium (M)*, *high (H)*, *very high (VH)*}. Secondly, five Gaussian fuzzy membership functions, whose centers are fixed respectively at {0, 0.25, 0.5, 0.75, 1}, and widths are randomly generated within (0,1]. Finally, the fuzzy membership function of each fuzzy rule is generated by randomly choosing one of five Gaussian fuzzy membership functions along with each feature. As such, the interpretable antecedent part of fuzzy rules can be assured, and the promising performance is still kept. Therefore, we prefer the random selection method [23, 34, 37, 40, 43] in this study.

Generally, the classification performance of a zero-order fuzzy classifier is worse than that of high-order fuzzy classifiers such as a first-order fuzzy classifier. However, it is too hard to give a clear interpretation for fuzzy rules of high-order fuzzy classifiers since too many parameters are involved in the consequent part of each fuzzy rule. On the contrary, a zero-order TSK fuzzy classifier has only one consequent vector $\boldsymbol{a}_k$ for multiple classification tasks in the consequent part of the kth fuzzy rule, whose value can be clearly interpreted as: the certainty degree of each element in $\boldsymbol{a}_k$ belonging to the corresponding class for multiple classification tasks. Thus, zero-order TSK fuzzy classifiers are more interpretable than high-order fuzzy classifiers, and we prefer them as sub-classifiers in the proposed classifier WEIFC.

Although zero-order TSK fuzzy classifiers have good interpretability and have earned great success in many application fields, they could not work well on multidimensional and even high-dimensional data due to the dimensionality curse [20]. In this case, zero-order TSK fuzzy classifiers often need so many fuzzy rules to achieve prescribed classification performance, which may inevitably cause severe deterioration of the interpretability of the whole zero-order fuzzy classifiers. The proposed classifier WEIFC will be designed to tackle this weakness.

3   The Proposed Classifier WEIFC

In this section, we will first state how to construct the proposed interpretable fuzzy classifier WEIFC and then give the corresponding training algorithm of WEIFC.

3.1 The Proposed Wide Structure

The design of the proposed interpretable fuzzy classifier WEIFC embodies the following motivations. Referring to [50], the interpretability of a TSK fuzzy classifier can be improved by reducing its model complexity. An effective way seems to simplify fuzzy rules by selecting the most important original features and ignoring the remaining ones. However, on the one hand, when a classifier ignores any original feature, the information loss contained in a dataset will inevitably be caused. On the other hand, due to the importance of each original feature may change, especially in each individual sub-classifier or dynamically changing environment, it is generally difficult to identify the most important features from the original features. Therefore, the fixed selection of the most important original features may not be preferable. Furthermore, as pointed out in [33], how to avoid the rule-explosion problem and reduce the complexity of each fuzzy rule on quite a lot of original features of data is also a crucial factor to be considered. After synthesizing all the above aspects, in this study, in order to address the above issues, we divide the original data space into several overlapping data subspaces in a bootstrapped manner. In addition, another advantage of doing so is that the diversity among sub-classifiers can be guaranteed. After building the antecedent parts of the fuzzy rules in all the sub-classifiers of WEIFC on their respective data subspaces in wide way, the corresponding consequent parts of all the sub-classifiers can be trained in parallel for only once without an individual aggregation step, which guarantees the fast training procedure and good interpretability of WEIFC.

Figure 1 illustrates the novel structure of WEIFC. According to Fig. 1, WEIFC first divides the original data space into several randomly overlapping data subspaces in a bootstrapped manner, and then the antecedent parts of the fuzzy rules in all the sub-classifiers are built on their respective bootstrapped data subspaces. That is to say, each sub-classifier is actually an interpretable zero-order fuzzy classifier on the corresponding bootstrapped data subspace of the original feature space. Below we state how the proposed fuzzy classifier WEIFC works. There exists a doubly randomness. The first randomness for each sub-classifier is to form the corresponding overlapping data subspace of the original features randomly in a bootstrapped manner [41, 42]. The second randomness is to use the random selection method to generate the antecedent parts of the fuzzy rules in all the sub-classifier on their respective data subspaces. For example, here suppose a q-dimensional data subspace $x = [x_1, x_2, \ldots, x_q] \in \mathbb{R}^q$, the obtained fuzzy rules in this sub-classifier of WEIFC on this data subspace can be expressed in the following form:

$$\text{IF } x_1 \text{ is high and } x_2 \text{ is low and} \ldots \text{and } x_q \text{ is very low} \quad \text{THEN } a \text{ for class } 2 \quad (5)$$

The corresponding antecedent part matrix can be formed after generating the antecedent parts of all fuzzy rules in a sub-classifier. Then, the obtained fuzzy rules can be expressed by the antecedent part matrix and the consequent part matrix (see dashed ellipses in Fig. 1).

More concretely, let us summarize the above training procedure in the following mathematical derivations.

Suppose input data $D = [x_1, x_2, \ldots, x_N]^T (\in \mathbb{R}^{N \times d})$ contains the total N input samples with d dimensions and the corresponding label set $Y = [y_1, y_2, \ldots, y_N]^T$ with

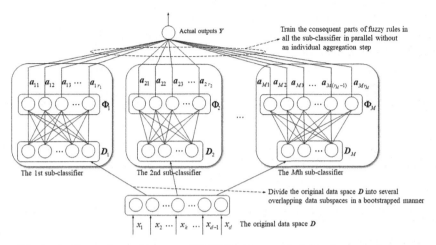

Fig. 1. An illustrative architecture of WEIFC without an individual aggregation step.

C classes. We assume WEIFC has the total M sub-classifiers in which the jth sub-classifier contains r_j fuzzy rules. As for the jth sub-classifier, firstly, WEIFC randomly generates the jth overlapping data subspace $\boldsymbol{D}_j \in \mathbb{R}^{N \times n_j}$ from the original features on $\boldsymbol{D}$ by choosing n_j $(< d)$ columns of $\boldsymbol{D}$ in a bootstrapped manner. Secondly, the corresponding IF-matrix $\boldsymbol{\Phi}_j \in \mathbb{R}^{N \times r_j}$ of the jth sub-classifier can be generated from $\boldsymbol{D}_j$ as

$$
\boldsymbol{\Phi}_j = \begin{bmatrix} \phi_1(\boldsymbol{x}_1) & \cdots & \phi_{r_j}(\boldsymbol{x}_1) \\ \vdots & \ddots & \vdots \\ \phi_1(\boldsymbol{x}_N) & \cdots & \phi_{r_j}(\boldsymbol{x}_N) \end{bmatrix} \tag{6}
$$

where $\phi(\boldsymbol{x})$ is Gaussian membership function and can be obtained according to Eqs. (3), (4) and the suggestion in [23, 40]. This procedure is repeated until all the sub-classifiers' antecedent part matrices are generated. Thirdly, after collecting all the antecedent part matrices denoted as $\boldsymbol{\Phi} = [\boldsymbol{\Phi}_1, \boldsymbol{\Phi}_2, \dots, \boldsymbol{\Phi}_M] (\in \mathbb{R}^{N \times \sum_{j=1}^{M} r_j})$, the actual output of such a WEIFC without any defuzzification can be expressed as

$$
Y = \boldsymbol{\Phi}\, a \tag{7}
$$

Please note, while the existing ensemble classifiers generally have an explicit aggregation step after generating each sub-classifier, Eq. (7) actually means an ensemble of the total M sub-classifier in an implicit rather than explicit aggregation way like averaging, weighting and majority-voting [25]. In essence, Eq. (7) is also a linear regression problem in which $a = [a_1, a_2, \dots, a_j, \dots, a_M]^T$, namely, a represents the consequent-part matrix $a \in \mathbb{R}^{(\sum_{j=1}^{M} r_j) \times C}$ respectively for the C-class classification task, where $a_j \in \mathbb{R}^{r_j \times C}$ represents the consequent part matrix of the jth sub-classifier.

Since the output in Eq. (7) is actually a linear regression problem, the analytical solution of a can be effectively by the extreme learning machine (ELM) [51] and least learning machine (LLM) [52–55]. By revealing the equivalence between ELM and ridge regression [51, 54], LLM is more flexible than ELM's initial pseudo-inverse-based version. Therefore, in this study, we prefer LLM to analytically solve the solution of a. According to [52, 54], LLM accomplishes its fast learning by solving the following optimal problem:

$$\arg \min_{a} : \|Y - \Phi a\|_2^2 + \lambda \|a\|_2^2 \tag{8}$$

where λ denotes the regularization parameter. Obviously, $a = [\Phi]^\dagger Y$, where $[\Phi]^\dagger$ denotes the pseudoinverse of Φ. In LLM, by using the following approximation [52–55] of $[\Phi]^\dagger$, the value of a can be analytically solved as follows.

$$a = (\lambda I + \Phi^T \Phi)^{-1} \Phi^T Y \tag{9}$$

where I denotes the corresponding identity matrix. Please note, when $\lambda \to \infty$, $(\lambda I + \Phi^T \Phi)^{-1} \Phi^T$ becomes $[\Phi]^\dagger$. Thus, WEIFC can quickly complete its training procedure only once without using an iterative update of a at a very slow speed.

Remark 1: From the structural perspective, there is a big difference between WEIFC and our recent works WL-TSK [37] and WIG-TSK [39]. On the one hand, while each sub-classifier of both WIG-TSK and WL-TSK works on the whole original data space, each sub-classifier of WEIFC works on the randomly overlapping data subspace of the original data space in a bootstrapped manner [41, 42]. On the other hand, in order to assure the ultimate performance of WL-TSK, WL-TSK takes an averaging aggregation (or majority-voting and weighting) on the outputs of all sub-classifiers. However, WEIFC indeed avoids an individual aggregation step. In particular, if the majority-voting or weighting strategy is taken, the whole ensemble's interpretability will deteriorate. However, such a case will never happen in WEIFC.

Remark 2: There is a big difference between WEIFC and our recent work WL-TSK [37] from the training perspective. WL-TSK can train each sub-classifier in a sequential or parallel way. In other words, each sub-classifier may be trained quickly by using the corresponding least learning machine LLM [52–55]. However, WEIFC trains all the consequent parts of fuzzy rules in all the sub-classifiers in parallel by only the least learning machine LLM.

Remark 3: According to the classical dropout [56], the number of selected features in each subspace in WEIFC may generally take $0.5d$, where d denotes the total number of original features. According to the random forest [42], it may generally take $\sqrt{d}$. As a result, the number of selected features in each subspace in WEIFC may be roughly within $[\sqrt{d}, 0.5d]$. In our experiments, we simply take it as $\sqrt{d}$ or $0.5d$. Note that, in order to assure an effective ensemble (cf. [42]), the features of different sub-classifiers should partly overlap with each other. Therefore, we may use a bootstrapped manner [41, 42] to divide the original features of input data.

3.2 B. Learning Algorithm and Computational Complexity

Here, we first present the learning algorithm of WEIFC, *i.e.*, Algorithm 1, and then discuss its computational complexity.

Remark 4: Different sub-classifiers may have different numbers of fuzzy rules. After considering easy parameter settings, we simply take the same number of fuzzy rules in each sub-classifier of WEIFC in our experiments.

The computational complexity of Algorithm 1 can be analyzed as follows. For step 2, it can be calculated as $O(Nn_j)$. The computational burden of steps 4 to 7 about the generation of the jth antecedent part matrix takes $O(N^2 n_j r_j)$. With the total M sub-classifiers of fuzzy rules, their computational complexity becomes $O(N^2 \sum_{j=1}^{M} n_j r_j)$. Then, step 9 requires $O(N \sum_{j=1}^{M} r_j)$. According to Eq. (9), the computational complexity of step 10 is calculated as $O(N(\sum_{j=1}^{M} r_j)^2)$. Step 11 requires $O(NC \sum_{j=1}^{M} r_j)$. Therefore, the computational complexity of Algorithm 1 becomes $O(N^2 \sum_{j=1}^{M} n_j r_j + N(\sum_{j=1}^{M} r_j)^2)$.

Algorithm 1: Training algorithm of WEIFC

Input: The training dataset $D = [x_1, x_2, \ldots, x_N]^T (\in \mathbb{R}^{N \times d})$, the corresponding label set $Y = [y_1, y_2, \ldots, y_N]^T (\in \mathbb{R}^{N \times C})$, the total M sub-classifiers, the total n_j input features of the jth data subspace and the total r_j fuzzy rules of the jth sub-classifier, $i = 1, 2, \ldots, N$, $j = 1, 2, \ldots, M$.

Output: the output $\bar{Y}$ of WEIFC, $a = [a_1, a_2, \ldots, a_M]^T$ and hence all the fuzzy rules in WEIFC.

Procedure:
1.   **for** j=1; $j \le M$ **do**
2.   Generate the jth bootstrapped data subspace $D_j \in \mathbb{R}^{N \times n_j}$ from D in a bootstrapped manner;
3.   **for** k=1; $k \le r_j$ **do**
4.   Calculate the values of fuzzy set of the kth fuzzy rules for each selected feature by Eq. (4)
5.   Calculate the values of the antecedent part of the kth fuzzy rules by Eq. (3)
6.   **end**
7.   Generate the jth antecedent part matrix Φ_j by Eq. (6)
8.   **end**
9.   Concatenate all the antecedent part matrices $\Phi = [\Phi_1, \Phi_2, \ldots, \Phi_M]$;
10. Solve a analytically by Eq. (9)
11. Calculate output $\bar{Y}$ by Eq. (7)

---

4 Experimental Results

In this section, in order to evaluate the practicability of the proposed WEIFC, we adopt the smartphone sensor-based human activity recognition (SSHAR) task for WEIFC. Thirteen state-of-the-art classification methods for SSHAR are taken as the comparative methods to fully evaluate the performance of WEIFC in the sense of classification testing accuracy. In subsection IV(A), we give the details of the commonly-used dataset human activity recognition (HAR) and the parameter settings of WEIFC. In subsection IV(B), we report the experimental results of all the adopted comparative methods on the data HAR in the sense of classification testing accuracies. All the experiments are carried out under a computer equipped Intel Xeon W-2102 2.90 GHz CPU and 16 GB memory.

4.1 Datasets and Parameter Settings

The adopted dataset HAR [57] is a commonly-used benchmark dataset for evaluating the performance of the classification methods for SSHAR [58], which is collected from signals from the accelerometer and gyroscope sensors embedded in a Samsung Galaxy SII smartphone. The accelerometer and gyroscope sensors are sampled at 50 Hz, and it records human activity from 30 volunteers between the ages of 19 and 48 years with the smartphone fixed at the waist. After preprocessing and segmenting the raw smartphone sensor signals using a fixed-length sliding window of 2.56s and 50% overlap, the dataset HAR consists of 10,299 samples, which are further divided into 7,352 training samples and 2,947 testing samples. Each sample has a total of 561 input features belonging to one of six categories, *i.e.*, *walking*, *upstairs*, *downstairs*, *sitting*, *standing* and *lying*. Table 1 lists the extracted features in dataset HAR [57] for the raw smartphone sensor signals.

Table 1. Extracted features in dataset HAR [57]

Domain	Extracted features
Time	Mean value, Standard deviation, Median absolute value, Maximum, Minimum, Signal magnitude area, Average sum of the squares, Interquartile range, Signal entropy, Autoregression coefficients, Correlation coefficient
Frequency	Largest frequency component, Weighted average, Skewness, Kurtosis, Energy of a frequency interval, Angle between two vectors

The parameter settings of WEIFC on data HAR are set as follows, referring to the strategy in the random forest [42], the number of features in each data subspace is set as $\sqrt{d}$, the number of sub-classifiers is set as 120, and the total number of fuzzy rules is set to be 60 for each sub-classifier. Besides, the regularization parameter λ for LLM in WEIFC is set to be 30.

Referring the experimental settings in [58], thirteen state-of-the-art classification methods for SSHAR are adopted to fully evaluate the classification performance of WEIFC. They are Gaussian random projection based ensemble ELM (GRP-E-ELM), HNN, FW KNN, FW NB, HF-SVM, Two-stage CHMM, SRC-SVD, FMM-CART, SAEs-c, J48-LR-MLR, Convnet, HCF Convnet, and tFFT Convnet. Their experimental results are cited simply from [58] for fair comparison.

4.2 Results and Discussions

Table 2 shows the testing accuracies of WEIFC and the thirteen state-of-the-art classification methods. The best testing accuracy is marked in bold in Table 2. As shown in Table 2, the testing accuracy of WEIFC is better than those of all the state-of-the-art classification methods except GRP-E-ELM, FMM-CART, HCF Convnet, and tFFT Convnet. Moreover, the testing accuracy of WEIFC is very competitive for those of two deep convolutional neural networks, *i.e.*, HCF Convnet and tFFT Convnet. WEIFC is slightly inferior to GRP-E-ELM in the sense of testing accuracy. However, GRP-E-ELM behaves like a black box, while WEIFC has good interpretability. These experimental results indeed demonstrate the practicability of WEIFC for SSHAR.

Table 2 Testing Accuracies of WEIFC and Thirteen Classification Methods on HAR

Methods	Testing accuracies	Methods	Testing accuracies	Methods	Testing accuracies
GRP-E-ELM	**97.35%**	FMM-CART	96.52%	Two-stage CHMM	91.76%
HNN	87.40%	SAEs-c	92.16%	SRC-SVD	95.00%
FW KNN	87.80%	J48-LR-MLR	93.55%	tFFT Convnet	95.75%
FW NB	90.10%	Convnet	94.79%	WEIFC	95.56%
HF-SVM	89.00%	HCF Convnet	95.75%		

5 Conclusion

In this study, a novel wide ensemble of interpretable TSK fuzzy classifiers WEIFC is proposed to encapsulate several zero-order TSK fuzzy sub-classifiers into a single structure without an individual aggregation step. As such, WEIFC trains all the sub-classifiers in parallel on their respective overlapping data subspaces obtained in a bootstrapped manner for only once without the explicit need for any aggregation. After applying the proposed WEIFC to smartphone sensor-based human activity recognition (SSHAR), compared with the thirteen state-of-the-art classification methods for SSHAR, the experimental results on the benchmarking dataset HAR show that WEIFC has better classification testing accuracy than most of them.

The future work may be focused on two aspects. In an implementation, how to quickly determine the parameter settings for WEIFC is an interesting topic to explore. In practice, how to develop imbalanced and/or stacked deep versions of WEIFC for imbalanced and even more challenging (e.g., large-scale) classification datasets is an ongoing topic.

References

1. Zadeh, L.A.: Fuzzy sets. Inf. Control **8**(3), 338–353 (1965)
2. Ying, H., Chen, G.: Necessary conditions for some typical fuzzy systems as universal approximators. Automatica **33**(7), 1333–1338 (1997)

3. Wong, S.Y., Yap, K.S., Yap, H.J., Tan, S.C., Chang, S.W.: On equivalence of FIS and ELM for interpretable rule-based knowledge representation. IEEE Trans. Neural Netw. Learn. Syst. **26**(7), 1417–1430 (2014)
4. Du, G., Wang, Z., Li, C., Liu, P.X.: A TSK-type convolutional recurrent fuzzy network for predicting driving fatigue. IEEE Trans. Fuzzy Syst. **29**(8), 2100–2111 (2021)
5. Yeganejou, M., Dick, S., Miller, J.: Interpretable deep convolutional fuzzy classifier. IEEE Trans. Fuzzy Syst. **28**(7), 1407–1419 (2019)
6. Wang, L.X.: Fast training algorithms for deep convolutional fuzzy systems with application to stock index prediction. IEEE Trans. Fuzzy Syst. **28**(7), 1301–1314 (2020)
7. Wang, W., Vrbanek, J., Jr.: An evolving fuzzy predictor for industrial applications. IEEE Trans. Fuzzy Syst. **16**(6), 1439–1449 (2008)
8. Karaboga, D., Kaya, E.: An adaptive and hybrid artificial bee colony algorithm (aABC) for ANFIS training. Appl. Soft Comput. **49**, 423–436 (2016)
9. Ishibuchi, H., Nozaki, K., Yamamoto, N., Tanaka, H.: Selecting fuzzy if-then rules for classification problems using genetic algorithms. IEEE Trans. Fuzzy Syst. **3**(3), 260–270 (1995)
10. Yeh, J., Su, S.: Efficient approach for RLS type learning in TSK neural fuzzy systems. IEEE Trans. Cybern. **47**(9), 2343–2352 (2017)
11. Chou, K.-P., Prasad, M., Lin, Y., Joshi, S., Lin, C.-T., Chang, J.: Takagi-Sugeno-Kang type collaborative fuzzy rule based system. In: 2014 IEEE Symposium on Computational Intelligence and Data Mining (CIDM), pp. 315–320. IEEE (2014)
12. Jiang, Y., Chung, F.L., Ishibuchi, H., Deng, Z., Wang, S.: Multitask TSK fuzzy system modeling by mining intertask common hidden structure. IEEE Trans. Cybern. **45**(3), 534–547 (2015)
13. Lin, C.-T., Pal, N.R., Wu, S.-L., Liu, Y.-T., Lin, Y.-Y.: An interval type-2 neural fuzzy system for online system identification and feature elimination. IEEE Trans. Neural Netw. Learn. Syst. **26**(7), 1442–1455 (2014)
14. Li, H., Wu, C., Shi, P., Gao, Y.: Control of nonlinear networked systems with packet dropouts: interval type-2 fuzzy model-based approach. IEEE Trans. Cybern. **45**(11), 2378–2389 (2015)
15. Lu, J., Zuo, H., Zhang, G.: Fuzzy multiple-source transfer learning. IEEE Trans. Fuzzy Syst. **28**(12), 3418–3431 (2019)
16. Wang, G., Zhang, G., Choi, K.-S., Lu, J.: Deep additive least squares support vector machines for classification with model transfer. IEEE Trans. Syst. Man Cybern. Syst. **49**(7), 1527–1540 (2017)
17. Chung, F.-L., Duan, J.-C.: On multistage fuzzy neural network modeling. IEEE Trans. Fuzzy Syst. **8**(2), 125–142 (2000)
18. Mantas, C.J., Puche, J.M.: Artificial neural networks are zero-order TSK fuzzy systems. IEEE Trans. Fuzzy Syst. **16**(3), 630–643 (2008)
19. Stavrakoudis, D.G., Gitas, I.Z., Theocharis, J.B.: A hierarchical genetic fuzzy rule-based classifier for high-dimensional classification problems. In: 2011 IEEE International Conference on Fuzzy Systems (FUZZ-IEEE 2011), pp. 1279–1285. IEEE (2011)
20. Gacto, M.J., Alcalá, R., Herrera, F.: Interpretability of linguistic fuzzy rule-based systems: an overview of interpretability measures. Inf. Sci. **181**(20), 4340–4360 (2011)
21. Yager, R.R.: On a hierarchical structure for fuzzy modeling and control. IEEE Trans. Syst. Man Cybern. **23**(4), 1189–1197 (1993)
22. Raju, G., Zhou, J.: Adaptive hierarchical fuzzy controller. IEEE Trans. Syst. Man Cybern. **23**(4), 973–980 (1993)
23. Zhou, T., Ishibuchi, H., Wang, S.: Stacked blockwise combination of interpretable TSK fuzzy classifiers by negative correlation learning. IEEE Trans. Fuzzy Syst. **26**(6), 3327–3341 (2018)
24. Joo, M.G., Lee, J.S.: Universal approximation by hierarchical fuzzy system with constraints on the fuzzy rule. Fuzzy Sets Syst. **130**(2), 175–188 (2002)

25. Hu, X., Pedrycz, W., Wang, X.: Random ensemble of fuzzy rule-based models. Knowl.-Based Syst. **181**, 104768 (2019)
26. Siami, M., Naderpour, M., Lu, J.: A choquet fuzzy integral vertical bagging classifier for mobile telematics data analysis. In: 2019 IEEE International Conference on Fuzzy Systems (FUZZ-IEEE),pp. 1–6. IEEE (2019)
27. Hoffmann, F.: Boosting a genetic fuzzy classifier. In: Proceedings Joint 9th IFSA World Congress and 20th NAFIPS International Conference (Cat. No. 01TH8569), vol. 3, pp. 1564–1569. IEEE (2001)
28. Deng, Y., Ren, Z., Kong, Y., Bao, F., Dai, Q.: A hierarchical fused fuzzy deep neural network for data classification. IEEE Trans. Fuzzy Syst. **25**(4), 1006–1012 (2016)
29. Shen, T., Wang, J., Gou, C., Wang, F.-Y.: Hierarchical fused model with deep learning and type-2 fuzzy learning for breast cancer diagnosis. IEEE Trans. Fuzzy Syst. **28**(12), 3204–3218 (2020)
30. Feng, S., Chen, C.P., Zhang, C.-Y.: A fuzzy deep model based on fuzzy restricted Boltzmann machines for high-dimensional data classification. IEEE Trans. Fuzzy Syst. **28**(7), 1344–1355 (2019)
31. Sarabakha, A., Kayacan, E.: Online deep fuzzy learning for control of nonlinear systems using expert knowledge. IEEE Trans. Fuzzy Syst. **28**(7), 1492–1503 (2019)
32. Zhou, T., Chung, F.-L., Wang, S.: Deep TSK fuzzy classifier with stacked generalization and triply concise interpretability guarantee for large data. IEEE Trans. Fuzzy Syst. **25**(5), 1207–1221 (2016)
33. Zhou, T., Ishibuchi, H., Wang, S.: Stacked-structure-based hierarchical takagi-sugeno-kang fuzzy classification through feature augmentation. IEEE Trans. Emerg. Top. Comput. Intell. **1**(6), 421–436 (2017)
34. Zhang, Y., Ishibuchi, H., Wang, S.: Deep Takagi–Sugeno–Kang fuzzy classifier with shared linguistic fuzzy rules. IEEE Trans. Fuzzy Syst. **26**(3), 1535–1549 (2017)
35. Wang, G., Zhou, T., Choi, K.S., Lu, J.: A deep-ensemble-level-based interpretable takagi-sugeno-kang fuzzy classifier for imbalanced data. IEEE Trans. Cybern. **52**, 1–14 (2020)
36. Wolpert, D.H.: Stacked generalization. Neural Netw. **5**(2), 241–259 (1992)
37. Qin, B., Chung, F.-L., Wang, S.: Biologically plausible fuzzy-knowledge-out and its induced wide learning of interpretable TSK fuzzy classifiers. IEEE Trans. Fuzzy Syst. **28**(7), 1276–1290 (2019)
38. Qin, B., Chung, F.-L., Wang, S.: KAT: a knowledge adversarial training method for zero-order takagi-sugeno-kang fuzzy classifiers. IEEE Trans. Cybern. **52**, 6857–6871 (2020)
39. Xie, R., Wang, S.: A wide interpretable Gaussian Takagi–Sugeno–Kang fuzzy classifier and its incremental learning. Knowl.-Based Syst. **241**, 108203 (2022)
40. Kuncheva, L.I.: How good are fuzzy if-then classifiers? IEEE Trans. Syst. Man Cybern. Part B (Cybern.) **30**(4), 501–509 (2000)
41. Hesterberg, T.: Bootstrap. Wiley Interdiscip. Rev. Comput. Stat. **3**(6), 497–526 (2011)
42. Biau, G.: Analysis of a random forests model. J. Mach. Learn. Res. **13**(1), 1063–1095 (2012)
43. Feng, S., Chen, C.L.P., Xu, L., Liu, Z.: On the accuracy-complexity tradeoff of fuzzy broad learning system. IEEE Trans. Fuzzy Syst. **29**(10), 2963–2974 (2021)
44. Kelly, D., Curran, K., Caulfield, B.: Automatic prediction of health status using smartphone-derived behavior profiles. IEEE J. Biomed. Health. Inf. **21**(6), 1750–1760 (2017)
45. Ferrer-Lluis, I., Castillo-Escario, Y., Montserrat, J.M., Jané, R.: Analysis of smartphone tri-axial accelerometry for monitoring sleep-disordered breathing and sleep position at home. IEEE Access **8**, 71231–71244 (2020)
46. Sung, G.M., Wang, H.K., Su, W.T.: Smart home care system with fall detection based on the android platform. In: 2020 IEEE International Conference on Systems, Man, and Cybernetics (SMC), pp. 3886–3890 (2020)

47. Chén, O.Y., et al.: Building a machine-learning framework to remotely assess parkinson's disease using smartphones. IEEE Trans. Biomed. Eng. **67**(12), 3491–3500 (2020)
48. Wang, S., Chung, F.-L., Hongbin, S., Dewen, H.: Cascaded centralized TSK fuzzy system: universal approximator and high interpretation. Appl. Soft Comput. **5**(2), 131–145 (2005)
49. Bezdek, J.C., Ehrlich, R., Full, W.: FCM: the fuzzy c-means clustering algorithm. Comput. Geosci. **10**(2–3), 191–203 (1984)
50. Trawiński, K., Cordón, O., Sánchez, L., Quirin, A.: A genetic fuzzy linguistic combination method for fuzzy rule-based multiclassifiers. IEEE Trans. Fuzzy Syst. **21**(5), 950–965 (2013)
51. Huang, G.-B., Zhou, H., Ding, X., Zhang, R.: Extreme learning machine for regression and multiclass classification. IEEE Trans. Syst. Man Cybern. Part B (Cybern.) **42**(2), 513–529 (2011)
52. Wang, S., Chung, F.-L., Wu, J., Wang, J.: Least learning machine and its experimental studies on regression capability. Appl. Soft Comput. **21**, 677–684 (2014)
53. Wang, S., Jiang, Y., Chung, F.-L., Qian, P.: Feedforward kernel neural networks, generalized least learning machine, and its deep learning with application to image classification. Appl. Soft Comput. **37**, 125–141 (2015)
54. Wang, S., Chung, F.-L.: On least learning machine. J. Jiangnan Univ. (Nat. Sci. Ed.) **9**, 505–510 (2010)
55. Wang, S., Chung, F.-L., Wang, J., Wu, J.: A fast learning method for feedforward neural networks. Neurocomputing **149**, 295–307 (2015)
56. Hinton, G.E., Srivastava, N., Krizhevsky, A., Sutskever, I., Salakhutdinov, R.R.: Improving neural networks by preventing co-adaptation of feature detectors. arXiv preprint arXiv:1207.0580 (2012)
57. Anguita, D., Ghio, A., Oneto, L., Perez, X.P., Reyes Ortiz, J.L.: A public domain dataset for human activity recognition using smartphones. In: Proceedings of ESANN, pp. 437–442 (2013)
58. Chen, Z., Jiang, C., Xie, L.: A novel ensemble ELM for human activity recognition using smartphone sensors. IEEE Trans. Ind. Inf. **15**(5), 2691–2699 (2019)

Prediction of the Facial Growth Direction: Regression Perspective

Stanisław Kaźmierczak[1] , Zofia Juszka[2] , Rafał Grzeszczuk[3] ,
Marcin Kurdziel[3] , Vaska Vandevska-Radunovic[4] , Piotr Fudalej[5,6,7] ,
and Jacek Mańdziuk[1(✉)]

[1] Faculty of Mathematics and Information Science, Warsaw University of
Technology, Warsaw, Poland
{s.kazmierczak,mandziuk}@mini.pw.edu.pl
[2] Prof. Loster's Orthodontics, Krakow, Poland
[3] AGH University of Science and Technology, Krakow, Poland
{grzeszcz,kurdziel}@agh.edu.pl
[4] University of Oslo, Oslo, Norway
vaska.vandevska-radunovic@odont.uio.no
[5] Jagiellonian University in Krakow, Krakow, Poland
[6] Palacký University Olomouc, Olomouc, Czech Republic
[7] University of Bern, Bern, Switzerland

Abstract. First attempts to predict the direction of facial growth (FG) direction were made half a century ago. Despite numerous attempts and elapsed time, a satisfactory method has not been established yet, and the problem still poses a challenge for medical experts. In our recent papers, we presented the results of applying various machine learning algorithms to the prediction of the FG direction formulated as a classification task, along with a preliminary discussion on its inherent complexity. In this paper, we summarize the previous findings and then delve into explaining the reasons for the FG estimation difficulty. To this end, we approach the task from a regression perspective. We employ Gaussian process regression (GPR) to investigate the predictive power of cephalogram-derived features in the estimation of the FG direction and to obtain a principled estimation of the regression uncertainty. Conducted data analysis reveals the inherent complexity of the problem and explains the reasons for the difficulty in solving the FG task based on 2D X-ray images. Specifically, to improve the regression performance, one needs to fit non-smooth regression functions, as smooth regression generally performs worse in this task. Even then, the estimated uncertainty remains large across all data points. These findings suggest a negative impact of noise in the available cephalogram-based features. We also uncover a clustering structure in the dataset that, to some extent, correlates with the source of annotations. The repeated landmarking process confirmed that the location of some landmarks is ambiguous and revealed that the consequent inaccuracies are significant in comparison to actual changes in growth periods. Overall, this translates to the weak explanatory power of the available cephalogram-based features in FG direction estimation.

© The Author(s), under exclusive license to Springer Nature Singapore Pte Ltd. 2023
M. Tanveer et al. (Eds.): ICONIP 2022, CCIS 1794, pp. 395–407, 2023.
https://doi.org/10.1007/978-981-99-1648-1_33

Keywords: Orthodontics · Facial growth prediction · Gaussian process regression · Machine learning

1   Introduction

Characteristics of FG - direction, intensity, and duration - are important in the treatment of congenital malformations and malocclusions. For example, patients with mandibular hypoplasia (i.e. when lower jaw is too small) and convex facial profile could benefit from horizontal growth of the mandible (i.e. lower jaw) while in patients with mandibular hypoplasia and straight facial profile vertical growth of the mandible could facilitate treatment of the malocclusion [6,9]. Therefore, the ability to predict FG before therapy is of practical importance because it can affect the effectiveness of treatment.

The aforementioned paucity of stable structures is related to the lack of a coordinate system within which the direction of growth can be unambiguously characterized. Both in research and clinical practice, different angular or linear measurements or proportions are used for facial classification. Unfortunately, the facial morphology or growth direction categorized as 'X' by a given measurement (labeling) can fall into a different category when alternative measurement (labeling) is applied.

Contribution. In this work, we approach the problem of FG direction estimation from a Bayesian regression perspective, complementing the previous work on classification models. Our main focus is to investigate the noise in cephalogram-based features and to quantify their explanatory power in the prediction of FG direction. The results demonstrate that the estimation of the FG directions is hindered by large regression uncertainty and the need to use nonsmooth regression functions, suggesting a negative impact of noise in the available cephalogram-based features. Apart from extending our previous results to regression models for FG, the main value of this work is a rigorous, formally grounded analysis of the sources of uncertainty in the considered data.

2   Related Literature

The first attempts to predict FG were made in the 1960s and 1970s – [4] proposed a structural method consisting in a qualitative assessment of seven morphological features on a single 2D radiograph, while [3] used statistical modeling for classification of facial types. Later, [5] developed a prediction system by adding mean annual velocities with predictions derived from a polynomial model of the population's growth curve, while [22] created prediction equations for identification of favorable vs. unfavorable growth patterns.

Unfortunately, the possibility of effective FG prediction was questioned by others [14], who observed that when previously proposed methods were used in different patient samples, their predictive power was limited and clinically irrelevant. Recently, the Italian team proposed to use cervical vertebrae maturation stage, sex, and chronological age as a curvilinear variable for the prediction of mandibular growth [8] and the American team suggested that anatomy of the mandible at a young age could predict the type of FG during adolescence [19]. Nevertheless, both approaches still need validation on independent samples to prove their efficacy.

An interesting alternative in the search for the method of prediction of FG can be the application of machine learning (ML) methods, which have been recently applied for automated identification of cephalometric landmarks on 2D radiographs [2], 3D computed tomographic (CT) images [10], or 3D magnetic resonance imaging [17]. ML methods were also used to determine the prognosis of patients with Class III malocclusion [13], to estimate the risk of the development of temporomandibular disorders [15], and to predict the outcome of orthognathic surgery [23].

In summary, the application of ML methods in clinical disciplines related to the treatment of craniofacial anomalies has been growing fast in recent years. However, to our knowledge, besides our recent attempts [11,12], no research focused on the FG prediction with ML methods has been presented yet.

3   Facial Growth Prediction

Prediction of the FG with ML methods is a novel setting. It was first addressed in our previous work [11]. Although there is no widely accepted set of measurements to assess FG direction, orthodontists can utilize the following *three central measurements*: SN-MP, FA, and PN-AN. Each of them corresponds to a slightly different aspect of growth. SN-MP is an angle between Sella-Nasion and Menton-Gonion Inferior lines. FA (facial axis) is an angle formed by Basion-Nasion and Gnathion-PTM. PN-AN is defined by the difference of distances from Point A and Pogonion to the line perpendicular to Porion-Orbitale and going through Nasion. FG direction can be described by one of three categories: *horizontal, vertical, and mixed.* Figure 1a depicts the sample X-ray photograph with landmarks and measurements used to create the predicted variables, while Fig. 1b and Fig. 1c some examples of horizontal and vertical growth, where all three measurements consistently point to the respective FG direction.

In our previous study [11], we thoroughly described the dataset. In short, we used material from two of the world's largest studies, a Norwegian study [7] and an American study [1], conducted until the mid-1980s. We filtered X-ray photographs of 639 patients at the age of approximately nine, twelve, and eighteen. As it is now considered unethical to periodically take X-ray images solely for research purposes, it is not possible to collect more extensive research material.

3.1   Face Normalization and Problem Definition

During the experiments, we considered three types of input data: *cephalometric* (ceph), *Procrustes* (proc), and *transformed coordinates* (trans). All of them have a common base which are cephalometric landmarks marked on the 2D X-ray images. Cephalometric data contains mainly angles. Since the raw landmark

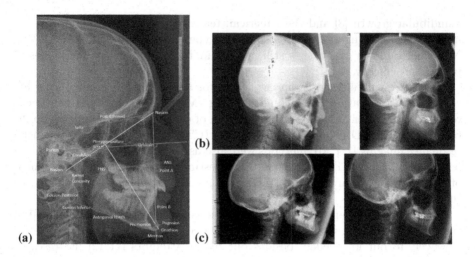

Fig. 1. Sample cephalograms. Figure (a) depicts marked landmarks, their names, as well as measurements used to create the predicted variables: SN-MP (blue), FA (green), PN-AN (orange). Figure (b) and (c) present horizontal and vertical growth, respectively. They illustrate the faces of two people in the age of 9 (left) and 18 (right). (Color figure online)

coordinates come from images in different scales, variously rotated and translated, we normalized them so that each meets the following requirements:

(1) A centroid of all landmarks is located at $(0, 0)$;
(2) A sum of distances between $(0, 0)$ and all transformed coordinates is equal to one;
(3) A sum of squared distances between a particular landmark and its average location is minimized across all landmarks and images.

Landmarks formed in the above way are called Procrustes coordinates and are commonly used in biological sciences [24]. However, the potential weakness of such representation is the lack of an anchor (all coordinates are relative). Thus, we proposed the third type of feature input which we called transformed coordinates. First, all raw coordinates are moved so that the Sella landmark is located at $(0, 0)$. Then rotation was performed to make Sella-Nasion line vertical. The main reason to unify the Sella-Nasion location is its far distance from the region of the chin (with landmarks Pogonion, Gnathion, and Menton), which presumably allows us to better notice the changes during its growth process.

Predicted variables are defined for each of the three measurements, SN-MP, FA, and PN-AN, by subtracting the value of a particular measurement at the age of 9 from the corresponding value at the age of 18. In the field of orthodontic, there is no standard, widely agreeable method of FG categorization. One of the possible approaches, which was adopted in our previous study, defines the target classes in the following way:

(I) The first class is created by instances whose values are lower than one standard deviation from the mean (*horizontal growth*);

(II) The second one, most numerous, contains samples located not further than one standard deviation from the mean (*mixed growth*);

(III) The third class constitutes instances greater than one standard deviation from the mean (*vertical growth*).

As a result, for SN-MP, FA, and PN-AN, the majority class contains 68.23%, 69.95%, and 74.80% instances, respectively. Let us denote the predicted variables as SN-MP(18-9), FA(18-9), and PN-AN(18-9).

3.2 Summary of Our Previous Results

In our previous work [11], we performed a comprehensive data analysis. It revealed a couple of problems related to the data that make the prediction task hard. Then, to predict FG, we employed a wide range of ML algorithms: decision tree, logistic regression, SVM, kNN, random forest, XGBoost, and a couple of multilayer perceptron architectures. We created a grid of experimental configurations that consisted of three data types (cephalometric, Procrustes, and transformed), five different periods in the input (data at the age of 9 (9), data at the age of 12 (12), difference between the values at the age of 12 and 9 (12-9), data at the ages of 9 and 12 (9, 12), data at the age of 9 and a difference between values at the age of 12 and 9 (9, 12-9)) and three predicted variables (SN-MP(18-9), FA(18-9), and PN-AN(18-9).

The first observation from the conducted experiments is that achieving an accuracy higher than the percentage of the most frequent class (MFC) became a challenge in the case of many configurations. Second, among all configurations with input from one timestamp, only two models beat MFC. It further evolved to the conclusion that 12-9 constitutes the best feature set. Finally, the best models for three predicted variables – SN-MP(18-9), FA(18-9), and PN-AN(18-9) exceeded MFC by 3.02%, 1.17%, and 0.45%, respectively. It could seem like a trivial achievement. However, one should be aware that the more the problem is imbalanced, the harder is MFC to be exceeded. We showed that in the case of evenly distributed classes, our models beat MFC (33% in this setting) by approximately 20 percentage points. Basing on the fact that all three measurements are, to some extent, correlated in the last set of experiments, we created an ensemble of three models forecasting SN-MP(18-9), FA(18-9), and PN-AN(18-9) to predict the most popular FG measurement – SN-MP(18-9). Eight different strategies for combining predictions of component models were tested, however, neither policy outperformed the single model predicting SN-MP(18-9).

In [12], we developed further research focusing on SN-MP measurement. Since SN-MP(12-9) is considerably correlated with the predicted variable, we suspected that a relatively small collection of features, including SN-MP(12-9), could bring a positive outcome. We created an empty set of attributes and added features one by one in a greedy way. The algorithm stopped very quickly – there was no statistically significant improvement in accuracy between models built on two and three attributes. The obtained score was 2.39% higher than the best reported in [11]. To further boost performance, a wide range of SMOTE-based data augmentation methods were tested. It improved the accuracy by an additional 0.4%. Finally, we showed that the undertaken problem is challenging for experienced clinicians as well.

4   Regression Analysis

The classification experiments summarized in the previous section indicate that predicting the type of FG direction is a difficult task, at least considering the features derived from cephalograms. To pinpoint reasons for this difficulty, in this section we attempt to uncover how well the cephalogram-derived features explain the changes in SN-MP, FA, and PN-AN measurements between the age of 9 and the age of 18. To this end, we fit non-linear regression models for the changes in these three measurements, using as explanatory variables features derived from the cephalometric, Procrustes and transformed coordinate measurements on cephalograms taken at the age of 9 and 12. The performance of these regression models can be seen as proxy to factors that limit the classification performance. Apart from quantifying which feature sets are predictive for the response variables, we also want to uncover the possible impact of noise in the data. We therefore, decided to employ regression models that allow us to encode clear prior assumptions about the smoothness of the regression function. Specifically, we fit the FG datasets using GPR [18, Chapter 15].

4.1   Experimental Setup

Results summarized in Sect. 3.2 indicate that the best feature sets – considering the classification performance – include measurements from both timestamps, i.e., at the age of 9 and the age of 12. Therefore, we focus our analysis on three variants of the features that include this information: measurements at the age of 9 and 12 (i.e. (9, 12) feature set), the difference between the two timestamps (i.e. (12-9) feature set), and measurements at the age of 9 together with the difference between the two timestamps (i.e. (9, 12-9) feature set). In each case, we separately fit the changes in SN-MP, FA, and PN-AN between the age of 9 and the age of 18.

Prior assumptions about the regression function in GPR are encoded in covariance functions. These functions contain hyper-parameters, e.g., variance in the Gaussian noise component. We follow a frequently used procedure for optimizing the hyper-parameters, where their values are chosen by maximizing the marginal likelihood of the data [18, Chapter 15.2.4]. As this is a non-convex optimization process, it is repeated 50 times with different initial hyper-parameter values. For each combination of the response variable, feature set, and covariance function, we fit 20 regression models to random splits of the respective dataset. In each case, a randomly selected 80% subset of the dataset is used for training, while the remaining 20% of the dataset is used for validation. We score the regression accuracy with the coefficient of determination over the validation set:

$$R^2 = 1.0 - \frac{\sum_{i=1}^{n} (y_i - \hat{y}_i)^2}{\sum_{i=1}^{n} (y_i - \bar{y})^2} \tag{1}$$

where y_i is the i-th value of the response variable, $\hat{y}_i$ is the regression prediction for that value, and $\bar{y}$ is the average value of the response variable over the validation set. Note, however, that we work in a Bayesian regression setting. Therefore, we do not have a single predicted value for an input data point, but instead a posterior predictive distribution over the predicted value. In the GPR, this posterior predictive is a Gaussian distribution with a closed-form solution for the mean and the variance [18, Chapter 15.2]. We take the mean of the posterior predictive as the predicted value and the standard deviation of the posterior predictive as the prediction uncertainty. We then report the average and the standard deviation of the coefficient of determination over 20 random splits. We also report distributions of the prediction uncertainty and prediction errors, as well as variance in the Gaussian noise component of the covariance function. These values were estimated with a 5-fold cross-validation.

4.2 How Well Cephalogram-Derived Features Predict FG Changes?

We begin the evaluation with two regression models that differ smoothness assumptions. The prior in the first model is constructed with an absolute exponential covariance function. This covariance function gives a prior over continuous but non-differentiable functions. The second model uses Matern covariance with smoothness parameter $\nu = 5/2$. This gives a prior over twice differentiable functions. See [21, chapter 4.2.1] for more details on these covariance functions.

Performance of the regression models, reported in Table 1, indicates that the available cephalogram-derived features are weak explanatory variables for the changes in SN-MP, FA, and PN-AN between the age of 9 and the age of 18. None of the models exceeded a coefficient of determination of $R^2 \approx 0.33$. Furthermore, regression with a smoother function gave inferior results across all experiments. Given that the predicted variables are changes in angles and distance on cephalograms, there is no inherent reason for explaining them with non-smooth functions. One likely explanation for the poor performance of smooth regression models is, therefore, the level of noise in the input features and the predicted variables. Next, the comparison of the regression performance across different feature sets indicates that the difference between the measurements at the age of 12 and the age of 9 plays an important role in the prediction.

To get a further insight into the obtained regression results, we quantified the variance of the predicted variables that is explained by a smooth regression over the (9, 12-9) feature set. To this end, we repeated the regression analysis using a covariance function that combines a prior over twice-differentiable functions and an explicit Gaussian noise component:

$$k(\mathbf{u}, \mathbf{v}) = \text{Matern}(\mathbf{u}, \mathbf{v}; \ \nu = 2.5) + \sigma^2 \cdot \mathbf{1}_{\mathbf{u}=\mathbf{v}} \tag{2}$$

Table 1. Coefficient of determination for GPR.

	Non-differentiable prior			Twice differentiable prior		
	12-9	9, 12	9, 12-9	12-9	9, 12	9, 12-9
	\multicolumn{6}{c}{Prediction of SN-MP(18-9)}					
1	ceph	ceph	ceph	ceph	ceph	ceph
	0.21 ± 0.06	0.20 ± 0.07	0.22 ± 0.07	0.09 ± 0.07	0.05 ± 0.08	0.15 ± 0.07
2	proc	proc	proc	proc	proc	proc
	0.26 ± 0.06	0.18 ± 0.05	0.26 ± 0.07	0.17 ± 0.08	0.08 ± 0.07	0.17 ± 0.08
3	trans	trans	trans	trans	trans	trans
	0.21 ± 0.07	0.09 ± 0.06	0.22 ± 0.07	-0.01 ± 0.02	0.01 ± 0.05	0.13 ± 0.06
	\multicolumn{6}{c}{Prediction of FA(18-9)}					
1	ceph	ceph	ceph	ceph	ceph	ceph
	0.23 ± 0.06	0.25 ± 0.07	0.26 ± 0.07	0.13 ± 0.07	0.07 ± 0.10	0.16 ± 0.07
2	proc	proc	proc	proc	proc	proc
	0.31 ± 0.07	0.26 ± 0.06	0.33 ± 0.09	0.20 ± 0.08	0.18 ± 0.07	0.23 ± 0.08
3	trans	trans	trans	trans	trans	trans
	0.24 ± 0.06	0.18 ± 0.06	0.31 ± 0.06	0.07 ± 0.09	0.11 ± 0.07	0.23 ± 0.08
	\multicolumn{6}{c}{Prediction of PN-AN(18-9)}					
1	ceph	ceph	ceph	ceph	ceph	ceph
	0.20 ± 0.09	0.20 ± 0.05	0.18 ± 0.08	0.09 ± 0.10	0.10 ± 0.06	0.10 ± 0.10
2	proc	proc	proc	proc	proc	proc
	0.11 ± 0.09	0.10 ± 0.06	0.13 ± 0.08	0.02 ± 0.10	0.01 ± 0.08	0.05 ± 0.08
3	trans	trans	trans	trans	trans	trans
	0.21 ± 0.06	0.11 ± 0.05	0.26 ± 0.06	0.02 ± 0.06	-0.01 ± 0.08	$\pm 0.19 \pm 0.07$

Table 2. Performance of GPR with a noise component in the covariance function.

	R^2	$\sigma^2/\mathrm{var}(y)$	R^2	$\sigma^2/\mathrm{var}(y)$	R^2	$\sigma^2/\mathrm{var}(y)$
	SN-MP(18-9)		FA(18-9)		PN-AN(18-9)	
ceph	0.29 ± 0.07	0.57 ± 0.01	0.32 ± 0.07	0.53 ± 0.03	0.20 ± 0.08	0.50 ± 0.05
proc	0.25 ± 0.06	0.30 ± 0.10	0.34 ± 0.09	0.34 ± 0.04	0.14 ± 0.08	0.34 ± 0.07
trans	0.19 ± 0.06	0.30 ± 0.10	0.28 ± 0.08	0.23 ± 0.06	0.22 ± 0.07	0.22 ± 0.04

The hyper-parameter σ^2 for the variance of the Gaussian noise component was fitted by maximizing the marginal likelihood of the data. Table 2 reports regression results for this covariance function and the estimated noise variance, relative to the variance of the predicted variable. Between 30% and 50% of the variance in the prediction variable is not explained by a smooth regression function.

Furthermore, a fit with an explicit noise component gives results broadly similar to the regression with non-differentiable functions. These results are compatible with the observed difference in performance between the smooth and the non-smooth regression models (Table 1).

Next, we focus on analysis of predictive uncertainty, i.e. the variance of the posterior predictive distribution for test inputs. To this end, we embed the input data points in $\mathbb{R}^2$ using t-distributed stochastic neighbor embedding algorithm [16] and then bin the embedded points. For each bin, we calculate the average prediction uncertainty of the points assigned to it (i.e., the average standard deviation of the posterior predictive distributions). We perform this analysis for the prior over continuous non-differentiable functions and the feature set that gave the best regression performance, i.e., (9, 12-9) (Table 1). Results are reported in Fig. 2. The estimated predictive uncertainty generally increases with the distance from the center of the dataset. That said, the uncertainty remains relatively large across the feature space: per-bin averages exceed 50% (SN-MP, PN-AN) to 70% (FA) of the mean magnitude of the predicted value.

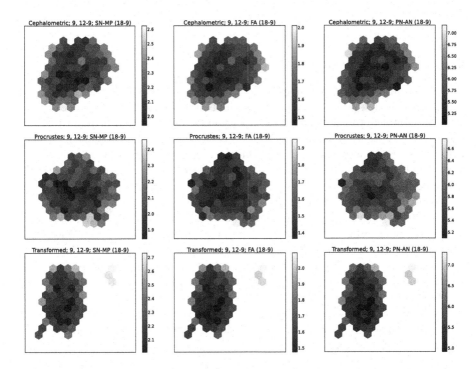

Fig. 2. Distributions of estimated regression uncertainty for (9, 12-9) feature sets.

Taken together, the comparative performance of smooth and non-smooth regression models, estimated Gaussian noise levels in the covariance function, and the distributions of estimated prediction uncertainties suggest that the regression performance in the evaluated datasets is limited by noise. A final finding worth mentioning in this context is the clustered distributions of data points in the transformed coordinates (Fig. 2, bottom row). Upon further investigation, the dataset forms distinct clusters in the feature space constructed with the measurements at the age of 9 or 12, but not in the feature space constructed from the difference between the two timestamps, namely (12-9) features (Fig. 3). The clusters correlate to some extent with the source of the original cephalograms.

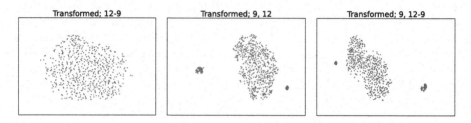

Fig. 3. Distribution of data points in the transformed coordinates

4.3 Further Analysis

As pointed in [20], the location of some landmarks is ambiguous, and it is impossible to mark such points very precisely. Thus, the data gathering process poses a source of noise. In the next set of experiments, we measured it quantitatively. Landmarking process was repeated for 30 cephalograms. The average Euclidean distance in the Procrustes space between the corresponding landmarks in matching cephalograms equaled 0.0076. For each patient that the above-mentioned cephalograms belong to, we measured (in the same way) the average distance between cephalograms at the age of 9 and 12, as well as between the age of 9 and 18. The respective values amount to 0.0092 and 0.0131, showing that inaccuracies arising from landmarking process are significant compared to the actual growth change which poses another problem in the FG prediction task.

Finally, we got a closer look at the data and discovered patients with relatively similar look at the age of 9 and 12, but significantly different at the age of 18. It other words, for the close values of input features, we have considerably different values of the predicted variable (cf. Fig. 4). Such cases confuse the model and make us hypothesize that sole landmarks at the age of 9 and 12 may not be indicative enough to create a strong predictive system.

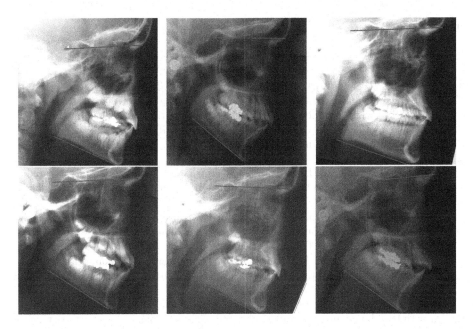

Fig. 4. Sample cephalograms of two patients (first and second row) at the age of 9 (left), 12 (middle) and 18 (right) years old presenting another reason for difficulties in growth prediction. Note that the SN-MP angle (between blue lines) is similar in both cases at the age of 9, but completely different at the age of 18. (Color figure online)

5   Conclusions

Previous work demonstrated that the classification of FG direction is a difficult task [11,12]. The main contribution of this work is a rigorous analysis of cephalogram-based FG data, which uncovers the sources of this difficulty. Specifically, the performance of the evaluated regression models shows that all variants of the dataset are best fitted with non-smooth regression functions. Furthermore, some of the considered coordinates display a clustering structure that, to some extent, correlates with the source of the cephalograms. It points to noise as a factor affecting the available cephalogram-based features. Overall, this translates to the limited explanatory power of available cephalogram-based features, explaining the previously reported difficulties in the classification of FG direction.

Acknowledgments. Studies were funded by BIOTECHMED-1 project granted by Warsaw University of Technology under the program Excellence Initiative: Research University (ID-UB). We would like to express our gratitude to the custodian of AAOF Craniofacial Growth Legacy Collection for the possibility to use the radiographs from Craniofacial Growth Legacy Collection.

References

1. American Growth Studies (1996). https://aaoflegacycollection.org/. (Accessed 13 Apr 2022)
2. Arik, S.Ö., Ibragimov, B., Xing, L.: Fully automated quantitative cephalometry using convolutional neural networks. J. Med. Imaging **4**(1), 014501 (2017)
3. Bhatia, S., Wright, G., Leighton, B.: A proposed multivariate model for prediction of facial growth. Am. J. Orthod. **75**(3), 264–281 (1979)
4. Björk, A.: Prediction of mandibular growth rotation. Am. J. Orthod. **55**(6), 585–599 (1969)
5. Buschang, P., Tanguay, R., LaPalme, L., Demirjian, A.: Mandibular growth prediction: mean growth increments versus mathematical models. Eur. J. Orthod. **12**(3), 290–296 (1990)
6. Efstratiadis, S.S., Cohen, G., Ghafari, J.: Evaluation of differential growth and orthodontic treatment outcome by regional cephalometric superpositions. Angle Orthod. **69**(3), 225–230 (1999)
7. El-Batouti, A., Øgaard, B., Bishara, S.E.: Longitudinal cephalometric standards for norwegians between the ages of 6 and 18 years. Eur. J. Orthod. **16**(6), 501–509 (1994)
8. Franchi, L., Nieri, M., McNamara, J.A., Jr., Giuntini, V.: Predicting mandibular growth based on cvm stage and gender and with chronological age as a curvilinear variable. Orthod. Craniofacial Res. **24**(3), 414–420 (2021)
9. Frye, L., Diedrich, P.R., Kinzinger, G.S.: Class ii treatment with fixed functional orthodontic appliances before and after the pubertal growth peak-a cephalometric study to evaluate differential therapeutic effects. J. Orofac. Orthop./Fortschritte der Kieferorthopädie **70**(6), 511–527 (2009)
10. Kang, S.H., Jeon, K., Kang, S.H., Lee, S.H.: 3d cephalometric landmark detection by multiple stage deep reinforcement learning. Sci. Rep. **11**(1), 1–13 (2021)
11. Kaźmierczak, S., Juszka, Z., Fudalej, P., Mańdziuk, J.: Prediction of the facial growth direction with machine learning methods. arXiv:2106.10464 (2021)
12. Kaźmierczak, S., Juszka, Z., Vandevska-Radunovic, V., Maal, T.J.J., Fudalej, P., Mańdziuk, J.: Prediction of the facial growth direction is challenging. In: Mantoro, T., Lee, M., Ayu, M.A., Wong, K.W., Hidayanto, A.N. (eds.) ICONIP 2021. CCIS, vol. 1517, pp. 665–673. Springer, Cham (2021). https://doi.org/10.1007/978-3-030-92310-5_77
13. Khosravi-Kamrani, P., Qiao, X., Zanardi, G., Wiesen, C.A., Slade, G., Frazier-Bowers, S.A.: A machine learning approach to determine the prognosis of patients with class iii malocclusion. Am. J. Orthod. Dentofac. Orthop. (2021)
14. Kolodziej, R.P., Southard, T.E., Southard, K.A., Casko, J.S., Jakobsen, J.R.: Evaluation of antegonial notch depth for growth prediction. Am. J. Orthod. Dentofac. Orthop. **121**(4), 357–363 (2002)
15. Lee, K.S., Jha, N., Kim, Y.J.: Risk factor assessments of temporomandibular disorders via machine learning. Sci. Rep. **11**(1), 1–11 (2021)
16. Van der Maaten, L., Hinton, G.: Visualizing data using t-sne. J. Mach. Learn. Res. **9**(11) (2008)
17. Maspero, C., et al.: Comparison of a tridimensional cephalometric analysis performed on 3t-mri compared with cbct: A pilot study in adults. Prog. Orthod. **20**(1), 1–10 (2019)
18. Murphy, K.P.: Machine learning - a probabilistic perspective. Adaptive computation and machine learning series. MIT Press (2012)

19. Oh, H.: Predicting adult facial type from mandibular landmark data at young ages. Orthod. Craniofacial Res. **22**, 154–162 (2019)
20. Perillo, M., et al.: Effect of landmark identification on cephalometric measurements: guidelines for cephalometric analyses. Clin. Orthod. Res. **3**(1), 29–36 (2000)
21. Rasmussen, C.E., Williams, C.K.: Gaussian processes for machine learning. Adaptive computation and machine learning series. MIT Press (2006)
22. Rudolph, D.J., White, S.E., Sinclair, P.M.: Multivariate prediction of skeletal Class II growth. Am. J. Orthod. Dentofac. Orthop. **114**(3), 283–291 (1998)
23. Tanikawa, C., Yamashiro, T.: Development of novel artificial intelligence systems to predict facial morphology after orthognathic surgery and orthodontic treatment in japanese patients. Sci. Rep. **11**(1), 1–11 (2021)
24. Zelditch, M.L., Swiderski, D.L., Sheets, H.D.: Geometric Morphometrics for Biologists: A Primer. Academic Press (2004)

A Methodology for the Prediction of Drug Target Interaction Using CDK Descriptors

Tanya Liyaqat[1(✉)], Tanvir Ahmad[1], and Chandni Saxena[2]

[1] Jamia Millia Islamia University, New Delhi, India
tanyaliyaqat791@gmail.com, tahmad2@jmi.ac.in
[2] The Chinese University of Hong Kong, Hong Kong SAR, China
csaxena@cse.cuhk.edu.hk

Abstract. Detecting probable Drug Target Interaction (DTI) is a critical task in drug discovery. Conventional DTI studies are expensive, labor-intensive, and take a lot of time, hence there are significant reasons to construct useful computational techniques that may successfully anticipate possible DTIs. Although certain methods have been developed for this cause, numerous interactions are yet to be discovered, and prediction accuracy is still low. To meet these challenges, we propose a DTI prediction model built on molecular structure of drugs and sequence of target proteins. In the proposed model, we use Simplified Molecular-Input Line-Entry System (SMILES) to create CDK descriptors, Molecular ACCess System (MACCS) fingerprints, Electrotopological state (Estate) fingerprints and amino-acid sequences of targets to get Pseudo Amino Acid Composition (PseAAC). We target to evaluate performance of DTI prediction models using CDK descriptors. For comparison, we use benchmark data and evaluate models' performance on two widely used fingerprints, MACCS fingerprints and Estate fingerprints. The evaluation of performances shows that CDK descriptors are superior at predicting DTIs. The proposed method also outperforms other previously published techniques significantly.

Keywords: Drug Target Interactions · CatBoost · CDK descriptors · Molecular fingerprints

1 Introduction

Drug target interaction (DTI) is a prominent task in drug discovery and research. It entails detecting possible links among chemical compounds and protein targets which acts as a guide in the preliminary phases of drug discovery and developmental research. Experiments carried out in wet labs are labor intensive and require a significant amount of money [22]. According to statistics, each novel molecular entity takes around 1.8 billion USD and the authorization of a novel drug application usually requires at least 9 years [8]. As a result, high-efficiency computational prediction techniques to investigate drug target interactions based on Machine Learning (ML) and Deep Learning (DL) have sparked a lot of attention in recent years [2]. The bonding of a medicine to a target's location resulting in the alteration of its functioning is considered as drug target interaction. Any chemical molecule that causes an alteration in the body's physiology

M. Tanveer et al. (Eds.): ICONIP 2022, CCIS 1794, pp. 408–419, 2023.
https://doi.org/10.1007/978-981-99-1648-1_34

when swallowed, ingested, or inhaled is referred to as a medication or medicine. On the other hand, targets consist of elements as nucleic acids or lipids, that are intended to modify. Ion channels, enzymes, nuclear receptors, and G-protein coupled receptors are among the most popular biological targets. To treat illness and ailments, the medicine inhibits the target's function in order to prevent certain catalytic processes from occurring in the human body. This is accomplished by preventing it from interacting with particular enzymes known as substrates. The drug discovery procedure that detects novel therapeutic molecules for targets relies heavily on DTI prediction [24]. Feature-based computational techniques for DTI prediction have gained significant attention over the years. The availability of the structural information of chemical compounds in the form of fingerprints or descriptors has played an important role. However, most studies consider fingerprints over descriptors. Hence, it becomes important to compare performance and identify better alternative. We provide more details about feature-based techniques in Sect. 2.

Considering the widely accepted ability of structure information of molecules, we aim to evaluate the performance of CDK descriptors against two widely used fingerprints, namely Molecular ACCess System (MACCS) and Electrotopological state (Estate) fingerprints. The proposed model utilizes Pseudo amino acid composition derived using amino-acid sequences of targets via *iFeature webserver* [4]. We use drug Simplified Molecular-Input Line-Entry System (SMILES) to obtain CDK descriptors, MACCS fingerprints and Estate fingerprints. The purpose here is to evaluate the impact of employing CDK descriptors for DTI prediction. We compare models' performance against two frequently used fingerprints, MACCS fingerprints and Estate fingerprints on benchmark data. This work mainly focus on extracting and feature processing, followed by a systematic prediction methodology based on machine learning. For example, in this case, we utilize the Categorical Boosting (CatBoost) classifier to make predictions. For validation, we compare our proposed model to several recently proposed models. The results reveal that the proposed DTI prediction model identifies drug-target interactions more accurately using CDK descriptors than MACCS and Estate fingerprints.

We organize the paper as follows. Section 2 offers an overview of computation approaches to DTI predictions and highlights recent methods closely related to our work. Section 3 provides the details about the datasets and feature encodings. Section 4 describes our proposed methodology and a brief overview of the CatBoost algorithm. Evaluation metrics and performance results are presented in Sect. 5 and Sect. 6 respectively. Finally, we conclude the paper in Sect, 7.

2 Computation Approaches to DTI Predictions

In this section, we provide an overview of computation approaches to DTI predictions and highlight some closely related work to our proposed methodology. The computational strategies for the prediction of DTIs can be broadly divided into **ligand-based**, **docking-based**, and **chemogenomic** approaches [11].

Ligand-Based. The rationale behind ligand-based techniques is that identical compounds bind to identical biological targets and have identical features. It starts with a single molecule or a group of chemicals known to be effective against the target and

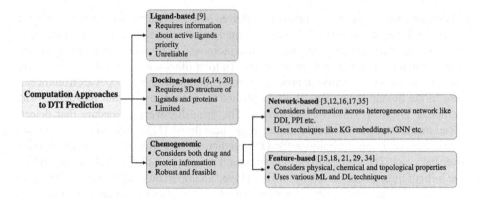

Fig. 1. A brief taxonomy of computational approaches to DTI prediction

it is further guided by the structure-activity relationships. However, there are certain drawbacks to this strategy. Because the protein sequence information is not employed in the prediction process, discovering new interactions reduces the connection across the identified ligand and protein families [9].

Docking-Based. The docking-based approach, on the other hand, uses the 3D shape of proteins and chemical compounds to determine their possibilities of interaction [6,14]. However, specific proteins like the membrane proteins have unknown 3D structures that make it less applicable [20].

Chemogenomic. The chemogenomic approaches use drug and protein information together to anticipate interactions. To infer probable interactions, a shared subspace is created by unifying the biochemical space of drugs and the genome space of targets. The main benefit of this method is that it utilizes a significant amount of biological data that is freely accessible from public repositories [33]. Chemogenomic approaches are roughly divided into **network-based** methods and **feature-based** methods. **Network-based** approaches integrate data like drug-drug interactions, protein-protein interactions, drug-disease interactions, and drug-target interactions from multiple sources into a single unified framework to boost DTI prediction [3,12,16,17,35]. For instance, Wan et al. [28] devised an end-to-end technique entitled *NeoDTI* to combine data from omics networks and learn topology that preserves the information of drugs and targets. Recent years have seen a fast growth of ML models based on knowledge graphs (KG). Mohammad et al. [19] suggest *triModel*, a model based on Knowledge Graph (KG) embeddings to derive novel DTI from the model's scores built by learning embeddings about drugs and targets from multi-modal heterogeneous data. On the other hand, **feature-based** approaches represent each drug target pair as an array of descriptors. Drugs and proteins are transformed into corresponding descriptors based on their chemical properties. Integration of individual features of drugs and targets forms the input to these approaches as a 1D array [15,21,34] (Fig. 1).

Most researchers prefer feature-dependent computation models to predict DTIs focussed on structural information of drugs based on molecular fingerprints that are bit strings indicating the existence of a specific substructure. For example, Han et al. [27]

Table 1. Qualitative details of the datasets.

Dataset	Drugs	Targets	Known interaction	Ratio of imbalance
Ion channel	201	204	1476	0.036
Enzyme	445	664	2926	0.010
Nuclear receptor	54	26	90	0.068
GPCR	223	95	635	0.031

present an automatic learning system called *LRF-DTIS* retrieving drug and target characteristics in the form of *PsePSSM* and molecular fingerprints employing lasso for feature selection, smote for handling imbalance, and random forest (RF) for predicting interactions. Wenyu et al. [18] suggest *PDTI-ESSB* turning all drug molecules into molecular substructure fingerprints and representing protein sequences as multiple features to express their evolutionary, sequential, and structural information. To prevent the drawbacks of sparseness and dimensionality curse, Wang et.al. [30] propose *MSPEDTI* which uses a Convolutional Neural Network to derive relevant low-dimensional features from the sequence and structural information defined in the form of PSSM and molecular fingerprints. Likewise, Wang et al. [31] propose a similar method using *PsePSSM* and *PubChem* fingerprints with feature weighted Rotation Forest. Sajadi et al. [25] introduce an interesting approach to handling the sparsity in the interaction matrix of drugs and targets through drug fingerprints. Wang et al. [29] use *MACCS* and *PAAC* for predicting DTIs with a novel method to create negative samples. Another way of capturing the structural information is molecular descriptors which are theoretically derived properties representing the physical, chemical, and topological characteristics of drugs. The majority of researchers use benchmark data to assess the effectiveness of their methods. We utilize the suggested benchmark data to evaluate our proposed method. In Sect. 3, we give a brief description about the data and feature representation for drugs and proteins.

3 Materials and Methods

3.1 Dataset Description

The gold-standard datasets used in this investigation are enzyme, Ion Channel (IC), Nuclear Receptor (NR) and G-Protein Coupled Receptor (GPCR), have been compiled by Yamanishi et al. [33] from the SuperTarget [10], BRENDA [26], DrugBank [32] and KEGG [13] repositories. The number of DTI pairs in these datasets after deleting the redundant information are 2926, 635, 1476, and 90, respectively. We consider each of these combinations as a positive interaction. To ensure a balance between positive and negative interactions, random under-sampling is applied to all pairs of DTIs to generate negative interactions. Table 1 displays the statistical data regarding these benchmark datasets.

3.2 Drug Feature Representation

In this study, molecular descriptors and molecular fingerprints convert the molecular structures of drugs into numerical form. For molecular descriptors, we use CDK descriptors derived from ChemDes[1], for molecular fingerprints, namely MACCS and Estate, we use the RDKit library[2]. The concept behind fingerprints is to define molecular structure using a library of molecular substructures, that translates a chemical compound into a bit vector of 0's and 1s by detecting whether a compound has a particular substructure or not. If the compound has that substructure, then only the bit at that position is put to 1 which results in a characterization of the molecular structure as a binary string. The number of molecular substructures in MACCS and Estate is 166 and 79 respectively, which is the size of the final binary bit vector. CDK descriptors, on the other hand, is an open-source platform for detecting and categorizing compounds using descriptor classes. The final size of the CDK descriptors is 275 and consists of autocorrelation descriptors, connectivity descriptors, constitutional descriptors, kappa descriptors, molecular properties, topological descriptors, WHIM descriptors, CPSA descriptors, geometrical descriptors, and quantum chemical descriptors.

3.3 Protein Feature Representation

PseAAC is a parallel-correlation-based method for delineating protein information that generates 20 + D features. There are various models based on amino acid compositions (AAC) that lack target sequence-order knowledge. Pse-AAC, introduced in [7] can be used to express both AAC and AA sequence order data. This technique is common in bioinformatics and related areas. Pse-AAC combines the core features of AAC with certain additional parts indicating a set of protein correlation factors and helps to improve model performance for multiple tasks. The expression for the features of PseAAC is as shown in Eq. 1.

$$P = [p_1, p_2, p_3, ... p_{19}, p_{20}, ..., p_{20+\lambda}]^T, \quad (\lambda < S), \quad (1)$$

where S corresponds to the size of the target sequence under consideration. The components are represented as shown below:

$$P_j = \frac{F_j}{\sum_{j=1}^{20} F_j + W \sum_{k=1}^{\lambda} \psi_j}, \quad 1 \le j \le 20, \quad (2)$$

$$P_j = \frac{W \psi_j}{\sum_{j=1}^{20} F_j + W \sum_{k=1}^{\lambda} \psi_j}, \quad 20 + 1 \le j \le 20 + \lambda. \quad (3)$$

Here, P stands for a vector of features, and W stands for a weight factor of 0.05. F_j shows amino acid occurrence frequency, ψ_j is the sequence correlation factor and λ represents information about the protein sequence order. In Eq. 2, for a single protein, AAC is expressed by 20 components, whereas sequence order is expressed by 20 + 1

---

[1] http://www.scbdd.com/chemdes/.
[2] https://www.rdkit.org/docs/GettingStartedInPython.html.

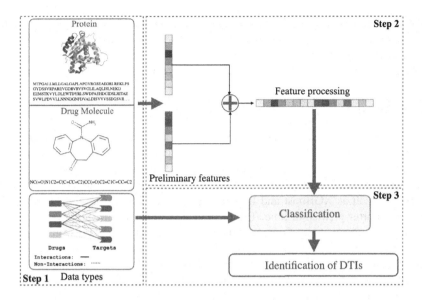

Fig. 2. Proposed methodology

to $20 + \lambda$ components, referred to as Pse-AAC shown in Eq. 3. For details about the ψ_j please refer [7]. For each protein sequence, we obtained a 50-D feature vector by setting the value lambda to 30. Rcpi [1], iFeature [4], and iLearn [5] are among the useful software tools for encoding protein sequences. Section 4 defines the work flow of DTI prediction and shows the use of PAAC in our proposed methodology.

4 Proposed Methodology

The proposed workflow of our DTI prediction model is as shown in Fig. 2. It is comprised of three main steps. The description of each step is as follows:

– **Step 1.** At first, we transform data into the corresponding values for which we represent each drug and target using their SMILES and amino acid sequences, respectively. Further, we use them to encode drug features and target features. For drugs, we use CDK descriptors, MACCS fingerprints and Estate fingerprints as features. For target protein, we use encoded features in the form of Pseudo amino acid composition (PseAAC).
– **Step 2.** In the next step, we process features from the input data. For each DTI pair, the drug features are concatenated with the target features to produce the final 1D array of features. The size of the array varies according to the drug feature under consideration. For instance, in the case of CDK descriptors, the length turns out to be 325. For MACCS and Estate fingerprints, it is 216 and 129, respectively. To normalize the range of independent attributes, we use the StandardScaler() function that converts the training and testing data to scaled representation. It accelerates calculations in machine learning techniques.

- **Step 3.** In the final step, we provide the processed features and existing DTIs to a classification model as input. We use the CatBoost algorithm to train a classifier. After this stage, we measured the performance of the trained model on a test dataset. We provide further details about the CatBoost algorithm in the following subsection.

4.1 CatBoost

Gradient boosted trees and Random forest is robust machine models for tabular heterogeneous data. CatBoost classifier is another open-source gradient boosting framework released in 2017 [23]. Although mainly designed to handle category features, CatBoost works on numerical and text data. According to the literature, it outperforms boosting algorithms such as XGBoost and LightGBM on a variety of datasets and has a substantially shorter prediction time. The technique is well-known for its use of ordered boosting to counteract overfitting and the use of symmetric trees for faster execution. During model training, a sequence of decision trees is built one after the other, with each succeeding tree having a smaller loss. In other words, each decision tree learns from its predecessor and influences the subsequent trees to increase its performance, culminating in a powerful learner. Gradient boosting trees are good at dealing with numerical data but struggle with categorical features. Both strategies require a large amount of memory and are computationally expensive. CatBoost, as a solution, uses target-based statistics to address categorical features, saving time and resources. To overcome overfitting, the CatBoost method employs an ordered boosting mechanism. After numerous boosting stages, traditional gradient boosting approaches use all the training samples to develop a prediction model. This strategy causes a prediction shift in the created model, resulting in a distinct form of target leakage problem. CatBoost eliminates the aforementioned challenge by utilizing an ordered boosting architecture. Furthermore, unlike standard learning classifiers, the CatBoost approach gracefully handles overfitting by employing many permutations of the training dataset, which emerges as the main reason for deploying its intelligence in the current work. Five-fold cross-validation is used to avoid data overfitting and for the appropriate application of CatBoost in the current DTI problem. We evaluate the performance of the created model on multiple performance metrics defined in the next section.

5 Evaluation Parameters

To evaluate and compare our proposed methodology with other methods, we use different metrics such as Precision, Sensitivity (or Recall), Accuracy, Mathews Correlation Coefficient (MCC), Area Under Curve (AUC), and Area Under Precision-Recall AUPR). The AUC and AUPR graphs are good choices for unbalanced data. Hence, most research uses it as a comparison criterion. The ROC curve demonstrates how well the trained model performs at different cutoffs. False positive rates are compared with actual true positive rates to form the curve. The AUC values range from 0 to 1, with higher values suggesting an effective model. As the AUC summarizes the curve with a range of cutoff values as a single score, the AUPR also does the same. The difference is that it shows the precision (y-axis) and recall (x-axis) for various probability cutoffs. The following are the definitions of other evaluation parameters used in this study:

$$Precision = \frac{TP}{TP + FP}, \tag{4}$$

$$Sensitivity = \frac{TP}{TP + FN}, \tag{5}$$

$$Accuracy = \frac{TP + TN}{TP + FP + TN + FN}, \tag{6}$$

$$MCC = \frac{TP * TN - FP * FN}{\sqrt{(TP + FP)(TP + FN)(TN + FP)(TN + FN)}}, \tag{7}$$

where TP means correctly labeled positive observations, FP implies wrongly labeled negative observations, TN means correctly labeled negative observations, and FN implies wrongly labeled positive observations.

6   Performance Evaluation

To evaluate the prediction capacity of our proposed approach, we use 5-fold cross-validation on all DTI networks, including IC, Enzymes, NR, and GPCR. We roughly divide the data into 5-folds and use four folds for the model training and the left-out fold for testing the model's performance. We repeated the process five times to get five different result sets and reported the mean values. Table 2 displays the experimental findings of five-fold cross-validation on various performance evaluators across all datasets.

Table 2 shows that we obtain the best accuracy of 0.8988 and the second best accuracy of 0.8929 using CDK descriptors on the enzyme and ion channel dataset, respectively. Results also show that the performance of CDK descriptors is better in most cases compared to MACCS and Estate fingerprints, which confirms that CDK descriptors are better at predicting the DTIs compared to these two widely used molecular fingerprints. Figure 3 shows the performance curves of the area under the ROC curve across all benchmark datasets.

6.1   Comparison with Previous Methods

To evaluate the proposed model's capacity for predicting DTIs in a logical manner, we contrasted it with earlier techniques using the gold-standard dataset and chose the AUC as the assessment measure since it best captures the model's performance. Table 3 aggregates the AUC values from prior approaches such as Yamanishi [34], DTCWT [21], Yang [15], Elastic net [27], RoFDT [31], AutoDTI++ [25] and MSPEDTI [30]. Table 3 clearly shows that the proposed model outperformed the prior technique across benchmark datasets. This shows that using CDK descriptors with the CatBoost classifier can significantly improve the capacity to anticipate DTIs.

Table 2. Obtained results using CDK descriptors, MACCS fingerprints, and Estate fingerprints across all datasets for different performance metrics.

Dataset	Feature	Accuracy	Precision	Recall	MCC	AUC	AUPR
Enzyme	**CDK**	**0.8988**	**0.9015**	**0.8954**	**0.7977**	0.9533	**0.9597**
	MACCS	0.8975	0.9013	0.89262	0.7915	**0.9548**	0.9595
	Estate	0.8822	0.8854	0.8783	0.7646	0.9468	0.9521
GPCR	**CDK**	**0.8409**	**0.8304**	**0.8567**	**0.6826**	0.8995	0.8967
	MACCS	0.8314	0.8178	0.8551	0.6650	**0.9063**	**0.9029**
	Estate	0.8196	0.8104	0.8346	0.6400	0.8818	0.8713
IC	**CDK**	**0.8929**	**0.8864**	**0.8997**	**0.7848**	**0.9539**	**0.9591**
	MACCS	0.8872	0.8793	0.8977	0.7750	0.9464	0.94767
	EState	0.8523	0.8409	0.8692	0.7058	0.9235	0.9174
NR	**CDK**	**0.8056**	0.7788	**0.8556**	**0.6155**	**0.8445**	**0.8376**
	MACCS	0.75	0.7560	0.7778	0.5101	0.8269	0.8342
	EState	0.7611	**0.7837**	0.7333	0.5332	0.8429	0.8327

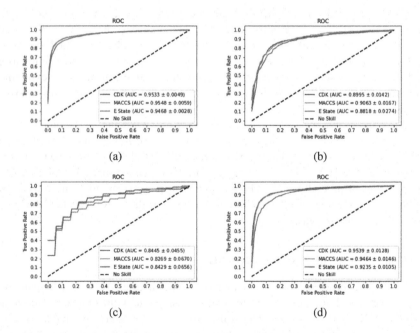

(a)   (b)

(c)   (d)

Fig. 3. Comparative analysis of the area under the ROC curves obtained using CDK descriptors, MACCS Fingerprints and Estate fingerprints across all datasets.

Table 3. Comparison of the proposed methodology with previous studies with respect to AUC values.

Methods	Enzyme	GPCR	IC	NR
Yamanishi [34]	0.821	0.811	0.692	0.814
Elastic net [27]	0.8605	0.7785	0.804	0.8418
Yang [15]	0.9529	0.8878	0.925	**0.8487**
DTCWT [21]	0.9498	0.8775	0.9270	0.7755
RoFDT [31]	0.9172	0.8557	0.8827	0.7531
AutoDTI++ [25]	0.90	0.86	0.91	**0.87**
MSPEDTI [30]	0.9437	0.8802	0.9088	**0.8663**
Proposed model	**0.9533**	**0.8995**	**0.9539**	0.8445

7 Conclusion

We presented a machine learning-based prediction model for DTIs. We use random under-sampling to deal with the imbalance of the datasets. To encode features such as CDK descriptors, MACCS fingerprints, and Estate fingerprints for drugs and PseAAC for targets, we use drug chemical structures and amino acid sequences. The objective of this research is to evaluate the impact of employing CDK descriptors for DTI prediction. We compare its performance against two frequently used fingerprints, namely MACCS fingerprints, and Estate fingerprints. The experimental findings reveal that CDK descriptors outperform the other two commonly used fingerprints. We use five-fold cross-validation criteria to get the results. The provided methodology is both practical and effective in forecasting DTIs, according to the comparative outcomes. We intend to expand our research in the future by taking into account novel target feature descriptors coupled with deep learning techniques.

References

1. Cao, D.S., Xiao, N., Xu, Q.S., Chen, A.F.: Rcpi: R/bioconductor package to generate various descriptors of proteins, compounds and their interactions. Bioinformatics **31**(2), 279–281 (2015)
2. Chen, R., Liu, X., Jin, S., Lin, J., Liu, J.: Machine learning for drug-target interaction prediction. Molecules **23**(9), 2208 (2018)
3. Chen, Z.H., You, Z.H., Guo, Z.H., Yi, H.C., Luo, G.X., Wang, Y.B.: Prediction of drug-target interactions from multi-molecular network based on deep walk embedding model. Front. Bioeng. Biotech. **8**, 338 (2020)
4. Chen, Z., et al.: ifeature: a python package and web server for features extraction and selection from protein and peptide sequences. Bioinformatics **34**(14), 2499–2502 (2018)
5. Chen, Z., et al.: ilearn: an integrated platform and meta-learner for feature engineering, machine-learning analysis and modeling of dna, rna and protein sequence data. Brief. Bioinform. **21**(3), 1047–1057 (2020)
6. Cheng, A.C., et al.: Structure-based maximal affinity model predicts small-molecule druggability. Nat. Biotechnol. **25**(1), 71–75 (2007)

7. Chou, K.C.: Prediction of protein cellular attributes using pseudo-amino acid composition. Proteins: Structure Function Bioinform. **43**(3), 246–255 (2001)
8. Dickson, M., Gagnon, J.P.: Key factors in the rising cost of new drug discovery and development. Nat. Rev. Drug Dis. **3**(5), 417–429 (2004)
9. Ezzat, A., Wu, M., Li, X.L., Kwoh, C.K.: Computational prediction of drug-target interactions using chemogenomic approaches: an empirical survey. Brief. Bioinform. **20**(4), 1337–1357 (2019)
10. Günther, S., et al.: Supertarget and matador: resources for exploring drug-target relationships. Nucleic Acids Res. **36**(suppl_1), D919–D922 (2007)
11. Jacob, L., Vert, J.P.: Protein-ligand interaction prediction: an improved chemogenomics approach. Bioinformatics **24**(19), 2149–2156 (2008)
12. Ji, B.Y., You, Z.H., Jiang, H.J., Guo, Z.H., Zheng, K.: Prediction of drug-target interactions from multi-molecular network based on line network representation method. J. Transl. Med. **18**(1), 1–11 (2020)
13. Kanehisa, M., et al.: From genomics to chemical genomics: new developments in kegg. Nucleic Acids Res. **34**(suppl_1), D354–D357 (2006)
14. Li, H., et al.: Tarfisdock: a web server for identifying drug targets with docking approach. Nucleic Acids Res. **34**(suppl_2), W219–W224 (2006)
15. Li, Y., Liu, X.z., You, Z.H., Li, L.P., Guo, J.X., Wang, Z.: A computational approach for predicting drug-target interactions from protein sequence and drug substructure fingerprint information. Int. J. Intell. Syst. **36**(1), 593–609 (2021)
16. Liu, Y., Wu, M., Miao, C., Zhao, P., Li, X.L.: Neighborhood regularized logistic matrix factorization for drug-target interaction prediction. PLoS Comput. Biol. **12**(2), e1004760 (2016)
17. Luo, Y., et al.: A network integration approach for drug-target interaction prediction and computational drug repositioning from heterogeneous information. Nat. Commun. **8**(1), 1–13 (2017)
18. Mahmud, S.H., Chen, W., Meng, H., Jahan, H., Liu, Y., Hasan, S.M.: Prediction of drug-target interaction based on protein features using undersampling and feature selection techniques with boosting. Anal. Biochem. **589**, 113507 (2020)
19. Mohamed, S.K., Nováček, V., Nounu, A.: Discovering protein drug targets using knowledge graph embeddings. Bioinformatics **36**(2), 603–610 (2020)
20. Opella, S.J.: Structure determination of membrane proteins by nuclear magnetic resonance spectroscopy. Annual Rev. Analytical Chem. (Palo Alto, Calif.) **6**, 305 (2013)
21. Pan, J., Li, L.P., You, Z.H., Yu, C.Q., Ren, Z.H., Chen, Y.: Prediction of drug-target interactions by combining dual-tree complex wavelet transform with ensemble learning method. Molecules **26**(17), 5359 (2021)
22. Paul, S.M., et al.: How to improve r&d productivity: the pharmaceutical industry's grand challenge. Nat. Rev. Drug Dis. **9**(3), 203–214 (2010)
23. Prokhorenkova, L., Gusev, G., Vorobev, A., Dorogush, A.V., Gulin, A.: Catboost: unbiased boosting with categorical features. In: Advances in Neural Information Processing Systems 31 (2018)
24. Sachdev, K., Gupta, M.K.: A comprehensive review of feature based methods for drug target interaction prediction. J. Biomed. Inform. **93**, 103159 (2019)
25. Sajadi, S.Z., Zare Chahooki, M.A., Gharaghani, S., Abbasi, K.: Autodti++: deep unsupervised learning for dti prediction by autoencoders. BMC Bioinformat. **22**(1), 1–19 (2021)
26. Schomburg, I., Chang, A., Ebeling, C., Gremse, M., Heldt, C., Huhn, G.: & schomburg, d. brenda, the enzyme database: updates and major new developments. Nucleic Acids Res. D **32** (2004)

27. Shi, H., Liu, S., Chen, J., Li, X., Ma, Q., Yu, B.: Predicting drug-target interactions using lasso with random forest based on evolutionary information and chemical structure. Genomics 111(6), 1839–1852 (2019)
28. Wan, F., Hong, L., Xiao, A., Jiang, T., Zeng, J.: Neodti: neural integration of neighbor information from a heterogeneous network for discovering new drug-target interactions. Bioinformatics 35(1), 104–111 (2019)
29. Wang, C., Wang, W., Lu, K., Zhang, J., Chen, P., Wang, B.: Predicting drug-target interactions with electrotopological state fingerprints and amphiphilic pseudo amino acid composition. Int. J. Mol. Sci. 21(16), 5694 (2020)
30. Wang, L., et al.: Mspedti: Prediction of drug-target interactions via molecular structure with protein evolutionary information. Biology 11(5), 740 (2022)
31. Wang, Y., et al.: Rofdt: Identification of drug-target interactions from protein sequence and drug molecular structure using rotation forest. Biology 11(5), 741 (2022)
32. Wishart, D.S., et al.: Drugbank: a knowledgebase for drugs, drug actions and drug targets. Nucleic Acids Res. 36(suppl_1), D901–D906 (2008)
33. Yamanishi, Y., Araki, M., Gutteridge, A., Honda, W., Kanehisa, M.: Prediction of drug-target interaction networks from the integration of chemical and genomic spaces. Bioinformatics 24(13), i232–i240 (2008)
34. Yamanishi, Y., Kotera, M., Kanehisa, M., Goto, S.: Drug-target interaction prediction from chemical, genomic and pharmacological data in an integrated framework. Bioinformatics 26(12), i246–i254 (2010)
35. Zheng, X., Ding, H., Mamitsuka, H., Zhu, S.: Collaborative matrix factorization with multiple similarities for predicting drug-target interactions. In: Proceedings of the 19th ACM SIGKDD International Conference on Knowledge Discovery And Data Mining, pp. 1025–1033 (2013)

PSSM2Vec: A Compact Alignment-Free Embedding Approach for Coronavirus Spike Sequence Classification

Sarwan Ali$^{(\boxtimes)}$ (iD), Taslim Murad (iD), and Murray Patterson (iD)

Department of Computer Science, Georgia State University, Atlanta, USA
{sali85,tmurad2}@student.gsu.edu, mpatterson30@gsu.edu

Abstract. The coronavirus SARS-CoV-2 is the cause of the COVID-19 disease in humans. Like many coronaviruses, it can adapt to various hosts and evolve into different variants. It is well-known that the major SARS-CoV-2 variants are characterized by mutations that happen predominantly in the spike protein. Understanding the spike protein structure and determining its perturbations are vital for predicting coronavirus host specificity and determining if a variant is of concern. These are crucial to identifying and controlling current outbreaks and preventing future pandemics. Machine learning (ML) methods are a viable solution to this effort, given the volume of available sequencing data, much of which is unaligned or even unassembled. However, such ML methods require fixed-length numerical feature vectors in Euclidean space to be applicable. For this purpose, we design two feature embedding techniques to convert spike sequences into a compact representation, which serves as input to various ML classifiers. Such embeddings are alignment-free, unlike some previous approaches, avoiding computationally expensive alignment and assembly pipelines. Our proposed embeddings, PSSM2Vec and PSSMFreq2Vec, combine the power of the position weight matrix for compactness, and k-mers to be alignment-free. Experiments on both SARS-CoV-2 and more general coronavirus sequence data show that the proposed embeddings yield better predictive performance, in most cases, than the baseline and state-of-the-art methods, and are also scalable to millions of spike sequences. We also show that in terms of runtime, PSSM2Vec is extremely efficient, which makes it applicable on datasets composed of millions of sequences. Using statistical analysis, we also show the compactness of the proposed feature embeddings compared to the existing methods.

Keywords: Sequence Classification · Coronavirus · Feature Embedding · Alignment-Free · k-mers · Position Weight Matrix

1 Introduction

The escalation of the COVID-19 pandemic since 2019 has gravely impacted the world, causing a global health crisis [1]. The severe acute respiratory syndrome

© The Author(s), under exclusive license to Springer Nature Singapore Pte Ltd. 2023
M. Tanveer et al. (Eds.): ICONIP 2022, CCIS 1794, pp. 420–432, 2023.
https://doi.org/10.1007/978-981-99-1648-1_35

coronavirus 2 (SARS-CoV-2) is the cause of the COVID-19 disease. Hundreds of millions of people have already been affected by this virus throughout the world making it more difficult to track and prepare an appropriate defense against.

Many studies indicate that SARS-CoV-2 was likely transmitted to humans from bats [2]. Coronaviruses (CoVs) cause various respiratory diseases and are broadly classified into five categories, namely alphaCoVs, betaCoVs, gamma-CoVs, alphaletoviruses and deltaCoVs, each of which infects various sets of hosts (*e.g.*, humans, camels, chickens, bats, etc.). As COVID-19 has been declared a zoonotic disease [3], understanding its host specificity can lead to a better understanding of SARS-CoV-2 and other coronaviruses [4]. This could help us to design an early warning system that could identify any future disease which has the potential to transfer from animals to humans before this happens.

In addition to adapting to new hosts, coronaviruses can quickly adapt new variants. Since the emergence of SARS-CoV-2, it has undergone many mutations, forming different variants [5]. The GISAID database[1] consists of a large number of diversified SARS-CoV-2 sequences due to the worldwide collection over time. Studying the behavior of these diversified sequences could enable tracing the growth of pathogens using genomic details (genomic surveillance). It could also help biologists to design vaccines that can help to eradicate the virus, and also prevent future pandemics.

Some effort has been done recently to classify and cluster sequences based on hosts [4,6] and variants [5,7,8]. Clustering approaches can help in identifying novel and rapidly growing variants, while classification can assist in keeping track of existing ones. Since the spike (S protein) sequence (see Fig. 1) of a coronavirus is the point of contact to the host cell, the spike region is often the focus in the literature (rather than the entire genome) for studying the behavior of coronaviruses, both in terms of variants and host specificity [6,9,10]. However, for a spike sequence to be a compatible input to machine learning (ML) models, it must be transformed into a fixed-length numerical representation, known as a feature vector. It is important to keep the length of these numerical vectors small as larger length results in more computational runtime, making it difficult to efficiently perform the underlying task [11,12]. There are many methods proposed in the literature to produce such a representation of spike sequences, such as one-hot encoding [6], k-mers based encoding [7], and position weight matrix based encoding [4].

ORF1ab(RdRp)	S	E	M	N

Fig. 1. The genome of a coronavirus is roughly 26 to 32 kb in length [13], comprising structural and non-structural proteins. The S region codes for the spike (structural) protein.

---

[1] https://www.gisaid.org/.

The position weight matrix (PWM) [14], also known as position-specific scoring matrix (PSSM) is utilized historically for the portrayal of biological sequences based motifs (patterns). In this paper, we propose two embedding methods, called PSSM2Vec and PSSMFreq2Vec that are alignment-free embeddings based on the PWM. Our contributions in this paper are the following:

1. We propose two different embeddings that are not only scalable, but also work with unaligned sequences, which makes it more applicable in practice.
2. We show that in terms of classification, the proposed embeddings outperform several baselines and state-of-the-art methods in most cases.
3. We perform statistical analysis on the embeddings to evaluate their compactness, which helps us understand the correlation of features to class labels.

The rest of the paper is structured as follows. Section 2 contains related work. Section 3 contains the proposed approach. Section 4 contains experimental setup and dataset statistics. Section 5 contains results and discussion. Section 6 concludes this paper.

2   Related Work

Embedding generation from the data is a popular approach in machine learning domain [15–21]. Various works have been presented for analyzing coronavirus spike sequences using classification with the help of machine learning algorithms. However, most of the previous classification approaches either lack scalability or generalizability. Some of them require globally aligned sequences, $i.e.$, of the same length, to use as input. An OHE (one-hot embedding) based approach is proposed [6] for predicting host specificity by transforming spike sequences into numerical vectors. Other algorithms for extracting a numerical representation of sequences are k-mers based (Spike2Vec) [7] and position weight matrix based (PWM2Vec) [4]. Although all three of these produce a fixed-length embedding of a sequence, they have their own drawbacks. For example, OHE possesses a curse of dimensionality challenge and does not capture all information on the order of amino acids [5,22]. Spike2Vec provides a more generalized and compact representation than OHE, but assigns an identical weight to each k-mer of a sequence to yield a frequency-based feature vector. PWM2Vec proved that assigning equal weight to each k-mer is too simple, as some k-mers carry more information than others. Similarly, the kernel matrix is a popular scheme used for sequence classification [23]. In this approach, a gram matrix is formed by calculating pairwise distance [24], and this matrix is used as input to kernel-based classifiers like SVM (Support Vector Machine). But due to high space complexity (storing kernel matrix), this method has little real-world usage.

3   Proposed Approach

We propose two different embedding methods to obtain a fixed-length numerical representation of aligned/unaligned spike sequences.

3.1 PSSMFreq2Vec

Although the goal of this paper is inspired by the idea of the PWM approach for finding patterns in sequences, we use the idea of PWM in a different way here. Given a sequence, we use the idea of k-mers to design a PWM and then assign a weighted value to each k-mer based on the values for different amino acids at different positions in the PWM. We then generate a fixed-length feature vector for all possible combinations of amino acids of length k and add the score from the PWM to the respective k-mer bin. All remaining entries of the vector will have a value of zero. In this way, we capture the locality information by using the k-mers and compute the importance of different characters' positions in the sequence. This type of weighted information cannot be computed by using the k-mers only. Finally, since PSSMFreq2Vec is still a (weighted) frequency vector, it does not rely on a global alignment. Combining these pieces of information in this way allows us to devise a compact, general, and alignment-free feature embedding, which can convert many types of sequence data to input for many different downstream ML tasks.

The summary of our proposed method, PSSMFreq2Vec, is shown in Fig. 2. It follows the given steps (from a to h) for generating a feature vector against a sequence. In step (a), a spike protein sequence is provided, which is used to extract k-mers in (b) ($k = 3$ is used in experiments). Further, in step (c), a position frequency matrix (PFM) is generated from these k-mers, which stores the count of each character of their position in the k-mers. The dataset used in the experiments contains 20 unique characters (represented by Σ, the set of amino acids) with $k = 3$, so the dimensions of PFM, in this case, is 20×3. In step (d), a position probability matrix (PPM) is generated by converting PFM values into column-wise probabilities. To obtain the PPM, we divide the count for a given character by the total count of characters in the column.

To avoid zero values in the PPM, a Laplace value (pseudocount) is added to every element, resulting in the matrix depicted in (e). A Laplace value of 0.1 is used in our experiments [25]. In (f), a position weight matrix (PWM) is produced from the Laplace-adjusted PPM by computing the log likelihood of each character $c \in \Sigma$ at a position i with the formula $W_{c,i} = \log_2(p(c,i)/p(c))$, where $p(c)$ is defined as $n(c)/61$ and $n(c)$ is the number of codons for each amino acid $c \in \Sigma$ and 61 is the number of sense codons.

We then calculate the absolute scores of each k-mer by summing up the individual scores from the PWM of every k-mer character with respect to their position in the PWM, resulting in the vector (g). In the last step (h), a feature vector of length $|\Sigma|^k$ is created, representing all the possible k-combinations of Σ. The feature vector consists of all zero values except for the positions representing the k-mers, which hold the absolute scores (computed in (g)) of the respective k-mers. The entire process is repeated for each spike sequence.

3.2 PSSM2Vec

This embedding approach is a more compact and generalized version of PWM2Vec [4]. Given a sequence, PSSM2Vec first designs the position weight

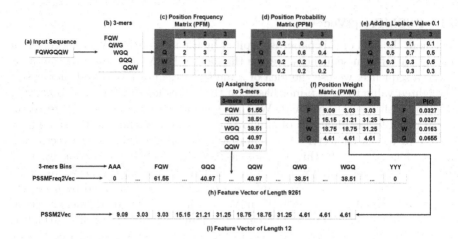

Fig. 2. PSSMFreq2Vec and PSSM2Vec flow chart. For PSSMFreq2Vec, we build a feature vector from a sequence by computing PWM from k-mers and creating a zero feature vector of length $|\Sigma|^k$ and updating its values accordingly. For PSSM2Vec, we build the vector by flattening the PWM matrix in step (f).

matrix (PWM) and then "flattens" (concatenates the rows) to obtain the resulting feature vector. The flowchart for PSSM2Vec is given in Fig. 2. Note that the steps from (a) to (f) are same as in PSSMFreq2Vec, but in the last step (I), the PWM is simply flattened to obtain a feature vector corresponding to the input sequence. Again, this process is repeated for each protein sequence.

4 Experimental Setup

This section discusses the datasets detail along with the description of evaluation metrics, ML models, and baseline models used for results comparison. The embedding methods are implemented in python and code is available online[2]. In this study, we use the following two datasets:

Coronavirus Host Dataset: It comprised of a set of spike sequences from different clades of the Coronaviridae family, along with metadata about the clade (genus/subgenus) of each sequence, but also about which hosts it infects. The Coronavirus Host dataset is extracted from both ViPR [4,26] and GISAID[3]. It comprised of the following Hosts/class labels (along with count of each host in the data): Bats (153), Bovines (88), Cats (123), Cattle (1), Equine (5), Fish (2), Humans (1813), Pangolins (21), Rats (26), Turtle (1), Weasel (994), Birds (374), Camels (297), Canis (40), Dolphins (7), Environment (1034), Hedgehog (15), Monkey (2), Python (2), Swines (558), and Unknown (2). In total, we extracted 5558 hosts along with corresponding spike sequences. Note that for the

---

[2] https://github.com/sarwanpasha/PSSM2Vec.
[3] https://www.gisaid.org/.

Coronavirus Host data, we also performed sequence alignment on all sequences so that we can run different baseline approaches that only work when all sequences have the same length. We then compare the results for the aligned and unaligned versions of this dataset in the results section.

SARS-CoV-2 Dataset: The SARS-CoV-2 dataset (extracted purely from GISAID), on the other hand, is a set of spike sequences from different variants of SARS-CoV-2, along with metadata about the variant of each sequence. This dataset comprised of following lineages/class labels (along with their class distribution): B.1.1.7 (976077), B.1.351 (20829), B.1.617.2 (242820), P.1 (56948), B.1.427 (17799), AY.4 (156038), B.1.2 (96253), B.1 (78741), B.1.177 (72298), B.1.1 (44851), B.1.429 (38117), AY.12 (28845), B.1.160 (25579), B.1.526 (25142), B.1.1.519 (22509), B.1.1.214 (17880), B.1.221 (13121), B.1.258 (13027), B.1.177.21 (13019), D.2 (12758), B.1.243 (12510), R.1 (10034). In total, we extracted 1,995,195 lineages along with corresponding spike sequences. The detail regarding lineages are given in [7].

4.1 Evaluation Metrics

W use the following evaluation metrics: Average Accuracy, Precision, Recall, F1 (weighted), Receiver Operating Characteristic curve (ROC) Area Under the Curve (AUC) with the "one vs. the rest" approach,and training runtime. We perform statistical analyses on different feature embeddings to evaluate the compactness of the information in the feature vectors using Spearman correlation and information gain, and also report the runtime needed to generate those feature embeddings. We use different linear and non-linear models for classification i.e. Support Vector Machine (SVM), Naive Bayes (NB), Multi Layer Perceptron (MLP), K-Nearest Neighbors (KNN), Random Forest (RF), Logistic Regression (LR) and Decision Tree (DT). For SARS-CoV-2 data, we only use 'linear' classification models such as Naive Bayes (NB), Logistic Regression (LR), Ridge Classifier (RC), and the Keras Classifier (KC) because of computational time issue on "Big Data".

4.2 Baseline Models

One Hot Embedding (OHE) [6]: In this method, a binary feature vector is designed for each alphabet Σ (where Σ contains "ACDEFGHIKLMNPQRSTVWY" characters) in the protein sequence, and the concatenation of all of these represents the sequence. In the binary vector, a 1 is only assigned to the corresponding character's location while all other have 0 value.

Spike2Vec [7]: For every spike sequence, this method generates sub-strings of length k (k-mers) and creates a frequency vector (Φ) containing the count of each k-mer occurrence in the sequence. Since in our experiments, $k = 3$, the length of frequency vector for the spike sequence dataset consisting of 20 unique alphabets is $20^3 = 8000$.

PWM2Vec [4]: This method generates embeddings for spike sequences based on the position weight matrix (PWM) concept [14]. It builds the PWM based on the k-mers of the sequences and uses PWM values as weights for the k-mers to construct the feature vector. A drawback of PWM2Vec is that it requires all input sequences to be of the same length (requires sequence alignment).

Approximate Kernel [24]: The method works by computing the distance between sequences using the number of matches and mismatches between characters (amino acids) from k-mers and designing the kernel (or gram) matrix. After computing the kernel matrix, classification can be performed by applying kernel PCA [27] (for the non-kernel based classifiers).

5   Results and Discussion

In this section, we present the classification results along with the statistical analysis to understand the compactness of feature vectors.

5.1   Classification Results

Table 1 and Table 2 shows the classification results of different embedding methods and classifiers on the Coronavirus Host dataset (for aligned and unaligned, respectively). An important behavior to observe is that PSSM2Vec outperforms all baseline methods despite having smaller feature vectors. The Spike2Vec and PSSMFreq2Vec are comparable in terms of predictive performance. Moreover, the performance of different embedding methods on unaligned sequences is better than (or sometimes comparable to) the performance on aligned sequences. This behavior shows that our alignment-free feature embedding methods are sophisticated enough to extract meaningful information from the spike sequences. Similarly, skipping the need to perform the computationally expensive step of sequence alignment could improve our model's overall runtime and make it more practically applicable in real-world scenarios. The training runtime is also minimum for PSSM2Vec compared to other methods because it has the smallest feature vector length. Therefore, we can conclude that on the Coronavirus Host data, PSSM2Vec outperforms all other existing methods in terms of predictive performance and runtime.

Table 3 shows the classification results of different embedding methods on the SARS-CoV-2 dataset ($\approx$1.9 million sequences). These results help to validate that the proposed embedding method is scalable to millions of sequences. We can observe that PSSMFreq2Vec outperforms all other embeddings methods, including PSSM2Vec, in terms of predictive performance. This is an interesting observation here, which indicates that with "Big Data", PSSMFreq2Vec is able to generalize more as compared to PSSM2Vec (which was not the case with the Coronavirus Host dataset). Although PSSM2Vec required less training runtime, its performance is on the lower side as compared to PSSMFreq2Vec.

Table 1. Performance comparison for different embedding methods and different classifiers on the Coronavirus Host (aligned) dataset. Best values are shown in bold.

Method	ML. Algo.	Acc.	Prec.	Recall	F1 (Weig.)	ROC AUC	Train Time (Sec.)
OHE [6]	SVM	0.82	0.83	0.82	0.82	0.83	389.128
	NB	0.67	0.80	0.67	0.65	0.81	56.741
	MLP	0.77	0.76	0.77	0.75	0.71	390.289
	KNN	0.80	0.79	0.80	0.79	0.78	16.211
	RF	0.83	0.83	0.83	0.82	0.83	151.911
	LR	0.83	0.84	0.83	0.82	0.83	48.786
	DT	0.82	0.83	0.82	0.81	0.81	21.581
Spike2Vec [7]	SVM	0.81	0.82	0.81	0.81	0.83	52.384
	NB	0.65	0.77	0.65	0.64	0.74	9.031
	MLP	0.81	0.82	0.81	0.81	0.77	44.982
	KNN	0.80	0.80	0.80	0.79	0.75	2.917
	RF	0.83	0.84	0.83	0.82	0.82	17.252
	LR	0.82	0.84	0.82	0.82	0.83	48.826
	DT	0.81	0.82	0.81	0.81	0.81	4.096
PWM2Vec [4]	SVM	0.83	0.82	0.83	0.82	0.83	40.55
	NB	0.37	0.68	0.37	0.33	0.69	1.56
	MLP	0.82	0.82	0.82	0.81	0.80	17.28
	KNN	0.82	0.80	0.82	0.81	0.78	2.86
	RF	0.84	0.84	0.84	0.84	0.83	5.44
	LR	0.84	0.84	0.84	0.83	0.83	43.35
	DT	0.82	0.81	0.82	0.81	0.82	3.46
Approx. Kernel [24]	SVM	0.78	0.79	0.78	0.77	0.78	16.67
	NB	0.62	0.66	0.62	0.61	0.72	0.19
	MLP	0.79	0.77	0.79	0.77	0.80	8.34
	KNN	0.85	0.84	0.85	0.84	0.80	0.24
	RF	0.82	0.81	0.82	0.81	0.83	1.95
	LR	0.76	0.77	0.76	0.74	0.83	3.80
	DT	0.77	0.77	0.77	0.77	0.82	0.27
PSSMFreq2Vec	SVM	0.83	0.83	0.83	0.82	0.81	50.72
	NB	0.64	0.74	0.64	0.61	0.75	5.90
	MLP	0.83	0.82	0.83	0.83	0.77	33.44
	KNN	0.80	0.80	0.80	0.80	0.75	65.20
	RF	0.84	0.85	0.84	0.83	0.81	11.42
	LR	0.84	0.85	0.84	0.84	0.81	57.55
	DT	0.81	0.82	0.81	0.80	0.79	7.50
PSSM2Vec	SVM	0.78	0.79	0.78	0.76	0.85	1.81
	NB	0.60	0.62	0.60	0.57	0.77	**0.15**
	MLP	0.81	0.81	0.81	0.80	0.89	13.70
	KNN	0.82	0.82	0.82	0.81	0.87	0.66
	RF	**0.86**	**0.86**	**0.86**	**0.85**	**0.91**	1.43
	LR	0.73	0.75	0.73	0.70	0.78	1.91
	DT	0.82	0.82	0.82	0.82	0.89	0.20

Table 2. Performance comparison for different embedding methods and different classifiers on the Coronavirus Host (unaligned) dataset. Best values are shown in bold.

Method	ML. Algo.	Acc.	Prec.	Recall	F1 (Weig.)	ROC AUC	Train Time (Sec.)
Spike2Vec [7]	SVM	0.84	0.84	0.84	0.83	0.87	45.36
	NB	0.69	0.77	0.69	0.67	0.79	6.02
	MLP	0.81	0.83	0.81	0.81	0.83	46.14
	KNN	0.80	0.81	0.80	0.79	0.79	1.97
	RF	0.84	0.85	0.84	0.84	0.85	10.21
	LR	0.84	0.85	0.84	0.84	0.87	31.00
	DT	0.82	0.83	0.82	0.82	0.85	2.54
Approx. Kernel [24]	SVM	0.79	0.80	0.79	0.77	0.78	18.18
	NB	0.60	0.66	0.60	0.57	0.73	0.07
	MLP	0.79	0.78	0.79	0.78	0.75	7.69
	KNN	0.86	0.85	0.86	0.862	0.76	0.21
	RF	0.82	0.82	0.82	0.81	0.78	1.80
	LR	0.76	0.77	0.76	0.74	0.76	2.36
	DT	0.78	0.78	0.78	0.77	0.75	0.24
PSSMFreq2Vec	SVM	0.82	0.82	0.82	0.81	0.84	51.32
	NB	0.67	0.74	0.67	0.64	0.78	6.19
	MLP	0.82	0.84	0.82	0.82	0.81	32.82
	KNN	0.80	0.80	0.80	0.79	0.78	46.85
	RF	0.83	0.83	0.83	0.82	0.84	11.70
	LR	0.84	0.84	0.84	0.83	0.84	33.09
	DT	0.81	0.82	0.81	0.81	0.81	5.79
PSSM2Vec	SVM	0.77	0.78	0.77	0.75	0.86	1.34
	NB	0.68	0.76	0.68	0.65	0.79	**0.14**
	MLP	0.81	0.81	0.81	0.80	0.86	11.72
	KNN	0.82	0.82	0.82	0.81	0.88	0.49
	RF	**0.87**	**0.86**	**0.87**	**0.865**	**0.92**	1.55
	LR	0.72	0.75	0.72	0.70	0.78	1.25
	DT	0.82	0.82	0.82	0.81	0.90	0.19

5.2 Evaluating t-SNE

We use the t-distributed stochastic neighbor embedding (t-SNE) approach [28] to evaluate the (hidden) patterns in the data. To see how well the data is preserved by t-SNE in 2 dimensions given different feature embeddings as input, we use k-ary neighborhood agreement (k-ANA) method [29]. The k-ANA test computes nearest neighbors in the original High Dimensional (HD) data and the Low Dimensional data (LD) (from t-SNE). It then takes the intersection of these to evaluate the number of neighbors on which both HD and LD agree. Using this intersection, a value $R(k)$ is calculated for evaluating the preservation of k-ary neighborhoods, and $R(k)$ is defined as follows: $R(k) = \frac{(n-1)Q(k)-k}{n-1-k}$,

Table 3. Variants Classification Results on the SARS-CoV-2 dataset for the top 22 variants (1995195 sequences). Best values are shown in bold.

Method	ML. Algo.	Acc.	Prec.	Recall	F1 (Weig.)	ROC AUC	Train Time (Sec.)
OHE [6]	NB	0.31	0.58	0.31	0.38	0.60	6576.10
	LR	0.57	0.51	0.57	0.50	0.58	191296.4
	RC	0.56	0.49	0.56	0.49	0.57	8725.96
	KC	0.59	0.55	0.59	0.54	0.60	120316.7
Spike2Vec [7]	NB	0.59	0.79	0.59	0.60	0.78	4410.27
	LR	0.88	0.89	0.88	0.87	0.86	140245.19
	RC	0.85	0.83	0.85	0.82	0.82	2985.94
	KC	0.88	0.901	0.88	0.87	0.86	53000.61
PWM2Vec [4]	NB	0.46	0.80	0.46	0.56	0.71	590.13
	LR	0.72	0.71	0.72	0.69	0.72	858.06
	RC	0.70	0.71	0.70	0.67	0.70	138.74
	KC	0.81	0.79	0.81	0.79	0.74	2287.41
PSSMFreq2Vec	NB	0.14	0.73	0.14	0.14	0.71	4605.95
	LR	0.88	0.89	0.88	0.87	0.86	281995.3
	RC	0.86	0.88	0.86	0.84	0.83	7659.69
	KC	**0.89**	**0.905**	**0.89**	**0.88**	**0.87**	90316.71
PSSM2Vec	NB	0.09	0.55	0.09	0.11	0.53	**42.56**
	LR	0.81	0.77	0.81	0.77	0.75	363.13
	RC	0.76	0.70	0.76	0.70	0.64	106.60
	KC	0.82	0.81	0.82	0.81	0.79	695.107

where $Q(k) = \Sigma_i^n \frac{1}{nk}|kNN(x_i) \bigcap kNN(x_i')|$. Similarly, $kNN(x)$ represents the set of nearest neighbors of x in high dimensions (HD). Moreover, $kNN(x')$ represents nearest neighbors in low dimensions (LD). The $R(k) \in [0,1]$ and higher value of $R(k)$ indicates better preservation of neighborhood in LD space. For our experiment, we have aggregated the $R(k)$ values for k from 1 to 99 and calculated the area under curve formed by $R(k)$ using the following expression: $AUC_{RNX} = \frac{\Sigma_k \frac{R(k)}{k}}{\Sigma_k \frac{1}{k}}$. The values of AUC_{RNX} for the baselines and proposed model are given in Table 4. We can observe that PSSM2Vec performs better than the other models for the Coronavirus Host dataset. This means that t-SNE is able to preserve the distance (hence the global structure of the data) between sequences more accurately using PSSM2Vec. For the SARS-CoV-2 data, PWM2Vec performs better than the other models. However, PSSM2Vec also performs comparably to PWM2Vec. Since PWM2Vec does not work with unaligned sequences, using PSSM2Vec becomes even more relevant as it works for both aligned and unaligned sequences. In general, since PSSM2Vec is better in terms of predictive performance, training runtime, and preserving the overall structure of data, we believe that it is more applicable in real-world scenarios for the classification of biological sequences.

To get a better idea about the overall time taken by each method to generate embeddings, we reported the feature vector computation runtime for different embedding methods in Table 5. We can again observe that PSSM2Vec takes very

Table 4. k-ary neighborhood agreement for $k = 1$ to 99.

Dataset	Method	AUC
Coronavirus Host	OHE	0.3914
	Spike2Vec	0.4054
	PWM2Vec	0.4169
	PSSMFreq2Vec	0.4029
	PSSM2Vec	**0.4417**
SARS-CoV-2	OHE	0.2248
	Spike2Vec	0.2549
	PWM2Vec	**0.2850**
	PSSMFreq2Vec	0.2554
	PSSM2Vec	0.2819

Table 5. Runtime for generating feature vectors using different methods.

Dataset	No. of Seq.	Method	Runtime
Coronavirus Host	5558	OHE	196.31 s
		Spike2Vec	1179.66 s
		PWM2Vec	1506.63 s
		Approx. Kernel	379.47 s
		PSSMFreq2Vec	908.12 s
		PSSM2Vec	48.25 s
SARS-CoV-2	2519386	OHE	> 3 days
		Spike2Vec	> 3 days
		PWM2Vec	> 3 days
		PSSMFreq2Vec	> 3 days
		PSSM2Vec	> 4 h

little time to generate in the case of both datasets. On the SARS-CoV-2 dataset, while other embedding methods took more than 3 days, PSSM2Vec just took 4.25 h to generate feature vectors for 1.9 million sequences.

5.3 Statistical Analysis

One way to evaluate the effectiveness of the feature embeddings is to analyze their compactness. For this purpose, we perform statistical analysis, including Pearson and Spearman Correlation. We compute the correlation values for different features of embeddings (corresponding to class labels) and report the fraction of attributes in each feature embedding having a high correlation corresponding to the class labels. The Pearson correlation values for different thresholds are reported in Fig. 3a (for the Coronavirus Host dataset). Similarly, the Spearman correlation values for different thresholds (ranging from −1 to 1) and embeddings are reported in Fig. 3b (for the Coronavirus Host dataset). We can observe that, overall, PSSM2Vec and PSSMFreq2Vec have the highest fraction of values for both Pearson correlation and Spearman correlation. This shows that more features in PSSM2Vec are highly correlated with the class label, demonstrating that these embeddings are the most compact. This compactness is also highlighted in terms of obtaining better predictive performance in terms of sequence classification (as given in Table 1 "for aligned data", Table 2 "for unaligned data" and Table 3 "for SARS-CoV-2 data"). In summary, we have the following properties of the PSSM2Vec: (i) it is better (or sometimes comparable) in terms of predictive performance, training runtime, and embedding generation runtime, (ii) it easily scales to millions of sequences, (iii) it works for both aligned and unaligned sequences, and (iv) it is better in terms of feature vector compactness (computed using Pearson and Spearman correlation). Therefore, we can conclude that in a real-world scenario, using PSSM2Vec is more appropriate than other embedding approaches for biological sequence classification.

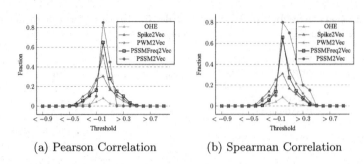

(a) Pearson Correlation   (b) Spearman Correlation

Fig. 3. Correlation values for Coronavirus Host data. (a) and (b) show the fraction of features having correlation values greater than or less than the thresholds (on x-axis). The fractions are computed by taking denominator as the size of embeddings (69960 for OHE, 8000 for Spike2Vec, 3490 for PWM2Vec, 8000 for PSSMFreq2Vec, and 60 for PSSM2Vec).

6   Conclusion

We propose two different alignment-free embeddings, called PSSM2Vec and PSSMFreq2Vec, to generate fixed-length feature vectors from spike sequences, which can be used as input for different ML algorithms. We show that these embeddings outperform the baseline methods in predictive performance and runtime. Moreover, we perform statistical analysis to evaluate the importance of features in the embeddings to understand the predictive behavior. Future extensions include assessing the performance of these embeddings on other viruses along with applying deep learning models to classify the embeddings.

Acknowledgements. The authors would like to acknowledge funding from an MBD fellowship to Sarwan Ali and a Georgia State University Computer Science Startup Grant to Murray Patterson.

References

1. Majumder, J., Minko, T.: Recent developments on therapeutic and diagnostic approaches for covid-19. AAPS J. **23**(1), 1–22 (2021)
2. Zhou, P., et al.: A pneumonia outbreak associated with a new coronavirus of probable bat origin. Nature **579**, 270–273 (2020)
3. Haider, N., et al.: Covid-19-zoonosis or emerging infectious disease? Front. Public Health **8**, 763 (2020)
4. Ali, S., Bello, B., Chourasia, P., Punathil, R.T., Zhou, Y., Patterson, M.: PWM2Vec: an efficient embedding approach for viral host specification from coronavirus spike sequences. Biology **11**(3), 418 (2022)
5. Ali, S., Sahoo, B., Ullah, N., Zelikovskiy, A., Patterson, M., Khan, I.: A k-mer based approach for sars-cov-2 variant identification. In: International Symposium on Bioinformatics Research and Applications, pp. 153–164 (2021)

6. Kuzmin, K., et al.: Machine learning methods accurately predict host specificity of coronaviruses based on spike sequences alone. Biochem. Biophys. Res. Commun. **533**(3), 553–558 (2020)

7. Ali, S., Patterson, M.: Spike2vec: an efficient and scalable embedding approach for covid-19 spike sequences. In: IEEE International Conference on Big Data (Big Data), pp. 1533–1540 (2021)

8. Tayebi, Z., Ali, S., Patterson, M.: Robust representation and efficient feature selection allows for effective clustering of sars-cov-2 variants. Algorithms **14**(12), 348 (2021)

9. Ali, S., Ali, T.E., Khan, M.A., Khan, I., Patterson, M.: Effective and scalable clustering of sars-cov-2 sequences. In: International Conference on Big Data Research (ICBDR), pp. 42–49 (2021)

10. Ali, S., Sahoo, B., Zelikovsky, A., Chen, P.Y., Patterson, M.: Benchmarking machine learning robustness in Covid-19 genome sequence classification. Sci. Rep. **13**(1), 4154 (2023)

11. Ali, S., Alvi, M.K., Faizullah, S., Khan, M.A., Alshanqiti, A., Khan, I.: Detecting ddos attack on sdn due to vulnerabilities in openflow. In: 2019 International Conference on Advances in the Emerging Computing Technologies (AECT), pp. 1–6 (2020)

12. Ali, S.: Cache replacement algorithm. arXiv preprint arXiv:2107.14646 (2021)

13. King, A.M., Adams, M. J., Carstens, E. B., Lefkowitz, E.J. (eds.): Order - nidovirales. Virus Taxonomy, pp. 784–794 (2012)

14. Stormo, G.D., Schneider, T.D., Gold, L., Ehrenfeucht, A.: Use of the 'Perceptron' algorithm to distinguish translational initiation sites in E. coli. Nucleic Acids Res. **10**(9), 2997–3011 (1982)

15. Ullah, A., Ali, S., Khan, I., Khan, M.A., Faizullah, S.: Effect of analysis window and feature selection on classification of hand movements using emg signal. In: SAI Intelligent Systems Conference (IntelliSys), pp. 400–415 (2020)

16. Ali, S., Shakeel, M.H., Khan, I., Faizullah, S., Khan, M.A.: Predicting attributes of nodes using network structure. ACM Trans. Intell. Syst. Technol. (TIST) **12**(2), 1–23 (2021)

17. Ali, S., Mansoor, H., Khan, I., Arshad, N., Khan, M.A., Faizullah, S.: Short-term load forecasting using ami data. arXiv preprint arXiv:1912.12479 (2019)

18. Ali, S., Mansoor, H., Arshad, N., Khan, I.: Short term load forecasting using smart meter data. In: International Conference on Future Energy Systems, pp. 419–421 (2019)

19. Ali, S., Zhou, Y., Patterson, M.: Efficient analysis of covid-19 clinical data using machine learning models. Med. Biol. Eng. Comput., 1–16 (2022)

20. Ali, S., Bello, B., Patterson, M.: Classifying covid-19 spike sequences from geographic location using deep learning. arXiv preprint arXiv:2110.00809 (2021)

21. Ali, S.: Information we can extract about a user from' one minute mobile application usage. arXiv preprint arXiv:2207.13222 (2022)

22. Ali, S., Ciccolella, S., Lucarella, L., Vedova, G.D., Patterson, M.: Simpler and faster development of tumor phylogeny pipelines. J. Comput. Biol. **28**(11), 1142–1155 (2021)

23. Ali, S., Sahoo, B., Khan, M.A., Zelikovsky, A., Khan, I.U., Patterson, M.: Efficient approximate kernel based spike sequence classification. IEEE/ACM Trans. Comput. Biol. Bioinf. (2022)

24. Farhan, M., Tariq, J., Zaman, A., Shabbir, M., Khan, I.: Efficient approximation algorithms for strings kernel based sequence classification. In: Advances in neural information processing systems (NeurIPS), pp. 6935–6945 (2017)

25. Nishida, K., Frith, M., Nakai, K.: Pseudocounts for transcription factor binding sites. Nucleic Acids Res. **37**(3), 939–944 (2009)
26. Pickett, B., et al.: Vipr: an open bioinformatics database and analysis resource for virology research. Nucleic Acids Res. **40**(D1), D593–D598 (2012)
27. Hoffmann, H.: Kernel pca for novelty detection. Pattern Recogn. **40**(3), 863–874 (2007)
28. Van der, M.L., Hinton, G.: Visualizing data using t-sne. J. Mach. Learn. Res. (JMLR) **9**(11) (2008)
29. Zhu, Y., Ting, K.M.: Improving the effectiveness and efficiency of stochastic neighbour embedding with isolation kernel. J. Artif. Intell. Res. **71**, 667–695 (2021)

An Optimized Hybrid Solution for IoT Based Lifestyle Disease Classification Using Stress Data

Sadhana Tiwari[✉], Ritesh Chandra, and Sonali Agarwal

Indian Institute of Information Technology, Allahabad, India
{rsi2018507,rsi2022001,sonali}@iiita.ac.in

Abstract. Stress, anxiety, and nervousness are all high-risk health states in everyday life. Previously, stress levels were determined by speaking with people and gaining insight into what they had experienced recently or in the past. Typically, stress is caused by an incidence that occurred a long time ago, but sometimes it is triggered by unknown factors. This is a challenging and complex task, but recent research advances have provided numerous opportunities to automate it. The fundamental features of most of these techniques are electro dermal activity (EDA) and heart rate values (HRV). We utilised an accelerometer to measure body motions to solve this challenge. The proposed novel method employs a test that measures a subject's electrocardiogram (ECG), galvanic skin values (GSV), HRV values, and body movements in order to provide a low-cost and time-saving solution for detecting stress lifestyle disease in modern times. This study provides a new hybrid model for lifestyle disease classification that decreases execution time while picking the best collection of features and increases classification accuracy. The developed approach is capable of dealing with the class imbalance problem by using WESAD (wearable stress and affect dataset) dataset, uses the Grid search (GS) method to select an optimised set of hyper parameters. It also applies a combination of the Correlation coefficient based Recursive feature elimination (CoC-RFE) method for optimal feature selection and gradient boosting as an estimator to classify the dataset, which achieves high accuracy and helps to provide smart, accurate, and high-quality healthcare systems. To demonstrate the validity and utility of the proposed methodology, its performance is compared to those of other well-established machine learning models.

Keywords: Lifestyle diseases · Stress detection · Imbalance class · Optimal feature subset · Parameter tuning · Machine learning classification

1 Introduction

Stress has become an increasingly widespread ailment as the modern world has gotten faster and faster. Stress levels in India are substantially greater than in

M. Tanveer et al. (Eds.): ICONIP 2022, CCIS 1794, pp. 433–445, 2023.
https://doi.org/10.1007/978-981-99-1648-1_36

many other countries; around 82% of Indians feel stressed [1]. The 35–49 year old age group is the most stressed. Stress is defined as a reaction to psychological, physiological, behavioural, and situational restrictions in combination. It's a stimulation state in which things run out of control and become extremely difficult. Regular stress can have a number of detrimental health repercussions [2]and it can be the root cause of various lifestyle diseases. Extreme levels of stress may be harmful to people's health and well-being, resulting in lack of sleep, high blood pressure (hypertension), depression, mental illnesses, and heart difficulties, among other things. Acute stress is temporary; but, when the degree of stress rises, it may develop into chronic stress, which is difficult to alleviate or even manage. These negative consequences impair an individual's health and well- being, as well as diminish overall efficiency, productivity, and peace of mind [3, 4].

Lifestyle illnesses are caused by a person's lifestyle or habits, or how they live their lives. There are various factors that have contributed to the fast increase of these diseases in recent years, including poor eating (junk food), lack of exercise, and addictive hazardous habits such as smoking and drinking. These illnesses are non- communicable by their very nature of spreading [5, 6]. These diseases are more likely to develop in the body if you live an irregular and unhealthy lifestyle. Long-term activity monitoring can aid in the treatment of lifestyle-related disorders such as stress, obesity, diabetes, and hypertension [7]. Frequent monitoring of many activities and physiological markers of the human body, including EDA, can also aid in the early detection of several chronic lifestyle disorders, including stress. IoT sensors, including as ECG, Galvanic skin response (GSR), Oxygen saturation (SPO2), and Accelerometer sensors, play a critical role in precise monitoring of physiological body factors connected to stress [8]. Monitoring environmental elements that might cause or treat any ailment, as well as monitoring other everyday activities and physiological indicators, are all big uses of IoT in the medical arena that have piqued the interest of researchers and medical experts [9]. This study proposes a novel low-cost and time-efficient machine learning approach for analysing an individual's stress. The following are the significant contributions of this study:

- Computation of a stress score in response to a questionnaire. The subject is not stressed if the stress score is less than the threshold number, and vice versa.
- Using the Synthetic Minority Oversampling approach (SMOTE) to handle the class imbalance problem to prevent biased findings.
- Using the Grid Search approach to optimise the model by selecting the optimum set of parameters.
- Introducing a novel CoC-RFE approach, which runs the feature selection algorithm to extract the most valuable characteristics and helps to remove the irrelevant features followed by execution of various machine learning methods to calculate the accuracy of the models.
- A hybrid classification model (CoC-RFE-GB) is proposed for better accuracy and performance.

The paper is organized as follows: The introductory details are explained in Sect. 1, and the reviewed relevant work in this field is discussed in Sect. 2.

The methodology of the work is described in Sect. 3. In Sect. 4, we performed a comparative analysis of classification results of each model based on statistical factors. Section 4.1 focuses on the in-depth graphical representation of the results. The last Sect. 5 contains concluding observations as well as recommendations for further research.

2 Related Work

To find the different parameters, methodologies, and models employed by the researchers, a thorough review of previous work was conducted. According to the Cigna 360 Happiness Survey 2019, India's stress levels are still very high when compared to other developed and developing countries and the sandwich generation, aged 35 to 49, is the most stressed, followed by the millennial generation. In contrast to the overall findings, 85% of Indian males and 82% of working women reported greater levels of stress. Overwork and financial concerns about personal health are the primary drivers of stress for women [1]. A research work proposed, ANN based hybrid model for stress and mental health detection of students aged between 18–35 uses GSR and HR values and achieves 99.4% accuracy. This work also predicts the stress levels of each subjects into four different classes [3]. Feng-Tso Sun et al. offer an activity-based mental stress inquiry approach based on continuous monitoring of vital body parameters related to stress employing ECG, GSR, and Accelerometer sensors. Twenty people were chosen to participate in a set of activities meant to assess a person's stress level. Because the heart rate fluctuates fast between activities, the findings were better when no ECG data was used. Later with inclusion of GSR sensor, the decision tree classifier with all features had the best classification accuracy (92.4%) [4]. A new stress sensor is designed using GSR which is controlled through Zigbee. 16 persons (8 men and 8 women) were chosen to participate in an experiment employing this newly built sensor. The GSR sensor is capable of recognising distinct emotional states of each user once the trial is completed, with a success rate of 76.56% [10]. Fitri Indra Indikawati et al. developed a customised stress inquiry system based on data obtained from IoT sensors in another study. The WESAD dataset is used to classify stress in this system. For classifying the data three machine learning classification models were used, out of them the random forest classifier provides the most accurate and consistent stress recognition, with accuracy ranging from 88% to 99% for 15 items [11].

Jennifer A. Healey suggested a new dataset based on physiological signals that includes variations in various body parameters from day to day. The original data was collected by evaluating young individuals in stressful situations such as rush hour or driving on highways, and numerous parameters were recorded, including ECG, EMG, HR, GSR, etc. The model for identifying a user's emotion level was created using the Python automated machine learning packages TPOT. The characteristics discovered in this unique dataset have an 81% success rate for all eight types of emotions and a 100% success rate for subsets of various emotion-based attributes [12]. Mario Salai et al. describe the findings of two studies done with the use of a low-cost heart rate sensor and a chest monitor for stress detection. The trial included 46 healthy volunteers, the majority of whom were students (27 men and 19 women; average age: 24.6 years). The experiment was split into two portions, each lasting 10 min, for a total of 20 min. For accurately identifying the stress, the accuracy, sensitivity, and specificity scores are 74.60 %, 75%, and 74.19 %, respectively [13].

Alberto Greco et al. presented a unique approach for electrodermal activity (EDA) analysis, which consists of changes in electrical characteristics of skin such as resistance, conductance, and voltage by utilising convex optimization techniques [14]. Another study found that using data collected by various wearable sensors, various machine learning and deep learning approaches are highly beneficial in the stress detection process [15]. K-Nearest Neighbour, Linear Discriminant Analysis, Random Forest, Decision Tree, AdaBoost, Gradient Boosting, and Kernel Support Vector Machine are some well-known models used for stress detection. Furthermore, a simple feed forward deep learning artificial neural network exhibiting high accuracy [16,17].

After reviewing several papers, it is identified that the data extraction and pre-processing of the raw data files is very tedious task. Another difficult challenge is to identify the most significant set of features from the dataset, as it contains many features and some of the features are really useful in the stress detection tasks and some are not. After getting the optimal set of features, we can reduce the execution time of the model. The major goal of this study is to develop a simple way for detecting stress levels in people, so that they may be alerted if their stress levels are excessive.

3   Material and Methods

This section presents the materials and procedures needed to conduct the experiment and calculate the results. This section covers the dataset description, hardware used for data acquisition, data preparation, and implementation of the proposed model.

3.1   Dataset Description and Hardware Used for Data Acquisition

The proposed method uses WESAD dataset [11,17] which is a publicly available dataset for wearable stress and affect detection. The data is recorded from 15 subjects using a chest (RespiBAN) and wrist (Empatica E4) worn devices. These sensors are used to record blood volume pulse, electrocardiogram, electro dermal activity, electromyogram, respiration, body temperature, and three-axis acceleration. Device Empatica E4 records the blood volume pulse (BVP), body temperature, electro dermal activity (EDA) etc. and device RespiBAN records electrocardiogram (ECG), EDA, respiration, temperature and 3-axis acceleration. Then 29 features are selected, which are related to BVP, EDA, temperature, respiration and their minimum, maximum and mean values. Apart from these, age and weight are also taken as features. The stress labels assigned across these data are taken as 0, 1, and 2.

3.2 Data Preparation

Data preparation includes the challenges associated in selection of various significant input parameters and data pre-processing phase.

1) **Selecting input parameters**

The frequent metrics discovered for predicting stress after evaluating several research publications are EDA, GSR, HRV, ECG, and others.

a) EDA (Electro dermal Activity)- According to the conventional EDA hypothesis, skin resistance fluctuates depending on the status of sweat glands in the skin. Skin conductance can thus be used to measure emotional and sympathetic reactions [16]. GSR is a measure that describes how sweat gland activity changes in response to changes in our emotional state [17]. The GSR is used to track variations in sweat gland activity or skin conductance over time. There is a link between GSR and stress levels, according to several research. The larger the conductance, lower the resistance, stronger sweat organ activity, and higher the value of GSR, the more stressed a person is [18].

b) HRV (Heart rate variability) - This is a measurement of the time difference between successive heartbeats, as shown in Fig. 1. The variance between subsequent heartbeats is low when a person is agitated or in fight-or- flight mode, i.e. HRV is low in panic circumstances. HRV, on the other hand, is high during relaxation, suggesting a healthy nervous system; a high HRV, on the other hand, shows balance. People with a low HRV value are more likely to be stressed, whereas those with a high HRV are more likely to be healthy [10].

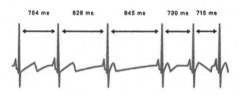

Fig. 1. Heart Rate Variability

c) ECG (Electrocardiography) - It is used to measure the electrical activity of the heart and its health. It detects various heart related issues like irregular heart rhythms. ECG generates a graph as output where time is on x-axis and voltage (amplitude) on y-axis.

Some other features can also be considered for the stress detection experiment, however, we must evaluate which features are most significant for our investigation. One of the most essential aspects used to identify stress is the galvanic skin response (GSR). In a study done by Villarejo et al., they were able to reach 76.56 utilising solely GSR characteristics [10].

3.3   Implementation of the Proposed Model

The proposed model's implementation has been broken down into two primary parts, named as stress score calculation part and accuracy computation using the proposed model as well as some existing ML models. In the first step a new algorithm is designed to automatic computation of stress score for automatic stress detection on behalf of some questionnaire. The second part of the model deals with the pre-processing issues, class imbalance concerns, and conducting feature selection on different sample sizes to produce an ideal feature subset and discover the best feature reduction strategies for the processed data and then classify these feature vectors using a fine-tuned set of hyper parameters.

a) Stress-score calculation

For primary level stress analysis, a stress score is computed for each participants by asking some basic questions using some questionnaire, whose response will help the physician to judge basic mental stress level of any person. After answering all questions the stress score is computed using Algorithm 1. The responses of each question can be marked in between 0 to 4 (where 0-never, 1-almost never, 2-often, 3-very often, 4-). After calculating the score the stress level of the person can be categorized into three classes which are low stress, moderate stress and high perceived stress.

Algorithm 1. Algorithm for Stress-score computation

Input : T1 Question ans score : value, T2 for checking, 0 never, 1 almost never, 2 sometimes, 3 fairly often, 4 very often. Check T4 = complete score.
For
Never : Score 0
Check T1
Goto
Sometimes : Score 2
Check T1
Goto
Fairly often : Score 3
Check T1
Goto
Very often : Score 4
Check T1
Now Calculate the stress score all T1 question after adding all the question score of individual person.
Check T4
If
T4 Score range (0 to 13) = low stress.
Else
T4 Score range (14 to 26) = moderate stress.
Else
T4 Score range (27 to 40) = high perceived stress.

---

b) Handle Class Imbalance problem

Class imbalance is one of the major issues that should be addressed carefully and efficiently during classification. Assume that if we are dealing with a binary class classification problem, where the bulk of the samples belong to one class and only a few examples belong to the other. As a result, if we perform classification using class imbalance data, the results may be skewed in favour of the majority class, because the majority class's contribution to the classification model will be greater than the minority class's and the model's performance will be affected. As a result, we adopted the SMOTE technique introduced by Chawla et al. in 2002 [19,20] to deal with the problem of class imbalance. The core idea behind this approach's to keep the class balanced by producing synthetic samples from the minority class. The synthetic random samples are generated using the k-nearest neighbour approach.

c) Feature reduction and selection of optimal subset of features

By finding the irrelevant and undesired characteristics, feature reduction helps to reduce the number of attributes in a huge data collection. This is essentially a data pre-processing step for large volumes of data. As illustrated in Fig. 2 the notion of feature selection indicates that we pick a subset of features or characteristics that assist in the creation of an efficient model to represent the selected subset of features [21]. By lowering the quantity of the input variables and identifying the ideal collection of features, the model's performance may be enhanced. Additionally, it is essential to reduce the computational cost and complexity of the model, as well as to improve prediction outcomes caused by overfitting. Four well-known feature selection strategies have been employed in this work: ANOVA f-test, Mutual Information (MI), Recursive Feature Elimination (REF), and Correlation coefficient. We examined all of these approaches using a variety of sample sizes, including 10, 20, 30, 40, and 50, and found that a sample size of 40 produces the best subset using all four strategies. c) Hyper parameter selection for selected features

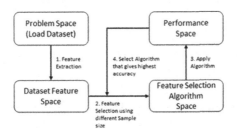

Fig. 2. Process of Optimal feature selection.

Hyper parameters are very important because they determine the overall behaviour of a machine learning model. The main goal of parameter tuning is to find the optimal set of hyper parameters which minimizes the predetermined loss function to get the best results. This is also necessary to avoid the

Algorithm 2. Pseudocode of correlation based RFE (CoC-RFE) feature selection algorithm

CoC-RFE (D, N, F, n) Input : D : Input Data; Dtrain: Training data; F: Original set of features, F= [f1, f2, f3,...,fn]; d: Dimension of feature; N: Size of population; C(Dtrain, F): Feature ranking technique.

Output: S_F: Optimal subset of features.
1. Initialize instance of the population
S_F = F
2. Compute correlation coefficient matrix R using features in F
3. Find out the contribution of each feature of F with the help of R
4. If correlation coefficient threshold $(C_f) <$ Threshold $(C\lambda)$ then
5. Discard the feature f_i from F_n
6. **Else**
7. Add the feature in S_F
8. while termination condition $(C_f < C\lambda)$ is not true do
9. **for** j = 1 to n do
10. Rank the feature S_F by applying C(Dtrain, S_F)
11. f_1 = Least important feature in S_F
12. Update the best position of the feature using Rank of features in S_F
13. $S_F = S_F - f_1$
14. **end for**
15. **end while**

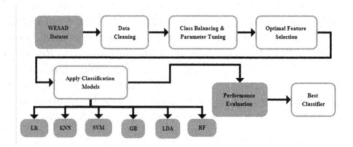

Fig. 3. Setup of the proposed work.

issues of overfitting and under fitting as no single value of parameters well suits all ML models. In this work, the Grid search (GS) method is used for hyper parameter tuning [22,23]. All the well-known machine learning models used in this experiment are trained by applying training data using a selected set of hyper parameters across each model. After that, evaluation of the model is done using the test data with the help of some statistical measures such as accuracy, f1-score, recall and precision etc. d) Model setup of the proposed model   This section develops a novel hybrid model, CoC-RFE-GB, that outperforms current machine learning models in terms of accuracy. Figure 3 depicts the planned CoC-RFE-GB system's work-flow diagram.

4   Result and Discussion

The primary goal of this research is to develop a new hybrid model, CoC-REF-GB (Correlation Coefficient- based Recursive Feature Elimination Gradient Boosting Classifier), that can address the class imbalance problem, overfitting and underfitting data problems, and optimal feature selection problem with increased accuracy and precision. It will take the lead in automating the process of stress detection for the human well-being by using IoT-based data. To choose the most acceptable machine learning classifier for the proposed model, a thorough comparison of six well-known models was conducted utilising a variety of performance assessment metrics that verify the classification result. The training - testing ratio used for this experiment is 70-30. Table 1 summarises the

Table 1. Comparison of various statistical measures between imbalanced, balanced and hyper tuned balanced dataset

S. No	Classifiers	Measures	Imbalanced dataset	Balanced dataset	Tuned balanced dataset
1	RF	Accuracy	89.41	90.07	91.72
		F1-score	0.89	0.91	0.91
		Precision	0.9	0.9	0.92
		Recall	0.89	0.9	0.91
2	LR	Accuracy	72.97	86.94	88.22
		F1-score	0.71	0.86	0.88
		Precision	0.71	0.87	0.88
		Recall	0.72	0.86	0.88
3	SVC	Accuracy	52.33	58.92	68.02
		F1-score	0.52	0.58	0.68
		Precision	0.52	0.58	0.67
		Recall	0.52	0.58	0.68
4	KNN	Accuracy	53.69	70.16	85.09
		F1-score	0.83	0.7	0.85
		Precision	0.54	0.7	0.84
		Recall	0.54	0.7	0.85
5	LDA	Accuracy	75.28	86.94	86.78
		F1-score	0.75	0.87	0.86
		Precision	0.76	0.87	0.87
		Recall	0.75	0.86	0.86
6	GB	Accuracy	86.36	90.07	90.88
		F1-score	0.86	0.9	0.9
		Precision	0.85	0.9	0.91
		Recall	0.86	0.9	0.9

statistical findings achieved throughout the experiment utilising the entire unbalanced dataset (processed dataset), the balanced dataset, and the hyper tuned balanced dataset. The experimental findings indicate that the newly proposed model achieves the maximum accuracy.

4.1   Accuracy of Various Classifier Using Feature Selection Techniques

Table 2 shows the performance of four well established feature selection techniques i.e. ANOVA f-test, Mutual Information (MI), Recursive Feature Elimination (REF), and Correlation coefficient used for finding the best subset of features to obtain best accuracy of the model. The performance of these existing feature selection techniques were compared to the newly designed CoC-RFE feature selection algorithm. The highest accuracy achieved from this novel hybrid model CoC-RFE feature selection method clubbed with GB classifier. Figure 4 represents the graph for accuracy achieved using the various feature selection methods applied with the GB classification model. It is visualized that the newly developed CoC-RFE hybrid feature selection approach attains the highest accuracy in comparison with the other techniques.

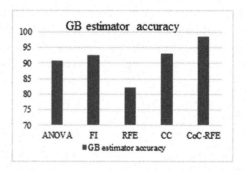

Fig. 4. Comparative analysis of GB estimator with various Feature selection techniques.

Table 2. Performance evaluation of various feature selection techniques

Feature selection method	Selected features	Accuracy	Optimal selected features
ANOVA f-test	10	80.21	40
	20	82.30	
	30	86.47	
	40	90.75	
	50	88.26	
Feature Importance	10	85.71	40
	20	87.11	
	30	88.79	
	40	92.43	
	50	92.43	
RFE	10	76.8	50
	20	76.8	
	30	79.9	
	40	82.24	
	50	85.1	
Correlation coefficient	10	82.19	40
	20	85.37	
	30	86.15	
	40	93.13	
	50	90.24	
CoC-RFE	10	94.70	40
	20	95.51	
	30	96.15	
	40	98.56	
	50	98.56	

5   Conclusion and Future Scope

Lifestyle diseases (for example, stress and related complications) are one of the greatest worldwide threats to the human population. As a result, it is critical to monitor several physiological characteristics continuously and in real time. Developing an appropriate model for smart healthcare services is a difficult but fascinating undertaking. Various uses of smart healthcare systems include monitoring blood pressure (BP), glucose levels, oxygen levels, skin conductance and resistance, and electrocardiography (ECG). This article offers a novel model for stress lifestyle disease classification that is capable of resolving class imbalance issues and overcoming overfitting and underfitting issues via the use of fine-tuned sets of hyper parameters. By picking the ideal subset of features, the model will lower the computational cost and complexity. The experimental findings indicate that the proposed model outperforms existing well-established machine learning classifiers in terms of accuracy across a variety of statistical metrics. This work can be improved using semantic web for making better decision making process in future. Additionally, this research may be expanded from an algorithmic and data analytics perspective.

References

1. Cigna 360 Well Being Study, https://m.economictimes.com/wealth/personal-fina nce-news/82-indians-bogged-down-by-stress-cigna-360-well-being-study/articlesh ow/68615097.cms. Accessed 24 Aug 2021
2. Sandulescu, V., Andrews, S., Ellis, D., Bellotto, N., Mozos, O.M.: Stress detection using wearable physiological sensors. In: Ferrández Vicente, J.M., Álvarez-Sánchez, J.R., de la Paz López, F., Toledo-Moreo, F.J., Adeli, H. (eds.) IWINAC 2015. LNCS, vol. 9107, pp. 526–532. Springer, Cham (2015). https://doi.org/10.1007/978-3-319-18914-7_55
3. Tiwari, S., Agarwal, S.: A shrewd artificial neural network-based hybrid model for pervasive stress detection of students using galvanic skin response and electrocardiogram signals. Big Data 9(6), 427–442 (2021)
4. Sun, F.-T., Kuo, C., Cheng, H.-T., Buthpitiya, S., Collins, P., Griss, M.: Activity-aware mental stress detection using physiological sensors. In: Gris, M., Yang, G. (eds.) MobiCASE 2010. LNICST, vol. 76, pp. 211–230. Springer, Heidelberg (2012). https://doi.org/10.1007/978-3-642-29336-8_12
5. An Introduction to Heart Rate Variability. https://support.ouraring.com/hc/en-us/articles/360025441974-An-Introduction-to-Heart-Rate-Variabilitytext=)20is20a. Accessed 20 Apr 2021
6. Tiwari, S., Agarwal, S.: Data stream management for CPS-based healthcare: a contemporary review. IETE Tech. Rev., 1–24 (2021)
7. Han, Y., et al.: A framework for supervising lifestyle diseases using long-term activity monitoring. Sensors 12(5), 5363–5379 (2012)
8. Tiwari, S., et al.: Classification of physiological signals for emotion recognition using IoT. In: 2019 6th International Conference on Electrical Engineering, Computer Science and Informatics (EECSI). IEEE (2019)
9. Rodrigues, M.J., Postolache, O., Cercas, F.: Physiological and behavior monitoring systems for smart healthcare environments: a review. Sensors 20(8), 2186 (2020)
10. Villarejo, M.V., Zapirain, B.G., Zorrilla, A.M.: A stress sensor based on galvanic skin response (GSR) controlled by ZigBee. Sensors 12(5), 6075–6101 (2012)
11. Indikawati, F.I., Winiarti, S.: Stress detection from multimodal wearable sensor data. IOP Conf. Ser. Mater. Sci. Eng. 771(1) (2020)
12. Healey, J.A.: Wearable and automotive systems for affect recognition from physiology. Dissertations Massachusetts Institute of Technology (2000)
13. Salai, M., Vassányi, I., Kósa, I.: Stress detection using low cost heart rate sensors. J. Healthc. Eng. 2016 (2016)
14. Greco, A., et al.: cvxEDA: a convex optimization approach to electrodermal activity processing. IEEE Trans. Biomed. Eng. 63(4), 797–804 (2015)
15. Zainudin, Z., et al.: Stress detection using machine learning and deep learning. J. Phys. Conf. Ser. 1997(1) (2021)
16. Deng, Y., et al.: Evaluating feature selection for stress identification. In: 2012 IEEE 13th International Conference on Information Reuse Integration (IRI). IEEE (2012)

17. Schmidt, P., et al.: Introducing WESAD, a multimodal dataset for wearable stress and affect detection. In: Proceedings of the 20th ACM International Conference on Multimodal Interaction (2018)
18. IMOTIONS – EDA/GSR. https://imotions.com/biosensor/gsr-galvanic-skin-resp onse-eda-electrodermal-activity/. Accessed 12 Mar 2021
19. Chawla, N.V., Bowyer, K.W., Hall, L.O., Kegelmeyer, W.P.: SMOTE: synthetic minority over- sampling technique. J. Artif. Intell. Res. **16**, 321–357 (2002)
20. Fernández, A., Garcia, S., Herrera, F., Chawla, N.V.: SMOTE for learning from imbalanced data: progress and challenges, marking the 15-year anniversary. J. Artif. Intell. Res. **61**, 863–905 (2018)
21. Visalakshi, S., Radha, V.: A literature review of feature selection techniques and applications: review of feature selection in data mining. In: 2014 IEEE International Conference on Computational Intelligence and Computing Research. IEEE (2014)
22. Syarif, I., et al.: SVM parameter optimization using grid search and genetic algorithm to improve classification performance. Telkomnika **14**(4), 1502 (2016)
23. Liashchynskyi, P., et al.: Grid search, random search, genetic algorithm: a big comparison for NAS. arXiv preprint arXiv:1912.06059 (2019)

A Deep Concatenated Convolutional Neural Network-Based Method to Classify Autism

Tanu Wadhera[1]📷, Mufti Mahmud[2,3,4](✉)📷, and David J. Brown[2,3,4]📷

[1] Indian Institute of Information Technology Una, Una, Himachal Pradesh, India
tanu.wadhera@iiitu.ac.in
[2] Department of Computer Science, Nottingham Trent University, Clifton Lane,
Nottingham NG11 8NS, UK
{mufti.mahmud,david.brown}@ntu.ac.uk, muftimahmud@gmail.com
[3] Computing and Informatics Research Centre, Nottingham Trent University,
Clifton Lane, Nottingham NG11 8NS, UK
[4] Medical Technologies Innovation Facility, Nottingham Trent University,
Clifton Lane, Nottingham NG11 8NS, UK

Abstract. Associating different brain regions relating to a particular neurological issue has emerged as an area of neuroimaging research. Deep learning algorithms have emerged as a promising approach to automate neural data processing for classifying traits or characteristics associated with a range of conditions. The present paper has worked on improving binary-classification accuracy of Autism Spectrum Disorder (ASD) by distinguishing ASD from Typically Developing (TD) individuals. A hybrid model is proposed concatenating VGGNet and ResNet-152 to fuse the most discerning heterogeneous features from both networks to build a strong feature vector for attaining high classification accuracy. The effectiveness of the proposed approach is demonstrated on ABIDE dataset, which showed an improvement over state-of-art classifiers in terms of accuracy (88.12%), sensitivity (91.32%), specificity (86.34%) and ROC (0.88), respectively, in classifying ASD and TD individuals.

Keywords: Autism · ABIDE · Fusion · Deep Learning · VGGNet · ResNet-52

1 Introduction

Autism Spectrum Disorder (ASD) – also referred to as 'Autism' in short - constitutes a diverse group of conditions related to brain development. It is one of the most prevailing neuro-development disorders among children. The disorder indicators usually grow gradually but exhibit more severe effects over time [29]. In India, 1 out of 69 children presents with autism. Growth is so high that by 2050, half of the children will be affected with ASD. Many conditions exhibit comorbidity with autism, including epilepsy which broadens the spectrum of the

M. Tanveer et al. (Eds.): ICONIP 2022, CCIS 1794, pp. 446–458, 2023.
https://doi.org/10.1007/978-981-99-1648-1_37

disorder. Autism has been classified as a behavioural disorder and is currently diagnosed via clinical assessment. New methods of diagnosis are required, providing additional objective information concerning the neural underpinnings of this cohort [7,13,18]. Thus, an accurate autism classification system is required to bring consistency in the definition and detection of autism, leading to the eventual improvement of the quality of life of those with autism. The present paper aims to distinguish ASD from the Typically Developing (TD) individuals to contribute toward making the objective identification of autism feasible.

There remain challenges – being able to accurately distinguish autism is quite impossible due to issues including unfitting (such as one-fit-all) and the subjective clinical methods associated with current diagnostic tools as specified in the literature. The existing techniques have presented behavioural markers and brain abnormalities as evidence of autism and generally fail to distinguish between ASD and TD individuals [8]. Computational scientists, with possibly little knowledge of psychology, analysed data collected from neuroimaging methods to draw interpretations for affected individuals. In recent years artificial intelligence (AI) has been applied in diverse problem domains to solve various challenging problems including student engagement [45], virtual reality exposure therapy [46], text classification [1,37,42,43], cyber security [3,17,24,57], neurological disease detection [10,19,39] and management [2,4,5,25,34,50], elderly care [12,36], biological data mining [32,33], fighting pandemic [6,9,28,31,40,41,47], and healthcare service delivery [11,16,27]. In particular, deep learning-based algorithms have shown significant potential further to augment computational approaches' role in the neuroscience domain. Researchers are working on deep learning methods to extract the requisite features directly from MRI, fMRI, X-ray, and other medical images [14,15]. Existing models primarily focus on binary classification to determine whether an individual has autism or not [20]. Deep learning models attempt to find the association of the features between neuroimaging data and labels of the data provided for classification. However, such models fail to train/map the new or unseen data.

Moreover, classification across different brain sites enabled via scanning or neuroimaging techniques is much more efficient than single-site-based data [21]. However, variations arising from using multiple sites add more noise due to equipment or data demographics. Deep learning techniques show promising results in classifying and identifying neurological disorders [22,23,26]. In such cases, deep learning models work better with the following development needs: (i) Large clinical datasets for achieving generalisation across populations, (ii) Variation in the classifier to accurately identify the classify the disorder, (iii) Variation in data characteristics for achieving high classification accuracy. Thus, to acquire highly accurate diagnostic tools, training them on large unseen datasets is mandatory [5]. Performance metrics and error measures, such as overfitting, are required to estimate the classifier's reliability for deployment in real-world scenarios. Consequently, the ABIDE dataset is explored in the present paper, where large data is collected from multiple brain sites to classify autism accurately.

In analysing neuro-signals, many studies have explored Convolutional Neural Networks (CNN) and have shown progress in software engineering and neuroimaging [32,33,35,38,39,44]. The combination of different algorithms has improved computational accuracy, time and assessment of large amounts of data [2,34]. Prior research studies combining brain imaging and deep learning methods have utilised several state-of-the-art techniques for the automated analysis of neurogenerative diseases [10,19,48,49,51,53–56]. Thus, the present paper has explored the development of an objective framework to analyse MRI data of individuals with autism to classify them from TD individuals accurately.

Towards that goal, the current work has the following contributions:

1. A hybrid approach is applied to extract the features from the brain MRI images using deep learning models and analyse the classification performance for the developed classification model based on accuracy, precision, sensitivity, f1-score, and receiver operating characteristic (ROC) to identify the potential of proposed classifier in the classification of ABIDE dataset.
2. We have employed different techniques of affine transformations for data augmentation to avoid the problem of overfitting and to enlarge the dataset for extracting discernible features from the images for better classifier training.
3. We have also compared the performance of the proposed classifier with the existing state-of-the-art classifier for ABIDE dataset classification for a coherent comparison.

In the rest of the paper, Sect. 2 reviews the related work, Sect. 3 describes the proposed model, Sect. 4 presents the results and discusses their usefulness, and finally Sect. 5 concludes the paper.

2 Related Work

Several works have been carried out using deep learning (DL) techniques to process high-dimensional MRIs to model neural patterns addressing a range of neural disorders [38]. Literature shows that the gold-standard ABIDE-I and II datasets have been explored with multi-channel deep attention neural network integrating different network layers, attention mechanisms and multimodal fused data, which classified 809 ASD subjects (ABIDE dataset), with an accuracy of 73.2% [52]. Similarly, a graph neural network containing different convolutional and pooling layers was proposed to process the neural connectivity matrix constructed from ABIDE dataset images that classified ASD with 79.7% accuracy [23]. These studies show that MRI appears to be a method that can provide information on brain connectivity in those with autism, helping to distinguish TD from ASD cases. Implementing emerging DL paradigms could improve detection consistency and ensure treatment quality. For efficient diagnosis, however, classification at different levels is mandatory to provide a prediction of this condition at an individual level [18,20]. Numerous autoencoders such as shallow, deep, denoising and scarce have been implied to extract the low-dimensional attributes from MRI recordings. A dense Long Short-term Memory (LSTM) network is deployed in a single layer which is forwarded to the sigmoid function for diagnosis of ASD. The network is further made dense by incorporating phenotypic information for a better diagnosis of ASD. In Convolutional neural networks (CNN), a network addressing multi-channels where each channel illustrates the connectivity of every neural voxel corresponding to the Region of interest (ROI), further integrated with additional convolutional, max-pooling and final fixed layers is utilised for a final decision in detecting ASD. A one-dimensional CNN network has been proposed to process the input matrix framing average values of time-series recordings for extracting the data non-linearities to diagnose ASD.

A semi-supervised graph CNN (GCNN) is formulated for ASD classification, where the imaging dataset is illustrated as nodes while the phenotypic information is considered as weights of the edges. Following the architecture, a bootstrapping GCNN is formulated to generate population graphs as "weak learners". A mean of learner values is evaluated to identify each of the classes. In the same line, several other neural networks, namely probabilistic, competitive, learning vector quantisation, and Elman NNs, have been proposed to identify the disorder phenotype. For example, a PNN trained upon functional connectivity scores acquired using Pearson's correlation between MRI and different brain regions has classified ASD with an accuracy of 90% [30]. On ABIDE dataset (505 ASD and 530 TD), a set of stacked auto-encoders are pre-trained to abstract out low-dimensional features, followed by a multi-layer perceptron in the final layer, which classified ASD with an accuracy of 70% [22]. The auto-encoder were trained to extract the features of low and high dimension. As per the requirement of fine-tuning, there are other deep learning-based classifiers, namely Visual Geometry Group Network (VGGNet) and Residual Neural Network (ResNet), which have outperformed various tasks and datasets related to image recognition. A VGGNet is a deep CNN design with numerous layers where the term "deep" describes the number of layers, with VGG-16 or VGG-19 having 16 or 19 convolutional layers, respectively. Such architectures have been utilised in object detection, image recognition and classification.

The present paper has used the VGG19 weight layer model to process the features from the MRI images [38]. In [52], the authors proposed an ASD screening method using facial images by applying VGG16 transfer learning-based deep learning to an ASD dataset of clinically diagnosed children sourced by the authors. Their model produced a classification accuracy of 95%, with 0.95 as its F1 Score. In [15], the authors focused on classification models applying the VGG16 algorithm of SVM classifier, CNN and Haar Cascade using OpenCV. They concluded that better accuracy of 90% is achieved from VGG16 as compared to other classification models. In addition, in [7], the authors set out to design a system based on autism spectrum disorder detection based on social media and face recognition. Their proposed Xception model achieved the highest accuracy of 91%, followed by VGG19 (80%) and NASNET Mobile (78%).

Similarly, the Residual Blocks idea was created by this design to address the issue of the vanishing/exploding gradient. A method known as skip connections is generally applied in this network. The skip connection bypasses some levels to link layer activations to subsequent layers. This creates a leftover block. These leftover blocks are stacked to create ResNet. The advantage of adding this type of skip connection is that if any layer hurts the architecture's performance, it will be skipped by regularisation. So this results in training a very deep neural network without the problems caused by vanishing/exploding gradient. The vanishing gradient issue is prevented with ResNet. Since the skip connections serve as gradient superhighways, the gradient can move freely. The fact that ResNet is available in versions like ResNet52, ResNet101, and ResNet152 is also among its primary justifications.

In [35], the authors suggested a 3D-ResNet for ASD classification that includes an attention subnet. The model combines the attention subnet and the residual module to hide the regions that are important or unnecessary for the classification during feature extraction. From the Autism Brain Imaging Data Exchange, sMRI was used to train and evaluate the model (ABIDE). A 5-fold cross-validation test results in a 75% accuracy. In [51], Tamilarasi & Shanmugam used the Convolution Neural Network (CNN) ResNet-50 architecture and obtained 89.2% accuracy. A reduced performance amongst different models proposed for the classification of ASD depends upon the training samples utilised for training, which differs in every study. Furthermore, different settings bring non-uniformity to the studies, making inter-comparisons quite less possible.

The CNN model's capacity to fit more complex functions grows as the number of layers does. Consequently, more layers promise improved performance. A residual neural network converts a plain network into its residual network counterpart by inserting shortcut connections. Considering their advantages, a concatenated structure is proposed in the present paper to attain a better classification of ASD.

3   Proposed Model

The MRI analysis includes various pre-processing steps such as registration, segmentation, bias correction and denoising. The manual analysis of MRI images is labour-intensive and influenced by various factors such as fatigue, attention and expertise of radiologists. However, analysis using deep convolutional networks reduce the time-consuming steps and extracts the patterns from raw images.

3.1   Dataset

The dataset, namely ABIDE [52], is a readily available neuroimaging dataset available to researchers. It contains data from the healthy controls, ASD and ADHD individuals. The present paper performs a multiclass classification to categorise the dataset into respective groups. The database is a result of the collaboration with 18 international sites worldwide, containing 1,112 digitised MRI images (Nifty format), which are collected from 539 ASD and 573 Typically Developing (TD) individuals aged between 7–64 years, as approved by the PCP community following Quality Assessment Protocols. The ABIDE data is beneficial for model generalisation and site variability, thus helping to avoid overfitting issues across different brain sites. In Fig. 1, the MRI images of the brain at other positions, namely sagittal, axial and coronal, are illustrated for reference.

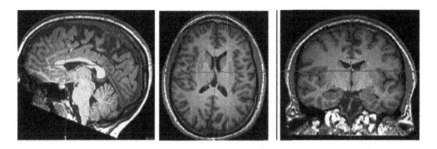

Fig. 1. Representation of ABIDE-MRI image in Sagittal (left), Axial (Middle) and Coronal (Right) format.

3.2 Methodology

The number of voxels utilised for imaging data classification is empirically selected, corresponding to 100, 200 and 400 voxels and exploiting sets which can prove best and optimal for image classification. In the present paper, the CC400 brain functional parcellation atlas has been used and analysed for classification. The atlas scheme constructed a matrix based on the ROI average time series, partitioning it into 400 different regions.

Figure 2 shows the model's block diagram where the neural network model is defined and complied with after importing the requisite libraries (classes and functions) and loading the dataset with o/p labels. Two models are considered for hybrid training of the data. The model construction depends upon the number of layers in the input, hidden and output layers. The Convolutional Neural Network architecture is designed efficiently by processing, correlating and understanding the massive data. It is a feedforward network with advanced architectures such as filter options, padding and strides [29]. CCNs are highly accurate and powerful classifiers, handling numerous features and parameters for classification. They constitute different parts, such as the convolutional layer, pooling layer, activation function, and fully connected and normalisation layers. The data is divided into three sets: training, validation (some portion of the training dataset) and testing. Afterwards, base class and utility functions (for example, fit) are used for compiling and training the model on the given dataset.

The steps and flow of the concatenated CNN framework of the model are shown in Fig. 3. The concatenation extracts all the necessary features via layers of the CNN from the dataset so that the final feature vector has distinct features for accurate data classification. In both CNN networks, the weights are initialised using the Glorot scheme, which can prevent a vanishing gradient.

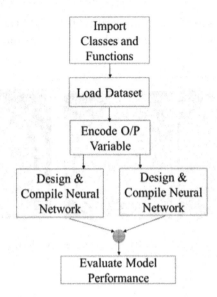

Fig. 2. Block diagram of the proposed model.

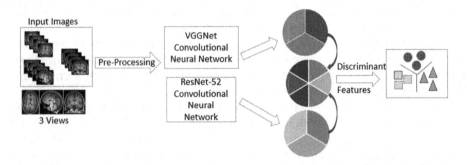

Fig. 3. Proposed Model – Concatenating VGGNet-19 and ResNet-52 CNN framework with SVM classifier.

4   Result and Discussion

The proposed model is run in the Keras framework and utilises a one-hot vector to encode the true labels of the class. The parameters of the two CNN models used in this work are trained on the features that can be influential in multiclass discrimination of multiple classes. A cross-validation scheme is used for training and testing with a 70:30 split of data. The activation function used is the softmax function. The learning rate during the training is fixed at 0.005, with 400 epochs in a batch size of 30. The input matrix is 396×396, with rows referring to each brain region. The number of filters used in CNN is 400, with sizes 1×396 to 8×396 (width of the filter = row of the connectivity matrix). The decision layer of concatenated CNN network to classify the individuals into ASD and TD groups are carefully selected after comparing different classifiers, namely, support vector machine (SVM), K-Nearest Neighbour (KNN), Logistic Regression (LR) and Deep Neural Network (DNN). The ROCs curves for different classifications are shown diagrammatically in Fig. 4A.

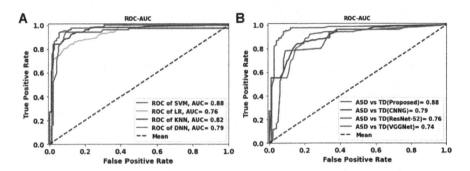

Fig. 4. A: ROC curves compare the classifier's performance in the decision layer with state-of-the-art classifiers. B: ROC curves compare the proposed model's performance with state-of-the-art classifiers.

The area under the curve for SVM is found to be 0.88, followed by KNN with a site of 0.82, a deep neural network with an area of 0.79 and logistic regression with an area of 0.76. Furthermore, the ROC curves distinguishing ASD and TD individuals for the proposed model have been compared with different developed state-of-art fully-developed deep learning models, namely VGGNet, ResNet-52 and CNNG (gated CNN), as shown in Fig. 4B.

The performance measures of the model and comparison with those from other existing studies are summarised in Table 1. The ABIDE dataset has numerous sensitive variations with coherence between multiple brain sites, which generally gets ignored by computational methods. On the contrary, the deep learning techniques deployed consider those variations, resulting in more accurate results in comparison with the other state-of-art techniques. The improvement in the classification results from the intricate layers in the raw data and the capacity of concatenated CNN to encode data variations to follow up the classification process. The proposed concatenated model shares the advantages of deep convolutional neural networks in their potential to extract features from MRI images. Furthermore, the most discerning features are concatenated to build a strong feature vector for classification.

Table 1. Comparison of the state-of-art machine and deep learning-based classifications with the Proposed Method on the ABIDE Dataset.

Ref.	Cls.	Sens.	Spec.	Acc.	ROC	CT
Heinsfeld et al., 2016	SVM	–	–	70%	–	Binary
Anderson et al., 2011	LOO	83%	75%	79%	–	Binary
Xing et al., 2018	CNN-EF	66.90%	69.94%	66.88%	–	Binary, MC
Eslami et al. 2019	DiagNet	68.03%	72.20%	70.30%	0.76	Binary, fMRI
Hao et al. 2020	Hi-GCN	67.20%	65.90%	68.40%	0.75	Binary, fMRI
Sherkatghanad et al. 2020	CNN-MLP	62.35%	72.35%	70.22%	0.75	Binary, fMRI
Jiang et al. 2022	CNNG	71.35%	79.25%	72.46%	0.79	Binary, fMRI
Proposed Model	CCNN	91.32%	86.34%	88.12%	0.88	Binary

Legend– Cls.: Classifier, Sens: Sensitivity, Spec: Specificity, Acc: Accuracy, CT: Classification Type, MC: Multichannel.

5 Conclusions

The present paper has studied and analysed the rationale of concatenating the features from the two CNN models with an aim to provide an efficient feature set for the accurate classification of autism. The concatenated CNN with SVM at the decision layer helped acquire a higher accuracy of 88.12%, with ROC showing the distinguishing ability for both classes as 0.88. The two networks utilised in the present paper are VGGNet-19 and ResNet-52, which have been chosen based upon their individual advantageous optimised attributes. The concept of fusion of two deep learning models achieving higher accuracy in ASD classification has illustrated the significance of the concatenation of models. In future, along with concatenation, the concept of a transfer learning approach can be utilised for improved multi-classification. An experimental study will also be designed to collect multimodal data to enhance model reliability.

Acknowledgement. This work is supported by the AI-TOP (2020-1-UK01-KA201-079167) projects funded by the European Commission under the Erasmus+ programme.

References

1. Adiba, F.I., et al.: Effect of corpora on classification of fake news using Naive Bayes classifier. Int. J. Autom. Artif. Intell. Mach. Learn. **1**(1), 80–92 (2020)
2. Ahmed, S., Hossain, M., Nur, S.B., Shamim Kaiser, M., Mahmud, M., et al.: Toward machine learning-based psychological assessment of autism spectrum disorders in school and community. In: Proceedings TEHI, pp. 139–149 (2022)
3. Ahmed, S., Hossain, M.F., Kaiser, M.S., Noor, M.B.T., Mahmud, M., Chakraborty, C.: Artificial intelligence and machine learning for ensuring security in smart cities. In: Chakraborty, C., Lin, J.C.-W., Alazab, M. (eds.) Data-Driven Mining, Learning and Analytics for Secured Smart Cities. ASTSA, pp. 23–47. Springer, Cham (2021). https://doi.org/10.1007/978-3-030-72139-8_2

4. Niamat Ullah Akhund, T.M., Mahi, M.J.N., Hasnat Tanvir, A.N.M., Mahmud, M., Kaiser, M.S.: ADEPTNESS: Alzheimer's disease patient management system using pervasive sensors - early prototype and preliminary results. In: Wang, S., et al. (eds.) BI 2018. LNCS (LNAI), vol. 11309, pp. 413–422. Springer, Cham (2018). https://doi.org/10.1007/978-3-030-05587-5_39

5. Al Banna, M.H., Ghosh, T., Taher, K.A., Kaiser, M.S., Mahmud, M.: A monitoring system for patients of autism spectrum disorder using artificial intelligence. In: Mahmud, M., Vassanelli, S., Kaiser, M.S., Zhong, N. (eds.) BI 2020. LNCS (LNAI), vol. 12241, pp. 251–262. Springer, Cham (2020). https://doi.org/10.1007/978-3-030-59277-6_23

6. AlArjani, A., et al.: Application of mathematical modeling in prediction of covid-19 transmission dynamics. Arab. J. Sci. Eng., 1–24 (2022)

7. Alsaade, F.W., Alzahrani, M.S.: Classification and detection of autism spectrum disorder based on deep learning algorithms. Comput. Intell. Neurosci. **2022** (2022)

8. Anderson, J.S., et al.: Functional connectivity magnetic resonance imaging classification of autism. Brain **134**(12), 3742–3754 (2011)

9. Bhapkar, H.R., Mahalle, P.N., Shinde, G.R., Mahmud, M.: Rough sets in COVID-19 to predict symptomatic cases. In: Santosh, K.C., Joshi, A. (eds.) COVID-19: Prediction, Decision-Making, and its Impacts. LNDECT, vol. 60, pp. 57–68. Springer, Singapore (2021). https://doi.org/10.1007/978-981-15-9682-7_7

10. Biswas, M., Kaiser, M.S., Mahmud, M., Al Mamun, S., Hossain, M.S., Rahman, M.A.: An XAI based autism detection: the context behind the detection. In: Mahmud, M., Kaiser, M.S., Vassanelli, S., Dai, Q., Zhong, N. (eds.) BI 2021. LNCS (LNAI), vol. 12960, pp. 448–459. Springer, Cham (2021). https://doi.org/10.1007/978-3-030-86993-9_40

11. Biswas, M., et al.: ACCU3RATE: a mobile health application rating scale based on user reviews. PloS One **16**(12), e0258050 (2021)

12. Biswas, M., et al.: Indoor navigation support system for patients with neurodegenerative diseases. In: Mahmud, M., Kaiser, M.S., Vassanelli, S., Dai, Q., Zhong, N. (eds.) BI 2021. LNCS (LNAI), vol. 12960, pp. 411–422. Springer, Cham (2021). https://doi.org/10.1007/978-3-030-86993-9_37

13. Di Martino, A., et al.: The autism brain imaging data exchange: towards a large-scale evaluation of the intrinsic brain architecture in autism. Mol. Psychiatry **19**(6), 659–667 (2014)

14. Du, Y., Fu, Z., Calhoun, V.D.: Classification and prediction of brain disorders using functional connectivity: promising but challenging. Front. Neurosci. **12**, 525 (2018)

15. Eslami, T., Mirjalili, V., Fong, A., Laird, A.R., Saeed, F.: ASD-DiagNet: a hybrid learning approach for detection of autism spectrum disorder using FMRI data. Front. Neuroinformatic. **13**, 70 (2019)

16. Farhin, F., Kaiser, M.S., Mahmud, M.: Towards secured service provisioning for the internet of healthcare things. In: Proceedings AICT, pp. 1–6 (2020)

17. Farhin, F., Kaiser, M.S., Mahmud, M.: Secured smart healthcare system: blockchain and Bayesian inference based approach. In: Proceedings TCCE, pp. 455–465 (2021)

18. Ganesan, S., et al.: Prediction of autism spectrum disorder by facial recognition using machine learning. Webology **18**, 406–417 (2021)

19. Ghosh, T., et al.: Artificial intelligence and internet of things in screening and management of autism spectrum disorder. Sustain. Cities Soc. **74**, 103189 (2021)

20. Guo, X., et al.: Diagnosing autism spectrum disorder from brain resting-state functional connectivity patterns using a deep neural network with a novel feature selection method. Front. Neurosci. **11**, 460 (2017)
21. Heinsfeld, A.S., et al.: Identification of autism spectrum disorder using deep learning and the abide dataset. NeuroImage: Clin. **17**, 16–23 (2018)
22. Huang, H., Liu, X., Jin, Y., Lee, S.W., Wee, C.Y., Shen, D.: Enhancing the representation of functional connectivity networks by fusing multi-view information for autism spectrum disorder diagnosis. Hum. Brain Mapp. **40**(3), 833–854 (2019)
23. Iidaka, T.: Resting state functional magnetic resonance imaging and neural network classified autism and control. Cortex **63**, 55–67 (2015)
24. Islam, N., et al.: Towards machine learning based intrusion detection in IoT networks. Comput. Mater. Contin **69**(2), 1801–1821 (2021)
25. Jesmin, S., Kaiser, M.S., Mahmud, M.: Artificial and internet of healthcare things based Alzheimer care during COVID 19. In: Mahmud, M., Vassanelli, S., Kaiser, M.S., Zhong, N. (eds.) BI 2020. LNCS (LNAI), vol. 12241, pp. 263–274. Springer, Cham (2020). https://doi.org/10.1007/978-3-030-59277-6_24
26. Jiang, W., et al.: CNNG: a convolutional neural networks with gated recurrent units for autism spectrum disorder classification. Front. Aging Neurosci., 723 (2022)
27. Kaiser, M.S., et al.: 6G access network for intelligent internet of healthcare things: opportunity, challenges, and research directions. In: Proceedings TCCE, pp. 317–328 (2021)
28. Kumar, S., et al.: Forecasting major impacts of covid-19 pandemic on country-driven sectors: challenges, lessons, and future roadmap. Pers. Ubiquitous Comput., 1–24 (2021)
29. Li, X., et al.: Pooling regularized graph neural network for fMRI biomarker analysis. In: Martel, A.L., et al. (eds.) MICCAI 2020. LNCS, vol. 12267, pp. 625–635. Springer, Cham (2020). https://doi.org/10.1007/978-3-030-59728-3_61
30. Lu, A., Perkowski, M.: Deep learning approach for screening autism spectrum disorder in children with facial images and analysis of ethnoracial factors in model development and application. Brain Sci. **11**(11), 1446 (2021)
31. Mahmud, M., Kaiser, M.S.: Machine learning in fighting pandemics: a COVID-19 case study. In: Santosh, K.C., Joshi, A. (eds.) COVID-19: Prediction, Decision-Making, and its Impacts. LNDECT, vol. 60, pp. 77–81. Springer, Singapore (2021). https://doi.org/10.1007/978-981-15-9682-7_9
32. Mahmud, M., Kaiser, M.S., McGinnity, T.M., Hussain, A.: Deep learning in mining biological data. Cogn. Comput. **13**(1), 1–33 (2021)
33. Mahmud, M., Kaiser, M.S., Hussain, A., Vassanelli, S.: Applications of deep learning and reinforcement learning to biological data. IEEE Trans. Neural Netw. Learn. Syst. **29**(6), 2063–2079 (2018)
34. Mahmud, M., et al.: Towards explainable and privacy-preserving artificial intelligence for personalisation in autism spectrum disorder. In: Proceedings HCII, pp. 356–370 (2022)
35. Moridian, P., et al.: Automatic autism spectrum disorder detection using artificial intelligence methods with MRI neuroimaging: a review. CoRR **2206.11233**, 1–51 (2022)
36. Nahiduzzaman, M., Tasnim, M., Newaz, N.T., Kaiser, M.S., Mahmud, M.: Machine learning based early fall detection for elderly people with neurological disorder using multimodal data fusion. In: Mahmud, M., Vassanelli, S., Kaiser, M.S., Zhong, N. (eds.) BI 2020. LNCS (LNAI), vol. 12241, pp. 204–214. Springer, Cham (2020). https://doi.org/10.1007/978-3-030-59277-6_19

37. Nawar, A., et al.: Cross-content recommendation between movie and book using machine learning. In: Proceedings AICT, pp. 1–6 (2021)
38. Niu, K., et al.: Multichannel deep attention neural networks for the classification of autism spectrum disorder using neuroimaging and personal characteristic data. Complexity **2020**, 1357853 (2020)
39. Noor, M.B.T., Zenia, N.Z., Kaiser, M.S., Mamun, S.A., Mahmud, M.: Application of deep learning in detecting neurological disorders from magnetic resonance images: a survey on the detection of Alzheimer's disease, Parkinson's disease and schizophrenia. Brain Inform. **7**(1), 1–21 (2020)
40. Paul, A., et al.: Inverted bell-curve-based ensemble of deep learning models for detection of covid-19 from chest x-rays. Neural Comput. Appl., 1–15 (2022)
41. Prakash, N., et al.: Deep transfer learning for covid-19 detection and infection localization with superpixel based segmentation. Sustain. Cities Soc. **75**, 103252 (2021)
42. Rabby, G., Azad, S., Mahmud, M., Zamli, K.Z., Rahman, M.M.: TeKET: a tree-based unsupervised keyphrase extraction technique. Cogn. Comput. **12**(4), 811–833 (2020)
43. Rabby, G., et al.: A flexible keyphrase extraction technique for academic literature. Procedia Comput. Sci. **135**, 553–563 (2018)
44. Rad, N.M., Furlanello, C.: Applying deep learning to stereotypical motor movement detection in autism spectrum disorders. In: Proceedings ICDMW, pp. 1235–1242 (2016)
45. Rahman, M.A., Brown, D.J., Shopland, N., Burton, A., Mahmud, M.: Explainable multimodal machine learning for engagement analysis by continuous performance test. In: Proceedings HCII, pp. 386–399 (2022)
46. Rahman, M.A., et al.: Towards machine learning driven self-guided virtual reality exposure therapy based on arousal state detection from multimodal data. In: Mahmud, M., He, J., Vassanelli, S., van Zundert, A., Zhong, N. (eds.) Proceedings Brain Informatics, pp. 195–209 (2022). https://doi.org/10.1007/978-3-031-15037-1_17
47. Satu, M.S., et al.: Short-term prediction of covid-19 cases using machine learning models. Appl. Sci. **11**(9), 4266 (2021)
48. Simonyan, K., Zisserman, A.: Very deep convolutional networks for large-scale image recognition. In: Proceedings ICLR, pp. 1–14 (2015)
49. Subah, F.Z., Deb, K., Dhar, P.K., Koshiba, T.: A deep learning approach to predict autism spectrum disorder using multisite resting-state fMRI. Appl. Sci. **11**(8), 3636 (2021)
50. Sumi, A.I., Zohora, M.F., Mahjabeen, M., Faria, T.J., Mahmud, M., Kaiser, M.S.: *f*ASSERT: a fuzzy assistive system for children with autism using internet of things. In: Wang, S., et al. (eds.) BI 2018. LNCS (LNAI), vol. 11309, pp. 403–412. Springer, Cham (2018). https://doi.org/10.1007/978-3-030-05587-5_38
51. Tamilarasi, F.C., Shanmugam, J.: Convolutional neural network based autism classification. In: Proceedings ICCES. pp. 1208–1212 (2020)
52. Tanu, T., Kakkar, D.: Strengthening risk prediction using statistical learning in children with autism spectrum disorder. Adv. Autism **4**(3), 141–152 (2018)
53. Wadhera, T., Kakkar, D.: Conditional entropy approach to analyze cognitive dynamics in autism spectrum disorder. Neurol. Res. **42**(10), 869–878 (2020)
54. Wadhera, T., Kakkar, D.: Multiplex temporal measures reflecting neural underpinnings of brain functional connectivity under cognitive load in autism spectrum disorder. Neurol. Res. **42**(4), 327–337 (2020)

55. Wadhera, T., Kakkar, D.: Modeling risk perception using independent and social learning: application to individuals with autism spectrum disorder. J. Math. Sociol. **45**(4), 223–245 (2021)
56. Wadhera, T., Kakkar, D.: Social cognition and functional brain network in autism spectrum disorder: insights from EEG graph-theoretic measures. Biomed. Signal Process. Control **67**, 102556 (2021)
57. Zaman, S., et al.: Security threats and artificial intelligence based countermeasures for internet of things networks: a comprehensive survey. IEEE Access **9**, 94668–94690 (2021)

Deep Learning-Based Human Action Recognition Framework to Assess Children on the Risk of Autism or Developmental Delays

Manu Kohli[1]([✉]) [iD], Arpan Kumar Kar[1] [iD], Varun Ganjigunte Prakash[2] [iD], and A. P. Prathosh[3] [iD]

[1] Department of Management Studies, Indian Institute of Technology-Delhi, Delhi, India
manu.kohli@dms.iitd.ac.in, arpan_kar@yahoo.co.in
[2] CogniAble, Gurgaon, India
varungp@cogniable.tech
[3] Department of Electrical Communication Engineering, Indian Institute of Science, Bengaluru, India
prathosh@iisc.ac.in

Abstract. Automatic human action recognition of children with machine learning and deep learning methods using play-based videos can lead to developmental monitoring, early identification, and efficient management of children at risk of neurodevelopmental disorders (NDD) and Autism Spectrum Disorders (ASD). Advancements in deep learning make it feasible to develop human action recognition models with large datasets, enhance clinician capacity, and improve access, affordability, and quality of care. However, data collection is challenging due to ethical, legal, and limited datasets of children with NDD and the enormous amount of human tasks involved in video annotation. Therefore, we propose a new method to overcome these challenges by training several deep learning models using a publicly available action dataset comprising adults performing various actions. We demonstrate the effectiveness of our multiple models to recognize similar actions of children in a custom-collected video dataset of children with NDD, ASD, and Typical development. Our method assist child psychologists in intelligently detecting children at risk of NDD and measuring their progress from their videos captured in the natural environment.

Keywords: Action recognition · Neurodevelopmental disorders · CNN · Autism Spectrum Disorder (ASD) · Deep neural networks (DNN)

1 Introduction

Increase in prevalence of Autism Spectrum Disorders (ASD) [28] and Neurodevelopmental delays (NDD) has made researchers interested in developing

M. Tanveer et al. (Eds.): ICONIP 2022, CCIS 1794, pp. 459–470, 2023.
https://doi.org/10.1007/978-981-99-1648-1_38

technology-driven solutions [5,34] for its early screening, risk assessments [12] and treatment monitoring.

Currently, children suspected of a developmental risk are confirmed with a diagnostic test performed by clinicians recording behavior observations and responses to stimuli initiated by referring to the gold-standard test such as ADOS and CARS-2 [4,19]. In diagnostic and assessment evaluations, various functional skills such as fine and gross motor skills, academic activities, and activities of daily living are measured for intervention formulation [14,30].

However, the current process of risk assessment and diagnosis of children with NDDs has several limitations: 1) lack of skilled therapists [11], particularly in geographically remote places, and 2) poor quality of detection, diagnosis, and intervention services [17,21], and 3) affordability and lack of data-based decision making. These limitations lead to a two-year delay between a family's developmental concern and diagnosis confirmation. The delay denies children early intervention services, most beneficial in the first three years when brain neuroplasticity is highest [15]. Delaying early intervention services may affect children's social, academic, and societal inclusion and achievement. Therefore, early detection and intervention are crucial for NDDs and ASD children. Lately, healthcare has increasingly adopted Machine Learning (ML) applications. Even though the application of ML in academic research has been evident since the middle of the 20th century, the higher adoption rate [1] can be attributed to three factors -1) improved computing capabilities, 2) multimodal data availability, and 3) the advent of deep learning methods [9]. Currently, academic research labs and enterprises have examined the application of AI and ML in three crucial areas: 1) the application of ML to predict the pharmacological properties of molecules for drug development; 2) applying pattern recognition and segmentation algorithms to medical images and behavioral videos to expedite diagnoses and disease progression tracking; and 3) using deep-learning (DL) on multimodal genetic and clinical data to identify disease onsets and develop predictive models [33]. The applications of ML are evident in ASD and NDD diagnosis, risk assessment [10,23,32,35], therapy recommendation, and personalization [16], aiming to optimize care, increase efficiency, and enhance the caregiver and family skills and produce significant outcomes. The rise in ML applications in the detection and management of ASD can be attributed to the availability of multimodal data from various bio-behavioral sources such as – 1) videos containing ASD behavioral traits [10,23,24,32,35], 2) audio [25], 3) facial expressions [2], and 4) electronic health record (EHR) data [26]. ML and DL models can be trained on multimodel data to develop innovations to detect and manage ASD. Further, researchers have collected multimodal data from hospital EHRs and built massive multimodal data lakes, allowing DL and ML algorithms to uncover clinically significant trends for ASD detection, longitudinal patient tracking, treatment recommendation, and personalization [16]. ML and computer vision (CV) have enhanced several facets of human visual perception to identify clinically relevant patterns in images and videos to classify actions of interest to assess and detect complex behavioral problems such as ASD [10,23,24,32,35,36]. However, one of the challenges in implementing CV in ASD detection and management is the high labor cost, significant human effort, and downtime in the manual video data annotation for actions of interest. We, therefore, propose to overcome this limitation by training DL models on a selected action class of interest available on publicly available annotated videos of typically developing (TD) adults. We then test the model on ASD children and evaluate the model's performance. Our objective in building the classifier is to detect the action of interest with high accuracy from trimmed videos. The study is structured with Sect. 2 describing in detail material and methods, Sect. 3.2 listing experiment and results, followed by discussion in Sect. 4 and conclusion in Sect. 5.

2 Material and Methods

Technological improvements in ML and DL methods have enabled the detection of human activities directly from a video stream [3]. These methods have contributed to the development of diagnostic and treatment monitoring innovations in the area of pediatric behavioral health. We are inspired by the DL architectures incorporating computer vision to analyze human actions of interest using the Human action recognition (HAR) framework. Therefore, we aim to use this in detecting and managing NDD and ASD. The structure of our methodology is as follows: Sect. 2.1 defines the study objective, Sect. 2.2 describes the dataset in detail, while Sect. 2.3 discusses the study methods.

2.1 Objective

To identify Human actions relevant for risk assessment, detection, and treatment monitoring of children with ASD and NDDs. The outcome of human action provides clinicians and therapists with actionable insights to assist through data-based recommendations and enhancing their workload capacity. Utilizing public action recognition datasets with similar action classes to implement and generalize action recognition for children for ASD risk assessment is the novel contribution of this paper.

2.2 Dataset

We develop the DL models on NTU action recognition dataset (NTU RGB+D 120) [18]. The dataset includes 120 actions of people (adults) performing daily actions (82), medical conditions (12), and two-person interactions (26), with 114480 short videos ranging from 2–4 seconds in length. We shortlisted actions in seven categories of interest that are clinically relevant to the NDD and ASD population and are used by clinicians to perform risk assessment, detection, and treatment monitoring.

2.3 Methods

We developed seven DL models on the adult NTU database. Additionally, we collected 283 videos from pediatric clinics and YouTube to validate the DL models on unseen real-world videos. These videos came from different environmental and camera settings and angles. The participants consisted of sixty children with ADHD/Speech Delay and six children with ASD diagnosed with gold-standard diagnostic tools and recorded their informed consent for video usage. In addition, two hundred and seventeen children's data was extracted from YouTube, and the diagnosis of these children was unknown. In addition, the videos of children had multiple resolutions, involved multiple people and objects with interfering actions in the background compared to the training videos.

3   Experiments and Results

The experiments were done in two stages. In the first stage, detailed in Subsect. 3.1, we developed the DL models on the NTU adult dataset. In the second stage, detailed in Subsect. 3.2, we validated the models on the ASD children dataset.

3.1   Development of DL Models

In the paper, we use a CV (Computer Vision) method and evaluate if the child can successfully perform the actions of interest. The success in performing specific actions of interest confirms that the child has the necessary motor, academic, Activity of Daily Living (ADLs), and instruction following skills. We assume that no action performance or incorrect action demonstration by the child are problems that are solved. Therefore a HAR framework can suggest based on clinician stimuli if action was performed successfully or if there was an incorrect or no response from the child. We identified 45 actions of interest in Table 1. The selected categories have semantically similar action classes (optical flow feature attributes are similar), given that both the public dataset and the target data distribution have similar attributes in optical flow space. This makes it possible to generalize the model's outcome on children's data [24]. We utilized 41808 videos from the NTU dataset [18] and grouped them into seven categories such as fine motor, gross motor, play, academic, daily living skills, medical conditions, and mutual interactions. These categories are used to analyze the skills of children for developmental risk assessment, treatment formulation, and tracking treatment progress [19,20].

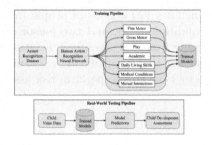

Fig. 1. Illustration of training and inference pipelines for child development analysis

Table 1. List of seven action recognition DL models with action labels

Category	No. of classes	Action labels (Action label number)
Fine Motor	5	Tear up paper (1), Open bottle (2), Rub two hands (3), Snap fingers (4), Put on a shoe (5)
Gross Motor	8	Clapping (6), Hopping (7), Nod head/bow (8), Hand waving (9), Point to something (10), Shake head (11), Cross hands in front (12), Arm swings (13)
Play	5	Play with phone/tablet (14), Play magic cube (15), Juggle table tennis ball (16), Bounce ball (17), Tennis bat swing (18)
Academic	7	Reading (19), Fold paper (20), Counting money (21), Staple book (22), Cutting paper (23), Writing (24), Ball up paper (25)
Daily Living Skills	5	Wipe face (26), Brush teeth (27), Cutting nails (28), Eat meal (29), Brush hair (30)
Medical Conditions	5	Sneeze/cough (31), Blow nose (32), Falling down (33), Yawn (34), Staggering (35)
Mutual Interactions	10	Punch/slap (36), Point finger (37), Shaking hands (38), Take a photo (39), Hugging (40), High-five (41), Pushing (42), Grab stuff (43), Hit with object (44), Exchange things (45)

Table 2. Training hyperparameters of action recognition models

Category	Output Classes	Clip length/ frames	Batch size	New step length	Optimiser	Initial learning rate	Epochs
Fine motor	5	32	8	2	SGD	0.001	30
Gross motor	8	32	8	2	SGD	0.001	115
Play	5	32	8	2	SGD	0.001	70
Academic	7	64	16	2	SGD	0.0005	90
Daily living skills	5	32	8	2	SGD	0.001	125
Medical conditions	5	64	16	2	SGD	0.0005	125
Mutual interactions	10	32	8	2	SGD	0.001	235

Fig. 2. Human action recognition neural network

Fig. 3. Training videos frames captured for various actions from NTU database

The child's skill level is indicated by his demonstration of various actions in a specific category, including ADLs. For instance, fine and gross motor action recognition demonstrates a child's ability to move their hands and legs to perform play and writing skills efficiently. Academic actions demonstrate a child's ability to engage with objects and perform fundamental tasks such as counting money, writing, and stapling a book. Detection of repeated medical conditions such as coughing, falling, or staggering enables a child to demonstrate medical issues in a natural environment to a doctor for timely treatment. The mutual interactions of a child, such as shaking hands, pushing, hitting, and exchanging objects, provide insight into his or her social interaction and ability to perform activities of daily living (ADLs). The training and real-world video inference pipeline is shown in Fig. 1. During training, we first collect the HAR task videos and split them into training and test sets. We trained seven DL models for each category, as listed in Table 1. For each category, we ensured the selection of nearly the same video count for every action within a category. Table 3 lists training and test video distribution for each model category. Each of the models was trained on the video sets using an action recognition neural network technique, and all the trained models were tested on the unseen test set (see Fig. 1).

We developed seven action recognition models based on a two-stream I3D architecture [29] with a ResNet [8] backbone initialized with Kinetics-400 [13] weights. Using 3D convolutional layers (like I3D) as opposed to 2D ones has been demonstrated to better capture temporal patterns and facilitate parameter learning for underlying architectures. The success of the two-stream architecture is a result of its exceptionally high performance on established benchmarks [3] and its efficiency for training, testing, and transfer learning on new video datasets. The two-stream architecture consists of spatial and temporal components as depicted in Fig. 2. The spatial stream convolutional network extracts information from individual RGB frames consisting of features related to how and where the objects, humans, and their appearance in the frame occur. The temporal stream convolutional network extracts information from the multi-frame optical flow [7] regarding the movement of humans or objects across subsequent frames. Each convolutional network consists of five convolutional layers, two fully connected layers with dropouts, and a softmax layer with the same stride and max-pooling layer parameters as described in [29]. The softmax prediction scores are fused by averaging method [29] to obtain the final prediction of action. In sum, the input to the model is the short video clip, and the output is the action label belonging to one of the seven action categories. We trained the seven models with their corresponding training and test samples and class labels, as shown in Table 3. We used one NVIDIA Tesla V100 GPU for training with a multi-threaded program running on 24 cores. Figure 3 shows a few examples of training videos. Upon multiple experiments for 20 epochs, each of 200 iterations (each iteration consists of random sampled videos of batch size from the training set), we selected the best hyperparameters for each model as listed in Table 2. Clip length is the number of input frames, new step length is the frame skip stride, and epoch is the number of times the model observes training clips with a certain batch size. The test accuracy of the models for fine motor, gross motor, play, academic daily living skills, medical conditions, and mutual interactions were 95.9, 98.9, 99.3, 73.9, 96.9, 95.2, and 97.5%, respectively (see Table 3). The following section will discuss our experiments and the model's performance on children's videos.

Table 3. NTU Dataset Action labels Training and Test set distribution

Category	Action label number	Training set per action label	Test set per action label	Train, test accuracy (%)
Fine motor	(1, 2, 3, 4, 5)	(829, 879, 802, 865, 795)	(76, 81, 102, 95, 110)	97.61, 95.91
Gross motor	(6, 7, 8, 9, 10, 11, 12, 13)	(809, 816, 806, 821,817, 808, 818, 865)	(96, 88, 98, 83, 87, 96, 86, 95)	99.60, 98.90
Play	(14, 15, 16, 17, 18)	(816, 867, 851, 868, 868)	(88, 93, 109, 92, 92)	99.80, 99.37
Academic	(19, 20, 21, 22, 23, 24, 25)	(816, 866, 854, 869, 855, 821, 868)	(89, 94, 106, 91, 105, 84, 92)	79.50, 73.98
Daily living skills	(26, 27, 28, 29, 30)	(818, 818, 860, 806, 819)	(86, 87, 100, 99, 86)	98.51, 96.94
Medical conditions	(31, 32, 33, 34, 35)	(810,862, 819, 864, 814)	(94, 98, 85, 96, 90)	98.71, 95.25
Mutual interaction	(36, 37, 38, 39, 40, 41, 42, 43, 44, 45)	(817, 803, 810, 849, 818, 857, 819, 883, 863, 869)	(87, 101, 94, 111, 86, 103, 85, 77, 97, 91)	98.41, 97.53

3.2   Validation of DL Models

We validated the seven action recognition models on 283 real-world videos of TD and ASD children performing various actions. The videos were annotated by expert clinicians, and ground-truth action label classes were recorded. Each video has an average duration of 5 s and was inferred by the seven DL models. If the prediction action label was correct compared to the ground truth action label and the prediction confidence score of the model ≥ 50%, it is then considered a correct prediction. Figure 4 shows a few example test videos of the children's

Fig. 4. Real-world test videos frames captured for various actions from children's database (with faces pixelated to protect privacy)

dataset. The test accuracy of children's videos for fine motor, gross motor, play, academic daily living skills, medical conditions, and mutual interactions were 87.5, 90, 72.4, 68.1, 76.9, 72.7, and 75.7%, respectively (see Table 4). We observed a few instances where our method performed inadequately. For example, there were differences in patterns of play performed by adults in the training set vs. children in the test set. Further, we observed that the model misclassified a few action videos, such as "play with phone/tablet" and "play with the magic cube." In these videos, adults used both thumb fingers of their hands to play on the phone, but the children held the phone in a different orientation and used all their fingers while playing, leading to misclassification. Also, adults solve/play with a magic cube by rotating it in different directions, whereas children bounce and flip them while playing. These misclassification instances necessitate significant data volumes to be included for training with various action representations. However, our models showed superior performance for many actions, such as "open a bottle," "put on a shoe," "clapping," "arm swings," "fold paper," "wipe face," "brushing hair," "sneeze," "falling down," "shaking hands," "hugging," and "hit with object" with more than 95% average confidence.

Future studies should train models on additional videos collected from children representing actions of interest in multiple demonstration ways to reduce misclassification. However, our study provides clinicians with a software tool that helps them comprehend children's cognitive and behavioral skills essential to establishing their risk of developmental delays or progress during therapy sessions. The CV-based HAR framework can automatically evaluate children's skills in seven categories without human intervention, reduce clinician decision-making biases, and enhance their capacity.

4   Discussion

Recent studies have discussed the application of neural networks to imaging data sets, drug characteristics, clinical diagnostics and genomics, computer vision for

Table 4. Model's validation on children dataset and test results

Category	Number of samples	Test accuracy
Fine motor	32	87.50%
Gross motor	40	90%
Play	29	72.41%
Academic	44	68.18%
Daily living skills	39	76.92%
Medical conditions	33	72.72%
Mutual interactions	66	75.75%

medical imaging, and Natural Language Processing for EHR [6,27]. Researchers have developed machine learning and computer vision algorithms that can use video recordings in controlled conditions to identify ASD behaviors automatically [22,31]. However, these methods heavily rely on expert annotation, might not be scalable, and do not test their algorithms on out-of-distribution samples for children, especially with NDDs. Further, the absence of high-quality, large volume labeled datasets, including ASD and NDD populations, with regulated data collection and ethical and legal norms are critical barriers to applying ML, DL, and CV methods for their detection and management.

Our proposed method can overcome the above-stated limitations in several ways. As a first step, we shortlisted human actions of interest. Our objective was to use the HAR approach to identify necessary skills of ASD and NDD children. We shortlisted seven action categories available in publically available datasets and traditionally used by clinicians to make assessments for detection and skill acquisitions of ASD children. Secondly, we developed DL HAR models on the videos of adults available in publicly recorded datasets in a controlled research setting. Thirdly we validated the model outcomes in a natural clinical environment, including ASD and TD children. The accuracy scores demonstrated mixed outcomes on classes of interest, demonstrating high accuracy on a few actions and modest on others. The modest results can be attributed to the fact that the DL models were trained on controlled environmental videos with the user performing actions in specific order leading to action biases. Therefore, the models performed modestly on test videos of children recorded in clinical or natural environments. For maximum benefit, care should be taken to train and test DL models with various actions performed in multiple ways. In the current study, we included limited samples of children with ASD, Speech delay, and NDD. Therefore future studies should include larger sample sizes of ASD and NDD populations using gold-standard tools. Further, to reduce bias and ensure the models' internal and external validity, there is an urgent need to conduct extensive clinical trials, including the collaboration of researchers and clinicians from different countries, backgrounds, and ethnicities. The objective of the collaboration should be to validate outcomes, identify the efficacy and detriments of model development, and devise methods to include children from diverse backgrounds in research studies. Further, HAR models have an inherent limitation to misclassifying similar action classes. Therefore care should be taken to have DL models consisting of the optimum count of action classes with minimum similarity to minimize misclassification and improve psychometric outcomes such as sensitivity, specificity, and accuracy.

5   Conclusion and Future Scope

We proposed a novel multi-model action recognition method trained on 45 actions to measure children's performance on the action of interest. We trained seven DL models on the NTU RGB video dataset on various adult actions to detect children with ASD and NDD. Our method is simple to implement and performs with modest to high psychometric outcomes on videos of actual children consisting of 283 videos of children that include complex video scenes. We propose three research avenues for the future: (1) develop new child-centric methods using multi-modal data of speech and video to evaluate diverse skills in joint attention, social communication, and repetitive/maladaptive behaviors for children with NDD; (2) include more action classes with behaviors and daily activities associated with children diagnosed with NDD from publicly available datasets; and (3) improve model deployment and production frameworks to provide rapid video inference without expensive and dedicated hardware resources (GPU).

References

1. Baker, S., Kandasamy, Y.: Machine learning for understanding and predicting neurodevelopmental outcomes in premature infants: a systematic review. Pediatric Res. (2022)
2. Carpenter, K.L., et al.: Digital behavioral phenotyping detects atypical pattern of facial expression in toddlers with autism. Autism Res. **14**(3), 488–499 (2021)
3. Carreira, J., Zisserman, A.: Quo vadis, action recognition? a new model and the kinetics dataset. In: 2017 IEEE Conference on Computer Vision and Pattern Recognition (CVPR), pp. 4724–4733 (2017)
4. Chlebowski, C., Green, J.A., Barton, M.L., Fein, D.: Using the childhood autism rating scale to diagnose autism spectrum disorders. J. Autism Dev. Disord. **40**(7), 787–799 (2010)
5. Cioni, G., Inguaggiato, E., Sgandurra, G.: Early intervention in neurodevelopmental disorders: underlying neural mechanisms. Developm. Med. Child Neurol. **58**(S4), 61–66 (2016)
6. Elbattah, M., Guerin, J.L., Carette, R., Cilia, F., Dequen, G.: Nlp-based approach to detect autism spectrum disorder in saccadic eye movement. In: 2020 IEEE Symposium Series on Computational Intelligence (SSCI), pp. 1581–1587 (2020)
7. Farnebäck, G.: Two-frame motion estimation based on polynomial expansion. In: Bigun, J., Gustavsson, T. (eds.) SCIA 2003. LNCS, vol. 2749, pp. 363–370. Springer, Heidelberg (2003). https://doi.org/10.1007/3-540-45103-X_50

8. Feichtenhofer, C., Pinz, A., Wildes, R.P.: Spatiotemporal residual networks for video action recognition. In: Proceedings of the 30th International Conference on Neural Information Processing Systems, NIPS 2016, pp. 3476–3484. Curran Associates Inc., Red Hook (2016)
9. Gupta, C., et al.: Bringing machine learning to research on intellectual and developmental disabilities: taking inspiration from neurological diseases. J. Neurodev. Disord. 14(1), 28 (2022)
10. Hashemi, J., et al.: Computer vision analysis for quantification of autism risk behaviors. IEEE Trans. Affect. Comput. 12(1), 215–226 (2021)
11. Hollis, C., et al.: Annual research review: Digital health interventions for children and young people with mental health problems - a systematic and meta-review. J. Child Psychol. Psychiatry 58(4), 474–503 (2017)
12. Hollis, C., et al.: the AQUA Trial Group: The impact of a computerised test of attention and activity (QbTest) on diagnostic decision-making in children and young people with suspected attention deficit hyperactivity disorder: single-blind randomised controlled trial. J. Child Psychol. Psychiatry 59(12), 1298–1308 (2018)
13. Kay, W., et al.: The kinetics human action video dataset. arXiv: 1705.06950 (2017)
14. Khowaja, M., Robins, D.L., Adamson, L.B.: Utilizing two-tiered screening for early detection of autism spectrum disorder. Autism 22(7), 881–890 (2018)
15. Klintwall, L., Eikeseth, S.: Early and intensive behavioral intervention (eibi) in autism. Comprehensive Guide Autism, 117–137 (2014)
16. Kohli, M., Kar, A.K., Bangalore, A., Ap, P.: Machine learning-based aba treatment recommendation and personalization for autism spectrum disorder: an exploratory study. Brain Informat. 9(1), 1–25 (2022)
17. Kornack, J., Persicke, A., Cervantes, P., Jang, J., Dixon, D.: Economics of autism spectrum disorders: An overview of treatment and research funding. In: Handbook of Early Intervention For Autism Spectrum Disorders, pp. 165–178 (2014)
18. Liu, J., Shahroudy, A., Perez, M., Wang, G., Duan, L.Y., Kot, A.C.: Ntu rgb+d 120: A large-scale benchmark for 3d human activity understanding. IEEE Trans. Pattern Anal. Mach. Intell. 42(10), 2684–2701 (2020)
19. Lord, C., et al.: The autism diagnostic observation schedule-generic: A standard measure of social and communication deficits associated with the spectrum of autism. J. Autism Dev. Disord. 30(3), 205–223 (2000)
20. Lord, C., Storoschuk, S., Rutter, M., Pickles, A.: Using the adi-r to diagnose autism in preschool children. Infant Ment. Health J. 14(3), 234–252 (1993)
21. Malik-Soni, N., et al.: Tackling healthcare access barriers for individuals with autism from diagnosis to adulthood. Pediatr. Res. 91(5), 1028–1035 (2021)
22. Nabil, M.A., Akram, A., Fathalla, K.M.: Applying machine learning on home videos for remote autism diagnosis: Further study and analysis. Health Informatics J. 27(1), 1460458221991882 (2021)
23. Ouss, L., et al.: Behavior and interaction imaging at 9 months of age predict autism/intellectual disability in high-risk infants with west syndrome. Transl. Psychiatry 10(1), 1–7 (2020)
24. Pandey, P., Prathosh, A., Kohli, M., Pritchard, J.: Guided weak supervision for action recognition with scarce data to assess skills of children with autism. In: Proceedings of the AAAI Conference on Artificial Intelligence, vol. 34, pp. 463–470 (2020)
25. Patten, E., Belardi, K., Baranek, G.T., Watson, L.R., Labban, J.D., Oller, D.K.: Vocal patterns in infants with autism spectrum disorder: Canonical babbling status and vocalization frequency. J. Autism Dev. Disord. 44(10), 2413–2428 (2014)

26. Rahman, R., Kodesh, A., Levine, S.Z., Sandin, S., Reichenberg, A., Schlessinger, A.: Identification of newborns at risk for autism using electronic medical records and machine learning. Euro. Psych. **63**(1) (2020)
27. Scassellati, C., Bonvicini, C., Benussi, L., Ghidoni, R., Squitti, R.: Neurodevelopmental disorders: Metallomics studies for the identification of potential biomarkers associated to diagnosis and treatment. J. Trace Elem. Med Biol. **60**, 126499 (2020)
28. Serenius, F., et al.: For the extremely preterm infants in sweden study group: neurodevelopmental outcomes among extremely preterm infants 6.5 years after active perinatal care in Sweden. JAMA Pediatrics **170**(10), 954–963 (2016)
29. Simonyan, K., Zisserman, A.: Two-stream convolutional networks for action recognition in videos. In: NIPS (2014)
30. Sundberg, M.L.: VB-MAPP Verbal Behavior Milestones Assessment and Placement Program: a language and social skills assessment program for children with autism or other developmental disabilities: guide. Mark Sundberg (2008)
31. Tariq, Q., Daniels, J., Schwartz, J.N., Washington, P., Kalantarian, H., Wall, D.P.: Mobile detection of autism through machine learning on home video: A development and prospective validation study. PLoS Med. **15**(11), e1002705 (2018)
32. Tariq, Q., et al.: Detecting developmental delay and autism through machine learning models using home videos of bangladeshi children: Development and validation study. J. Med. Internet Res. **21**(4), e13822 (2019)
33. Uddin, M., Wang, Y., Woodbury-Smith, M.: Artificial intelligence for precision medicine in neurodevelopmental disorders. NPJ Digital Med. **2**(1), 112 (2019)
34. Valentine, A.Z., Brown, B.J., Groom, M.J., Young, E., Hollis, C., Hall, C.L.: A systematic review evaluating the implementation of technologies to assess, monitor and treat neurodevelopmental disorders: A map of the current evidence. Clin. Psychol. Rev. **80**, 101870 (2020)
35. Young, G.S., et al.: A video-based measure to identify autism risk in infancy. J. Child Psychol. Psychiatry **61**(1), 88–94 (2020)
36. Zhang, L., Wang, M., Liu, M., Zhang, D.: A survey on deep learning for neuroimaging-based brain disorder analysis. Front. Neurosci. **14**, 779 (2020)

Dynamic Convolutional Network for Generalizable Face Anti-spoofing

Shitao Lu[1], Yi Zhang[2], Jiacheng Zhao[3], Changjie Cheng[4],
and Lizhuang Ma[1,4(✉)]

[1] East China Normal University, Shanghai, China
lusto993@163.com, lzma@cs.ecnu.edu.cn
[2] Zhejiang Lab, Hangzhou, Zhejiang, China
zhangyi620@zhejianglab.com
[3] Zhejiang University, Hangzhou, China
3180103606@zju.edu.cn
[4] Shanghai Jiao Tong University, Shanghai, China
cjcheng@sjtu.edu.cn

Abstract. With the increasing of face presentation attacks from unseen scenarios, domain generalization of face anti-spoofing (FAS) task has drawn much attention. Recent researches mainly focus on seeking a generalized feature space via various training strategies. However, few of them pay attention to the convolution operation which directly affects the extraction of features. In this work, we concentrate on the dynamic convolution kernels and propose a novel framework for generalizable face anti-spoofing. Specifically, Dynamic Domain Convolution Generator (DDCG) is proposed to generate the input-dependent convolution kernels which can adapt to samples from different domains. Moreover, an asymmetric center mining is designed to make only real faces more compact in the feature space, but not for the fake ones. Both of above methods can help to achieve a more generalized class boundary in the target domain. Comprehensive experiments and visualizations illustrate that our model is effective and competitive with alternative state-of-the-art methods.

Keywords: Face anti-spoofing · Domain generalization · Dynamic convolutional layer

1 Introduction

In recent years, face recognition technique has facilitated our daily lives in the fields of access control, mobile payment, etc. However, plenty of presentation attacks like photos and videos make the face recognition system vulnerable. To deal with such threats, face anti-spoofing techniques are proposed against various attacks. FAS models usually take a face image or video as input and then distinguish whether it is a real face or fake one.

Early FAS researches focus on traditional hand-crafted features such as texture-based methods (e.g., LBP [1,6], HOG [9,31], SIFT [21], etc.) and

M. Tanveer et al. (Eds.): ICONIP 2022, CCIS 1794, pp. 471–482, 2023.
https://doi.org/10.1007/978-981-99-1648-1_39

temporal-based methods (e.g., eye blinking [20], rPPG [11,14,15], etc.) With the strong representation abilities of deep networks, deep feature-based FAS methods [17,30,32,33,36,37] gradually emerge and surpass traditional methods.

Despite the state-of-the-art performance in intra-dataset testing scenarios, generic FAS methods may have poor performance when faced with cross-dataset testing scenarios. That is because the model only fits on the source domains so that it has limited ability to deal with the data from target domain where the imaging conditions and face identities are different to source data. To this end, domain generalization is introduced into FAS and different datasets are usually regarded as diverse domains. Various methods have been proposed to restrain the influence of the domain gap.

Shao et al. [25] and Qin et al. [22] utilized meta-learning to simulate the domain shift in training phase. Such DG methods mainly focus on training strategies aiming to align final features to a domain-agnostic space without altering model parameters like convolution kernels in the testing phase. These convolution kernels fitting on source domains have limited ability to adapt to the target domain. Jia et al. [8] proposed the asymmetric triplet loss which treats real faces from various domains as single category and fake ones in different domains as distinct categories. That is because the real faces always have more similar patterns than fake ones which have different attack types and imaging conditions. However, it merely considered the relative distances between real and various fake faces in source domains without considering the intra-class distance.

To deal with aforementioned limitations, we proposed a framework with Dynamic Domain Convolution Generator (DDCG) module and Asymmetric Center Mining to achieve generalizable FAS. Firstly, DDCG aims to dynamically generate adaptive convolution kernels for each sample based on the shallow features and domain information. What's more, asymmetric center mining helps to better learn the pattern of real faces and seek a more generalized feature space. Our contributions can be summarized as follows: 1) From a novel perspective, we propose to dynamically generate input-dependent convolution kernels to make the network adapt to various domains. 2) We design an asymmetric center loss to achieve more compact real face representation which can further improve the generalization. 3) We conduct comprehensive experiments to verify the effect of proposed methods and achieve quite competitive results on popular test settings.

2   Related Work

2.1   Face Anti-spoofing

Face anti-spoofing researches could be roughly divided into handcrafted-feature-based methods and deep-feature-based ones. The handcrafted features like LBP [1,6], HOG [9,31] and SIFT [21] are followed by a traditional classifier to distinguish attacks. Recently, various deep-feature-based methods [16,35] have been proved to perform better than traditional ones. R-PPG signals [11,14,15] aim to capture the subtle changes on faces. Yu et al. [33,34] design special network structures to extract more discriminative features.

Although these methods achieve good results in intra-dataset test settings, the performance may become poor under cross-dataset test settings. To tackle this problem, more attention is paid to the domain generalization (DG) scenario of FAS task. Shao et al. [24] and Jia et al. [8] leveraged adversarial training to learn a domain-agnostic feature space. Shao et al. [25] and Qin et al. [22] utilized meta-learning to make the model generalize better to unseen domains. Special network structures [33,34] and adaptive normalized technique [12] were also designed to improve generalization. Although these DG frameworks have achieved good performance, their parameters of convolutional layers are fixed after training which is experimentially not optimal when faced with unseen domains. Our method focuses on dynamic convolution kernels which can adaptively extract discriminative features for each sample according to its domain information.

2.2 Dynamic Convolutional Layer

Convolutional layers are basic blocks of deep neural networks. Several researches have been carried out to study dynamic convolutional layers. Yang et al. [29] learned specialized convolution kernels for each sample. Liu et al. [3] aggregated multiple parallel convolution kernels based on attention weights. Such alterable convolutional layers increase the size and capacity of the model without sacrificing efficiency.

3 Methodology

3.1 Overview

Since fixed convolution kernels are not flexible to the target domain, we argue that using dynamic convolution kernels is a better strategy to adapt to the unseen feature distribution of target data. To this end, as illustrated in Fig. 1, we propose the dynamic domain convolution generator for generalizable FAS tasks, which can dynamically generate adaptive convolution kernels for each sample to relieve the influence of domain gap during feature extracting stage. What's more, since the discrepancies are much smaller among real faces than the fake ones, it is unreasonable to use the same strategy to align them in the feature space. Therefore, we proposed the asymmetric center mining to further make real faces more compact in the feature space. Finally, combined with asymmetric triplet loss [8], the dynamic domain convolution generator and asymmetric center mining could better deal with samples from target domains, leading to a generalizable FAS model.

3.2 Dynamic Domain Convolution Generator

In traditional convolutional layers, the convolution kernels are used unaltered for testing samples after training. While in the domain generalization scenario,

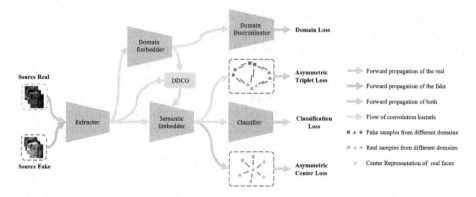

Fig. 1. An overview of the proposed framework. Real and fake faces from different datasets are fed into the feature extracter to get shallow features. The domain embedder embeds shallow features into domain features. Then, the DDCG module generates adaptive convolution kernels for the semantic embedder according to shallow features and domain features. The domain discriminator and classifier are used to predict the domain label and semantic label respectively.

the fixed convolution kernels trained with source domains have limited ability to extract discriminative features for faces from unseen domains. Motivated by Condconv [29], we attempt to generate adaptive convolution kernels to deal with the domain shift. Firstly, discriminative domain information is drawn from each sample. Concretely, assume M source datasets could be achieved during training and each dataset contains both real and fake faces. Firstly, the feature extracter extracts shallow feature maps U_i from the input face x_i. Then, the domain embedder further encodes U_i into domain feature z_i^d and the domain discriminator is used to predict the domain of z_i^d. The domain loss can be formulated as Eq. 1, where $y_i \in \{0, 1, ..., M-1\}$ donates the domain label of x_i.

$$\mathcal{L}_{domain} = - \sum_{(x_i, y_i)} y_i log(Dis(Dom(Ext(x_i)))) \qquad (1)$$

Since z^d contains discriminative domain information, it could further be used to guide the generation of convolution kernels. As shown in Fig. 2, DDCG module takes shallow features and domain features as input and generates the adaptive kernels. Based on U, a group of convolution kernels $K \in \mathbb{R}^{H \times H \times C}$ (H and C donate the kernel size and number of channels respectively) are generated according to Eq. 2, where W_1 and W_2 are learnable matrices in fully connected layers and g, δ, σ donate average pooling function, ReLU function and sigmoid function respectively.

$$K = F_{gen}(U) = \sigma(W_1 \delta(W_2 g(U))) \qquad (2)$$

Since the convolution kernels should be adaptive for samples from various domains, we mine the domain information to generate scaling weight for each

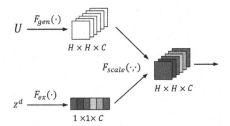

Fig. 2. Illustration of the dynamic domain convolution generator.

kernel. Although testing samples come from unseen domains, the domain embedder can also extract domain-related information to guide convolution kernels in a scaling way. Inspired by SENet [7], we calculate the scaling weights through Eq. 3, where W_3 and W_4 are learnable matrices in fully connected layers.

$$s = F_{ex}(z^d) = \sigma(W_3\delta(W_4 z^d)) \tag{3}$$

Finally, the dynamically generated convolution kernels $\widetilde{K} = \{\widetilde{k}_1, \widetilde{k}_2, ..., \widetilde{k}_C\}$ is obtained according to Eq. 4, where $F_{scale}(\cdot, \cdot)$ donates the channel-wise multiplication and k_c is the c-th kernel of K.

$$\widetilde{k}_c = F_{scale}(k_c, s_c) = s_c k_c \tag{4}$$

The architectures of feature extracter and embedder (detailed in Table 1) in our framework have been widely used in FAS tasks [8,25]. In this work, we generate convolution kernels only for conv2-1 so that the additional cost of parameters and calculation are completely acceptable.

3.3 Asymmetric Center Mining

According to [8], real faces are collected by directly imaging real people in any domain while attack types and collecting ways of fake faces varies. For this reason, the distribution discrepancies of real faces are relatively smaller than those of fake faces from different domains. Therefore, it's easier to aggregate features and seek a generalized feature space for real faces. To this end, Jia et al. [8] proposed asymmetric triplet loss to separate the features of fake faces while aggregating the real ones from different domains. Concretely, real faces from different domains are combined into a single category and fake faces from M domains are regarded as M disparate categories. The asymmetric triplet loss function is then applied to the $M + 1$ categories:

$$\mathcal{L}_{triplet} = \sum_{z_i^a, z_i^p, z_i^n} (\|z_i^a - z_i^p\|_2^2 - \|z_i^a - z_i^n\|_2^2 + \beta) \tag{5}$$

where the anchor feature z_i^a and positive feature z_i^p belong to the same category (real or fake), while z_i^a and negative feature z_i^n come from different categories. The hyper-parameter β donates the margin which is set to 0.1 in this work.

Table 1. The structure details of feature extracter and embedder.

Feature Extracter			Feature Embedder		
Layer	Chan./Stri.	Out.Size	Layer	Chan./Stri.	Out.Size
Input			Input		
image			pool1-3		
conv1-1	64/1	256	conv2-1	128/1	32
conv1-2	128/1	256	pool2-1	-/2	16
conv1-3	196/1	256	conv2-2	256/1	16
conv1-4	128/1	256	pool2-2	-/2	8
pool1-1	-/2	128	conv2-2	512/1	8
conv1-5	128/1	128	avg pooling		
conv1-6	196/1	128	fc2-1	1/1	1
conv1-7	128/1	128			
pool1-2	-/2	64			
conv1-8	128/1	64			
conv1-9	196/1	64			
conv-10	128/1	64			
pool1-3	-/2	32			

Although the asymmetric triplet loss aligns real and fake features in an easier way, samples from unseen domain are still likely to be mispredicted. Therefore, we utilized center loss [28] and further proposed the asymmetric center mining which forces real face features to be closer to a center in the feature space. In this way, we compel the model to better learn the similar patterns of real faces from different domains. With the cooperation of asymmetric triplet loss, real face features will be aligned in a smaller region of the feature space leaving more space for various types of fake faces which is more reasonable in reality. The asymmetric center loss is formulated as Eq. 6:

$$\mathcal{L}_{center} = \sum_i \|z_i^{real} - v\|_2^2 \tag{6}$$

where $v \in \mathbb{R}^q$ donates the learnable class center of real face features.

Above all, the total loss of our framework is formulated as Eq. 7, where $\mathcal{L}_{cls}$ is the binary cross entropy classification loss for the FAS task and γ is set to 0.005.

$$\mathcal{L}_{total} = \mathcal{L}_{cls} + \mathcal{L}_{domain} + \gamma \mathcal{L}_{center} + \mathcal{L}_{triplet} \tag{7}$$

4   Experiments

4.1   Experimental Settings

Datasets. To evaluate the effectiveness of the proposed model. We conduct experiments on four public FAS datasets, *i.e.*, MSU-MFSD (denoted as M) [27], CASIA-MFSD (denoted as C) [38], OULU-NPU (denoted as O) [2] and Idiap

Table 2. Comparison results on three-to-one cross-dataset testing.

Method	O&C&M to I		O&C&I to M		O&M&I to C		I&C&M to O	
	HTER (%)	AUC (%)	HTER (%)	AUC (%)	HTER (%)	AUC (%)	HTER (%)	AUC (%)
MS_LBP [19]	50.30	51.64	29.76	78.50	54.28	44.98	50.29	49.31
Auxiliary(Depth) [15]	29.14	71.69	22.72	85.88	33.52	73.15	30.17	77.61
MMD-AAE [10]	31.58	75.18	27.08	83.19	44.59	58.29	40.98	63.08
MADDG [24]	22.19	84.99	17.69	88.06	24.50	84.51	27.98	80.02
SSDG-M [8]	18.21	**94.61**	16.67	90.47	23.11	85.45	25.17	81.83
RFM [25]	17.30	90.48	13.89	93.98	20.27	88.16	16.45	91.16
DRDG [13]	15.56	91.79	12.43	95.81	19.05	88.79	15.63	91.75
D^{2}AM [4]	15.43	91.22	12.70	95.66	20.98	85.58	15.27	90.87
ANRL [12]	16.03	91.04	10.83	**96.75**	17.85	89.26	15.67	91.90
SSAN-M [26]	**14.00**	94.58	10.42	94.76	16.47	90.81	19.51	88.17
Ours	15.08	93.30	**9.58**	**96.75**	**13.33**	**92.04**	**12.33**	**94.98**

Table 3. Comparison results on two-to-one cross-dataset testing.

Method	M&I to C		M&I to O	
	HTER (%)	AUC (%)	HTER (%)	AUC (%)
LBPTOP	45.27	54.88	47.26	50.21
MADDG	41.02	64.33	39.35	65.10
SSDG-M	31.89	71.29	36.01	66.88
DRDG	31.28	71.50	33.35	69.14
ANRL	31.06	72.12	30.73	74.10
Ours	**30.00**	**76.28**	**28.61**	**77.05**

Replay-Attack (denoted as I) [5]. We select three of them as the source domain for training and the remaining one as the target domain for testing. Totally, there are four testing tasks which could be donated as: O&C&M to I, O&C&I to M, O&M&I to C and I&C&M to O. The differences like background and illumination within and between datasets make the these tasks challenging to FAS models.

Implementation Details. Our experiments are conducted via PyTorch on GTX 2080Ti GPUs. We extract frames from videos in mentioned datasets and then crop the face region with a face detector. Face images are all resized to $3 \times 256 \times 256$ with RGB channels. Our models are trained with SGD optimizer. The learning rate is initially set to 0.01 and halves every 100 epochs. For comparison, we calculate the Half Total Error Rate (HTER) and the Area Under Curve (AUC) which are popular evaluation metrics in recent FAS researches.

4.2   Comparison Results

As shown in Table 2, the proposed method outperforms alternative methods on three cross-domain settings in terms of both HTER and AUC. On the remaining O&C&M to I setting, our method also achieves competitive results. What's more,

Table 4. Evaluations of each component.

Method	HTER (%)	AUC (%)
Ours w/o ddcg & center	16.67	90.27
Ours w/o ddcg	13.33	93.50
Ours w/o center	14.44	93.30
Ours	**12.33**	**94.98**

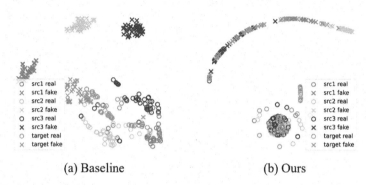

(a) Baseline   (b) Ours

Fig. 3. The t-SNE visualizations of features extracted by baseline model (a) and our framework (b) on I&C&M to O setting.

we also conduct harder experiments with more limited source domains (only two source datasets are available during training). Concretely, Idiap and MSU are utilized for training and the remaining CASIA and OULU are used for testing respectively. As shown in Table 3, our method also performs much better than previous methods in more challenging settings which convincingly shows the great generalizability of our model.

4.3   Ablation Study

To verify the effect of each proposed component i.e., the dynamic domain convolution generator (donated as ddcg), and the asymmetric center mining(donated as center), we conduct ablation experiments on the I&C&M to O setting. It is easy to learn from Table 4 that significant improvement is achieved compared to the method without ddcg and asymmetric center mining. Moreover, the performance degrades whichever component is moved. Above comparison results verify the effectiveness of each proposed components.

4.4   Visualization and Analysis

We visualize features output by the semantic embedder via t-SNE [18]. As shown in Fig. 3, the model optimized only by the classification loss and asymmetric triplet loss is regarded as the baseline (a). Figure 3(b) shows the final feature

real   fake

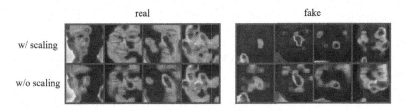

w/ scaling

w/o scaling

Fig. 4. Grad-CAM visualizations of features after the dynamic convolutional layer.

space of our framework. Compared with the baseline, the real face features from source domains are more compact and have a clear center thanks to the asymmetric center loss. Under the cooperation with the classification loss, features of fake faces look like a curve which is far from the source real ones. Moreover, the boundary between real and fake faces from target domain of our framework is much clearer than that of the baseline. Above observations verify that our model is further promoted to learn the similar patterns of real faces and achieves better generalization ability on the target domain.

Further more, to show the interpretability, we visualize the class activation map of features output by the dynamic convolutional layer using Grad-Cam [23]. As shown in Fig. 4, where the visualized faces are all from the target domain, after equipping domain information guided scaling, the dynamic convolutional layer can better capture the liveness cues from real faces which should not be detected in fake ones. On the other hand, the domain information can help promoting the extraction of liveness cues of real faces and restrain that of fake ones.

5   Conclusion

In this paper, we propose the Dynamic Domain Convolution Generator (DDCG) module and Asymmetric Center Mining to improve the generalization ability of the face anti-spoofing model. The DDCG module generates adaptive convolution kernels for each sample according to its domain information which provides our model with more flexibility especially on the target domain. The asymmetric center mining further aggregates real faces of different domains in the feature space. Extensive experiments on popular test settings prove that both of our contributions can lead to better generalization.

Acknowledgments. This work is supported by National Key Research and Development Program of China (2019YFC1521104), National Natural Science Foundation of China (No. 61972157, 72192821), Shanghai Municipal Science and Technology Major Project (2021SHZDZX0102) and Shanghai Science and Technology Commission (21511101200, 22YF1420300).

References

1. Boulkenafet, Z., Komulainen, J., Hadid, A., et al.: Face anti-spoofing based on color texture analysis. In: 2015 IEEE International Conference on Image Processing (ICIP), pp. 2636–2640. IEEE (2015)
2. Boulkenafet, Z., Komulainen, J., Li, L., Feng, X., Hadid, A.: OULU-NPU: a mobile face presentation attack database with real-world variations. In: 2017 12th IEEE International Conference on Automatic Face & Gesture Recognition (FG 2017), pp. 612–618. IEEE (2017)
3. Chen, Y., Dai, X., Liu, M., Chen, D., Yuan, L., Liu, Z.: Dynamic convolution: attention over convolution kernels. In: Proceedings of the IEEE/CVF Conference on Computer Vision and Pattern Recognition, pp. 11030–11039 (2020)
4. Chen, Z., et al.: Generalizable representation learning for mixture domain face anti-spoofing. In: Proceedings of the AAAI Conference on Artificial Intelligence, vol. 35, pp. 1132–1139 (2021)
5. Chingovska, I., Anjos, A., Marcel, S., et al.: On the effectiveness of local binary patterns in face anti-spoofing. In: 2012 BIOSIG-Proceedings of the International Conference of Biometrics Special Interest Group (BIOSIG), pp. 1–7. IEEE (2012)
6. de Freitas Pereira, T., Anjos, A., De Martino, J.M., Marcel, S.: LBP − TOP based countermeasure against face spoofing attacks. In: Park, J.-I., Kim, J. (eds.) ACCV 2012. LNCS, vol. 7728, pp. 121–132. Springer, Heidelberg (2013). https://doi.org/10.1007/978-3-642-37410-4_11
7. Hu, J., Shen, L., Albanie, S., Sun, G., Wu, E.: Squeeze-and-excitation networks. IEEE Trans. Pattern Anal. Mach. Intell. 42(8), 2011–2023 (2020)
8. Jia, Y., Zhang, J., Shan, S., Chen, X.: Single-side domain generalization for face anti-spoofing. In: Proceedings of the IEEE/CVF Conference on Computer Vision and Pattern Recognition, pp. 8484–8493 (2020)
9. Komulainen, J., Hadid, A., Pietikäinen, M., et al.: Context based face anti-spoofing. In: 2013 IEEE Sixth International Conference on Biometrics: Theory, Applications and Systems (BTAS), pp. 1–8. IEEE (2013)
10. Li, H., Pan, S.J., Wang, S., Kot, A.C.: Domain generalization with adversarial feature learning. In: Proceedings of the IEEE Conference on Computer Vision and Pattern Recognition, pp. 5400–5409 (2018)
11. Li, X., Komulainen, J., Zhao, G., Yuen, P.C., Pietikäinen, M.: Generalized face anti-spoofing by detecting pulse from face videos. In: 2016 23rd International Conference on Pattern Recognition (ICPR), pp. 4244–4249. IEEE (2016)
12. Liu, S., et al.: Adaptive normalized representation learning for generalizable face anti-spoofing. In: Proceedings of the 29th ACM International Conference on Multimedia, pp. 1469–1477 (2021)
13. Liu, S., et al.: Dual reweighting domain generalization for face presentation attack detection. arXiv preprint arXiv:2106.16128 (2021)
14. Liu, S.-Q., Lan, X., Yuen, P.C.: Remote photoplethysmography correspondence feature for 3D mask face presentation attack detection. In: Ferrari, V., Hebert, M., Sminchisescu, C., Weiss, Y. (eds.) ECCV 2018. LNCS, vol. 11220, pp. 577–594. Springer, Cham (2018). https://doi.org/10.1007/978-3-030-01270-0_34
15. Liu, Y., Jourabloo, A., Liu, X., et al.: Learning deep models for face anti-spoofing: binary or auxiliary supervision. In: Proceedings of the IEEE Conference on Computer Vision and Pattern Recognition, pp. 389–398 (2018)
16. Liu, Y., Stehouwer, J., Jourabloo, A., Liu, X.: Deep tree learning for zero-shot face anti-spoofing. In: Proceedings of the IEEE/CVF Conference on Computer Vision and Pattern Recognition (CVPR), June 2019

17. Liu, Y., Stehouwer, J., Liu, X.: On disentangling spoof trace for generic face anti-spoofing. In: Vedaldi, A., Bischof, H., Brox, T., Frahm, J.-M. (eds.) ECCV 2020. LNCS, vol. 12363, pp. 406–422. Springer, Cham (2020). https://doi.org/10.1007/978-3-030-58523-5_24
18. Van der Maaten, L., Hinton, G.: Visualizing data using t-SNE. J. Mach. Learn. Res. **9**(11), 2579–2605 (2008)
19. Määttä, J., Hadid, A., Pietikäinen, M., et al.: Face spoofing detection from single images using micro-texture analysis. In: 2011 International Joint Conference on Biometrics (IJCB), pp. 1–7. IEEE (2011)
20. Pan, G., Sun, L., Wu, Z., Lao, S.: Eyeblink-based anti-spoofing in face recognition from a generic webcamera. In: 2007 IEEE 11th International Conference on Computer Vision, pp. 1–8. IEEE (2007)
21. Patel, K., Han, H., Jain, A.K., et al.: Secure face unlock: spoof detection on smartphones. IEEE Trans. Inf. Forensics Secur. **11**(10), 2268–2283 (2016)
22. Qin, Y., et al.: Learning meta model for zero-and few-shot face anti-spoofing. In: Proceedings of the AAAI Conference on Artificial Intelligence, vol. 34, pp. 11916–11923 (2020)
23. Selvaraju, R.R., Cogswell, M., Das, A., Vedantam, R., Parikh, D., Batra, D.: Grad-CAM: visual explanations from deep networks via gradient-based localization. Int. J. Comput. Vision **128**(2), 336–359 (2020)
24. Shao, R., Lan, X., Li, J., Yuen, P.C.: Multi-adversarial discriminative deep domain generalization for face presentation attack detection. In: Proceedings of the IEEE/CVF Conference on Computer Vision and Pattern Recognition, pp. 10023–10031 (2019)
25. Shao, R., Lan, X., Yuen, P.C., et al.: Regularized fine-grained meta face anti-spoofing. In: Proceedings of the AAAI Conference on Artificial Intelligence, vol. 34, pp. 11974–11981 (2020)
26. Wang, Z., et al.: Domain generalization via shuffled style assembly for face anti-spoofing. In: Proceedings of the IEEE/CVF Conference on Computer Vision and Pattern Recognition, pp. 4123–4133 (2022)
27. Wen, D., Han, H., Jain, A.K., et al.: Face spoof detection with image distortion analysis. IEEE Trans. Inf. Forensics Secur. **10**(4), 746–761 (2015)
28. Wen, Y., Zhang, K., Li, Z., Qiao, Yu.: A discriminative feature learning approach for deep face recognition. In: Leibe, B., Matas, J., Sebe, N., Welling, M. (eds.) ECCV 2016. LNCS, vol. 9911, pp. 499–515. Springer, Cham (2016). https://doi.org/10.1007/978-3-319-46478-7_31
29. Yang, B., Bender, G., Le, Q.V., Ngiam, J.: CondConv: conditionally parameterized convolutions for efficient inference. In: Wallach, H., Larochelle, H., Beygelzimer, A., d'Alché-Buc, F., Fox, E., Garnett, R. (eds.) Advances in Neural Information Processing Systems, vol. 32. Curran Associates, Inc. (2019)
30. Yang, J., Lei, Z., Li, S.Z., et al.: Learn convolutional neural network for face anti-spoofing. arXiv preprint arXiv:1408.5601 (2014)
31. Yang, J., Lei, Z., Liao, S., Li, S.Z.: Face liveness detection with component dependent descriptor. In: 2013 International Conference on Biometrics (ICB), pp. 1–6. IEEE (2013)
32. Yu, Z., Li, X., Niu, X., Shi, J., Zhao, G.: Face anti-spoofing with human material perception. In: Vedaldi, A., Bischof, H., Brox, T., Frahm, J.M. (eds.) European Conference on Computer Vision, pp. 557–575. Springer, Cham (2020). https://doi.org/10.1007/978-3-030-58571-6_33
33. Yu, Z., Qin, Y., Zhao, H., Li, X., Zhao, G.: Dual-cross central difference network for face anti-spoofing. arXiv preprint arXiv:2105.01290 (2021)

34. Yu, Z., Wan, J., Qin, Y., Li, X., Li, S.Z., Zhao, G.: NAS-FAS: static-dynamic central difference network search for face anti-spoofing. IEEE Trans. Pattern Anal. Mach. Intell. **43**(9), 3005–3023 (2021)
35. Yu, Z., et al.: Searching central difference convolutional networks for face anti-spoofing. In: Proceedings of the IEEE/CVF Conference on Computer Vision and Pattern Recognition (CVPR), June 2020
36. Zhang, K.Y., et al.: Structure destruction and content combination for face anti-spoofing. In: 2021 IEEE International Joint Conference on Biometrics (IJCB), pp. 1–6. IEEE (2021)
37. Zhang, K.-Y., et al.: Face anti-spoofing via disentangled representation learning. In: Vedaldi, A., Bischof, H., Brox, T., Frahm, J.-M. (eds.) ECCV 2020. LNCS, vol. 12364, pp. 641–657. Springer, Cham (2020). https://doi.org/10.1007/978-3-030-58529-7_38
38. Zhang, Z., Yan, J., Liu, S., Lei, Z., Yi, D., Li, S.Z.: A face antispoofing database with diverse attacks. In: 2012 5th IAPR International Conference on Biometrics (ICB), pp. 26–31. IEEE (2012)

Challenges of Facial Micro-Expression Detection and Recognition: A Survey

Rajesh Dwivedi[1(✉)] and Deepak Kumar[2]

[1] Indian Institute of Technology Indore, Indore, India
rajeshdwivedi@iiti.ac.in
[2] Mahamaya Polytechnic of Information Technology, Hathras, India
waytodeepak3@gmail.com

Abstract. Facial expressions are mainly divided into two broad categories micro-expression and macro-expression. During human interaction, both macro-expression and micro-expressions, as well as intermediate expressions, are present. Macro gestures are deliberate in design and cover large areas of the face. The duration of macro-expression is 1/2 to 4 s, while micro expressions are automatic in nature, having a period of 65 milliseconds to 500 milliseconds and revealing the mind's genuine emotions. Micro-expression covers minimal face area. Detection of macro-expression is pretty much straightforward and easily identified due to the short retention period. A lot of research has been done for macro expression recognition, and almost 95% accuracy has been achieved. A significant part of the research has also been done for micro-expression recognition by the extension of the macro-expression recognition approach, but still, the researcher lacks to achieve better accuracy. This research paper discusses the challenges of micro-expression detection and recognition. Few methods that cover these challenges are also discussed, but these methods also have some limitations that can be considered for future work.

Keywords: Facial micro-expression · Micro-expressions recognition · Feature extraction · Deep learning

1 Introduction

A micro expression (ME) is a brief expression of the face of one's genuine emotions that is very difficult to see because it only exists for a fraction of a second, sometimes as fast as .04 s. In most cases, the person who has sent a little expression is either oblivious to the fact that they did so or would prefer to keep the emotion hidden. Detection of micro-expression in real-time is challenging as it lasts a fraction of a second [1]. The expression that retains on the face for up to two seconds and is detectable by humans through muscular movements of the face in real-time is known as macro expressions. Hence micro expression and macro expression are the two categories of facial expression. One can easily pretend their emotions; therefore, macro expressions not be able to reveal the true emotions, while micro-expressions reveal one's genuine emotion most of the time due to their shorter retention time and spontaneous occurrences on the face. Hence, now a day's, micro-expression is a very trending research topic for detecting true emotions [21].

Due to the self-educated ability of Deep learning, it is commonly used in image processing fields such as pattern recognition, natural language processing, computer vision, and facial expression recognition, among others. Most existing micro-expression recognition approaches are based on hand-crafted methods like LBP-TOP [25]. Still, for increasing the accuracy [5], the Convolution Neural Network (CNN) method of deep learning is the most popular technique for micro-expression recognition [2].

When someone tries to mask his/her feelings, the flow of that emotion can always appear on that person's face. The flow can be restricted to a single area of the face (a mini or subtle expression), or it can be a short expression, known as a micro expression, available across the entire face.

ME's are very hard to detect, so Ekman et al. [7] has developed ME training instruments to identify and respond to micro-expression. According to Ekman et al. [7], human emotions are classified into seven universal emotions, i.e., disgust, surprise, rage, happiness, sorrow, fear, and contempt. In addition, the Facial Action Coding System (FACS) was implemented by action units (AU's) to describe facial expressions, but the accuracy achieved to detect micro-expression using action unit is 47%. Hence further research is required.

The rest of the paper is organized as follows: Sect. 2 elaborates on the major challenges of micro-expression recognition. Section 3 presents the micro-expression recognition process. Section 4 illustrates how facial features are extracted. Section 5 provides a quick overview of the current limitations of various state-of-art methods of ME recognition. Finally, Sect. 6 concludes with a look at the future and the conclusion.

2   Major Challenges During Micro-Expression Recognition

2.1   Climate Deviation

Climate deviation [27], requiring lighting variation and head-pose variation, is the most daunting part of ME acknowledgment. When researchers try to identify the features using state-of-the-art methods, most of the features are highly dependent on the intensity of the pixel changes. If there is poor or uneven illumination, estimating exact features is very difficult. Similarly, a small head movement significantly affects the changes in the face component; hence micro-expression accuracy is also affected.

2.2   The Unconstrained and Refined Motion of Facial Movement

On behalf of state-of-art methods study, the low elegance and spontaneity of facial expression may be a significant obstacle [27] that makes feeling recognition non-distinguishable through the naked eyes. An innovative motion descriptor named as Local Motion Patterns (LMP) [26] was proposed by researchers. This approach deals with irregularities and noise caused by the features of the face (skin reflection, skin smoothness, and elasticity) during abstracting facial motion information and enhances the accuracy of ME recognition. Different morphological approaches [26] are also used to detect subtle facial movement motions.

2.3 Imbalanced Dataset for Normal Situations

There are a couple of openly accessible datasets [8] that emphasize on ME acknowledgment, for example, Chinese Academy of Sciences Macro-Expressions and ME (CAS(ME)2), Chinese Academy of Sciences ME (CASME), Chinese Academy of Sciences ME 2 (CASME II), and Spontaneous Micro-articulation Corpus (SMIC). In a controlled environment with even lighting and no head movements, tests of available datasets are typically conducted. Therefore, in typical circumstances, well-tested calculations using these datasets could not be rational and satisfy an interest in the dataset.

2.4 In the Implementation of Deep Learning (High Level Representation)

In deep learning algorithms, state-of-the-art high-level representations in ME are derived from the convolution neural network (CNN) [2]. Data shortages in high-level representations forcefully limit the power of the deep learning approach. Different approaches, like data augmentation or transfer learning, have been proposed to reduce this limitation; still, the accuracy is very low. Hence, improvement is required in a high-level approach for unconstrained ME recognition to achieve better accuracy.

3 Micro-Expression Recognition Process

The micro-expression recognition process is divided into the following fundamental steps:

3.1 Preprocessing

Preprocessing is the pre step for ME recognition [16]. The micro-expressions are very short in time and very low in intensity. Therefore, normalization of the input data is required for the extraction of sufficient details of micro expression. After normalization, noises are removed through low pass filtering approaches. In ME recognition, preprocessing includes face detection, face registration, magnification of motion, and temporal normalization.

3.2 Face Detection

This step extracts the faces from the image through image segmentation and a template matching approach.

3.3 Face Registration

The step of face registration aligns a face detected with a reference face [16]. The face registration process is done before feature extraction, so small head pose, and illumination variations can be handled during ME recognition. Major work on face registration that has been done till now can be classified as landmark points and generic approaches.

3.4 Motion Magnification

Due to the short retention time, it is challenging to detect ME facial movements. Motion magnification techniques [3] are then applied to improve the distinguishing powers between various gestures. The Eulerian video magnification (EVM) approach is widely used to magnify subtle movements by improving motion variations. EVM magnifies both motions and colors. Recently a new method has been developed that identifies facial expressions on behalf of an innovative Local Motion Patterns (LMP) feature. The motion distribution is locally analyzed to distinguish stable movement patterns from noise. Indeed, there is still a lack of magnification work to date.

3.5 Temporal Normalization

To normalize video lengths, the Temporal Interpolation Model (TIM) approach [22] is widely used. It is explicitly designed to resolve subtle, spontaneous phrases that are accidental and difficult to detect reliably. TIM is also used to delete redundant faces without feelings. However, the efficacy of recognition success is not improved by this approach. In the meantime, Le Ngo et al. [14] reported that at regularly spaced locations, TIM partially removes redundant information without knowledge of sparse information in the frame that could be removed unintentionally. Thus, Sparsity-promoting dynamic mode decomposition was suggested to address the disadvantages of TIM. Sparsity-promoting dynamic mode decomposition (DMDSP) offers better results compared to TIM.

4 Feature Extraction

Extraction of facial features is a two-step operation i.e.; Feature detection and feature representation, which are discussed in detail in subsequent subsection.

4.1 Feature Detection

A feature is any piece of information that must be computed in order to complete some specific task related to an application. Detection of features is a low-level processing procedure, usually performed as the first image operation. It analyzes each pixel to identify the feature. Few feature detection methods are summarized below-

Facial Action Coding System (FACS): The FACS [10] is based on a physiological system for systematically classifying all facial movements. The FACS of Ekman and Friesen offers an objective way to calculate the facial muscles function from video image frames of faces. An Action Unit is a name given to each observable facial movement feature. There are 46 separate action units defined by Ekman and Friesen, each corresponding to displacement in a specific muscle or muscle group and producing facial feature deformations that can be identified in the image.

Active Appearance Models (AAM): AAM [4] is a model matching approach of statistics, where a representative training set takes over the variability of form and texture. The training supervisor is given a collection of images with landmark coordinates appearing in all images. In the sense of face analysis, the model was first proposed by Edwards, Cootes, and Taylor [6]. The method is commonly used for medical image interpretation and for matching and monitoring faces. The algorithm uses the difference between the current appearance estimate and the target image to derive an optimization process. The current residuals are calculated to match an image, and the system is used to predict adjustments to the current parameters, leading to a good match. A successful overall match is obtained in a few iterations, even from low starting estimates. AAMs, from their training package, learn about the valid forms and strength variation.

Active Shape Models (ASM): The ASM [4] algorithm is a simple and powerful way of comparing a new image with a collection of points managed by a shape model. In active shape models, the shape variability is learned through observation, as suggested by Cootes et al. [12]. Once again, ASM is an analytical model of the shape of the object that iteratively deforms to match an illustration of the object in a new image. This technique depends upon a number of points being represented by each object or image structure. A boundary, inner features, or even external features, such as the Centre of a concave portion of the border, can be identified. The points are put in the same way on each training set of examples of the object. Analyzing the statistics of the positions of the labelled points yields a "Point Distribution Model (PDM)". This model provides average point positions and has some parameters that regulate the key variation modes found in the training set.

Discriminative Response Map Fitting (DRMF): There are significant shape and appearance variations in registering and tracking a non-rigid object. DRMF [4] is based on texture which depends upon shape initialization. DRMF performs well in the generic face-fitting scenario as a discriminatory regression-based process. DRMF is used in each ME video clip to identify facial feature points in the first frame facial region. In the facial Multimedia Tools Appl area, DRMF found 68 feature points. Thirty-six regions of interest (ROI) are labeled with the help of FACS, and the facial area is separated.

Optical Flow Vectors: The optical flow vector identifies the object's motions by detecting the Spatio-temporal intensity of pixels between two image frames. As per the Lucas-Kaneda [4] approach, the pixel displacement between the two nearest frames is minimal and almost constant. The optical flow method provides better results in face alignment than the image-domain-based method. Optical flow is typically extracted and analyzed for cropped and preprocessed images to distinguish head pose and face variations. The study is used raw images to estimate optical flow and discard head pose movements as the input and total Variance (TV-L1) optical flow estimation where L1 is the gradient standard.

4.2   Feature Representation

Feature representation is classified into two categories: single-level and multi-level. In single-level representation, the features are directly extracted from the video sequence. In multi-level representation, the input video sequence is transformed into another domain before feature extraction; then, some other features are extracted for ME recognition.

In facial expression recognition, feature representation is either geometric or appearance-based. Geometric-based representation deals with the shapes and locations of facial landmarks. In contrast, appearance-based representation deals with texture as well as intensity information caused due to emotions such as wrinkles and other patterns. In dealing with lighting changes and misalignment errors, it has been discovered that appearance-based features outperform geometric-based features. Features focused on geometry cannot be as robust as features dependent on appearance as they require accurate procedures for detecting and aligning landmarks. For these comparable reasons, representations of appearance-based features have become more common in literature documents. Some feature representation approaches are discussed subsequently.

Local Binary Pattern (LBP) and Its Variant: LBP [13] is the baseline evaluation method among all appearance-based feature representation methods. It describes the local texture pattern with binary code along a circular area and is encoded into the histogram. In literature, we found that LBP on three orthogonal planes (LBP-TOP), the extension of the LBP method, is most widely used as a baseline evaluation method among the available dataset like SMIC, CASME, CASME II.

Further, the various LBP-TOP variant for ME was proposed. One is Local Binary Pattern with six intersection points (LBP-SIP) proposed by Wang et al. [23], where only six intersection points of 3 orthogonal planes are considered for constructing the binary pattern as neighbor points. LBP-SIP is better in performance in comparison to LBP-TOP because it removes redundant information. Local Binary Pattern with Mean Orthogonal Planes (LBP-MOP) was developed by Wang et al. [24] where the LBP characteristics were concatenated using only three mean images, which are the temporal pooling result of the image stacks along the three orthogonal images. LBP-MOP is more efficient than LBP-SIP because it reduces computation time. Some interesting developments have been made in recent works. An extension of the binary pattern called the spatio-temporal binary pattern of Radon local (STRBP) was suggested by Huang-Huang and Zhao [11], which uses transforming Radon to obtain robust shape characteristics. LBP and its variant are implemented in holistic images, which contain too much redundant information in feature histogram. Hence, further optimization methods like Robust Principal Component Analysis (RPCA) can be used to reduce redundancy.

Optical Flow Method and Its Variant: The visible motion of individual pixels on the image plane, is known as optical flow [9]. It also functions as a good approximation of the actual physical motion projected onto the plane of the image. Many optical flow estimation methods assume that a pixel's color/intensity is invariant under the displacement from one video frame to the next. A succinct explanation of both the regions of the picture undergoing motion and the speed of motion is given by optical flow. Optical flow computing is sensitive to noise and changes in illumination in operation. In facial detection recognition, A reliable optical flow method has been widely used for displacement calculation using the concept of brightness conservation. Liong et al. [15] suggested an ex- tension of optical flow, which calculates subtle changes in facial motion, similar to optical flow. He also identified an optical strain map (OSM) from the magnitude of optical strain weight (OSW) and optical strain function (OSF), as well as the hybrid version of these two functions. Since ME recognition is highly dependent on the movement of the facial part, an extension of the focused optical flow (HOOF) histogram is proposed. On the other hand, the HOOF histogram is easily influenced by lighting changes. Happy and Routray, therefore, implemented a fuzzy-centered optical flow histogram (FHOOF) to address the drawback of HOOF. While FHOOF is an invariant of illumination, FHOOF's assigned weight is highly reliant on the different MEs' motion magnitudes, which vary from sample to sample. To address this drawback, the authors have implemented a Fuzzy Histogram of Optical Flow Orientations (FHOFO). As motion magnitude is ignored, recognition accuracy increases. In comparison with HOOF and LBP-TOP, FHOOF and FHOFO achieved remarkable results. Meanwhile, Xu et al. [19] used the Facial Dynamics Map (FDM), which uses optical flow estimation to measure movement between frames and classify movements of ME sequences. Liu et al. [17] inserted Main Directional Mean Optical-flow (MDMO) for ME recognition. The MDMO is a locally-focused optical flow that originates in a specific area of interest. It handles the small head movement and is invariant to illumination variation.

Histogram of Oriented Gradient Method and Its Variant: A large intensity changes occur in and around the edges and corners. These intensity changes can be used to identify subtle motion. The gradient method [20] is mainly used to identify the gradient magnitude, which identifies the subtle motion information. Robert K. McConnell [18] introduced the Histograms of Directed Gradients

Table 1. Methods used to handle climate deviation

Existing Methods	Limitations
LBP and it's variant	The motion of the facial component and action unit are unknown.
Optical flow and gradient methods	Better in accuracy in comparison to LBP and it's variant but fail to identify motion information i.e., cannot handle head pose variation

Table 2. Methods used to handle Unconstrained and refined motion of facial movement

Existing Methods	Limitations
Local motion pattern and morphological patches	Identify the motion information but fails to handle climate deviation, i.e., illumination variation and head pose movement.
Optical flow and gradient methods	Better in accuracy in comparison to LBP and it's variant but fails to identify motion information i.e., cannot handle head pose variation

Table 3. Imbalanced dataset for normal situations

Existing Methods	Limitations
SMIC, CASME CASME-II and CAS(ME)^2	All the datasets are available in controlled environment; hence popular algorithm fails with existing dataset for a realistic situation

(HOG), where the first step consists of obtaining horizontal and vertical derivatives by filtering the kernel image. The gradient directions and magnitudes are then measured to construct the histogram. Histogram of Image Gradient Orientation (HIGO) is another method defined. HIGO has lower complexity than HOG and is a simpler version of HOG. In the case of spatio-temporal feature extraction, 3D HOG and 3D HIGO were expanded from 2D HOG and 2D HIGO with three orthogonal planes instead of the XY plane used in 2D approaches.

5   Limitations of Existing Methods of Feature Descriptors

In this section, we presented the limitation of various existing methods and some examples of existing imbalance datasets. Table 1 and Table 2 show the existing methods which are used to handle climate deviation and unconstrained and refined motion of facial movement, respectively. A few examples of imbalanced datasets are shown in Table 3.

6 Conclusion

In this paper, we focused on the current challenges like environment factor, imbalanced dataset, spontaneous and subtle motion recognition for improving ac- curacy of micro-expression recognition and provide different methods to handle the challenges, but these methods also have some limitations or challenges that give the motivation for future research. We also discussed the problems that researchers faced during the implementation of deep learning approaches for automatic detection of ME, i.e., scarcity of sample data. Hence geometrical transformation and data augmentation techniques can also be used for future work to improve the accuracy.

References

1. Allaert, B., Bilasco, I.M., Djeraba, C.: Micro and macro facial expression recognition using advanced local motion patterns. IEEE Trans. Affect. Comput. **13**(1), 147–158 (2019)
2. Ayyalasomayajula, S.C., Ionescu, B., Ionescu, D.: A cnn approach to microexpressions detection. In: 2021 IEEE 15th International Symposium on Applied Computational Intelligence and Informatics (SACI), pp. 345–350. IEEE (2021)
3. Bai, M., Goecke, R., Herath, D.: Micro-expression recognition based on video motion magnification and pre-trained neural network. In: 2021 IEEE International Conference on Image Processing (ICIP), pp. 549–553. IEEE (2021)
4. Ben, X., et al.: Video-based facial micro-expression analysis: A survey of datasets, features and algorithms. IEEE Trans. Pattern Anal. Mach. Intell. **44**(9), 5826–5846 (2021)
5. Dwivedi, R., Kumar, R., Jangam, E., Kumar, V.: An ant colony optimization based feature selection for data classification. Int. J. Recent Technol. Eng **7**, 35–40 (2019)
6. Edwards, G.J., Taylor, C.J., Cootes, T.F.: Interpreting face images using active appearance models. In: Proceedings Third IEEE International Conference on Automatic Face and Gesture Recognition, pp. 300–305. IEEE (1998)
7. Ekman, P., Friesen, W.V.: Facial action coding system. Environmental Psychology & Nonverbal Behavior (1978)
8. Esmaeili, V., Mohassel Feghhi, M., Shahdi, S.O.: A comprehensive survey on facial micro-expression: approaches and databases. Multimed. Tools Appl. **81** 1–46 (2022). https://doi.org/10.1007/s11042-022-13133-2
9. Fan, L., Zhang, T., Du, W.: Optical-flow-based framework to boost video object detection performance with object enhancement. Expert Syst. Appl. **170**, 114544 (2021)
10. Freitas-Magalhães, A.: Facial Action Coding System 4.0-Manual de Codificação Científica da Face Humana. Leya (2022)
11. Huang, X., Wang, S.J., Liu, X., Zhao, G., Feng, X., Pietikäinen, M.: Discriminative spatiotemporal local binary pattern with revisited integral projection for spontaneous facial micro-expression recognition. IEEE Trans. Affect. Comput. **10**(1), 32–47 (2017)
12. Iqtait, M., Mohamad, F., Mamat, M.: Feature extraction for face recognition via active shape model (asm) and active appearance model (aam). In: IOP Conference Series: Materials Science and Engineering. vol. 332, p. 012032. IOP Publishing (2018)

13. Karanwal, S., Diwakar, M.: Od-lbp: Orthogonal difference-local binary pattern for face recognition. Digital Signal Process. **110**, 102948 (2021)
14. Le Ngo, A.C., See, J., Phan, R.C.W.: Sparsity in dynamics of spontaneous subtle emotions: analysis and application. IEEE Trans. Affect. Comput. **8**(3), 396–411 (2016)
15. Liong, S.T., See, J., Wong, K., Phan, R.C.W.: Less is more: Micro-expression recognition from video using apex frame. Signal Process.: Image Commun. **62**, 82–92 (2018)
16. Liu, K.H., Jin, Q.S., Xu, H.C., Gan, Y.S., Liong, S.T.: Micro-expression recognition using advanced genetic algorithm. Signal Processing: Image Commun. **93**, 116153 (2021)
17. Liu, Y., Du, H., Zheng, L., Gedeon, T.: A neural micro-expression recognizer. In: 2019 14th IEEE international conference on automatic face & gesture recognition (FG 2019), pp. 1–4. IEEE (2019)
18. McConnell, R.K.: Method of and apparatus for pattern recognition (Jan 28 1986), uS Patent 4,567,610
19. Miao, S., Xu, H., Han, Z., Zhu, Y.: Recognizing facial expressions using a shallow convolutional neural network. IEEE Access **7**, 78000–78011 (2019)
20. Ochango, V.M., Wambugu, G.M., Ndia, J.G.: Feature extraction using histogram of oriented gradients for image classification in maize leaf diseases. Int. J. Comput. Inform. Technol. **11**(2)2279–0764 (2022)
21. Qu, F., Wang, S.J., Yan, W.J., Li, H., Wu, S., Fu, X.: Cas (me) [2]: a database for spontaneous macro-expression and micro-expression spotting and recognition. IEEE Trans. Affect. Comput. **9**(4), 424–436 (2017)
22. Shi, Z., Xu, X., Liu, X., Chen, J., Yang, M.H.: Video frame interpolation transformer. In: Proceedings of the IEEE/CVF Conference on Computer Vision and Pattern Recognition, pp. 17482–17491 (2022)
23. Wang, Y., See, J., Phan, R.C.-W., Oh, Y.-H.: LBP with Six Intersection Points: Reducing Redundant Information in LBP-TOP for Micro-expression Recognition. In: Cremers, D., Reid, I., Saito, H., Yang, M.-H. (eds.) ACCV 2014. LNCS, vol. 9003, pp. 525–537. Springer, Cham (2015). https://doi.org/10.1007/978-3-319-16865-4_34
24. Wang, Y., See, J., Phan, R.C.W., Oh, Y.H.: Efficient spatio-temporal local binary patterns for spontaneous facial micro-expression recognition. PLoS ONE **10**(5), e0124674 (2015)
25. Wei, J., Lu, G., Yan, J., Liu, H.: Micro-expression recognition using local binary pattern from five intersecting planes. Multimed. Tools Appl. pp. 1–26 (2022). https://doi.org/10.1007/s11042-022-12360-x
26. Zhang, L., Arandjelović, O.: Review of automatic microexpression recognition in the past decade. Mach. Learn. Knowl. Extract. **3**(2), 414–434 (2021)
27. Zhou, L., Shao, X., Mao, Q.: A survey of micro-expression recognition. Image Vis. Comput. **105**, 104043 (2021)

Biometric Iris Identifier Recognition with Privacy Preserving Phenomenon: A Federated Learning Approach

Harshit Gupta[1]([⊠]), Tarun Kumar Rajput[1], Ranjana Vyas[1], O.P. Vyas[1], and Antonio Puliafito[2]

[1] IIIT Allahabad, Allahabad, India
{rsi2020501,mit2020078,ranjana,opvyas}@iiita.ac.in
[2] University of Messina, Consorzio Interuniversitario Nazionale per l'Informatica (CINI), Messina, Italy
apuliafito@unime.in

Abstract. As technology is getting advanced day by day, the concern of security, authentication, and identification are also becoming important in every domain. Apart from other identifiers used for authentication, a biometric identifier is a quantitative assessment of a person's bodily characteristics, which is effectively used to authenticate or corroborate the identification. Biometric identity is significantly more difficult to forge by attackers. With different biometric identification systems like fingerprint identification, face detection etc., Iris recognition is also an essential and most efficient biometric identification system which uniquely identifies a person's identity. Also, the data corresponding to Iris identification is very sensitive and is supposed to be used in a very secure manner. The work aims here is to develop a privacy preserving and powerful Convolution Neural Networks (CNN) model for Iris recognition in a federated learning approach. The said approach provides privacy to the user data because there is no sharing of data with the central server, unlike the traditional machine learning approach where data from all clients are required to be stored on central server. The work implemented in this paper simulated the CNN model in a privacy-preserving manner. The result provides the performance of the model for different combinations of participating clients and global rounds.

Keywords: Federated Learning · Convolution Neural Network · Hough Transformation · Daugman's Rubber Sheet Model

1 Introduction

Protecting personal information is getting difficult as technology pervades every part of modern life and our society becomes increasingly computerised. Passwords and keys were long thought to be enough for data security, but they now appear to be more ineffective in the face of sophisticated hacker attacks. In a

M. Tanveer et al. (Eds.): ICONIP 2022, CCIS 1794, pp. 493–504, 2023.
https://doi.org/10.1007/978-981-99-1648-1_41

company's security system, passwords are, in fact, the weakest link. This is due to the fact that they may be shared, and even those with high entropy can be cracked using a variety of techniques. Recent stories of network security breaches and identity thefts reinforce the need for a solid authentication technique. In continuation to this, bio-metric-based security seems to be the efficient way which proves an individual's identification. So due to this, it has also become essential [4]. Bio-metric qualities, like iris, voice, fingerprints, gait etc., are intrinsic and unique to each individual [3].

Iris recognition technology is being employed as a form of biometric identification that can accurately authenticate an individual's identity. For the iris recognition, front portion of the eye is read since the iris is located at the front portion of the eye and to obtain the same high-performance UV camera is needed. It is important to note that iris recognition is not the same as retina recognition [5].

Various machine learning techniques are being used to implement security solutions, and the majority of them require a centralised dataset, which is often accomplished by transmitting data created on a client to a remote server. This is important in terms of data privacy and data management, as a big data infrastructure is required to analyse massive volumes of data in order to train the models. But it could be dangerous to share such critical data with a data centre as it might be misused by a third party, or it may go through data breaches, which could compromise the user's privacy. These are the prominent issues in traditional machine learning-oriented solutions. So to get rid of this setback, a different machine learning setting, i.e. Federated Learning [13], is introduced.

Federated Learning (FL) uses a distinct method and can work alongside standard AI applications like image classification, recommendation systems, and natural language processing [14]. In FL, the local model is implemented and trained at every client and model updates/gradients obtained from these clients are shared with centralized server instead of the client's data [1].

The Convolutional Neural Network (CNN) technique for feature extraction and Softmax activation as a classifier are used to improve the performance of iris recognition.

The paper is organized as follows: Sect. 2 presents an overview of existing literature on the proposed work, while Sect. 3 describes the federated approach for secure recognition of the iris model. Section 4 describes the results obtained after the simulation. Finally, the conclusion is summarized in Sect. 5.

2   Literature Review

The work in **Lubos Omelina and Jozef Goga and Jarmila Pavlovicova and Milos Oravec and Bart Jansen** [8], examines the available iris imaging databases. The authors concentrated on the accessibility and popularity of datasets. Six distinct RQs were raised. A total of 158 distinct datasets were found, but only 81 of them were truly available. The whole list may be found in the supplemental materials. Authors discovered that the CASIA database is the most often mentioned dataset in various works. They organised a comprehensive description of the available databases, identifying common qualities, pros and cons of the different databases. Lastly, the authors provided several recommendations for developing an iris database based on their assessment.

In **Lingjuan Lyu and Han Yu and Qiang Yang**, authors highlighted how, despite the unique qualities of federated learning, this paradigm has yet to be extensively adopted. Furthermore, only a few papers have focused on communication and privacy problems. As a result, several research gaps in federated learning still need to be filled, such as participant heterogeneity, clustering approach, the dynamic association of participants with clusters, hierarchical design, and so on [17].

In **Zhang, W., Lu, X., Gu, Y., Liu, Y., Meng, X., & Li, J.**, authors suggested the FD-Unet, a robust iris segmentation scheme. Initially, according to them, an overall performance of a system will be improved if an appropriate process of segmentation of the iris is used. After testing the model that was suggested, they found that it is able to perform better comparatively in extracting features. They got 97.36 percent, 96.74 percent, and 94.81 percent using three distinct datasets, namely CASIA Iris v4,ND IRIS 0405 , UBIRIS v2.

In **Arora, S., & Bhatia, M. S.**, the authors presented the validation of an individual's identification, and the recommended technique of iris recognition adopted a deep learning methodology. They employed the Circular Hough transform for iris localisation, followed by automatic feature extraction using CNN from localised iris input picture areas, and finally, the Softmax classifier was used to classify the dataset into one of 224 classes.They found that by selecting appropriate optimisation approaches and parameters, the performance of their model is affected very much; hence they achieved 98% accuracy with fine-tuning.This network was not tweaked to operate with additional real-world data.

The work in **Nguyen, K., Fookes, C., Ross, A., & Sridharan, S.**) discusses the difficulties encountered during the iris identification phase. CNN characteristics that were initially taught for object identification may be applied efficiently for the iris recognition issue, according to their research. CNN features that have been pre-trained for object identification can be employed successfully for the recognition of iris. DenseNet achieves the greatest peak recognition accuracy of the five CNNs. They obtained recognition accuracy in two big iris datasets, ND-CrossSensor-2013 and CASIA-Iris-Thousand.

In **Liu, M., Zhou, Z., Shang, P., & Xu, D.**, to increase the ratio of signal to noise, fuzzing the region that was beyond the given boundary, Adoption of triangular fuzzy median and averages smooth filters has been proposed by them. Fuzzy triangular filters are quicker and easier to measure. Through the use of fuzzy operations, the modified pictures were utilised for training deep learning approaches, which increased recognition accuracy and sped up convergence. For recognition of iris, to provide the framework of DL they recommended using F-capsule and F-CNN. In general, fuzzy image training outperforms training on the raw picture. It uses data sets generated by the standard lens with two distinct sensors instead of being intended to study the impact of different capture devices.

In **Thomas, T., George, A., & Devi, K. I.** the presented technology allows for less restricted imaging circumstances for iris recognition. The iris pictures may, in fact, be compromised by some noise or factors like inappropriate lighting, blurring of image etc. In comparison to Hough modified iris localisation and Daugman's approach, ellipse fitting by RANSAC, which stands for Random Sample Consensus, produced a decent result. Peak Side Lobe Ratio is the similarity metric used for template matching (PSR). Only a small number of iris photos were used to assess the method on the WVU iris database, but it showed encouraging results for both iris borders.

In **Menon, H., & Mukherjee, A.**, while addressing both identity and verification difficulties, they look at the benefits of employing dynamic characteristics compared to manually created features constructed using improved deep residual network models. They tackled the problem of iris recognition by using a network created for a different objective. Finally, in addition to increasing accuracy, CNN may be effectively employed to eliminate several weaknesses in conventional biometric systems. More study is required to determine how deep networks may be used effectively in biometric applications to produce beneficial outcomes in terms of accuracy and security.

The authors in **Gupta, Harshit, P., M., K., Vyas O. P and Puliafito, Antonio** presented the federated learning approach for risk prediction in insurance domain. The work is done in a privacy preserving manner where users participated in collaborative training of global risk prediction model by keeping their personal data private and safe. The work has shown the good results for model training in the proposed FL approach.

From the previous studies, it has been observed that traditional machine learning models are able to achieve promising results, and their performance is highly dependent on the quality and size of the data. It is very necessary to have large centrally aggregated Iris datasets for training traditional Iris recognition algorithms. However, acquiring and sharing iris datasets has grown to be quite challenging because of the rising data privacy issues and legal limitations. To overcome such issue, a novel approach, i.e. Federated Learning (FL) approach is proposed which has the capability of privacy-conscious collaborative learning for iris recognition models. With the help of this approach, organisations with small datasets are able to learn or take advantage of large datasets in a collaborative manner without accessing those datasets.

The proposed approach in this paper promotes privacy and security to the training data of a machine learning model. It eliminates the need to maintain a large centralised database. Especially when there is a failure to back up the data elsewhere, centralising databases raises the danger of data loss and also it exposes the risk of losing the centralised point to intruders. Since the main idea in federated learning is to share weights and not the actual data, security is promised to data.

3   Methodology

This section describes the federated approach for secure recognition of the iris model. The work presents a Federated Learning Based Iris Recognition System Using Convolutional Neural Networks [15]. The original dataset which is taken for simulation is insufficient for feature extraction. Hence, three types of operations are performed on it to create a new dataset. These operations are Image Acquisition, Iris Segmentation, and Normalization. A client-server architecture is used in the federated learning environment. Multiple clients train their respective models under the supervision of a central server. The local models are then shared with the central model and aggregated. The aggregated model is now shared with all clients, and the process is kept on repeated until we get the optimal model. The local models, on the other hand, all employed CNN for feature extraction and softmax as classifier [15].

3.1   Dataset

In the proposed work, the CASIA Iris dataset - Interval subset of version 4 is used. It has 249 subjects. For each subject, there is a left and right folder, each containing around 10 high-resolution grayscale images. There is a total of 345 classes for such 249 subjects [8]. A total of 2639 images in present in the entire dataset. Each of the 2639 images has of resolution of 320×240. Figure 1 represents the data samples for Iris Recognition.

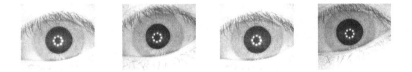

Fig. 1. Original Data Sample for Iris Recognition

3.2   Data Preparation

In Fig. 1, the samples shown are original images without any preprocessing operation. These data can not be directly applied to the simulation; hence they are gone through Image Acquisition, Iris Segmentation and Normalization process where **Image Acquisition** represents the capturing a high-quality sequence of iris images of the subjects by high-performance devices like sensors and cameras. The concern is more on iris here, and then additional preprocessing might be applied in order to increase quality and obtain photos with appropriate clarity and resolution [9]. Instead of acquiring ocular pictures, the CASIA-IrisV4 is employed here. The main difficulty was isolating the target iris from a complicated backdrop that included other undesired parts of the eyes [10]. So The next stage in iris identification is **Iris segmentation** [6], which is a procedure that isolates only the concerned iris part. To identify the circular iris area, the work takes advantage of Hough Transformation [11], which is a method for calculating the geometric object's parameters (lines, curves, circles etc.) in a picture. The iris and pupil region's centre coordinates and radius can be determined using the circular Hough transform. This technique [11] is commonly used to discover the forms of things using a voting mechanism among the given classes.

The iris part in the proposed work is circular in nature which can be represented by the following Eq. 1. Where (x_c, y_c) are coordinates of center and r is radius.

$$x_c^2 + y_c^2 = r^2 \tag{1}$$

To identify the border of iris and sclera, gradients are measured in the vertical direction, which reduces the impact of the horizontally oriented eyelids [6]. When executing a circular Hough transform, vertical gradients being used to locate the iris border reduces the impact on the eyelids. For proper localization, not all circle edge pixels are required. Here circular localization's accuracy is not the only thing that improves, but it also improves efficiency since there are fewer edge locations in the Hough space where votes may be cast. Figure 2 represents the process of iris segmentation with the help of Hough Transformation.

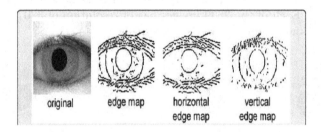

Fig. 2. Segmentation of Iris with help of Hough Transformation.([6])

After the segmentation stage, **Normalization** is done, in which the circular iris area is processed into a fixed-size block which is geometrically rectangular. The Rubber-sheet model [12] of Daugman's is the most used process for normalisation of iris, that converts the iris to a block that is rectangular in shape over a doubly dimensionless polar coordinate system that is non-concentric [6].The normalisation method creates iris areas with the same dimensions that are constant, resulting in two pictures of the same iris taken under conditions that are different, having distinctive characteristics at the same spatial position. The iris area is translated into an array with 2d dimensions that are horizontal and equivalent to the angular resolution and a dimension that is vertical and corresponds to the radial resolution [6]. The processed dataset sample is shown in Fig. 3.

Fig. 3. The data sample after the data processing operation is performed

3.3 Privacy Preserving Model Training Approach: Federated Learning

Federated learning is an ML setting that enables data scientists to train statistical models utilising sensitive user data without having to submit it to a central server [2]. It is a distributed training method in which training and testing take place locally (at the edge), and only meta-data is transmitted to a central server. The locally trained model's updates are transferred to the global server, where the updates get aggregated.

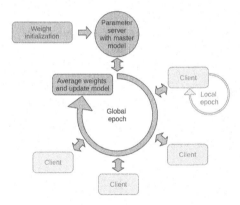

Fig. 4. Flowchart showing the aggregation of local model's weights. [16]

Figure 4 shows the flow diagram of the federated learning averaging algorithm. For aggregating all the local model updates, the FedAvg algorithm [2] is used. FedAvg is Google's first pure fl algorithm which runs in the global server. There are also various averaging algorithms, including "FedProx," "FedMa," "FedOpt," "Scaffold", etc. Each FedAvg cycle aims to lower the model's global weights w, which is represented as the mean of the weights obtained from local device loss.

$$min f(w) = \sum_{k=1}^{N} p_k F_k(w) \tag{2}$$

3.4   Feature Extraction

The most crucial phase in recognition of iris is the features extraction [6]. In this work, the Convolutional Neural Network (CNN) [7] is used for the extraction of features from the normalised iris image.

The functioning of CNN is comprised of input, hidden and output layer. Image is input fed via input layer. The hidden layer is responsible for convolution, pooling, Rectified Linear Unit, dropout Layer, and normalisation. The output layer provides the subject id name (label).

In CNN, the first layer is always a convolutional layer, with the input being a photo in the case of the first community layer [6] or a characteristic map from the preceding layer. To produce the output characteristic maps, the input is convolved [7] with the filters, known as kernels. The output of the convolution can be written as,

$$x_j^l = f\left(\sum_{i \in M_j} x_i^{l-1} + k_{ij}^l + b_j^l\right) \tag{3}$$

where,
x_j stands for the set of output characteristic maps, M_j for the set of enter mappings, k_{ij} for the convolution kernel, and b_j for the prejudice term. The length of the output characteristic map is determined by,

$$O = \frac{w - K + 2P}{S} + 1 \tag{4}$$

Where O : is output height, W : is enter height, K : is clear output length, P: is padding, and S: is stride. The amount of padding to use, P, can be determined in the following way:

$$P = \frac{K - 1}{2} \tag{5}$$

As it performs linear operations at some point during the convolution process, the Rectified Linear Unit layer [7], also known as the activation layer, was created to inject some non-linearity into the device. As a result, it comes after each convolution layer. This layer effectively sets all of the low activation values to zero. Also, this layer helps in resolving the vanishing gradient issue. For multi-class classification, the ReLU works well. Instead of ReLU, the sigmoid function [6] can be utilised for binary classification.

After this, there are pooling layers which can reduce the dimension of the feature maps. The feature map created by a convolution layer has features and these are summarised by the pooling layer. Hence further operation will be applied to summarised features. As a result, the model becomes more resistant to changes in the feature's positions in the input picture. After pooling, there is a dropout layer. Its basic principle is that entry variables with a high likelihood of being activated or dropped out are deactivated or dropped out, allowing the individual neurons to focus on activities that are less dependent on their surroundings [6].

In CNN, between the convolution layer and ReLU layer, there is a Batch Normalisation layer, which enables the network layers to learn more independently, and the output of the previous layers is normalised using this. In training following things are performed:

Calculation of mean and variance of layer inputs

$$\mu_n = \frac{1}{m+2} \sum_{i=1}^{m} x_i \qquad (6)$$

$$\sigma^2 = \frac{1}{rn} \sum_{i=1}^{mw} (x_i - f_{13})^2 \qquad (7)$$

Equation 7 and Eq. 8 represents the mean and variance. Then normalization of layer inputs is performed as represented in Eq. 9.

$$\hat{x}_i = \frac{x_i + \mu_B}{\sqrt{\sigma_B^2 + \varepsilon}} \qquad (8)$$

Then to obtain output of batch normalization layer, scaling and shifting is performed.

$$y_i = \gamma \hat{x}_i + \beta \qquad (9)$$

γ and β are learned during the training.

3.5   Classification

The classification consists of assigning the predicted labels to the input images. The label encoding is performed for the corresponding output, which varies between 0 to n-1. In order to get the predicted multinomial probability distribution in the output layer, the Softmax Activation Function is exploited.

$$\sigma(\mathbf{z})_i = \frac{e^{z_i}}{\sum_{j=1}^{K} e^{z_j}} \qquad (10)$$

$\mathbf{z}$: vector fed to softmax function. z_i : elements of $\mathbf{z}$, e^{z_i} represents standard exponential function is applied to z_i.

K is number of classes and $\sum_{j=1}^{K} e^{z_j}$ represents normalization.

The output of the model is in the form of a vector with the size of a total number of labels or classes we have, and the value tells weather the image belongs to that class or not.

An output vector that is generated by the model has the same size of the input vector, i.e. the number of classes and its value tells us the class the input image belongs to.

4 Results and Discussion

In the proposed work, a federated learning approach is applied to classify the different classes of the iris dataset. Simulation is performed by using a CNN model. It is observed that the result of the entire simulation heavily depends on the number of clients participating in the training process and the number of rounds being performed between the local model and the global model. Thus, in this work, the simulation is performed with varying combinations of clients and rounds, e.g. 2 clients with 2,3, & 5 rounds, 3 clients with 2,3, & 5 rounds and 5 clients with 2,3, & 5 rounds. The accuracy and loss for each combination are recorded. The graphical representation of the obtained accuracy and loss for the varying number of clients and executed rounds are shown in Fig. 5 & Fig. 6. In the simulation, the minimum number of the round is 2, and the maximum round is 5 because after 05 number of rounds, the accuracy of the model become stable.

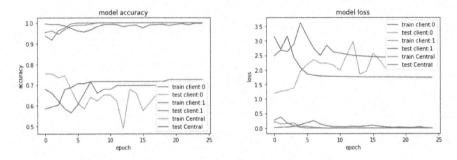

Fig. 5. Graphical Representation of Accuracy(Left Side) and Loss (Right Side) for 02 Clients and 02 Rounds

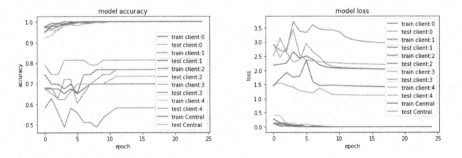

Fig. 6. Graphical Representation of Accuracy (Left Side) and Loss (Right Side) for 05 Clients and 05 Rounds

Figure 5 represents the accuracy and loss for the simulation with 02 clients and 02 rounds whereas Fig. 6 represents the accuracy and loss for the simulation with 05 clients and 05 rounds.It can be observed that the accuracy increases and the loss decreases when a simulation is performed with specific parameters (e.g. clients & rounds).

To get the best combination of clients and rounds for better performance, a comparison is shown in Table 1 where accuracy as a performance metric is represented for different client and round based simulation. In the table it can be seen that the best performance of the model is obtained when the number of the participating clients is 05, and the total number of rounds is 05, having an accuracy of 83 percent. Also, the worst results in terms of accuracy (68 per cent) is when the total participating clients is 03 and the number of rounds is 02.

Table 1. Performance Comparison of Different Combinations of clients and rounds in Simulation.

Number of Clients	Number of Rounds	Accuracy
2	2	70
2	3	76
2	5	81
3	2	68
3	3	70
3	5	75
5	2	75
5	3	78
5	5	83

5 Conclusion

The work provides a secure image classification approach utilizing a CNN model to improve the performance of existing frameworks with respect to privacy. Tests were conducted on the CASIA Iris V4 dataset to assess performance.The findings shows that the major setback in traditional machine learning approaches is getting vanished by preserving confidential user data. Also the work proves the efficacy and validity of the proposed technique in image classification.

The work currently is only be able to perform Iris classification in a privacy-preserving federated learning fashion. Moreover, this work could be further extended into developing a system which is able to extract higher quality input image features and by changing the optimization strategies to speed up the convergence of the cost function in order to improve classification results and training effect.

References

1. Gupta, H., Patel, D., Makade, A., Gupta, K., Vyas, O., Puliafito, A.: Risk Prediction in the Life Insurance Industry Using Federated Learning Approach. In: 2022 IEEE 21st Mediterranean Electrotechnical Conference (MELECON), pp. 948–953 (2022)
2. Hu, K., Xia, M., Lu, M., Weng, L.: Federated Learning: A Distributed Shared Machine Learning Method. Hindawiy. **47**, 1–20 (2009)
3. Umer, S., Dhara, B.C., Chanda, B.: A Noble Cance-lable Iris Recognition System Based on Feature Learning Technique. Elsevier Information Sci. **406** (2017)
4. Naseema, I., Aleemb, A., Togneric, R., Bennamoun, M.: Iris recognition using class-specific dictionaries. Elsevier Comput. Electr. Eng. **62**, 178–193 (2016)
5. Galdi, C., Nappi, M., Dugelay, J.: Multimodal authentication on smartphones: Combining iris and sensor recognition for a double check of user identity. Patt. Recogn. Lett. **82**144–153 (2016), https://www.sciencedirect.com/science/article/pii/S0167865515003190, An insight on eye biometrics
6. Azam, M., Rana, H.: Iris Recognition using Convolutional Neural Network. Int. J. Comput. Appl. **175**, 24–28 (2020). http://www.ijcaonline.org/archives/volume175/number12/31505-2020920602
7. Albawi, S., Mohammed, T., Al-Zawi, S.: Understanding of a convolutional neural network. In: 2017 International Conference On Engineering And Technology (ICET), pp. 1–6 (2017)
8. Omelina, L., Goga, J., Pavlovicova, J., Oravec, M., Jansen, B.: A survey of iris datasets. Image Vision Comput. **108** 1–20 (2021)
9. Mishra, V., Kumar, S., Shukla, N.: Image Acquisition and Techniques to Perform Image Acquisition. SAMRIDDHI : A J. Phys. Sci. Eng. Technol. **9**, (2017)
10. Zuo, J., Ratha, N., Connell, J.: A new approach for iris segmentation. In: 2008 IEEE Computer Society Conference On Computer Vision And Pattern Recognition Workshops, CVPR Workshops, pp. 1–6 (2008,7)
11. Verma, P., Dubey, M., Verma, P.: Hough Transform Method for Iris Recognition-A Biometric Approach. Int. J. Eng. Innov. Technol. (IJEIT). **1** (2012)
12. Daugman, J.: High condence visual recognition of persons by a test of statistical independence. Patt. Anal. Mach. Intell. IEEE Trans. **1** (1993)
13. Li, Q., et al.: A Survey on Federated Learning Systems: Vision, Hype and Reality for Data Privacy and Protection. CoRR. abs/1907.09693 (2019), http://arxiv.org/abs/1907.09693
14. Aledhari, M., Razzak, R., Parizi, R., Saeed, F.: Federated Learning: A Survey on Enabling Technologies, Protocols, and Applications. IEEE Access. **8** 1–1 (2020,1)
15. Ahmed, L., Ahmad, K., Said, N., Qolomany, B., Qadir, J., Al-Fuqaha, A.: Active learning based federated learning for waste and natural disaster image classification. IEEE Access. **8**, 208518–208531 (2020)
16. Preuveneers, D., Rimmer, V., Tsingenopoulos, I., Spooren, J., Joosen, W., Ilie-Zudor, E.: Chained Anomaly Detection Models for Federated Learning: An Intrusion Detection Case Study. Appl. Sci. **8** 2663 (2018,12)
17. Lyu, L., Yu, H., Yang, Q.: Threats to Federated Learning: A Survey. CoRR. abs/2003.02133 (2020). https://arxiv.org/abs/2003.02133

Traffic Flow Forecasting Using Attention Enabled Bi-LSTM and GRU Hybrid Model

Nisha Singh Chauhan[ID] and Neetesh Kumar[(✉)][ID]

Indian Institute of Technology-Roorkee, Roorkee 247667, India
{nisha_sc,neetesh}@cs.iitr.ac.in

Abstract. In the past few years, Machine Learning (ML) techniques have been seen to provide a range of Intelligent Transportation Systems (ITS) related solutions. Avoiding traffic jams is one of the most challenging problems to solve globally. In this paper, the use of ML techniques to forecast traffic flow to avoid congestion and redirect vehicles to reduce travel time, waiting time, pollution, and fuel consumption are explored. Deep hybrid models, in particular, have become effective ways to predict traffic flow. The temporal and periodic aspects of the traffic data cannot be effectively captured by the layered architecture used by the majority of hybrid models. Therefore, this work proposes a hybrid deep learning model of two distinct modules to extract the temporal and periodic characteristics from the traffic data. In order to learn the temporal properties of the traffic data, first module makes use of a Bi-LSTM whereas the second module is developed using GRU to extract the periodic properties of the traffic data. Additionally, a novel attention mechanism named confined attention is added to the first module to enhance the performance of the model by concentrating solely on the most recent pertinent data in the traffic flow sequence. The performance of the proposed model is evaluated using a publicly available real-world data set and compared with many existing methodologies for traffic flow prediction. As a result, a drop in the average value of Mean Absolute Error (MAE), Mean Absolute Percentage Error (MAPE), and Root Mean Squared Error (RMSE) for all of the prediction horizons is observed, which is ranged from 9.2%–29%, 4.1%–54.2%, and 5.9%–20.6%, respectively.

Keywords: Traffic flow prediction · Deep learning · Hybrid models · Bi-LSTM · GRU · Attention

1 Introduction

Predicting traffic congestion is one of the most challenging issues in cities worldwide. The advance congestion prediction offers significant benefits like minimization of carbon emissions, fuel costs, travel time, and waiting time that substantially benefit the environment, individuals (drivers/pedestrians), and the overall economy. One critical Intelligent Transportation Systems (ITS) solution to

M. Tanveer et al. (Eds.): ICONIP 2022, CCIS 1794, pp. 505–517, 2023.
https://doi.org/10.1007/978-981-99-1648-1_42

address issues with traffic congestion is traffic flow prediction. The goal of traffic flow prediction is to make predictions about future traffic conditions based on previous data. This can help drivers plan their journeys more efficiently and help traffic control agencies develop strategies to avoid potential congestion. The traffic flow forecast is divided into short-term and long-term predictions based on temporal granularity. The traffic flow prediction can exhibit apparent instabilities with a short duration granularity. This makes forecasting short-term traffic patterns more difficult than long-term ones [1]. Various traffic flow prediction methods have been presented through time to predict traffic. These models can be broadly divided into: parametric, non-parametric, and hybrid models [2]. Time series data are the foundation for parametric statistical models. In such models, the link between the independent and dependent variables is probably known, and the model's performance can be reasonably consistent by capturing the periodicity and recurrence of traffic flow. Instead of making strict theoretical assumptions about the traffic flow, non-parametric models use data to determine the model structure. Since parametric methods cannot represent stochastic and nonlinear traffic flow features, non-parametric models have become increasingly popular in traffic flow forecasting. Machine Learning (ML)-based methodologies are relatively common among non-parametric approaches. ML-based approaches better match the nonlinear properties of the traffic data and requires fewer knowledge about the relationship between various traffic patterns.

Deep learning algorithms have recently gained a lot of momentum in ITS. The prediction performance of such systems is constrained since the deep learning-based models for traffic forecasting now in use have few restrictions [3]. Several intricate hybrid deep learning models have performed better than deep neural networks. Hybrid models have been proved to be significantly better in capturing the temporal and periodic characteristics of the traffic data and improving the performance [2]. Thus, for traffic flow prediction, hybrid models gained much attention from researchers. Zhaowei et al. [4], proposed a hybridized model of Long Short-Term Memory (LSTM) and Bidirectional LSTM(Bi-LSTM) to predict the short-term traffic flow, and comparative results indicated the better performance of the model. Zheng et al. [5] used LSTM along with other sub-models to capture the medium and long-term features of the traffic data to make the forecast. Autoregressive Integrated Moving Average (ARIMA) and LSTM were used together by Lu et al. [6] to predict the traffic flow, where ARIMA was used to capture the linear features, and LSTM was responsible for extracting non-linear features. Graph Convolutional Network (GCN) along with LSTM, was presented by Li et al. [7] where GCN aimed to map observation stations onto a graph and drove spatial features and traffic flow correlations. The output of the GCN was then sent to the LSTM module to capture temporal dependencies effectively. A combination of Stacked Auto Encoder (SAE) and LSTM was also proposed in [8] in which LSTM is used to learn historical patterns and extract shallow information from time series. From this study, it is observed that the LSTM and Bi-LSTM are widely adopted machine learning models which are used to capture the temporal and periodic features of the traffic data. Further, compared to LSTM, Gated Recurrent Unit(GRU) has similar performance with fewer parameters, this makes GRU more demanding in future research [19], and the use of GRU in hybrid models, to predict short-term traffic flow, has not been rigorously explored yet. Motivated by this, we explore a best-suited hybrid model for short-term traffic flow prediction using GRU, BiLSTM, and LSTM models with an efficient attention mechanism to obtain higher prediction accuracy. The significant contributions of this work are itemized as follows.

- This work explores short-term traffic flow prediction problem for time-series data and proposes a hybrid machine learning model to improve the traffic flow prediction accuracy.
- A BiLSTM-GRU hybrid deep learning model is proposed that captures the temporal and periodic characteristics of the traffic data separately, and then, the extracted features are concatenated to make predictions. The Bi-LSTM is employed to retrieve the temporal features whereas the GRU is used to capture the periodic characteristics.
- As the traffic flow at any point is heavily influenced by recent data. Therefore, to emphasize more on the nearest data, a confined attention mechanism is designed and incorporated into the Bi-LSTM module. This allows the model to focus on more relevant features of the input data in order to estimate traffic flow with higher accuracy.
- To analyze the performance behaviour of the model, a set of experiments are conducted on publicly available real world dataset [9]. Further, the performance of the model is compared with several baseline models: Support Vector Regression (SVR) [10], K-Nearest Neighbours (KNN) [11], GRU [20], LSTM [12], Bi-LSTM [13] and LSTM-BiLSTM [14]. As an outcome, the average reduction in the value of MAE, MAPE, and RMSE for all the prediction horizon lie in the range from 9.2%–29%, 4.1%–54.2% and 5.9%–20.6%, respectively.

2   Related Work

This section explores the state of the art methods for short-term traffic flow prediction. ARIMA and ARIMA-based models are well-known parametric methods to predict traffic flow. The ARIMA model was proposed by Ahmed et al. [15] to forecast the traffic, and the results proved better performance than moving-average, double-exponential smoothing, and Trigg and Leach adaptive models. Further, the Kohonen network and ARIMA were combined for traffic flow prediction, where Kohonen improved the performance of the ARIMA method [16]. It was observed that the parametric models were incapable of capturing the complex spatial, and temporal characteristics of the traffic flow. Therefore, the non-parametric approaches like KNN methods, SVR, and Artificial Neural Networks (ANNs) were widely adopted for traffic flow prediction [3]. Nevertheless, these methods have a shallow structure that restricts them from detecting hidden patterns in extensive traffic data. This led to the popularity of deep learning models that used multiple-layer architecture to extract intrinsic features from raw data [3]. In recent years, the adoption of hybrid models to anticipate traffic flow has increased dramatically. Recently, an improved GRU neural network was proposed by Shu et al. [19] using Bidirectional GRU to predict the traffic flow. The proposed model performed better than traditional LSTM and SAE. Furthermore, a combination of LSTM and GRU was also proposed by Miao et al. [21] in which multiple units of LSTM and GRU models were stacked together to make the predictions. An improved LSTM model was also proposed by Ma et al. [14] to increase the accuracy of short-term traffic flow prediction for time-series data. In this model, a Bi-LSTM model was integrated to combine the advantages of sequential data with the long-term reliance on forward LSTM and reverse LSTM. In the same-line, another hybrid model was proposed by Huang et al. [18] in which CNN was used to capture the spatial features whereas Convolutional LSTM (ConvLSTM) was used to capture the temporal characteristics with a time-dependent attention mechanism improved the model's prediction.

Based on the above study, it is observed that the LSTM, BiLSTM, and GRU are the key performing models, and the use of GRU in hybrid models, to predict short-term traffic flow, has not been rigorously explored yet. Therefore, this work explores a best-suited hybrid model for short-term traffic flow prediction via possible different combinations of GRU, BiLSTM, and LSTM models in order to obtain better prediction accuracy.

3   Proposed Approach

The Proposed Architecture of the Model: In this work, a novel hybrid deep learning model is proposed to make traffic flow predictions at a particular point of interest. The model consists of two modules; one module is employed to capture the temporal features of the traffic data, and the second module extracts the periodicity in the historical data. Figure 1b represents the abstract view of the proposed model architecture.

The temporal and periodic features are extracted using independent modules. The obtained characteristics are then concatenated together to be given as input to the dense layers that perform the final predictions. Since the Recurrent Neural Network (RNN) based models are commonly used for traffic flow prediction, the combination of GRU and Bi-LSTM emerged with good results after experimenting with many models. Thus, a GRU and Bi-LSTM hybrid model is proposed, in this study, for traffic-flow prediction. In this hybridization, first module is a Bi-LSTM that captures the temporal features of the traffic data, whereas the second module is GRU, which captures the periodic elements from the input data. Next, the extracted features are concatenated and passed through the dense layers to perform the predictions. A confined attention mechanism is also used with the Bi-LSTM module to emphasize the relevant information in the input, and ignores unnecessary data. As an outcome, this further elevates the performance of the proposed model.

Components of the Proposed Model

Bidirectional LSTM (Bi-LSTM): LSTM was introduced to reduce the problem of long-term dependency found in Recurrent Neural Networks. A single

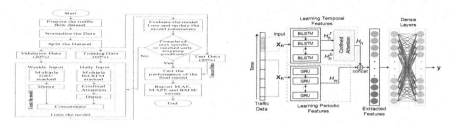

(a) Flow-graph of the proposed traffic flow prediction model.   (b) Architecture of the proposed model to predict traffic flow.

Fig. 1. Flow Graph (Left) and Architecture(Right) of the proposed model. BiLSTM: Bidirectional Long Short Term Memory; GRU: Gated Recurrent Unit.

LSTM unit consists of an input gate, forget gate, and output gate. Equations 1–5 shows the computation of hidden state (h_t) of a LSTM cell. In Eq. 1, f_t represents the output value of the forget gate, σ is the sigmoid function, h_{t-1} is state of the latest hidden layer, and x_t is current input at time t. The output of the input gate is given by Eq. 2. Equation 3 represents the updated cell state, whereas the equation of output gate is given by Eq. 4.

$$f_t = \sigma(W_f \cdot [h_{t-1}, x_t] + b_f) \tag{1}$$

$$i_t = \sigma(W_i \cdot [h_{t-1}, x_t] + b_i) \tag{2}$$

$$C_t = f_t \cdot C_{t-1} + i_t \cdot \tanh(W_c \cdot [h_{t-1}, x_t] + b_c) \tag{3}$$

$$o_t = \sigma(W_o \cdot [h_{t-1}, x_t] + b_o) \tag{4}$$

$$h_t = o_t \cdot \tanh(C_t) \tag{5}$$

A Bi-LSTM model is made up of two unidirectional LSTMs, of which one is used for learning the input sequence in the forward direction, whereas the other is used to remember the sequence in the reverse direction. Figure 2a shows the structure of the Bi-LSTM model. Since the Bi-LSTM architecture consists of two LSTMs, the equation of the hidden state of Bi-LSTM can be given as:

$$h_t = h_t^f \oplus h_t^b \tag{6}$$

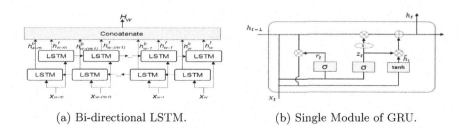

(a) Bi-directional LSTM.   (b) Single Module of GRU.

Fig. 2. Structure of a Bidirectional LSTM (Left) and Single Module of GRU (Right).

where, h_t^f and h_t^b represent the hidden state of forward and backward LSTM, respectively. In this paper, Bi-LSTM is used to capture both temporal and periodic characteristics of the traffic flow data separately. Multiple Bi-LSTM units have been stacked together to form the neural network.

Gated Recurrent Unit (GRU): Dzmitry Bahdanau and Kyunghyun Cho proposed the GRU model as an evolutionary model of the LSTM model in 2014 [20]. It is an enhanced RNN that uses an update gate and a reset gate to tackle the problem of vanishing gradients in a typical RNN. The update gate assists the model in determining how much historical data (from earlier time steps) should be forwarded in the future. The reset gate determines the amount of information to forget from the past. The update gate and reset gate for time step t can be calculated using Eqs. 7–10.

$$z_t = \sigma(W_z \cdot [h_{t-1}, x_t + b_z]) \tag{7}$$

$$r_t = \sigma(W_r \cdot [h_{t-1}, x_t + b_r]) \tag{8}$$

$$\tilde{h}_t = \tanh(W_z \cdot [r_t \odot h_{t-1}, x_t] + b_h) \tag{9}$$

$$h_t = (1 - z_t) \odot h_{t-1} + z_t \odot \tilde{h}_t \tag{10}$$

A single GRU unit is shown in Fig. 2b. In the proposed model, GRU is used to extract the periodic features of the traffic data. Multiple GRU units are stacked together which receives X_w, as input and outputs the hidden state H_w.

Attention: We propose a novel attention mechanism called confined attention, focusing on the recent hidden states while calculating the context vector. To achieve this, we consider a window (p) that decides the number of recent hidden states to consider while calculating the context vector. Thus, the context vector H_h is the weighted sum of the output of Bi-LSTM network (H_h^f and H_h^b), and it can be calculated as follows:

$$H_h = \sum_{k=1}^{p} \alpha_k H_{h-(k-1)} \tag{11}$$

where, $H_h = H_h^f \oplus H_h^b$, and p is the number of hidden states considered to calculate the context vector. The weight α_k can be computed as:

$$\alpha_k = exp(s_k) / \sum_{k=1}^{p} exp(s_k) \tag{12}$$

$$s_h = tanh(W_s H_h + b_s) \tag{13}$$

Here, s_h is the alignment score which is calculated using Eq. 13. Figure 3 shows the integration of confined attention in Bi-LSTM.

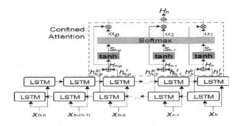

Fig. 3. Bi-LSTM with Confined Attention.

Feature Fusion: In this work, concatenation is used to combine the temporal and periodic features. The output from the Bi-LSTM (with attention) module (H_h), and Bi-LSTM module (H_w) are concatenated together to form a feature vector given by Eq. 14.

$$H^{concat} = concat(H_h, H_w) \tag{14}$$

This feature vector is the final input to the dense layer. The dense layer uses linear activation, which outputs the predicted traffic flow (y).

$$y = H^{concat}W^y + b^y \tag{15}$$

where, W^y and b^y are learnable parameters.

4 Performance Evaluation

Dataset: The dataset is obtained from the Performance Measurement System [9] sponsored by the California Department of Transportation. The traffic flow dataset was collected using several sensors at I980 Street, District 4 in Oakland city (located in an urban area) ranging from September 11th, 2017, to March 4th, 2018, including weekdays and weekends. The road contains three lanes; therefore, the traffic flow of all the lanes has been combined for the prediction. The traffic data is aggregated every 5 min; therefore, for a single day, there are 288 timestamps. The entire dataset is divided into three parts: training (60%), validation (20%), and test (20%) sets which assist in improving the generalization error of the proposed model.

Training Configuration: During training, the aim is to find such parameters that minimize the error between actual and estimated traffic flow. In the proposed model, the loss function $(E(\theta))$ is the Mean Squared Error (MSE) given by Eq. 16.

$$E(\theta) = \underset{\theta}{argmin}(\frac{1}{m}\sum_{i=1}^{m}(y^i - Y^i)^2) \tag{16}$$

Here, m represents the total number of samples in the dataset, y^i is the actual traffic flow, and Y^i is the estimated traffic flow. Equation 17 represents the prediction function Y^i.

$$Y^i = h_\theta(X_h^i, X_w^i) \tag{17}$$

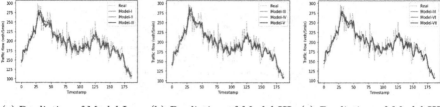

(a) Prediction of Model-I vs Model-II vs Model-III.

(b) Prediction of Model-III vs Model-IV vs Model-V.

(c) Prediction of Model-III vs Model-VI vs Model-VII.

Fig. 4. Comparison of the performance of the proposed modules from 5:00 AM to 9:00 PM for a day.

As the accuracy of a deep neural network not only depends on the size of the Neural Network (NN) but also on the number of training epochs. If the number of epochs increases, the backpropagation training of NN may lead to overfitting. To avoid this, we have used 20% dropout, which helps in reducing overfitting and improving the generalization error. The models are built on jupyter notebook using TensorFlow, Keras, and Pandas package with Python. The model is trained using various hyperparameters: the *batch size = 32, learning rate (μ) = 0.01*, and *number of epochs = 200*.

Performance of the Proposed Model: In this section the performance behavior of different versions (model-I, model-II, model-III, model-IV, model-V, model-VI, and model-VII) of the proposed model are thoroughly analyzed. The proposed model consists of two modules: First module is used to capture the temporal characteristics by taking past 15 time-steps i.e., 75-minutes of the traffic data. Whereas, the second module takes past one-week data and is used to extract the periodic features and predict the traffic in the next five minutes. Since the LSTM can successfully capture the time dependent data, therefore initially, both the modules are constructed using LSTM that is named as model-I. The LSTM model has more parameters as compared to GRU; therefore, GRU has recently been utilized to uncover temporal correlations in traffic data for traffic flow prediction. Motivated from this, the LSTM modules in model-I is replaced by GRU modules which makes model-II. According to [13], LSTM learns the input sequence only in the forward direction, whereas Bi-LSTM has the ability to learn the input sequence both directions i.e., in regular order and reverse order. This indicates the performance of Bi-LSTM can be better than LSTM. Therefore, in model-III both the modules are replaced by Bi-LSTM units. Figure 4a presents the comparative study of model-I, model-II and model-III for 5 min prediction from 5:00 AM to 9:00 PM (during the peak hours) where model-III seems to be closer to the real data. Further, in model-IV, a combination of LSTM and GRU is used where the first module is a LSTM module and the second module is a GRU. In model-V, Bi-LSTM is used along with LSTM where Bi-LSTM is used to capture the temporal features and LSTM is used to capture periodic

Table 1. Comparison of different proposed modules for traffic flow prediction.

Model Name	Modules	MAE	MAPE (%)	RMSE
Model-I	LSTM-LSTM	12.20	12.92	16.58
Model-II	GRU-GRU	11.83	13.96	15.84
Model-III	BiLSTM-BiLSTM	11.61	12.57	15.75
Model-IV	LSTM-GRU	12.43	16.57	16.29
Model-V	BiLSTM-LSTM	12.20	15.20	16.19
Model-VI	BiLSTM-GRU	11.59	12.18	15.73
Model-VII	BiLSTM-GRU with Attention	**11.45**	**11.84**	**15.60**

features. From Fig. 4b, it can be observed that prediction of model-III is effective and quite close to the real data, in comparison to model-IV and model-V, during the peak hours of a day. In model-VI, Bi-LSTM is combined with GRU to capture the features and predict the traffic flow. It is observed that model-VI makes better predictions than model III shown in Fig. 4c. The confined attention concentrates on the relevant information and ignores the irrelevant information. Therefore in model-VII, the confined attention mechanism is introduced on the top of the Bi-LSTM module. From this, it can be observed that the predicted value of model-VII is closer to actual value as compared to model-III and model-VI. This proves the effectiveness of the confined attention in improving the prediction performance of the model. At the end, the model-VII is the final model which uses Bi-LSTM along with the proposed confined attention in the first module (to extract temporal features) and GRU in the second module (to extract periodic features).

Table 2. Comparison of proposed model with other existing approaches for predicting the traffic flow.

Prediction Horizon	Metric	SVR	KNN	LSTM	GRU	BiLSTM	LSTM-BILSTM	Proposed
5 min	MAE	14.131	14.056	12.180	12.139	12.006	11.952	**11.457**
	MAPE%	24.749	14.521	12.537	13.359	12.084	12.003	**11.841**
	RMSE	17.664	17.474	16.462	16.352	16.313	16.236	**15.609**
15 min	MAE	17.987	16.298	14.467	14.220	14.038	14.038	**13.158**
	MAPE%	36.882	16.045	14.979	15.111	14.476	14.835	**13.320**
	RMSE	22.049	22.047	19.400	19.038	19.069	18.879	**18.166**
30 min	MAE	24.629	18.809	17.833	17.287	17.082	16.846	**16.141**
	MAPE%	39.710	17.970	17.405	17.197	15.793	16.031	**15.193**
	RMSE	30.733	25.785	23.628	23.060	23.170	22.771	**22.080**
60 min	MAE	26.638	25.138	24.936	24.178	23.546	21.984	**17.100**
	MAPE%	35.753	27.094	26.265	26.537	20.256	24.289	**19.662**
	RMSE	33.501	32.500	32.419	31.716	31.861	28.956	**25.118**

Comparison with Baseline Models: For the above set of experiments, Table 1 presents a comparative summary of MAE, MAPE, and RMSE values of all the seven models. From this study, it is observed that the value of MAE and RMSE of model-II are reduced by 3% and 4.4%, respectively, whereas MAPE is increased by 7.4% in comparison to model-I. Further, the values of MAE, MAPE, and RMSE are dropped by 1.8%, 7%, and 0.5%, respectively in model-III as compared to model-II. Model-IV and model-V perform poorly as compared to model-III. Compared with model-III, the MAE, MAPE, and RMSE values of model-IV are increased by 6.5%, 24%, and 3.3%, respectively. Whereas model-V witnesses an increase in MAE, MAPE, and RMSE by 4.8%, 17%, and 2.7%, respectively, compared with model-III. Finally, model-VI performs better than model-III with a reduction of MAE, MAPE and RMSE values by 0.2%, 3.1%, and 0.1%, respectively as compared to model-III. Further, model-VII drops its MAE by 1.2%, MAPE by 2.7% and RMSE by 0.8% as compared to model-VI.

SVR uses Radial Basis Function (RBF) as the kernel function. Compared to SVR, the proposed model performs better as the average values of MAE, MAPE, and RMSE for all the prediction horizons are dropped by 18.9%, 52.1%, and 11.6%, respectively. KNN used euclidean distance as the distance metric and seemed to perform better than SVR. This improvement may be because the traffic at a particular point is highly related to the traffic in the nearby history. Compared to KNN, a reduction in the average values of MAE, MAPE, and RMSE for all the prediction horizons by 18.4%, 18.4%, and 10.6%, respectively was observed. Since LSTM can capture the temporal features of the given data, it performs better than SVR and KNN. However, the proposed model outperforms LSTM as the average values of MAE, MAPE, and RMSE, for all the prediction horizons, are reduced by 5.9%, 5.5%, and 5.1%. As compared to GRU, the MAE, MAPE and RMSE values of the proposed model are dropped by 5.6%, 11.3%, and 4.5%, respectively. Comparing the performance of Bi-LSTM with the proposed model, the average values of MAE, MAPE, and RMSE for all the prediction horizons are reduced by 4.5%, 2%, and 4.3%, respectively. LSTM-BiLSTM model has been recently been proposed in which the author presented a stacked architecture that has both LSTM

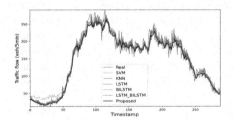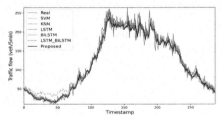

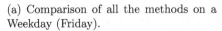

(a) Comparison of all the methods on a Weekday (Friday).

(b) Comparison of all the methods on a Weekend (Sunday).

Fig. 5. Comparison of all the methods on a Weekday (left) and Weekend (right).

and Bi-LSTM modules that captures the complex traffic features [14]. Consequently, the LSTM-BiLSTM model performs better than previous models. Comparing LSTM-BiLSTM and the proposed model, it is observed that the proposed model has marginally improved the performance with the drop in MAE, MAPE, and RMSE values by 4.1%, 1.3%, and 3.8%, respectively. Figure 5 shows the comparison of the proposed model with state of the art methods. It is observed that the prediction of the proposed model is closer to the real data than the other models.

Further, to evaluate the consistency of the proposed model, the predictions were carried out for longer horizons, i.e., 15 min, 30 min, and 60 min, and the results are compared with other baseline methods shown in Table 2. As an outcome of this study, the proposed model captures the temporal features of the traffic data using the Bi-LSTM modules and periodic features using GRU. The confined attention mechanism further improves the performance by concentrating on the relevant data for the prediction. Hence, the proposed model outperforms all the other models with the average reduction in MAE, MAPE, and RMSE values, for all the prediction horizons, in the range of 9.2%–29%, 4.1%–54.2%, and 5.9%–20.6%, respectively.

5   Conclusion and Future Work

This work proposes a hybrid deep learning model for short-term traffic flow prediction with two modules. First module is a Bi-LSTM along with a new attention mechanism named confined attention that captures the temporal characteristics of the traffic data. The second module is a GRU module that extracts the traffic data's periodic features. To analyze the performance of the model, a set of extensive experiments were conducted. Further, the proposed model was compared with the set of baseline state of the art methods. The proposed model may not be efficient enough for a complex road network as the model is trained on straight road senors traffic data that is rarely influenced by the traffic on another road. Thus, in future work, we aim to design a model in a more complex scenario in which the traffic data generated from multiple intersecting road-lanes, can be used to predict the traffic flow. We also aim to include external features that affects the traffic flow which may assist in improving the prediction performance of the model.

Acknowledgement. This work was supported by the Science and Engineering Research Board (SERB), Department of Science and Technology (DST), Government of India, under the Project through Software Defined Controlled and Dynamic Traffic Load Balanced Scheduling Framework for the IoT Enabled Intelligent Transportation System (ITS) under Grant EEQ/2019/000182.

References

1. Wang, P., Hao, W., Jin, Y.: Fine-grained traffic flow prediction of various vehicle types via fusion of multisource data and deep learning approaches. IEEE Trans. Intell. Transp. Syst. **22**(11), 6921–6930 (2020)
2. Tedjopurnomo, D.A., et al.: A survey on modern deep neural network for traffic prediction: trends, methods and challenges. IEEE Trans. Knowl. Data Eng. **34**, 1544–1561 (2020)
3. Zheng, H., et al.: A hybrid deep learning model with attention-based Conv-LSTM networks for short-term traffic flow prediction. IEEE Trans. Intell. Transp. Syst. **22**(11), 6910–6920 (2020)
4. Zhaowei, Q., et al.: Short-term traffic flow forecasting method with MB-LSTM hybrid network. IEEE Trans. Intell. Transp. Syst. **23**(1), 225–235 (2020)
5. Zheng, G., et al.: A joint temporal-spatial ensemble model for short-term traffic prediction. Neurocomputing **457**, 26–39 (2021)
6. Lu, S., et al.: A combined method for short-term traffic flow prediction based on recurrent neural network. Alexandria Eng. J. **60**(1), 87–94 (2021)
7. Li, Z., et al.: A hybrid deep learning approach with GCN and LSTM for traffic flow prediction. In: 2019 IEEE Intelligent Transportation Systems Conference (ITSC). IEEE (2019)
8. Wang, X., Wei, X., Wang, L.: A deep learning based energy-efficient computational offloading method in Internet of vehicles. China Commun. **16**(3), 81–91 (2019)
9. Dua, D., Graff, C.: UCI Machine Learning Repository. University of California, School of Information and Computer Science, Irvine, CA (2019). http://archive.ics.uci.edu/ml
10. Feng, X., et al.: Adaptive multi-kernel SVM with spatial-temporal correlation for short-term traffic flow prediction. IEEE Trans. Intell. Transp. Syst. **20**(6), 2001–2013 (2018)
11. Zhang, L., et al.: An improved K-nearest neighbor model for short-term traffic flow prediction. Procedia-Soc. Behav. Sci. **96**, 653–662 (2013)
12. Zhao, Z., et al.: LSTM network: a deep learning approach for short-term traffic forecast. IET Intell. Transp. Syst. **11**(2), 68–75 (2017)
13. Xie, W., et al.: Variational autoencoder bidirectional long and short-term memory neural network soft-sensor model based on batch training strategy. IEEE Trans. Industr. Inform. **17**(8), 5325–5334 (2020)
14. Ma, C., Dai, G., Zhou, J.: Short-term traffic flow prediction for urban road sections based on time series analysis and LSTMBILSTM method. IEEE Trans. Intell. Transp. Syst. **23**(6), 5615–5624 (2021)
15. Ahmed, M.S., Cook, A.R.: Analysis of freeway traffic time-series data by using Box-Jenkins techniques. Transp. Res. Rec. **722**, 1–9 (1979)
16. Van Der Voort, M., Dougherty, M., Watson, S.: Combining Kohonen maps with ARIMA time series models to forecast traffic flow. Transp. Res. Part C Emerg. Technol. **4**(5), 307–318 (1996)
17. Zhao, J., et al.: Short term traffic flow prediction of expressway service area based on STL-OMS. Physica A Stat. Mech. Appl. **595**, 126937 (2022)
18. Huang, X., Tang, J., Yang, X., Xiong, L.: A time-dependent attention convolutional LSTM method for traffic flow prediction. Appl. Intell. **52**, 17371–17386 (2022). https://doi.org/10.1007/s10489-022-03324-7
19. Shu, W., Cai, K., Xiong, N.N.: A short-term traffic flow prediction model based on an improved gate recurrent unit neural network. IEEE Trans. Intell. Transp. Syst. **23**(9), 16654–16665 (2021)

20. Bahdanau, D., Cho, K., Bengio, Y.: Neural machine translation by jointly learning to align and translate. arXiv preprint arXiv:1409.0473 (2014)
21. Miao, F., Tao, L., Xue, J., Zhang, X.: A queue hybrid neural network with weather weighted factor for traffic flow prediction. In: 2021 IEEE 24th International Conference on Computer Supported Cooperative Work in Design (CSCWD), pp. 788–793. IEEE (2021)

Commissioning Random Matrix Theory and Synthetic Minority Oversampling Technique for Power System Faults Detection and Classification

Ayush Sinha[1]([✉])(iD), Shubham Dwivedi[2], Sandeep Kumar Shukla[3](iD), and O. P. Vyas[1](iD)

[1] Indian Institute of Information Technology Allahabad, Prayagraj, India
{pro.ayush,opvyas}@iiita.ac.in
[2] University of Hildesheim, Hildesheim, Germany
dwivedi@uni-hieldeshiem.de
[3] Indian Institute of Technology Kanpur, Kanpur, India
sandeeps@cse.iitk.ac.in

Abstract. The fast paced innovation in communication and computation capabilities has laid the foundation of sophisticated transformation from legacy power systems to smart grid (SG) infrastructure. So, Providing the effective protection to the distribution lines against the power system faults is crucial for smart grid stability, however it totally depends upon the accurate detection and classification of line fault category. In recent years, Data driven perspective evolved on machine learning classification models are in practice for cyber attack detection. Though the classification accuracy suffers since contingency or anomalous data transcends rarely than normal data in the power flow analysis. This paper presents a complete approach starting from the contingency data generation using Random Matrix Theory (RMT) and Synthetic Minority Oversampling Technique (SMOTE) and ending with the power fault detection and classification. The proposed method uses power flow analysis of the current signals and applied Objective cost sensitive support vector machine (OCSSVM) for the detection and applies decision tree for the correct faults classification in the smart grid infrastructure. Faults investigated in the paper include line to ground (LG) fault, double line (LL) fault, three phase fault with ground (LLLG) and double line to ground (LLG) fault. To support the effectiveness, the proposed method is applied to IEEE-9 and IEEE-14 node test feeder. Finally, we juxtapose the results in terms of accuracy with the state of the art models and established the efficacy of proposed method.

Keywords: Decision tree · Power system fault · Fault Data · Line Fault classification

---

Supported by C3i Hub IIT Kanpur, India.

M. Tanveer et al. (Eds.): ICONIP 2022, CCIS 1794, pp. 518–529, 2023.
https://doi.org/10.1007/978-981-99-1648-1_43

1 Introduction

Protection of lines used for distribution of electricity against undefended faults is a crucial and important task due to vulnerabilities present in power system. Protective relay system is installed in power system with main motive as to identify and detect anomalous signals available in the infrastructure which eventually leads to faults. However protective relay systems requires fast and speedy detection and classification of fault categories to enable protective strategies for power lines. Recently soft computing techniques fascinate the researchers to develop methods based on past historical data to correctly identify, detect and classify the power fault. The approaches that are followed in these methods tend to be trained with training data that are derived from historical power system data, which further classified into supervised and semi-supervised category. Supervised models decipher the patterns of data samples with and without the presence of attacks scenario to find orchestrate measurements, while semi-supervised models learn just from the non-attacked readings and the models treat any fluctuation of the learned data patterns as cyber-attacks. Deep consensus regarding operating of power systems is rather the objective of ever approach used. With these models the main issue was with the historical measurement database which when uniformly sampled directly then the sporadically distributed contingency data is probable to be missed out, which is more crucial and phenomenal for the learning mechanism of a model based on machine learning techniques.

So following the approach that was used by Chen et al. [2], a data preparation method is proposed based on RMT and SMOTE technique to solve the stated issue. We followed a phased approach working with chen et al.'s [2] model while forming a consensus with Yongxin et al. [1] on RMT. Our Initial directives for phase one was to have a relative model with respect to chen et al. [2], that will further benefit in the optimization of different approaches that will be followed. A cost sensitive approach as utilized in [3] which overrides the epical margin maximization through the minimization of the number of selected features, but excising upper bounds on the false negative and positive rates. This approach was later improved by adding the construction of the classification rules of the cost sensitive support vector machine(CSSVM) with an objective cost associated with each sample to achieved a more dependable classifier known as objective cost sensitive support vector machine (OCSSVM). The Second phase dealt with further classification of the faulty data that was classified into a different fault categories as defined in 2 which was achieved by using decision tree algo. in a similar approach as it was used by bala et el. [21] but instead of using wavelet transformation we will be using a fault simulation approach with PMU measurements for classification. The rest of the paper is organised as: Sect. 2 states the background work, Sect. 3 depicts how to model the historical data using RMT, and explains about the contingency data detection, extraction as well as generation of synthetic data. This section also elaborate the brief about the machine learning models used for this research work along with the error techniques applied. In the last, Sect. 4 states about the methods used along with the advantage of using SMOTE and RMT for this experiment and Sect. 5 shows the experimental setup with the concluding remarks in Sect. 6

2 Literature Survey

To acquire an uninterruptible power supply framework, it is vital for a system to recognize various kinds of faults as fast as possible to protect it from complete power outages utilizing different procedures. Ozay et al. [5] proposed a series of semi-supervised online decision making framework along with feature level fusion algorithms for detection of False Data Injection (FDI) attacks in varied scenarios. This approach as not able to define the propagation of effects of fault in the system that is why He et al. [6] focused on detecting the tampering of measurement data by using a framework that combines state vector estimators and convolutional deep belief networks, this approach did tackle the propagation of error however one cannot state the type of fault with the said approach.

The approach by [8] utilize a feed-forward neural network model to identify attacks in distribution but the proposed method is not applicable in a coordinated attack situation that causes immediate power system stability issues. Through our literature review, we found that one of the crucial issues that were faced was the class imbalance [23] situation, the faulty data was mostly imbalanced compared to that of a stable one. This motivates us to go for a data-driven approach for fault detection and classification in the SG. To avoid the impact due to the presence of bad data, the RMT is applied to the proposed approach [2]. The advantage of using RMT is it tackles both the problem of propagation and class imbalance situation in the simulation runs.

Further in [4] the proposed objective cost was not integrated with traditional mis-classification costs (sample-based cost and class-based cost) which in turn does not help in considering the objective cost that is based on the inherent properties of the sample itself and on the mis-classification cost that is for the specific domain knowledge, simultaneously. So, we added the SMOT to overcome the situation that arises due to this.

Descriptions of Line Faults: An electrical fault may be understood as the deviation of measurement vectors from their nominal values or states. Power system equipment or lines carry normal measurements vectors under day to day scenario which results in a safer and smooth functioning of the grid. The occurrence of faults in the system creates a skewed measurement vector. Our paper includes a thorough investigation of all the unsymmetrical faults witnessed in the IEEE test bench.

LG: One of the most common faults is a single line-to-ground (LG) fault, different experiences state that this fault is one of the most prominently occurring ones, That is around 70–80% all the fault occurrence in a power system. This fault generally occurs after a short circuit which creates a path between the line and ground.

LL: When a live conductor comes into proximity of another live conductor it gives rise to a line to line fault (LL). Generally, natural cause such as Heavy winds leads for this fault during which overhead conductors may come in contact while swinging. They occur in the range of 15–20% of total reported faults.

LLG: LLG refers to the double line to ground faults, where two lines and ground come into contact. These come under the severe faults category and the occurrence of these is about 10% as compared to the total system faults.

3 Approach for Contingency Data Generation and Detection

3.1 Application of RMT and SMOTE

A matrix with random variables as entries is considered as a random matrix. For a k-dimensional random matrix $\mathbf{M}$ having real eigenvalues $\lambda_i^{R}(j = 1, 2, 3 \ldots, k)$, one can characterize the Empirical Spectral Distribution (ESD) of this matrix as

$$F_n^{R}(x) = \frac{1}{k} \sum_{j=1}^{k} V \left\{ \lambda_j^{R} \leq x \right\}, x \in \mathbb{R} \tag{1}$$

where function $V\{\cdot\}$ acts as an indicator which returns 1 when the condition is true, else returns 0. The Empirical Spectral Distribution(ESD) of different types of random matrices has particular attributes [9] associated with them. For instance, a random matrix M having a non-Hermitian nature is considered herein Eq. (5)

$$\tilde{\mathbf{Y}}_i \in \mathbb{K}^{C \times J}(j = 1, 2, 3 \ldots, M) \tag{2}$$

here the entries of the matrix are independent and are also identically distributed retain a mean of $\mu = 0$ and variance being $\sigma^2 = 1$.

Considering (5) if the ratio of $c = C/J \in (0, 1]$ is constant while $C, J \to \infty$ then the Empirical Spectral Distribution of their standard matrix product ($\tilde{P}$) will be converging to its Limit Spectral Distribution (LSD) and is defined by the expression:

$$f(\lambda) = \begin{cases} \frac{1}{\pi c M} |\lambda|^{\frac{2}{M} - 2} (1 - c)^{\frac{M}{2}} \leq |\lambda| \leq 1 \\ 0 \qquad \text{otherwise} \end{cases} \tag{3}$$

Equation 6 shows a clear representation of a ring area that lies within the complex plane while holding its geometric properties, this characteristic specifically belongs to Empirical Spectral Distribution and is also called the Ring Law. For the calculation of the standard matrix product $\tilde{P}$ of M random matrices $\tilde{\mathbf{Y}}_j$, the singular value equivalence matrix $\tilde{\mathbf{Y}}_{u,i}$, of each $\tilde{\mathbf{Y}}_j$ has to be initially calculated by

$$\tilde{\mathbf{Y}}_{u,j} = \sqrt{\tilde{\mathbf{Y}}_1 \tilde{\mathbf{Y}}_j^{\top}} \mathbf{Z} \tag{4}$$

where $\mathbf{Z} \in \mathbb{K}^{C \times C}$ signifies a Haar unitary matrix. For any $C = 2^c$ $(c \in \mathbb{C}^*)$, that belongs to the family of C Haar functions $h_w(t), w = 0, 1, \ldots, C - 1,$, which is defined within the range $t \in [0, 1]$ as

$$h_0(t) = \frac{1}{\sqrt{c}} \quad w = 0 \tag{5}$$

$$h_w(t) = \begin{cases} \frac{2^{r/2}}{\sqrt{c}} & w > 0, \frac{(s-1)}{2^r} \le t < \frac{(s-0.5)}{2^r} \\ \frac{-2^{r/2}}{\sqrt{c}} & w > 0, \frac{(s-0.5)}{2^r} \le t < \frac{s}{2^r} \\ 0 & \text{otherwise} \end{cases} \tag{6}$$

where r and s are two variables that are natural numbers. The variables r and s and function index w follows a relationship defined as $w = 2^r + s - 1$. The said relationship can be proved for any given w, that the corresponding r and s are both uniquely determined. The generation of C-dimensional Haar unitary matrix $\mathbf{Z}$ can be obtained with the sampling of C values from each Haar function $h_w(t)$. At $t = k/C, k = 0, 1, 2 \ldots, C - 1$ the sampling points for generation are required to be selected. Thus, the obtained Haar unitary matrix Z is expressed as:

$$\mathbf{Z} = \begin{bmatrix} h_0(0) & \cdots & h_0(t) & \cdots & h_0(C-1/C) \\ \vdots & & \vdots & & \vdots \\ h_w(0) & \cdots & h_w(t) & \cdots & h_w(C-1/C) \\ \vdots & & \vdots & & \vdots \\ h_{C-1}(0) & \cdots & h_{C-1}(t) & \cdots & h_{C-1}(C-1/C) \end{bmatrix}$$

The product of all the M singular value equivalence matrices is calculated after they are obtained, with the help of following equation

$$\mathbf{p} = \prod_{j=1}^{m} \tilde{\mathbf{Y}}_{u,j}$$

Normalizing each row vector $p_j (j = 1, 2, \ldots, C - 1)$ of $\mathbf{P}$ yields

$$\tilde{p}_j = \frac{p_j}{\sqrt{C}\sigma(p_j)}$$

where the standard deviation regarding the row vector p_i is represented by $\sigma(p_j)$. Thus, the standard matrix product $\tilde{\mathbf{P}} = (\tilde{p}_1, \tilde{p}_2, \ldots, \tilde{p}_C)^{\mathrm{T}}$ can be formed. Even though, a necessary theoretical condition for the ESD of $\tilde{\mathbf{P}}$ converging to (6), is considering the dimension of the random matrices $\tilde{\mathbf{Y}}_j$ which has to be tending towards ∞, which will lead to a more accurate convergence outcome which is obtained [11], if the dimension of the matrix lies within the range of tens and hundreds. The assumption that the entries of $\tilde{\mathbf{P}}_j$ are independent and identically distributed is a must for the ring law to be established, which in turn can be used for the purpose of detection of the contingency data that disrupts the distribution of normal data. In other words, the Ring Law will not be valid if contingency data exists, which then makes (6) no longer tenable.

A Haar unitary matrix with a particular dimension of $C = 2^c (c \in \mathbb{C}^*)$, is hard to achieve as the different types of electrical quantities considered is $C' = pq$ which is amassed by the phasor measurement units, i.e., the capacity of $\hat{x}^{(t)}$ refer to Eq. (1), is not necessarily equivalent to 2^c. If $C' \ne 2^c$, then the dimension of the vector $\hat{x}^{(t)}$ obtained by PMU must be reduced to value nearest to 2^c $(c \in \mathbb{C}^*)$ in order to perform matrix multiplication (7).

Measurements generally have electric field coupling or magnetic field coupling existing between them. As an example one can point out the redundancy in the vector $\hat{x}^{(t)}$ obtained by PMU, This can be reasoned as a consequence of recording three-phase load and voltage magnitude data of each phase belonging to the same bus under normal operating conditions which leads to Identical values. Accordingly, dimension reduction approach is considered for the removal of redundant data in order to have the total number of electrical quantities $\tilde{x}_{mn}$ equivalent to C' while it satisfies 2^c without compensating much of the significant information. For this purpose, the paper uses a correlation matrix for the determination of redundant data within different types of PMU data.

When the value of the correlation coefficient lies in the interval of $[-1, 1]$,, it signifies the degree of linear correlation among variables. The higher value of the correlation coefficient signifies more linear correlation, i.e., greater redundancy among the variables. Representation of the correlation coefficient for two-variable A and B is as

$$r(A, B) = \frac{\text{Cov}(A, B)}{\sqrt{\sigma^2(A) \cdot \sigma^2(B)}} \tag{7}$$

where $\text{Cov}(A, B)$ is the co-variance of X and B, and $\sigma^2(A)$ $\sigma^2(B)$ are the variances of the A and B respectively.

Considering the row vectors of the source matrix φ, there are redundant values that are obtained by recording the same type of measurements under similar operating conditions. The correlations between every two of the C types of measurements are considered, then we can obtain C^2 correlation coefficients to generate the correlation matrix, and can be expressed as

$$\mathbf{R} = \begin{bmatrix} r(1,1) \cdots r(1,2) \cdots r(1,c) \\ \vdots \qquad \vdots \qquad \vdots \\ r(2,1) \cdots r(2,2) \cdots r(2,c) \\ \vdots \qquad \vdots \qquad \vdots \\ r(c,1) \cdots r(c,2) \cdots r(c,c) \end{bmatrix}$$

where $r(m, n)$ is the correlation coefficient for the m-th and n-th measurement entity. From the Eq. 7, it can be deduced that $r(m, m) = 1$ and $r(m, n) = r(n, m)$. We reduce the dimension C', by sorting of the entries in the upper triangular (except the diagonal element) in an iterative manner and removing any one of these measurements having the highest correlation coefficient until we found $C' = 2^c$

Generation of synthetic samples are carried out according to the following approach: Initially, calculation of the difference between the feature vector of the sample which under consideration and its nearest neighbor is carried out, then a random number is selected which belongs within the range of 0 and 1, then this selected random number is multiplied with the difference calculated above, the result obtained is then added to the same feature vector that was under consideration. The followed procedure then leads to a random point that is selected along the line segment between the two specific features. This approach effectively forces the decision region of the minority class to become more general. For each instance x_i in minority class, SMOTE searches its k nearest neighbors and one neighbor is randomly selected as x' (we call instances x_i and x' as seed sample). Then a random number between [0,1] δ is generated. The new artificial sample x_{new} is created as:

$$x_{new} = x_i + (x' - x_i) \times \delta$$

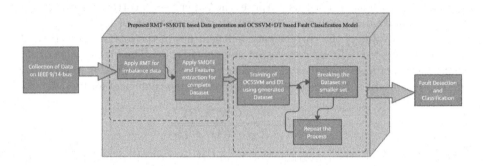

Fig. 1. Block Diagram of Proposed Model

4 Proposed Methodology: Detection and Classification of Line Faults

We have proposed the below steps for detection of faults in the power line Fig. 1:

1. Different IEEE bus architectures are considered, then different types of unsymmetrical faults are simulated between sections of transmission lines and buses.
2. Stable values of different electrical measurement vectors of corresponding buses are generated with the Matpower.
3. The equivalent structures of buses are established in Matlab to simulate faulty data corresponding to base values considered in the stable scenarios.
4. Different electrical measurement vectors are recorded, including phase angles of the voltage, the three-phase magnitudes and the current phase of the transmission line.
5. Stable and Faulty data sets were labeled accordingly.
6. RMT and SMOTE are used to tackle the issue of fault class imbalance.
7. Different Algorithms were fed with raw as well as curated Data-sets to record the progress.

5 Experiment and Analysis

5.1 Classification of Power System Faults Using Binary Classifier

The experiment was carried out in a phased manner so for the preparation of data used in phase 1, an IEEE 9-bus system and a 14-bus System, as shown in Fig. 1 and Fig. 2 respectively were implemented in MATLAB Simulink [28]. For 9 bus we deployed Six Three-Phase V-I Measurement components to replicate PMUs installed in power systems. Similarly, for 14 bus we deployed. 11 Three-Phase V-I Measurement components. For each PMU in 9-bus system, we recorded 18 different electrical quantities such as the magnitudes and related to voltage and current, Similarly for 14 bus 28 such electrical measurements are recorded. For example, the PMU at Bus 5 records the measured magnitudes and phase angles of the voltage phasor v_5 and the current phasors i_{75} and i_{54}. With the help of simulation, around 12000 groups of measurement vectors are gathered, which contains about 3300 of those contingency values defined above (L-G, L-L-G, L-L).

The contingency value set is considered according to [32] through which one can see the what type of contingency occur normal and which doesn't, hereby taking the ratio values as 65% for L-G, 22% for L-L-G and 13% for L-L which was considered as Data set 1.0, that contained only binary classes, the test bench for this data base was OCSSVM [4] which was used only to create a match-up system in consensus with Chen et al.'s [2] system of OCSVM, the produced results are depicted in Table 1. In comparison with this, we have shown the result in Table 2 as per given by author in [2]. Then we have compared our result as shown in Fig. 2 and established the accuracy of OCSSVM algorithm on proposed data model dataset 1.0. However later Deadset 1.0 was considered as meagre database with limited information to fault identification only rather than analysing the type of fault. This motivate us to go for further making of dataset 2.0 with a labelled fault category as explained in the next section.

5.2 Classification of Power System Faults Using Rule Based Decision Tree

In continuation to Data-set 1.0 which does not have the labelled fault category, we made an extension Dataset 2.0 which consists of 4 classes i.e. Stable(33750),

Table 1. Performance of Optimal Cost Sensitive Support Vector machines on Dataset 1.0

Iterations	10	150	300	600	850	999
IEEE_9 Bus						
FPR	11.96	10.53	8.22	5.46	3.62	2.72
FNR	12.94	7.54	6.63	5.55	4.83	4.48
IEEE_14 Bus						
FPR	16.95	14.56	11.30	8.81	4.21	2.82
FNR	17.96	16.02	12.74	7.04	6.19	4.89

Table 2. Performance of One Class Support Vector machines as per [2]

No.	1	2	3	4	5	6	7	8	9	10
IEEE_9 Bus										
FPR	4.35	4.45	4.05	4.55	4.10	4.50	4.35	4.65	5.05	4.05
FNR	3.40	4.00	4.20	2.70	3.40	3.30	2.70	4.80	2.20	3.60

Method Quality Parameters	IEEE 9 Bus RMT+SMOTE	IEEE 14 RMT+SMOTE	IEEE 9 bus[2] RMT+ADASYN
FPR	2.72	2.82	4.35
FNR	4.48	4.89	2.70

Fig. 2. Comparison with existing approach

LG(6750), LL(2813), LLG(1687) which further needed synthetic data set so as to tackle the problem of imbalanced data. To tackle this situation, we used synthetic technique SMOTE only on faulty data and eventually generated LG(1750), LL(813), LLG(687) data, so the total data set came out to be around 40,000. In the experiment, a total of 28 electrical values are measured, which includes the voltage and current magnitudes and phase angles. Only faulty data was generated through Simulink as stable data was available using Matpower [26,27]. A tolerance value of 1% was kept so as to emulate real-world scenarios. Later the data set after pre-processing was used with CNN, OCSSVM, Decision Tree and random forest for comparative studies and the result is stated in Table 3. From the table we have shown that our used model outperforms to other classifiers.

Table 3. Comparison of Fault detection with State-of-the-art on Dataset 2.0

Algorithm	IEEE 9-bus	IEEE 14-Bus
CNN [15]	87.68	83.42
OCS-SVM [2]	91.73	90.21
Random Forest [21]	94.0	97.0
Decision Tree (Our Approach)	95.8	97.6

6   Conclusion

To respond against the cyber attack, machine learning based classification approaches are well in advance and established. However, the methods rely on a good amount of contingency data for the training purpose which rarely occurs. So this work addresses the issue in a complete sense i.e. starting from data generation to the power fault detection and finally, the exact classification and thus can be considered as a complete solution for a power system. This experiment for this research work probes detection and classification of faults on the distribution line. We have used RMT and SMOTE as a data generation method for the generation of contingency data and generated 33750 stable and 11250 contingency data that contains various fault categories. For the fault detection, we used a modified OCSSVM model that gives FPR as 2.72 and FNR as 4.48 for the IEEE-9 bus system as compared to state of the art model that gave FPR as 4.05 and FNR as 3.60. To prove the efficacy of the proposed model, we have also tested the algorithm on the IEEE-14 bus system and find the FPR as 2.82 and FNR as 4.89. In extension to fault detection, we have also classified the correct fault on the generated data and achieved the accuracy of 95% on IEEE-9 bus and 97% on IEEE-14 bus and juxtaposed our result with state of the art techniques and shows the better performances. As a future scope of this work, we are planning for fault isolation and hardening scenario which would eventually lead to a smart grid restoration mechanism.

Funding. The work is partially funded by Department of Science and Technology(DST), and C3i-Hub (Indian Institute of Technology Kanpur), India for the Risk Averse Resilience Framework for Critical Infrastructure Security (RARCIS) project.

References

1. Xiong, Y., Yao, W., Chen, W., Fang, J., Ai, X., Wen, J.: A data-driven approach for fault time determination and fault area location using random matrix theory. Int. J. Electr. Power Energy Syst. **116**, 105566 (2020). ISSN 0142-0615. https://doi.org/10.1016/j.ijepes.2019.105566
2. Chen, H., Wang, J., Shi, D.: A data preparation method for machine-learning-based power system cyber-attack detection. In: International Conference on Power System Technology (POWERCON), pp. 3003–3009 (2018)
3. Benítez-Peña, S., Blanquero, R., Carrizosa, E., Ramírez-Cobo, P.: Cost-sensitive feature selection for support vector machines. Comput. Oper. Res. **106**, 169–178 (2019). ISSN 0305-0548, https://doi.org/10.1016/j.cor.2018.03.005
4. Yu, S., Li, X., Zhang, X., Wang, H.: The OCS-SVM: an objective-cost-sensitive SVM with sample-based misclassification cost invariance. IEEE Access **7**, 118931–118942 (2019)
5. Ozay, M., Esnaola, I., Vural, F.T.Y., Kulkarni, S.R., Poor, H.V.: Machine learning methods for attack detection in the smart grid. IEEE Trans. Neural Netw. Learn. Syst. **27**(8), 1773–1786 (2015)
6. He, Y., Mendis, G.J., Wei, J.: Real-time detection of false data injection attacks in smart grid: a deep learning-based intelligent mechanism. IEEE Trans. Smart Grid **8**(5), 2505–2516 (2017)
7. Pan, S., Morris, T., Adhikari, U.: Classification of disturbances and cyber-attacks in power systems using heterogeneous time-synchronized data. IEEE Trans. Industr. Inf. **11**(3), 650–662 (2015)
8. Khanna, K., Panigrahi, B.K., Joshi, A.: AI-based approach to identify compromised meters in data integrity attacks on smart grid. IET Gener. Transm. Distrib. **12**(5), 1052–1066 (2017)

9. He, X., Ai, Q., Qiu, R.C., Huang, W., Piao, L., Liu, H.: A big data architecture design for smart grids based on random matrix theory. IEEE Trans. Smart Grid **8**(2), 674–686 (2015)

10. Gonzales, R.C., Woods, R.E., Eddins, S.L.: Digital Image Processing. Prentice Hall, New Jersey (2002)

11. Qiu, R.C., Antonik, P.: Smart Grid Using Big Data Analytics: A Random Matrix Theory Approach. Wiley, New York (2017)

12. James, G., Witten, D., Hastie, T., Tibshirani, R.: An Introduction to Statistical Learning: with Applications in R. Springer, New York (2013). https://doi.org/10.1007/978-1-4614-7138-7

13. He, H., Bai, Y., Garcia, E.A., Li, S.: ADASYN: adaptive synthetic sampling approach for imbalanced learning. In: 2008 IEEE International Joint Conference on Neural Networks (IEEE World Congress on Computational Intelligence), pp. 1322–1328. IEEE, June 2008

14. Chawla, N.V., Bowyer, K.W., Hall, L.O., Kegelmeyer, W.P.: SMOTE: synthetic minority over-sampling technique. J. Artif. Intell. Res. **16**, 321–357 (2002)

15. Min, F., et al.: Fault prediction for distribution network based on CNN and Light-GBM algorithm. In: 14th IEEE International Conference on Electronic Measurement & Instruments (ICEMI), Changsha, China, 2019, pp. 1020–1026 (2019). https://doi.org/10.1109/ICEMI46757.2019.9101423

16. Lu, X., et al.: Fault diagnosis for photovoltaic array based on convolutional neural network and electrical time series graph. Energy Convers. Manag. **196**, 950–965 (2019). ISSN 0196-8904, https://doi.org/10.1016/j.enconman.2019.06.062

17. Tuballa, M.L., Abundo, M.L.: A review of the development of smart grid technologies. Renew. Sustain. Energy Rev. **59**, 710–725 (2016)

18. LeCun, Y., Bengio, Y., Hinton, G.: Deep learning. Nature **521**, 436–444 (2015). https://doi.org/10.1038/nature14539

19. Sundararajan, A., Riggs, H., Jeewani, A., Sarwat, A.I.: Cluster-based module to manage smart grid data for an enhanced situation awareness: a case study. In: Resilience Week (RWS). San Antonio, TX, USA 2019, pp. 81–87 (2019). https://doi.org/10.1109/RWS47064.2019.8971817

20. da Costa, C.H., et al.: A comparison of machine learning-based methods for fault classification in photovoltaic systems. In: IEEE PES Innovative Smart Grid Technologies Conference - Latin America (ISGT Latin America), Gramado, Brazil 2019, pp. 1–6 (2019). https://doi.org/10.1109/ISGT-LA.2019.8895279

21. Bala, P., Dalai, S.: Random forest based fault analysis method in IEEE 14 bus system. In: 2017 3rd International Conference on Condition Assessment Techniques in Electrical Systems (CATCON), Rupnagar, pp. 407–411 (2017). https://doi.org/10.1109/CATCON.2017.8280254

22. Yao, W., Gao, X., Liu, S., Zhang, Y., Wang, X.: A CNN-based fault section location method in distribution network using distribution-level PMU data. In: Xue, Y., Zheng, Y., Rahman, S. (eds.) Proceedings of PURPLE MOUNTAIN FORUM 2019-International Forum on Smart Grid Protection and Control. LNEE, vol. 585, pp. 623–633. Springer, Singapore (2020). https://doi.org/10.1007/978-981-13-9783-7_51

23. Davagdorj, K., Lee, J.S., Pham, V.H., Ryu, K.H.: A comparative analysis of machine learning methods for class imbalance in a smoking cessation intervention. Appl. Sci. **10**(9), 3307 (2020)

24. Nimankar, S.S., Vora, D.: Designing a model to handle imbalance data classification using SMOTE and optimized classifier. In: Sharma, N., Chakrabarti, A., Balas,

V.E., Martinovic, J. (eds.) Data Management, Analytics and Innovation. AISC, vol. 1174, pp. 323–334. Springer, Singapore (2021). https://doi.org/10.1007/978-981-15-5616-6_23

25. Mohammadpourfard, M., Sami, A., Seifi, A.R.: A statistical unsupervised method against false data injection attacks: a visualization-based approach. Expert Syst. Appl. **84**, 242–261 (2017)

26. Zimmerman, R.D., Murillo-Sanchez, C.E.: MATPOWER (Version 7.0) [Software] (2019). https://matpower.org

27. Zimmerman, R.D., Murillo-Sanchez, C.E., Thomas, R.J.: MATPOWER: steady-state operations, planning and analysis tools for power systems research and education. IEEE Trans. Power Syst. **26**(1), 12–19 (2011)

28. Simulink Documentation: Simulation and Model-Based Design. MathWorks (2020). https://www.mathworks.com/products/simulink.html

29. Nicholson, A., Webber, S., Dyer, S., Patel, T., Janicke, H.: SCADA security in the light of cyber-warfare. Comput. Secur. **31**(4), 418–436 (2012)

30. Roop, D.W.: Power System SCADA and Smart Grids (2015)

31. Breiman, L.: Random forests. Mach. Learn. **45**(1), 5–32 (2001)

32. Goswami, T., Roy, U.B.: Predictive model for classification of power system faults using machine learning. In: TENCON 2019–2019 IEEE Region 10 Conference (TENCON). IEEE (2019)

33. Ozay, M., Esnaola, I., Yarman Vural, F.T., Kulkarni, S.R., Poor, H.V.: Machine learning methods for attack detection in the smart grid. IEEE Trans. Neural Netw. Learn. Syst. **27**(8), 1773–1786 (2016). https://doi.org/10.1109/TNNLS.2015.2404803

34. Chen, H., Wang, J., Shi, D.: A data preparation method for machine-learning-based power system cyber-attack detection. In: International Conference on Power System Technology (POWERCON) 2018, pp. 3003–3009 (2018)

35. He, X., Ai, Q., Qiu, R.C., Huang, W., Piao, L., Liu, H.: A big data architecture design for smart grids based on random matrix theory. IEEE Trans. Smart Grid **8**(2), 674–686 (2017). https://doi.org/10.1109/TSG.2015.2445828

Deep Reinforcement Learning with Comprehensive Reward for Stock Trading

Qibin Zhou$^{(\boxtimes)}$, Tuo Qu, Yuntao Han, and Fuqing Duan

Beijing Normal University, Beijing, China
201921210056@mail.bnu.edu.cn

Abstract. Stock trading is one of economically research hotspots. In the past decades, many researchers used machine learning methods to simply predict the short-term price of stocks or long-term trend of stocks. However, only by comprehensive consideration of these two we can better reduce the risk of stock trading. This paper models stock trading as an incomplete information game, and proposes a deep reinforcement learning framework for training trading agents. In order to make well use of the temporal relation of stock data, we select the most advanced Temporal Convolutional Network and Transformer network as the policy network in deep reinforcement learning, and use TRPO and PPO for policy optimization. We propose a reward function that integrates short-term stock price prediction and long-term stock trend prediction with controllable risks to compute the utility of the agent action, which allows the agent to learn low risk trading strategies. The trading experiment in the standard & poor 500 ETF (S&P500 index) validates the proposed deep reinforcement learning method, and the experimental results show that the strategies by the proposed method in economic indicators (Maximum drawdown, Sharpe Ratio, Return Curve) are better than the S&P500 ETF baseline strategy.

Keywords: Incomplete Information Game · Stock Trading · Deep Reinforcement Learning · Policy Optimization · Transformer

1 Introduction

Stocks are issued for a company to raise funds for its own development, and they are transferred, traded and circulated at the stock market. Investors usually formulate stock trading strategies based on their perception of the stock market. With the increasing of investors, the stock market becomes competitive, and the investors want to obtain more information to make reasonable investment strategies. Hence, most investors model the stock market with machine learning algorithms [1,2], which can help investors to make decisions to increase return and

Supported by National Key Research and Development Project under Grant 2018AAA01008-02.

reduce risk. However, stock market are affected by many factors such as government policy, investor's expectations, global economic situations and correlations with other markets. As Anish and Majhi described [19], stock markets are a complex, evolutionary and nonlinear dynamic system whose prediction is considered a challenging task. A stock prediction model usually takes time-series data from past prices or information from news media as input, and predicts stock trends by analyzing past market behavior [5]. With the excellent performance of deep learning in many other fields, deep neural networks are increasingly being used to model stock markets due to their strong nonlinear representation capability [4–6]. However, the stock price changes are non-stationary, and often include many unexpected jumping and moving because of too many influencing factors. So deep neural networks used for simple price regression are prone to be over-fitting, which makes the stock price prediction unreliable [6]. Recently, some researchers [10–18] try to use deep neural networks combined with reinforcement learning to train agents, which make dynamic decisions by exploring the unknown stock market environment. For example, Azhikodan et al. [22] used a deep deterministic policy gradient-based neural network model to train trading agents, along with a deep recurrent convolutional neural network for market sentiment analysis from the financial news. They proved that DRL is capable of learning the tricks of stock trading. Liu et al. [17] developed the FINRL library, which simulates trading environments across various stock markets, including NASDAQ-100, DJIA, S&P 500, HSI, SSE 50, and CSI, incorporates trading constraints such as transaction cost, market liquidity and the investor's degree of risk-aversion, and provides state-of-the-art DRL algorithms such as DQN, DDPG, PPO, SAC, A2C, TD3, etc. Although deep reinforcement learning has shown promising results in stock trading, training a good agent is still challenging due to incomplete market environment information. The agent needs a powerful strategy network model and a reasonable reinforcement learning optimization algorithm to learn the key information of stock market. This paper proposes a deep reinforcement learning method that can maximize the learning effect of a single agent in the stock market. We model stock trading as an incomplete information game and use DRL to optimize the agents based on the solution method of the incomplete information game. In order to make well use of the temporal relation of stock data, we select the most advanced Temporal Convolutional Network TCN [9] and Transformer network [8] as the policy network, which can better extract the informative features from time-series stock data. We design a reward function that enables the agent to learn the short-term stock price and the long-term stock trend, so that the agent can make a reasonable decision by combining these two key characteristics. Moreover, a risk control factor is introduced into the reward function, and the agent is trained based on the variance of risk tolerance.

2   Method

Stock trading can be seen as an incomplete information game between an agent and the stock market environment. The deep reinforcement learning framework for stock trading is shown in Fig. 1. It includes two parts: one part is the policy network of the agent, which outputs the probability distribution of the strategy actions. The other is the policy network optimization with a reinforcement learning algorithm during the interacting between agent and environment.

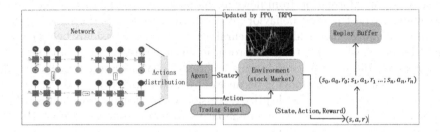

Fig. 1. framework of deep reinforcement learning in stock trading

2.1 Policy Network Model

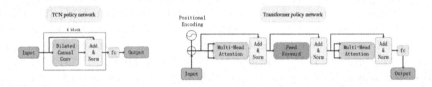

Fig. 2. policy network model

Stock trading prediction is a classical time series prediction task, and it needs to make use of the temporal correlation of the stock price changes. Several network models like Recurrent Neural Network (RNN), Long Short-Term Memory network (LSTM), Temporal Convolutional Network (TCN) and Transformer network are specially designed for modeling time series data. However, LSTM and RNN are extremely computationally intensive, since they cannot perform massive parallel processing due to their memory mechanism. Moreover, the long term information they store is limited. TCN uses the convolutional structure to extract features and captures time dependent information by using causal convolution and dilated convolution. TCN can not only capture local information, but also is good at capturing data relation in long time series with parallel processing. Transformer model adopts the encoder- decoder structure and self-attention mechanism. The network architecture supports massive parallel processing, while the self-attention components can learn the self-correlation information of the stock price sequence. Compared with LSTM and RNN, TCN and Transformer showed better performance on multiple tasks. Therefore, we use TCN and Transformer to build policy network.

TCN and Transformer are designed mainly for Seq2Seq tasks. Because stock trading is not a Seq2Seqe task, we modify the original TCN and transformer architecture as the policy network. Figure 2 shows the TCN network we use, the output of the Seq2Seq task is changed to output y which is the probability distribution of the actions in stock trading. Figure 2 shows the transformer we use. We only use the encoder module in transformer, where the multi-head attention module can extract different position information of a sequence and calculate the correlation between different positions of the sequence. Next to the multi-head attention module, a position-wise fully connected feed-forward network is used transform the attention features to the probability distribution of the actions.

2.2   Policy Network Optimization by RL

Since stock trading is an incomplete information game, the stock price may rise or fall in the same state, and thus the value function in the same state is different, which often makes the value based method difficult to converge stably. The counterfactual regret minimization algorithm [7] is commonly used to find the Nash equilibrium strategy of incomplete information games. It calculates the probability distribution of actions by accumulated regret values. Therefore, the policy based RL is more appropriate for learning stock trading strategies, because it is similar to the counterfactual regret minimization algorithm in principle.

Assuming consecutive $T + 1$ trading operations starting from the state s at a certain trading moment to be a complete episode, then τ_s is the episode formed from state s. In such an episode the agent continuously interacts with the environment to form a sequence $\tau_s = \{s, a, s_1, a_1, \ldots s_T, a_T\}$, with a reward r_t obtained for each action a_t, and R is the total reward obtained by a complete episode. The agents' objective is learning strategy π by maximizing a value function $V_\pi(s)$, which is an expected return of the strategy π in the state s. The objective is learning strategy π by maximizing a value function $V_\pi(s)$.

$$V^*(s) = \max_\pi \; V_\pi(s) \tag{1}$$

$$V_{\pi(\theta)}(s) = \sum_{\tau_s} R(\tau_s) P_\pi(\tau_s), \quad R(\tau_s) = \sum_{t=1}^{T} \gamma^t r_t \tag{2}$$

$$P_\pi(\tau_s) = P(s) \prod_{t=1}^{T} P_\pi(a_t|s_t) P(s_{t+1}|s_t, a_t) \tag{3}$$

where $P_\pi(\tau_s)$ is the probability distribution of τ_s, γ is discount factor, $0 \leq \gamma \leq 1$, $P_\pi(s_{t+1}|s_t, a_t)$ can be obtained by counting history stock data.

Therefore, the policy network can be continuously updated according to the gradient ascent with learning rate α as follows.

$$\theta = \theta + \alpha \nabla V_{\pi(\theta)} \tag{4}$$

As in [21], in order to make the strategy converge stably during training of the policy network, an advantage function $A_{\bar{\pi}}(s, a)$ is used to replace $R(\tau_s)$.

Assume N episodes are sampled by Monte Carlo sampling. The average return of N sampled times is taken as the baseline, and the difference between the return of each episodes and the baseline is taken as the advantage return of (s_t, a_t).

$$A_{\bar{\pi}}(s_t, a_t) = R(\tau_t) - \frac{1}{N} \sum_{n=1}^{N} R(\tau_n) \tag{5}$$

where $\bar{\pi}$ is the last updated strategy, and it is used to sample state s_t and action a_t, τ_t is the episode starting from state s_t.

Then the expected return V_π becomes as follows:

$$V_\pi = \sum_\tau A_{\bar{\pi}}(s_t, a_t) P_\pi(\tau_t) \tag{6}$$

$$\nabla V_{\pi(\theta)} = \frac{1}{N} \sum_{n=1}^{N} \sum_{t=t_n+1}^{t_n+T} A_{\bar{\pi}}(s_{t_n}, a_{t_n}) \nabla \log P_{\pi(\theta)}(a_t|s_t) \tag{7}$$

where θ in strategy π is a variable and $P_{\pi(\theta)}(a_t|s_t)$ is the output of the policy network, and the others can be obtained after sampling by the $\bar{\pi}$.

Generally, policy based RL has two flaws. The first is that strategy π is updated by data that must be sampled based on the latest policy $\bar{\pi}$, resulting in low efficiency of sampling data. The second is that the learning rate needs to be set manually. If the learning rate is not appropriate, the updated strategy will become worse the previous strategy. Proximal Policy Optimization (PPO) [20] can well determine the step-size. Meanwhile, it uses an approximate data distribution for the real distribution estimate, which makes it achievable to use the data sampled by previous policy to update the policy. Assuming that the data distribution approximate to the real data distribution P_π is $q_{\bar{\pi}'}$, where $\bar{\pi}'$ is the previous policy, then the expected return V_π can be written as

$$V_{\pi(\theta)} = \sum_{\tau_t} A_{\bar{\pi}'}(s_t, a_t) q_{\bar{\pi}'}(\tau_t) \frac{P_{\pi(\theta)}(\tau_t)}{q_{\bar{\pi}'}(\tau_t)} \tag{8}$$

$$\nabla V_{\pi(\theta)} = \sum_{\tau_{t_n}} q_{\bar{\pi}'}(\tau_{t_n}) \sum_{t=t_n+1}^{t_n+T} K\mu A_{\bar{\pi}'}(s_{t_n}, a_{t_n}) \nabla \log P_{\pi(\theta)}(a_t|s_t) \tag{9}$$

$$K = \frac{P_{\pi(\theta)}(a_t|s_t)}{q_{\bar{\pi}'}(a_t|s_t)}, \quad \mu = \frac{P_{\pi(\theta)}(s_t)}{q_{\bar{\pi}'}(s_t)} \tag{10}$$

Since P_π and $q_{\bar{\pi}'}$ should be as close as possible, the KL divergence can be used as the constraint condition. Then integrate Eq. (10), and the expected return V_π becomes:

$$V_{\pi(\theta)} = \sum_{(s_t, a_t)} KA_{\bar{\pi}'}(s_t, a_t) - \beta div_{KL}(P_{\pi(\theta)}, q_{\bar{\pi}'}) \tag{11}$$

where div_{KL} is the KL divergence, β is a hyperparameter which is difficult to be set. Since an inappropriate β leads to non-convergence, a function clip is defined to replace KL constraint.

$$clip\left(K\right) = \begin{cases} 1 + \epsilon, \, if \; K > \; 1 + \epsilon, A_{\bar{\pi}'}\left(s_t, a_t\right) > 0 \\ 1 - \epsilon, \, if \; K < \; 1 - \epsilon, A_{\bar{\pi}'}\left(s_t, a_t\right) \leq 0 \\ K, \qquad\qquad\qquad\qquad else \end{cases} \qquad (12)$$

where ϵ is the hyperparameter, and is set to 0.2 in the experiment. Then the PPO objective function is as follows:

$$V_{\pi(\theta)} \approx \sum_{(s_t, a_t)} \min\left(K A_{\bar{\pi}'}\left(s_t, a_t\right), \; clip\left(K\right) A_{\bar{\pi}'}\left(s_t, a_t\right)\right) \qquad (13)$$

Then the policy network can be updated by substituting Eq. (13) into Eq. (4).

Similar to PPO, Trust Region Policy Optimization (TRPO) [21] is a method that can monotonously improve the strategy. TRPO optimizes the strategy $\pi\left(\theta\right)$ by maximizing the objective value function $V_{\pi(\theta)}$ under constrained conditions based on the trust area in $\bar{\pi}'$.

$$V_{\pi(\theta)} = \sum_{\tau_{t_n}} q_{\bar{\pi}'}\left(\tau_{t_n}\right) \sum_{t=t_n+1}^{t_n+T} \frac{P_{\pi(\theta)}\left(a_t|s_t\right)}{q_{\bar{\pi}'}\left(a_t|s_t\right)} A_{\bar{\pi}'}\left(s_{t_n}, a_{t_n}\right), s.t. div_{KL}\left(P_{\pi(\theta)}, q_{\bar{\pi}'}\right) < \delta \qquad (14)$$

where δ is an adaptive constraint. Then the policy network can be updated by substituting Eq. (14) into Eq. (4). Before next update of the policy network, the old policy $\bar{\pi}'$ is updated by current policy $\pi\left(\theta\right)$. In our experiment, given an initial value δ_0, δ is adaptively adjusted in the learning process as Eq. (15), which means the constraint is enhanced if the KL divergence is very different, otherwise the constraint is weaken.

$$\delta = \begin{cases} 0.5 \; * \delta, \, div_{KL}\left(\pi_{old}, \pi\right) \leq 0.01 \\ 2 \; * \delta, \quad div_{KL}\left(\pi_{old}, \pi\right) > 0.01 \end{cases} \qquad (15)$$

2.3 Proposal Reward Function

Here, we discuss how to calculate the reward r_t after taking an action a_t in the state s_t. In order to improve the anti-risk ability, we propose a reward function that enables the agent to learn the short-term stock price and the long-term stock trend. Thus the agent can comprehensively consider the possible profit and loss for action at the current moment. The problem of daily stock trading (short-term trading) can be transferred into predicting whether the stock open on $T+1$ trading day is higher than the stock open on T trading day. The reward for learning short-term stock open is as follows:

$$r_{short} = \begin{cases} O_{T+1} - O_T \; if \; action \; is \; buy \\ O_T - O_{T+1} \; if \; action \; is \; sell \end{cases} \qquad (16)$$

where O_T is stock open on the T trading day, O_{T+1} is stock open on the $T+1$ trading day. Long-term stock price trend is evaluated by the average change trend of stock prices in the next 20 trading days after the T trading day. We use linear regression to fit the stock price trend in the next 20 trading days as follow:

$$O_T = k_0 + k_1 T \tag{17}$$

where k_1 is the average change trend of stocks in the next 20 stock trading days. The reward for learning long-term stock trend is calculated as:

$$r_{long} = \begin{cases} k_1 * O_T & if \ action \ is \ buy \\ -k_1 * O_T & if \ action \ is \ sell \end{cases} \tag{18}$$

The comprehensive reward is as follows:

$$r_t = \begin{cases} VA & if \ VA > 0 \\ VA - \varphi & if \ VA < 0 \end{cases} \tag{19}$$

$$VA = \alpha r_{short} + \beta r_{long} - O_T * L \tag{20}$$

where L is a rate of commission charge for each buy or sell action, α and β are hyperparameters and $\alpha + \beta = 1$. If $\alpha = 1, \beta = 0$, the trained model becomes a short-term stock prediction model. If $\alpha = 0, \beta = 1$, the trained model becomes a stock trend prediction model. $\varphi \ (\varphi \geq 0)$ is a hyperparameter that controls the risk of trading. If the risk tolerance for trader is low, φ can be set as large as possible, which will make agent reduce the probability of choosing higher-risk actions.

2.4 Sentiment Analysis of Stock

Stock sentiment analysis is of great significance in financial market research. Since stock data has a lot of noise, it is not possible to obtain a effective policy based only on stock fundamental indicators and stock price technical indicators MACD. To solve this problem, this paper adds a BERT-based Chinese stock comment sentiment indicator [27]. We concatenate the sentiment indicator into stock data as neural network input.

We used the Chinese pre-training model trained by Google and the dataset to get a sentiment model. Then we use the sentiment model to compute the sentiment indicator.

3 Experiment

We select the Standard & Poor's 500 (S&P500) data set, which is widely used in stock trading system test, to verify the proposal method. The S&P500 and S&P500 index reflect the trend of the US stock market. The datetime, open, close, high, low, volume of each stock at different time frequency (e.g. 5 min, 10 min, 1 h, 1 day, etc.) can be obtained.

3.1 Evaluation Criterion

Accuracy. According to the known stock price information, the policy evaluation can be converted into the accuracy evaluation of the classification task. More precisely, given the stock price data during a period of stock trading days, the action every stock trading day taken by the agent is compared with the best action determined by known stock price information to compute the "f1 score" classification accuracy.

Maximum Drawdown (MDD). A drawdown refers to an investment or fund declining from peak to trough during a specific period, and it is computed as the percentage between the peak and the subsequent trough. In a long period, there will be several drawdowns, and the largest drawdown will be selected as the maximum drawdown, which is an important risk indicator in investment analysis. It is mainly used to measure the loss rate of an investment in the worst case as follows:

$$MDD = \frac{MA - MI}{MA} \tag{21}$$

where MA is the peak of the maximum drawdown, MI is the trough of the maximum drawdown.

Sharpe Ratio. The sharpe ratio is a classic indicator that comprehensively takes into account both returns and risks. It mainly evaluates the rate of return that can be obtained under a fixed tolerable risk. In other words, the risk needs to be assumed under a fixed expected return. It is calculated as:

$$SharpRatio = \frac{E(R_p) - E\left(\bar{R}_p\right)}{\sigma_p} \tag{22}$$

where $E(R_p)$ is the expected return rate of the investment, $E\left(\bar{R}_p\right)$ is the expected return rate of risk-free investment, σ_p is standard deviation of the investment's excess return.

Maximum Drawdown (MDD). A drawdown refers to an investment or fund declining from peak to trough during a specific period, and it is computed as the percentage between the peak and the subsequent trough. In a long period, there will be several drawdowns, and the largest drawdown will be selected as the maximum drawdown, which is an important risk indicator in investment analysis. It is mainly used to measure the loss rate of an investment in the worst case as follows:

$$R_T = (C + R_{T-1}) * H * CR - (C + R_{T-1}) * L, \ CR = \frac{O_{T+1} - O_T}{O_T} \tag{23}$$

where H is holding position ($H \in \{1, \ 0.5, \ 0.25, \ 0\}$), CR is Change Ratio of stock, O_{T+1}, O_T and L have the same meanings as (27).

3.2   Implentation Details

The experiment uses Python development tools on the keras platform, and runs on 64-bit operating system (Linux Ubuntu), with 128G of RAM and Nvidia GTX 2080ti. 256 samples as a batch-size are randomly selected from the replay buffer to train the policy network each time, the learning rate is set to 0.00025, the optimization method is ADAM, and the discount factor γ is set to 0.99. In training agents, the Eq. (19) is used to calculate the reward. The commission charge rate is set to 0.15%. The risk-free annual rate of return is 2% to calculate the sharpe ratio. S&P500 stocks and S&P500 index from 2010 to 2019 are used as training data, while those in 2020 as test data. The initial investment amount is set to 1. We use

We task the Buy-Hold strategy [21] for S&P500 index during a period of time as the baseline strategy (BS) to compare with our agents' strategy. It is a strategy model commonly used in long-term investment and is usually used as a benchmark to evaluate the profitability of investment strategies.

3.3   Results and Discussion

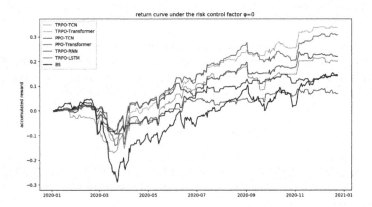

Fig. 3. Under the risk control factor $\varphi = 0$, the cumulative return curve of different agents on the S&P500 index in 2020

We train 4 agents by using TCN and Transformer as the policy network with TRPO and PPO used for policy optimization respectively. For comparison, 2 agents are trained with TRPO by using the two neural network models, RNN and LSTM as the policy network, and one agent using baseline strategy is also presented. The return curve of each agent is shown in Fig. 3. We can see that the cumulative returns of the four agents using TCN and Transformer are better that those of the other three agents using RNN, LSTM and baseline, while the performance of the agents using RNN and LSTM is not much different with the performance of the baseline strategy after the networks converge, which shows that compared with RNN and LSTM, TCN and Transformer can more effectively extract key information from the sequence to make decision as well as they can extract more essential characteristic information and make agents get better strategy.

In 2020, due to the impact of the COVID, there are several circuit breakers in the U.S. stock market which cause the stock market crashing. From Fig. 3, we can conclude that our agents can learn to cut losses in time when the stock market falls sharply, enter the stock market in time when the stock market recovers, and rise to obtain a higher rate of return. These indicate that the proposal reward function enables the agent to integrate the short-term stock price and the long-term stock trend of the stock characteristics to obtain a lower-risk strategy. Table 1 shows the other evaluation indicators (MDD, sharpe ratio, return ratio) under various risk for baseline and the agents using TCN and Transformer.

Table 1. The performance of different strategies in various evaluation criterions under various risk control factor.

φ	S&P500 index in 2020	accuracy	Maximum drawdown	Sharpe ratio	Return ratio of year
–	BS	–	33.78%	0.545	14.49%
0	TRPO-TCN	79.3%	17.42%	1.089	20.11%
	TRPO-Transformer	86.54%	14.56%	1.912	33.7%
	PPO-TCN	78.69%	10.42%	1.274	21.95%
	PPO-Transformer	84.98%	12.07%	1.798	30.75%
50	TRPO-TCN	44.92%	11.69%	1.337	18.74%
	TRPO-Transformer	49.33%	9.41%	2.187	20.84%
	PPO-TCN	44.99%	10.05%	1.299	17.68%
	PPO-Transformer	50.04%	10.15%	1.866	21.3%

From Table 1, we notice that affected by the risk control factor φ, in order to reduce the risk of trading, the agent will reduce the times of trading, so that the agent doesn't take action when the growth rate for stock is low, resulting in a relatively low classification accuracy in $\varphi = 50$. According to the sharpe ratio, maximum retracement rate and annual return, we can see from Table 1 that the policy network using the transformer network is better than the policy network using the TCN network. From the perspective of various indicators, the performance of the policy networks optimized by the TRPO and those by PPO is not much different, but the agents trained by TRPO are better than the agents trained by PPO in more indicators. When the risk control factor φ is large, the agent learns a more conservative strategy, obtaining a better return with a lower MDD, and more importantly the sharp of ratio is as high as 2.187. It indicates that the agent has learned the strategy of obtaining higher return under lower risk. When $\varphi = 0$, the MDD of the TRPO-Transformer algorithm is 14.56%. When $\varphi = 50$, the MDD of the TRPO-Transformer algorithm is

9.41%. These prove that the risk control factor φ can make the agent well learn a lower risk strategy. More importantly, we can see that the performance of these agents in all evaluation indicators is much better than the baseline. From the experiment analysis above, we conclude that the proposal method is effective for stock trading and can be used for stock trading in different countries.

4   Conclusion

Stock trading is one of economically research hotspots. This paper models stock trading as an incomplete information game, and proposes a deep reinforcement learning framework for training trading agents. In order to make well use of the temporal relation of stock data, we select the most advanced Temporal Convolutional Network and Transformer network as the policy network in deep reinforcement learning. A reward function that can learn short-term stock prices and long-term stock trends is proposed, and it allows the agent to learn low risk trading strategies by integrating two important features of the stock market. We also add a risk control factor to enable the agent to learn trading strategies under different risks. Traders can choose the agent with different ability to resist risks, according to their own risk tolerance. The trading experiment in the standard & poor 500 ETF (S&P500 index) validates the proposed deep reinforcement learning method. The method can be extended to other countries' stock markets, even futures markets and foreign exchange markets.

References

1. Zhang, Y., et al.: Stock market prediction of S&P 500 via combination of improved BCO approach and BP neural network. Expert Syst. Appl. **36**, 8849–8854 (2009)
2. Man Chon, U., Rasheed, K.: A relative tendency based stock market prediction system. In: 2010 Ninth International Conference on Machine Learning and Applications, Washington, pp. 949–953 (2010)
3. Rapach, D.E., Strauss, J.K., Zhou, G.: International stock return predictability: what is the role of the United States. J. Finance 46 (2012)
4. Graves, A.: Sequence transduction with recurrent neural networks. In: International Conference of Machine Learning (ICML) (2012)
5. Iqbal, Z., et al.: Efficient machine learning techniques for stock market prediction. Engineering Research and Applications (2013)
6. Chen, K., et al.: A LSTM-based method for stock returns prediction: a case study of China stock market. In: IEEE International Conference on Big Data IEEE (2015)
7. Murekachiro, D.: A review of artificial neural networks application to stock market predictions. Network and Complex Systems (2016)
8. Akita, R., Yoshihara, A., Matsubara, T., Uehara, K.: Deep learning for stock prediction using numerical and textual information. In: International Conference on Computer and Information Science (ICIS) (2016)
9. Burch, N.: Time and space: why imperfect information games are hard. Ph.D. thesis, University of Alberta (2017)
10. Vaswani, A., et al.: Attention is all you need. In: Neural Information Processing Systems (NIPS) (2017)

11. Bai, S., et al.: An empirical evaluation of generic convolutional and recurrent networks for sequence modeling. arXiv preprint arXiv:1803.01271 (2018)
12. Li, X., Li, Y., Zhan, Y., Liu, X.-Y.: Optimistic bull or pessimistic bear: adaptive deep reinforcement learning for stock portfolio allocation. arXiv preprint arXiv:1907.01503 (2019)
13. Meng, T.L., Khushi, M.: Reinforcement learning in financial markets. Data 4(3), 110 (2019). https://doi.org/10.3390/data4030110
14. Li, Y., Ni, P., Chang, V.: Application of deep reinforcement learning in stock trading strategies and stock forecasting. Computing 102, 1305–1322 (2020)
15. Yuan, Y., Wen, W., Yang, J.: Using data augmentation based reinforcement learning for daily stock trading. Electronics 9(9), 1384 (2020). https://doi.org/10.3390/electronics9091384
16. Wu, X., Chen, H., Wang, J., Troiano, L., et al.: Adaptive stock trading strategies with deep reinforcement learning methods. Inf. Sci. 538, 142–158 (2020)
17. National University of Singapore, Singapore, Trung Hieu, L.: Deep reinforcement learning for stock portfolio optimization. IJMO 10(5), 139–144 (2020). https://doi.org/10.7763/IJMO.2020.V10.761
18. Badr, H., Ouhbi, B., Frikh, B.: Rules based policy for stock trading: a new deep reinforcement learning method. In: 2020 5th International Conference on Cloud Computing and Artificial Intelligence (2020)
19. Liu, X.-Y., et al.: FinRL: a deep reinforcement learning library for automated stock trading in quantitative finance. arXiv preprint arXiv:2011.09607 (2020)
20. Carta, S., et al.: A multi-layer and multi-ensemble stock trader using deep learning and deep reinforcement learning. Appl. Intell. 51, 889–905 (2021)
21. Carta, S., et al.: Multi-DQN: an ensemble of Deep Q-learning agents for stock market forecasting. Expert Syst. Appl. 164, 113820 (2021)
22. Anish, C.M., Majhi, B.: Hybrid nonlinear adaptive scheme for stock market prediction using feedback FLANN and factor analysis. J. Korean Stat. Soc. 45, 64–76 (2016)
23. Schulman, J., Levine, S., Moritz, P., Jordan, M.I., Abbeel, P., Wang, J.: Trust region policy optimization. In: International Conference on Machine Learning (2015)
24. Wang, Y., He, H., Tan, X., Gan, Y.: Trust region-guided proximal policy optimization. In: Conference and Workshop on Neural Information Processing (2019)
25. Azhikodan, A.R., Bhat, A.G.K., Jadhav, M.V.: Stock trading bot using deep reinforcement learning. In: Innovations in Computer Science and Engineering (2019)
26. Xu, Y., Yang, C., Peng, S., Nojima, Y.: A hybrid two-stage financial stock forecasting algorithm based on clustering and ensemble learning. Appl. Intell. 50(11), 3852–3867 (2020). https://doi.org/10.1007/s10489-020-01766-5
27. Li, M., Chen, L., Zhao, J., Li, Q.: Sentiment analysis of Chinese stock reviews based on BERT model. Appl. Intell. 51(7), 5016–5024 (2021). https://doi.org/10.1007/s10489-020-02101-8

Deep Learning Based Automobile Identification Application

Pattanapong Chantamit-o-Pas[✉], Pattanayu Sangaroon, and Jukkapat Srisura

School of Information Technology, King Mongkut's Institute of Technology Ladkrabang,
Ladkrabang 10520, Bangkok, Thailand
{Pattanapong,61070309,61070281}@it.kmitl.ac.th

Abstract. Today, the high competition among domestic automobile manufacturers is intense situation than previous years. This result gives advantages in a good variety of brands, models, engine sizes and appearances. This can cause some critical issues in recognizing and recalling a car by manufacturer. In addition, an owner may modify some parts of original vehicle such as the head bumper, the rear bumper, and the head light. This modification also affects the people who are looking for pre-owned cars. Despite the fact, the details are mismatch with the vehicle registration book that issued by the Department of Land Transport. From this incident, the researchers implemented a convolutional neural network (CNN) in the identification of vehicle characteristics to reduce the ambiguity for each car's models. The researchers conducted experiments using five algorithms. SVM, ResNet34, ResNet50 and Inception-ResNetV2. The researchers set up a library of two car models, Toyota Hilux and Honda Civic sedan and Civic Hatchback, including models from past ten years ago until the present. The images are of 224×224 pixels. The data are categorized into two sets, a training set has 1,449 images which is counted as 80% of total images and a testing set is having 362 images which is about 20% of total. The total images are 1,811 and 26 Classes. Our experiments compared the accuracies of SVM, ResNet34, ResNet50, and Inception-ResNetV2, which came out to be 21.4%, 55.5%, 66.6%, and 92.8% respectively. As a result, Inception-ResNetV2 outperforms among all other methods.

Keywords: Automobile image · Image Recognition · Convolutional Neural Network

1 Introduction

Today, the competition among domestic car producers is stronger than before. This impacts many brands, models, engine sizes and looks. This leads to difficulty in identifying and recognizing each car model. Most manufacturers tend to modify internal and external equipment each year, as known as facelift or minor change. To make the model modern, the manufacturer has to enhance its functionality and appearance. This substantially modification raises the number of car images and its value. Some of them

M. Tanveer et al. (Eds.): ICONIP 2022, CCIS 1794, pp. 542–552, 2023.
https://doi.org/10.1007/978-981-99-1648-1_45

are still resembled the model since it was built up. The facelift does not involve customers who buy new cars but may confuse those who plan to buy a pre-owned one. In taking a used car, the crucial considerations are the appearance and the features of the car. Apart from the details noted in the Department of Land Transport registration book of each vehicle, the actual appearance of a car can be altered by its former owner. The modification involves parts such as the head bumper, the rear bumper, or the head light. This can confuse customers who plan to buy used cars as the resemblance make it harder to precisely identify the model in spite of taking the retails in the registration book. In term of the insurance company, an identification of the model of the car to claim to the insurance company. They need to know about the car model before ordering spare parts and maintenance. That prevents order mistakes of parts. Furthermore, the modification perplexes the task of the police when a car is involved in a crime.

From the matter indicated above, there have been a number of researchers who suggested the application of a convolutional neural network (CNN) in identifying a car. CNN is design to extract the feature of complicated data, data that are not well organized and unstructured data, such as images. In most cases, VGG16 is employed with the using Kernels 3x3 to resize image in categorization and identification of the required image property. The researchers used Deep Learning Algorithm to develop prediction models such as ResNet34, ResNet50 and Inception ResNet V2, by using multi-layer neural network. The first layer is the input layer while the last layer is the output one. In the interest of getting the correct vehicle information such as make, model and year, the researchers created a library of two models, Toyota Hilux and Honda Civic, containing models up to ten years back. The application part for user interface was written in Python on Flutter Framework. The application is simple and easy to use to facilitate the searching for car models. The application is convenient for people who are looking for used cars as well as practical for car related criminal investigation and car theft.

The rest of this paper is organized as follows. Section 2 reviews convolutional neural network technique in automobiles. Section 3 discusses the process and methodology. Section 4 discusses the outcomes of the experiments, and the entire work is concluded in Sect. 5 of this paper.

2 Convolutional Neural Network and ITS Extensions

Machine Learning is a tool that supports the prediction of future events by analyzing a large number of existing data and gives outcome and the machine is capable of learning by itself. It can find an approach with smallest error as well as can learn from new input data and can be self-learning.

Supervised Learning categorizes and gives the outcome in advance and then use the sample data to train the model using the defined algorithm. It is aimed to predict the future outcome. When learning evolves, it can input new data, which have not been known to the machine before, to facilitate the machine learning and predict the future event.

2.1 Convolutional Neural Network

Convolutional Neural Network (CNN) is a multi-layer neural network with a specific structure designed to heighten its capability in extracting complex features from data. It is highly suitable for problems related to perceptual tasks as it is often used to extract features from data which are not well ordered or do not have a specific structure such as images. In most cases, VGG16 is used while Kernels 3X3 is used in classifying and identifying the characteristics of images [1, 2].

2.2 Deep Residual Network

Deep Residual Network is a new basic form of Convolutional Neural Network (CNN) that recognizes images by applying the principle of Deep Residual Network (ResNet). That is the introduction of a shortcut that connects to a layer not immediately above or below it.

The procedure of ResNet uses the remaining blocks as shortcuts between layers in order to reduce unwanted effects in the neural network. This is obtained by cutting down the number of layers by skipping some. By hopping across one or more layers, there will be some blocks left. These blocks are the fundamental parts of Deep Residual Network (ResNet) as in Fig. 1.

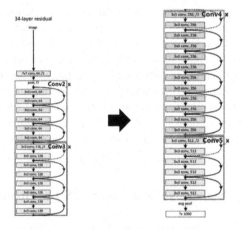

Fig. 1. The procedure of Deep Residual Network Architectures (ResNet) [3]

From Fig. 2, the significant aspect of the operation in Deep Residual Network (ResNet) is the circumvention of layers. Nevertheless, there can be situations when the variable x and the function F(x) do not share the same dimension because in the Convolution state, image can turn into ones of different resolutions. For example, an image of size 32Í32 in 3Í3 Convolution state will output an image of size 30Í30. Also from the variable W, the mapping approach is Linear Projection and W is the variable that support the consolidation of x and F(x) into one input and forward it to the next layer [4–7].

$$y = F(x, \{W_i\}) + W_s x. \tag{1}$$

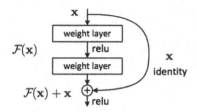

Fig. 2. Residual learning: a building block.

3 Car Classification and Detection

Many cars classification and detection research have been widely applied in image processing techniques such as CNN, Deep learning, and machine learning. Specially, they considered the evaluate damages and estimate the repair cost instantly in a problem domain of insurance company. The characteristics of machine learning and deep learning algorithm can help to solve for car classification and insurance company. Basically, a captured automobile image is a common resource to use for image processing techniques. These are able to evaluate and estimate costs for car accidents. The image processing techniques have been used to analyze with a large scope for automation. They consider the classification of car damage, but some part of the car has fine granular [8, 9].

CNN models have several algorithms that contain VGG16, VGG19, ResNet, and Inception-ResNetV2. These can classification/detection, which can be used to capture car accidents. The performance of model can the adoption of fast, scalable, and end-to-end trainable convolutional neural networks make it technically feasible to recognize vehicle damages with large computer vision based on deep convolutional networks. It started with pre-train process that re-size the image to avoid overfitting. The model will learn general features. These are useful to improve the performance of the model [10].

VGG16 and VGG19 algorithm analysis can be done by car damaged detection. These techniques extract an image from real-world dataset. The location of car part and severity detected and decrease claim leakage of insurance companies [11].

Moreover, the amount paid of insurance companies had close to a million dollars per year. The expert argue that Artificial Intelligence (AI) has huge advantage. It can be able to solve in problem domain for insurance industry. They need to an automatically detect damages in automobiles, classified their severity level, locate of spare part, and visualize of car by extract locations. The inception-ResNetV2 approach used to implement. These is contain pre-train model, which is followed by a fully connected neural network, and achieve to higher performance in features extraction [12].

However, smartphone has been used to capture automobiles to complete views. Image segmented technique use to analyze into parts, each of which has an area adjacent to others. Each area represents a part of the object in the image. Segmentation process is deemed complete only when the object is entirely partitioned. The result of the segmentation is the indicator of success in the analysis process such as identified in car part, identified in damage parts, evaluation of each part, and cost estimate [13].

4 Models

We confirm the meaning of Deep Learning and its operating principle. This also includes other models used in this research, such as SVM, ResNet34, ResNet50, Inception-ResNetv2. The aspects and the fitness for application in the research are also examined.

To develop car image classification in our mobile application, the CNN technique is used. The CNN consists of five parts including input layer, convolutional layer, pooling layer, rectified linear unit, fully connected layer, and Softmax. The briefly detail in each part is summarized as follows:

- The basic of CNN that read image from source to input layer. Therefore, convolutional layer is designed to extract feature detector or kernel from the input image.
- The Rectified Linear Unit (ReLU) is non-linear activation function. It is reducing the computing time and overfitting problem. This function transforming the feature map from the convolutional layer to be the non-linear feature map. This work used this too detailed information.
- Max Pooling layer is a layer to convert the image into spatial invariance and construct a compact feature representation. In our work, we used to reduce the size of image and make it robust to a variety of size, rotation, and shift.
- Fully connected layer employs learning from source with multiple level of abstraction by computational models that are associated with multiple processing layers. This method intended to discover complex structure in big data set by using the feed forward neural networks algorithm to predict the result. Each layer derives from the computation of node and weight of connections among nodes, and each transform represents one level, which will be the input for the next (see Fig. 3).

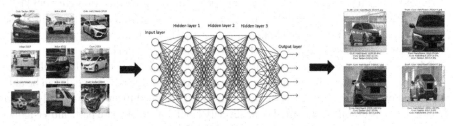

Fig. 3. Fully Connection of model

- Softmax function is used to calculate the probability of each class. That used the maximum probability value and selected the answer.

Our car image classification model used in our application is implemented by using Keras model with weights pre-trained from ImageNet as explained in [14].

5   Experiment and Discussion

5.1   Experimental Setup

The researchers have collected the dataset for the development of the model from a database that stores 1,811 images in car dataset with image resolution of 224 × 224 pixels. There are cover to two car models in Thailand from past 10 years. That include Toyota Hilux (van) and Honda Civic (Car in C-Segment – Hatchback and Sedan) from 2012–2021. Therefore, the dataset has 26 classes, which cover main model and sub-model such as Hilux 2015, Hilux 2019, Civic Sedan 2012, Civic hatchback 2020, Civic Sedan 2020 and so on. Among these, 1,291 images (80%) are for training purpose while 520 (20%) ones are for testing (see in Fig. 4).

For data preparation, the images are classified into classes according to the brand, model, and year of vehicles as the input data have not been categorized yet.

Fig. 4. A Sample car dataset

The result of image training through all models that uses our dataset to learn and distinguish by training result of 80% and testing result at 20% of distinguish dataset. The classification of automobiles result showed as follows:

5.2   Experimental Results

As shown in Fig. 5, it depicts the accuracy of ResNet34, ResNet50, and Inception-ResNetv2 in the training data and the validation data. It is evident that the training accuracy is low in the beginning and gets higher when the training is executed. The validation accuracy rises only slightly as the training continues and becomes constant thereafter due to the limited size of the data.

Figure 5(a) display the accuracy graph of ResNet34. The accuracy of the first part of the training is apparently low and it scores higher as the training goes on.

Figure 5(b) display the accuracy graph of ResNet50. Similar to those of ResNet34. The accuracy of the first part of the training is apparently low and it scores higher as the training goes on.

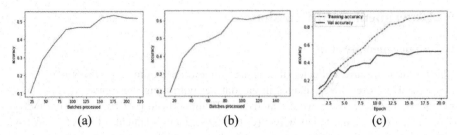

Fig. 5. The accuracy graphs of (a) ResNet34, (b) ResNet50, and (c) Inception-ResNetv2

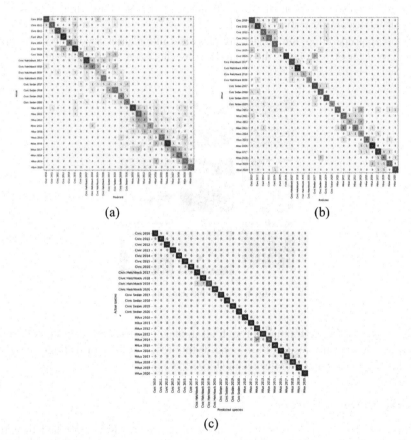

Fig. 6. Confusion matrix of (a) ResNet34, (b) ResNet50, and (c) Inception-ResNetv2.

In Fig. 6, the matrix table expands that both horizontally and vertically illustrates sample of dataset in both models. The amount of rows and columns are determined by the number of type of automobiles in ResNet50 and also shows the performance of recognition.

Support Vector Machine (SVM) is another algorithm for data classification and analysis. It is based on getting the coefficient of the equation to construct a boundary between the data that are input into the learning process. It focuses on the lines that divides data into groups (Hyperplane). SVM is favorable for data of small to medium sizes. The result shows the accuracy of the prediction from unseen data. Using SVM accuracy is at 0.21 (see in Table 1).

Figure 6(c) shows the accuracy of Inception-ResNetV2. The accuracy of the first part of the training is low and it becomes higher and reaches a constant level as the training continues.

In Fig. 6, the matrix table expands that both horizontally and vertically illustrates sample of dataset in both models. The amount of rows and columns are determined by the number of type of automobiles in Inception-ResNetv2 and also shows the performance of recognition.

5.3 Evaluation and Application

To prove the performance of our model, this research also did comparison of five models: SVM, CNN, ResNet34, ResNet and Inception-ResNetV2. The researchers set up a library of two car models, Toyota Hilux and Honda Civic, set batch size = 64 and image size to 224 × 224 pixels. The data are categorized into two sets, set train having 1,449 images in 26 classes. Our experiments compared the accuracies of SVM, ResNet34, ResNet50, and Inception-ResNetV2, which came out to be 21.4%, 55.5%, 66.6%, and 92.8% respectively. All models share the same goal that is to identify a car in the most efficient way. The result from testing shows that the most accurate one is inception-ResNetV2 (see in Table 1).

Table 1. Compares The Accuracy and Losses of all models.

Model	Accuracy	Loss
SVM	0.214	5.83
ResNet 34	0.555	1.33
ResNet 50	0.666	1.08
Inception-ResNet V2	0.928	0.23

As the researchers have developed a model to identify a vehicle and ultimately achieve an applicable and most efficient model. In the analysis, we built up an application so that users can use it conveniently. The application analyzes and processes the input that is the image taken by the user. There show instructions to capture the car's position such as the front, headlight, body, rear, and angle of the car (see in Fig. 8(b)). The application then analyzes and processes the output using the model developed by the researcher. The output is as follows (see in Fig. 7 and 8).

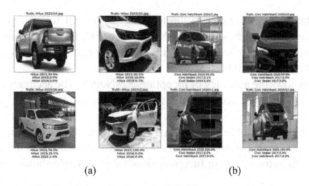

(a)   (b)

Fig. 7. The result of car classification among brands.

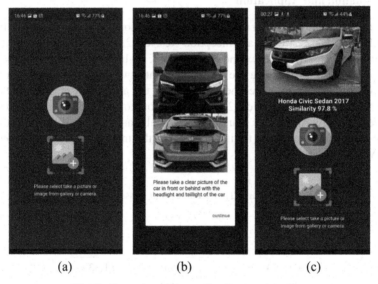

(a)   (b)   (c)

Fig. 8. Examples of the application user interface

6 Conclusion

The researchers conducted detailed studies about the process and method of developing a model to be as efficient and precise as possible in order to identify a vehicle according to the objective and goal in this research. That is to facilitate the second-handed car buyers who do not have much knowledge about automobiles to perceive and understand reliable information about particular cars that they are interested in. It can also assist relating officers in identifying the make, model and year of a vehicle when there is a car-related crime or a car theft.

In the development of the model, the researchers performed experiments on five algorithms, namely SVM, ResNet34, ResNet50 and Inception-ResNetV2. All models share the same goal that is to identify a car in the most efficient way. The result from testing shows that the most accurate one is Inception-ResNetV2.

The application that was developed in this research can run on Android and was written in Python. It has two main functions, the prediction of the outcome of the deep learning algorithm and the function of taking a photo to input to the application, which will process the image and give out the result. The photograph taking function also contains instructions on the suitable angle for taking a photo so as to step up the accuracy of the system.

One frequently encountered problem is when data are classified into classes, the size of data is too small in each class. This is a drawback when it is being input to the model. When the researchers selected the most efficient model, its accuracy on mobile application dropped slightly compared to the result of the testing on website. In future, researchers plan to extend the comprehensiveness of vehicles to include more brands, more models and more number of years.

References

1. Qassim, H., Verma, A., Feinzimer, D.: Compressed residual-VGG16 CNN model for big data places image recognition. In: 2018 IEEE 8th Annual Computing and Communication Workshop and Conference (CCWC), pp. 169–175 (2018)
2. Tammina, S.: Transfer learning using VGG-16 with deep convolutional neural network for classifying images. Int. J. Sci. Res. Publ. (IJSRP) **9**, 143–150 (2019)
3. Simonyan, K., Zisserman, A.: Very deep convolutional networks for large-scale image recognition. arXiv preprint arXiv:1409.1556 (2014)
4. He, K., Zhang, X., Ren, S., Sun, J.: Deep residual learning for image recognition. In: Proceedings of the IEEE Conference on Computer Vision and Pattern Recognition, pp. 770–778 (2016)
5. Bishop, C.M.: Neural Networks for Pattern Recognition. Oxford University Press, Oxford (1995)
6. Ripley, B.D.: Pattern Recognition and Neural Networks. Cambridge University Press, Cambridge (2007)
7. Venables, W.N., Ripley, B.D.: Modern applied statistics with S-PLUS. Springer, Heidelberg (2013). https://doi.org/10.1007/978-0-387-21706-2
8. Patil, K., Kulkarni, M., Sriraman, A., Karande, S.: Deep learning based car damage classification. In: 2017 16th IEEE International Conference on Machine Learning and Applications (ICMLA), pp. 50–54 (2017)
9. Kalshetty, J.N., Hrithik Devaiah, B.A., Rakshith, K., Koshy, K., Advait, N.: Analysis of car damage for personal auto claim using CNN. In: Shakya, S., Balas, V.E., Kamolphiwong, S., Du, K.-L. (eds.) Sentimental Analysis and Deep Learning. AISC, vol. 1408, pp. 319–329. Springer, Singapore (2022). https://doi.org/10.1007/978-981-16-5157-1_25
10. Dwivedi, M., et al.: Deep learning-based car damage classification and detection. In: Chiplunkar, N.N., Fukao, T. (eds.) Advances in Artificial Intelligence and Data Engineering. AISC, vol. 1133, pp. 207–221. Springer, Singapore (2021). https://doi.org/10.1007/978-981-15-3514-7_18
11. Kyu, P.M., Woraratpanya, K.: Car damage detection and classification. In: Proceedings of the 11th International Conference on Advances in Information Technology, pp. Article 46. Association for Computing Machinery, Bangkok, Thailand (2020)

12. Dhieb, N., Ghazzai, H., Besbes, H., Massoud, Y.: A very deep transfer learning model for vehicle damage detection and localization. In: 2019 31st International Conference on Microelectronics (ICM), pp. 158–161 (2019)

13. Pasupa, K., Kittiworapanya, P., Hongngern, N., Woraratpanya, K.: Evaluation of deep learning algorithms for semantic segmentation of car parts. Comp. Intell. Syst. (2021)

14. Gulli, A., Pal, S.: Deep learning with Keras. Packt Publishing Ltd, Birmingham (2017)

Automatic Firearm Detection in Images and Videos Using YOLO-Based Model

Sourav Mishra$^{(\boxtimes)}$ and Vijay K. Chaurasiya$^{(\boxtimes)}$

Indian Institute of Information Technology Allahabad, Prayagraj,
Uttar Pradesh, India
{rsi2019005,vijayk}@iiita.ac.in
http://profile.iiita.ac.in/vijayk

Abstract. In this day and age, we are witness to ever increasing gun violence all around the world. Technology has surpassed all human beliefs where each person can be easily tracked through their mobiles or through the fortitude of CCTV cameras available all across public properties and areas. There is a need to stop gun violence to protect people's Right to Live. There are several instances appearing in the news daily about deaths caused due to gun violence. An alarm based system can be introduced which tracks the publicly available CCTV footage to look for guns in the open and raise appropriate alarms. In order to achieve this a robust model to identify and classify firearms automatically from videos is required. The aim of this paper is to describe a YOLO-based model which is highly effective in recognizing firearms in videos and mark them in the video such that the model can be further used for further applications such as raising alarms, tracking human beings with firearms etc.

Keywords: Gun Violence · Robust · Alarm · YOLO · Footage

1 Introduction

Over the years, the increase in population in urban areas put pressure on the legal bodies to prevent and control the crime rates in the cities. The real-time information of crime scenes and monitoring of weapons used in public is necessary. And also the crime rates because of guns are very critical all around the world. Although it is legal to keep firearms in some countries, monitoring is still required for its use in public. Gun violence is one of the greatest public health crises of the present time. Deep learning is a part of artificial intelligence that is known to imitate the human brain working to perform any action and imitates the patterns to get the required results. Video surveillance for real-time detection of weapons in public areas is a very great effort in the prevention and detection of criminal activities. Behavioral cloning is a process of reproducing human performed tasks by a deep neural network. We achieve this by training the neural network with the data of the human subject performing the task.

1.1 Yolo Algorithm

YOLO, which stands for You Only Look Once, is a fast and one of the most popular object detection convolutional neural networks (CNNs) algorithms. It is good to use for real-time detection with not much loss of accuracy. The difference between a detection and recognition algorithm is that the latter cannot detect the position of any object while a detection algorithm can detect many objects within the same picture. A complete image is applied to a single neural network to split it into smaller boxes to get the confidence score of each region. This helps detect whether an object is present or not in that particular region (Fig. 1).

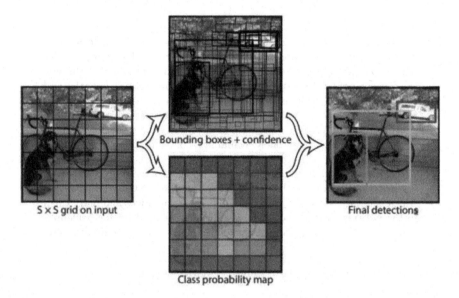

Fig. 1. The picture forms a grid that will predict the bounding boxes and a score to determine the presence of an object in a particular square box. There are five parameters to find out the confidence score and to find the presence of an object along with the parameters like accuracy, precision, and exactness. If there is no object in the square box, then the score becomes zero, and if it is equal to the Intersection Over Union, then the object is present.

YOLOv1: Only a part of the complete image is used for the detection of bounding boxes. The drawbacks of using YOLOv1 was that it was very difficult to detect objects which were smaller in size and were grouped together.

YOLOv2: An improved version of YOLOv1 that contains Darknet-19 architecture as a backbone, a better resolution classifier, and batch normalization. Darknet-19 contains the top 19 layers which are the same as the 1024 layer of the YOLOv2 network and then attached appended with a 1×1 convolution of

1024 filters. The YOLOv2 outperformed Faster RCNN with ResNet and SSD and ran at a higher speed. The drawbacks may be said as non-sampling, no residual blocks, and no skip connections.

YOLOv3: It uses a different variation of Darknet, containing 53 convolutional layers. The DarkNet-53 takes the place of the DarkNet-19 feature extraction network of YOLOv2 and contains a network of 53 layers consisting of 3×3 and 1×1 filters with residual skip connections. Its drawback was COCO benchmarks have a higher value of IoU which is used for the detection rejection than Yolov3. Also while training, images are resized to a fixed size ratio, which leads to increased batch size and multiple GPU training. Unfortunately, right now it is not possible to keep the aspect ratio of images and batch them for the TensorFlow object detection. These fixed aspect ratios which are fed and used by the models also affect memory usage and inference times.

YOLOv4: The architecture of YOLOv4 has a backbone of CSPDarknet53, a YOLOv3 head, and a PANet path-aggregation neck. It involves the implementation of the new architecture in the Backbone and the modifications in the neck which led to the improvement of the mAP (mean Average Precision) by 10% and the number of FPS (Frame per Second) by 12%. Also, it is easier to train this neural network on a single GPU.

Over the past decade, the Internet of Things (IoT) market has been experiencing explosive growth and by 2023, there will be 25 billion connected devices. The old ways, methods, and strategies need to be changed with the increasing number of data and technologies for reliable investigation which will help to ensure trust and authenticity. These IoT systems incorporated with the digital investigation process helps the legal agencies and Law Enforcement Agencies for accumulating digital records and evidences. The greatest technology of this century is object detection and recognition. As per the statistics [14], the death rate increases by 1.7% in 18 years, with more than 15,000 homicides per day. The legal bodies are always in the research of making public places safer so that they can bring safety and peace to the citizens. The Yolo algorithm can be used to detect weapons in real-time. This algorithm can also be used on thermal images of people with concealed weapons. The real-time video images can help to take quick action by the police against any criminal activities and also to identify the criminals.

In this paper we have tried to propose a surveillance system which will alert us if there are people who are carrying weapons without access or licenses. However establishing a full working system will require a combination of various facets of the government and industries. We start this off by building a model which can automatically predict the prevalence of a firearm in a video footage. The model will be adept at identifying firearms with high precision and run in real time. In this paper we will provide the method of building such a model and we will also attach the results produced from its implementation.

2   Related Work

In 1805, Legendre proposed a regression analysis technique i.e. Least Square Method. This technique provides a line between the independent and dependent variables as best as possible. In the year 1809, Gauss used this method for predicting the unknown circular object which had been seen around the sun by using planetary recordings. Most of the time comets, and later extend to explore small planets. In 1821, this work had been extended by Gauss by introducing the Gauss-Markov hypothesis. In the work published in 2018 [14], the researcher classifies and detects the utilized various systems like YOLOv2, CNN which is a sliding window-based, convolutional networks (R-FCN), faster region-based CNN. The result showed that features of CNN give comparatively better performance than the traditional algorithms. The X-ray images were used. In [16], the researchers use the ImageNet dataset to train and model this detection system. A faster RCNN with VGG-16 based classifier was applied on YouTube videos and resulted in a mean average precision (mAP) of 84.21%. In 2019, the research work [16] made use of the Yolov3 algorithm for gun detection where the researcher created an image dataset containing guns with various locations and adjustments by their selves and blended it with the ImageNet dataset. For better results and to evaluate the Yolov3 algorithm, the model is trained and validated. The results show that Yolov3 is faster in speed than the Faster RCNN. In 2020, the paper [17] implements multiple object detection algorithms, which are suitable for traffic and surveillance applications. Multiple object detection is a key capacity for most computer and AI (Artificial Intelligence) vision systems. For the dataset of video, accuracy was 99% and for the dataset of images, accuracy was 98%. Also, this model was conducted on DSP and FPGA [17]. Bhatt et al. suggested a dataset where the resolution was less with very dim light and they were streaming from CCTV in real-time frame per second. Most of the prior work done was on recognizing pictures and recordings of good quality as a result those models were prepared on high-quality datasets, it isn't conceivable to at that point distinguish and protest the determination in real-time. The comes about are analyzed after preparing and testing models on distinctive datasets [18]. Several researchers have done firearm detection using fuzzy classifiers [8] and an ensemble of neural networks [9].

3   Methodology

We want to develop a model which will be able to automatically identify guns from a video or a photo. To achieve this we need to develop a module which will take images as input and output images with bounding boxes around guns. This leads us to develop a Deep learning based model to perform this task. Any such model requires data that can be trained on. We have used images of firearms available online to train our model. We have also used 3d synthetic images to enhance the model. These synthetic images are 3 dimensional computer generated images which capture the same image from different angles and different lighting conditions. These images provide an extra edge to the model in regards to gun identification. Once the required data is collected, we will have to train the model. Now a question arises regarding which base model is to be chosen. As explained in the Literature Review, several options were explored and finally the YOLO model was selected. This is followed by training of the model. Once the model is trained we test the model on unseen data. Once the model has reached a satisfactory stage with regards to accuracy, we need to develop a module to read video input. Video Input has to be read frame by frame and each frame has to be fed into the model and the output has to be displayed. We need to ensure that the model is able to handle videos in real time. Normal real time videos run at 24 FPS. The model has to be fast enough to handle 24 images per second (Fig. 2).

3.1   Analysis

Model Selection. We have selected the YOLO v4 model for the task of object identification and classification. Since this model is supposed to classify images, a lot of convolution layers is expected. As you can see in the picture, only the last few layers are fully connected layers. Each convolution layer uses Leaky-ReLU as the activation function. On top of it, each convolution layer is followed by a max-pooling layer. All the convolution layers have filters of size 3×3 with stride = 1, on the other hand all the max-pool layers have filter size of 2×2 with stride = 2.

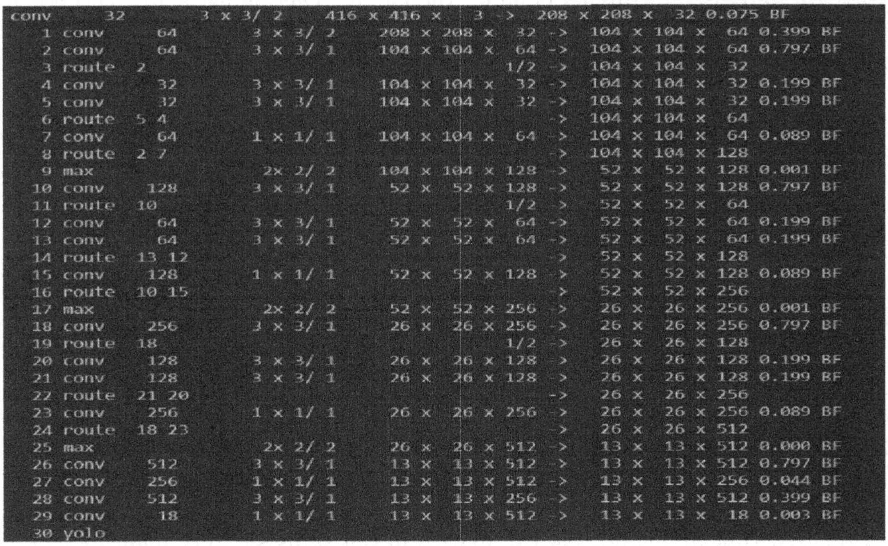

```
   conv       32        3 x 3/ 2     416 x 416 x    3  ->  208 x 208 x   32 0.075 BF
 1 conv       64        3 x 3/ 2     208 x 208 x   32  ->  104 x 104 x   64 0.399 BF
 2 conv       64        3 x 3/ 1     104 x 104 x   64  ->  104 x 104 x   64 0.797 BF
 3 route  2                                      1/2   ->  104 x 104 x   32
 4 conv       32        3 x 3/ 1     104 x 104 x   32  ->  104 x 104 x   32 0.199 BF
 5 conv       32        3 x 3/ 1     104 x 104 x   32  ->  104 x 104 x   32 0.199 BF
 6 route  5 4                                          ->  104 x 104 x   64
 7 conv       64        1 x 1/ 1     104 x 104 x   64  ->  104 x 104 x   64 0.089 BF
 8 route  2 7                                          ->  104 x 104 x  128
 9 max                  2x 2/ 2      104 x 104 x  128  ->   52 x  52 x  128 0.001 BF
10 conv      128        3 x 3/ 1      52 x  52 x  128  ->   52 x  52 x  128 0.797 BF
11 route  10                                     1/2   ->   52 x  52 x   64
12 conv       64        3 x 3/ 1      52 x  52 x   64  ->   52 x  52 x   64 0.199 BF
13 conv       64        3 x 3/ 1      52 x  52 x   64  ->   52 x  52 x   64 0.199 BF
14 route  13 12                                        ->   52 x  52 x  128
15 conv      128        1 x 1/ 1      52 x  52 x  128  ->   52 x  52 x  128 0.089 BF
16 route  10 15                                        ->   52 x  52 x  256
17 max                  2x 2/ 2       52 x  52 x  256  ->   26 x  26 x  256 0.001 BF
18 conv      256        3 x 3/ 1      26 x  26 x  256  ->   26 x  26 x  256 0.797 BF
19 route  18                                     1/2   ->   26 x  26 x  128
20 conv      128        3 x 3/ 1      26 x  26 x  128  ->   26 x  26 x  128 0.199 BF
21 conv      128        3 x 3/ 1      26 x  26 x  128  ->   26 x  26 x  128 0.199 BF
22 route  21 20                                        ->   26 x  26 x  256
23 conv      256        1 x 1/ 1      26 x  26 x  256  ->   26 x  26 x  256 0.089 BF
24 route  18 23                                        ->   26 x  26 x  512
25 max                  2x 2/ 2       26 x  26 x  512  ->   13 x  13 x  512 0.000 BF
26 conv      512        3 x 3/ 1      13 x  13 x  512  ->   13 x  13 x  512 0.797 BF
27 conv      256        1 x 1/ 1      13 x  13 x  512  ->   13 x  13 x  256 0.044 BF
28 conv      512        3 x 3/ 1      13 x  13 x  256  ->   13 x  13 x  512 0.399 BF
29 conv       18        1 x 1/ 1      13 x  13 x  512  ->   13 x  13 x   18 0.003 BF
30 yolo
```

Fig. 2.

The output of the yolo consists of three layers. Each layer has 5+N attributes, where N is the number of classes. Here is what each entry in the output means:

1: CentreX
2: CentreY
3: Width
4: Height
5: Confidence that object is present in that bounding box
6: Probabilities of the object belonging to each of the N classes

The output of yolo consists of three layers with each layer containing 5+N entries. The yolo algorithm works by dividing the image into a grid of fixed length. The dimension of these grids determines the size of the object that can be detected. For example, if we wanted to spot the pigeons in the image and if we divide the image into a grid of 13X13 we may not be able to detect the pigeons that are close to one another because there will be multiple pigeons in a grid. On the other hand, had we split the image into 52X52 grids there is a very good chance that no two pigeons are in the same grid. This technique improves the accuracy of the model. So, the three layers correspond to outputs after dividing the image into 13X13, 26X26 and 52X52. This makes sure that we are recognizing both smaller and bigger objects.

Dataset. We have used two datasets to train our model. Images from [10] were initially used to train the model. After using these images, images obtained from [13] were used to further enhance the model. These images are synthetic in nature i,e they are computer generated 3 dimensional images which are used to enhance the model. A total of 22,000 images were used to train our model.

Training. As explained 22000 images were used to train the model. However, all images were not used at a single stretch. We divided the images into 5 batches and performed 5 rounds of training. The details and observations from each round of training are explained below.

Round 1. We used the open-source dataset [10] to perform training in this round. The dataset contains 3000 images with the bounding box annotations of guns in the images. We trained the YOLO model with these images. After one round of training, we validated the model with some unseen pictures and the results can be seen in Fig. 3. The network was able to easily detect the guns which are big and clearly visible but failed to detect the guns in the moderately difficult images. When we tried to find the reason for this under-performance, we realized that about 60% of the images in our data-set were plain images of guns.

Fig. 3.

Fig. 4.

Round 2. We decided to retrain the model in order to correct the mistakes of the model. This time, we removed all the images which contained only guns. This led to only images which were realistic in nature. The logic behind doing this was to remove any hidden over-fitting towards the plain-gun images. 1000 images were used in this round. Figure 4 shows the predictions obtained after the second round of training.

Round 3. Though the results obtained with validation images were better, there was still scope to improve the accuracy of the model. We explored other ways to increase the accuracy of the network. We found that doing some basic image transformations and augmentations like, scaling, rotation, shearing, cropping can increase the accuracy [12]. The transformations applied are shown below (Figs. 5, 6, 7, 8 and 9).

Fig. 5. Scaling involves resizing the input image to produce images of different sizes. Result of applying scaling on the sample image is shown.

Fig. 6. Image Rotation is the process of rotating input images to produce new images at different angles. Result of rotation on a sample image is shown.

Fig. 7. Shear Transformation a mathematical operation that preserves the volume of an image but shifts each point in the image. Result of performing shear transformation on sample image is shown in the top two images. **Exposure** is the amount of light per square unit of an image that can be manipulated to either make it darker or lighter. Result of changing exposure on an image can be seen in the bottom two images

Fig. 8. Random Salt and Pepper Noise Here we are adding random noise to the image as real world images might not always be clear and noise-less.

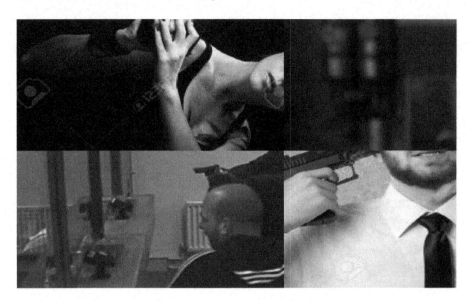

Fig. 9. Mosaic is a combination of multiple images and different angles. An example of a mosaic image is shown.

So we enhanced our data-set by applying those transformations on the images that were already present in our data-set. 9000 images were developed using the above techniques. Then we refined the weights in round-2 by performing transfer learning on these transformed images. Figure 10 shows the results of the predictions after this round.

Fig. 10.

Round 4. We then used synthetic images from [13] to train the model. Synthetic images are computer generated 3 dimensional images which portray the same scene from different angles and directions and in different physical settings. These images are useful as real world data-sets are limited and we require a large number of images to train the model. 6000 Synthetic images were used to train the model in this round. After training we observed that though these images were useful for the model to train upon, performing an entire round of training only on synthetic images led to slight skewing of the model. Hence, we decided to perform one final round of training.

Round 5. This is the final round of training for the model. Here we used a mix of synthetic and real images to train the model. 3000 images were used to train the model here. The mix of real and synthetic images provided a good balance to the model.

Video Input Module. We implemented sequential video reading from input followed by processing each frame of input video. The flowchart on the left of Fig. 11 explains this process. This helped us process videos at 19 FPS. However real time videos run at 24 FPS. Hence we needed a new approach to solve this. The main cause of this problem is that reading the video input is an I/O operation which takes more time. Hence, we thought of using multithreading. We created 2 threads and let 1 thread take the video input and feed the frames into a queue and use the other thread to take frames from the queue and feed it into the model. The flowchart on the right of Fig. 11 shows the operation. We found a significant increase in the frame rate of the video and found that videos were processed upto 42 FPS (Fig. 12).

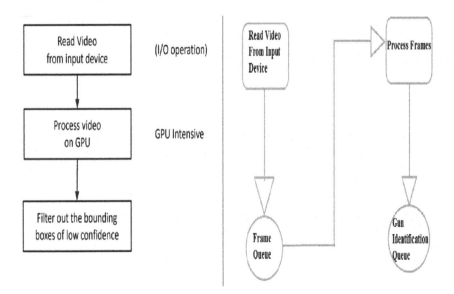

Fig. 11.

Fig. 12. After the model was completely trained, it was evaluated on unseen images obtained from various sources online. Some of the results obtained are shown

We managed to improve the robustness of the network using a variety of techniques as described above. Since we had to create bounding boxes of guns, there is no automatic way for testing of the model and its accuracy. Hence we performed manual testing where we fed unseen images into the model and verified if the output is correct or not. Model was accurate upto 85% during manual testing.

4   Conclusion

Gun violence is a major threat to the safety of society. Weapon Detection is the foremost need to curb the crimes and aid the law-enforcement to track, suspect and identify criminals on this basis. This will help them to take prompt action which in turn will save more lives. The model described in this paper is only the tip of the iceberg. The YOLO v4 model acts as an efficient object detection and identification model which has produced very good results considering the limited data available online in public forums. The video input module developed is of great use as it can process videos upto 42 FPS ensuring that the module with the model described can be deployed in real world scenarios and can be made to run in real time.

References

1. Hubel, D.H., Wiesel, T.N.: Receptive fields and functional architecture of monkey striate cortex. J. Physiol. **195**, 215–243 (1968)
2. Viola, P., Jones, M.: Rapid object detection using a boosted cascade of simple features. In: CVPR (2001)
3. Girshick, R., Donahue, J., Darrell, T., Malik, J.: Rich feature hierarchies for accurate object detection and semantic segmentation. In: CVPR (2014)
4. Girshick, R.: Fast R-CNN. Microsoft Research (2015)
5. Ren, S., He, K., Girshick, R., Sun, J.: Faster R-CNN: towards real-time object detection with region proposal networks (2015)
6. He, K., Gkioxari, G., Dollar, P., Girshick, R.: Mask R-CNN. Facebook AI Research (FAIR) (2017)
7. Redmon, J., Divvala, S., Girshick, R., Farhadi, A.: You only look once: unified. realtime object detection University of Washington, Allen Institute for AI, Facebook AI Research (2015)
8. Grega, M., Matiolański, A., Guzik, P., Leszczuk, M.: Automated detection of firearms and knives in a CCTV image (2015)
9. Egiazarov, A., Mavroeidis, V., Zennaro, F.M., Vishi, K.: Firearm detection and segmentation using an ensemble of semantic neural networks. Digital Security Group University of Oslo (2020)
10. Dataset. https://www.kaggle.com/atulyakumar98/gundetection
11. Fuentes, A., Im, D.H., Yoon, S., Park, D.S.: Spectral analysis of CNN for tomato disease identification. In: Rutkowski, L., Korytkowski, M., Scherer, R., Tadeusiewicz, R., Zadeh, L.A., Zurada, J.M. (eds.) ICAISC 2017. LNCS (LNAI), vol. 10245, pp. 40–51. Springer, Cham (2017). https://doi.org/10.1007/978-3-319-59063-9_4
12. Shorten, C., Khoshgoftaar, T.M.: A survey on image data augmentation for deep learning, pp. 7–9 (2019)
13. Dataset. https://www.edgecase.ai/articles/worlds-first-synthetic-gun-detection-dataset-from-edgecase-ai
14. Akcay, S., Kundegorski, M.E., Willcocks, C.G., Breckon, T.P.: Using deep convolutional neural network architectures for object classification and detection within x-ray baggage security imagery. IEEE Trans. Inf. For. Secur. **13**(9), 2203–2215 (2018)
15. Olmos, R., Tabik, S., Herrera, F.: Automatic handgun detection alarm in videos using deep learning. Neurocomputing **275**, 66–72 (2018)
16. Warsi, A., Abdullah, M., Husen, M.N., Yahya, M., Khan, S., Jawaid, N.: Gun detection system using Yolov3. In: 2019 IEEE International Conference on Smart Instrumentation, Measurement and Application (ICSIMA), pp. 1–4 (2019). https://doi.org/10.1109/ICSIMA47653.2019.9057329
17. Kumar, B., Punitha, R., Mohana, C.: YOLOv3 and YOLOv4: multiple object detection for surveillance applications. In: 2020 Third International Conference on Smart Systems and Inventive Technology (ICSSIT), pp. 1316–1321 (2020). https://doi.org/10.1109/ICSSIT48917.2020.9214094
18. Bhatti, M.T., Khan, M.G., Aslam, M., Fiaz, M.J.: Weapon detection in real-time CCTV videos using deep learning. IEEE Access **9**, 34366–34382 (2021). https://doi.org/10.1109/ACCESS.2021.3059170
19. Brownlee, J.: A Gentle Introduction to Transfer Learning for Deep Learning (2017). https://machinelearningmastery.com/transfer-learning-for-deep-learning/

20. Evolution-of-Yolo. https://towardsdatascience.com/evolution-of-yolo-yolo-versio n-1-afb8af302bd2
21. Goodfellow, I., et al.: Generative adversarial nets. Adv. Neural Inf. Process. Syst., 2672–2680 (2014)
22. Lin, M., Chen, Q., Yan, S.: Network In Network (2013). arXiv:1312.4400
23. An open source dataset under Creative Commons Attribution-ShareAlike 4.0 International License. https://github.com/ari-dasci/OD-WeaponDetection
24. Simonyan, K., Zisserman, A.: Very Deep Convolutional Networks for Large-Scale Image Recognition (2015). arXiv:1409.1556
25. Hashmi, T.S.S., Haq, N.U., Fraz, M.M., Shahzad, M.: Application of deep learning for weapons detection in surveillance videos. In: 2021 International Conference on Digital Futures and Transformative Technologies (ICoDT2), pp. 1–6 (2021). https://doi.org/10.1109/ICoDT252288.2021.9441523
26. India sees the third-highest firearm-related deaths in the world by Joe Myers https://theprint.in/india/india-sees-the-third-highest-firearm-related-deaths-in-t he-world/274576

Author Index

M. Tanveer et al. (Eds.): ICONIP 2022, CCIS 1794, pp. 567–569, 2023.
https://doi.org/10.1007/978-981-99-1648-1

Printed in the United States
by Baker & Taylor Publisher Services